Selected Letters of
VANESSA BELL

Also by the Author:

Bloomsbury Pie: The Making of the Bloomsbury Boom

Selected Letters of
VANESSA BELL

Edited by
REGINA MARLER

Moyer Bell

Wakefield, Rhode Island & London

Published by Moyer Bell

First Edition

LIBRARY OF CONGRESS
CATALOGING IN PUBLICATION DATA

Bell, Vanessa, 1879-1961.
[Correspondence. Selections]
Selected Letters of Vanessa Bell / edited by
Regina Marler. -- 1st ed.

p.   cm.

Originally published : New York : Pantheon
Books, c1993.
Includes bibliographical references and index.
1. Bell, Vanessa, 1879 - 1961 -- Correspon-
dence. 2. Painters -- England -- Correspon-
dence. 3. Bloomsbury group. I. Marler,
Regina, 1964- . II. Title.
ND497.B44A3   1998
759.2 [B]--dc21   98-2755
ISBN 1-55921-261-6   CIP

Printed in the United States of America
Distributed to the trade by Publishers Group West, 1700
Fourth Street, Berkeley, California 94710
(510) 658-1444

*This book is dedicated with affection and respect
to the family of Vanessa Bell:
Angelica Garnett, Quentin Bell, and Anne Olivier Bell*

*and to
Bernadette Fraser of Rodmell,
whose audacity made it possible.*

CONTENTS

Illustrations follow pages 150 and 342.

LUDENDORFF BELL

"Museum 5596."

"Can I speak to Mrs Bell?"

"I am afraid Mrs Bell is out."

"But you are Mrs Bell; I am your brother George."

"I am afraid Mrs Bell is out."

"But Vanessa, I know your voice; this is George Duckworth."

"I am afraid Mrs Bell is out."

"But, confound it, you *are* Mrs Bell."

"I am afraid Mrs Bell is out."

Sir George slammed down the receiver.

It was not often that Vanessa employed an imaginary parlourmaid, and there were times when she would have responded kindly enough to almost any caller; but at that moment she had no time for anyone save the agreeable young woman who reclined naked upon a sofa. Her middle years were made happy by her ability to employ a model and to preserve those sacred hours that were dedicated to work with the help of a fictitious domestic. It was the lack of any such assistance which had brought her into sad collision with Lydia Lopokova, who was soon to become Mrs Maynard Keynes. Lydia, charming, and welcome almost everywhere, started with the enormous advantage of living in the same house as Vanessa; she needed no telephone, she was universally welcome, and she wandered innocently into the studio for a chat at almost any time of day. In the end Vanessa made what she called "a statement"—her statements sometimes sounded more like ultimatums—and her working hours were saved, but not without some protests from Mr Keynes. This incident and others earned for Vanessa the reputation of a dragon, a terrible monster who guarded the life-room with fire and flames. I doubt whether she did much to contradict the popular legend. Nevertheless, since I did for a time work beside her, I feel it is right to say that her reputation was not entirely deserved. On two occasions I saw her throw up her morning's work in order to assist a friend in trouble. On the first occasion it was in fact a woman who had fallen into debt and other difficulties and needed sympathy; on the second, it was a last-minute theatrical crisis in which the fate of a ballet embodying the work of Blake, Vaughan Williams and Gwen Raverat was in peril. That morning Vanessa and I found ourselves painting innumerable ballet dresses in order to be ready for that night's performance. It has to be remembered that here Vanessa was responding to one of the occasional emergencies of a fellow artist. Lydia Lopokova's friendly incursions resulted from a more or less constant need to communicate, to discuss, perhaps for the hundredth time, the genius of dear Maynard, the infamy of Diaghilev, of Massine, and in fact of nearly everyone connected with the ballet in London, and the undeniable differences which might be discovered between the climate of Russia and that of England, as also between their languages, their literature and their polity. A less dedicated painter than Vanessa might have discovered, as she did, that her capacity for responding to conversational openings such as these diminished rapidly.

A time came when she decided that she no longer needed a house, or rather part of a house, in Gordon Square. In the late twenties she moved into a studio at No. 8 Fitzroy Street adjacent to one Duncan Grant had taken over from Sickert at the beginning of the decade. They were huge, tall rooms looking onto a back alley and communicating with the street by means of a clanking metallic passageway. Here there was ample studio space, with room enough for a sleeping and dining area, a bathroom, and a kitchen: here too one child could be accommodated at a time, and here an imaginary parlourmaid could be employed to deal with the outside world.

I think that in many ways the time that Vanessa spent at No. 8 Fitzroy Street was the happiest of her life, although her happiness ended abruptly in 1937.[1] The earlier years of that decade were years in which Duncan's success, always as important to her as her own,

---

[1] I.e., when her son Julian was killed in Spain.

was continually growing. She saw a good deal of her children in London and a great deal of them at Charleston. Although she claimed that Bloomsbury had come to an end in 1914, there was still a good deal of it that she could see either in London or in Sussex. Those of Duncan's friends who bored her could be entertained in his part of the building. It says a good deal for her character that Duncan's lovers usually ended by becoming her intimate friends.

Like her sister Virginia, Vanessa was always anxious to dispense as far as possible with servants; the very nice woman who came in to help with domestic chores was rapid and inconspicuous. Vanessa made breakfast and lunch for herself and Duncan on the studio stove, and sometimes a more substantial meal in the evenings. She worked until the light failed, when she would sometimes design decorations or write letters. After dinner she and Duncan would often go to a movie.

Today when we think of her, I suspect that we refer to Marcel Gimond's study of her head. It is a gravely beautiful, an Olympian head, but neither the sculptor's intention nor his medium allow us to suppose that it is a head that might be distorted by laughter or by distress; and yet in thinking of Vanessa I do see her thus transformed. My elder brother, speaking with unconscious prescience, likened her to Demeter, a goddess who with terrible velocity could change from summer to winter. My earliest memories are of her summer laughter, specifically of an evening seated on a bench in Gordon Square when she told us how children were made and born, an account which she made so overwhelmingly droll that I rolled helpless with mirth off the bench.

W. B. Yeats once told Vanessa that she had supernatural gifts. A stern rationalist, she rejected the idea with indignation. I think that it was more generally felt that, although far from stupid, she was not an intellectual, and this I think was true and is not incompatible with the fact that she was on affectionate terms with the owners of brilliant minds—Keynes, Strachey, Fry, and indeed her sister. But one was always being mildly surprised by her erudition. I had never suspected that she had any Latin until my brother was preparing to enter a public school and she was able to introduce him to Virgil.

But it was in the domestic and managerial line of business that she excelled. It was here that she excited the admiration of Maynard Keynes, even though he sometimes suffered as a result of her regulations. It was he who called her Ludendorff Bell, comparing her to the Prussian commander of terrifying efficiency who manipulated the armies of Germany with such verve and skill as very nearly to break the Allied lines in 1918. She was called upon to exert these talents, which were indeed diplomatic rather than military, when in 1916 she, Duncan Grant, David Garnett, servants, children and a dog arrived at Charleston Farmhouse in order to comply with and perhaps evade the conscription laws of that year. The group was soon to be enlarged by the addition of a governess, her daughter, and her lover, and by the birth of my sister Angelica. Maynard Keynes used the house as a weekend retreat, Mr and Mrs Woolf came over from Asheham, Lytton Strachey arrived and made improper suggestions to the boys on the farm. With the coming of peace, my father would often arrive, bringing with him a number of charming strangers. Duncan, who always had an unlucky talent for attracting the lunatic and criminal classes, brought one hapless young man who believed himself to be the lineal descendant of the pharaoh Tutankhamen, and another, less sympathetic, who specialized in building illicit stills. Maynard brought catamites who ranged from the absolutely charming to the perfectly appalling. Altogether we made an unstable compound which needed to be handled with intelligent dexterity.

In a house inhabited by difficult, temperamental individuals, where machinery consisted of a hot-water system quite as difficult and temperamental as any of the inhabitants, no motorcar, no telephone and no serious shops within six miles, the mere mechanics of housekeeping must have been formidable: but to placate, assuage, reason with or charm all the inhabitants and yet to go on painting their portraits or, what might seem better, some distant landscape, was surely a feat of considerable magnitude.

No doubt Maynard was right when he told Vanessa that she might command armies; but of course they would have bored her to tears. Better to command households, and this I think she must have enjoyed as one enjoys anything that one does well; much better to stay in the nursery. But I am sure that she was happiest away from the world, painting in her studio.

Quentin Bell

ACKNOWLEDGMENTS

For permission to publish the letters of Vanessa Bell, I am greatly indebted to Angelica Garnett, copyright holder, and to Professor Quentin Bell, executor of Vanessa Bell's literary estate. Without the additional trust and support of Anne Olivier Bell, editor of Virginia Woolf's diaries, I could not have completed this book.

Many institutions have supplied me with information and access to their holdings of Bell letters. I am especially grateful for the assistance of Jennifer Booth, Louise Ray, and all the staff of the Tate Gallery Archive, London; Dr. Michael Halls and his successor, Jacqueline Cox, modern archivists at King's College Library, Cambridge; the late Dr. Lola Szladits and her successor, Francis O. Mattson, and the staff of the Berg Collection, New York Public Library; Elizabeth Inglis of the University of Sussex Library; and Robin Harcourt Williams, librarian and archivist to the Marquess of Salisbury, for preparing a typescript of Vanessa Bell letters in the Cecil of Chelwood Papers at Hatfield House. For permission to publish letters in their collections, I would like to thank the Tate Gallery Archive; King's College Library, Cambridge; the Berg Collection, New York Public Library; University of Sussex Library; the British Library; the Harry Ransom Humanities Research Center, University of Texas at Austin; the Houghton Library, Harvard; Cambridge University Library; Princeton University Libraries; Trinity College Library, Cambridge; and the Beinecke Rare Book and Manuscript Library, Yale University.

Many Bell letters remain in private collections. For permission to study and in some cases publish letters in their possession, I wish to thank Frances Partridge, Nigel Nicolson, Angelica Garnett, Quentin and Anne Olivier Bell, Igor and Annabel Anrep, Michael and Alison Bagenal, Baron Hutchinson of Lullington, the Marquess of Salisbury, and Lieutenant Colonel Sir John Baynes. My special thanks go to Henrietta Garnett, for allowing access to the Duncan Grant papers, and to C. H. W. Parish of MacFarlanes, Solicitors, for the great fun of uncovering over sixty Vanessa Bell letters in the miscellaneous luggage and trunks housing the uncatalogued Bussy family papers.

My work was supported in part by a grant from the Office of the Vice President for Research at Arizona State University. Renée Marler and Phil Malone provided room and board in the crucial (and ever-lengthening) final months of this project. Other thanks are due Christopher Naylor and the staff of Charleston Farmhouse; Anthony Bradshaw of the Bloomsbury Workshop; Dr. Frances Spalding; Kenneth Pople; John W. Bicknell; Lord Kennet; Christine Hepworth; and Judith Lowry of the Argosy Bookstore, New York. For support and encouragement at an early stage of this project, I thank Professors Thaïs Morgan, Marjorie Lightfoot, and O. M. Brack of the English Department at Arizona State University. Eternal gratitude goes to Renée Guillory, who assisted with annotation. My agent, Maia Gregory, has been an invaluable advocate throughout the past year. To Shelley Wanger of Pantheon Books, my thanks and respect.

Final acknowledgment is reserved for Melissa DuBose: unflagging editorial assistant, brave chauffeur, trusty companion, and matron of the arts.

A NOTE ON THE TEXT

Vanessa Bell's punctuation was impressionistic and rhetorical. She favored an all-purpose punctuation mark, something between a comma and a dash, and used a modified plus sign as an ampersand. Frequently, she omitted relevant punctuation. The paragraph, for instance, was a structure foreign to her. Since Vanessa was an artist rather than a writer, and my principal aim is to render her words more accessible, I have normalized her punctuation to early-twentieth-century English standards and written out "and." Readers will find I have used a very light hand in these corrections. It seemed out of keeping with Vanessa's prose style and the speed at which she wrote to impose the punctuation of an English teacher onto the letters of a Post-Impressionist artist.

Some spelling variants have been retained: "sate" for "sat" and "eat" for "ate," where they occur; also "moonlight" for "moonlit." Harmless variants in the spelling of some names have also been retained, but for the most part, spelling is silently corrected.

Editorial additions and explanatory notes occur within brackets, as do suggested readings of illegible words; Vanessa's marginalia appear within angled brackets.

Some letters have been abridged, an unhappy but necessary action to reduce repetition and to make room for as many interesting letters as possible. Omitted material is frequently domestic in nature, long lists of potential dates for visits, for instance, or complaints about servants (though plenty of these are retained). No letter is abridged for any other reason.

For brevity, easily recognizable initials are used in the footnotes: VB is Vanessa Bell, even before her marriage, just as Virginia Stephen is VW. JMK is John Maynard Keynes. Vanessa's childhood home, 22 Hyde Park Gate, is abbreviated as HPG. Standard abbreviations for canonical works of Bloomsbury scholarship are employed (e.g., VWLII, 239 refers the reader to the *The Letters of Virginia Woolf*, edited by Nigel Nicolson and Joanne Trautmann, vol. II, p. 239). A selected bibliography follows the text.

BIOGRAPHICAL INTRODUCTION

You have a touch in letter writing that is beyond me. Something unexpected, like coming round a corner in a rose garden and finding it still daylight.

> —Virginia Stephen to Vanessa Bell,
> August 10, 1908 (VWLI, 349)

By the way, Vanessa sent me a splendid description of [Jean Cocteau's ballet] "Parade"; and as the next day I was lunching with Picasso, & Cocteau and Satie, his collaborators, I read it aloud, translating as I went, and it had an immense success.

> —Clive Bell to Virginia Woolf,
> November 23, 1919 (Sussex)

From the rainbow of inks available to her, Vanessa Bell—avant-garde painter and decorator, sexual revolutionary, brazen colorist—chose black. In her old age she took to a blue Biro ballpoint pen, but not very well. There was in this remarkable woman a streak of formality and reserve—the hand that unswervingly chose black ink—coexisting with great tolerance, irreverence, and wit. Each of these letters, selected from over twenty-five hundred that survive, offers a casual self-portrait. Collectively, they present a larger picture of Vanessa Bell's mind and character, of her progression as a modernist and as a female artist, and of her central role in the social and aesthetic life of Bloomsbury.

Celebrated and maligned with equal ferocity, Bloomsbury is the best-documented literary and artistic coterie in twentieth-century Britain. Its philosophical cornerstone was personal liberty, especially sexual liberty and freedom of expression, coupled with an emphasis on personal relationships and an appreciation for the arts. When Thoby Stephen, Vanessa's younger brother, went up to Trinity College, Cambridge, in 1899, Leonard Woolf, Clive Bell, Lytton Strachey, and Saxon Sydney-Turner were among the first students he met. By 1902, most of these men had been elected to the Apostles, a secret society of intellectually stellar undergraduates from Trinity and King's colleges. The novelist E. M. Forster left Cambridge in 1901 but kept his connection with the Apostles, as did the artist and critic Roger Fry and the critic Desmond MacCarthy, two names associated with Bloomsbury but of an older generation. In 1903, John Maynard Keynes was elected to the Apostles, and—with the later addition of Thoby's sisters, Vanessa and Virginia, and the artist Duncan Grant— the nucleus of Bloomsbury was complete. Its name came afterward, of course, from that district in London where Vanessa chose to settle after the death of her father in 1904.

The Bloomsbury group tended toward agnosticism, pacifism, and mild socialism, but as individuals they spanned the political spectrum.[1] The writer and editor Leonard Woolf began his career in the Ceylon Civil Service—"ruling blacks," as his wife Virginia liked to put it— but the experience made him a committed Fabian socialist and anti-imperialist. John Maynard Keynes, then an economist for the Treasury, enraged his pacifist friends one evening during the First World War by suggesting that no one could be a true conscientious objector. He redeemed himself after the Versailles peace conference, however, by resigning his Treasury post to write *The Economic Consequences of the Peace* (1919),[2] a denunciation of the Versailles Treaty and its emphasis on heavy German reparations. He underscored his argument with withering character sketches of President Woodrow Wilson and French statesman Georges Clemenceau. Years later, Keynes accepted a peerage—anathema to Bloomsbury—but again redeemed himself

---

[1]Thoby Stephen is hardest to place, since he died at the age of twenty-six, but he can be said to represent Establishment values far more than any other Bloomsbury figure. He was tall and manly, with a strong character, in the prep-school sense of fair play and duty. At Cambridge he bridged the distance between Clive Bell, a sportsman with a taste for French literature, and his more scholarly friends.
[2]Most of the book was written at Charleston, Vanessa's country home, in August and September 1919.

by founding the Arts Council. Vanessa's husband, Clive Bell, voted Tory, like any country gentleman, and kept the table stocked with pheasant and partridges during the Second World War. He was, nevertheless, an outspoken pacifist, a sexual libertine and *bon vivant,* and an advocate for what seemed the most pernicious experiments—Cubism, for instance—in modern art. In the course of a heated literary correspondence in the 1920s, George Bernard Shaw called Clive "a fathead and a voluptuary."

Most of the contradictions within Bloomsbury are represented in microcosm in Vanessa Bell's own character. After her marriage, and especially during her love affair with Roger Fry, she indulged herself in ribald humor and gossip, always *au courant* with Maynard Keynes' or Lytton Strachey's love affairs with Duncan Grant, or Duncan's romance with her brother Adrian. She and her sister Virginia attended the 1910 Post-Impressionist ball in skimpy togas, in homage to Gauguin's Tahitian women. At another prewar party, Vanessa's insecurely fastened blouse fell away and she danced uninhibitedly naked to the waist. Yet this is a woman who later found herself unable to tell her adolescent daughter the most basic facts about sex.

Though political talk bored her, Vanessa's letters make it clear she was anti-Tory and antimonarchy. She voted Labour, even when she disliked the candidate, but could not endure her servants' conversation for more than a few minutes. She was instinctively feminist, easily shrugging off Edwardian London's expectations for a woman of her class. Yet she preferred male company, and once told Marjorie Strachey, an ardent suffragist, that she found women "more hysterical" than men. In her early years, she also showed a bias toward male artists, perhaps in reaction against the amateur women painters whose works hung beside her own in the New English Art Club and other venues.

From 1910 through the First World War, Vanessa's painting and decorative work placed her in the vanguard of British modernism. She was represented in Roger Fry's legendary Second Post-Impressionist Exhibition and codirected the Omega Workshops, a bold attempt to combine Post-Impressionism and interior design. Her work was praised in Paris and London, but despite her successes, Vanessa worried about succumbing to "the usual female fate": that people would find (or invent) too much of her lover Duncan Grant's influence in her work. From about 1911, Duncan and Vanessa frequently worked side by side, painting the same subjects. Her paintings are often more formally innovative, while his show a greater range of subject matter, as well as a whimsical license foreign to Vanessa's work, or which she may have felt she could not afford. No matter how significant Vanessa's personal and artistic achievements were, she nourished a kernel of disbelief in herself—the legacy of her Victorian girlhood. She once remarked to Duncan that as soon as a collector expressed interest in a particular painting, she began to hate the thing, and then to doubt the collector's taste.

Vanessa was educated at home and learned the art of letter writing from her half-sister, Stella Duckworth. Also from Stella, perhaps, she acquired a sense of the letter as a gift, a "proof of love." To her children, her sister, her lovers, Vanessa wrote almost daily. On the whole, her reserve and shyness argued against written declarations of affection; she preferred to entertain, keeping up a teasing, ironic tone. She excelled in narratives of domestic chaos and embarrassment. She was forever spilling her inkpot down the front of her skirt, then describing the mess. In this, as well as in her attitude toward her painting, her lack of vanity is striking. It shows up in her family photograph albums too. Few beautiful women would keep as many awful, blurred snapshots of themselves, clothes disheveled, eyes half-shut, hair drooping into their mouths. Compared to the 1902 studio portrait of Vanessa by G. C. Beresford, the family photographs show how unconventional she really was, and how daring her choices.[3]

Vanessa often illustrated her letters, sketching her latest composition, or a friend's unflattering hat, or sometimes a dolphin—from her nickname—by the signature. "Dolphin" dates from Vanessa's youth in Hyde Park Gate and is said to refer to her slow, undulating walk, stopping and starting again. She called Virginia "Goat" or "Billy Goat," her childhood nicknames, well into adulthood, and from "Billy Goat" evolved "William," then "Sweet William." Virginia is also "Ape" or "the Apes," another nursery name that lingered into adulthood; Virginia sometimes signed herself "Mandrill" in letters to Leonard Woolf. To Duncan, "Dolphin" gave way to "Beaver" or "Rodent," less flattering but equally affectionate sobriquets. While "Dolphin" is purely sensual, though, "Rodent" gives a hint of Vanessa's mournful aspect, burrowing against Duncan for love and reassurance, making do with whatever he could give her.

[3]The other exceptional aspect of Vanessa Bell's family albums is the dozens of photographs of her children naked—running in the garden, posing as cherubs, leaping onto guests. Vanessa sometimes painted from these photographs, but they are now a convincing testimony of the liberal atmosphere of the Bell family holidays and country life.

Surrounded all her life by professional writers, Vanessa tended to denigrate her writing skills. Certainly she was not above occasional verbal infelicities, reporting for instance that her first baby had "lovely blue eyes which the nurses think will stay there." Virginia, who adored her sister's letters, nonetheless took a malicious pleasure in Vanessa's famous mixed metaphors (e.g., "It's the last feather in the camel's cap"), and liked to contrast their talents, giving herself all the verbal and intellectual skill and Vanessa the intuitive, maternal qualities. "Virginia since early youth has made it her business to create a character for me according to her own wishes," Vanessa complained to Clive.[4] Yet Vanessa was in some respects complicit in these myths. In her letters, especially to Virginia, she maintained a steady self-mockery, presenting herself as unintellectual and uninformed.[5] She enjoyed describing the 1915 dinner party at which she turned blithely to a Mr. Asquith, then prime minister, and asked if he was interested in politics. To some extent her self-mockery masked a genuine lack of confidence, but it was also a carefully constructed comic façade. Curiously, Vanessa's letters—the rare instance when she shares Virginia's medium—display a dramatic streak that the sisters have in common and which appears nowhere in Vanessa's artwork.

The bulk of Vanessa's letters were deposited in the Modern Archives at King's College, Cambridge, in the late 1970s as part of the Charleston Papers (most of which are now owned by the Tate Gallery Archive). These frank and detailed letters to Roger Fry, Clive Bell, and others have proven to be a gold mine for scholars of Bloomsbury, especially biographers. But while brief quotations published out of context may help illuminate the figures surrounding her, they cannot represent Vanessa herself with any depth. My hope is that this larger sample of her letters does so.

Since Frances Spalding's 1983 biography of Vanessa Bell is still readily available, this introduction will be brief and basic, covering only Vanessa's early years. Readers familiar with the Stephen family and life at Hyde Park Gate should feel free to begin with the letters themselves.

From about the age of ten, Vanessa's physical countenance was established—her large, deeply lidded grey eyes and full, curved lips, her

---

[4]From an unpublished letter of June 25, 1910, at the Tate Gallery Archive.
[5]In her letters to Virginia, Vanessa's self-mockery takes the additional function of neutralizing the sisters' rivalry. Having decided from an early age that Virginia would be the writer, Vanessa the artist, they zealously protected their chosen spheres.

low and melodious voice. She was a grave, responsible child, comfortable in her role as the eldest. Once after their mother's death, when the Stephen children were walking in the garden at night, they heard their aged father call to them repeatedly from the house. When he asked later if they had heard him, only Vanessa spoke the painful truth. Her action betrays not only her honesty but a hint of premature cynicism, the root of her dry, mocking wit in later life.

Vanessa Stephen was born into a class once clearly defined: well-educated people, not wealthy, but with enough inherited capital to pursue the vocations of their choice. Her extended family was duty-minded and, unlike Vanessa's agnostic parents, conventionally religious. They occasionally married into the aristocracy, but more often selected spouses from among their family friends, contributing further strands to a minutely woven society of civil servants and men of letters.[6] Vanessa's paternal grandfather, Sir James Stephen, was colonial under secretary of state. His second son, Sir James Fitzjames Stephen, was an eminent lawyer and political theorist. Leslie Stephen (1832–1904), Vanessa's father, abandoned his profession as a Cambridge mathematics don when he realized he had lost his faith (at the time, Cambridge still required ordination of its Fellows). He moved to London and threw himself into an energetic career as a journalist and later editor of the *Cornhill Magazine* and the *Dictionary of National Biography,* contributing almost four hundred individual biographies to the DNB before exhaustion forced him to retire at the age of fifty-nine. At his peak, he was capable of producing eight-thousand-word essays in a single night. Leslie Stephen's capacity for hard work is just one of several traits inherited by his children. He also suffered serious mood swings and hypersensitivity and, as a boy, had displayed a fondness for poetry that his parents found puzzling and tried to curb.

Even as an adult, Leslie scribbled small animals in his letters and the margins of his books. Noting Vanessa's drawing abilities (nurtured, like her letter writing, by Stella), he arranged for her first art lessons at age fifteen from Ebenezer Cooke, much influenced by Ruskin. Vanessa's mother, Julia Stephen (1846–95), may also have encouraged Vanessa's artistic training, though not perhaps to the point of a profession.

Julia's mother, Maria Jackson, had been the fourth of seven beau-

---

[6]Vanessa's maternal relations were distinctly more colorful, and more aristocratic, than the Stephens.

tiful Pattle sisters. Sociable, resourceful women, they were raised in Calcutta but educated at Versailles, home of their maternal grandmother, Thérèse Blin de Grincourt. Several Pattle sisters displayed an uncommon interest in the visual arts. They were frequently painted, and one of them (incidently, the most imperious and least beautiful sister), Julia Margaret Cameron, having been presented with a camera for her fiftieth birthday, produced some of the finest and most evocative portraits of the nineteenth century. It is said she once wandered off absentmindedly while Carlyle and Tennyson, posed according to her wishes, waited out a rainstorm under a tree. In her day, Julia Cameron's photographs were criticized for seeming out of focus, though this was part of her deliberate attempt to push beyond "mere conventional topographic Photography." In her unpublished autobiography, "The Annals of My Glass House," she wrote:

> When I have had such men before my camera my whole soul has endeavored to do its duty towards them in recording faithfully the greatness of the inner as well as the features of the outer man. The photograph thus taken has been almost the embodiment of a prayer.

Though Vanessa would never have described her own work in such spiritual terms, her great-aunt's disregard for mimetic representation was not unlike her own. This may partly explain why Julia Cameron's photographs were among the few inherited works of art that Vanessa hung at Gordon Square in early Bloomsbury days.

Julia's father, John Jackson, was a leading physician at the Medical College in Calcutta. He stayed on for several years, devoted to his practice, after his wife Maria left in 1848 for reasons of health, bringing her three daughters to be raised at the Kensington home of their aunt Sarah and her husband, Thoby Prinsep, a retired Anglo-Indian administrator. Little Holland House was a kind of weekend retreat for the mid-Victorian cultural elite. On a given Sunday, Disraeli, Carlyle, Tennyson, and Rossetti might arrive for tea and croquet. Sarah Prinsep and her sisters had a gift for putting great men at their ease, a certain playful deference combined with maternal warmth and solicitude. G. F. Watts lived at Little Holland House for many years, and Julia was not only painted by him and other artists, including Edward Burne-Jones, but was also frequently photographed by Julia Margaret Cameron. There she met the novelist Thackeray and his daughters, the youngest of whom, Harriet (Minny), married Leslie

Stephen in 1867. In the same year, Julia married the handsome barrister Herbert Duckworth.

Both were passionate unions, and both ended tragically. In 1870, Herbert Duckworth reached into a fig tree and burst an unsuspected abscess. He died almost immediately, leaving Julia with two young children, George (1868–1934) and Stella (1869–97), and a third, Gerald (1870–1930), born six weeks after Herbert's death. Julia was just twenty-four. She fell into deep mourning, which lasted for years, permanently altering her character. Feeling that no happiness was left for her, she devoted herself completely to the care of the sick and needy.

Minny and Leslie had a daughter, Laura, in 1870, but within a few years she began to display signs of mental deficiency. It is difficult now to determine how much this deficiency was exacerbated by Leslie's insistence that Laura was simply a "wayward" child, and by his repeated and angry attempts to make her behave. In any case, it was a heartbreaking situation, and even more so when Minny, again pregnant, died suddenly in 1875 after a seizure.

Although Julia Duckworth's friendship had principally been with Minny's sister, the writer Anne Thackeray, she extended her sympathy to Leslie Stephen. Aside from their grief, they had in common their agnosticism and their work ethic. The most essential factor to their union, though, may have been Leslie's emotional neediness, coupled with Julia's compulsion to care for others. Even after their marriage in March 1878 and the birth of their children, Julia was frequently away on charitable missions, especially those involving nursing. She wrote several essays and children's stories but published only one short book, *Notes from Sick Rooms* (1883), which asserts, among other useful minutiae, that "the origin of crumbs in bed has never excited sufficient attention among the scientific world."[7]

Vanessa was Leslie and Julia's first child, born May 30, 1879, followed the next year by Thoby, whom Vanessa adored, then in 1882 by Virginia, and finally by Adrian in 1883. No. 22 Hyde Park Gate, Kensington, was already full of children, three Duckworths and Laura Stephen, but the little Stephens formed a clique within the household. They were physically separated, also, occupying the day and night nurseries in the upper two stories of the house. Laura had in fact a

---

[7]Professors Diane Gillespie and Elizabeth Steele have published Julia's writings in *Julia Duckworth Stephen: Stories for Children, Essays for Adults* (Syracuse, N.Y.: Syracuse University Press, 1987).

nurse of her own, not only to feed and clothe her but to help control her sudden bursts of violence—scissors flung into the fireplace, wild tantrums. The little Stephens were closest to their half-sister Stella, who idolized Julia, emulating her selflessness. "Stella was always the beautiful attendant handmaid," Virginia wrote, "feeding her mother's vivid flame, rejoicing in the service, and making it the central duty of her life."[8] Julia acknowledged to Leslie that she was especially hard on Stella, since she considered the girl part of herself.

Like Little Holland House, 22 Hyde Park Gate attracted luminaries: the writers Henry James and George Meredith, and the American ambassador James Russell Lowell (Virginia's unofficial godfather) were frequent visitors. The younger Stephens soaked up the grown-ups' conversation during tea and dinner. Alone, the children read *Titbits* and *Punch* faithfully, as well as the novels of George Eliot and Charlotte M. Yonge. In winter they skated on the Round Pond in Kensington Gardens. When the surface thawed, they sailed toy boats across it, and played cricket nearby. Vanessa remembered their thrill at finding the corpse of a small black dog there in the high grass. At home, the children took lessons in history, Latin, French, and mathematics from their parents and Stella. Leslie, recognizing her gifts, gave Virginia the run of his extensive library.

The atmosphere at Hyde Park Gate was palpably intellectual compared to Little Holland House, and would have made the Pattle sisters' "aesthetic" interests seem merely frivolous. Although Vanessa met some artists, such as Watts and Charles Furse, through her family, she felt out of place among her aggressively literate siblings, and shy of her talent in such a different sphere. "When she won the prize at her drawing school," Virginia recalled,

> she hardly knew, so shy was she, at the recognition of a secret, how to tell me, in order that I might repeat the news at home. "They've given me the thing—I don't know why." "What thing?" "O they say I've won it—the book—the prize you know."[9]

The house itself was no consolation to Vanessa: tall and dimly lit, crowded with dark, spindly furniture and indifferent paintings.

Most of the younger Stephens' favorite childhood memories were set at Talland House, St. Ives, Cornwall, where the family spent each

[8]VW, *Moments of Being*, 42.
[9]VW, *Moments of Being*, 30.

summer. Leslie, a great walker, led his children briskly through the countryside and taught them to swim in the ocean. In the afternoon the children played cricket—Rupert Brooke and his brother were frequently among the players—and, after dinner, laid out rags soaked in rum and treacle to trap moths. Late at night, they would creep outside with lamps to secure their captives. Virginia Woolf's novel *To the Lighthouse* (1927) so effectively evoked those summers, and the characters of Leslie and Julia Stephen, that Vanessa found it painful to read.

Julia might reasonably have relaxed a little at St. Ives, despite her large household. But even here, she visited the neighborhood poor and sick, delivering food baskets. Her exhaustion was obvious, and in photographs from the 1880s she looks much older than her forty-odd years.

In May 1895, just before Vanessa's sixteenth birthday, Julia Stephen died of influenza. Well-intentioned aunts and cousins—a sea of mourning black—flooded Hyde Park Gate, bent on comforting the orphans. Virginia suffered her first nervous breakdown at this time. Stella, trying to conceal her considerable grief, quietly assumed her mother's household duties. Leslie, however, did everything but conceal his pain, and his constant emotional displays and demands for sympathy alienated his children, especially Vanessa. Only Stella remained patient and consoling. When, despite Leslie's grumbling, Stella married the solicitor John (Jack) Waller Hills in 1897, Vanessa was expected, as the next female in line, to take over responsibility for the servants and the household books.

In some ways, Vanessa made an excellent housekeeper: competent and efficient, her mind elsewhere. She unfailingly cared for Virginia, who was still recovering from Julia's death. But unlike her mother and Stella, Vanessa was unmoved by Leslie Stephen's moods and rages. On more than one occasion, unable despite all economies and reasoned arguments to convince him that they were not approaching bankruptcy, she conspired with the cook to doctor the household books. After Stella's sudden death of peritonitis three months after her wedding, Vanessa had no close female advisors, no one to intercede for her with Leslie. She developed a steely determination. Her one aim was to get her domestic duties over with, so that she could return to her art.

No wonder George Duckworth questioned Vanessa's candidacy for Victorian womanhood. Since their mother's death, he had taken it upon himself to prepare Vanessa for Society, coercing her into attending dinners and dances, alternately pleasing and embarrassing her with expensive gifts—an opal necklace, an Arab mare. When she rebelled, he burst into tears or kissed her. George's physical affection for Vanessa and Virginia has excited much speculation in the last five years, and indeed caused a small uproar of disbelief when first exposed by Quentin Bell in his 1972 biography of Virginia Woolf. From Vanessa's letters and Virginia's autobiographical essays, it is clear that George forcibly kissed and embraced his half-sisters, presumably with an erotic motive, perhaps unconscious. But there is no evidence to support more focused sexual advances.[10] George Duckworth's greatest crime was conventionality, coupled with only average intelligence. He meant well, but he was a major factor in the misery of Vanessa's home life.

As the voice of propriety, George was especially irritating during Vanessa's first romance. After Stella's death in 1897, her widower, Jack Waller Hills, spent each weekend with the Stephens in the house in Gloucestershire they had rented for the summer holidays, and then took Vanessa and Virginia with him to stay at Corby Castle, his parent's home near Scotland, and pursued a close friendship with them. Jack was a very different young man from George or Gerald Duckworth, or even from Thoby. Virginia has described Jack's welcome frankness about sexual matters, for instance, and what a revelation male desire was to her and Vanessa. Comforting Jack in his tremendous grief, Vanessa found herself becoming attracted to him. Her feelings were reciprocated. Aunt Mary Fisher somehow got wind of this and sent warning letters to Hyde Park Gate. George was alerted. Even Virginia, Vanessa's staunch ally, mentioned George's worries to her. Though Jack Hills had political ambitions and was thus unlikely to pursue an engagement to his dead wife's half-sister,[11] the furor over her private life roused Vanessa's defenses, and contributed to her uncertainty that in an ideal life, there was no place for Aunt Marys.

From 1896 to 1900, Vanessa studied at Sir Arthur Cope's art school in South Kensington and in 1901 was accepted into the Royal Academy Schools. Despite what would later come to be her contempt for the academy, these were exhilarating years. The calm, detached ob-

---

[10]Some evidence in fact contradicts the sexual-abuse theory. George Duckworth's caresses often took place in public, for instance, and the sisters did not seem to distinguish these from his private embraces.
[11]The marriage would not have been permitted under English law in any case, and the couple would have had to be married abroad.

servation of the life room, the absorption with pure form, became as necessary to her as food. It was here she found her first artist friends and received criticism from such established painters as Sargent. Above all, there were no needy or prying relations, no George Duck-worth. She had no responsibilities but the work itself.

For Vanessa the death of Leslie Stephen in February 1904 was the effective end of the Victorian era. Her immediate impulse was to escape Kensington and all it represented. Though she must at times have felt insecure—there were, after all, no models for the sort of domestic revolution she planned—her letters reveal only her unwav-ering determination to find a better way of life, one not founded on convention—above all, a life conducive to art. Within a year of Leslie Stephen's death Vanessa had taken 46 Gordon Square, Bloomsbury, and moved there with the younger Stephens.

It was at Gordon Square that the group known as Bloomsbury came into existence, but Vanessa's letters take up the story before this point and are more evocative than any summary.

CHRONOLOGY

1879	*May 30*	Vanessa Stephen born at 22 Hyde Park Gate, Kensington.
1880	*September 8*	Julian Thoby Stephen born.
1882	*January 25*	Adeline Virginia Stephen born.
	Summer	The Stephen family spends the first of twelve summers at Talland House, St. Ives, Cornwall.
1883	*October 27*	Adrian Leslie Stephen born.
1894	*February*	Virginia and Vanessa stay with the painter G. F. Watts in Guildford, Surrey.
1895	*May 5*	Death of Vanessa's mother, Julia Stephen (née Jackson).
1896		Vanessa begins drawing classes, first with Ebenezer Cooke, then with Sir Arthur Cope, R.A.
1897	*July 19*	Death of Vanessa's half-sister, Stella Hills.
1899	*October 3*	Thoby enters Trinity College, Cambridge, soon meeting Leonard Woolf, Saxon Sydney-Turner, Clive Bell, and Lytton Strachey.

1901	*September*	Vanessa enters the Royal Academy Schools.
1902	*April*	Vanessa and her half-brother George Duckworth go to Rome and Florence for three weeks, returning at news of Leslie Stephen's ill health.
1903	*March*	Vanessa stays with G. F. Watts.
1904	*February 22*	Sir Leslie Stephen's death from cancer.
	April–May	The Stephen children travel in Italy. Vanessa, Virginia, and Violet Dickinson stop in Paris on their return, where Clive Bell entertains them. Visits to the studios of Rodin and Gerald Kelly.
	October	Vanessa leaves the Royal Academy Schools and studies briefly at the Slade School of Fine Art. Also, she orchestrates the Stephens' move to 46 Gordon Square, Bloomsbury.
	December 14	Virginia's first publication (an unsigned book review) appears in *The Guardian*.
1905		Vanessa meets Duncan Grant, a cousin of Lytton Strachey's.
	February 16	Thoby starts his "Thursday Evenings."
	April	Vanessa exhibits for the first time, in the summer exhibition at the New Gallery, London. Her painting (a portrait of Lady Robert Cecil) attracts a portrait commission from a stranger.
	August	Clive Bell proposes to Vanessa and is rejected.
	October	First meeting of Vanessa's "Friday Club." Their first exhibition is held a month later.
1906	*July 31*	Vanessa rejects Clive's second marriage proposal.
	September–October	The Stephens and Violet Dickinson travel in Greece; Vanessa is ill.

	November	Vanessa and Thoby both confined to bed at 46 Gordon Square; Violet Dickinson ill at her home at Welwyn. On the 20th, Thoby Stephen dies of typhoid fever.
	November 22	Vanessa accepts Clive's third marriage proposal.
1907	*February 7*	Marriage of Vanessa and Clive at St. Pancras Registry Office, Bloomsbury.
	April	The Bells honeymoon in Paris. Thereafter, they both visit Paris frequently, usually once or twice a year.
	December 21	First meeting of the Play Reading Society at 46 Gordon Square: the Bells, Virginia and Adrian, Lytton Strachey, and Saxon Sydney-Turner.
1908	*February 4*	Birth of Julian Heward Bell at 46 Gordon Square.
	June–July	Vanessa exhibits three paintings with the Friday Club.
	July	Vanessa exhibits at the Allied Artists' Association at the Albert Hall.
1909	*June*	Vanessa exhibits *Iceland Poppies* (1909) at the New English Art Club; the piece is praised by Walter Sickert, who writes to Vanessa: "Continuez!"
1910	*January*	The Bells renew their acquaintance with Roger Fry.
	February 25	Roger Fry talks to the Friday Club.
	Summer	Vanessa exhibits with the Friday Club and the New English Art Club.
	August 19	Quentin Claudian Stephen Bell born at 46 Gordon Square.
	November 8	Opening of Roger Fry's First Post-Impressionist Exhibition ("Manet and the Post-Impressionists") at the Grafton Galleries, London.

1911	*February*	Vanessa exhibits with the Friday Club.
	April	The Bells, Roger Fry, and H. T. J. Norton travel in Turkey. Vanessa suffers a miscarriage and begins a love affair with her nurse, Roger. Virginia travels from London to help Vanessa home.
	July 3	Leonard Woolf, on leave from the Ceylon Civil Service, dines at 46 Gordon Square.
	November	Virginia and the Bells take the lease of Asheham House, Beddingham, Sussex.
1912	*January 11*	Leonard Woolf proposes to Virginia, who stalls.
	February	Vanessa exhibits four works, including "Design for Screen," with the Friday Club.
	May 29	Virginia agrees to marry Leonard.
	July	Vanessa represented in Roger Fry's "Exposition de Quelques Indépendants Anglais" at the Galerie Barbazanges, Paris.
	August	Vanessa's first sale: *The Spanish Model,* bought by the Contemporary Art Society for five guineas; On August 10 Virginia and Leonard marry.
	October	Roger Fry's Second Post-Impressionist Exhibition opens; Vanessa represented by four paintings, including *The Spanish Model.*
1913	*March*	Vanessa represented in the first exhibition of the Grafton Group, held at the Alpine Club Gallery.
	July 8	Roger Fry's Omega Workshops open at 33 Fitzroy Square, Bloomsbury. Vanessa and Duncan Grant are company directors.

1914	*January*	In Paris, Gertrude Stein takes Vanessa and others to the studios of Picasso and Matisse, where Vanessa meets these artists for the first time; Vanessa exhibits six works, including a screen, in the second exhibition of the Grafton Group.
	Spring	Vanessa contributes a mosaic floor for the Omega decoration of Lady Ian Hamilton's home at 1 Hyde Park Gardens, London.
	May	Vanessa exhibits five paintings in the "20th Century Art Exhibition" at Whitechapel.
1915		Vanessa, in love with Duncan Grant since 1913, begins a physical relationship with him.
	May	Costume exhibition at the Omega Workshops.
	Spring–Summer	Vanessa at Eleanor House, West Wittering, Sussex. In August she takes the Grange, Bosham, Sussex.
1916		Vanessa's first one-artist exhibition, a small show at Omega.
	Spring–Summer	Vanessa with Duncan Grant and David Garnett at Wissett Lodge, Halesworth, Suffolk.
	October	Move to Charleston Farmhouse, Firle, Sussex.
1917	*May*	Vanessa shows five copies at the Omega Workshops "Copies" exhibition.
	July	First publication of the Hogarth Press, *Two Stories* by Leonard and Virginia Woolf.
	September	Vanessa well represented in "The New Movement in Art," shown at Birmingham and the Mansard Gallery, London.
	November	Vanessa's work shown with others' at the Omega Workshops.

1918	*August*	Six Bell paintings included in "Englische moderne Malerei" at the Kunsthaus, Zurich.
	September–October	Duncan and Vanessa decorate Maynard Keynes' sitting room at 46 Gordon Square.
	December 25	Angelica Vanessa Bell, the child of Duncan and Vanessa, born at Charleston.
1919		Closure of the Omega Workshops; Vanessa joins the London Group, thereafter exhibiting regularly with them. This year she and Duncan begin to decorate Maynard Keynes' rooms at Webb Court, King's College, Cambridge (completed 1922).
	March	Vanessa rents James Strachey's flat at 36 Regent Square, London, for one year.
	Summer	Meetings with Derain and Picasso in London.
	November	London Group exhibition.
1920		Vanessa moves to 50 Gordon Square.
	March 4	First meeting of the Memoir Club.
	Spring	Vanessa exhibits with others in Paris at Charles Vildrac's gallery.
	May	Travels to Rome with Maynard Keynes and Duncan. They stay with Bernard Berenson in Florence and visit Picasso in Paris.
	November	Vanessa, Duncan, and Robert Lotiron exhibit watercolors at the Independent Gallery, London.
1921	*February*	With Duncan, Vanessa decorates Adrian and Karin Stephen's rooms at 50 Gordon Square.
	March	Vanessa contributes to "Some Contemporary English Artists" at the Independent Gallery.
	October	With Duncan and her family, Vanessa takes La Maison Blanche, St. Tropez.

1922		Vanessa moves back to 46 Gordon Square.
	February	Vanessa takes a Paris studio for one month.
	June	Vanessa's first major one-artist exhibition, at the Independent Gallery: 27 paintings shown, which sell well.
1923	*May*	Vanessa travels in Spain with Roger Fry and Duncan.
1925		Vanessa moves to 37 Gordon Square.
	January	With Duncan, Vanessa decorates the loggia at Moon Hall, Gomshall, Surrey, home of Peter Harrison.
	March–April	Vanessa and Duncan decorate Raymond Mortimer's drawing room at 6 Gordon Place, Bloomsbury.
	October	Vanessa represented in "Modern Designs in Needlework" at the Independent Gallery.
1926	*May*	Vanessa becomes a founder member of the London Artists' Association, showing with them at the Leicester Galleries and, later this year, exhibitions in Berlin, New York, and Pittsburgh.
	May–June	Tour of Italy with Duncan.
	October	Vanessa and Duncan decorate Clive Bell's flat at 50 Gordon Square.
1927	*January–May*	Vanessa and her family take the Villa Corsica, Cassis.
	May 5	Publication of Virginia's novel *To the Lighthouse,* based on the Stephen family summers at St. Ives.
	August	Vanessa and Duncan decorate the garden room of the Château d'Auppegard, near Dieppe, the home of Ethel Sands and Nan Hudson.

1928		Vanessa acquires a ten-year lease of La Bergère, Cassis, in exchange for funding its renovation; regular visits until the onset of war. Also, Vanessa takes a studio (which doubles as her pied-à terre) at 8 Fitzroy Street, adjoining Duncan's.
	November	Vanessa exhibits with the LAA at the Marie Sterner Galleries, New York.
1929	*January–February*	To Germany, Austria, and Prague with Duncan.
1930		With Duncan, decorates Penns-in-the-Rocks, Withyham, Sussex, the home of Lady Gerald Wellesley.
	February	One-artist exhibition at the Cooling Galleries; catalogue introduction by Virginia Woolf.
1931	*December*	Vanessa included in an exhibition of Allan Walton textiles at the Cooling Galleries.
1932		Vanessa executes decor for *High Yellow,* performed by the Camargo Ballet.
	January 21	Death of Lytton Strachey.
	June	"Recent Paintings by Duncan Grant, Vanessa Bell, and Keith Baynes" at Thos. Agnew & Sons, London.
	December	With Duncan, Vanessa decorates and furnishes a music room at the Lefevre Gallery; Virginia guarantees sales of £60, and does end up buying several items.
1933	*January*	Vanessa designs decor and costumes for Frederick Ashton's ballet *Pomona,* performed by the Sadler's Wells Ballet.
1934		Vanessa designs decor for Ethel Smyth's ballet *Fête Galante.*
	March	One-artist exhibition at the Lefevre Gallery.
	September 9	Death of Roger Fry.

	October	Vanessa's decorated pottery for Foley China is shown in "Modern Art for the Table" at Harrods.
1935	*January 18*	Virginia's play *Freshwater* performed at Vanessa's Fitzroy Street studio: Vanessa plays her great-aunt, the Victorian photographer Julia Margaret Cameron.
	Summer	In Rome; Vanessa commissioned to design panels for a room on the R.M.S. *Queen Mary.*
	August 29	Julian Bell leaves for a teaching position in China.
c. 1936–37		With Duncan, Vanessa decorates the Chelsea home of Nan Hudson and Ethel Sands.
1937	*January*	Vanessa represented in "British Contemporary Art," Rosenberg & Helft, London.
	March	Julian Bell returns from China in hopes of fighting in Spain with the International Brigade.
	May	One-artist exhibition at the Lefevre Gallery; Vanessa visits Picasso in Paris while he is working on *Guernica.*
	July 18	Death of Julian Bell in Spain. Vanessa receives the news by telephone at Fitzroy Street on July 20.
1938		With Duncan, teaches informally at the Euston Road School.
	Autumn	Publication by the Hogarth Press of *Julian Bell: Essays, Poems and Letters,* edited by Quentin and Vanessa Bell.
1939		Vanessa and Duncan join the Mural Society, exhibiting in its first show at the Tate Gallery; they spend 1939–45 at Charleston.

1940		8 Fitzroy Street studios destroyed by an incendiary bomb. Most of Vanessa's early work is lost.
1940–43		With Duncan and Quentin Bell, Vanessa designs and executes murals for the parish church at Berwick, a village near Charleston. Decorations consecrated in the summer of 1943.
1941	*June*	Vanessa exhibits with Frank Dobson and Algernon Newton at the Leicester Galleries.
	March 28	Suicide of Virginia Woolf.
	July	Opening of Miller's Gallery in Lewes, Sussex; the Bells and Duncan are active in its support.
1942	*Spring*	Marriage of Angelica Bell and David Garnett.
	June	Vanessa represented in "Robert Colquhoun and Notable British Artists" at the Lefevre Gallery.
1944	*February*	"Cinderella" decorations at Devonshire Hill School in Tottenham, executed by Duncan and Vanessa, opened by Maynard Keynes.
1946		Vanessa and Duncan contribute large decorative panels to the "Britain Can Make It" exhibition.
	April	Death of Maynard Keynes.
1947–60		Frequent trips to France and Italy with Duncan, often in the company of Edward Le Bas.
1948	*May*	Death of Adrian Stephen; Vanessa becomes the last surviving member of her family.
1949		Vanessa joins the committee of the Edwin Austin Abbey Memorial Trust Fund for Mural Painting.

1951		Vanessa contributes *The Garden Room* (1951) to the "60 Paintings for '51" exhibition sponsored by the Arts Council.
1952	*February*	Marriage of Quentin Bell and Anne Olivier Popham; Vanessa later moves into a flat at 26a Canonbury Square, Islington, vacated by Olivier.
1953		Exhibition at Ferens Art Gallery, Hull, by past members of the LAA; Vanessa sits on the jury for the Prix de Rome awards.
1954		Vanessa joins and exhibits with the Royal West of England Academy at Bristol.
1955		Duncan and Vanessa take the 28 Percy Street flat vacated by Saxon Sydney-Turner.
1956	*February*	One-artist exhibition at the Adams Gallery, London.
1959		Vanessa suffers from bronchial pleurisy; Tate retrospective of Duncan Grant's work.
1961	*April 7*	Vanessa dies at Charleston of heart failure, following an attack of bronchitis.
	April 12	Burial in Firle churchyard.
1962		Death of Saxon Sydney-Turner.
1964		Death of Clive Bell.
1969		Death of Leonard Woolf.
1978	*May 9*	Death of Duncan Grant; buried beside Vanessa in Firle churchyard.

Selected Letters of
VANESSA BELL

CHAPTER ONE

1885–1906

Few of Vanessa's earliest letters survive. There are some to her parents, so early that they constituted writing lessons; several to Thoby, away at school; none to Adrian; none to her Fisher, Vaughan, or Stephen cousins. If she kept a childhood diary (Virginia suggested as much at the beginning of her own 1897 diary), it too is lost. All but a handful of her twenty-five hundred or so extant letters were written in adulthood. This gives us a curious image of Vanessa, who seems to emerge from a brief childhood fully developed: capable, sardonic, resolute. At age eighteen Vanessa was responsible enough to assume her half-sister Stella's duties as woman of the house, in charge of servants, ordering meals, keeping accounts, presiding every afternoon at the tea table. In between these tasks she carved out hours for sketching and study, defending her time as best she could from the well-meaning persistence of George Duckworth and his society matrons.

But in fact, as she herself noted, Stephens were late developers. The letters in this chapter show an ambitious art student, beginning to voice her ideas, though still dependent on her teachers' praise. She may quote the Victorian painter G. F. Watts with amusement, but she quotes John Singer Sargent with reverence. Her closest relationship was with her sister Virginia. Their correspondence in these years is amorous and unguarded. And when, after Sir Leslie's death in 1904, Vanessa organized the move from respectable Kensington to a then unfashionable Bloomsbury address, her motivation was largely aesthetic. She longed for white walls. Dark, cluttered Victorian decor was the principal enemy; only later did her moral sense rebel.

Changes came slowly. At 46 Gordon Square, Bloomsbury, Vanessa's closest friends were Thoby's Cambridge colleagues, writers and civil servants, all male. The etiquette of the Victorian drawing room remained crisply intact: when Vanessa declined Clive's second marriage proposal, she addressed him as "Mr Bell." Margery Snowden, her friend from the Royal Academy Schools, was her only intimate beyond Old Bloomsbury.[1] Gradually, Vanessa sought the company of other artists, and started the Friday Club in 1905 to break the stranglehold of literature and philosophy over her social life. Though the group overlapped a little with Thoby's Thursday Evening crowd, it was still an occasion set aside for the discussion of Vanessa's own great passion—art—rather than, say, the nature of Good. She began to exhibit her work. She accepted fewer invitations from her aunts and cousins.

These were not uproarious years, however. Vanessa remained a respectable young woman, silent in company, conventionally (though often untidily) dressed,[2] and still very much Virginia's caretaker.

Thoby Stephen died of typhoid on November 30, 1906. Two days later Vanessa accepted Clive's third proposal. Like the move to Gordon Square, this was partly an instinctive decision—flight from pain—and partly a measured step into a new life.

BERG

---

[1]"Old Bloomsbury" refers simply (or not so simply) to the prewar Gordon Square crowd, those who regularly attended Thoby's Thursday Evenings, or remained close to the Stephens after Thoby's death. Few scholars would offer the same list of Old Bloomsbury members, and in fact the Bloomsberries (a phrase coined by Molly MacCarthy in about 1910) themselves often disagreed. Very roughly, Old Bloomsbury includes Thoby, Adrian, Virginia and Vanessa, Clive Bell, E. M. Forster, Saxon Sydney-Turner, Lytton Strachey, Maynard Keynes, Leonard Woolf, Roger Fry, Desmond and Molly MacCarthy, H. T. J. Norton, possibly Marjorie and James Strachey, possibly Sydney Waterlow, and a few figures not later linked with Bloomsbury, such as Hilton Young, Charles Tennyson, and Robin Mayor.
[2]Many years later, Rebecca West remarked that both Virginia and Vanessa always looked as if they had been pulled through a hedge backward before going out.

I-1. To Leslie Stephen[1]

[Summer c. 1885]   *[Brighton]*

Dear Father,

Ginia and Thoby rode in a goat carriage. I rode on a donkey called Black Bess, Thoby's was Polly, Ginia's was Topsy. I went down on the beach and picked up a shell and got a white bit of glass I found, But Georgie took me nearly right into the sea, he did; and I got up on a wall and Georgie went round to see if he could try and get up but he couldn't, and Georgie lifted me up on the wall, and thats how I got up, and I tried to pull Georgie up, but I couldn't because he was too heavy, of course. Granny[2] has given us some chocolates, and we got some airballs ourselves first Ginia's was busted, then Thoby's was busted and then Ginia busted mine. I had some Mutton for dinner and some very hot potatoes and some Tapioca pudding.

We can see the see as well as when we're at the lodgings. I told Georgie I thought Ginia had a nice 'spectatle ride this morning. I say that Adrian's a nice pretty little boy. Georgie and Gerald are very agravaking boys. Goodbye I send you a kiss. I send my love to Rob and to Spot and to Spot's puppy. I like him.

Vanessa Stephen Butterfly

BERG

[1]This letter is printed without corrections.
[2]Maria Jackson (1818–92), Vanessa's maternal grandmother, spent her final years in Brighton.

I-2. To Thoby Stephen

Monday [November 1896]   *22, Hyde Park Gate, S.W.*

My dear Tobs,

I meant to write to you when we were at Boulogne[1] but somehow I never did. We got back yesterday after a beastly crossing. I dare say you wouldn't have minded it, but Georgie and I thought it horrible. It's very nice to hear English spoken by everyone and to be able to be rude again. French people are dreadfully polite. You have to take off your hat and make a little bow if you go into a shop or railway carriage! We went to Amiens one day and saw the Cathedral[2] there. An old woman took us right up to the top of it and it was rather giddy climbing about on narrow ledges and looking down on the roofs of houses. We took a lot of photographs, but we haven't had time to develop any yet. We had chocolate and rolls in our rooms at about 8.30, luncheon at 12 of about 6 courses, and dinner at 7. On Saturday we went to a very improper French play. The ladies looked as if they were almost entirely naked with only thin muslin skirts, though they really had on tights of course. On Sunday we went to mass. The French are most disgusting people I think. They never seem to wash and they spit everywhere and always.

I don't know if you will have got your caramels yet. I hope they won't all have stuck together, but I expect they will have.

Your loving
Nessa

KCC

---

[1] In November 1896 VB, VW, and George Duckworth traveled for a week in northern France with George's aunt Minna Duckworth. I am indebted to Olivier Bell for suggesting the date of this letter.
[2] Amiens Cathedral of Notre Dame, begun 1220.

I-3. To Thoby Stephen

Feb. 6th, 1901   22, *Hyde Park Gate, S.W.*

My dear Thobs,

I couldn't write to you last night as I meant to, as we all went off to the pantomime.[1] I had a very uncomfortable journey home, sustained by your muffins. They really were most comforting. You might send a line to say how you are. Don't go and get pneumonia now. I'm afraid this shows that you ought to be very careful always about catching cold. I hope you had some amusing visitors after I left.

It is most disappointing that none of the photographs of the Funeral[2] that I took have come out. The Frena[3] went wrong somehow and they were not even taken.

I have been at the studio all today where I am drawing my Academy[4] figure. It's very dull and I'm doing it very badly, so I don't expect I shall even get my first drawings accepted. I don't know where I shall hide my head then.

Boo[5] has gone to the play with Gerald tonight. Tomorrow I rather hope she will go. Poor Gerald's horror you can imagine when he found she was taking her lizard to the play under her dress! It always comes out too when it hears music—and its habits are *disgusting*.

I must stop as the letters are going.

Your loving
Nessa

KCC

[1]*The Sleeping Beauty and the Beast* (music by J. M. Glover, libretto by J. H. Wood and A. P. Collins), a pantomime at Drury Lane.
[2]Of Queen Victoria (1819–1902). The funeral procession on February 2, 1901 passed through Hyde Park, where the Stephen children were most likely to have seen it.
[3]The Frena (introduced by R. and J. Beck, London, in 1892) was the ancestor of all film-pack cameras; the camera box carried a pack of forty films separated by opaque papers. At this time Vanessa developed her own film and prints.
[4]The Royal Academy of Arts (founded 1768) at Burlington House. Prospective students were required to submit four drawings, "one of an undraped antique sculpture, a life-size drawing of a head and arm done from life, a drawing from an antique figure anatomized to show the bones and the same anatomized to show muscles and tendons, all of which had to be correctly labelled" (Spalding, *Vanessa Bell*, 33). VB was one of twenty students accepted in 1901 into the Painting School of the Royal Academy of Arts.
[5]Cordelia Fisher, first cousin to Vanessa on her mother's side.

I-4. To Clive Bell[1]

Sep. 10th, 1902   *Fritham House, Lyndhurst [Hampshire]*

Dear Mr Bell,

I hope you are able to imagine the excitement and joy that your partridges have caused here, as I am quite unable to describe it. Thank you very much indeed for them. It is most kind of you to have provided both such delicious food and such a splendid topic of conversation.

I really ought to thank you too for your Collins,[2] which was received with great applause and which ought to be shown as a model to all our other visitors. I hope you will prove its sincerity by coming here again some day, in spite of the probabilities of sudden death in the pony cart and the certainty of endless discussion of one subject.[3]

Thank you again for the partridges.

Yours sincerely,
Vanessa Stephen

TATE

I-5. To Margery Snowden

Sunday [March 15, 1903]   *[Limnerslease, Guildford][1]*

My dearest Margery,[2]

I have just been having a long lecture upon Art, and I think I had better write it down before I forget it all. After breakfast I went into

[1]This is VB's first extant letter to Clive.
[2]A thank-you note.
[3]Probably art.
[1]Country home of the painter George Frederic Watts (1817–1904), long acquainted with both VB's parents. VB and George Duckworth spent the weekend there.
[2]Margery ("Snow") Snowden (1878–1966), an artist, studied painting at the Royal Academy Schools with Vanessa and became her closest friend for several years.

8

the studio. Mr Watts is painting a huge tree trunk covered with ivy. "That's going to be sent to the Academy as a protest against Impressionism. You see every leaf is cleanly painted. There's no smearing, and cleanness is a great quality. Now what do you mean by style?" I gibbered feebly something about its being one's individual expression. "No. Now I'll tell you what it is. If you look at the lines around any form in nature you will see that they all tend to return on themselves, and those which make the smallest circle are poor and those which suggest the largest are fine. Look here at the Venus of Milo[3] and the Theseus and Ilyssus.[4] You see how the lines stretch out into space, and in this cast of an arm, though it is a fine arm, the forms are rounder and therefore not so grand. They won't teach you that in the schools, but I found it out for myself years ago and now I always follow it up in my paintings. You will find it a rule for deciding whether a thing has style or not. Now Rubens, though he has great vigour and movement and is admirable for those things, has not that quality at all, his forms are all rounded and like bubbles. Colour one can give no rule for—it's a matter of taste. Now look at this"—he showed me a painting of a bit of wood with brilliant green trees and grass—"Do you think it's beautiful? Well, there's no warm colour in it at all, it's all cold and I think that's the most difficult thing to make harmonious. Now this sunset makes it look crude and of course it's much easier to make these warm colours into a picture. Perhaps there's some reason for it. They suggest warmth and the blood circulating and all that sort of thing. If flesh were cold and like alabaster it would give one no pleasure, but when one sees a rosy child one wants to take it in one's arms and cuddle it." He showed me a portrait of a woman with an armful of roses. "There you see what I mean about movement. All the movement I have tried to suggest is in the thing itself, in the circulation of the blood beneath the skin and the sort of indefiniteness that makes you wonder after looking at it for a time whether it really is quite still or not. Of course Sargent's[5] portraits are much greater in technical ability, and this makes no direct appeal to you as they do, but with him the movement is always in the attitude, and though his people jump you feel that they are quite incapable of

[3]*Aphrodite of Melos* (c. 150–100 BC), Louvre, Paris; popularly known as the *Venus de Milo*.
[4]The *Ilissos* and *Theseus* (so-called) are figures from the east pediment of the Parthenon, British Museum, London.
[5]John Singer Sargent (1856–1925), American painter based primarily in London, where he was celebrated for his portraits of the wealthy and fashionable.

jumping. They have no blood in them. Still I admire him for his great ability. The great mistake of modern art is that they try to make things too real. As soon as the Greeks began to imitate nature exactly they began to go down—and yet nothing can be finer than their finest work.

... When I paint a picture I want to give a message and I care comparatively little about how good the art is—but only comparatively little because after caring for art all my life I can't say I don't care for it. I have known all the great men of my time—Tennyson, Browning, Carlyle, Rossetti, Fred Walker,[6] Burne-Jones[7]—and I think Rossetti was the greatest genius of them all. Millais[8] was more loved than anyone—he was so hearty and kind. Once at a dinner party he was heard to say in a loud voice (with Lady Millais there): 'I don't suppose any married man exists who hasn't at one time wished his wife dead!' "

I really think I have put down all I can remember of his sayings about Art. I don't know that they really come to much and perhaps they will only bore you. Still you told me to write. He's a very kind old gentleman and has quite a sense of humour. I haven't had much real talk with him since this morning as we went out this afternoon, but I have put in scraps of what he said at meals. I daresay I shall remember a lot more when I see you. He has long—and I think most comical—talks with Georgie on the future of the Empire, as I don't think either of them know much about it, and he has given him notes on Education to put in order, written chiefly as he is getting out of his bath, and which G[eorgie] says explains the sort of thing they are.

I'm afraid you won't have a letter on Monday morning, as I couldn't get my other sent off today and shall have to post them both in London tomorrow. But I daresay it will excite the Milmans[9] even more to see

[6]The painter and illustrator Frederick Walker (1840–75).
[7]Edward Coley Burne-Jones (1833–98), painter and designer. An outspoken critic of "modern" trends in art, especially French art.
[8]Sir John Everett Millais (1829–96) married Effie Gray in 1854, after her first marriage, to John Ruskin, had been annulled.
[9]Margery was staying with the Milmans, family friends of the Stephens. Sylvia Milman studied painting with Margery and Vanessa at the Royal Academy Schools. She was a granddaughter of Henry Hart Milman (1791–1868), dean of St. Paul's.

two bulky envelopes arriving together, especially as I shall see you before you can get them!

Your loving
Nessa

I-6. To Margery Snowden

[October–November, 1903]   *[22, Hyde Park Gate, S.W.]*

[First page missing] . . . Sargent is teaching most astonishingly well at the R.A. How I wish you were there. He gives lessons as you said he did, that would apply to any painting. They're chiefly about tone. He insists upon thick paint and makes one try to get the right tone at once. Apparently the drawing is to be got entirely by painting thickly the different tones, which doesn't sound very clear. He generally tells me that my things are too grey. The one thing he is down upon is when he thinks anyone is trying for an effect regardless of truth. He squashed Miss Roxby and Miss Clague—or however she's spelt—for it the other day.[1] He told Miss Clague she was simply trying to paint a pot-boiler, which was unnecessary as she wasn't going to sell her painting, but she didn't seem to mind at all. He told Miss Everett he couldn't see the use of painting as she did, with thin half-tones and a ridge of thick paint for the light. Of course there are many minor lights whom he squashes. I am only trying to think of the more prominent ones, to please you! Miss Ouless is working in another room so I never hear her lessons. I don't think anyone has had any praise, though at first he seemed to take a good deal of interest in Miss Price-Edwards, but I believe it quickly went off. She always does

[1]Of VB's fellow female students at the R.A., it is notable that many of them went on to exhibit their work widely. Daisy Radcliffe Beresford, née Clague, exhibited at the R.A. and elsewhere until 1938. Miss Catherine Ouless had a career as a painter of landscapes and portraits. Miss Ethel F. Everett, a portrait painter of children, exhibited at the R.A. and other leading London galleries through the 1920s, as did Sylvia Whitham (née Milman), and Margery Snowden.

begin very well and then seems to spoil her work. I told you how he squashed Miss Wolford, didn't I? She was quite subdued by it.

I have just remembered. Do you want to send up anything for the medal?[2] If so, write at once, as they have to go up on Saturday. If I don't hear from you I will give in the things you sent up for 2nd term. I am sending one figure and Sylvia [Milman] one head. You needn't fear either of us as competitors!

Your loving
VS

TATE

I-7. To Margery Snowden

Wednesday [April 6, 1904]   *Grand Hotel, Venice*[1]

My dearest Margery,

It does seem ages since I saw you off at the station. So much has happened since then that I don't know where to begin. However the longer I wait the harder it will be, so I will write to you now. We had a fairly uneventful journey here, straight through, and arrived at Venice at about 12 on Saturday night, very dirty and tired and wondering where we should sleep, as Gerald had had no answer to his letter to the manager of this hotel. You can imagine our feelings when a man from the hotel met us and said there were no rooms to be had and that Venice was crowded. We telephoned to the other large hotels—no rooms anywhere. At last we were told that we might get some of a sort at a small hotel and we set off in a gondola in the hope. It was a moonlight [sic] night luckily, as except for the moon, the canals were practically in complete darkness. There were no lights in any windows and only an occasional gas lamp. It was quite an alarming journey really. We none of us had ever been to Venice before

[2]Awarded at the annual R.A. Schools Prize-giving.
[1]Sir Leslie Stephen died of cancer on February 22, 1904. To escape the funereal atmosphere at HPG following his death, the Stephen children with George Duckworth spent a month in Pembrokeshire, then traveled with Gerald Duckworth for a month in France and Italy.

or could speak a word of Italian, and there we were in the middle of the night on a dark canal with all our valuables beside us, gliding along in dead silence, with no other noise to be heard but the occasional splash of an oar. The gondolas are all painted black and looked very mysterious and funereal. Do you appreciate the situation? I thoroughly enjoyed it, and expected a dark figure to jump out from some doorway or our gondolier to shoot down a side canal and demand money—but when one came to think of it Thoby and Adrian would be more than a match for most gondoliers. We did get to a hotel at last and got very small and uncomfortable rooms, but we were quite glad of any place that we could sleep by that time. We had to stay there for two nights as Venice is crowded and it was with great difficulty that we did in the end get rooms here. The Goat [Virginia] and I are now at the top of the hotel, which is rather nice, as there is a lift, and we look out over nice tiled roofs to the mountains, and we also get the sunset.

We are hard at work seeing pictures and churches, but of course we haven't seen very many yet. There are simply heaps to be seen, and every street and canal seems to have dozens of things that one wants to stop and look at . . .

I really don't know how to describe the pictures here. They are simply gorgeous. Tintoretto is the greatest. One gets no idea of him in London or anywhere else that I have been to, but here all the churches and galleries are full of him. His finest pictures are enormous things. There's a huge crucifixion which takes up the whole of one wall and is quite splendid, and there are several others.[2] I shall bring back some photographs to show you as its useless to try to describe them.

We spend our mornings seeing pictures, and the afternoons churches. Most of the churches are full of pictures too. I expect I shall get new ideas of painting. The worst of it is that all the pictures in the churches and some in the galleries are in such a bad light. Of course there is nothing by Velasquez here—I wish I could see him [beside] the Venetians. They have much more idea of decoration and seem to think nothing of personal character, or hardly anything. Tintoretto's portraits are dull and he doesn't seem to have taken any interest in them, but his large pictures are simply splendid in colour

[2]Tintoretto remained a favorite painter of VB's. She may have been referring to the *Crucifixion* in his scenes from the life of Christ at the Scuola di San Rocco (1565–87).

and composition, and there's a tremendous sort of force about them. Titian's large paintings here are very fine too, but they don't seem to be quite as great as Tintoretto's. There are beauties by Bellini and Carpaccio. Ruskin[3] raves about them, but I don't think he's any good at all as a critic, though he's generally amusing. He never cares for anything unless it is a symbol or has several deep meanings, which doesn't seem to me to be what one wants.

Mr Crofts sent me quite a nice letter and also a grand notice signed by Poynter and Mr Eaton to say that I was fit to profit by the use of foreign galleries, but it's no good at all apparently.[4] I suppose it is meant to use if one wants to copy. Anyhow I have to pay my franc.

How I wish you were here. Write and tell me what you're doing. I have done no painting. When do you go back to London? Has W.[5] appeared again? I want to know everything that is happening to you.

I hope you won't have to pay for this letter but I have written sheets.

Your loving
VS

TATE

I-8. To Margery Snowden

[April 25?, 1904]   **Palace Hotel, Florence**

My dearest Margery,

This is only to tell you that we go on Wednesday to Siena for two nights, then to Genoa for one night and then to Paris. We haven't time here as long as we meant to. Violet Dickinson[1] has been here with us for the last week, and she had to get back to London the

---

[3]The writings of John Ruskin (1819–1900) had been a formative influence on VB's art. Her first drawing teacher, Ebenezer Cooke, had studied under Ruskin at the Working Men's College in the 1850s.

[4]Ernest Crofts, R.A. (1847–1911), was keeper of the Academy Schools. Sir Edward Poynter (1836–1919) was at this time president of the Royal Academy. (Sir) Frederick Eaton (1838–1913) was secretary-registrar of the R.A. from 1873 until his death.

[5]Probably Mr. Watson, a suitor of Margery's.

[1]Violet Dickinson (1865–1948), a family friend of the Duckworths who, in 1902, became VW's closest friend.

week after next, so we are going with her as far as Paris. It seems rather a pity not to stay here longer, but on the other hand it is a chance to get Violet to travel with, as I don't think the Goat and I should manage very well alone. It's such a long journey and we can't talk the language, and have a good deal of small baggage which makes travelling difficult. So we shall go to Paris, getting there on the 1st of May and staying there I think till about the middle of May. Write to me there, % Cooks Office,[2] 1 Place de l'Opéra, Paris, and write soon. I don't know why you haven't before. In fact you have really been rather bad about it.

We have been confining a great deal of our attention to shopping lately. One can get lovely old frames and such things here are very cheap. When one thinks of what one has to pay for a new frame in London and how much nicer these old ones are it seems absurd not to get these when one can. So I have got one or two, but of course there is the difficulty of carting them home. I have also got some very nice drawing-books with vellum covers, and real old paper, which is much nicer than any modern paper and quite cheap. I have done no painting at all. It's hopeless to try to.

I shall have such heaps to tell you when I see you about all the places here. It has been rather rainy lately, but we have managed to do a good deal. There is one of the finest portraits here that I have ever seen by Titian, of a man in black.[3] It's quite splendid. We went one day to see Miss Paget who writes under the name of Vernon Lee— I expect you have heard of her. She's very clever, but what interested me is that she has got a portrait of herself by Sargent, and several other sketches by him.[4] The portrait is extraordinarily like, and it was interesting to see her beside it, as I hardly know any of the people he has painted. Certainly this was very like, though done when she was much younger, and she's rather ugly but very clever looking.

Do write quickly.

Your loving
VS

TATE

[2] The travel agency Thomas Cook & Son.
[3] Very likely his *Portrait of a Gentleman*, also known as *The Englishman*, Palazzo Pitti, Florence.
[4] The novelist Violet Paget (1856–1935) was a friend of Sargent's. He completed at least two portraits of her. The one VB saw was painted in 1881 and is now at the Tate Gallery, London.

I-9. To Margery Snowden

Monday night [May 2, 1904]   *Hôtel du Quai d'Orsay, Paris*

My dearest Margery,

I am going to see you so soon that I feel that I must write to you. Isn't that a good reason? I think we shall be at home in a week now. Thoby and our lady courier[1] leave on Wednesday. I think George is probably coming here for next Sunday and if he does we shall go back with him on Monday. I think anyhow we shan't stay longer than that, so I shall really see you very soon.

I got your letter today. I do understand so well all you say, and I even know what you mean when you say that you really thought I didn't care. I have felt exactly the same thing myself. I can remember very clearly once at Cope's[2]—about 6 years ago I suppose—being quite wretched and wishing that I could be Miss Bulley or Miss Cholmley[3] or anyone in the world except such a wretched being as I was, not because I was so unhappy especially, but I felt so utterly mean and despicable. I looked around the room and thought that any one of the people working there must despise me. The feeling goes off, but I have had it again and quite lately, and I have come to think that one must really treat it as a sort of physical thing. I think one must simply force oneself to turn one's mind to other things, and in time it becomes very easy to and one gets rid of such ideas. After all they are quite unreasonable and so one must fight against them, but I know it's very difficult to. It's very nice of you, dear old beast, to say that I am sensible and cheer you up, but you don't know what a fool I feel. I only wish I could be of any use. What a blessing it will be to see you again. Don't think of your depressions again for another week and then we will talk them all out.

One thing I see you and I must do some day. We must come and work here. Your[4] little friend Bell is here. Thoby is staying with him, as he lives in rooms here, and he knows a lot of the young artists and

---

[1]Violet Dickinson.

[2]Arthur Cope's art school in South Kensington, where VB studied from 1896 to 1901.

[3]Margaret Bulley, the art historian, later Mrs. G. W. Armitage. Miss Cholmley is unidentified.

[4]Margery Snowden circled this word and wrote above it: " 'Your'! pure hypocrisy. MKS."

tells us of all the latest geniuses. I went today to see one of them called Kelly.[5] He is only 24 and has 5 pictures in the Salon[6]—but somehow it didn't depress me! He is very clever and just now is evidently entirely under the influence of Whistler. It amuses me to see these things. He paints much better than I could, but I don't mind. I think I am beginning to know what I want to do, and as it's not the same quite as what I think I can see that these other people are trying to do, I don't mind how well they succeed! In fact I am quite pleased when they do.

Good Lord, it is awful work seeing people's pictures. I never know what to say. Mr Kelly was very shy, and his shyness took the form of talking abruptly and fast and making rather bad jokes and praising his own things extravagantly, so I didn't know what to say. His father was there, a nice old clergyman. I talked to him and left Thoby and Bell and the Goat to talk to his son. The father turned out to have known Father at Cambridge, and was very nice indeed about him, so I liked talking to him. What an odd world it is. In the end he asked his son if I might come and watch him paint tomorrow morning. The poor wretch couldn't say no and I had to pretend that I should be delighted, as I am going, but I don't know what on earth I shall do or say. However he is going to paint the father, which will make it easier. Anyhow it is very interesting to see a Paris studio. I want to go over Julian's[7] or some such place. I have been to the Salon, which is much the same as the R.A., though I think the average is higher. But much the best thing is the Lord Ribblesdale by Sargent,[8] and there are some beautiful Whistlers. Furse[9] seems to be getting more praise than ever. The Sargents sound very good, and I should think the one you describe would give you a lot of hints for Mrs Tatham [older friend of Margery's]. I believe I suggested doing her in that way a long time ago! I think it would be very nice to keep her quiet and black and grey and have a red curtain, but you must get exactly the right red.

[5]Gerald Kelly (1879–1972), later president of the Royal Academy.
[6]The official exhibition, sponsored by the Société des Artistes Français of the French Academy. By this date, the Salon was being undermined by its more daring rivals, the Salon d'Automne (founded in 1903 by Matisse, among others) and the Salon des Indépendants.
[7]The Académie Julien, founded 1873.
[8]Lord Ribblesdale (1902), now at the Tate Gallery, London.
[9]Charles Wellington Furse (d. 1904), an early influence on VB's painting. He died later this year of tuberculosis. His widow was Katharine Symonds, sister of Madge Vaughan (see p. 22, note 3).

. . . I shall be glad to get back and to see you. When shall I? On Tuesday? It sounds so nice to say that as it makes me really feel near. Goodbye my old creature.

Your loving
VS

TATE

I-10. To Virginia Stephen

Oct. 25th [1904]   *46, Gordon Square, Bloomsbury*

Beloved William,[1]

This paper delights both me and Thoby. Is this the only cheap kind you ordered? as all they have sent besides is some white very thin super-fine paper, and I thought you ordered some cheap small grey. Perhaps it is still to come.

I had your letter this morning. I must say you do write rather good letters! Violet even calls them "brilliant" but then her taste is peculiar. I went to see her this morning and stayed to lunch with her. We talked of you a good deal as you might guess and she was very charming. She is longing to visit you, but may not be able to come early next week, as Ozzy[2] has not yet returned and she wants to be at home when he does, but she is writing herself. Thoby and I went to tea with Sir Herbert where we met Harry and Barbara N.[3] She looked

[1]On the day after their return from Paris, VW, still grieving deeply for her father, experienced a mental breakdown, one symptom of which was a violent mistrust of VB. Soon not even three nurses could control VW, and she was removed to Violet's home at Burnham Wood, Welwyn, where she remained all summer. During October, she stayed with her aunt Caroline Emilia Stephen (1834–1909) at Cambridge. VB wrote to her daily.
[2]Oswald Eden Dickinson (c. 1868–1954), the younger of Violet's two brothers. He lived with Violet.
[3]Sir Herbert Stephen, 2nd baronet, and his brother Harry, who took over the baronetcy at Sir Herbert's death in 1932, were Vanessa's first cousins on her father's side. Harry Stephen was a judge of the High Court of Calcutta. He married Barbara Nightingale later that year.

quite pretty, but I think it was because she had on a large hat and the light being above, her face was in shade. She was quite nice and is a great friend of Miss Cake's, with much the same views I should think of Art. She admires Charles Shannon[4] very much and is going to be painted by him. I can't imagine how she will survive Stephen furniture, etc. As it was today, Harry asked her if she liked some tea cups—of which he has 30 in India. They were hideous and she said so—and it turned out that they were his own special choice. Everything else will be to match. Harry has not changed. He is coming to see me tomorrow morning, but we shall have nothing to say to each other.

I will do my best to bring all you ask for tomorrow. Fred sounds charming and I am glad you think he will do the Life well.[5] It must be a great help to him to have you to talk to. Of course you understood Father better than anyone else did and I hope you will write something that Fred can quote or even put in entirely. I am sure you could.

Now I am going to give you a sort of lecture as usual, poor little beast, but I want you to have time to think it over before I see you. I went to see Savage[6] this morning to ask about your sleeping. I hadn't expected to see him, but I did. He has given me a medicine which I shall bring. He was quite charming and I had a long talk about you. I do think he understands you very well and not many people do. I told him about your writing something to help Fred and he quite approved of it. The one thing he said which I want you to think about is that he thought you ought to stay out of London and preferably at Cambridge for 2 months. I know this will horrify you, but I will tell you what he said and you must judge for yourself. He said that your fortnight in London had brought you very near another serious breakdown and had undone a great deal of the good of your time at Teversal,[7] that you were quite clearly not yet strong enough to stand London. He said that even if you keep very quiet, which it

[4]Charles Shannon (1863–1937), lithographer and painter. Miss Cake is unidentified.
[5]Sir Leslie's official biographer was Frederic W. Maitland (1850–1906), Downing Professor of the Laws of England at Cambridge. He had asked VW to contribute a note on Sir Leslie's final years with his children, and to read the correspondence between Leslie and Julia, selecting appropriate passages for the book.
[6](Sir) George Savage (1842–1921), specialist in mental disorders, consultant to Sir Leslie Stephen.
[7]VW joined her siblings for a holiday in Nottinghamshire in September before her convalescence at Cambridge.

is difficult to do, the atmosphere of hurry and noise must affect you. I told him that you got bored and irritated at Cambridge, but he said that that would happen to a certain extent anywhere now and was really partly because you were not well yet. He said that your not being able to sleep showed that you were not right and that you needed all possible quiet and rest to make up for the want of sleep. He told me several details of how your days should be spent, such as resting and lying down before dinner, most of which I think you do, but I can tell you those when I see you. The one important thing was about staying away, and that he did say most strongly. He said that you had told him that you would do anything to get well—and that in his opinion you ought not to be in London yet. He also said that you were not to be forced to do anything, [but] that you must decide for yourself after thinking over his advice. After he had talked to me he said "There is one thing I want to tell you most seriously—I will have no fees." I said he must let us pay him, as we had taken up so much of his time and could do nothing in return, but he then pointed to the photograph he has of Father, and said that he was proud to do anything for his children, and that the only thing he cared about was that you should get well. It was quite extraordinarily nice of him, when one thinks of his being about the greatest man on his subject in England and what his time is worth. He wants to see me again on Friday to hear how you are getting on.

Now my own beloved monkey—don't go and imagine that I *want* you to stay away. I am very lonesome without you and miss you terrible bad. At the same time I do think, after Savage's extraordinary kindness, that we ought to consider what he says. I feel that I would willingly spend the next 2 months in a dungeon if at the end of that time we could give up all thought of your having to be specially careful. Unluckily my being dungeoned would do no good.

Your letter written on a sofa has just come like an answer to this. I know how you long to be here, but all I can say is, think it over well. You must decide these things for yourself now and think of what will happen in the long run. One thing is that if you are going to write something for Fred, surely it would be easier for him and for you if you were near him. You could have regular hours for writing and need see very little of Nun.[8] You know I do think it's very kind of her to have you and to be ready to have you for any length of time. It would be a great bore to *me* to have a niece of mine in that way!

[8] The Stephen children's nickname for Caroline Stephen.

However I won't try to argue or advise you. I only wanted to tell you what Savage said so that you may make up your mind and not decide in a hurry. We can talk it all over when I see you. I shall come by the 3.10, getting in at 4.27, and will come straight to the Porch[9] where I hope you will keep some tea for me . . .

Your
VS

BERG

I-11. To Virginia Stephen

Sunday [October 30(?), 1904]   *46, Gordon Square, Bloomsbury*

Beloved Monkey,

I hope for a letter from you tomorrow morning. I had none yesterday, but perhaps you hardly had had time to write since I saw you. I do long to hear that you are sleeping better. It must make such a difference. I have been most virtuous today. I spent the morning in struggling with the study. One wades through books which seem to get more and more confused. As Thoby is away I can't do more than collect different kinds roughly together, but that takes one all one's time. I suppose some day they will be done. Certainly books are wonderful things. Even I—though you may hook your learned nose at me in disdain—after spending some time grubbing amongst them, get to feel a great affection for the scrubbiest and most backless volume. I suppose it's from living in a book loving family. I feel happy and content sitting on the floor in an ocean of calf.

. . . George *did* come to tea yesterday! He was looking very well and beaming. He now calls me "Darling" every two minutes—otherwise there is no change. He is still capable of laughing at Margaret[1] and his in-laws, which is a good thing. Margaret seems to spend all

[9]Caroline Stephen's Cambridge home.
[1]George Duckworth had married Lady Margaret Herbert in September 1904.

her day on the sofa. They have not got a house yet. He thought this [house] quite charming.

Your
VS

I-12. To Virginia Stephen

Oct. 31st [1904]   *46, Gordon Square, Bloomsbury*

Beloved William,

I have just had your letter written on the sofa. My poor little monkey, I'm afraid you have been very bad. I do hope you have been keeping quiet. You know it is really important to rest at such times— not only on the day itself but for the first few days. [Nurse] Traill told me it was most necessary that you should. It may have made a difference to your sleep. Perhaps that will get better now it's over, but I am bothered about that.[1]

I haven't seen Beatrice[2] but I hope I shall soon and shall hear how you seemed. I have just had a letter from Madge—delighted to have you.[3] I wrote to her as I thought it would be more polite if I did too, and I suggested that I should come with you for a day or two just to see them and see that you were comfortable, so perhaps I might. She says we're not to let such delightful plans fall through, that you shall have a kitchen table in your room and do just what you like, play with the children or be a hermit. It all sounds as if it might be what you would like. She says there are no bores! I have just been dining

---

[1]Like many women of their class at this time, VB and VW treated menstruation as an illness. Both usually spent the first day of their period in bed, whether or not they felt unwell, and rearranged visits and travel to avoid exertion while menstruating. As a result, their letters to each other are full of references to their periods.

[2]Lady Beatrice Thynne (1867–1941), daughter of the 4th marquis of Bath, was part of Violet Dickinson's social circle in Somerset, and became a friend of Virginia's.

[3]Margaret (Madge) Vaughan (1869–1925), daughter of John Addington Symonds, and married to the Stephens' cousin William Wyamar Vaughan.

alone with Violet and Ozzy. Violet wants to go to Cambridge on Saturday. They were full of inquisitiveness about you. Ozzy is really very nice—quite simple and friendly. Violet as usual charming.

I don't at all fear that you and Fred will say too much, though I own that I was a little alarmed by his wanting to have so many family letters. However it's you who read them first and of course it's necessary for him to know everything, even if he makes no use of it. I am glad that I shall never be celebrated enough to have my life written. It wouldn't matter to oneself though. But there's something horrible to me, which I expect the true literary mind does not feel any sympathy with, in any third person's reading what was meant to be only between two. I shall burn all my letters someday.

I think I shall come by the same train on Wednesday.

Your
VS

BERG

I-13. To Margaret Vaughan

Nov. 16th [1904]   *46, Gordon Square, Bloomsbury*

My dearest Madge,

Virginia will arrive on Friday, but I am afraid alone. You will think that my promise of coming is never to be kept, but it is a great disappointment to me not to come now and I shall certainly come as soon as I can and you will have me. I suggested coming with her really because I thought that she would not be allowed to travel alone, but now the doctor says she can quite well and as I could only stay for a day or two, I think I had better not come now. I have just begun work at the Slade[1] and there are still many things to do in this house, so that it would have been difficult to come now in any case. Don't think me faithless. It is more disappointing to me not to see you and your house than it can be to you not to have me!

[1]The Slade School of Fine Art, opened in 1871, was at this time considered the most important art school in the country. Its teaching was heavily influenced by the New English Art Club.

Ginia is much better, and is now quite able to walk alone, so don't bother about her in that way if it's ever difficult for anyone to go with her. I think it is really good for her to walk alone sometimes. May I tell you the extra things she has and which she ought to go on with? I hope it won't mean giving you a lot of trouble. She has a glass of milk in the morning at 11, hot chocolate when she goes to bed, and a cup of tea when she is called. The only difficulty now is sleep. She has been sleeping much too little. She has a medicine to take, and the D[octor] says that if she sleeps very badly she is to have mulled wine. This she hates, and won't take it unless it is absolutely necessary. I hope it won't be, and that your air will make her sleep well. You'll think me a fearful old hen! But now that she is getting better I am very anxious that she should go on getting better and be quite well enough to start London after Christmas. There's no fear of making her think too much about her own health. She never thinks or talks of it unless one makes her. In all other ways she leads a perfectly ordinary life, with as much fresh air as possible and working all the morning. She is tremendously interested in everything and very cheerful and happy. The danger is really that her mind should become too active rather than not active enough, and one has to be careful if anything *not* to stimulate her. Of course her brain must have work, and so her regular morning's work is good for her, but she ought to rest alone after tea and a little after luncheon if possible.

You don't mind my telling you all these things do you? I wish I could see you and talk instead. It will be a joy to her to be with you. She says she has always wanted a real chance of seeing you, and she is full of interest in your wild country. She loves children too. I will write and tell you her train tonight. Could you order something to meet her? I suppose Settle is the station.

Your loving
VS

KCC

I-14. **To Margaret Vaughan**

Tuesday [November 29, 1904]   46, *Gordon Square, Bloomsbury*

My dear Madge,

I have waited to answer your letters till Ginia had come back. It was so good of you to write. She seems to me to be very well, and I am most grateful to you for having looked after her and had her for so long.

Don't be afraid that I shall quote what you say as "comic." I know you think us all very critical, but really I don't think we criticize unfairly, and we certainly don't laugh at people behind their backs and treat them affectionately to their faces. So don't even be afraid that we shall talk of your "fads"! Ginia has talked to me of you and Will [Vaughan] only in the most appreciative way and I do think that the safeguard with her is that she always does see the real good in people. She is too clever not to find a great many people bores, and I think she often enjoys giving vigorous expression to feelings which though true are always temporary, but when one knows her ways one can always tell how much is permanent and how much will change and I think I can honestly say that I have never heard her say a really unkind thing about anyone. So I don't think the criticism matters. Everyone who has brains must be critical when they are young. She is sure to get more tolerant, and even now it does come partly from having a high standard in most things.

I quite agree with you that she should not lead an invalid life, and the more independent she can be the better. At the same time I do think that just now she seems better than she really is, and that only someone who has seen her all through her illness can quite tell what sort of stage she is in. Of course she is always highly strung, but it is natural to her to sleep well, and I hope it will come back. Father always slept splendidly and in most ways she is extraordinarily like him. So I think that just now one has to insist upon her taking care in small ways as one finds from experience how much difference they make to her. I don't mean from all this that you didn't make her keep to them. From her account she led a most healthy life with you and I think you must have been *too* conscientious when you told me that you hadn't followed my instructions! In fact altogether her visit to you has been a real delight to her, as she always wanted to know you well, and she has come back full of your charms! Of course she loved the children and was very much interested in their different characters.

I think you are quite right when you say that she ought to lead her own life and I am most anxious for her to do so, but up to the time of her illness it was impossible not to interfere a good deal in physical ways because she had rather morbid ideas on the subject of health and would have allowed herself to get ill if one had not prevented her. In fact I think her illness in the end did come partly from her not having looked after herself in the small ways that one can only judge for oneself about. Now she has had such a fright that I hope and believe she will be much more sensible than she used to be and will be really independent, but until she is perfectly well one has to go slowly and run no risks and that is why I sometimes bother her in small ways. I don't want to do so for a moment longer than is absolutely necessary, for I hate dependence in anyone—apart from the fact that I don't enjoy myself having to be always on the lookout for her. Besides I think it only leads to unhappiness all round.

I feel that I have given you a fearful long answer to your letters. In the end I want to tell you how glad I am that Ginia has had the chance of knowing you and to thank you for all you have done. You have given her a great deal of pleasure and it has been a great help to me to know that she was with you.

Your loving
VS

KCC

I-15. To Virginia Stephen

Dec. 7th [1904]   *46, Gordon Square, Bloomsbury*

Beloved William,

I'm sure you can't have been eating enough. I heard from Madge and she said that you had eaten very little there, as they only had a temporary cook. You see the pain in your back comes simply from your nerves not having enough nourishment, and you must make yourself eat. Violet said that the first day at luncheon you had nothing but fish—I mean no meat. My monkey, do be sensible. It does worry me so dreadfully to think that you don't look after yourself, and I do think that though you are sensible in theory about yourself and you don't apply it in practice. You have such a horror of making a fuss about yourself, but really it's much wiser to recognize the fact that you aren't strong in some ways and to look out for them, and I should feel a great respect for you if you did. Now I won't go on lecturing, but tell me how you are when you write.

I went to see Violet this afternoon and found her simply full of your praises. Of course her taste may be peculiar, but she thinks your writing most wonderful. She said she had sat and howled over the life of Caroline Emilia.[1] You must send it to me to read. She thought you would undoubtedly be a great writer one day. Your things are so well thought out—fresh and original and interesting. You always have something to say on any subject and your writing is so living. Is that enough for you? She really thinks you a genius. Isn't it strange? Madge says you came as a boon and a blessing to them (like the pen)[2] with your delightful mind, so finely trained and your curious penetrating personality—to say nothing of your affectionateness. Really! William I shall borrow your green eyes in my old age.

I haven't dared to show my works to Tonks[3] yet, but I think I must on Friday.

When are you coming back? on Saturday? Or do you want me to come for Sunday? I could, only I rather want to go to the R.A. prize-giving on Saturday. I'm afraid I can't get you a ticket for it as I'm not a student now. But tell me what you want me to do as I needn't go there . . .

How do you get on with Headlam?[4] I like him, but I think one can have the artistic temperament without flirting. That part of it is unnecessary and I think rather degrading don't you? Not that I'm

---

[1] Unfortunately lost.
[2] "They come as a boon and a blessing to men,
   The Pickwick, the Owl, and the Waverly Pen."
(Advertisement)
[3] Henry Tonks (1862–1937), VB's teacher at the Slade.
[4] Walter Headlam, the poet and scholar, was a lecturer in Classics at Cambridge. Violet Dickinson also considered him a flirt. For his brief interest in VW, see QBI, 124–25.

afraid of my pure-minded William flirting, but I don't much like it in him.

Now I must stop.

Your

VS

BERG

I-16. To Margery Snowden

Jan. 11th [1905]　　　　　　　*46, Gordon Square, Bloomsbury*

My dearest Margery,

I am living in the hope of your return this week. You were a good beast to write me such a nice long letter . . .

I wish you hadn't so many worries and that I knew more about them.

Burn my letters—don't leave them about!

I am in a fix about work and want you badly. I have decided not to go back to the Slade at all because I think I should waste my time there either in drawing or painting, but at this moment I have nothing to do here. I want to start on you and on Lady Robert[1] as soon as possible and I mean to get a model and do a picture of some kind. I think firelight, but I'm not sure. Do you think I'm wise not to go back to the Slade? I mean if I am bold enough to write to Tonks at the end of the term and say that I have been trying to follow his advice and work by myself and ask him to look at my things.

If you want to paint me by sunlight you easily can here and I think it would be great fun in the drawing room perhaps. As for your Xmas number of Jill[2] I don't see that it need be at all Xmas numbery. It depends much more on how you do it than on the subject. Whether

[1]Lady Robert Cecil, née Eleanor Lambton (1868–1956), third daughter of the 2nd earl of Durham. Lady Robert met the Stephen girls in 1903 through Violet Dickinson and was an early supporter of their professional endeavors. This commissioned portrait was VB's first piece to be exhibited, in the 18th Summer Exhibition (1905) of Works by Living Artists at the New Gallery.
[2]Jill Snowden, Margery's sister.

one liked it or not no one could call that painting by Lenbach of a woman with a kitten[3] Xmas numbery, and many paintings by Reynolds I should think might be described so as to sound commonplace and yet be painted in such a way that no one would think them so. So do Jill with a kitten and blue ribbons if the fancy takes you that way. It is a true character of her, or part of her.

I am longing to start on you and have several ways in my head. I think your remark about the portrait of Father by Watts[4] being better than one by Sargent could be is most likely true, but then I think it's finer than any now on show. Still one ought to judge him by his best and not his worst. But it does annoy me to see anyone with real talent and capabilities deliberately neglecting the art of painting and using it only as a half-learned language. It ought to be such a fine thing in itself and there's no excuse for anyone not doing it as well as he can if he does it at all. It really would not be difficult to paint like Watts (this is quite serious) if one didn't try to get something more out of paint than he thought worth while, and if one had a certain amount of artistic feeling and had looked a good deal at the Venetians. Having done these things, which it doesn't need a great genius to do, one ought to begin the real work of mastering oil paint, and then one might have some chance of doing fine work. One thing that consoles me always in painting is that I believe all painting is worth while so long as one honestly expresses one's own ideas. One needn't be a great genius—all the second-rate people are worth having so long as they're genuine, because of course one always must have something of one's own to say that no one else has been able to say—and that's always interesting—but the moment one imitates other people one's done for. It's allowable while one's a student, learning the language and trying to find out what one does think of it all, but when one once starts alone one must be oneself. I'm sure all these wise reflections are not particularly original but you see I'm giving the subject some attention now that I've cast off the Slade, and as usual you get the benefit. Don't snub me by silence—and come soon.

Your
VS

---

[3]Unidentified. Could VB have been thinking of Franz von Lenbach's *Fritzi Scheff mit Pudel* (1890), Stadtmuseum, Munich?
[4]G. F. Watts' portrait of Sir Leslie hung for many years at Hyde Park Gate, but was not accorded a place of honor at Gordon Square. VW took it with her to Fitzroy Square after her sister's marriage.

I enclose a priceless first proof of a silver point [etching]. The bad drawing is not because I can't draw (as you might think) but because I at first found it difficult to see what I was doing. So the result was not brilliant.

TATE

I-17. To Virginia Stephen

Tuesday [April 4, 1905]   *46, Gordon Square, Bloomsbury*

Beloved Wombat and William,

I was enormously excited by your letter, and even a land rat like myself, as you impertinently called me, can appreciate the romance of the sea.[1] Didn't you long to be Whistler? You will be rather cross at my not having gone yet, but it's Mrs Snowden's[2] fault. We go tomorrow and even so shall have more than a fortnight away, so you ought to be satisfied. I haven't yet quite settled whether we cross to Dieppe or Havre, but I think Dieppe. Anyhow I hope to have letters forwarded from you.

I can well understand that many of your passengers must have succumbed, and you and Adrian are evidently as good as you thought you would be. Anything more horrible than a gentle roll—however I won't think of it as I shall be in it myself tomorrow. I am beginning to get excited at the prospect of foreign lands again. It will really be great fun.

Since I wrote to you I have been to Sargent's studio. Elena, Mr Rathbone, Miss Lüling and I went.[3] The great man was most affable and remembered me and said he knew me well from the Academy, so I was satisfied, as I had been afraid I should have to thrust myself on to his memory. I want to get to know him well enough to ask him

[1]At the end of March 1905, Virginia and Adrian journeyed by sea to Portugal, then visited Seville and Granada in Spain. VB went to France with Margery Snowden.
[2]Margery Snowden's mother.
[3]Elena Rathbone (1878–1964). She later married Bruce Richmond, editor of the *Times Literary Supplement* (hereafter *TLS*). Mr. Rathbone was her father. Miss Lüling is unidentified.

for criticism. His pictures are quite wonderful, but as you'll see them all at the Academy (if you return alive) I won't describe them. Elena asked a great deal after you, as does everyone, and they all seem to think that you two are the most casual and erratic travellers. Gerald has quite made up his mind that you will lose the boat somewhere.

My poor Wombat. How are you really? You do seem to be in another hemisphere altogether, and I only hope you look after yourself. Don't lay up seeds of future disease and do be a hedonist as you say you are. I am going to be [one] on my travels. I shall think of nothing but my own pleasure.

Snow comes here tonight for the night.

I find that my finances are in a most flourishing state. In some wonderful way I have a balance of £160! I can't think why, but as I am so rolling I shall invest in objects of art without scruple if I come across them, which will be great fun. Also when you come back you *must* let me repay you Snow's £10. I simply insist upon it. But that can wait till you return. I have also this moment had a letter from George sending me a cheque for £5—so I am more rolling than ever.[4]

I wonder if you will get this letter and when. I shall send it to Seville on the chance. How is Wombat behaving without his Maria? Is he lonely or is he a happy beast? I do wish I could see his furry face looking up at me over the bed clothes. When do you get to bed my animal? And do you really eat enough? I wish I knew truthfully how you are. This is a very dull letter but really Bloomsbury does seem dull when one thinks of Spain. Are you bull-fighting?

You wrote me a most poetic account of the Cornish cliffs which reminds me that Nelly said casually the last time I saw her that you ought to be painted but that there was no one alive now with *poetry* enough to do it!

> *Your*
> *Maria*

[Postscript on envelope:] T. says A. is to bring back his hat safe and to look out for kestrels.

BERG

---

[4]A very rough estimate of the values of these amounts today would be: £160 = £7667 (about $13,417 at an exchange rate [current in mid-1992] of $1.75 to the pound sterling); £10 = £479 ($838); £5 = £239 ($418).

I-18. **To Virginia Stephen**

April 13th [1905]   *Hôtel d'Angleterre, Caen [France]*

Beloved William and Wombat,

To my joy I found a letter signed by William and Wombat's mark waiting here for me yesterday sent on from London. It was the first I had had since your letter from Havre and I was thankful for news. This must go to Lisbon, as I don't think I should be in time for the other places. I have written to Seville and to Lisbon before, but it's quite a chance whether you get any of my letters. I hope you won't go on imagining Thoby in bed with diptheria, etc., for as far as I know he is fat and flourishing, as I am too, and Snow and I are enjoying life after our own peculiar fashion. You seem to be most energetic sightseers. We on the contrary have done no real sightseeing at all. I think today we shall go and see the two churches here, and in the evening we're going to a service where they seem to be going to have good music! in a beautiful old church.[1] I don't believe we shall get to Rouen, as we are going on south to Granville and Mont St. Michel.

We came here yesterday from Honfleur which was a charming little place with real Cornish fishing boats. We passed through country with quantities of apple blossom out against the sea, but I expect your Spanish coast will spoil you for tamer scenery. My land rat blood can think with nothing but horror of your tossing off the coast. Have you never really felt ill at all? I am already thinking with dread of our 7 hours back from Havre.

My poor Wombat, I wish I knew how your fur was really looking. You ought to be pining for a real petting by the time you get back, and perhaps—*if* you have been good—there's no saying but you may get it. I keep on thinking that this letter will probably be read by Spanish officials which restrains my otherwise demonstrative pen. Also by the time you get this I suppose you will be within 3 days of seeing me again. Do you go back to Liverpool or stop at Southampton? Let me know exactly when you do arrive. Gordon Square is being well cleaned up and the Hyde Park Gate mantelpiece is being put in. I wish that rat Adrian had written to me. He might have given me a

[1]VB could have attended a service with music at the church of St. Nicholas in Caen.

truthful account of your state, for I don't altogether trust your complete rest cure description. However I have to make up my mind to be philosophical and hedonistical.

Thoby tells me the water works have burst in Madrid and the mob is rioting. I'm thankful you aren't going to be there. I hope the rioting isn't elsewhere too. Poor little monkeys are so easily trampled on and squashed. Do keep well, my Wombat. What a lot we shall have to talk about.

Your
Maria

BERG

I-19. To Margery Snowden

Sunday [August 13, 1905]   *Trevose View, Carbis Bay [Cornwall]*

My dearest,

Your letter was such a blessing. Did I write you a *very* silly letter?[1] I think I must have, but since writing to you I have come of my own accord to take a more sensible view of things, and now with the help of your letter I think I am quite reasonable. Also I think a change of scene is a great help! We had had about enough of London.

I don't think there is any harm in my telling you that the person who was worrying me with his love affairs was Jack,[2] so you see he has a certain amount of right to. But after all it's not fair to say that he was worrying me, for he had kept it to himself for more than a year, and now there is nothing to be done for the lady has refused him and he can't possibly see her till the winter, if then. But you know how anxious I am that he should marry, and so naturally this is rather

---

[1]Early in August, CB proposed marriage to Vanessa. She rejected him and joined her siblings on a nostalgic trip to Cornwall. Her "silly" letter to Margery has not survived.

[2]John (Jack) Waller Hills (1867–1938), solicitor and Conservative M.P. In 1897 he married Stella Duckworth, Virginia and Vanessa's half-sister. Though she died three months after the wedding, Jack remained friendly with the Stephen family. He did not remarry until 1931.

tiresome. And as it has gone on already more than a year it looks as if it were serious—at any rate more so than an ordinary "affection of the nerves." I can only hope that it may not be quite hopeless, but as to that I am rather in the dark. However I don't think he is or has been really unhappy, so I'm not going to bother.

As for the other affair,[3] as you say, I can't help it. I was stupid not to see what was going to happen, but even if I had I don't think I should have behaved differently, for I didn't flirt. I might have been less friendly, but that would have been difficult and unpleasant for everyone, and also unless this particular man is unlike every other, it is highly probable that by this time next year he will have turned to fresh diversions. I can't bring myself to take his unhappiness very seriously, for I *have* had some experience of men! I think really my being worried was chiefly because of the selfish reason that a comfortable and easy and friendly state of things had to come to an end. Also when one is actually asked by a man to marry him, even though one has no feeling at all of that kind oneself, one is obliged to think rather more seriously about it than one has done before. It really seems to matter so very little to oneself what one does. I should be quite happy living with anyone whom I didn't dislike—(and I think I like this man quite as much as you like Mr Watson!) if I could paint and lead the kind of life I like. Yet for some mysterious reason one has to refuse to do what someone else very much wants one to. It seems absurd. But absurd or not, I could no more marry him than I could fly—so there's an end of it and I'll turn to sensible pursuits and wait to have sensible intercourse with him again until he has recovered his senses and fallen in love with someone else.

Doesn't that strike you as a reasonable state of mind? You see you have done me a lot of good and I feel that I ought not to have written you such a stupid letter before. But I know that you will never fail me when I really want help and so I can't resist asking for it.

How I wish you could come here. This house is new and hideous and the furniture is of the worst lodging house description, but the place is most beautiful. You can't think how odd it is to come here after 10 years. There are some changes of course, but it is all astonishingly the same and we feel as if we had never been away. You can't imagine the colour of the sea here. It is quite unlike any other, and the country altogether is beautiful, very wild and bare. I mean to paint a great deal. I have established myself in my room much as we did in our hotels and mean to paint sunsets from the window. We

[3] I.e., CB's proposal.

look out across the bay, and the sun sets just behind the headland to the left, so that one gets most lovely effects on the sea. . . .

As for my foundation scheme, I didn't explain properly. You see, in the first place I think that my kind of painting must be done more or less directly, partly because of its being thick, but also because (this is the important point) it seems to me almost impossible to get good colour by putting one layer of, say, grey over another layer of grey. But you can get good colour by putting one layer of grey over another of red or brown. I believe this is true and not only an idea of mine. Therefore you see as I want to have thick paint in the end my method would be this: Prepare a canvas with a red ground. Sketch in the drawing in any neutral colour, then paint quite directly and leave it. If I paint the whole thing in rather thickly on a new canvas and then want, in order to get a good surface, to go over it again (for I am sure that a good surface can only be got either by quite direct and very thick paint, right at once as to drawing tone and colour, like Sargent, or by a greater or smaller number of layers), I should by putting more or less the same colours on the top of the first painting lose the freshness entirely.

You see my method is the same as Whistler's, only he used many more layers than I should because he painted very thinly—which I can't, now at any rate, get myself to do. But the important point, which I believe I haven't realised before, is that he didn't put the right colour on at once. It was probably almost a monochrome to start with and I suppose he only got the right colour at the end. I expect that the most beautiful surface is got his way, but I can't paint thinly enough to do that for one thing, and also in sketching I am not sure that it would be possible. Have I made myself clear? I don't want you to experiment on your Creswick⁴ though. Do it thoroughly with a view only to the prize and send me the sketches soon. I think I shall really have to come to you in the autumn if your family will have me!

I am ashamed of the length of this letter. Do write soon or I shall think you are bored, and really I am becoming almost as tiresome as a man! I won't do it again.

What a wise and sensible and consoling old animal you are.

Your loving
VS

TATE

⁴A painting for the Royal Academy's Creswick competition.

I-20. To Clive Bell

Monday [September (?) 1905]   *46, Gordon Square, Bloomsbury*

Dear Mr Bell,

Thank you very much for your letter and suggestion. As a matter of fact, my first idea was that we should meet regularly in private houses, then on talking it over we grew more ambitious.[1]

I have been to see some rooms this afternoon in Beauchamp Place, a turning out of the Brompton Rd. The rooms I saw were some of them in ordinary small lodging houses, and some over shops, but they were all very small. One would get two opening into each other, one *very* small, and the other about half the size of the study here, for about £25 a year, but then the larger room could only be used by us on the one evening a week and in the afternoons one would have to use the small room. The other rooms I saw were more expensive but we could use them always. I am afraid though that they would all be too small. I see in the *Studio* an advertisement of two rooms to let at £20 a room at Somerset Chambers, next to Somerset House on the west side.[2] Do you think it would be worth asking about them? They tell one to apply to 151 Strand. I am afraid they will probably be very small rooms and they aren't in South Kensington, but if you don't think it sounds quite impossible, should you be able to look at them as you are fairly near? You see I am making use of you.

It seems to me on the whole unlikely that we shall get a room for the price we want to give and big enough, so to come back to your suggestion, the more I think of it the more I think that it might be best to begin in that way. Anyhow you might suggest it tomorrow, and objections are sure to pour in. The chief one seems to me to be that, as you say, we should have to eradicate politeness. We can get to the point of calling each other prigs and adulators quite happily when the company is small and select, but it's rather a question whether we could do it with a larger number of people who might not feel that they were quite on neutral ground. I suppose there are many other objections, but there are also great advantages in this

[1]The Friday Club, founded by VB for the discussion of the fine arts, had its first official meeting on October 13, 1905. They held annual exhibitions in London until the First World War.
[2]Approximate values: £25 = £1,198 ($2,096); £20 = £958 ($1,676).

plan. It would be much cheaper of course, and we could do with fewer members. I should say that we ought to stick to the plan of having an occasional exhibition and for that we should have to hire a room specially for a short time.

Don't go and see the Strand rooms if they sound to you out of the question. It's quite a random shot of mine and I really only tell you of them to convince you of my selfishness in practice as well as theory. It's quite enough to ask you to come here at the hottest hour of the day to lend me your moral support! Without it I should give in at once to all "celebrity" suggestions.

Yours very sincerely,
Vanessa Stephen

TATE

I-21. To Virginia Stephen

Sunday [April 15, 1906]   *Gale, Chelwood Gate, Uckfield*

Beloved Billy,

A nice long letter from you this morning which I read at my solitary breakfast. You certainly *are* rather a genius, don't you think so? Of course I don't. Naughty Billy, to get up a flirtation in the train. You really aren't safe to be trusted alone. I know some lady will get a written promise of marriage out of you soon and then where will you be? It was lucky you had Gurth [the family dog] to look after you.

I continue my peaceful and lazy existence here. Your instincts are all wrong, for you see Billy, it is whispered that you aren't *entirely* a monkey. I do hardly any work. Lord R.[1] went to church this morning, and I could only do a little to the background without him. I am in

---

[1]Lord Robert Cecil (1864–1958), created Viscount Cecil of Chelwood in 1923; husband of Nelly Cecil. After her 1905 portrait of Nelly, VB was invited back to paint Lord Robert.

a tolerable state of conceit, having as usual thrown all rules to the winds and abandoned all method and order. I enjoy chaos. It would not be the joys of Harrogate[2] which would keep me from you but the slow progress of my painting here—but I hope to leave on Thursday. But I get on quite happily here. This afternoon was spent sitting out. It is like August when one is out of the wind, and we were all thoroughly lazy and happy, when to our dismay a motor arrived with a party from Brighton. I haven't yet discovered their names beyond that they were a Mr and Mrs W. and two daughters, one married to some relation of the Thynnes.[3] We had to be polite and give them tea, after which Nelly and I went for a little walk and talked about the difference it made to have beautiful people to live with. Nelly is really artistic and has very good taste, with occasional lapses, as when she said how beautiful you were, but perhaps she didn't mean it. She thought you would be spoilt if one tried to dress you fashionably, as I told her George used to try to make us, and said you were perfect as you are— very odd—so different from what I always tell you. She also thinks you choose very nice colours for your dresses. In fact I'm getting bored with you.

I wish I weren't such an ignoramus. I've come to the conclusion that staying away is a very severe test for one's general intelligence and it's appalling to find how little I've got. If I were to do it often I should try to get educated. It's rather a difficult position with Nelly deaf, for I have to talk a good deal to Lord R. and I know nothing about politics which I suppose are what really interest him. However he can but think me stupid. I have a very high opinion of him. Do you get any food? And what is your joke about hoarseness? I suppose there is one, but I don't take that allusion. Also Billy, do remember that I don't know Greek. I suppose *Hailé*[4] is Greek, isn't it? Or Hindu? or Monkey language? I don't want to miss any gems so please explain. It comes after a sarcastic sentence about the attractions of Harrogate, and apparently is a sentence in itself.

Have you had any correspondence? I have had none except a line from Waller about nothing but the weather.

Well goodbye my Monkey. Give my love to Madge and tell her I

---

[2]After completing the portrait, VB planned to stay with Margery Snowden at her home at 21 Granby Road, Harrogate.
[3]The Thynnes of Longleat were aristocratic friends of Violet Dickinson. The W.'s are unidentified.
[4]*Hailé* may have been χαῖρε: hail, welcome, farewell. VW had studied Greek under the tutelage of Janet Case from 1902 through about the end of 1903.

couldn't find or hear of a housemaid (if you think of it) though I asked several people, and Sophy and Maud had no stray relations.[5]

Don't get ill whatever you do. I haven't much faith in you.

Your
Maria

BERG

I-22. To Lady Robert Cecil

Friday [April 20, 1906]   21 *Granby Road, Harrogate*

My dear Nelly,

I hope it is snowing with you. Here it is cold and horrible and altogether beastly. I am in a thoroughly spiritual and inartistic atmosphere and I find it rather hard to live up to!

I did so enjoy your material way of life and I hated leaving you yesterday. I wanted very much to stay on. I think you and Lord Robert ought each to be painted every other year. Next year it will be your turn. In time I shall be able to do you quite by heart and shan't want *any* sitting, so it won't interfere with your other doings, and the paintings will get more and more spiritual. I hope you aren't going on with that argument without me to keep you to the point. Besides if you do Lord Robert will have got all his ideas too clear and will squash everyone else at the Friday club.

I hope Violet will have a try at him on Sunday. It will make her kinder to *my* portrait. I believe I ought to have done more to the hands. What do you think? Of course the whole is only a sketch but I think perhaps the hands are too sketchy even for the rest.

I go to Virginia's lodgings[1] tomorrow. The natives here look with suspicion upon my elaborate route to Giggleswick and I see that I

---

[5]Sophia Farrell. Maud, a housemaid.
[1]VW spent about a fortnight in April at lodgings near the Vaughans in Giggleswick, Yorkshire.

shall probably give in weakly and go by Leeds, but I shall struggle against it.

I do wish I were still with you.

Your affectte
Vanessa Stephen

HATFIELD

I-23. To Clive Bell

Monday [July 30, 1906]   46, *Gordon Square, Bloomsbury*

Dear Mr Bell,

You have given me a very difficult thing to do, for you know that I can't express myself very well on paper. First I must say the worst I have to say. I do not feel that I can marry you now. You ask me to give my opinion whether there is the slightest chance of my changing my mind in the course of the next year or two. If you are unconventional, what am I? According to all rules I am sure I ought simply to tell you to go to Germany and never think of me again, but the fact is that I trust you so entirely that I am going to try and tell you quite honestly what I think and feel. I believe more will be gained by my doing so than if I treated you with "frigid politeness."

When you asked me to marry you last year it was really a great surprise to me, for to be honest, at the risk of being thought hypocritical, I had always taken it for granted that you thought me rather stupid and quite illiterate, and were only polite to me because of the rest of the family. Then I thought I had behaved very badly to you and had never taken the trouble to see what you were really feeling. So I was very unhappy about it all last summer and I thought you would probably want to avoid me as much as possible in the future. To make this easier for you, I told Thoby about it so that he should not press you to come here.

Now this summer I suppose I have simply been behaving very selfishly. I tried at first to behave as I suppose anyone with a strong character would behave, but I soon came to the conclusion that I knew you too well to make pretence and that if I was to see you at all I must talk to you naturally and freely. I think it is a question whether I ought to see you at all. For you see if marriage were only a question of being very good friends and of caring for things in the same way, I could say yes at once. I like you much better than I like anyone else (other man, I suppose I ought to say!) outside our family, and I am sure that our friendship means quite as much to me as it can to you. But I suppose that something more is wanted which now I don't feel. Therefore our being friends is a very good arrangement for me and only pure gain. Ought I to tell you that it's very bad for you? I am not pretending that I don't think that it gives you pleasure, but after all there is more for you to think than of the question of your immediate pleasure.

I suppose by the time you have read all this you will see that I am thoroughly weak and also that I am quite incapable of telling you coherently what I think. I don't want to be enigmatic as usual, but it really only means that I haven't the strength of mind to be clear and decided. So I put the burden on to you. I don't now feel for you or for anyone else what I imagine one ought to feel for the person one marries. I always enjoy seeing you and talking to you. If I were thinking only of my own pleasure I shouldn't hesitate to see you. But I do feel quite seriously that you ought to do what in the end is likely to be best for you and I don't feel capable of deciding that.

I feel that this whole letter is a fraud, for what can you say? But in spite of the fact that I know you have perfectly good cause for heaping any abuse you like on me, I still think that we know each other too well for me not to give myself away to you. So there it is. My sense of humour seems to have abandoned me.

The only other thing I want to say is how extraordinarily unselfish and generous I think you have been all through—much too much so. It has made me the opposite . . .

Yours very sincerely,
Vanessa Stephen

TATE

I-24. To Margery Snowden

Thursday [November 1, 1906]   *46, Gordon Square, Bloomsbury*

Dearest,

Here I am safe and sound and thinking of you.[1] Your letter touched me so. You old dear. Why should you be so fond of me? I don't know. We are in a turmoil here. First George met us at Dover and told me he had a nurse waiting for me here, which made me so cross. But when we got here we found poor old Thoby in bed with a high temperature. I hope it will be nothing. Other people seem to be having the same thing. But the nurse can attend to him, which is a mercy.

Meanwhile I have been put to bed, and have seen the doctor whom George also insisted upon providing. You see I am well looked after! He says there is nothing wrong with me now, but I am to stay in bed tomorrow—bother it. Tonight I am too much excited at getting back to be able to go to sleep quietly, which they seem to think I ought to do. Besides I am worried about Thoby. Oh dear, how I long to see you. Will you really come up soon and see me? You don't know how I have wanted you and I have such *heaps* to tell you. I shall leave this open and add the latest news of Thoby tomorrow.

Friday. Thank goodness Thoby is better and the doctor thinks the worst is over and he hopes he will get better now. He's more comfortable. It seems to have been a very sharp attack of some kind, but there is no reason why it should be anything bad. So that is a relief. Now to satisfy your mind about myself. He says—the doctor I mean—that I am to stay in bed and rest as much as possible which I am doing. There's nothing the matter with me except that I am tired, which is natural after travelling 3 days and . . . [last page missing]

TATE

[1]In September, VW, VB, and Violet Dickinson joined Adrian and Thoby in Greece. VB was ill almost from her arrival. On the first of November she returned to London very ill with appendicitis, to find Thoby in bed with typhoid—wrongly diagnosed as malaria. As she recovered, he grew worse.

I-25. To Clive Bell

Wednesday [November 7, 1906]   *46, Gordon Square, Bloomsbury*

Dear Mr Bell,

I asked Adrian to tell you to come at 3 if you could tomorrow, but now I am going to try to write to you instead, because I don't think it would be fair to either of us if I were to see you while I feel so good for nothing. Adrian will have told you I expect that the doctor wants me to have a rest cure, and though I hate it, I really feel so tired that I suppose I must give in. I'm not to be made to begin though until Thoby is really better, and at first I want to explain to you why I wrote as I did from Constantinople.

I'm afraid I shall have to be rather solemn, and tiresome. I don't know exactly what I said to you when I wrote in the summer. I'm sure it was all very confused, but the simple meaning as of course you saw was that I didn't know my own mind. What I didn't understand then but have come to see quite clearly since is that if I go on seeing you in London as I did last summer I shall probably never make up my mind. You see I don't want to marry in the abstract and so there's no reason why I should want to make a change as long as I could go on seeing you as I did then, and as long as I thought only of my own feelings. But I can't quite do that, and I do feel that to see you constantly while I am uncertain is very unsettling to myself, and it seems to me that in every way it would be best if you were to go away—I thought for a year. Do you think me too brutal? What I wanted to suggest was that the thing should be put aside for the present—that is for as long as it would only be possible for me to see you in London, and that then, if you want to, you should come and stay with us in September—we shall probably be somewhere in the country. By that time, if you still want it, I can give you a definite answer, and if you stay with us, you are much more likely to get disillusioned about me than if you see me on my best behaviour on Thursday evenings.[1]

I have tried to look at the question from the point of view of some third person and I honestly believe you would find it best to do as I have said.

---

[1] I.e., at Thoby's weekly gathering of friends.

But of course I know that it is quite likely that all this may seem to you absurd and if so you must say so, for you see even if you do as I think best I can't give you any promise now and so I haven't the least right to ask you to do anything. Also I don't want you to be unselfish because I am ill and do what you don't think right yourself. Will you say truthfully if you would rather that we both gave up now all thoughts of anything else and agreed definitely to see each other in future as friends only? I feel that for me that is the only alternative to the other course and you must do exactly as you choose in deciding which we are to follow.

What I am going to say now is I know very impertinent. I wish that, if you decide to go away, you would work at something. I don't mean that I in the least want you to go in for any particular profession—in fact I can't imagine you being a successful barrister or man of business! But I do think you would be happier and would most likely think less of the Stephen family if you were producing some kind of work and not only adding to your knowledge. Besides I think brains are so badly wanted that people who possess them haven't the right to let them be of no use. I haven't the courage to go on being impertinent.

One more thing I want to say is, don't worry about me and don't imagine that you have in any way helped to tire me. This illness is I know simply the result of getting very much tired by nursing Virginia two years ago and it had to come sooner or later. I suppose it's true as they all tell me that I have got off cheaply, and I am quite sure that all I want is a rest and that I shall be perfectly well by Christmas. Perhaps for the first time in my life I shall now do some reading! You can get news of me from Adrian, who is really more sensible about illness than the rest of my family and who has been most charming to me. I haven't seen Thoby but I hope he's going on very well. I hope you'll forgive me for being so tiresome.

Yours very sincerely,
Vanessa Stephen

TATE

I-26. To Margery Snowden

Tuesday [November 20, 1906]   *46, Gordon Square, Bloomsbury*

My dearest Margery,

You will know before you get this.[1] I can only send my love and say what I know you will want most to hear, that I am taking every care I can of myself so as to be as little trouble as possible. The end was very peaceful and I saw him twice yesterday.

Your
VS

Wednesday

This wasn't sent yesterday. We all slept last night. Write to me when you can.

TATE

I-27. To Margaret Vaughan

Dec. 11th [1906]   *[Cleeve House, Melksham, Wiltshire]*[1]

Dearest Madge,

Now that I am allowed to write letters I must tell you how much I cared to have both yours. Why should your words jar on me? It is what I feel myself in a way—that is, I think I do understand that happiness is good and that sorrow more than one can help is altogether a pity. Perhaps it is made very easy for me to say and feel this now, but even if it had not been made easy for me I hope I should have known it to be true. I do feel that Thoby's life was not wasted. He was so splendidly happy, in these last two years especially, with everything ahead of him, full of the best possibilities and able to see con-

[1]Thoby Stephen had been operated on for a suspected perforation on November 17 and died the morning of the twentieth.
[1]Home of CB's parents.

stantly all the people he most cared for, that sorrow does seem selfish and out of place, more than with most people. But I as yet can hardly understand anything but the fact that I am happier than I ever thought people could be,[2] and it goes on getting better every day.

I hope I may see you somehow after we go back to London, early in January . . .

Your loving
VS

KCC

I-28. To Virginia Stephen

Dec. 14th [1906]   *[Cleeve House, Melksham, Wiltshire]*

Beloved Monkey,

Two letters from you yesterday, which was an unlooked for piece of luck. I can't make out your posts. They seem varied. However it may be more interesting. My letters probably arrive with dull regularity, like the news they give. My letter yesterday was tiresome I know, and I will have made you swear, nothing but questions stuck in at odd corners.

I had to go for a drive with Lorna[1] yesterday morning. We get on very well and talk quite easily to each other though, like you, I have to sit up on my hind legs all the time. I really find it just as difficult to do as you do, but I must say most of my day is spent not at all on my hind legs but clunking over trees on all fours and with my tail waving talking to Clive. Have any other engaged couple ever seen each other in the way we have I wonder? We must have talked hard to each other for 7 to 8 hours a day for the last 3 weeks and yet we never seem to have time enough. I get morbid sometimes and think I must be boring him or that it is all too wonderful to be true and that some awful catastrophe must happen, but after all I

[2]On November 22, VB had accepted CB's third marriage proposal.
[1]Lorna Bell, one of CB's two sisters.

suppose it is true isn't it. What does your philosophical mind think, Billy? . . .

Take great care of yourself and Wombat.

Your
Maria

BERG

CHAPTER TWO

1907–1910

On February 7, 1907, Vanessa married Clive Bell at St. Pancras Registry Office in Bloomsbury. Many of the letters in this chapter are written from Cleeve House, Seend, the home of Clive's parents. This mock-Jacobean Victorian mansion, principally decorated with animal trophies and highly polished brass, offended Vanessa on every level. Together with Clive's cheery, sporting family, it was an unending source of misery for her, a monument to English respectability and bad taste. In later years, she avoided visits whenever possible.

A year after her marriage, Vanessa gave birth to her first child, Julian Heward Bell. Motherhood would prove to be one of Vanessa's strongest points, but for the moment, thanks to Julian's nurses, it did not appreciably affect her work or social life. The greatest influence in the latter sphere may have been Thoby's death. Virginia has written that, were it not for the death of her father, there would have been "no writing, no books." In a sense, Thoby's death as well liberated his friends from conventionality. Under his sobering influence, they would never have begun those experiments in living that now characterize Bloomsbury.

Christian names begin to appear in the letters[1]—though not without

[1]It is difficult now to convey the weight of Edwardian social convention on the lives of even these skeptical, irreverent young people. Men were expected to call their male friends by their surnames all their lives. Visitors to Gordon Square in these days would have been struck by the informality even before they noticed other irregularities.

conscious deliberation on Vanessa's part—and the affectionate banter she once used only with Virginia now finds its way into her other letters. Her frank style and bawdy language especially endeared her to her homosexual friends, such as Lytton Strachey. I think it is safe to say that at this time, no other middle-class woman in London wrote letters like Vanessa's.

But the most wrenching change in these years is conspicuously absent from Vanessa's letters. On holiday at Cornwall in April 1908, Clive and Virginia—frustrated by Vanessa's increasing absorption with her infant—began a long flirtation that came dangerously near a love affair. Clive's objective was simple, "no less and . . . not much more than a delightful little infidelity, ending up in bed" (Quentin Bell, *Virginia Woolf* I, 138). But Virginia's motivation had far more to do with Vanessa than with Clive.

Though this complicated affair² has been addressed by other writers, its significance to the sisters' relationship cannot be overstated. Virginia had at first thought Clive unworthy of her sister. She felt also that Vanessa's marriage betrayed their own intimacy. "We have been your humble Beasts since we first left our isles," Virginia wrote to Vanessa on the eve of her marriage, "and during that time we have wooed you and sung many songs . . . in the hope that thus enchanted you would condescend one day to marry us. But as we no longer expect this honour we entreat that you keep us still for your lovers, should you have need of such" (VWLVI, 493). Vanessa was quite prepared to continue their close relationship. It was Virginia who could not reconcile herself to the new situation. Although it began as silly sibling rivalry and pettiness, her flirtation with Clive took on the dimensions of a revenge tragedy, in which Virginia, as the wronged suitor, played out a role she knew would ruin her.

Instead of the sisters' amorous correspondence, Virginia now sent most of her caresses through Clive: "Give my love to my sister, and, if you like, kiss her left eye, with the eyelid smoothed over the curve, and just blue on the crest" (VWLI, 290); "Kiss her, most passionately, in all my private places—neck—, and arm, and eyeball, and tell her— what new thing is there to tell her? how fond I am of her husband?" (VWLI, 325). Virginia does not love Clive, but rather appropriates his privileged position near Vanessa. In this equation his caresses become hers, and she remains her sister's lover.

²*Affair* is Virginia's term and does not imply a sexual relationship, as it would today.

In reality, of course, the equation fell apart. Vanessa grew worried, then resentful, watching Clive open his brilliant missives from Virginia. The affair put an end to Vanessa's extended honeymoon with Clive, and to her romance with Virginia. After a few pained letters, in which she adopts the suppliant tone which was traditionally Virginia's, Vanessa cools to an affectionate, concerned, but implacable elder sister. According to Vanessa's daughter Angelica Garnett: "It was an episode that left behind a permanent scar. Years later, seeing them together, in spite of their habitual ironic affection and without any idea of the cause, I could see in their behaviour a wariness on the part of Vanessa, and on Virginia's side a desperate plea for forgiveness" (AVG, 28).

In January 1910, the Bells caught sight of the artist and critic Roger Fry on the station platform at Cambridge. Though they were no more than acquaintances, they discovered on the train a mutual fascination with modern French art. And when Vanessa's second son, Quentin, born in August, was ill for weeks, she found Roger to be interested and sympathetic. That November the Bells attended "Manet and the Post-Impressionists," the first of Roger Fry's two famous Grafton Gallery exhibitions. Whereas Duncan Grant, as an art student, had seen Fauvist Matisses in Paris in 1907 and barely noticed them, by 1910 the Bloomsbury painters were more than ready for Post-Impressionism. "That autumn of 1910," Vanessa wrote later, "is to me a time when everything seemed springing to new life—a time when all was a sizzle of excitement, new relationships, new ideas, different and intense emotions all seemed crowding into one's life. Perhaps I did not realise then how much Roger was at the centre of it all" (quoted in Spalding, *Vanessa Bell*, 92–93).

II-1. To Virginia Stephen

Tuesday [July 30, 1907]   *Seend*

My Billy,

I wish you weren't back in London again but ferreting about into all the good smells here with your little black nose. We had the arrival of the rest of the family to keep us alive yesterday, all managed as you may imagine with great common sense and calmness. Dorothy[1] seems to be if anything the better for her journey. How do they manage it? I have not seen her yet. Two nurses invade the house, which makes me feel quite at home, though it is a blessing that I have not to go in and talk to them. The doctor is quite nice but I should think he'd find life here rather dull.

We are really very well off for we have now established ourselves in Clive's dressing room, where we spend the morning. I paint and he writes and we see no one until lunch, and we go out alone together in the afternoon, when the rest of the family always have exercise of some kind to occupy themselves with. So we shall see very little of them except at meals and for about an hour after dinner every night.

I have begun to write my biography.[2] I don't think you will find me a rival to you, Billy. The literary style will be mixed and discursive. I find that I shall have so much to say that it will take me years to write.

[1]Dorothy Bell, CB's sister.
[2]Not extant.

51

Did you see Miss Noel?[3] I hope you gave her my love. I feel I ought to be polite to her. If she's going to be in London in the winter I must see her. I am prepared to believe that she is really very nice as you think for I can't say I know her at all.

I hope I shall hear from you tomorrow my monkey.

Take care of yourself and don't starve or do anything foolish. I know you aren't at all to be trusted and I see quite plainly that you'll have to take up your abode with me again before very long. Aunt Goat will be a feature of my establishment and probably essential to the happiness of the nursery.

Your
Maria

Your letter has come by the afternoon post. A charming letter, Billy. I'll write tomorrow.

BERG

II-2. To Virginia Stephen

Wednesday [July 31, 1907]   *Cleve House, Melksham, Wilts*

My Billy,

I had a letter from you after writing to you yesterday, a very nice one all about the probable charms of my babies. I'm inclined to take a more cheerful view of them myself in consequence and I daresay they'll be full of whimsicalities and charms and we shall be a delightful family, where you will feel really domesticated and at home. The domestic strain in you is very odd. How do you account for it? Perhaps it's the sign of real genius. If you were only very clever you wouldn't care for such things.

I have just had a letter from Snow saying that owing to a financial crisis of hers, she won't be able to pay any visits this summer and

[3]Irene Noel (1869–1956), daughter of Frank Noel of Achmetaga, Euboea. She had entertained the Stephens (but not Vanessa, who was ill at Athens) on their September 1906 visit to Greece.

can't come to Rye[1]—so at present we have no one in prospect but Walter Lamb and Lytton Strachey, and possibly Saxon[2] at the end of September. Have you got your visitors arranged at all definitely yet?

It poured omnibuses and elephants yesterday all the afternoon and hailed too. I went for my first drive in the pony cart after tea but we were drenched and had to come in. I'm afraid my pony cart won't come off very well.

They have been rather worried about Dorothy for the last few days as she has had a high temperature every afternoon, but the doctor doesn't seem to think much of it and expects it to stop in a day or two. It's a good thing you aren't here, Billy, with your hatred of the hospital atmosphere, for talk of diseases is the only variation on talk of the weather.

How is Adrian getting on? I suppose he goes to you on Friday. My husband is going to write to you soon I think. I am reading Lavengro[3] whom I like. Is it true that Thackeray was in love with Granny?[4] I ask for the purposes of my biography!

I hope Wombat will get to Rye before the 26th. Otherwise I shall find him on the road and shall have to pick him up and put up with his company most of the way. But I suppose he started some time ago.

Love to the singeries [Virginia].

> *Your*
> *Maria*

Your letter just come, which I will answer tomorrow.

BERG

---

[1]In August of this year Adrian and VW stayed at the Steps, Playden, near Rye in Sussex. The Bells joined them on August 26, renting Curfew Cottage in Rye. Snow did manage to visit them.
[2]Saxon Arnold Sydney-Turner (1880–1962), civil servant, educated at Trinity College, Cambridge, and a core member of Bloomsbury. At Cambridge he was elected to the highly select Cambridge Conversazione Society (founded 1820), usually called the Apostles. Walter Lamb (1882–1968) lectured in classics at Cambridge. In July 1911 he proposed marriage to Virginia, who rejected him. Giles Lytton Strachey (1880–1932), biographer and essayist, was educated at Trinity College, Cambridge; like Sydney-Turner, an Apostle and a core member of Bloomsbury.
[3]George Henry Borrow's novel *Lavengro: The Scholar, the Gypsy, the Priest* (London: John Murray, 1900; originally published 1851).
[4]Pure speculation, although Thackeray knew the Pattle sisters well and appreciated their beauty.

II-3. To Virginia Stephen

Saturday [August 3, 1907]   *Cleeve House, Melksham, Wilts*

My Billy,

It's really absurd of you to imagine I'm ill when I don't write, for you yourself sometimes sin. How do I know that you mayn't be concealing all kinds of diseases alone in Fitzroy?[1] You at any rate know that my husband would act with great practical common sense in any emergency, wouldn't he Billy? whereas Goodness knows what you wouldn't be up to.

I suppose [nurse] Traill thought you looking very ill or something, didn't she? You can speak openly, for, according to your commands, your letters are now private. Traill may have smells of hay about her— of course they'd make me sneeze—but she certainly does make one think of all kinds of horrible things and people. I suppose I shall never see her again which is a mercy, but you will be burdened with her for life. She is a warning against ever making friends with hospital nurses.

As you may see, Billy, I do as I foresaw I should, write very dull letters from this place, but you know how my days are spent. This morning I painted Clive, having refused to drive into Devizes with Mrs Bell,[2] and then came down to the family lunch. I shall soon devote a chapter of my biography to family life. What shall I do with my family of 4 when they grow up? I'm beginning to think 2 will be enough. Do you think we shall gradually fall into all the old abuses and that I shan't have any idea what my children are like or what they want to do? I am honestly terrified sometimes of the responsibility of having any children. I'm not sure it doesn't mean hanging the most terrific millstone round one's neck. What do you think? I can look at it calmly now but when I have them I shall probably be so unreasonably fond of them that it won't strike me in that light, but all the same I doubt if I shall be a good parent. I think I shall probably hate the practical part too much. Think of taking them to the dentist and looking after them when they've measles. I suppose I can turn it all on to you though?

[1] Adrian and VW had taken a house together at 29 Fitzroy Square, Bloomsbury.
[2] Hannah Bell, CB's mother.

Take care of yourself my monkey. Do go out and take the air and eat enough. What did you say to Fanshawe?[3]

Your
Maria

BERG

II-4. To Virginia Stephen

Monday [August 5, 1907]   *Cleeve House, Melksham, Wilts*

My Billy,

I wonder how you are passing your solitary bank holiday. It's a beastly day anywhere, but I daresay you like being a hermit and I hope you're writing a long letter to me full of *your* views, not Waller's, on family life. Not that I didn't enjoy Waller's too, but I feel sure your odd mind is stored with clear wisdom on the subject and I think of how I fished in it last year walking round the garden with the fear of toads in my heart!

In about 3 weeks now we shall be in Rye, thank God. I don't mean to complain of this as much I may seem to, but Clive and I agree that it is depressing and hope our children will get on each others' nerves and have all kinds of peculiarities which will have to be treated and humoured and keep us and them alive. Will you take a small country house with us some day, somewhere in country with a good character to it, so that we can come there or send our family there instead of letting them come and get all their instincts blunted here? I have a terror of the inheritance that may await the poor little beasts in the form of Bell conventionalities. How can they escape? Stupidity seems to overwhelm one when one lives with it, and to be quite impregnable.

I see that Clive has taken up the only possible attitude and the one that I always ought to have taken up with George. One ought to go one's own way without argument or fuss and without attempting to

[3]H. C. Fanshawe, editor of *The Memoirs of Anne, Lady Fanshawe, 1600–72* (London: John Lane, 1907), which VW had reviewed in the *TLS* on July 26, 1907; he sent twelve pages of protest to the *Times*.

make the stupid see one's point of view, and when asked to do things one does not want to do one ought to give a half jocular refusal and stick to it, which is the only way of baffling them. I haven't had to put this into practice but I shall lay it down as a guide for future conduct. It really surprises me to find out how utterly impossible it is to make the average understanding see what one is driving at. One thing I see will be impossible, and that is to send our offspring here alone much. There's no knowing what wouldn't happen to them.

This letter will not go till tomorrow morning, there being no second post out today. I am very lazy and inflict grumbles upon you, Billy, chiefly because I can't paint. My brains too seem to have deserted me. Lorna has gone off to watch cricket! Dorothy had indigestion two days ago and is not going out in consequence, though she is better again. Mrs Bell worries a good deal about her and spends her days I think at small jobs. Mr Bell[1] is very busy over I don't know what and Clive writes a good deal and reads. So now you know just how we pass our time and I feel that we are typical of all the country households in England.

Do I write very dull and depressing letters? I must stop now as it is time for tea and punctuality is a virtue in this house. So good night, Sweet William.

Your
Maria

BERG

II-5. To Virginia Stephen

Tuesday [August 6, 1907]   *Cleeve House, Melksham, Wilts*

My Billy,
    Your Sunday letter did not reach me till this morning. It seems at last to be getting warm and we have even been led by wild imagination to talk of the heat of last year as compared to that of the year '81. But generally it is the winter of the year '82, or whatever it is, that absorbs conversation. Today the doctor goes, which I am rather sorry

[1]William Heward Bell, a successful colliery owner, father of CB.

for, as though stupid he is nice and at any rate talk of his cases is more amusing than the weather.

Clive had a letter from Sydney-Turner at Bruges[1] this morning. He hopes that we have thought of a name for him, so I am going to write to "My dear Saxon" in a day or two. I see that Saxon will soon become the most natural name for him. He seems to be staying at the most select and expensive hotel.

How are you Billy? Are you being sensible or shall I soon have to nurse you through a nervous breakdown? I am most flourishing and for the last 3 nights have not been sick, so I hope that is now coming to an end, which it ought to do by now. It's a great mercy.

I have washed my hair and am extremely furry. Would you like to stroke it?

Have you heard what George's plans are? Clive says that if he were to go to Rye he thinks we could hardly go there too. However I see no reason for taking such an alarmist view of the position. I suppose they will go to Bretby or some other seat, and in any case I look forward to being at Curfew Cottage, Rye, this day three weeks.

My biography is not fit to be read and has not got much forwarder lately. It's simply a jumble at present of all the people and incidents I can remember up to the age of 14. Why don't you write yours? Have you finished your Life of Violet[2] yet? If so do send it to me, and any other works I haven't seen. I wish you would Billy.

Love to the singeries.

Your
Maria

BERG

[1]Sydney-Turner returned from Bruges later in the month to spend a holiday with VW and Adrian at The Steps, Playden.
[2]See "Friendships Gallery" in *Twentieth Century Literature,* vol. 25, nos. 3/4 (Fall/Winter 1979), edited and with an introduction by Ellen Hawkes.

II-6. To Virginia Stephen

Wednesday [August 21, 1907]   *Cleeve House, Melksham, Wilts*

My Billy,

I have been rather bad about writing to you, I'm afraid. The posts seem to go at such awkward hours here. I'm always just missing one, and now I've only time for a line. However of course I've no news, so if I wrote pages you wouldn't get much benefit from them. You write charming letters to me Billy and I think your muse must be pleased with you now and smiling upon your genius. Is your Life [of Vanessa]¹ as good as your letters?

Mr Bell has gone off to Paris and the rest of us sit here, dull as ditchwater and I gape with my beak open waiting for your drops of crystal to be poured in daily. Clive got the drop today, and I got a letter from Snow! Jill's baby does not seem to have arrived yet, at least it hadn't 10 days ago.

Now I must stop I suppose. You'll swear at me for treating you so badly.

Your
V.B.

BERG

II-7. To Margaret Vaughan

Feb. 17th [1908]   *46, Gordon Square, Bloomsbury*

My dearest Madge,

Your jacket is delightful and I think the colour most beautiful. I was very much surprised at getting a present for myself, and really you oughtn't to bestow one on my son¹ too, though as you know all warm coverings are most welcome.

¹Now published as "Reminiscences" (*Moments of Being*).
¹Julian Heward Bell, born February 4, 1908.

How much I wish you could look in and see us. We are both flourishing and Julian came into the world shouting healthily and has continued to do so ever since, whenever he thinks food or attention are due to him. He is very tall and large but not fat and he has tremendously long fingers and toes. I think he is like Clive but one doesn't know if all likenesses aren't one's imagination. He has large blue eyes which the nurses think will stay there and a good deal of hair, which is not very fair but is getting fairer, and a very nice complexion and ears!

The only characteristics he has shown are greed and a great interest in light. You must come and see him for yourself. I find it quite as difficult to describe him as it would be to describe a grown-up to anyone who had never seen him.

I am going to get Elsie [a nurse] to come in about a fortnight when he will be a month old and shall keep on this nurse for a week after that. Don't forget the nursery rules you promised me! This nurse is very sensible and I pick her brains on the subject of babies and all to do with them whenever I can, so I hope to get properly started.

> *Your loving*
> *Vanessa*

KCC

II-8. To Virginia Stephen

Saturday [April 11, 1908]   *Cleeve House, Melksham, Wilts*

My Billy,

I must write tonight in order to get this sent off tomorrow morning early. Are you enjoying life without me? I hope you feel the difference, or are you too much engrossed in me as a subject for your art to be able to think of me in the flesh? I am reading your life of Violet again and really find it very witty and brilliant (what should I have said?) but I wonder more and more how you ever dared to show it to her. It brings me back to the rarified culture and free talk which is so congenial to me and is a solace from talk of Julian and the winter of '81.

You can imagine that I play the part of the proud mother even less well than I did that of the engaged young lady, but on the whole the baby provides a very useful topic of conversation on which we can all discourse for some time without fear of running onto Art or Religion. I look at these surroundings and feel thankful that he is still too young to know the difference between ugliness and beauty and in fact rather enjoys the many shining brass knobs which meet the eye everywhere. But it will be awful when we have to educate his taste and point out how hopelessly wrong everything here is. Poor little wretch, he's been howling all day and so perhaps he knows more than we think. I'm going to begin his one bottle now and shall soon increase it to two, I think, for really my milk shows signs of being too little.

Did you have Pernel[1] to lunch and get anything interesting out of her? I look forward to a letter from you tomorrow, full of gems.

I have had a piece of true Stephen wit today in the shape of a letter addressed to Julian Bell Esq. Inside is a sheet of paper "with J.A.S.'s compliments" and a very small visiting card printed with "Mr James Alexander Stephen."[2] Isn't it what you'd expect?

I haven't had a petting to speak of since I've been here, and no doubt you've been revelling in your genius (?).

Your
V.B.

BERG

II-9. To Virginia Stephen

Sunday [April 19, 1908]   *Cleeve House, Melksham, Wilts*

My Billy,
    I had your description of the Vaughans today and also your M.S. [VW's Life of Vanessa]. It is very virtuous of me to sit down and write

---

[1]Joan Pernel Strachey (1896–1951), university don, and principal of Newnham College, Cambridge, 1923–41, a sister of Lytton Strachey's.
[2]This was perhaps a joke sent by Vanessa's cousin Harry Stephen, whose son James was also a newborn baby.

to you now instead of reading it as I am tempted to do, but as I must catch the early post to you tomorrow if you're to have a letter at all I must write this evening.

We dined on Friday with the Raven-Hills[1] and I believe Clive gave you some description of the proceedings there. Mrs R.H. is really amusing and also most wildly improper in conversation. Talk of freedom in talk. She stops at nothing. Different methods of stopping children and the joys of married life were freely discussed and notes compared by her, Mrs Armour[2] and myself, and I quite enjoyed myself as you will believe. Also I see that I can get some useful tips from Mrs Raven-Hill as to the best methods of checking one's family and I mean to make use of the dance at Devizes for the purpose, though as she is very deaf I shall probably cause a scandal.

Today we have been lunching with the Armours, who are very nice but not exciting. Still it is a mercy to escape the Sunday dinner here.

You seem to have had an interesting conversation with Lytton. Did you talk of the great B[illy]'s works? I shall probably write to you at length tomorrow and tell you my opinion of my Life—I see it will be an absorbing work and probably your master-piece so far. I think in future you will have to keep me supplied with works of yours whenever I am here, for contact with your wits lifts me out of this dead level of commonplaces and I sniff the air like an old war horse and snort with delight. You have your uses, Billy. Oh God, what a world, as you used to say. However, Friday will come. I'm sorry to write such dull letters but what is one to do in Wiltshire while you are sniffing the smells of St Ives? I hope you didn't lose either of your familiars [dogs] on the way.

Your
V.B.

BERG

[1]Leonard Raven-Hill (1867–1942), a *Punch* artist and political cartoonist, and his wife Annie were country neighbors of the Bell family at Seend. She had been CB's first lover, and he was soon to renew his relations with her.
[2]G. D. Armour (1864–1949) was a *Punch* illustrator and painter, particularly of hunting scenes. The Armours also lived in Wiltshire.

II-10. To Virginia Stephen

April 20th [1908]   *Cleeve House, Melksham, Wilts*

My Billy,

I have been reading your M.S. and so has Clive. I believe he has many small criticisms to give you. I have marked two places only I think which I will show you. I cannot give you real criticism of course but I think it is extraordinarily interesting. I like the part about Mother best. It seems to me that you really get into your stride when you begin to write about her, and I think, as far as I can tell, that you have given a very good idea of her—much the best I have seen. I think you also give a very true idea of Stella, but she is more difficult to get hold of. Some of your phrases about her bring her back to me very vividly, but it is impossible for me to know quite what they would mean to anyone who didn't know her. But I should think you have made her a very real person and also have given the relationship between the two very well. Of course I can only talk as do laymen about a portrait and tell you whether I think it like or not. My word, what a scene of gloom it becomes after the tragedies! I felt plunged into the midst of that awful underworld of emotional scenes and irritations and difficulties again as I read. How did we ever get out of it? It seems almost too ghastly and unnatural now ever to have existed. One is even inclined to think dull commonplaceness better, but perhaps it was chiefly George's commonplaceness that made it so awful. I hope no one will ever have to go through it again. I am longing to go on and have more to read, for the relations between me and Waller will be most interesting! I think you have got the whole thing remarkably well constructed, especially considering what a forest of people and events you had to clear out and put in order. You have got them all very well together and the whole story moves on in good order and is an artistic whole—so it seems to me. I shall tell you much more when I see you, but I leave all literary criticism to Clive.

I had your letter from St Ives this morning. *Don't* give up the best bedroom, for you will want it to sit in probably and Clive and I shall want separate rooms. He tried here sleeping in the dressing-room, but gave it up as he couldn't get to sleep again after once being waked by Julian, so will you get us another room? As we shan't want a large double room you had much better keep the one you are in, in case you want to write in it.

We shall get to St Ives at 7.10 on Friday. Will you order a short vehicle to bring me and the nurse and baby from the station with one box and perambulator, and unless they should arrive beforehand also another two boxes, Julian's cradle and bath? These last we shall send off in advance so they may come before we do, but if not we shall find them at St Ives and bring them up with us.

Poor Billy, I am giving you practical jobs which you hate, although you do despatch them with great brilliance—but I don't think there is anything else.

I suppose your landlady will send up my nurse's meals to her room. Otherwise there is nothing unusual.

I shall look for your handsome red tie and soft nose at St Ives— Oh God, what a joyful sight.

Your
VB

BERG

II-11. To Virginia Stephen

May 4th [1908]   *Trevose House [Cornwall]*

My Billy,

Your journey sounds rather terrible. It will be the very devil with Julian, even if we do book seats. I wonder why on earth the trains should be full now. However, I will book seats and trust to God. The best of the weather departed with you and it now alternately mists or is rather stuffy and grey. I had a letter from Saxon yesterday and today I have sent him a pot of cream, as he seemed to relish yours so much. The poor little man ought to be fed upon Cornish cream and sent to the Scillys for a month or two. I suppose he was only away about 3 days.

Your imaginary conversation by the rhododendrons has not yet taken place.[1] It is sad to see how we miss you. This morning Clive managed painfully to limp down to Hambyn's where we bought our tea. Of course I won't say why he had to limp,[2] and now we have come struggling back from the beach, where I did a sketch of the sea and your dog tormented a family of children to let him join their games. We talk of you and all your pranks and idiosyncrasies and gen———eral charms. I wonder what *you* have said about us—"Of course Nessa was quite taken up with the baby. Yes, I'm afraid she's losing all her individuality and becoming the usual domestic mother, and Clive—of course I like him very much, but his mind is of a peculiarly prosaic and literal type. And they're always making moral judgements about me. However they seem perfectly happy and I expect it's a good thing I didn't stay longer. I was evidently beginning to bore them."

Now Billy, on your honour haven't you uttered one of those sentiments? You seem to have started already on your gaieties.

Your
VB

I think I shall bring your leavings with me as they'd make such a large parcel. I doubt if they'd go by post, and I don't suppose you want any of them at once.

BERG

II-12. To Virginia Stephen

Thursday [July 30, 1908]   *Cleeve House*

My Billy,
    At this moment, it being soon after 10 and Thursday evening, you I suppose are sitting in the midst of the most rarefied culture in

---

[1]Not recorded.
[2]CB fell and injured himself running after VW's train with a book she'd left behind.

London, with Saxon, Lytton and no doubt Hilton Young[1] all hanging upon your words. I, on the other hand, am listening to Lorna's description of a bazaar she has been to and a raffle she has won (I can do it with one small lobe of one lovely little ear) and the speculations of the Bell family as to the weather tomorrow when the whole village of Seend is going to feed and drink and dance here. Isn't it a pathetic picture? Clive I believe is writing to you too, so you see we both turn to you for relief.

After you had gone yesterday George appeared, very fat and very much pleased with himself. I can't think why he came. He only stayed a few minutes, having been to call on you first, and he had no news.

We caught our train [to Seend], of course. There was never any real hope of losing it. We found Julian well, but he's rather unhappy with his teeth—change of milk. Dorothy is much better, and all else is as usual. The country is a dark green and dusty like its inhabitants, but I will say for it that it smells delicious and is very quiet—when Julian lets it be.

I hear that the Vicar's Close at Wells is the most charming place— old 14th century houses, very becoming to you and Gurth.[2]

Shall we meet at Bath on Thursday? We have been threatened with Lorna's company when we go to Bath and so are choosing Thursday as a day when we know she will have to attend a large garden-party, and shall say that you can only go then.

I have inspected my studio, which I see will make time pass much more quickly here, and will provide a room with empty walls of a pleasant [cool?] duck's egg green on which I shall rest my eyes when they smart too much under the combination of new art and deer's hoofs here. Oh God, this life amazes me more and more. Mr Bell is now getting sleepy over his one bit of literature during the day—the Cornhill with your article in it[3]—(he has not told me what he thinks of it). Mrs Bell is reading I don't know what, a thick black book, probably a novel from the library. Lorna has just gone to bed with

---

[1]Edward Hilton Young (1879–1960), politician and poet, educated at Trinity College, Cambridge; Liberal M.P. for Norwich, later Conservative M.P. for Sevenoaks, raised to the peerage as Baron Kennet in 1935. Hilton was a regular at Gordon Square Thursday Evenings, and was at this time hesitantly courting Virginia.

[2]VW was about to spend a fortnight in Wells with her two dogs, Hans and Gurth.

[3]"John Delane," *Cornhill Magazine,* June 1908, a signed article based on *The Life and Letters of John Thadeus Delane* (London: John Murray, 1908). It was this book that CB gallantly fetched for VW as her train started out of St. Ives Station.

many yawns. How can people waste their lives like this? It goes on all the year round, all the time that we in London are wondering whether we are growing old and railing against Saxon's dullness. Now Mr Bell is quite asleep. Can it be your article he is reading? After all I don't know that it much matters that people spend their lives like this, but it is monstrous and criminal, isn't it, that *we* should have to spend any portion of ours in this swamp and fog? I must say that since I have been here there have been one or two interludes—but why should they be interludes?

Did Lytton propose to you this afternoon?[4] And did he say I could send you his poems? I would rather you married him than anyone else, but perhaps on the whole your genius requires all your attention.

I hope tomorrow for a ray of light from the outer world in the shape of a letter from you. You won't get this till tomorrow night, as I didn't write in time to send it by the afternoon post and so it won't go out till tomorrow morning.

Goodbye, my monkey. If you were here, perhaps I'd kiss you.

Your
Maria

II-13. To Virginia Stephen

Tuesday [August 11, 1908]   *Cleeve House*

My Billy,

I had a charming long letter from you this morning with flattering hints of rose-gardens and daylight round corners and I don't know what all.[1] I purr all down my back when I get such gems of imagery thrown at my feet and reflect how envied I shall be of the world some

---

[4]He did not. His eventual proposal came in February 1909.
[1]Cf. Virginia Stephen to VB [August 10, 1908]: "You have a touch in letter writing that is beyond me. Something unexpected, like coming round a corner in a rose garden and finding it still daylight" (VWLI, 349).

day when it learns on what terms I was with that great genius, the creator of Valentine Ambrose and his wife Helen (?) and that original character—will none of my suggestions do? Polly, Sarah, Daphne— I can't think of anything at this moment.[2] I wish we were having evening walks and planning our autumn doings. Perhaps Siena or Florence will provide a good setting.

I didn't mean by saying that Hilton Young was jocose to reflect upon his seriousness of purpose—which I daresay is deadly and de-termined—but rather upon him himself. His humour is laboured and rather like an elephant in a china shop and I can't imagine it very well-mated to your wit, for which we all gave you so many marks. I don't think I'd like him for your husband but then whom should I? I should like Lytton as a brother in law better than anyone I know, but the only way I can perceive of bringing that to pass would be if he were to fall in love with Adrian—and even then Adrian would probably reject him. But I expect you haven't yet exhausted all the charming young men in the world, and I know we are near the end of another stage and you soon will be married. Can't you imagine us in 20 years' time, you and I the two celebrated ladies, with our families about us, yours very odd and small and you with a growing reputation for your works, I with nothing but my capacities as a hostess and my husband's value to live upon? Your husband will probably be dead, I think, for you won't have boiled his milk with enough care, but you will be quite happy and enjoy sparring with your clever and cranky daughter. I'm afraid she'll be more beautiful than mine, who I know will take after the Bells. When mine is on the road[3] I shall refuse to come here and shall see you every day and gaze at the most beautiful of Aunt Julia's[4] photographs incessantly. Do you think Belinda Bell would be quite impossible? I am rather taken with the name at present and I believe it would suit her character rather well . . .

> Your
> VB

BERG

[2]Over the several drafts of *Melymbrosia*, VW's working title for *The Voyage Out*, Valentine Ambrose's name changed finally to Ridley Ambrose, and VW settled on Rachel Vinrace for her heroine's name.
[3]On the way; i.e., when I am pregnant.
[4]Julia Margaret Cameron (née Pattle) (1815–79), the famous Victorian photographer. She was VB's great-aunt.

II-14. To Virginia Stephen

Aug. 13th [1908]   *Cleeve House, Melksham, Wilts*

My Billy,

I don't know why you had no letter from me one day, for I have certainly written to you every day, if not oftener, and that in spite of the fact that to one of my letters Clive will get the answer probably. It must be the fault of the post.

Have you had bad toothache and have you had it again? If so you had better go to Tisdall [their dentist] during the one or two days you are in London before we go to Italy, for it will be awful if you have it there. Poor little beast. I hope it's all right again.

I had a long and amusing letter from Adrian this morning. He seems to find a good deal of interest in watching Saxon's ways. He is apparently taken for an imbecile by the inhabitants[1] for to all their remarks he replies "Um-m-m" and smiles. He also has a habit of sitting silent for some time and then looking up sharply and saying "Yes, well, I think, on the whole perhaps it may be," or "I don't know. I don't know at all." I can quite imagine him with his old man's habits and little peculiarities. I am really afraid he is becoming fossilized. I had another letter from him a day or two ago, entirely taken up with an inventory of the smoking room in which he was sitting. It's really too odd. Even at his dullest I shouldn't have expected him to write such dull letters. It seems to me to show that his old age is more deeply rooted than I had thought, for it cannot be only social if his letters show it.

Has Hilton Young written and come and proposed yet?[2] At this moment you may be refusing him, but no, after dinner it is not likely.

I suppose you'll go to your bathless cottage at Manorbier.[3] You'll get very dirty, Billy, and I don't think I shall be able to kiss you as much as usual for some time after.

You ask what kind of letters I like. What can I say but one thing? Of course what I really like is flattery and affection, but you may

---

[1] Adrian and Saxon were at Bayreuth for the annual Wagner Festival.
[2] Not until May 1909 did Hilton Young propose to Virginia, in a punt at Cambridge.
[3] In mid-August VW went from Wells to Manorbier, Pembrokeshire.

write a good deal about your novel too—a good deal more than you do.

I have written a mortuary letter too to old Dodder,[4] but I didn't know what to say.

Thank God my nurse comes home tomorrow. I look forward to Saturday.

Your
VB

BERG

II-15. To Virginia Stephen

Friday [August 21, 1908]   *Glencarron Lodge, Achnashellach,*
Ross-shire [Scotland][1]

My Billy,

... We arrived this morning at Inverness soon after 9, and there breakfasted, and then we came on slowly reaching this place at about 1. The house is about 2 minutes from the station and on the high road, but both station and high road are small and derelict. The station in fact is a private one and we ourselves have to give orders for the train to stop at it. The Scotch in talking to one say "Will Mrs Bell like me to unpack for her?" and are like old Nurse to look at—ugly. Clive and I found that Mr Bell and Mr Greg[2] were out shooting and so we had a cold luncheon alone and then went for a short walk, during which Clive killed three rabbits. Oh Billy! poor little furry beasts. It surpasses my imagination entirely, this wish to kill—does it yours? Of course another animal with fur such as a monkey would feel for them. I have no particular feeling for them, but I don't understand why anyone gets any pleasure from killing them. However

---

[4] Old Dodder is Dorothea Stephen (1871–1965), Vanessa's first cousin, whose sister Helen (b. 1862) had died August 9, 1908.
[1] VB's first and final shooting party with her husband.
[2] T. T. Greg, a friend of CB's, and author of a little book of essays on wine, *Through a Glass Lightly* (London: Dent, 1897), reprinted from the *Pall Mall Gazette* and *National Observer*.

they do, and I can keep out of the way of seeing the slaughter in future . . .

Saturday

They have all gone off to shoot or to fish and I am left to spend my morning alone. I am going to be motored out to lunch with Clive and his party who are grouse-shooting. It's very cold, and how I am ever going to sketch I don't know, for I see that it will always be either icy or the midges will be intolerable. I shall take refuge in painting some beasts for a "crawler" for Julian. They will be cut out in red twill and sewn onto a white ground by Dorothy. The effect will be hideous I should think, but Dorothy has so often asked me to do it that I feel I must, and perhaps a wombat likes such things to crawl on. Does it?

There is an atmosphere of undiluted male here. How you would hate it! If only you were here we should now light a fire and sit over it talking the whole morning, with our skirts up to our trousers. You would say "Now what shall be talk about?" and I if I were tactful would say "Our past," and then we should begin and discuss all our marvellous past and George's delinquencies, etc., and so come to our present and then on to your future and whether and whom you would marry, and then at last to the one great subject. "Now what do you really think of your brains, Billy?" I should say with such genuine interest that you'd have to tell me and we should probably reach the most exalted spheres. Why aren't you here? This is a vast house and a small monkey could be put away anywhere. I feel it to be a lost opportunity. I am feeling extremely garrulous and can only give vent to it in this remarkably unsatisfactory way. Mr Greg asked me if I wrote and I said "No, only letters, but my sister writes for the Times" . . .

Your
V.B.

BERG

II-16. To Virginia Stephen

Aug. 25 [1908]   **Glencarron Lodge, Achnashellach, Ross-shire**

My Billy,

I had 3 letters from you yesterday! But I deserved them for I hadn't had a line since I'd been in this desert land . . .

I read your letters over and decided with Clive that when they are published without their answers people will certainly think that we had a most amorous intercourse. They read more like love-letters than anything else. Certainly I have never received any from Clive that could compare with them, but then his, as you may imagine, were always worded with the greatest restraint. I like love-letters. The more passion you put in the better, Billy. Soon you will know just how to suit my taste in letters. I am greedy for compliments and passion.

What do you mean by my "irrational and inarticulate passions"?[1] All my passions are perfectly reasonable and only inarticulate when they are thought unreasonable. What is the good of pointing out Snow's virtues to you when the mere mention of them makes you storm against her limitations? As for Julian, you spend a day in his company and mine and I will tell you exactly why and when his ways seem to me charming and endearing. I am in reality the most critical and rational of all the Stephens and you by far the most magnanimous.

You ask me to tell you what Scotland is like, but you only have to look at any Landseer[2] to know. The hills are so plainly cut out of card-board, with hard edges clear against each other or the sky, that they are like nothing so much as the sham landscape at the Franco-British.[3] It would drive me almost as mad as does the Seend drawing-room to live opposite them always. Sometimes one gets a glimpse of

[1] Though VW's letter has not survived, this is without doubt a reference to one of her frequent jabs at VB's legendary maternal instincts (legendary in part because of VW's myth-making).
[2] Sir Edwin Landseer (1802–72), popular painter and sculptor; a favorite of Queen Victoria. He frequently painted Highland scenes.
[3] The Franco-British exhibition at Shepherds Bush (summer 1908) was a significant step in the movement of English artists and critics away from the Academy and toward modern French art. The sham landscape is John Brett's *Val d'Aosta*, which the critic Robert Ross considered "the most astonishing landscape in the English School." He argued that it violated every canon, and might have been "the frontispiece for a tract on the prevention of cruelty to landscape" (*Burlington Magazine* 13:198).

better things in certain lights or on grey days, but generally they give one no aesthetic pleasure at all. The pleasure one does get from Scotland is, as Sheep[4] says, of the senses. The heather smells delicious and the clear water looks extraordinarily pleasant . . .

I doubt if I shall ever come to Scotland again. I could not stand more than 10 days of it in any case and my plan for the next year, if Clive wants to come here, is that I, with Julian, should spend the time with you and Adrian. You see if Clive came here the Bells could not but think it natural that I should prefer to be with my family than with them, and of course I should take Julian with me wherever I went. However Clive most likely won't want to come here either and in that case I hope we should all join in some country house. One thing is quite clear to us both. Julian can never be allowed to spend more than a week or so alone at Seend. Evidently all their ideas about bringing up children are conventional and tiresome, and I don't see how that awful atmosphere of Sunday and best clothes could fail to affect a child left alone in it at any age over a year. Poor little wretches, they so easily become conventional and lose their individual charm. It reminds me of George and all those horrors when I hear them saying that it is good for a child to go to parties and put on clean clothes for company.

I hope I shall have a letter from you today, but the post doesn't come till the afternoon when I shall be out. I believe Clive gave you some good practical advice as to what to take to Italy. I shall be able to come and overhaul your arrangements on Wednesday, but if your good woman is so overcome by your loveliness that she wants to wash for you, for God's sake, let her. Then you may have a good stock of clean things to start abroad with. I shall take a few medicaments, but not much. We can easily get things there. Take warm underclothing— winter combis and cholera belts[5] and warm drawers. This reminds me of Violet. I feel very much as if we were setting off for Greece again . . .

Your
VB

BERG

[4]Mary Sheepshanks (c. 1870–1958), effective principal of Morley College, a night school for working people in South London. She employed VW to teach a weekly literature class.
[5]Combis are combination underwear. Cholera belts are warm, cummerbundlike articles, often made of wool or flannel.

II-17. To Margery Snowden

Sep. 18th [1908]   *Grand Hotel, Perugia [Italy]*[1]

My dearest Margery,

In your last letter to me you said that you had only had a post card from Paris. This is my third *letter* to you. I hope by now you have got the others. They were very dull, but still I may as well have the credit of having written them, for at any rate it meant that I was not neglectful of you.

We came here on Tuesday and find ourselves in a large modern hotel with every luxury and a horrible atmosphere of waiters and British tourists—very unlike our little Sienese *pension*. Also there are some English people called Fletcher.[2] We met them in Siena. (I know them in London quite well—that is to say, they are great friends of the Booths and very like them and I have met them constantly at the Booths, Pollocks,[3] etc.) We came suddenly upon them. They were at a short distance and when the alarm was given I turned suddenly, hoping foolishly to avoid them forever, and gazed into the nearest shop window. Unluckily it was a tallow-chandler's and so the device was obvious. The next time we met we bowed and were met by a very cold and frigid nod in return. Of course we met them at every church and picture gallery after that, and so anxious were they to show that they wished to avoid us at least as much as we to avoid them, that on several occasions they actually fled before us, leaving the most starred of Baedeker's [the travel guidebook] objects of interest unvisited. I thought they were carrying things to rather an absurd length and took care to bow politely whenever they did not make it impossible by turning their backs and hurrying away. Now they have come to this hotel and encounters in passages daily are inevitable and awkward.

---

[1] The Bells and VW toured Tuscany in September, returning in October after a week in Paris.

[2] Despite their impressive connections, the Fletchers are an elusive tribe and I am unable to trace them with certainty.

[3] Booths and Pollocks featured large in VB's childhood. Charles Booth, ship owner and social scientist (*Life and Labour of the People in London,* 1905), was a friend of VB's parents and employed George Duckworth for ten years as his unpaid private secretary. Sir Frederick Pollock (1845–1937), jurist and professor of jurisprudence at Oxford, 1883–1903, was a founder with Leslie Stephen of the "Sunday Tramps," an informal group of Sunday walkers.

Apart from them we do not like this as well as Siena, but then that was peculiarly attractive. We have come upon no good churches yet, but there is a good collection of pictures, with some very beautiful Peruginos. There is a small chapel too entirely decorated with frescoes by him.[4] In fact I have found Perugino altogether the most surprising of painters here and at Siena, for I had very little idea from the Nat. Gallery[5] that he was so good. He can be very bad too but sometimes at his best he gets most lovely colour and very beautiful, simple and spacious composition.

I have probably given you a worse idea of this place than it deserves, for in reality we have not yet explored it enough to know what it is like and besides there are very beautiful views to be had of the country all round. It is very high up and built on steep hills, as I suppose all these little Italian towns are. In fact our chief causes of discontent are the too respectable character of the hotel and the want of a place to have tea, such as we had at Siena.

There is an old and ugly lady here, I should say she was about 65, and she has in tow her mother, who must in consequence be about 85 at least. She is morose and infirm and her bedroom is next door to ours. We hear her muttering imprecations and growling at her unfortunate daughter, whose life has evidently been sacrificed to her. Shall I shock you if I tell you of her form of oath, when her unfortunate daughter happens to offend her? "G—d d—mn you" she shrieks at her—I think dashes may make it less shocking . . .

Your
V.B.

TATE

[4]The Audience Chamber of the Collegio del Cambio, 1500.
[5]The National Gallery, Trafalgar Square, London, home to the nation's art collection (at its present location) since 1838.

II-18. To Margery Snowden

Oct. 21st [1908]   *46, Gordon Square, Bloomsbury*

My dearest Margery,

I think it is comparatively a long time since I have written to you, which I hope you have taken as a mark of displeasure at your not coming to stay with us. Of course I don't consider your excuses good ones, but still I see that, such as they are, they must be accepted. You will have to come after Christmas instead, but I am very cross at not having you now.

I have been feeling this last week just as if I had been plunged back 3 years. For one thing I had a pathetic last appeal from Dobbin[1] to go to the Friday Club meetings, to which I have answered, perhaps rather cruelly, that if she were in my place she would know how difficult it is to tear oneself away from one's husband and a warm fire after dinner! Then there has been the reappearance of Henry Lamb.[2] He is very much improved in manner and has lost many of his youthful affectations. As before, I find him delightful to talk to, for he is one of the very few people who will talk intelligently about painting to me. I wish he lived in London, but he is just off to Edinburgh to do a portrait. Then he will come back to London but I am afraid not for long. However I shall see something of him then, for the Goat has commissioned him to do a drawing of me. He came yesterday afternoon and did two preliminary sketches. One was very good, I thought, both as a drawing and as a likeness. He is now very much under the influence of John.[3] His drawings are much freer than they were and have lost that rather unpleasant hardness. We had a long talk about painting, or at least we talked in scraps for a long time for I was sitting. He is now painting without any medium (like

---

[1]Dobbin (sometimes Dobbins) is Mary Creighton, daughter of the bishop of London; she studied painting with VB at the Academy Schools.
[2]Henry Lamb (1883–1960), painter, a follower of Augustus John (see note below), and on the fringes of Bloomsbury until the First World War. He was a younger brother of Walter Lamb. One of his best-known paintings is the portrait of Lytton Strachey (1914) now at the Tate.
[3]Augustus John (1878–1961), Slade-trained painter famous in the first two decades of the century for his bohemian lifestyle and his independence from the mainstream of English art. His reputation is currently eclipsed by that of his sister Gwen John (1876–1939), whose work VB sometimes admired.

us), and is using no black. His blacks he makes with blues, reds and greens—an expensive method. He too found as I did that it was impossible to mix every time for a small painting, but thinks that in a large one it might be a good plan to mix all the broad masses, with which I agree. Does this shop [talk] interest you I wonder? I find it absorbing and I also found to my pleasure that Henry Lamb did not depress me about my own work as he used to do. Not that he saw any of mine or talked of it, but I felt that I had my own point of view and was not swamped by him. Of course too he is older and does not talk in the violent extremes that he used to.

I have been painting rather well too, lately! Or so I think. I have done a still life which is perhaps rather ugly but well painted, and now I have asked Marjorie Strachey[4] to sit to me and have had my

[4]Marjorie Colville Strachey (1882–1964), teacher, a sister of Lytton Strachey. Also known as "Gumbo."

first sitting today. I am interested in it so I shall tell you about it at the risk of boring you. She is sitting leaning forward in black with a black hat on. She is sitting on our green sofa, which comes behind her across the picture. At the back is the wall with a jar of yellow chrysanthemums. I want to make all the background look some way off, and she is to be sitting in front in a sort of half tone, with light coming in at the back on the wall and chrysanthemums, like this, without the splodge! ⟨There will be light on her hand and a good deal of shadow about the pot and flowers which will also cast shadows on the wall.⟩ I think I may have to put the edge of a picture or something on the wall where the splodge is, but I am going to work at the composition of the background tomorrow. I shall only do small and unimportant things at the same time, so I hope to make this a success. I think my very careful still-life painting will come in usefully, and as Marjorie Strachey is very ugly (perhaps that's too harsh but you have seen her) I shan't be nervous about doing her justice as I generally am with the Goat.

Have you begun your thing of Hal[5] and how are you doing him? You will have to work very hard now if you want me to believe that you really couldn't come to us.

By the way, to add to the effect of having gone back 3 years, Nina is coming to see me on Friday! She calls herself now Euphemia Lamb![6] Do write soon and are you really quite well?

Your
V.B.

TATE

[5]Unidentified.
[6]Nina Forrest, an extremely attractive but friendless young woman, was rescued by Henry Lamb from a forced betrothal and moved with him to London in 1905, when he abandoned his medical training in Manchester to become an artist. They married in 1906, but separated soon after. "Euphemia" was Lamb's pet name for Nina.

II-19. To Clive Bell

Nov. 4 [1908]   *46, Gordon Square, Bloomsbury*

My dearest Clive,

There was a letter waiting from you last night and another this morning. Are you really better? You sound so in your second letter. The first was melancholy, poor little Master. I am simply besieged by people. I don't know why they suddenly seem to swarm. Ottoline[1] asks us both or me alone to dine tomorrow night to meet the Birrells.[2] I am going though I daresay it will be political and dull. She says it's not a party and I'm not to dress, so I don't know what to wear. Katharine Stephen wants to come and see me on Friday afternoon early. Your father wants to come tomorrow afternoon. Gwen Darwin[3] comes then too, as she's going on to dine at Fitzroy [with Virginia]. Walter Lamb wants to come to us for Saturday night! Altogether it's rather a whirl.

I had both Gwennie and Marjorie S[trachey] to lunch today and then we went on to the concert which was of course a seething mass of Fletchers, etc. Aunt Anny with Billy who quite obviously and intentionally cut me and was very rude.[4] He must be cross at our neglect of them. She was quite polite and friendly. Ottoline was there, and Katie[5] who wants to come and see me. Then I went back to Fitzroy with the Goat, Marjorie and Gwenny, and now I am just come home and am writing this Aunt Mary–like[6] letter before Lytton comes. I must keep all gossip till I see you.

[1]Lady Ottoline Violet Anne Morrell (née Cavendish-Bentinck) (1873–1938), society hostess and patron of contemporary art. Her parties at Bedford Square and Gower Street, Bloomsbury, and at Garsington Manor, near Oxford, are now legendary, along with her eccentricities of dress and decor. Her twins were born May 18, 1906: the girl, Julian, survived, but the boy died three days later.
[2]Augustine Birrell (1850–1933), author and Liberal statesman. He was at this time chief secretary for Ireland. His wife Eleanor (née Locker) (d. 1915) was the widow of Tennyson's second son Lionel.
[3]Gwen Darwin (1885–1957), daughter of Sir George Darwin, professor of astronomy at Cambridge, and granddaughter of Charles Darwin. She was a painter and wood engraver, and in 1911 married the painter Jacques Raverat.
[4]"Aunt" Anny is the writer Anne Thackeray Ritchie (1837–1919), sister of Sir Leslie Stephen's first wife Harriet. Billy is her son William.
[5]Lady Katherine Thynne, who married Lord Cromer in 1901.
[6]Anxious upholder of respectability and convention, Aunt Mary Fisher (1841–1916), a sister of Julia Stephen, had long been a source of uncomfortable disrespect for VB and VW.

Gwenny is very young and she and Marjorie together made me feel most completely middle-aged. They argued as to whether wrong and stupidity were the same thing. M. is cleverer than G., but you can imagine the crudities of their talk. What shall I talk to Lytton about tonight? After all he can go very early if he's bored or unwell, but I feel very flighty, uncertain, patchy and absent-minded without you. It is melancholy waking to a foggy, cold London morning, turning over lonely in bed and then thinking that it will be no easier to get up in half an hour and so making the plunge. The bathroom looks so deserted too and I think, well, the day after tomorrow I shall be feeling wildly excited. Why don't you write me a *very* long affectionate letter?

Dolphin's in disgrace.

> *Your*
> VB

TATE

II-20. To Lytton Strachey

[March 8, 1909]   *[The Lizard, Cornwall]*

Dear Lytton,[1]

How are you feeling after your Sunday with Sheepshanks, etc? I wish you would consider how charming we should be compared to them if you spent next Sunday here, but I don't think I can pretend that you'd enjoy it much. Perhaps the weather is better, it's very mild really, though there is sometimes a tearing wind, and sometimes rain. Still in the sun and out of the wind it's delicious. But this house of course is very uncomfortable. I didn't realise it last time. The food is rather scanty and nasty and here we are with Julian and Gurth. Adrian has been sunk in gloom ever since he arrived. I am amazed at his state of languor. Virginia says it's quite normal. If so I would almost marry Hilton Young, no, I suppose not quite, but he has been literally sitting

---

[1]On February 17, Lytton had proposed to Virginia and been accepted. They both realized their mistake, however, and the engagement was immediately dissolved. VW joined the Bells in Cornwall on about March 2.

in an arm-chair with his eyes shut all Saturday, Sunday and today, except for two short walks of at most 1/2 an hour each. He occasionally grumbles at the weather or the food and last night he roused himself for 10 minutes to explain to us how we had all combined to sit upon him in his youth and how much misery he has had in life. He doesn't even read, and I can't make out why he's come. Clive says the Stephen family are very depressing. He himself is extremely active and goes for long walks and Virginia and I pursue a middle course. I suppose it's very healthy. As a matter of fact we are all, except Adrian, really very cheerful.

I wish you'd send me your sentimental poem. I think I could get into a sympathetically sentimental mood here and should appreciate it.

> Yours affect'ly,
> V.B.

BRITISH LIBRARY

II-21. To Virginia Stephen

Friday [March 12, 1909]   *The Lizard*

My Billy,
    You do seem to be having a most dismal time.[1] How is Adrian really? I suppose you would tell me the truth.

The weather has improved here. It is still cold but there isn't so much wind and we went for a walk, and it was really very beautiful. You tell me to describe the look of things, but how can I? Besides I'm not basking on a cliff as you imagine, like a seal. If I were a seal, as I believe you imagine me to be, I should no doubt bask in all weathers. Being only a dolphin, I need the sun.

Today it was all grey with only one brilliant streak of light in the distance. I kept thinking of how various painters would have treated it and I flattered myself that I saw how it ought to be treated but I

---

[1] VW was back in London with Adrian. Her letter suggesting a "dismal time" is not extant.

could not do it. A melancholy watercolour of a sunset is my only achievement. You writers, however, do not know the joy of experimenting in a new medium, especially in one of which one is quite ignorant. One seems to come upon so many unexpected capacities in oneself.

Tonight Clive and I have had a lengthy argument about Tono-Bungay.[2] Have you read it? Do do so and send me your candid and detailed opinion, for I am curious to know what other people think. Clive and I are so different in our views, and I cannot express mine.

Our stores have come, to our joy. We get more attention and even hot lunches now that you have gone. You will be sorry to hear that I have inflicted a gash on the inside of the joint of my first right-hand finger to the injury of my handwriting. It is not otherwise serious. Do send me long letters. They are badly wanted.

Your
VB

BERG

II-22. To Virginia Stephen

Saturday [April 10, 1909]   *Cleeve House*

My Billy,
No letter from you by either post today. Why don't you write? I have only had one scant post card from you since we've been here, and no news of your plans or anything. I saw the Quaker's death in the Times today,[1] which makes it all the odder that I don't hear from you. I hope I shall tomorrow morning. I suppose you have heard from Katharine.[2] I have had no letters at all. I don't know what to write about to you, for the days are monotonous to a degree. Clive is very happy sitting in the sun like a salamander. I have spent most of today

[2]H. G. Wells' *Tono-Bungay* (London: Macmillan, 1909).
[1]Caroline Emilia Stephen died April 7, 1909.
[2]Katharine Stephen, VB's first cousin, had been especially close to Caroline Emilia and inherited much of her property. VB and Adrian received £100 each (today approx. £4,520/$7,910), VW a legacy of £2500 (approx. £113,025/$197,793).

wondering why I don't hear from you and consoling myself by the reflection that Sophy[3] would probably let me know if you had influenza or anything else. Clive suggests that you may have gone off to Cambridge but I think it highly improbable.

I feel that I am writing in a rather complaining spirit, but really you don't know how much one depends on small things here. Like all Stephens, as we said the other day, my sense of proportion gets lost in solitude, for here one is practically in solitude as far as anything one wants from one's fellow creatures goes. I hardly see Clive alone, and besides I feel that we are both oppressed by the family weight. I know that, according to you, I am too much oppressed by it, but I can't help it. Also I feel really sorry that the Quaker is dead. She was far the best of our relations, and a link with the past as they say. I somehow always thought that she would weep over us all in our graves.

Your
VB

BERG

II-23. Lytton Strachey

Wednesday [April 28, 1909]   *32, Via Romana, Florence*[1]

Dear Lytton,

How charming it would be if you were lying on the verandah outside our windows now. I can't help thinking your doctor was wrong in forbidding you to come to Florence. We had a very easy journey out, stopping one night in Milan, and here we are in a palatial room about as big as both the drawing rooms at Gordon Sqre. However the food isn't very good, which might be a drawback to you. As we came along

[3]Sophia Farrell (c. 1861–1942), cook at HPG. She moved to Bloomsbury with the Stephen children, but eventually left for the more traditional household of George Duckworth.
[1]The Bells traveled to Florence and Milan with VW. Her continuing flirtation with CB strained the trio however and, after a quarrel, she left alone for England on May 9. The Bells stayed on another fortnight.

in the train a row of naked boys saluted us. We travelled out with an unbelievable English party, one of Dr. Lunn's,[2] Sarah and Alfred, a middle-aged couple with a dutiful niece and another young lady. We had secured the corners, so they had to sit bolt upright all night. Alfred sat next me, pressing me tightly into my corner with his waterproof jacket. He lit matches at intervals to see the time and rattled mysterious papers. Can you imagine what it was like, after spending the night so, when at about 3 A.M. they decided to have breakfast and produced from a basket oranges, eggs and shortbread?

Here the Germans are worse than English and I realise the horrors of a German invasion when they plant their fat backs between me and the Botticellis,[3] which really are the most beautiful pictures in the world. I believe you don't appreciate him.

Our *pension* has some awful females, but two young men who sing you might flirt with. They walk past our windows on their way to their baths every morning and there are strange goings on on the verandah at all hours of the night. There might be still stranger if you were here. All the windows almost open onto it. I am finishing the Liaisons.[4] It is getting too tragic, but it is absorbing. Why did I never read it before?

I hope you'll write and say how you are. Virginia has been rather unhappy because she was told by Dorothea Stephen[5] the other day that her writing was ladylike and empty, but she is beginning to cheer up. I suppose Saxon has been visiting you.

Your
V.B.

BRITISH LIBRARY

[2]Dr. Henry Lunn (1859–1939), a travel agent and founder of the Hellenic Travellers Club.
[3]At the Uffizi Gallery.
[4]Pierre Choderlos de Laclos, *Les Liaisons Dangereuses* (1782), a Bloomsbury favorite.
[5]"Old Dodder," VB's first cousin, sister of Katharine Stephen. This criticism may have been voiced during VW's lunch with Dorothea after Caroline Emilia's funeral.

II-24. To Virginia Stephen

May 16 [1909]   *32, Via Romana, Florence*

My Billy,

Whether you write two letters a day or not, I only get one a day, so continue your practice. Is Ottoline becoming my rival in your affections? I am suspicious. You will have a desperate liaison with her I believe, for I rather think she shares your Sapphist tendencies and only wants a little encouragement.[1] She once told me that she much preferred women to men and would take any trouble to get to know a woman she liked, but would never do the same for a man. If I had not brutally said that I generally preferred men, what might not have happened?

What is this mysterious exhibition at the Grafton,[2] I am curious to know? It cannot be the New English for that is to be in Suffolk St. We saw the John I think in his studio when it was half finished. It looked then as if he had already spoilt it by painting too long upon it. I cannot of course say yet whether I should agree with your acute criticisms. As for Mary Davis,[3] whose work I think but am not sure I know, I am inclined to be sceptical. But we shall see.

We spent this morning at the Accademia, which of course you did not half see. I come more than ever to the conclusion that the Primavera[4] is one of the greatest pictures ever painted.

We had lunch yesterday with Rezia.[5] Pasolino was there and actually told Clive that although he thought George charming he quite saw that he was a fearful snob. The Herberts[6] had stayed in Rome and

[1]Ottoline Morrell's romance with Bloomsbury equaled Virginia's romance with the aristocracy, but at no time was Lady Ottoline a "Sapphist."
[2]The Grafton Galleries, London, which often exhibited the works of the New English Art Club, and which would host Roger Fry's First and Second Post-Impressionist exhibitions in 1910 and 1912. The current exhibition was called "Chosen Pictures."
[3]Lady Mary Davis (née Halford) (1866–1941), principally a painter of silk fans. She exhibited regularly at the R.A.
[4]The celebrated allegorical painting by Botticelli, c. 1478.
[5]Principessa Lucrezia (Rezia) Corsini (née Rasponi) (1879–1971), friend of the Stephens and Duckworths in HPG days. "Pasolino" is Guido Pasolini, Rezia's cousin.
[6]The Duckworths' cousins on their father's side were Herberts. Herbert was the family name of the earls of Carnarvon. Elsie, widow of the fourth earl, was a great friend of George's and he married her stepdaughter, Lady Margaret.

Pasolino had tried to be polite to them, but they had given themselves great airs and were intolerable. He thought George must have been much influenced by them.

Last night as we sat on our verandah we saw a fire-fly. Wasn't it romantic? It looked very ghostly, a tiny white point of flame floating about in the garden. I thought at first it must be your disembodied spirit come to visit me.

It was really hot at last and is still. We are going up to call on the Berensons[7] this afternoon. This time next week I shall be in England and very nearly in London.

We have been at last given our long expected invitation to stay with the Freshfields[8] in June. Clara Pater[9] has also written asking me to go and see her. I shall go when we are back. Go on writing [here] till Wednesday morning.

Your
VB

BERG

II-25. To Lytton Strachey

Aug. 26 [1909]   *Cleeve House, Melksham, Wilts*

Dear Lytton,

You seem to have vanished, but I hope you are recovering and are out of prison.[1] Is your cure as full of temptations as we thought it would be? I had a terrible dream of you in a vast house full of cubicles in each of which there was supposed to be one young man. There was a sudden raid by the police and each young man was found to

[7]At I Tatti, the Florence home of the art critic Bernard Berenson and his wife.
[8]The Freshfields were old family friends of the Stephens in Kensington; they had a country house in Sussex.
[9]Clara Pater, sister of Walter Pater, and VW's first tutor in Greek.
[1]Lytton spent August and part of September at Badenstalten, a health spa at Saltsjöbaden, near Stockholm. His traveling companions were Daisy McNeil, an aunt of Duncan Grant's who ran a private nursing home at Eastbourne, and her patient Miss Elwes, a woman devoted to Duncan's mother.

have a boy in with him. You were taken in the act and sent to prison, but only for Saturday to Monday, as it was a "first offence." Is there any truth in this? I had a letter from Pippa[2] which seemed to imply that you were surrounded by ugly females, which I suppose is more likely to be true.

We have just come here after a perfectly solitary August in London. I had an unfortunate encounter with Walter Lamb at the end of his Clifton term,[3] but perhaps it would be more discreet not to tell you of it. [Two lines heavily scored over.] No, I get into too many scraps when I write or talk of him, so I will scratch it out.

Will you come and stay with us at Studland Bay between Sep 16th and 30th? It is a place near Poole Harbour, and sounds attractive country, but I must warn you that we shall be in lodgings, probably uncomfortable ones. I only know that the rooms are rather small. If it is fine it won't so much matter, as there is a large beach very near. Virginia is going to be in other lodgings there, I hope for the whole time. She has sent me long accounts of Saxon at Bayreuth.[4] He seems to have been unusually lively and has himself written very often to me and Clive, sometimes in verse. Adrian has been in a state of irritation with both the others—Saxon sang in his sleep and Virginia was too enthusiastic. They come back at the end of the week.

I have scratched out the only interesting sentence in this letter!

Your
VB

BRITISH LIBRARY

[2]Philippa Strachey (1872–1968), proponent of women's rights, an elder sister of Lytton. In 1907 she organized the first significant women's suffrage march through London.
[3]Walter Lamb worked as assistant master at Clifton College, Bristol from 1907 to 1909 while continuing to lecture in classics at Cambridge.
[4]VW had joined Adrian and Saxon on their annual pilgrimage to the Wagner Festival.

II-26. To Virginia Stephen

Thursday [September 2, 1909]   *Cleeve House, Melksham, Wilts*

My Billy,

I get time to read your letters and even to enjoy them while Julian is out in his pram. I have not written to you for some days, for I thought it was no use writing later than Sunday to Dresden and no use to write to Fitzroy Sq. till today. Nothing has happened meanwhile except that I have got through more than half my time of being nursemaid for which I am rather thankful . . . .

Your theories of art[1] are very interesting, of course. I don't see how you use colour in writing, but probably you can do it with art. The mere words gold or yellow or grey mean nothing to me unless I can see the exact quality of the colour, but I suppose if you do it well you convey that. But I don't see how you can ever count upon the reader getting just the right impression, as you can in a painting, when it comes to describing the looks of things. Perhaps you don't really describe the looks but only the impression the looks made upon you.

In any case your art seems to be progressing and ascending, while mine is under the heel of moo-cows.[2] It will spring up I hope at Studland. I can't for the life of me tell you what I meant about Holmes,[3] and I rather suspect I was wrong and that you just hit the mark. I should have abused his sentimentality. Perhaps it was more Americans than Holmes that I disagreed about. I suppose father liked his sentimentality. How odd that he should have had me and Adrian for children. I often feel singularly boorish and crude. But here I feel subtle and clever and almost a genius. Unluckily the feeling is not so pleasant as you might suppose. It is only contrast with Lorna and Dorothy that makes me feel so, and it would be truer to say that I

---

[1]VW and her party moved from Bayreuth to Dresden, where they admired the Italian and Dutch painters represented in the Dresden Gallery. Though two of VW's letters to VB from Dresden survive, the third, which VB here answers, does not.

[2]The infant Julian's name for Vanessa.

[3]VW had reviewed *Oliver Wendell Holmes* by Lewis W. Townsend (London: Headley Brothers, 1909) in the *TLS* on August 26. Cf. VB to Virginia Stephen, Friday (August 27, 1909): "I have got your Holmes article and will keep it in case you want it. What do you think of it? I feel incompetent to judge . . . but I don't feel as if I should agree with what you say of him—if I had read his works, which I haven't" (Berg).

feel like a dolphin stranded high and dry, lashing about to find some water.

When one first comes here, one thinks, well they really aren't so bad, there are virtues in vegetables and one has plenty to say oneself. But gradually with no nourishment from without, one's own stream of talk runs dry, and one lapses into silence, and then the awful torrent of commonplaces on tennis and the weather—oh Lord! how much can be said on the weather!—a subject I have never known you and I to mention to each other—overwhelms one and one can do nothing but subside into gloom. But I forgot that you once told me I ought not to complain! Still I really have some right to now, for I don't even see Clive much—hardly ever alone—now that I have Julian, so it is unrelieved family. What a mercy it will be to get away . . .

VB

BERG

II-27. To Duncan Grant

Mar. 16 [1910]   *46, Gordon Square, Bloomsbury*

Dear Duncan,

I am sending you tomorrow two cholera belts. Don't laugh at me. They really may be useful if you do get a chill. I don't suppose you'll want them otherwise, and if you don't use them you can always give them back to me at the end of your travels. Lytton made off with the two others I once possessed, so I shall be quite glad to have this pair returned to me in time if you don't want them.

I expect that Keynes has made all the preparations and is taking plenty of medicines, and that in consequence all my grandmotherly advice was superfluous and officious. All the same, when I think how everybody refrained from giving us advice before we set out for the East[1] because they thought somebody else would do so, I make bold to be superfluous and officious. I thought last night that the word

[1] I.e., on the Stephens' ill-fated 1906 trip to Greece.

diarrhoea would shock Philip[2] too much—Virginia had already shouted "after-birth" at him—but what I wanted to say was if you do get it, as everyone does, don't at once stop it with chlorodyne, as Thoby and Adrian did, but take castor oil and rest and feed on sloppy foods. Also take a supply of Bromo. It's quite easy to carry decently really, though I have visions of masses tumbling out of coat pockets at all moments. Don't wash your teeth in ordinary water, but get some mineral water. It doesn't really cost much and it's quite as bad to wash your teeth in plain water as to drink it.

I can't think of any other good advice to give you, except that I wouldn't myself go to the Palace Hotel at Athens again. It may be all right now but it was horrid when we were there. The Hôtel d'Angleterre was stodgy, but I think quite healthy. I enclose £2, in case it's convenient to get cloaks or anything else.

Your
VB

HENRIETTA GARNETT

II-28. To Virginia Stephen

Thursday [June 23, 1910]   *46, Gordon Square, Bloomsbury*

My Billy,

I have just seen Savage.[1] He was going to write to you himself, and so you will probably know his opinion before you read this. I had given him in my letter as accurate an account as I could of how you are and said that I thought you were better but still had numbness and headache when anything unusually tiring happened. I told him that you were, I thought, prepared to do anything rather than go on being not quite well very much longer when you had had a bad day, but that when you felt better you were very sanguine and thought

[2]Philip Edward Morrell (1870–1943), lawyer and liberal MP.
[1]During the spring of 1910, VW traveled with the Bells to Cornwall, to Studland in Dorset, and to a rented house near Canterbury in her efforts to shake off the headaches which foreboded another bout of insanity. In July she entered Burley, a mental nursing home at Twickenham, for a rest cure.

yourself almost well. Savage said that he had considered the whole matter most easefully and had come to the conclusion that he had tried half-measures long enough. He said he had done his best with them and thought it was too risky to go on with them any longer and that you would never get quite well unless you had a rest cure. I asked him whether that was his honest opinion and he was most decided about it. Then he said that he did not think you could have a cure in London at this time of year because it was so stuffy. I suggested some place like Hampstead and he said that he would find out and make all arrangements. He thought he knew of a very good place at Richmond, kept by a lady he knows where you could have a modified cure and be within easy reach. He does not think the most severe type of Weir Mitchell[2] treatment necessary, but thinks that you ought to have what he calls slightly modified treatment for a month. He said that he would try to get it arranged by the beginning of next week and would let you know when to come up and see him before beginning it. He wants you to come up and go straight to the cure from Canterbury. He said he supposed that on some days you felt quite well and on others bad again.

I think I have told you everything he said as far as I can remember it. I am afraid, unless you happen to have a headache, that you will be inclined to think it all absurd, but I am quite sure that Savage took it most seriously and was convinced that your only way of complete recovery was this. I certainly did not give him too bad an account of you and I thought that he evidently understood your state.

Does this all sound very matter of fact and brutal? I am not really but I thought I had better tell you just what happened. I know how horrid it is but I am sure Savage thought that you would only go on in this unsatisfactory way indefinitely unless you did something drastic. It does seem a pity that he didn't decide this sooner, but I think he had wanted to give gentle measures a fair trial.

I went on my way home to Fitzroy and couldn't find your books anywhere. I looked in all your rooms and the drawing-room and study and I think I must have seen them if they had been there.

I saw Saxon last night. He was evidently highly flattered at your invitation and I thought in a flutter of gratified vanity which he tried to conceal under a mask of incapacity to find out your station or trains. I was kind enough to tell him West Canterbury and I suppose

[2]The American doctor Weir Mitchell pioneered in the 1880s the "Rest Cure," a strict though very popular treatment involving seclusion and long periods in bed.

he can really look out trains. But he didn't come home with us, so I only saw him for a few minutes. Ottoline was there and kissed her hand to me across the theatre, a salute which I hadn't the grace or self-confidence to return. She came in the next interval to talk to me and ask after you. She herself evidently thinks she has exactly the same disease—and perhaps she has. She has long wisps of hair all over her eyes and looked very much distraught. She had only just come to London, which she finds too exhausting, and she is to go abroad almost at once for 2 months. She wished you could go with her and thought you would have a good effect upon each other as she is—outwardly—calm. I saw rows of Booths and Milmans, but no one else to talk to. Duncan of course came home with us, but I felt *de trop*. I must leave some of my gossip to tell Clive. I have had no letter from you yet and only one from him.

Do write to me and tell me how you are and whether there is anything else you want to know about what Savage said—but I think I have told you all. Our interview was short as he already had all the facts from my letter and had clearly made up his mind. I have written immediately on coming in, so as not to forget anything. It seems a very long time since I saw you and I feel in an oddly widowed position here. Certainly Adrian would in some ways be a weight to live with, but he is very kind and polite to me and compliments me on having ice on the butter.

Your
V.B.

BERG

II-29. To Clive Bell

Thursday [June 23, 1910]   *46, Gordon Square, Bloomsbury*

My dearest Clive,

I have told the Goat what Savage said, so I will not repeat it to you. He was very serious and quite decided and I am sure I was right in thinking that she could not get well going on as she is doing. I hope she won't be in a fearful state about it, but I suppose that depends upon how she happens to be feeling. But in any case it may be a relief to have a definite opinion. I only wish we had got it before.

Savage has taken all arrangements upon himself and was very kind and friendly. Of course all the difficulties and tiresome things will be discussed by you both, and I feel that there's not much use in my pointing out the other side from this distance. I am only anxious that the Goat shouldn't think that I have in any way tried to make Savage suggest a rest cure, of which I do see all the disadvantages very clearly, and also that she should realise how serious he thought it. I saw that he really wouldn't have advised it even now if he had thought anything else possible, and I do believe in his opinion.

Now I will tell you such of my adventures as I haven't already told Virginia.

I went to the Friday Club with Adrian yesterday. The Puvis de Chavannes are disappointing.[1] I thought them quite dull. Peter Studd's[2] sketch is much the best. The whole show was on the whole a great deal better than I had expected and better than any other we have had. One young man of 17 I marked down as promising. His name is Mark Gertler[3] and he has two rather remarkable paintings, remarkable really only considering his age, but I think he may be going to be good. Your little Viscountess[4] has a watercolour called "The Christening," two parents holding up a baby to a crucifix from which rays of light fall on it, highly intense and I thought not very good. Gwenny has a great many wood-cuts, of which several have been sold, some to Will Rothenstein.[5] She is of course delighted. They are exceedingly dramatic. Corpses and dancers on gravestones, etc. Some have merit. There are several more or less good drawings, and a great many bad ones. Poor Sylvia has been all rejected but one small still life and is said to feel it acutely. Dolphin has two still lifes. Her

[1]Pierre Puvis de Chavannes (1824–98), influential French muralist. VB would have also seen his work at the Franco-British Exhibition in 1908 and at the National Gallery.
[2]Arthur Peter Studd (1863–1919), trained at the Académie Julien in Paris and at the Slade.
[3]Mark Gertler (1891–1939), English painter born of poor Polish-Jewish parents. Later a member of the New English Art Club (hereafter NEAC) and the London Group.
[4]Unidentified; possibly a brief romantic interest of CB's. (Catalogues from Friday Club exhibitions are extremely scarce, unfortunately, and this one seems not to have survived.)
[5]Sir William Rothenstein (1872–1945), painter, writer, and teacher, later principal of the Royal College of Art (1920–35).

beach at Studland[6] was rejected, but the still lifes are hung in the best place. But in between them, and in the principal place of honour, is hung a sketch by Duncan which I thought far better than anything else, including the Puvis's. It is really very good indeed, very well drawn and a beautiful composition, of women carrying loads on their heads.[7] I was very much impressed by it and really think that he may be going to be a great painter. There seems to me to be something remarkably fine in his work, and in the grand manner. He is certainly much the most interesting of the young painters.

We came home to tea when who should appear but Harry.[8] Adrian was there of course and our talk was rather difficult I thought. Julian came down and we went into the square. Harry stayed till 7.15, my dinner-time, but Adrian was there nearly all the time so I hardly saw him alone, you'll be sorry to hear. Lytton is at Hampstead but in bed, and will probably be sent out of London again as soon as he's better. We talked about Cambridge and a good deal about the Goat's state. Norton was rather distressed about it, tell her, and thought we were mad not to insist upon a rest cure, and that she was equally mad not to insist upon having one. He wasn't at all affectionate to me and twitted Adrian upon his affair with Duncan, which I don't think A. much liked . . .

But Dolphin does want you back very badly. She feels very odd and forlorn having to arrange everything for herself and Saturday even seems a long way off. Still I see that the Goat must be considered, as I'm afraid she'll hate the idea of the cure when it comes to the point.

I am longing for news of you. You wrote me a nice letter yesterday but your poor little bed-fellow is so lonely of a morning. If you're away till Monday it will be nearly a week since I've seen you . . .

Dolphin rubs your orange whiskers with her snout and offers her tail to be stroked.

V.B.

TATE

[6]See plate viii, bottom.
[7]*Lemon Gatherers* (1910), bought by Vanessa Bell, and now at the Tate.
[8]H. T. J. Norton (1886–1937), Cambridge mathmetician and Apostle, much attracted to VB. Also a special friend and financial supporter of Lytton Strachey's who dedicated *Eminent Victorians* (1918) to "H.T.J.N."

II-30. To Virginia Stephen

July 17 [1910]   *46, Gordon Square, Bloomsbury*

My Billy,

I heard what I expected from Clive, that you are seducing the household of the hitherto respectable Miss Thomas[1] and that your own lusts are increasing at the same time. Perhaps you find massage inducive to lust. I can imagine it might be. Really, what with your cultivation of Sapphism with a Swede at Twickenham and Lytton's of Sodomism with Swedes in Sweden,[2] which apparently is the breeding-house of vice, you will be a fine couple worthy of each other when you both come out. I believe he went to his home yesterday. But apparently Miss T. herself has a pure and even, to my sceptical mind, slightly sentimental, passion for you. With tears in her eyes she told Clive how after a winter of discontent *you,* etc., etc. But I will leave Clive to tell you himself. I had gathered a good deal from her letters to me which always speak of you with bated breath as a privilege and an angel of unselfishness—until I feel my cynical sisterly hairs rising down my back and I wonder where *your* red ones can be concealing themselves. But you are evidently a huge success and I expect to see a troupe of lunies and their keepers dancing attendance on you in the autumn.

Meanwhile, what has happened to us since Thursday? Clarissa[3] has not appeared and I do not now expect her to be kind enough to do so for weeks. I see it was fatal to take any precautions about her and she will have been frightened off indefinitely. Duncan came to lunch on Friday, as did also Clive's editor. Clive is to begin his editing [of the *Athenaeum*] on the 25th for 3 weeks only. We have seen no one else but Adrian and Saxon who both came to lunch yesterday. They

---

[1]Jean Thomas, proprietor of the nursing home at Twickenham. A devout Christian, she became enamored of VW, occasionally attempting to convert her. Later in the year she accompanied VW on a walking tour in Cornwall.

[2]Lytton Strachey was again in Sweden at the Saltsjöbaden sanatorium for a ten-week cure. He arrived on July 18, not the sixteenth, as Vanessa suggested.

[3]Actually, Quentin Claudian Bell, born August 19, 1910. The arrival of a second male child threw the Bells into confusion. He was hastily named "Gratian," a uniformly unpopular choice. Saxon Sydney-Turner scoured the Latin dictionary for help, suggesting "Viggo" and "Crippen." "Claudian" was transitional to "Quentin."

were made to play catch all the afternoon which kept them livelier than anything else could have done, but did not lead to much that would interest you—or indeed anyone else. Adrian went back to tea so as to sit to Duncan afterwards, and Sylvia appeared here. Mr Milman had been as meek as a lamb about her plans of independence, and it is settled that she is to live by herself in a flat in the autumn.

We are going this afternoon to a farewell tea with Ottoline. They leave England early tomorrow morning. I shall have no scene with her, as I shall not see her alone. I suppose we shall hear tomorrow what Savage has arranged for your doings this week. No doubt you will see Clive at any rate. I wish your headaches would quite disappear. Don't cajole Miss T. too much into letting you do whatever you like. I have to leave a space so that Clive may insert some vanity and therefore I will stop now.

Your
V.B.

[Paragraph by CB about his articles in the *Athenaeum* omitted.]

BERG

II-31. To Clive Bell

Oct. 9 [1910]   *Harbour View, Studland*

My dearest Clive,

You sounded rather melancholy in your letter this morning, but I hope by now you are travelling through that lovely French country on your way to Paris and beginning to get excited at the prospect. If it is like this it must be divine. I never saw such weather. We sat on the beach this morning with books which we didn't open. It is now about 4. I have been kept in waiting for the doctor. He has just been and thinks Claudian going on quite well. His inside is not perfectly right yet, but he thinks it will get so and that all is going on well. We are giving him more milk successfully so I hope he will soon get less skinny. I don't quite know what to do about going home, but I think we must anyhow stay till Wednesday. The doctor comes again on Monday, and I can't settle definitely till he has been. It seems rather absurd too to go in this weather but London will be tempting I expect after the Goat has gone. She says her head is in [a] very good state now and she slept well here last night. She has walked in to Swanage this afternoon, principally to have tea.

We have had no very interesting talk since I wrote. In fact, after our first outbursts we have been rather silent. Last night we sate over the fire sleepily and we have only indulged in wandering reminiscences about our pasts. You might have found them enlightening if you had been here, but not very, I think.

I have a card from Carfax for a Private View of works by Albert Rothenstein.[1] You will be able to see such things in their true light I expect after Paris. Oh dear, I own I should rather like to be in that exciting atmosphere where people really seem to realise the existence of art. What fun it would be if we were wondering now where we should dine, and sitting looking at those beautifully neat and amusing little females walking in front of us. But I am quite happy here and we will go there before long. I make my mouth water by thinking about it all. Perhaps you'll come back quite determined that we must go and live there.

You ought to have had Dolphin with you to recognize Binyon,[2] Foolish Peak. Julian has quite realised that you are in Paris and how you get there. He is looking very well and is most irrepressible, dancing all over the place and chasing me all the way up from the beach. I was talking today about the dead leaves and he reminded me how I used to scatter rose petals for him on the floor in London. It must have been at least 3 months ago. We have no letters of interest, a long one from Jean [Thomas] of course, and I have a sort of Collins from Alice.[3] How is your cold?

V.

TATE

[1]Albert Rothenstein (1881–1953), painter, younger brother of Sir William, anglicized his name to Rutherston at the onset of the war in 1914. He had his first one-artist exhibition at the Carfax Gallery in 1910.
[2]Laurence Binyon (1869–1943), of the British Museum, poet and lecturer on oriental art.
[3]Alice Waterlow (née Pollock), at this time the wife of the diplomat Sydney Waterlow (1878–1944), a friend of CB's at Trinity College, Cambridge. The Waterlows, with VW, had joined the Bell family at Studland in September. In 1911 Sydney separated from Alice and proposed to VW.

CHAPTER THREE

1911–1914

This chapter begins and ends with a love affair, actually two. In April 1911 the Bells traveled to Turkey, meeting Roger Fry and H. T. J. Norton on the way. Vanessa assumed she would be paired with Norton while the art critics debated the merits of mosques, but (to Norton's dismay) instead found herself frequently alone with Roger, painting and talking. She had already discovered his unique empathy and open-mindedness, and now she learned what a delightful and adventurous companion he made. His energy astonished her. At Brusa, Vanessa suffered a serious miscarriage, bringing with it physical and mental collapse. The little town had no doctor and Clive was flustered by even the thought of illness. Roger stepped in, competently nursing and comforting Vanessa until Virginia arrived to help carry her back to London by the Orient Express. Sometime at Brusa, Roger and Vanessa realized they were in love.

Loving Roger meant that Vanessa could share her ideas, almost as soon as they occurred to her, with one of the most daring critics of this century. She was intimately involved with his Second Post-Impressionist Exhibition in 1912 and with the July 1913 foundation of the Omega Workshops (she, Roger, and Duncan Grant were co-directors). Her artistic experimentation found a new outlet in the Omega's decorative work, and she applied what she learned to her paintings. Concurrent with her great artistic growth, however, was her increasing fondness and admiration for Duncan Grant, then in love with her brother Adrian.

Adrian lived at 38 Brunswick Square in a strange ménage concocted by Virginia in 1911 to save money and enable the occupants to work freely. She took the second floor (what Americans would consider the third), Adrian the first, and Maynard Keynes a pied-à-terre on the ground floor. Leonard Woolf, on leave from the Ceylon Civil Service, moved into the top floor. By the end of January 1912, Leonard was in love with Virginia and had proposed marriage. Vanessa encouraged the match, urging Virginia to ignore all trivial concerns, such as Leonard's Jewishness, and to marry only for love. On May 29, Virginia accepted him, and Vanessa—though remaining an advisor—gratefully began to shift responsibility for her sister's health and happiness to Leonard.

Even with that burden lifted, Vanessa had more than enough to occupy her time and attention in this period: her continuing recovery from her miscarriage; negotiating a friendship with her husband; raising two young boys; starting the Omega; loving Roger; and establishing herself in the vanguard of British art, among the first to venture into pure abstraction. Her most creative years as an artist coincided with the most chaotic period in her personal life. To add to the confusion, sometime early in 1913 Vanessa discovered she was deeply in love with Duncan Grant.

III-1. To Roger Fry

June 23 [1911]   *46, Gordon Square, Bloomsbury*

My dear Roger,

I wrote to you yesterday but the letter was too dull and tiresome to send. Pehaps this will be no better but it shall go anyhow, if only to tell you how glad I was of yours this morning. I kept it to myself, although it was very discreet.

I heard all about Virginia's visit to you[1] from her. She too enjoyed it very much and said you were charming, and that she was very much surprised by the beauty of the place. It made my mouth water to hear of your walk, but soon I shall be going that walk with you. Why shouldn't I have been there to hear you talk about me? Do you think I should have been shy? You must know me too well for that! You might have discussed the qualities of my inmost soul or body without making me blush, and Virginia is equal to saying anything to anybody's face.

What a gloomy two days it has been. I hope Julian will get through his pageant safely.[2] Virginia and Adrian walked out after luncheon to see the coronation[3] and Adrian at any rate saw it all quite easily. They gave a gloomy report. Duncan on the other hand thought it very beautiful, with the grey sky, and charming Chinamen lolling back in

---

[1] RF and VW had recently exchanged visits: he to Little Talland House, her villa at Firle, Sussex; she to his house, Durbins, at Guildford.
[2] Julian Fry (1901–1984), RF's son, was involved in a local pageant to celebrate the coronation.
[3] Of George V (1865–1936).

their carriages smoking cigarettes. But perhaps he was a little prejudiced in favour of it all by his intense admiration for the Duchess of Devonshire's footman, who was the most exquisite creature he had even seen. Also the Prince of Wales stirred him a little! He doesn't seem to be changing his tastes very quickly, does he?

He and I have decided to emulate Gill[4] and paint really indecent subjects. I suggest a series of copulations in strange attitudes and have offered to pose. Will you join? I mean in the painting. We think there ought to be more indecent pictures painted, and you shall show them at your show.

Oh dear, today you're going to Miss Sands[5] and I shan't see you till Tuesday, shall I? and Snow is not coming here till Tuesday and then only stays one night, so we can't have you as I had half hoped. I want to talk to you for several weeks on end about painting and I want to enlarge upon my theories of composition in front of your paintings. They were very vague and confused when I did talk to you. Will you give me your lectures to read? I think they might be good for me and would also perhaps save me from telling you things you know already.

I have written to Studland. By the way, if you could get rooms for most of you, we shall have one room at any rate in our house that you could use. You'd probably be quite near the others. It wouldn't be impossible for you just to sleep with us, would it? I do hope something will be found.

I'm afraid I gave you rather a dose of grumbling when I saw you, but it didn't mean that I was worse. Only I'm getting so sick of not being quite well, and this half-baked existence is beginning to make both me and everything else seem so unreal to me. I asked [Doctor] Lankester when he thought I could work again, but he would only treat the question as a bad joke. I think I must try to see Craig[6] again next week. It would be easier if I knew something definite. I am really going on quite well. I've had better nights and my affairs are fairly normal. The neuralgia has been rather bad at times but it doesn't last bad very long.

When I think about you I begin to try to draw you, but luckily only

[4]Eric Gill (1882–1940), sculptor, writer, typographer.
[5]Ethel Sands (1873–1962), American painter. She studied and exhibited in Paris, then, moving to London, became a founding member of the London Group in 1913. Her lifelong companion was the American painter Nan Hudson (1869–1957).
[6]Dr. Maurice Craig, a nerve specialist.

in the air. I know the shape of all of you pretty well now, even your hands I think I know almost as well as you know mine. I don't talk about them as much but perhaps I have felt them even more intimately. Do you think so? I was very happy after you'd gone the other day, thinking of you. It was such a blessing that you didn't have to rush off quite so early. Very soon now we shall be established I hope in Mr MacKenzie's[7] house, and then we shall be able to spend whole days together and I shall agree with Pamela[8] in disliking your London days.

Is Miss Sands horribly skilful and do you really think I can ever do anything to make up for my complete lack of skill? There's a nice fishing question for you to answer.

Perhaps I'll enclose a note for Edith.[9]

Your
Vanessa.

I can't read your address. I must send this to Guildford.

TATE

III-2. To Roger Fry

Sunday [July 2 1911]   *46, Gordon Square, Bloomsbury*

My dear Roger,

It is tantalizing to hear your voice at the other end of the telephone and not be able to see you. I wanted to see you try to look disturbed when I insinuated such disturbing things as I did yesterday. It always makes a peculiar look come into your eyes which I enjoy. Have I ever told you of it? You look very much on the alert and rather wicked, and your mouth takes a very nice shape, drawn back over your teeth a little. If you looked in the glass more you'd know what I mean.

I forgot to say yesterday that I hoped Edith didn't mind my having

[7]VB's landlord at Millmead Cottage, Guildford, where she stayed in August.
[8]Pamela Fry (1902–1985), RF's daughter.
[9]Edith Burroughs, an American woman whose husband had been a colleague of RF's at the Metropolitan Museum. She had a slight flirtation with RF, quashed by VB.

made you late. I really am sorry that I did. I don't behave nearly as well as she does, but I *did* get just a little jiggery yesterday. I suppose I shall at times until I quite recover. It was all right afterwards and luckily, having seen Edith now, I know that she will be too nice to blame either of us for it, only I wish I hadn't again cut short your time with her. But I won't do such things when I'm perfectly well again. Please give her my love and tell her I'm sorry.

Who kissed my toes? What will you give me if I tell you? I will only say now that it was done with almost if not quite as much pleasure (and of the same kind!) as you showed. Now you can think that over till I see you.

As I told you, I followed your advice to try to be kinder to men with Walter Sickert,[1] and as a result I had a long and intimate and interesting conversation with him after Clive had gone to catch his train. As a beginning, it was so successful that I think I shall certainly continue your method. He gave me an astonishing account of his love affairs and we discussed love and marriage. He said he should accept the next person who proposed to him, but he was too old to do the proposing himself. Do you think I may take that as a hint that I have only to hold out my hand to him—or is that too much à l'Ottoline? Then we talked of painting and I actually got some compliments without fishing! Not very big ones to be sure, but as you know I'm so modest that anything pleases me. He wants me to go to his school, but you don't think that would be a good thing, do you? I'm not sure, for I shouldn't do anything he told me to unless I happened to agree with it and probably he could teach one a lot in some ways. Still I hate any kind of teaching. (I am here overcome by the thought that my letters to you are apt to "burble on" and be "very dull." This one seems to be going to. I must make it so indiscreet that you'll have to destroy it at once.)

To return to Walter Sickert. I liked him better than I have ever done before and was impressed by the ease with which I can, by remembering your advice, get onto intimate terms with a man at once. It would take me years with a woman. Men are certainly much simpler.

. . . I didn't have Lytton after all last night but Adrian came and confided to me the difficulties and loves of his life. I think he's really a little in love with Duncan, which is perhaps the best thing for him

[1]Walter Sickert (1860–1942), influential painter, member of the NEAC and the inspiration of the Camden Town Group. At this time he was teaching painting in the Fitzroy Street studio once used by Whistler and which Duncan Grant would later occupy.

to be. Duncan is coming tonight and has something private and important to say to me! He has wanted to talk to me for some time but finds it difficult to see me alone! No, you needn't wriggle and sharpen your eyes. I know what it is and it's nothing to do with me. But I must be discreet and not tell you what it is.

Talking of discretion—*do* be careful—this is only a general warning—what you ever tell Virginia. I found that she had told Adrian, which means Duncan, *all* about the Ottoline affair.[2] She hadn't only given him a general sketch but had told him every detail. It doesn't matter, I think, as Adrian tells me that Duncan is really safe and doesn't repeat things to the Stracheys, but of course we don't know whom else V. may not have told. I thought she was to be trusted over this after the special warnings I gave her, but evidently one can't run any risks with her. Isn't it awful? I'm thankful I've never told her anything about you.

Now this letter *has* burbled on and isn't very indiscreet. What shall I do to make it so? I want you and I love you. You took my latch key from me. I didn't put that there as a bad joke. It's really my habit of mind. Also did you understand that you were to sleep here on Thursday whatever happened? Will you? Oh Roger, I really am too patchy, even for you, cockchafer[3] though you be. If only you were going to be here all today and tonight.

Vanessa

TATE

III-3. To Roger Fry

Wednesday [July 5, 1911]   *46, Gordon Square, Bloomsbury*

[Heading:] This can be read at leisure.

My dear Roger,

If, when you get to Paris, you have doubts as to whether you ought to have stayed with me today you may give them up when you get

---

[2]On the eve of his departure for the Continent (and hence to Turkey with the Bells), RF and Lady Ottoline fell into bed together, rather to his surprise. On his return from Brusa, though, he accused Lady Ottoline of circulating a rumor that he was in love with her. Whether she did so is in question, but the quarrel effectively ended their friendship.

[3]A beetle of the family Scarabaeidae.

this, for I don't know how I should be feeling this evening if I hadn't had you with me all day. A few minutes after you had gone Clive telephoned from Cambridge to ask whether I very much wanted him to come back as he could only just with a rush possibly catch his train. Your commands to me were so strong in my mind that I called up all my natural selfishness and asked him to try to come. But I then found that even if he did catch it he wouldn't get home till after 11, by which time it wouldn't be much use, so I said it wasn't worth while trying, and he's not coming till tomorrow morning. He made me promise to send for either Lankester or Saxon if I felt bad. But I shan't feel bad, and if I did I think writing to you is a better remedy than either of the others. Lankester would no doubt laugh at me for feeling anything, and Saxon would sit silent. No, I think his real niceness might make him take trouble, but I don't know how to get at him even if I wanted him.

You see, you must put up with a long and straggly letter from me because I've no other way of passing the time. The evening paper of course hasn't come. Doesn't all this sound most dreadfully pathetic? Well, it is really meant to show you how very necessary you were to me today. I told Clive that you had stayed because I had felt I couldn't be alone so long, and he was very penitent. Only I am a little amused when I think that I should otherwise have been alone from this morning till tomorrow and yet I shall I know be blown up if I stay up an hour longer than usual some night soon. What odd ideas people have of what's good for one. Am I writing a really nasty letter? I suppose so, but you see I can't read much and I haven't any work at present. Besides I do just at this moment want to talk to you and if I do so I must write what I think, nice or nasty. My thoughts aren't *all* nasty though. How good you were to me today. You didn't let me feel how annoyed you really must have been at the whole situation. Perhaps after all Ottoline is a little right about "those dreadful people" with whom you spend so much of your time. When I think how really precious I have always thought your time to be—even when I didn't know you much—how obvious it is that everyone you know is always clamouring for bits of it. How much I resent your wasting it as you do on being nice to people whom I don't consider worth it. Then even I, impudent as I am, sometimes feel abashed to think how we calmly intrude ourselves into your days, upsetting them and putting you out by our incompetence and stupidities. Really, this is honest, I do feel ashamed. I can say this for you can't answer it more than if it were an after-dinner speech.

Oh Roger, how horribly I want you. I can say it now I'm ill. I know when I'm well I shan't be allowed to, but just now I do have privileges, don't I? Besides what nurse was ever so good as you, and one must recognise good technique if it's not to be wasted on one. You seem to know so exactly what I want, physically and mentally. How do you do it? Being with you is like being on a river and being with most people is like driving a jibbing horse along a bumpy road.

But what's the good of trying to tell you what it's like to be with you? The only good is that it keeps me happy this evening and won't do you any harm beyond giving you another letter to wade through. Still I wish I *could* tell you a little. I sometimes wonder if you really have any idea of all you have given me, not only of how you have helped me through this, but of all the rest. You know you have given me something quite new and very large and beautiful. Though you profess not to care about beauty, you can't get away from it. You *are* beautiful, both you and your character and your whole view of life, and I, who don't pretend to be so silly as not to like it, feel that it has made and will make the most tremendous difference to me to be allowed to come so near it and feel it and know it. It will make everything better for me and spoil nothing. I wish, for the moment, that my "vision" would become literary so that I might see the words in which I could tell you what I feel. At this moment I could paint you, so that perhaps you would see something of what I mean. At least I think I could but I dare not look at my picture too closely, and after all it may be all wrong, and almost certainly would be quite unrecognisable.

This solitary evening had almost resulted in some kind of love letter, hasn't it? Now don't leave it lying about. If you *want* to show it to any other of your ladies you may. I don't mind what you do as long as you do it on purpose. But don't give anyone too many ideas beforehand as to what I'm like (I know you'll have to give some) as I want to make a favourable impression for myself some day.

Vanessa

TATE

III-4. To Saxon Sydney-Turner

Aug. 20 [1911]   *Cleeve House, Melksham*

My dear Saxon,
  I hope you won't think,
As I'm writing in pencil and not in ink,
nor yet in prose, nor in poetry either,
My letter'll be interesting more than another,
Which last may be taken to come from Scotch blood.[1]
Even then it won't rhyme but I can't think what would.
I started so boldly and now I'm o'ercome
By a sense of incompetence, making me dumb.
We came here last Monday and now we're laid low
By the heat and the strokes [?] and the moans of a cow.
I believe the poor beast from her calf has been weaned.
At any rate, night is made hideous at Seend.
There's nothing to tell you. I sit in the garden
And nothing more mighty [?] than needles do harden
My fingers. I'm working on Duncan's design
For a chair that I fear will not even be mine,
But Keynes's. He stayed with us at Millmead Cottage[2]
And gave us some gossip, but all of an old age.
We lived in a whirlpool of people and chatter,
But Adrian and Clive will have told all the latter.
I heard from Virginia. She bathed with her Brook.[3]
And now they're at Firle. For what next must we look?
My rhymes will not carry me down this next sheet.
And so I must stop. I hope we shall meet
At Studland. Good-bye. That is, farewell.
Your affectionate friend,

                                                            Vanessa Bell

MICHAEL BAGENAL

[1]I.e., her Stephen origins in Aberdeenshire.
[2]Where VB had lodged early in August, to be near RF at Durbins.
[3]Rupert Brooke (1887–1915), the Cambridge poet, whom VW visited at the Old
Vicarage, Grantchester. They swam naked by moonlight in the Granta.

III-5. To Clive Bell

Oct. 11 [1911]   *46, Gordon Square, Bloomsbury*

My dearest,

Your letter and card to Julian came last night. I'm glad you have cheered up and I hope you met Roger and Duncan last night and got my telegram and didn't have any moments of gloom over my letter. I'm still in bed and feeling quite well, though I think these blessed affairs are rather more than they were last time. But perhaps they'll stop early and anyhow it's such a blessing to have them instead of a baby. I've had a visit from Lankester today. He thought me looking very well, as usual of course, and had nothing else much to say. I think he disapproves rather of Paris, but I told him firmly that I was going.¹ He's coming again tomorrow to see Julian's rupture.

Virginia and Adrian came to dinner last night. A new discovery has been made, or did I tell you about the rooms in Fitzroy Sq? Anyhow, there are two magnificent rooms to be had in the large house with the urns for £90 a year, and over them is a flat of 4 rooms. There are a man and his wife in the house to do all the cleaning, etc. V. thinks of taking the two large rooms, and Adrian and Duncan could get the others at a reduction if they took them all—that is for about £65.² They haven't yet seen the upstairs rooms as they're inhabited, but they're very much inclined to take them and it certainly sounds the best I've heard of. The question now is about Sophy. She could be housed there and a small kitchen could be had, which, if she were shared by V. and A., would probably come cheaper than feeding out. This morning V. broached the great question to her and was met by dignified silence, or almost silence. She would not commit herself but was inclined to be tearful. I don't much believe she'll go into such quarters. Maud, anyhow, has been definitely told, through Sophy, that she must go. V. had an awful time of it and Sophy made matters very difficult by her dignified restraint. "I suppose you mean

¹In the first week of October VB was still recovering from her miscarriage, but had had reason to suspect she might again be pregnant. CB (still physically involved with VB) and RF waited in Paris for news. A few days later she was able to report in the negative.
²They did not take this house. See the following letter.

that you don't want me, Miss Geenia," upon which of course V. said that she couldn't bear to lose her.

I have a few small items of gossip. The Raverats[3] are in London. Jacques is nervous again and can't live in Paris. At this point Woolf[4] appeared and I have had a long visit from him. I like him very much. He is of course very clever and from living in the wilds seems to me to have got a more interesting point of view than most of the "set" who seldom produce anything very new or original. He thinks we ought to visit the East. The colour is amazing and one's animal passions get very strong and one enjoys one's body to the full. We discussed our set and young Cambridge and the neo-pagans. I can't remember the other bits of gossip I had. I don't think they were very interesting, and chiefly about the Neos. I have had a letter from Harry [Norton] who is in bed with saddle-sores. Isn't it the kind of thing he would go to bed with? He wants me to go to tea with him which perhaps I shall do tomorrow. He says that he's only going to Cambridge for week-ends up till Christmas as he doesn't mean to work much—which rather alarms me. I *shall* have a stormy winter, shan't I? But the old lady says Dolphin must expect troubles if she keeps too many males on her hands.

Do you really miss your Dolph, my legitimate male? Or are you quite content now that you have the other two to keep you company? I'm looking forward to Paris enormously. This time next week I shall be actually there I hope. Julian shrugged his shoulders with delight at your card. He's been sitting with me in bed. I told him he was a terrible storyteller because he inserted some long fable about Dr Lankester having opened the letter box but not come in, so he said "I'm a liar." I asked him why he told lies and he said his trousers made him. I've heard from your mother who has been trying to buy him a highwayman's coat,[5] but luckily such things aren't made now, so she wants me to get him one.

Give my love to Roger and Duncan. Are they doing any sketching?

---

[3]Gwen Raverat (née Darwin) and her husband Jacques (1885–1925), French painter, both members of the so-called "neo-Pagan" circle around Rupert Brooke.
[4]Leonard Woolf (1880–1969), writer and publisher, educated at Trinity College, Cambridge, elected an Apostle in 1902. He had just returned from seven years in the Ceylon Civil Service.
[5]A descriptive term. According to Anne Olivier Bell, a waisted, full-flared, long-skirted, high-collared double-breasted overcoat.

Shall you all be glad to see me next week or is it nicer to be a party of males? It seems to be my fate to find myself abroad with 3 males.

Your
Dolph

TATE

III-6. To Virginia Stephen

Thursday [October 19, 1911]   *Café Napolitain, Paris*

My Billy,

I got here without adventure yesterday and as usual feel very much at home and contented in Paris. Roger and Duncan haven't arrived yet. They'll probably come tonight. So I haven't been able to discuss any of your schemes[1] with Duncan yet and you won't hear what he thinks till about Saturday I suppose. However I hope you may be in a less wild state of turmoil then when I saw you and that you're proceeding with Asheham.[2]

As for us, we're in a huge state of excitement having just bought a Picasso for £4.[3] I wonder how you'll like it. It's "cubist" and very beautiful colour, a small still life. We've also bought me two hats and a great deal of underclothing. That's not bad for the first day, is it? Tomorrow when Roger and Duncan are here we shall see some pictures. We've seen Morrice[4] but no one else yet. Our hotel is comfortable and very quiet, which is a blessing. Paris is pandemonium. All the streets are up and the crowd is terrific, but I enjoy it. They all seem so irresponsible, and the clothes are amusing, and one gets a great sense of holiday.

[1]VW was trying to negotiate a new living arrangement and proposed sharing a house, cook, and housemaid with Adrian, JMK, and DG. In the final scheme (carried out at 38 Brunswick Square), Leonard Woolf also shared the house.
[2]See p. 114, n. 3.
[3]*Pots et Citron* (1908); it was sold in the 1960s and a copy by Quentin Bell hangs at Charleston.
[4]J. W. Morrice, Canadian painter, a friend of CB's from his Paris days, 1904–5.

It's almost impossible to write with this pen and hardly any ink. Do write and tell me if any more brilliant ideas as to housing yourselves have struck you. Either expensive rooms or a house with its disadvantages seem to me the only alternatives. I'm sure you'll never put up with cheap rooms.

If I were you I really should warehouse and travel for a time. London seems to me too tiresome and without beauty at this moment. But of course I don't want you to.

Your
V.B.

BERG

III-7. To Virginia Stephen

[October 20, 1911]   *Le Rat Mort [Café, Paris]*

My Billy,

We are dining here before going to a play. Roger and Duncan turned up last night and we spent this morning looking for young geniuses at the autumn salon. Before starting I had an awful vision of Ottoline. A woman passed the hotel door, tall and dressed in floating violet robes, but it wasn't really Ot. But a few minutes later, as we stood at the doorway, Ot in person drove past us, looking ill and haggard. She stared at us with rather a fearsome and gloomy stare, and I suppose we shall have to go and see her soon.

There were no very exciting pictures at the salon, but several very good ones. Then we have been to see O'Conor.[1] It all seems very much as it used to be. I brought here your article in the Nation.[2] Roger says he likes it very much. It's just what he wanted to get said. He thinks it a great advantage to have art criticism written by those

[1]Roderic O'Conor (1860–1940), Irish painter, another friend from CB's Paris days.
[2]A review of *The Post Impressionists* by C. Lewis Hind (London: Methuen, 1911) appeared in *The Nation* on October 14. Andrew McNeillie, the editor of VW's essays, does not firmly attribute this piece to her.

who know nothing about it.* For my part, I couldn't see any art criticism in it. However it seemed to meet with Duncan's approval too. He has no views on the house question as far as I can see, but I can only give him a confused account of all your various ideas. I haven't heard from you yet but may find a letter when I get in to-night.

Have you heard that Henry and Nina are being accused of scandal by some strange man and woman! O'Conor had an advertisement warning them of it from the Daily Telegraph. I suppose nothing will happen.

I must stop. They're getting so restive.

Your
V.B.

*[In Roger's hand:] This isn't at all what I said but you can read between the lines and allow for Vanessa's artistic distortion.

BERG

III-8. To Roger Fry

Nov. 23 [1911]   *46, Gordon Square, Bloomsbury*

My dear,

. . . I wish you could go to the Sangers[1] tomorrow night. We're dining there. Perhaps you could sleep there too, so as to come here early on Saturday. I only wish I could ask you to sleep here. I am tempted to, but I suppose we must be on the safe side at present and as I shall see you all Saturday and Sunday, perhaps we'd better not risk anything. Clive goes I think at about 10 on Saturday, so we could have a nice long morning together.

Roger—aren't you jealous—Duncan came to tea yesterday and a

---

[1]Charles Sanger (1871–1903), Chancery barrister, was an Apostle and a friend of Bertrand Russell's at Trinity College, Cambridge. He and his wife Dora (*née* Pease) formed friendships with Old Bloomsbury through younger Apostles like Lytton Strachey, Leonard Woolf, and H. T. J. Norton.

number of things happened to stir your jealousy! First we invented a new art, the art of covering boxes with a most beautiful lacquer of different colours and painted with figures. The result is exquisite, though the process, which we intend to keep secret, may be painful. Then Duncan asked me to sit to him. But very likely that won't come off. Perhaps you could paint me at the same time, which might console you. And then—what do you think happened? I had my bath in his presence! You see he wanted to shave and I wanted to have my bath (he stayed to dinner) and he didn't see why he should move and I didn't see why I should remain dirty, and Clive was there and didn't object—and so! But I'm afraid he remained quite unmoved and I was really very decent. I felt no embarrassment and I think perhaps it was a useful precedent!

Are you painting today I wonder? I'm writing to you instead, and *that* ought to remove all trace of jealousy, for I wouldn't stop painting for anything else. I think I've done all I can to the chrysanthemums and they're not very interesting.

We went to the New English yesterday. My word, what a show! Of course Steer[2] is quite done for, and the John seemed to me to be some rather sentimental drawings badly put together, with no feelings for the whole, and the child is beastly.[3] As for Henry Lamb, I'm not quite clear what I think of him. It's simply too deadly—academic drawing, niggled and polished up to the last point, without life or interest, very skilful, and utterly commonplace and second-hand in idea. Miss [Gwen] John seemed to me much more interesting than anyone. I suppose Holmes[4] is good, but Clive thought him much better than I did. I don't see anything very genuine in it. Still it's irreproachable.

I *mustn't* write you letters of art criticism though! Why can't we go to these things together? Then you'd get the benefit of my views not on paper.

My dear, I love you. That's more worth saying, and I realise it more and more every day. How you have changed everything for me, all the things I most care for. What an extraordinary person you are. When I see you in your own house I understand that even better. I do like seeing you among the things you have chosen yourself. They

---

[2]Philip Wilson Steer (1860–1942), a founder of the NEAC. At one time considered progressive, after 1895 his work became gradually more conventional.
[3]Painting unidentified.
[4]Charles Holmes (1868–1936), later director of the National Gallery (1916–28).

all seem, like you, full of quite peculiar charm and rightness. Wouldn't it have been a pity if I could never have told you any of these things which I have always felt to some extent, and I suppose I couldn't have said them unless you knew that I loved you.

Your
Vanessa

TATE

III-9. To Leonard Woolf

Jan. 14 [1912]   *Springvale, Niton [Isle of Wight]*[1]

Dear Leonard,

I am writing to tell you that Virginia has told me about her talk with you and also to say how glad I shall be if you can have what you want.[2] You're the only person I know whom I can imagine as her husband, which may seem to you a rash remark, considering how little I know you. However I have faith in my instincts, at any rate as far as they imply what I think of you. Besides that, which perhaps isn't very important, I shall be so glad if you don't go back to Ceylon. It seems absurd that we shouldn't get the benefit of your existence.

Here I am in your despised Isle of Wight, which certainly is a bit smug, but I think rather suited to me in my present state. Still I shall be glad to be in London again where I hope I may at last settle down to normal existence.

---

[1]VB took a short holiday alone at Niton, receiving visits first from RF, then VW.
[2]Since his return from Ceylon, and especially after moving into 38 Brunswick Square on December 4, 1911, LW had fallen in love with Virginia. On January 11 he proposed marriage. She was not yet ready to accept him, but considered the matter more seriously than any previous proposal.

You're coming to Asheham,[3] aren't you, for our house-warming party?

Don't bother to answer this.

Yours
Vanessa Bell

SUSSEX

III-10. To Clive Bell

Jan. 15 [1912]   *Springvale, Niton [Isle of Wight]*

Dearest,

I have just had your long letter full of excitements of the chase. How you induced one of those respectable carriage horses to jump fences I can't imagine. I wish I had been jumping fences with you, though I shouldn't have liked the return to Lorna and Dorothy. Skin tights hardly sound to me the right clothing for Sylvia,[1] but I suppose they were.

We have been very quiet and well behaved here. Roger is better but was still too feeble or *débile* as I call him, which makes him very cross, to do much. However we took two walks (I lie down virtuously after tea so as to go out in the afternoon) and encountered a very angry farmer called Peach who wouldn't let us go through his fields. There are some very good cliffs here and the climate is soft and warm in spite of grey weather inclining to rain. Last night we heard the voice of the siren—it was fearsome, but didn't last very long. We have been going to bed very early, before 11 generally.

Roger has been trying to paint me, so far without much success, and I think will now turn his attention to a still life instead. He's also writing articles and reviews. I have been looking at Holmes' Rembrandt[2] and come to the conclusion that at his best (in the etch-

---

[3]VB and VW had recently acquired the lease of Asheham (spelled "Asham" by VW and LW), an isolated house in a fold of the downs on the east side of the Ouse Valley in Sussex.
[1]Probably Sylvia Raven-Hill, the attractive daughter of CB's former mistress.
[2]Charles Holmes' *Notes on the Life of Rembrandt* (1911).

ings) he was about as good as Cézanne. In most of them he is nothing like so great. Perhaps you as usual are right, but he *is* very great at moments. I must get the Athenaeum at Ventnor tomorrow when I go to meet the Goat, and give you my valuable criticism,[3] though as I don't know the Lysistrata they may not really be very valuable.

Roger is staying on here I think till Wednesday. He really wasn't well enough to go back today and thought if he didn't go today he could stay over Tuesday so I shan't be alone at all. He has just seized my paper to tell you a foolish remark (I mean *his* remark is the foolish one). Mine of course was expressive and sensible. Do tell me all about the changes at Gordon Sq. Are you fond of me?

> *Your*
> *Dolph*

[In Roger Fry's hand:] Vanessa's latest—she was describing a conversation with someone and said "of course I had my tail up my sleeve all the time." I laughed and she tried to mend it to "my sleeve in cheek" and finally got into such impossible attitudes that the thing had to be given up.

> *Roger*

TATE

III-11. To Virginia Stephen

Tuesday [May 17, 1912]   *Hotel Manin, Milan*
                                  Rue Manin 7–9 [Italy][1]

My Billy,

Here we are again at the blessed old Hotel Manin. I feel as if I had known Milan and the Manin all my life. We had a few hours in Paris yesterday and helped Roger with the hanging of the show,[2] which

[3]CB reviewed *The Lysistrata of Aristophanes acted in Athens in the year B.C. 411*, translated by Benjamin Bickley Rogers, in the *Athenaeum* of January 13, 1912. The essay is reprinted in CB's *Potboilers* (1918).
[1]The Bells and RF spent most of this month in Milan, Bologna, and Florence.
[2]A small exhibition of avant-garde English art, held at Percy Moore Turner's Galerie Barbazanges in the Rue Saint-Honoré.

seems as if it might be successful. They won't hang Duncan's Mars and Venus on account of its indecency. The pictures altogether looked much better than I thought they would, all except the Camden Town group,[3] which collapsed. We met Doucet[4] and Vildrac[5] there and afterwards were taken off to dine with the Vildrac family. It was rather amusing.

I am now surrounded by just the kind of people you want for Mel[6] I'm sure. English tourists, old and middle-aged women, married and single. I wish I could give you examples of their conversation. "Shall we go by rail to Genoa?" "Oh no, no." "Not go by rail to Genoa? You didn't mean to go by motor to Genoa?" "Oh yes, certainly." "*Not* in *this* weather?" "Oh yes." The glass[7] is going up. "If you want to see the distance, Mary, it is in that map. Yes. We were talking of rail, weren't we?" etc., etc. They were quite silent all through dinner but have now woken up and are buzzing about, very ugly and drab.

I have had the misfortune to soak my new dresses in turpentine, which rather spoils their freshness. I shouldn't notice it myself but Clive would unluckily. Roger joins us here tomorrow and we go to Bologna either then or the next day. One of the females has dropped all the newspapers on the floor with a bang. Her sister aged 60 looks at her with reproach. They're all much excited about a party of 2 Booth-like young ladies with their mother in a white shawl and two Italian young men. The young ladies, who are as innocent as lambs, are thought to be very giddy and are suspected of being in the lounge with the young men . . .

I suppose you are sitting in the sun at Asheham while we shiver in Italy. Give Leonard my love. I must write to him soon I think, which will be self-sacrificing of me for I shan't get an answer.

Clive has not talked much of the affair, but thinks you are certain to get engaged to him soon. I don't know why he has suddenly come to this conclusion unless it's because of L's giving up Ceylon,

[3]The Camden Town Group, formed in 1911, inspired by Sickert and in reaction to the Royal Academy and NEAC. Members included Augustus John, Harold Gilman, Charles Ginner, Spencer Gore, and Duncan Grant. In 1913 they merged with other groups to form the London Group.
[4]Henri Doucet (d.1915), French artist. He later worked at the Omega Workshops.
[5]Charles Vildrac (1882–1971), French dramatist, poet, and art dealer.
[6]*Melymbrosia*, VW's working title for *The Voyage Out*, not published until 1915.
[7]I.e., barometer.

which did rouse his suspicions. Write and tell me all about your doings.

Your
VB

III-12. To Virginia Stephen

Sunday [June 2, 1912]   *46, Gordon Square, Bloomsbury*

My Billy,

I think I *won't* lunch with you tomorrow. Perhaps you'll ask me another time to some lunch or dinner alone with you two, but I think I had better come back to lunch tomorrow.

I have had a talk with Clive, about which I will tell you when I see you. He suddenly and for no reason asked me point blank whether you had seen his letters to Adrian, so I said yes. I will tell you what else happened tomorrow, as we had some talk which is too long to write about.

Well, I'm afraid I was very inexpressive today, but although I had expected it,[1] it was somehow so bewildering and upsetting when I did actually see you and Leonard together that I didn't know how to say what I felt. You do know, however, Billy, and Leonard too, that I do of course care for you. I won't say more than for anybody, but in a way that's quite special to you. Your happiness does matter frightfully to me and I do now feel quite happy about you, which really means that I think Leonard one of the most remarkable and charming people I know. I am looking forward very much to having him for a brother-in-law.

Goodnight, my dear couple, before I get too doddering. It's a great

[1]On May 29, Virginia had told Leonard that she loved him and would marry him.

blessing to think how happy you are. It does make the whole difference to one's life, doesn't it?

Your
VB

BERG

III-13. To Roger Fry

June 5 [1912]   *46, Gordon Square, Bloomsbury*

My dear,

Another nice long grumblesome letter from you this morning which gave me your right address too, so I can write you safely, and if my other letters have gone astray you won't miss much.

I think I should like your Ida.[1] She sounds very human. People who get on with beasts always seem to me human. We are all in something of a vortex here, at least I find it is so after the peace of our travels. London is full. Everyone is wanting to know about Virginia's engagement. If you *didn't* get my other letters you won't have heard of that.

June 6. I began this yesterday and had to leave off. Roger, I do want you so badly. You don't know how often I have wanted you since that night at Genoa. I wish life could be as simple as you and I would make it. I have been at Brunswick[2] a good deal, too much for the smoothness of life here. It's very funny, but really they are much more resented [by Clive] than you are. Perhaps it's as well, only it makes things difficult.

We started on our return with the tremendous quarrel you may or may not have heard about vaguely from my other letters.[3] It has blown over but has left Clive rather sore. He won't see much of the couple and I think resents my doing so, but it has so far been difficult to

---

[1]Ida Cresswell (née Widdrington), RF's first love.
[2]Virginia and Leonard's residence (with Adrian, Duncan, and JMK).
[3]CB had expressed his growing frustration and anger with Virginia, whom he was still half in love with, in acerbic letters to his friends. Adrian allowed Virginia to read these and both she and LW were incensed. CB, in turn, was furious at having his letters passed around.

help it. Well I daresay it will all be ancient history by the time you get this so I won't go on about it. I'll tell you about my painting instead. I went yesterday to paint Duncan's model but she didn't turn up, so we got Woolf to sit for an hour instead. I saw D.'s and Etchell's decoration,[4] which I think very good—no one else does. It's not finished and wants a good deal doing in places, but bits are very good. It's extraordinary how indistinguishable they become. I suppose their general colour schemes have a great deal in common. Duncan seems to have been doing not much else but that and the dresses[5] which I haven't seen.

(This letter spent the night in my bag in company with Julian's chocolate.)

I have been painting my nursery scene, which is rather comic, but I am just in an exciting stage as I flatter myself that I am painting in an entirely new way (for me). Probably you'll think it exactly like everything else I've ever done. I am trying to paint as if I were mosaicing, not by painting in spots, but by considering the picture as patches, each of which has to be filled by one definite space of colour, as one has to do with mosaic or woolwork, not allowing myself to brush the patches into each other. It's amusing to make these experiments even if they don't succeed. I think this one ought to give one something of the life one seems to get with mosaic. I don't know if it will.

I haven't heard definitely but I don't believe our murals can even have been accepted![6] Duncan seems to have taken them in charge. He didn't get them framed and I have my suspicions as to whether he ever got them to the right place. Anyhow Woolf's mother,[7] the only person who seems to have been to the show, saw nothing of the kind there. It will be rather a blow to poor Aitken[8] if Duncan and Etchells aren't even hung!

[4]Frederick Etchells (1886–1973), artist and architect, trained at the Royal College of Art and in Paris. He was close to the Bloomsbury painters from about 1911 to 1913, and briefly an Omega artist. His decoration with DG was a mural in Maynard Keynes' ground-floor room at 38 Brunswick Square, featuring a street scene of an accident between two horse-drawn cabs.
[5]From October through December 1912 DG was engaged in costume designs for a Granville-Barker production of *MacBeth* (never staged). The dresses mentioned here may have been preliminary sketches.
[6]For an exhibition at Crosby Hall, London, of designs for mural painting and for the decoration of schools and other public buildings. There is no evidence that the Bloomsbury painters were included.
[7]Marie Woolf (née de Jongh) (c. 1848–1939), LW's widowed mother.
[8]Charles Aitken (1869–1936), director of the Whitechapel Art Gallery, and later director of the Tate and founder of its modern foreign wing.

I have got myself a new coat, a long blue cloth one for everyday wear, with a large white triangle in front. I'm not at all sure you'll approve.

What a damned dull letter, but I'm wishing I were in France. Are you having a very good time with Doucet I wonder? How terrified I should be of painting with him. I hope you're not coming back before you really need, though I should rather like you to dine with me on the 10th, but that's impossible unless you come back at once. It strikes me that this letter may be too late for you, but I'll send it on the chance.

Your
VB

TATE

III-14. To Roger Fry

Sunday [July 21? 1912]　　　　　*Cleeve House, Melksham, Wilts*

My dear,

It's a very long time I believe since you've had the pleasure of a letter from me, and now you'll hardly get this before you see me. You were in disgrace yesterday for you looked out our train wrong from Newbury. It really left a few minutes after the other got in and we got to Devizes at 4.40 instead of 5.50. However it didn't much matter as we went and had tea in Devizes and hadn't very long to wait afterwards till the carriage fetched us. I was very glad to see the children again, othewise the depressing atmosphere of this place is already stealing over me and I found myself last night counting the number of dinners I should have to eat here. Still, I can also compare my misery of last year during those dinners with my comparative cheerfulness this!

Clive said he couldn't stand Newington[1] and was thankful to get to Seend, where at least one could be "jolly." I own I'm degenerate enough to prefer the refined Ethel and Nan, where at any rate one

[1]Newington House, Oxfordshire, the home of Nan Hudson and Ethel Sands.

can enjoy free talk. All the same I was a little alarmed at their excessive elegance and 18th century stamp. It isn't what we want even for our minor arts, is it?[2] Won't they import too much of that? Of course I know they're useful, but I do think we shall have to be careful, especially in England where it seems to me one can never get away from all this fatal prettiness. Can't we paint stuffs, etc., which *won't* be gay and pretty? I see how easy it would be to turn out yards of very fanciful and bright and piquant things, and I don't see what else that couple can do. I daresay you're right in using them, but although I don't go to Clive's lengths I must say that seeing them in their own chosen surroundings did give me rather the creeps, at least when I thought of bringing that into anything to do with art. Does that sound priggish?

I had an awful time though, Roger, when the things came back from Cardiff.[3] Not about my own works, which weren't ever very brilliant specimens, but about Duncan's. It seemed to me suddenly that he had collapsed. I thought that I could see that he had never since done anything nearly as good as the early one we have, that the Queen of Sheba[4] was not only a failure because he had gone on and spoilt it, but that the whole conception was really sweet and too pretty and small, that the Whippet, which I had thought better, was not really very much, and that the dancers on the hill was only better because he hadn't carried it far. I thought that the usual English sweetness was coming in and spoiling all. I am saying horrid things, and I think it's very likely that it's only that I was in a bad mood at the moment. But I also thought perhaps I think all this now because I have been seeing all those French pictures since seeing the Cardiff ones before. Perhaps these look so bad by comparison with Derain, Picasso, Matisse, etc. I want you to come and put them in their right place again. It's too awful if everyone turns out a failure, and if even Duncan, at his age, is already going for less fine things than he did. Anyhow I shall have a lot to say to you on the subject! You'll tell me I'm bumbling on if I write any more about it.

My dear, I am thinking of the nice time we're going to have. Does the thought of it excite you too? I shall telephone to you when we

[2]RF had been discussing with various artists and collectors a proposed project that eventually became the Omega Workshops. Nan Hudson and Ethel Sands were not included in the final scheme.
[3]An exhibition at Cardiff Castle, National Museum of Wales.
[4]The Bells owned *Lemon Gatherers* (1910). It and *The Queen of Sheba* (1912) are now at the Tate.

get back on Tuesday, but don't stay in or anything, as if you aren't there when I telephone I will try again later. I want you to choose my present with me and then you shall come back, and I shall see you properly. Keep from the 15th onwards as free as you can.

Your

V.B.

TATE

III-15. To Clive Bell

Aug. 15 [1912]   *46, Gordon Square, Bloomsbury*

Dearest,

I have a most astonishing piece of news to give you. I have sold a picture! Doesn't that startle you? And you will be still more astonished when you hear who has bought it. The Contemporary Art Fund![1] This morning Aitken and Bobby Ross[2] suddenly appeared to see the Duncans. (Duncan had told Aitken they were here.) They didn't like the dancers, and want Roger to let them have the Queen of Sheba. They didn't like the Whippet either. Then Ross asked me how much I wanted for my Spanish lady.[3] I didn't know what to ask or whether he really wanted to buy it, but I thought I'd better stick to low prices, so I said £5.5.0. and he said he'd buy it for the C.A.S. It's rather comic isn't it? Perhaps it will be an advertisement and help me to sell.

Then Ross wanted to know if we'd think of selling the John. I said I thought we would, for about £600. He said that the Johannesburg

---

[1]The Contemporary Art Society, originally proposed at the Morrells' Bloomsbury home in 1909 and formally established in May 1910 with the aim of purchasing modern art, especially (but not exclusively) by British artists. Works were then loaned and/or given to public collections. Early members included Clive Bell, D. S. MacColl, Charles Holmes, Roger Fry, the Morrells, Arthur Clutton-Brock, Robert Ross, and Charles Aitken. Still an important and active organization.

[2]Robert Baldwin Ross (1869–1918), art dealer and writer, director of the Carfax Gallery from 1900 to 1908 and at this time on the staff of the *Morning Post*. He was Oscar Wilde's literary executor.

[3]Painted in 1912 and now in the collections of the Leicestershire Museums and Art Galleries.

gallery want a John and have given him £500. He would have to screw them up to £600, but meanwhile he asked if we would give him the refusal. I said yes, as that only means telling him before we sell to anyone else. I said of course I couldn't say anything definite without asking you.

Roger turned up to lunch. He thinks we ought to ask Lord Howard de Walden £750 for the John and play him off against Johannesburg.[4] Perhaps you think we'd better not sell at all yet. Anyhow we evidently can if we want to. I must say I would rather possess a Cézanne or some modern French painting.

You see I spent a very business-like morning . . .

I heard this morning that the children are well and that Julian told a visitor who admired Quentin's [red] hair that if Mabel[5] would only brush it, his hair would become that colour too! I shall soon have first hand news of them to send you which is a blessing. I hope you slept last night. I did like a top from about 11 to 9. No news of the couple. Now I must pay some bills and try to clear things up a bit.

Dolphin

TATE

III-16. To Virginia Woolf

Aug. 19 [1912]   *From the Reading Room,*
The Civil Service Co-Operative Society Ld.,
28, Haymarket, S.W.

My Billy,

I have ¾ of an hour to spend in the waiting room here and you shall have the benefit of it. You may have been surprised by the wild telephone message you must have received from that ghoul at B[runswick] Sq[uare], but the fact was that we read in the papers

[4]Thomas Evelyn Scott-Ellis, 8th Baron Howard de Walden (1880–1946), writer, sportsman, and patron of the arts. In the end, Johannesburg did buy the Bells' Augustus John painting *The Childhood of Pyramus* for £600 (£25,692/$44,961).
[5]Mabel Selwood, nurse.

some days ago that there was an outbreak of typhoid at Avignon. I meant to tell you when I wrote but quite forgot. Roger, who was spending Sunday with me at Asheham said we must somehow let you know, and so he bicycled into Lewes and telephoned with great difficulty to Florry [servant] who seemed to be paralyzed with terror. I have come up this morning to do some odd jobs and meet the children at Paddington this afternoon. I went to B. Sq. this morning but found you had left last night. I got your addresses though.

It was stupid about the Austro-Hungarian [a missed appointment] but the telephone seemed to blame. I must give Leonard some business messages. First I will master his instructions about Kings B.W.[1] and carry them out. Am I to take rooms on my own responsibility if there are any to be had or would that be going too far? Then, Roger would be delighted to have him as secretary to the Grafton.[2] He had not thought of him as he thought there was no chance of his doing such a job. He is very glad to get him and thinks he will be better even than Desmond.[3] He is going to write about it. He (L.) need not be there till Oct. 8th about, but you will get full details from Roger.

Your honeymoon in the Quantocks[4] sounds very wintry, but apparently internal warmth made up for the outside cold. I wish you'd send me details to enliven my solitude.

It is very damp and grey at Asheham, but as you may imagine I am very busy inside the house, putting up curtains, etc. I have just been getting a bright reddish orange stuff for curtains for the sitting room, to be lined and bordered with mauve, and a set of Badminton to be played in front of the house, which will be good practice for tennis and will I hope keep the males happy. In fact it is all going to be as charming as I can get it so as to make Clive want to keep it on.

[1]King's Bench Walk, Inner Temple. Eventually, the Woolfs took rooms at Cliffords Inn, off the Strand.
[2]The Second Post-Impressionist Exhibition, expanded to include English and Russian art, opened October 5, 1912, at the Grafton galleries. LW took this position, manning a desk at the gallery and bearing the brunt of public outrage at Post-Impressionism. For his description of the show and public response, see pp. 93–96 in *Beginning Again* (London: Hogarth Press, 1963), the third volume of his autobiography.
[3]Desmond MacCarthy (1877–1952), literary journalist and drama critic, educated at Trinity College, Cambridge. He had known the Stephens since HPG, and had acted as secretary to the First Post-Impressionist Exhibition in 1910.
[4]After their marriage ceremony on August 10, the Woolfs spent two nights at Asheham, then honeymooned at the Plough Inn, Holford, in the middle of the Quantock Hills. The next week they left for a six-week tour of Provence, Spain, and Italy.

Sophy is very amiable, bent on showing her superiority to Jessie,[5] I think. Wonderful new egg dishes appear at every meal. She and Maud seem very happy and think it a beautiful place, and she was very much touched by Leonard's post card. I also was very much pleased by his letter, extraordinarily false though his idea of my character seems to be. *Of course* I should have expected him to be in the 7th heaven of delight and happiness and would never think of quibbling in the way he suggests. As long as the ape gets all he wants, doesn't smell too much and has his claws well cut, he's a pleasant enough bed-fellow for a short time. The whole question is what will happen when the red undergrowth sprouts in the winter?

Are you really a promising pupil? I believe I'm very bad at it. Perhaps Leonard would like to give me a few lessons. But of course *some* people don't need to be so skilful, at least that's my theory.

The Stores[6] atmosphere is making me daft. I must go and have luncheon.

I do envy you going to Spain. I'd give a good deal to be going there too.

Your
V.B.

BERG

III-17. To Virginia Woolf

Aug. 23 [1912]   *Asheham House, Rodmell, Lewes*

My Billy,

You might think I had time to write letters here, but if so you are much mistaken. I lead the busiest of lives. Down at 9 punctually, then dinner to order, which means a long talk with Sophy, who tells me what she thinks of you and Leonard—very flattering to *him* of course—and how she thinks you eat better when you are helped, and

---

[5]Vanessa's servant. Sophy Farrell normally worked for VW now.
[6]I.e., the Civil Service Co-operative Stores, originally catering to members only, but by this date open to the general public.

don't have to cut your own helpings. "Like the Master,[1] Miss Nessa. Miss Geenia doesn't like to be bothered with those things." So tell Leonard to do the carving. Then I give Julian his reading lesson! and wonder how anyone ever learns that BAT spells bat with so many appalling difficulties in the way. Then I have to talk a little to Quentin, and then perhaps I paint, when curtain-making allows of it, but I haven't really embarked on much painting yet. Julian has lunch with me, which means that it takes about 1½ hours, and I can't settle down to write letters after lunch, and then you see comes tea and the children again, and then I read my Times of yesterday and after dinner all the really important letters have to be written, and then in odd moments there is my dog! He is the most loveable and attractive creature, large and beautiful, and the exact image of Gurth, a size larger. And he chases the sheep whenever we aren't looking. We have named him Rob. I see he will be a great addition to our lives.

Don't trust to local information about typhoid at Avignon. It's to the interest of the natives to make out that there is none, and they always do. I remember at Bologna even the doctor would hardly admit that malaria was ever known at Ravenna, and when there was cholera last year in Italy no Italian would allow it. Don't run even a slight risk. It's not worth it. I do envy you abroad. I now get quite homesick for foreign parts. Even if they're not really better than England there's something so free and irresponsible in one's life in them. I wish I were going to meet you in Spain . . .

Tell L. that from certain minute signs I, with my eye of experience, come to the conclusion that you are very happy, probably more so than you have ever been. Am I right? If he'll write to me perhaps I shall be able to give an opinion on his state too.

V.B.

[1]Sir Leslie Stephen.

III-18. To Leonard Woolf

Sep. 21 [1912]   *Asheham House, Rodmell, Lewes*

My dear Leonard,

It is the most gorgeous September day. Saxon, Clive and I are sitting on the terrace. Indoors with the windows shut sit Oliver Strachey and Norton in the thick of an aesthetic discussion. I am too lazy even to paint and so I will write to you. When I went in to fetch paper and pen just now I heard something about emotions and "if you look at *any* picture" and I wondered if you and Mrs Woolf (as she is now popularly known) were right. But those people aren't the painters themselves of whom you complained. Good heavens, it does seem odd that that should go on perennially whether one's there or not, and one knows that Norton hasn't and never will have the remotest conception of any of the things he's talking about. Well I suppose it's exercise for the brain.

I hope you aren't at this moment in bed at Ravenna, but you have treated me very badly in the way of letters lately and I see I must never give you praise in that direction again. In fact you have proved to me clearly that my methods are the right ones and that I do well to with-hold the torrents that would naturally gush from my lips. I charitably put down Mrs W.'s silence to the fact that she's too happy with a really sympathetic and admiring companion to think willingly of wholesome discipline. But as for you, after your awful description of a night with the apes I can hardly imagine why *you* don't write to me. I am happy to say it's years since I spent a night in their company, and I can't conceive anything more wretched than it sounds. It would be bad enough to know they were in the next bed with all their smells and their whines and their wettings, but to have to change beds with them and all the rest of it—a coal hole would be more to my taste. So now you know what I think.

I am today having a large square flower bed dug and manured, and as soon as it's wet enough I shall have flowers sent from Seend and plant them. Otherwise not very much has been done to the garden since you saw it. The front lawn is used as a playground by the children and is not changed. I hope to enlarge the terrace if I can get anyone to help, but that's doubtful. Clive goes to London most of next week to see to his part of the Grafton show,[1] and most likely, I shall go up

[1]CB selected the English work in the exhibition, choosing paintings by VB, DG, Frederick and Jessie Etchells, Henry Lamb, Wyndham Lewis, Stanley Spencer, Bernard Adeney, and Spencer Gore, and sculpture by Eric Gill.

too for a day or two to help with the hanging. Roger is in the thick of it all and the troubles are beginning. Pictures and hangings won't arrive, but that's all inevitable. Duncan has done the poster, which is rather fine. We expect a lively autumn with visits probably from Matisse and Vildrac and other distinguished foreigners. I am also proposing to give 3 evening parties to introduce young women to the house. Once introduced it is hoped that Clive will find no difficulty in doing the rest.

Sophy appeared yesterday from Seaford where she says she is very comfortable and has met and talked to Lisa Stillman (tell Mrs W.).[2] Today the children have gone to spend the day with her. Saxon's sciatica (he thinks) is hardly if at all better. He plays Badminton however and actually said last time he came that he had seldom been so happy as he was here. He woke in the morning without a headache and was very talkative.

I envy you very much in Italy now but I doubt if it's more beautiful than this. The trees here are amazing colour. Well I don't expect to be answered or to get any attention from either of you for the next 2 years.

Your
V.B.

SUSSEX

III-19. To Roger Fry

Oct. 12 [1912]   *Asheham House, Rodmell, Lewes*

[Heading:] There is no hurry about reading this.
My dear,
    It was horrid leaving you standing on the platform waiting for your train, and I was afraid that you would lapse into feeling frightfully

---

[2]Lisa Stillman, portraitist, daughter of the Pre-Raphaelite painter Marie Spartali and the American painter W. J. Stillman, whose courtship had been encouraged by Julia Stephen. She lived at Ditchling, Sussex.
Sophy may have been on holiday at Seaford.

tired and worried again as soon as I had gone! Such is my conceit. I just caught my train at Brighton owing to my pushing my way through the luggage gate without a ticket, and when I got to Lewes I met with disaster—that's to say I didn't get all my flowers. I found Clutton Brock's[1] waiting all right at the passenger station. The goods dept., they told me, shut at 4 on Saturdays. I secured an angelic porter, most sympathetic, who first telephoned for a taxi for me, then telephoned to the goods people to ask them to let me in. I went there and found an even more angelic clerk, who said they had had my telegram at 5 after all the men who knew where the parcels were had gone. He had been looking for them ever since without success. He would be delighted to let me in to look too but was afraid it would be useless. So I went in to the most wonderful huge space, lighted by two lamps, with lots of boxes and hampers and great bales waiting to be fetched. It was so beautiful, but unluckily I could find nothing in the dark. When I got there I found no railway notices of goods arrived, so I can only suppose that your things and those from Seend and the bulbs have not yet come . . .

I have just had dinner for which I cooked myself a sausage and eggs. It was odd to be cooking my own solitary meal. Mrs Funnell[2] was so much upset at the idea of my sleeping alone here "what with all those goings on at Eastbourne—it makes one wonder what will happen next," that she insisted upon coming to sleep here . . .

Oh Roger, it was delicious today in spite of sordid surroundings, like a little water when one was very thirsty. In fact I think perhaps the sordid surroundings are like the Matisse.[3] I mean one has to fall back on the really important things. I have always had a taste for love-making in the midst of quite ordinary things. It turns them into something else. Not that it wouldn't be divine to do it in Asia Minor, too.

Roger, if you get ill in France, which I think you quite well may, for you'll really feel worse when the strain is taken off I expect, you're to send for me without thinking twice about it. If you just telegraphed for me there could be no question but that I'd have to go and illness

---

[1]Arthur Clutton-Brock (1868–1924), art critic of the *Times*. Possibly VB was collecting flower bulbs from her friends for the garden at Asheham.
[2]The shepherd's wife, who lived in a nearby cottage and "did" for the residents of Asheham.
[3]Possibly a reference to one of the thirty Matisse paintings included in the Second Post-Impressionist Exhibition.

is always enough excuse for any aberrations. You see Joan[4] couldn't leave the household and go to you and there'd be no one else but me to send for. I'm really rather afraid of your being ill, for you never looked so tired as you did today. Adrian and Duncan would be no good at looking after you and it would be all right for me to come with them there. But I don't want you to get ill. It would give me the devil of a time till I got to you even if there were nice moments then.

You see I've got nothing to do but write to you. That's why you're having this long letter which most likely you won't have time to read. I am meditating upon the extraordinariness of the world. It does get odder and odder. When I think that 2 years ago I hardly knew you. Quentin was 2 months old about, and I was fearfully worried about him and one evening you came to dine and for a few minutes I was alone with you while Clive went down to fetch the wine. You asked me about the baby, and I said he had been very ill and you told me that you had had fearful times with Julian [Fry] when he was a baby. I had a sort of inkling then that you would be sympathetic and understand. No one else that I cared about had been and I had had to keep most of my worries to myself. But I was still too ill at ease with you really to talk to you and I suppose I didn't realise much all that winter except that I was always happy when I knew you were coming, as you did begin to do fairly often.

Do you know that even that spring, when we went abroad, I thought that I should probably pair off with Harry and you with Clive, and it was quite with surprise that I found on the journey out and in Constantinople that I wanted to talk to you much more than to him. I think I suddenly saw then that it would be possible to have some quite new relation with you, some much more complete sympathy than I had ever had with anyone. But I didn't speculate at all as to what you felt for me. I only took it for granted that you liked me, and then those unfortunate worries with Harry took up most of my attentions. Only I knew that I was very glad of any reason which made me stick to you and not to him! My dear, why *am* I writing all this? I shall put a large notice at the top to say you're not to bother to read it. Oh God, having got so far I upset the ink (I'm writing on my knee) all over the rug, the carpet, the door, the wall—it's too awful—and hardly any over the letter which wouldn't have mattered! Well, one must be philosophic over such things, but you never saw

[4]Joan Mary Fry (1862–1955), one of RF's sisters, kept house for him at Guildford. A Quaker and a very sheltered woman, she disapproved of Vanessa.

such a splash. It's put an end to all the nice things I was going to say, but you know Roger, I love you. I love you. Do you know how much?

V.

TATE

III-20. To Clive Bell

Dec. 27 [1912]   *46, Gordon Square*

Dearest Puck,[1]

I sent you a scrawl to catch the country post[2] this afternoon. I hope it didn't sound too gloomy. My inside has been making me rather wretched all day but I think it's getting all right now and as I have been sensible and stayed in bed I hope to be quite recovered tomorrow. As I told you yesterday this weather is really too awful for anything. I am longing as I suppose everyone is for a little sun, and feel inclined to join the Daily Mirror lady at Scarborough.[3] I have had a letter from Madge who wants to know if I have measles as Janet developed them after coming here. That at least I haven't got. I had a bad moment wondering whether the children could have got them from her, but have decided that it was too long ago that she was here.

Sat[urday]. I was interrupted yesterday by Duncan who came in and lay on the floor and talked in a desultory but cheering way of the Mausoleum Book[4] and how we are to turn my studio into a tropical forest with great red figures on the walls, a blue ceiling with birds of paradise floating from it (my idea), and curtains each one different. This is all to cheer us through London winters. Duncan also

---

[1]A variation on Peak, VB's habitual name for CB.
[2]VB continued to suffer setbacks in her recovery from the 1911 miscarriage. This Christmas, she sent CB and the children alone to Seend while she convalesced in Bloomsbury.
[3]The *Daily Mirror* had reported an intrepid female assaying the icy sea at Scarborough.
[4]An account of his early life and marriage, written by Leslie Stephen for his children after the death of Julia. Edited by Alan Bell and published in 1977 by the Oxford University Press.

wants a bath let into the floor but I told him that was à la Leighton House,[5] which made him rather cross.

He didn't leave till 8, and as I was in the middle of dinner in came the Woolves, so I never got my letter to you finished. They seemed very happy, but are evidently both a little exercised in their minds on the subject of the Goat's coldness. I think I perhaps annoyed her but may have consoled him by saying that I thought she never had understood or sympathised with sexual passion in men. Apparently she still gets no pleasure at all from the act, which I think is curious. They were very anxious to know when I first had an orgasm. I couldn't remember. Do you? But no doubt I sympathised with such things if I didn't have them from the time I was 2. They can go to Asheham any day I like to go they now say . . .

I'm afraid you're having rather a dose of the babies, aren't you. Do they take up too much time? I hope Julian's spiked toy isn't one which he could really hurt himself badly with. Don't let him have anything that he could fall onto and hurt his face again, but of course you won't. I sometimes think of such horrors in bed but they are quite fantastic. I expect Mabel is really very careful but I always have a dread of spikes. They creep in unnoticed. The most peaceable toys suddenly develop them.

. . . Give my love to those babies. I dreamt of them all last night but I had 3 all as like as 2 peas, rather to my disappointment, and all boys. I have written a silly scribble for Julian, more for my own satisfaction than his! Peak darling, I'm very sorry if I have written gloomily, but you'll forgive Dolphin. I'm really better today.

[unsigned]

TATE

[5]The Kensington home, now a museum, of Frederic Leighton (Baron Leighton) (1830–96), distinguished Victorian painter and sculptor and President of the Royal Academy.

III-21. To Leonard Woolf

Jan 22 [1913]   *Asheham House, Rodmell, Lewes*

My dear Leonard,

I will return your article[1] with this if I can find an envelope big enough for it—if not, I hope it won't matter if I keep it a day or two longer. I have given it to Clive and to Duncan to read which I hope was not indiscreet of me. Clive I think is answering it. I don't think I can sign it, for I don't entirely agree, but I'm not sure I can tell you why I don't. I agree with you that representation, and imitation too, for that matter, are not incompatible with great art, but it seems to me clear that if the chief aim or if one of the principle aims of an artist is to imitate or to represent *facts* accurately (is there any difference?) it is impossible that he should also produce significant form, or whatever you like to call it. Does Clive say more than this? I haven't read his article again, but my impression was that that was what he meant. It is clearly possible to use imitation or representation in producing a great work of art, but it can't be the object of a great artist to tell you facts at the cost of telling you what he feels about them.

Then I don't think I agree with you in your account of the way in which one looks at a picture (but that may be my blindness). I often look at a picture—for instance I did at the Picasso trees by the side of a lake[2]—without seeing in the least what the things are. I saw trees, but never dreamt of a lake or lakes [?] although I saw certain colours and planes behind the trees. I got quite a strong emotion from the forms and colours, but it wasn't changed when weeks afterwards it was pointed out to me by chance that the blue was a lake. This happens as often as not. The picture does convey the idea of form, of what you call secondary form I suppose, but not the idea of form associated with anything in life, but simply form, separated from life. As a matter of fact we do first feel the emotion and then look at the picture, that is to say, look at it from the point of view of seeing its tertiary form— at least I do. The reason I think that artists paint life and not patterns

[1]Unidentified and probably unpublished.
[2]This painting is difficult to identify with certainty, but Clive Bell's review of the Second Post-Impressionist Exhibition in the *Burlington Magazine* 22:226–30 mentions that one of Picasso's works was hung beside a painting by Derain entitled *Trees by a Lake*. Possibly VB confused the artists.

is that certain qualities in life, what I call movement, mass, weight, have aesthetic value. But I doubt if those qualities have anything to do with the emotions you mean in your last sentence. At any rate feelings about them can be expressed without the artist's saying any-thing about the emotions of life—as I understand you to mean "life." However I may be wrong about your meaning. I think it's all very confusing and one wades into such quagmires when one embarks on this subject that I thank my stars I needn't really bother about it.

. . . I have I think quite recovered. Anyhow I'm quite as well as I was before I got bad, so I don't see why I shouldn't come back to London. However I shall see Craig next week and see what he says.

I am rather surprised at your account of Jean's opinion,[3] for she certainly told me the opposite. Why has she changed? I hope you'll get something definite from Savage. After all he does know Virginia and ought really to be the best judge. I suppose Craig can't tell as much without having seen her or knowing her at all. Do tell me what Savage says.

How is the beard?[4] The fringe is visible but not very long yet.

Your
VB

SUSSEX

III-22. To Roger Fry

Feb. 6 [1913]   *Asheham House, Rodmell, Lewes*

My dear,

You will be seeing Clive today and hearing all our doings and so perhaps you won't want a letter from me. All the same you're going to have one just to pay you out for all the *horrid* things you said to

---

[3]LW was seeking advice from VB and various medical advisors on whether VW's mental and physical health would be endangered by maternity. Savage argued in favor of motherhood, Craig against. VB consulted Jean Thomas, who at first thought it might be good for VW.
[4]LW's beard was short-lived. Perhaps VB had cut a fringe ("bangs" in America) to compete with him.

me in your letter this morning. Well, I see Duncan has been making mischief between us. Now what conceivable motive could he have for doing such a thing? Can you guess? I merely told him that you didn't altogether approve of the watercolour I thought best. Evidently the rumour will be set afloat that you have given up any small belief you may once have had in my talents, and as Duncan is well known to be above all things generous—I can't go on with this lengthy exposition but you see where it ends—you with Melian,[1] I with Duncan. Eh? Who'll get the better of that bargain? But you have chosen your bed, and a precious bony one it will be I should think. Melain's b. can't be very soft, is it? And as for her b.'s, I know what they're like, all withered and hanging down, no youthful spring about them! Ha, ha—Am I nasty enough yet?

I am writing to you instead of painting. Perhaps that helps me to be bitter. I hoped it was going to be really fine and that I could go out and finish my watercolour of Mrs Funnell's cottage and the road, but it's cold and grey. I can't go on with my still-life till it's dry, and I haven't the energy to pound off alone to do a drawing of that barn we saw. I wish I were going to lunch with you and Miss Stein,[2] but I shall meet her some day no doubt if she takes to Clive.

. . . Will Clive tell you I wonder of our great scheme for a combined dinner to you and advertisement of the group? (Why shouldn't Miss Stein give money?) We propose to get up a Bohemian dinner to you, given by all the grateful young artists, about the middle of July, at the Italian restaurant in Gt. Portland St. (I think) where the Butler Erewhon dinners were given.[3] We should get all your disreputable and some of your aristocratic friends to come, and after dinner we should repair to Fitzroy Sq., where would be seen decorated furniture, painted walls, etc. There we should all get drunk and dance and kiss. Orders would flow in and the aristocrats would feel sure they were really in the thick of things. If properly done, it seems to me it might be a great send off for the business. By the end of the summer we should have a lot to show and orders could be delivered in the autumn. What do you think?

[1]Florence Melian Stawell (1869–1936), classical scholar and lecturer at Newnham College, Cambridge.
[2]Gertrude Stein (1874–1946), brilliant American expatriate writer and patron of the arts, resident in Paris from 1903. RF had known her since at least 1907. Her collection (begun with her brother Leo) of paintings by Cézanne, Matisse, and Picasso was at this time unrivaled in Europe.
[3]Untraced.

I am thankful the Grafton is over. I hope it means not quite such a rush for you. As for the Liverpool show,[4] don't put yourself out too much for them.

I have had a very affectionate letter from Virginia, so I suppose for the moment there is peace. I have also heard from Snow who is going to hear you lecture at Leeds[5] and wants to know if you're going to abuse the old masters! What very queer notions people have. I hope you'll enlighten them a little and don't forget what Snow looks like in case she tries to talk to you.

Now shall I end this nasty letter with a few words of affection and tell you how much I want you, and that I'm really very dependent on you and think you're the most charming and loveable creature under the sun? But you may be in Melian's arms when you get this and I, alas, am not in Duncan's, but all alone in the depths of Sussex. So perhaps I'd better not say anything of the kind.

Are you going to paint your railway scene for the group's show, or what will you have for it? I suppose I shall have to come to Guildford before long and choose your things and tell you what to do. I don't see why between now and Easter you shouldn't do quite a lot of painting and perhaps most of it might be done at Gordon Sq. Shall we paint the Square?

But I have got so realistic.

Your
V.

TATE

III-23. To Virginia Woolf

Feb. 6 [1913]   **Asheham House, Rodmell, Lewes**

My Billy,

You do seem to have gone back to the 90s with a vengeance. How incredibly antediluvian it all sounds. I think I prefer to hear about it

---

[4]The Second Post-Impressionist Exhibition, a smaller version of the Grafton show, held at the Sandon Society, Liverpool.
[5]On Sunday, February 16.

all than to be in it, but still I am rather hurt that you didn't wait for me [to return] to give the dinner at the Cock to which you promised to invite me. The least you can do now is to write and tell me all about it.[1]

I don't know when I shall see you. Are you going to Leeds next Sunday [for Roger's lecture] or what? We shall come back I think on Thursday or Friday. My affairs are due next week which makes us a little uncertain as to the exact day, but I expect it will be one of the two. We shall on the whole be rather sorry to go. The weather has been rather better lately and this place is very beautiful. Lots of crocuses are out, chiefly yellow I regret to say, which I'm afraid is the fault of my Dutchman,[2] and the daffodils are all sprouting. Rows of tulips are coming up, there are quantities of violets and a few snowdrops. Some days are like warm spring. On the other hand it generally pours and blows like the devil. I see the country has immense advantages, especially as regards work, but I suppose we never shall really make up our minds to retire to it.

Clive has gone to London today to lunch with Roger, Duncan, and Miss Stein. Roger was here Sunday and the air is teeming with discussion on Art. They think they are gettting further. I don't know. Roger's views of course are more mature than ours. He is at one pole and Clive at the other and I come somewhere in between on a rather shaky foothold, but none of us really agree with Leonard, whatever he may say to the contrary, and Duncan tells me it is a gross libel to say that he does either. So your husband had better reconsider his position, I think. We shall go on till doomsday I suppose.

Duncan's art is supposed to be improving, and I think his latest works are very good. There is hope after all that he may be the long-looked-for British genius. I hear that Etchells is just settling in London, so he will be upon us when we return. It will be very odd to come back to the thick of things again.

Have you settled anything about your plans for the future now you've had all the conflicting advice[3] or are you still vague?

Your
VB

BERG

[1]Although VW's letter is lost, we do know that she asked her old friends Violet and Ozzy Dickinson to dine at the Cock on January 22, 1913.
[2]The gardener.
[3]Regarding whether to have children.

III-24. To Virginia Woolf

May 3 [1913]   *Albergo d'Italia, Urbino*[1]

My Billy,

I have only just got your letter from Ravenna. Roger, Duncan and I came here yesterday in the hope of finding a lovely little country town where we might paint. Clive stayed on at Ravenna till today and has now arrived bringing your letter with him. Here we are in the most horrible place, as I begin to see all mountain people and places are horrible. It is cold and raining. The people are dour and hostile. The hotel is dirty and everyone cheats. They are breaking down the wall outside my bedroom door, and we are therefore going on tomorrow to Spoleto and then to Rome. The weather had been getting lovely and so we hope to get into warmth again in the plains.

I see I had been unjust to you as you had written to me, but I don't know what had happened to your letter. It seems to have been broken open and glued together again with ink, and is in a horrid mess. I wish I could see the result of my gardening at Asheham. I hope Sydney sees that he was wrong if it is really what you describe.[2] Who is the lunatic who has planted the Christmas trees?[3] It's too ghastly to think of Marny and Emma[4] dreading the summer evenings. Why don't they commit suicide at once and end their boredom. You will have Lisa [Stillman] on you soon and will I hope write me an account of her visit.

The best place we have been to was Ravenna, where I could have stayed happily for some time. We have now bought large quantities of crockery, stuffs, etc., mostly to be sold at Fitzroy Sq. We also discovered a genius, a young man of exquisite beauty and a charming smile, called Dante Paradiso, from whom Duncan bought two enor-

---

[1]This year VB's Italian holiday included a new companion, DG, as well as CB and RF.

[2]Perhaps a reference to Sydney Waterlow's praise of VB's latest contribution to the Novel Club (a precursor to the Memoir Club). Waterlow had stayed with the Woolfs at Asheham on April 26 and 27.

[3]As a wedding present for the Woolfs, Jean Thomas and an anonymous well-wishing "lunatic" in her care had planted two pines squarely in front of the Asheham windows.

[4]The Woolfs had received a visit at Asheham on April 23 from Margaret (Marny) and Emma Vaughan, VB's unmarried cousins.

mous painted wooden figures,[5] and Clive a large oil painting. Roger has commissioned him to do another, and boxes for the shop too! You can imagine the activities and otherwise of the party. Roger is up with the lark, does many sketches, sees all the sights, and he and Clive are indefatigable in their attributions and historical discoveries. I can't say I listen to much, and after Padua I struck at sightseeing and now refuse to see more than one thing a day. I find that Duncan sympathises with me and if he and I had the conduct of the party in our hands we should settle down somewhere for a month and spend most of our time loafing. Perhaps it's as well we can't.

We have seen today one of the best pictures in the world, a very beautiful Piero della Francesca,[6] so it has been worth coming here in spite of all the horrors of the place.

One of my principal amusements is reading Roger's family letters, which throw amazing light on their lives and characters. I should like to quote from one of them but it is thought too dangerous.

What is Sydney's latest love affair? Molly[7] apparently thinks it too horribly sordid but does not go into details. However as she says you know about it I think you might hand it on. Also tell us about the divorce case.[8] I hope Leonard did go to it.

My love was not repulsed.[9] I fear it was not even noticed. But then *I* don't *brusquer* matters in the way some people do. Give my love to Leonard and tell him I think he might write to me soon even if he is a successful novelist.[10] Write to Hôtel de Milan, Monte Citorio, Rome. We shall probably be there till Tue. the 11th or 12th.

Your
VB

BERG

[5]Still in the studio at Charleston.
[6]Possibly Piero's celebrated *Flagellation*, in the Ducal Palace at Urbino.
[7]Molly MacCarthy (neé Warre-Cornish) (1881–1953), writer, wife of Desmond MacCarthy.
[8]Sydney Waterlow's divorce from his wife Alice was granted in May 1913. Soon afterward, he married Margery Eckhard.
[9]By Duncan Grant.
[10]LW's *The Village in the Jungle* (London: Edward Arnold, 1913) was reviewed favorably and twice reprinted before the end of the year.

III-25. To Clive Bell

Tuesday [August 12, 1913]   *Weating Grange [Brandon]*[1]

Dearest,

We had rather an awful evening yesterday, though there were intervals of sunshine in the morning. By night however everything had got soaked through and even the tents were dripping inside. Roger made us some delicious toasted cheese, which you wouldn't have found consoling, on his Duck oven, and we sat in a tent and kept up our spirits by singing catches. I was glad I had arranged to sleep at the farm, and did sleep like a top till 9 AM. Today luckily has been lovely again, warm and sunny, and we have all got dried up. Adrian spent the afternoon romping with Noel and Daphne,[2] so I hope he was happy. Roger of course has been painting hard. They are all now playing tip and run and I am sitting over the fire keeping watch on a wonderful stew R. has made with a chicken, bacon, potatoes, a touch of apple, mint, etc.! We also had an omelot [*sic*] made by him for lunch.

I have had a rather pathetic letter from Molly who said she had a temperature, so I'm afraid her time here did her no good. Woolf has written to say that they weren't going to Asheham till Monday on account of her affairs, so it will be sharp work getting them out by the 25th. However I shall simply assume that we are going there then. She imagines herself to be quite well again but is still not sleeping very well. I wish we were all healthy young women like the O[livier]s.

Maynard has gone to London today for one night. Ka[3] didn't come yesterday but may do so in a day or two. I think I shall be back on Friday or Saturday probably. Roger is a great success with the young

---

[1]A summer camp at Brandon in Norfolk, organized by some younger "Neo-Pagan" friends.

[2]Noel (1892–1969) and Daphne (1889–1950), the youngest of the four daughters of Sir Sydney Olivier, Fabian socialist and colonial administrator. Adrian was unsuccessfully in love with Noel.

[3]Katherine ("Ka") Laird Cox (1887–1938), educated at Newnham College, Cambridge, where she became a close friend of Rupert Brooke's and later, disastrously, his lover.

women, who seem to find him a great acquisition. I hope I shall hear from you soon. The children are flourishing.

Your
V.B.

TATE

III-26. To Virginia Woolf

Aug. 28 [1913]   *46, Gordon Square, Bloomsbury*

My Billy,

This letter is going to be a lecture, for Leonard says you think you are being made to eat unnecessarily. You may think it absurd of me to think I know anything about it at this distance, but I don't think it is, for you know I have had plenty of experience of you in the past and when I saw you in London I could tell quite well what state you were in. It was perfectly clear to me that you were in that same sort of badly nourished state that you were in that first time at Welwyn,[1] not nearly so bad as that, for of course you aren't quite incapable now as you were then of using your brain at all. But you are in the less bad state when you sometimes worry frightfully and feel as if your brain were working round and round, and are miserable. At other times you think there is nothing the matter.

I understand these states better now than I did then from having been through them myself. I found it difficult then to believe that all your states of misery would go when you got nourished again, but I took Savage's word for it that you would and found it to be true. When I got into the same state myself,[2] I found it quite impossible often to believe it at all, but I did have the sense, which you must have now, to go by other people and not by my own feelings. No one will tell you to eat if it's not necessary. Why should they? It *is* most

[1] VB refers to VW's serious breakdown after the death of Sir Leslie in 1904, when she stayed for three months at Violet Dickinson's home in Burnham Wood, Welwyn.
[2] VB suffered mental instability after her 1911 miscarriage and in a lesser form for many months afterward.

necessary and is the only way of preventing you from getting really bad. Now Billy do be sensible and don't make things difficult for Leonard, but realise that at this moment he is far more sensible than you are, and trust him to know how to get things right. You know, when you were bad before, you thought just as you do now, that we were all mistaken, that there was nothing the matter and that it was cruel to make you eat. But you know now we were right and so must take it on trust again that we are right until you can feel it for yourself. Don't bother to write but tell L. to send me a line.

Your
VB

BERG

III-27. To Leonard Woolf

Thursday [September 11, 1913]   *Asheham*

My dear Leonard,

Your telegram was a great relief,[1] Evidently, I think, now things are going on well and it is just a question of great care. I rather hope too that there won't be much trouble from the complications, but anyhow I suppose that is not serious. It means good nursing and that she will get. You will of course have done this, but to satisfy my mind, will you tell the nurses, now that there is returning consciousness, to turn out the room carefully and remove everything that *could* be dangerous, scissors, knives, etc. and of course drugs. You can't take too many precautions, and however unlikely it seems it is conceivable that she might take a nurse unawares, jumping up and perhaps hurting herself

[1]Since the beginning of July 1913, VW had been increasingly depressed and unwell. A short stay in Jean Thomas' Twickenham nursing home on Savage's advice did not help, and on September 9 she and LW consulted new doctors, who advised a lengthy rest cure. That night, while LW was briefly out, VW took a lethal dose of Veronal, a sleeping aid. Vanessa was summoned, along with doctors and nurses, and joined Ka Cox (who had discovered Virginia unconscious) at VW's bedside. At 9 A.M. the following morning she was pronounced out of danger, but remained unconscious all that day.

before they could stop her. It will all become a routine soon and you will feel safe, but it mustn't be relaxed.

I do hope you are going to rest all you can now, for the strain will still be great. I meant to ask you, does it add to your bothers to write daily to me? Do tell me this honestly my dear, for if I didn't hear I should just take it for granted things were going on well. I know you would tell me if they weren't, and you mustn't have any strain that can be avoided.

I have talked to Adrian about Sophy and he is quite ready to let you have her, so I will write to her tonight or tomorrow. I am sending this to Lewes this afternoon.

I shall come up to the consultation with Belfrage when you want me, and if it would be useful I could come and help to get you to Forest Row.[2] But that we can see about. Also of course I can easily come there from London to see you anyhow if not her. We could meet outside the house. You will be so easy to get at, which is a great blessing.

Give my love to Ka, and tell her I am seeing about a design for her. How I do wish I could be of more use to you. Having one's own family to think about is so incapacitating.

Your
V.B.

SUSSEX

III-28. To Roger Fry

Sep. 18 [1913]   *Asheham*

My dear Roger,

First business. The size of the screen[1] is 34 in. × 31 in. I am going on working at it and getting much quicker I think but I certainly

---

[2]Dr. Sydney Belfrage (1871–1950), the Bell's family physician, who looked after VW for the next six months. George Duckworth had lent the Woolfs his country home, Dalingridge Place, near Forest Row, Sussex.
[1]Possibly a firescreen.

shan't have it done in time. Still I think it's quicker than cross-stitch, and it's more amusing to do. We have been working hard at the panels[2] today and I think we shall get them finished tomorrow. On the other side you'll find a rough idea of mine but as it's only from memory and my pen wouldn't work perhaps it doesn't do justice! The young lady is dressed in yellow, the young gentleman in dark blue, with a pale green shirt front, and the background is in venetian red ridges, but I don't think they're very realistic. We're leaving a good deal of white in ridges so as to give brilliance and there are black lines too between the colours. Marjorie thinks them hideous and that we shall be stopped by the police, but I can't see what she means. She is in a very vigorous mood and roaring health, full of Dalcrose.[3] She dressed up in black tights and did her exercises for us and says it is a new art and has given her new life. She is going back to Germany for a year. God! I don't think I could do it even for a new art and a new life. She is an odd contrast to Molly. Last night we sang all the popular songs we could remember. Would you have enjoyed it?

It is now after dinner and they are doing it again so letter writing is not easy. In fact I think I've been very clever to write to you at all and I hope my last letter *was* nice enough. Roger dear, you mustn't be so pathetic. What with your age and Wadsworth and Jones[4] and all the rest of it, it's too awful! I know you do devil for us and it does seem wretched that you should be lunching with Jones while we're painting in the country. How damnable.

I can't go on with Gilbert and Sullivan being shouted at me. My inside has recovered well, you'll be glad to hear.

Your
V.

I can't make any criticisms on your prospectus, only I thought you ought to ask people to come to the [Omega] showrooms more plainly.

TATE

[2]VB painted one of three panels for the Omega's Ideal Home Exhibition room. Her design is now at the Victoria and Albert Museum. Alternately, VB may have produced her panel for the front of the Omega Workshops.
[3]Emile Jacques Dalcroze (1865–1950), Swiss music teacher. With French psychologist Edouard Claparide, developed eurythmics, a whole-body approach to rhythm. He opened many schools to propound his theories. Though he did not teach at all of his schools, he did so at the one established in London in the 1920s.
[4]Edward Wadsworth (1889–1949), painter. Employed at the Omega Workshops until the Ideal Home Rumpus (see the following letter). Jones is uncertain.

III-29. To Roger Fry

Sunday [October 12, 1913]   *46, Gordon Square, Bloomsbury*

My dear Roger,

We have had a day of it! This morning Molly telephoned to say that they had had the enclosed circular letter from Lewis, Etchells and Co.[1] which you had better read at this point as it will explain matters. It is so absurd that perhaps you'll think it unnecessary to do anything but laugh about it. On the other hand, Molly evidently thought you must somehow have given them cause to be very angry, and Desmond thought that your enemies would be only too glad to get hold of any story against you and would be delighted at a split in the Omega, and that you ought to defend yourself. Duncan and Adrian came round here, and D. and I decided that we had better see Etchells and try to get him to see that whether they were right or not, they had behaved monstrously in writing this letter without first accusing you to your face. We went to see him this afternoon and talked for nearly 2 hours. He was incredibly stupid and could hardly be made to see our point at all. When he did see it he simply said that he didn't agree. He brought up a long tale of grievances of how he had gradually become convinced against his will of your meanness. Evidently he had been storing up small things which had at last been brought to a point by this. It is all such a muddle that one couldn't convince him of anything. But I don't think either he or the others will give in at all, or that there is any use in trying to get them to.

Desmond has been here for some hours, and he and Clive have concocted these letters which are the sort of thing they think you might say in reply. Etchells had written to Rutter to ask him for your letter, which I only hope *didn't* say that Etchells had no paintings!

[1]Four Omega artists (Wyndham Lewis, C. J. Hamilton, Frederick Etchells, and Edward Wadsworth) had distributed to Omega shareholders a letter arguing (a) that RF secured the decoration of the "Post-Impressionist" room at the Ideal Home Exhibition by a trick, appropriating for the Omega a commission from the *Daily Mail* originally intended to be shared between Wyndham Lewis, Spencer Gore (not an Omega artist), and the Omega, and (b) that RF kept from Frederick Etchells the knowledge that Frank Rutter of the Leeds Art Gallery wanted some of Etchells' work for a London exhibition. For a detailed discussion of the controversy and its fallout, see "The Ideal Home Rumpus" by Quentin Bell and Stephen Chaplin and related essays in *The Bloomsbury Group*, ed. S. P. Rosenbaum (Toronto and Buffalo: University of Toronto Press, 1975).

Apparently he had several, and both he and Lewis are sending to the Dore,[2] so anyhow they have taken no harm.

Then Desmond thought that I, as I am supposed to be in charge at the O[mega] had better see the Daily Mail man[3] tomorrow and get him to say what happened at your interview with him. After I have seen him and got his statement, which I will send on to you, you could write your letter, if you think it all right.

We have been discussing this all at great length today and now Leonard, who is here, is rather against your taking any notice of it. I think it rather depends on whether Rutter and the Daily Mail produce clear evidence. If they do, there are at any rate those two questions of fact about which they can be shown to be quite mistaken, and perhaps it would be better to leave out the rest. I have put alternative suggestions on the letter suggested. However it may of course be better not to answer in any case. You will have to settle this as you think best. It's the most awful nuisance, but after all you have got rid of Etchells and Wadsworth.

Etchells was going to send you a list of the people to whom they had sent their circular. Oh God, what utter idiots they are. It seems almost incredible. I have no other news as our day has been spent discussing this affair which I hope will seem to you happily remote and unreal. You can imagine how we have enjoyed ourselves over it! . . .

[unsigned]

[Postscript in Clive Bell's hand:] It seems to me just possible that we have all rather lost our heads over this area row. I wonder whether it wouldn't be best to let the whole thing slide—for a time at any rate. We could then see what was happening. After all, why should you wrangle with four grubbly little ill-bred painters? The whole thing's a matter of character, and surely yours is good enough to stand a little scurrilous rhetoric . . .

TATE

[2]The Dore Gallery, London.
[3]A Mr. Craston. What becomes apparent in retrospect is that two commissions for the Ideal Home room were made: one by Mr. Craston, who spoke with RF at the Omega and never mentioned individual artists, and another by an unknown representative of the *Daily Mail* who, on the advice of critic P. G. Konody, approached Spencer Gore in July 1913 and specifically requested that he, Wyndham Lewis, and the Omega decorate the room. Gore took this news to the Omega and left a message with DG, the only person present. Given DG's absentmindedness, the message was probably never passed on to RF.

III-30. To Roger Fry

Oct. 13 [1913]   *46, Gordon Square, Bloomsbury*

My dear Roger,

It was very difficult to write to you yesterday for, as I expect you saw, I was in a crowd, and they all wanted to know what I was saying and to add remarks of their own. Well, now I must tell you what has happened today about this silly affair. Clive had a letter from Lewis this morning, written to explain *his* position. He said the facts were beyond dispute, then he abused you, and then said he hoped Clive would not be alientated from him. Clive went out this afternoon and in Bond St. whom should he run into but Lewis, who came forward and said "I hope you're not much upset!" "Oh no," said Clive, "not in the least." They then had a long talk walking about Bond St. and Piccadilly. Lewis expained that he had to use politics to defend himself, that he had his way to make, etc. Clive pointed out that their letter had been a silly and "suburban" affair which would convince no one of anything but the folly of the writers. Lewis then tried to put all the blame of the letter on the others and said it wasn't the sort of thing he liked doing. "I hope my colleagues were not hurt by any remarks about Prettiness," he said. He had not wished to put in that sort of thing.[1] Clive seems to have made him feel rather foolish and found out that they are all longing for you to reply. Lewis was very much disappointed that you had not rushed back from France at once! What they would really like would be an action for libel. It seems quite clear now that the best thing is to do nothing. It is quite evident that no one will believe anything they say and that they will be crushed more by silence than any reply . . .

Your

V.

TATE

[1]The seceding artists had taken the opportunity of their Round Robin letter to lambast the style of the Bloombury painters and to assert their own importance: "This family party of strayed and Dissenting Aesthetes, however, were compelled to call in as much modern talent as they could find, to do the rough and masculine work without which they knew their efforts would not rise above the level of a pleasant tea-party" (quoted in Rosenbaum, 337).

III-31. To Roger Fry

Tuesday [October 14, 1913]   *46, Gordon Square, Bloomsbury*

My dear,

I see I never enclosed the letters we suggested you should write. Here they are, though perhaps not of much use now. I went this afternoon to see Mr Craston of the Daily Mail at Olympia! He was very friendly and entirely upheld your statement of course. In fact he said he couldn't understand how the people at Carmelite House[1] could have given any commission, for he wasn't at Carmelite House but had offices elsewhere and knew nothing about them. He said that the names of Lewis and [Spencer] Gore hadn't been mentioned in his interview with you and that the commission had been given directly to the Omega. He was delighted to come forward and say this, so I gave him definite questions written out to be answered and he is going to send me a letter saying this. So we shall have complete evidence on one point . . .

Robinson[2] came and talked to me very seriously this morning about Jessie [Etchells]. He says she is disloyal to the O[mega] and only works for her bread and butter, that she will most likely spread dissension among the apprentices and will report things to [her brother] Fred that he may use against us, that it is bad business to have anyone disloyal in the place and he wants her discharged. Also he says Winnie[3] is a little jealous of her getting more pay! However I don't think there's really any harm they *can* do us that they have not already done, nor do I really think Jessie is likely to try to do active harm even if she isn't very keen. I said I certainly couldn't take any steps without asking you and that I thought her too valuable as an artist not to keep her . . .

[1]Headquarters of the *Daily Mail*. The exhibition offices were at Olympia, Kensington.
[2]Charles Robinson, business manager of the Omega.
[3]Winifred Gill, a Slade-trained artist, formally Joan Fry's secretary at Guildford.

I'm very glad Doucet is so charming. Give him my love and say I hope he's soothing you after all these wild beasts here.

The Anreps[4] are coming to dinner—I must stop. Oh Lord!

Your
V.

TATE

III-32. To Roger Fry

Sunday [late October 1913]   *46, Gordon Square, Bloomsbury*

My dear,

I suppose as you leave your aristocrats tomorrow I had better send this to Failand.[1] We went to the pottery,[2] Adrian, Duncan and I, as A. was very curious to come too. It is a fascinating place and so beautiful itself. The old potter was late of course, but we tried our hands at potting while waiting for him. I wished I could have gone on for hours. It's very difficult of course but I don't for a moment believe the 7 years story. 7 months would be more like it. Of course that old gentleman might well take 7 years, but he's obviously quite stupid and would have no natural instinct to help him. I couldn't help thinking even now that one would do the finishing much better than he does. We stayed till 5 and did about 10 or 11 pots, 2 or 3 pretty good I think. Then we left him to copy some again, but I doubt if he'll have done it decently. If he could it would be a good thing as I

[4]Boris (1883–1969) and Helen Anrep (née Maitland) (1885–1965) were not actually married until 1918, after the birth of their second child, Igor. Much later, Helen became a close friend of VB's. Boris organized the Russian contribution to the Second Post-Impressionist Exhibition; after World War I he was considered Europe's leading mosaicist. His most prominent surviving work is the vestibule floor of the National Gallery in London (executed 1928–33). Another impressive, if less well known, work is in Westminster Cathedral.

[1]Failand House, near Bristol, the home of RF's parents, Sir Edward (1827–1918) and Mariabella Fry (née Hodgkin, 1833–1930).

[2]In Mitcham, Surrey. According to Winifred Gill, the Mitcham potter (not George Schenk, who would have been too old) was called up for war service, after which most Omega pottery was produced by Roger Carter of Poole from prototypes by RF.

think we have enough variety of shapes now. Mr Schenck gave us some clay to bring home and said if we liked to model some figures he would cast them for us for a shilling or two and we could have them baked with the rest. So I have spent hours today trying to model a figure, which of course is most exciting, but I doubt if I'm much good at it. I shall be very curious to see what Duncan makes of his lump. The potter may be able to come next Saturday for the whole day. They'll let you know if he can.

I have no other news you see, except that Desmond came to dinner last night. Molly is still in bed with influenza but he seemed very cheerful and stayed till past 1. However I was so tired and sleepy after the pottery that I went to bed before 11, after he had told us several short stories. Tonight Adrian and Saxon are coming to supper.

I wonder if you had a delightful time with the Ilchesters[3] and fell in love with some exquisite aristocratic woman of the world such as you really like, with a fashionable figure and wonderfully cut dresses that quite put in the shade my coral velvet—and *just* the right amount of scent![4] Well, you will have 2 days to get over it with your sisters to look at.

Your
V.

TATE

III-33. To Leonard Woolf

Dec. 1 [1913]   *46, Gordon Square, Bloomsbury*

Dearest Leonard,

I have had a great many answers to my advertisement for a nurse [for Virginia], but nearly all write from the country, and I don't think it's possible to engage anyone without seeing them, though I am

---

[3]The family of Giles Stephen Holland Fox-Strangeways, 6th earl of Ilchester (1874–1959), landowner and historian, with a strong interest in the arts. His family home was at Melbury, near Dorset.
[4]VB herself did not use perfume, although—or perhaps because—she had an acute sense of smell.

strongly tempted by one quite illiterate Nurse Budkin who has nursed an admiral and a member of the Royal Family. I have also had an interview with a woman from Mrs Hunt[1] who told me in 5 minutes the whole history of her husband's life and death, and I expect more from another registry office tomorrow. No one has come from Nurse Read's place.[2]

It is evidently quite easy to get what you want and perhaps as she's only to sit up at night it isn't frightfully important that she should be anything but able to keep awake. However if no one comes from the Nurses' Co-op tomorrow I'll do my best to choose from the Registry Offices as one is really able to tell very little from letters.

I wonder how you're getting on. I'm afraid I've been a very long time getting V.'s dress, but the dress maker has been busy, and I hope she won't think it too frightful when it does come. But I think it was rather rash to trust to my taste in colour. I am getting a new dress for myself too, coral velveteen, but that's an evening one.

Lytton's staying here for 2 or 3 days but I haven't seen him yet as he's dining with Henry [Lamb]. Tomorrow night we have a dining party to which I'm not looking forward much consisting of Ka, Adrian, Daphne O[livier], Bobbie Ross, Sydney and Mrs S. W.[3] Did you hear about him? He failed to penetrate her! and she's had to go to a nursing home to be penetrated or enlarged or something! You were right you see. But we'll hope it will be all right now. Anyhow they're dining with us tomorrow.

Your
VB

SUSSEX

---

[1]Mrs. Hunt operated a domestic agency at 86 High Street, Marylebone.
[2]Nurse Read managed the Nurses' Co-operative Society.
[3]Sydney Waterlow had recently married his second wife Margery (née Eckhard). It was rumored in Bloomsbury that he was impotent.

III-34. To Duncan Grant

Jan. 14 [1914]   *46, Gordon Square, Bloomsbury*

My dear Duncan,

I am having my 2000th (?) miscarriage[1] today and so I will write to you. It has come on early, which is rather a blessing as it will let me get to Paris in time to see the Cézannes. I shall come on Friday I think, but you will be gone I suppose. It's a bore about your play.[2] I should have thought of coming in February instead, but I expect a visit from my old friend Snow just about then, so it seems better to stick to this time. Also I want to see the Cézannes. It won't be long I expect before one will have to go to Germany or Finland to see any more, so one had better take one's chances now.

That devil Marjorie. It's just like her to say such things, just what she did to us. The fact is she's so much afraid of saying the wrong thing if she says anything about Art that she has to invent these absurd by-products which she hopes will be amusing enough to distract one's attention from the barrenness of her mind. But it doesn't. God. Why won't Stracheys ever give themselves away? Which is ungrateful of me, for Oliver actually did screw himself up to write me an enthusiastic letter about my big picture at the Alpine Club.[3] I thought it was really very nice of him for he must have hated doing it.

The show there seems to be a great success. Dora Sanger has bought your Nepi, and I believe Roger's sister is going to buy one of your other pictures. Hilton Young has bought the town by Marchand. I expect more will be sold, and Hamnett[4] has been taking about £1 in shillings. So I should think we might almost pay expenses. There have been lots of notices, mostly quite good. Of course your Adam and

---

[1]A joke between VB and DG for her period.
[2]DG had designed costumes for Jacques Copeau's ballet *Twelfth Night*, which opened in May at the Théâtre du Vieux Colombier in Paris.
[3]The first exhibition of the Grafton Group, including paintings (shown anonymously) by several Omega artists. VB showed *Woman and Baby* (1913), a six-foot-square canvas (now lost) that hung at RF's home in Guildford. Oliver Strachey (1874–1960), one-time Indian Railway official and cryptographer, was the elder brother of Lytton and James. In 1911 he married Ray Costelloe, sister of Karin Stephen, Adrian's wife.
[4]Nina Hamnett (1890–1956), painter, employed at the Omega Workshops. Walter Sickert and RF helped promote her work, and she became RF's mistress (and Sickert's) for a time.

Eve[5] is a good deal objected to, simply on account of the distortion and Adam's standing on his head. In fact I think it's rather upsetting how people *won't* consider what matters. When they praise it's because of the human feelings displayed and when they blame it's because of non-representation. I had a visit from the Raverats the other day who were in an absurdly muddled state of mind I thought. They objected very much to A. and E. because of the distortion. Why couldn't you get the design without it? So I said why should you? Jacques sat and thought for about 10 minutes while Gwen waited like a figure by Rodin staring at her feet, and at last said that was unanswerable in theory but that as a matter of fact one ought to find a safe middle line between distortion and realism and stick to that. They seemed very much excited about it all but hopelessly confused. I believe distortion is like Sodomy. People are simply blindly prejudiced against it because they think it abnormal.

Adrian was here last night and amused us very much about Woolf's novel.[6] He is furious about it and will find it difficult to meet Woolf in consequence! I hadn't really thought that the description of him was meant to be so uncomplimentary—it was so obviously superficial—but he had been made angry enough to send in Woolf a bill for £70! He also thinks the whole thing very unpleasant and that it oughtn't to be published. I have heard from Woolf however that the publishers have written to ask him for another novel and he is sending it to them to read, though saying that he won't pledge himself to publish it. But if Adrian's bill comes in at the same moment he certainly will publish it, so there may be a fine family row soon! And even if it's not published, relations will be strained, according to Adrian!

We went to the pottery on Saturday. The old man was late of course and so we did some pottery and Roger, I need hardly tell you, did actually produce a small pot! He would evidently master the centreing in a week or two and that's the main difficulty. Even I then managed to produce a thing which would have been all right if it hadn't got too thin at one side just at the end, and then Roger did quite a pretty little cream jug. The old potter was rather patronising about them, but it's evident I think that in a few weeks one could learn how to

[5]Now in JMK's former rooms at King's College, Cambridge.
[6]*The Wise Virgins* (London: Edward Arnold, 1914), an autobiographical novel based on LW's courtship of Virginia. No one is depicted favorably, and the book nearly estranged LW from his own family.

produce pots of some kind. We were so much excited by our success that we have quite determined we must get a wheel. I think I shall have one here.

I am now rather cross because the design I did for silk Roger doesn't think will do and he wants to make it into something different himself, and also a design I did for the Kevorkian Counter[7] is not thought suitable, so I have wasted a good deal of time, which is annoying. But I suppose he may be quite right and one must run these risks. What annoys me is I have started a large picture which I should otherwise have been working at. It has no human interest this time, but may turn out to be a Judgment of Paris! That's doubtful however. Perhaps one is very foolish to start more large pictures, but this one is only about 4½ ft. × 3½ ft.

Molly is coming to lunch and to Paris with us, probably with me on Friday, but possibly with Clive on Thursday. The scandal may prevent that. Which word reminds me that there are many more things I might tell you, but I think this letter is already too long.

Yours
VB

HENRIETTA GARNETT

III-35. To Duncan Grant

Feb. 25 [1914]   *46 Gordon Square*

My dear Duncan,

It sounds too beastly, your having to wait on in Paris, for most likely the play will only be put off again I suppose. I think you ought to come back and then Copeau can send for you to come out again when it's really settled, paying your expenses. He ought to do that anyhow. Do be strong minded and say you can't stay on indefinitely. I wonder if you have got a studio and are painting. That would make things better, but anyhow it's probably not so easy to work as it would

---

[7]Kevorkian was a Persian art dealer specializing in Near Eastern art. He also collected modern French art and was a supporter of the Omega.

be here. You aren't missing the pots here for they haven't come yet. Roger has gone off to Mitcham with the Princess[1] today. I thought it more tactful not to go too, also I saw that now he has really managed to pot himself he wouldn't be able to stand letting me do it incompetently while he looked on. Only half a kiln full has been done yet so he will be able to turn out plenty more. He arranged to have some jugs, basins, etc., done at the Potteries and got what look like much better colours from them.

What did Lytton say to you that was so beastly? He was very affable here but he spent most of his time out seeing Henry, etc. Is he making love to you now or what? I suspect him of wanting to have another affair with you, but you'll only snub him. Poor old George[2]—I should think his remarks will by their ineptitude destroy his friendship with you. I can't make out what they're all about. However there's no doubt it's really a great compliment to have a picture so much abused. I expect you will make people thoroughly angry for some time to come now, which is a good thing. The Friday Club has a show on which seems to be meeting with universal praise. It seems to me utterly hopeless. Bomberg[3] has two striking pieces and Nevinson has several very clever works. There are a great many very bright, enthusiastic, lively young painters, all making experiments, but it seemed to me that they were all simply trying to be up to date and that not one of them was in the least an artist. Of course I may have been prejudiced by the fact that nearly every second picture is a biblical scene. The young are reverting to Pre-Raphaelitism really, with all the moral and literary part of it as strong as ever.

Do come back soon. It's so depressing to have no good painters about. There's a compliment for you. Did you go to see Picasso? I gave Snow your love and she was rather pleased. She is beginning to discuss Christianity with me. I am trying to disprove the Resurrection! The novel club[4] was great fun as Desmond has begun a new novel,

[1]Princess Mechtilde Lichnowsky (1879–1958), writer and patron of the arts; wife of the German ambassador. She named the six printed linens (among them the print "Mechtilde") designed and sold by the Omega.
[2]George Leigh Mallory (1886–1924), educated at Magdalene College, Cambridge, and much admired by the Bloomsbury homosexuals for his looks. He became a schoolteacher and died climbing Mt. Everest.
[3]David Bomberg (1890–1957) and C. R. W. Nevinson (1889–1946) considered themselves at this time the "English Cubists." They were members of the newly formed London Group.
[4]The Novel Club was a collective attempt to draw from Desmond MacCarthy his long-awaited literary masterpiece. It failed; on one occasion he delivered a brilliant improvisation from behind an open briefcase ostensibly containing a manuscript.

but there's no room to tell you about that now. Have you seen Clive's book?[5]

Your
VB

HENRIETTA GARNETT

III-36. To Duncan Grant

Thursday [March 5, 1914]   *46, Gordon Square*

My dear Duncan,

I do wish we could come over and see the Cézanne exhibition, but we think we mustn't, though it seems rather absurd. But perhaps Roger will get them all for the Grafton next winter. I rather wish we had paid our visit to Paris now instead of in January, but as we did so then, and considering the state of our finances, we feel we must restrain ourselves.

If you get a room in Paris it looks as if you would settle down there indefinitely. I hope you won't. There's a great deal for you to do here, some quite amusing things for the Omega. The pots may come at any time. They are certain to in a few days I think and you'll be very badly wanted for them. Then I am doing what may be rather fun to do, a pavement in Lady Ian Hamilton's house[1] in a sort of rather large mosaic. I did a design for a stained glass window for her which was rejected in favour of Roger's, but it is going to be turned into the mosaic instead with some alterations, and I hope to do it mostly myself. Then I am also doing another screen, a twofold one which is always rather fun to do. Roger is very much depressed about the O[mega] at present. It is possible that Kevorkian is going bankrupt, in which case we shall lose a good deal over him, and no one is buying just now. However I think it's too soon to hope for a steady flow of business.

Snow is still here but goes tomorrow. Have you heard of our return

[5]*Art* (London: Chatto & Windus, 1914).
[1]At No. 1 Hyde Park Gardens, London.

to the fold? which means Ottoline's fold. She has asked us to her Thursday evenings! It's very queer but I suppose she thought it absurd to go on any longer. It seems to me strange to have decided that at the end of 3 years nearly. Perhaps she feels too deserted now that Henry [Lamb] has gone and Lytton has become cold. There is one tonight but I'm not sure if it would be tactful to go the first time.

Clive and I went to lunch with the Raven-Hills at Richmond on Sunday and she gave me a great lecture on dress. She showed me all her clothes and finally tried most of them on. Clive came to her bedroom and she got off her clothes down to her drawers and skipped about with a great deal of coyness. You would have enjoyed it thoroughly but the most extraordinary sight was finally when she wanted to go on the po[2] (Clive had left the room) and her skirt was too tight to do it in the ordinary way and she got into the most extraordinary attitude, something like this [sketch], kneeling on the floor, but I don't think I've given the effect very well. Only it really would have been a very good thing to paint, as her legs somehow made a very good design and her blouse was bright yellow, carried out by the other yellow touches. With some of the children's chalks I have managed to make it very realistic.

I have had a very charming present from Simon[3] of a little paper book with a very pretty cover painted by him in watercolours in return for the Rainbow cup, which however I think you really deserve most credit for, as you carted it out there.

Have you recovered from your grippe? You seem anyhow to be capable of enjoying Copeau. I am very much flattered by the admiration for my scarf, also by your still wearing it. We think the sort of picture buying club you described such a good idea that we want to start one like it here. The idea for ours is that it should consist of about 10 people who should each put in £10 a year for 10 years and that at the end of the time the pictures bought in the first year should be sold by auction and so on every year for another ten years. Do you think it a good idea? You are to be allowed to give a picture worth £10[4] instead of money if you like, if you will join. The pictures

[2]Chamber pot.
[3]Simon Albert Bussy (1869–1954), French painter, trained at the Ecole des Beaux-Arts in Paris under Gustave Moreau; fellow pupils were Rouault and Matisse, who became a close friend. In 1903, Bussy married Dorothy Strachey, a sister of Lytton.
[4]In today's terms, about £432/$756.

are to be bought mainly because one thinks they will go up in value, but also when one thinks them good.

It's to be called the Christian Dining Society,[5] chiefly to spite me.

Your
VB

Roger has sent you a cheque to the Hôtel d'Univers et du Portugal which he hopes you've got.

HENRIETTA GARNETT

III-37. To Clive Bell

Wednesday [March 18, 1914]   *Asheham House, Rodmell, Lewes*

Dearest,

I don't know when I shall get back tomorrow as it partly depends on when Leonard arrives. It's lovely here but the Goat has her affairs, unluckily. However I'm going now to the post. There are three dogs barking for me, though we have barricaded them out with great difficulty with a mosquito net and cardboard and rabbit wiring. Still they have succeeded in adding one more to the 3 already broken panes of glass through which the wind cuts like a knife. The cat comes in with a squeaking mouse in its mouth. Oh God, country life with animals is too trying. The lambs are rather nice but noisy.

The house is crowded with picturesque hangings and the walled garden is being planted with vegetables. Large boxes of growing plants fill all corners. I really can't stand the dogs any longer and must go, so goodbye.

Your
V.

Will you open this or your *little* lady's letter first?[1]

TATE

[5]One of several schemes proposed to support contemporary art. The Christian Diners did buy and sell art for a year or two, but as the Contemporary Art Society fulfilled the same function in a more businesslike way, it petered out.
[1]Probably Molly MacCarthy, whose affair with CB ended in early 1915.

III-38. To Duncan Grant

Wednesday [March 25, 1914]   *46, Gordon Square, Bloomsbury*

My dear Duncan,

Your basket of oranges and lemons came this morning. They were so lovely that against all modern theories I suppose I stuck some into my yellow Italian pot and at once began to paint them. I mean one isn't supposed nowadays to paint what one thinks beautiful. But the colour was so exciting that I couldn't [resist] it. I took what was left round to the Omega for Roger this afternoon and no doubt he'll soon be doing likewise. It was very clever of you I think to send them on stalks.

We had a most successful time in Paris. Molly was very nice to travel with and very knowing about Paris shops. She and I are going to revolutionize our dress. Rose took us to Lafayettes',[1] where the clothes are very pretty and absurdly cheap. There we had our measurements taken and told them to send us catalogues from which we are to choose models and have dresses made to fit us. I have already ordered a black velvet dress for £1–8– and we hope to have a large stock of the Paris dresses of the latest cut in future.

We had a very exciting time with pictures. We went to see Gertrude [Stein] and she took us to Picasso's studio.[2] I forget if you've seen him. I thought him perfectly charming and quite easy and simple. His studio was wonderful. You go in one of the worst new art German buildings, and inside there is the frieze of the Parthenon all the way up the stairs and then you go into the studio which is large and very light, and has a small room opening out of it with a wonderful view over a great cemetery and an enormous space. The whole studio seemed to be bristling with Picassos. All the bits of wood and frames had become like his pictures. Some of the newest ones are very lovely I thought. One gets hardly any idea of them from the photographs, which often don't show what is picture and what isn't. They are amazing arrangements of coloured papers and bits of wood which somehow do give me great satisfaction. He wants to carry them out in iron. Roger recommended aluminum, which rather took his fancy. Of course the present things are not at all permanent. He also showed us a lot of paintings he had done when he was 10 which were rather

[1]Galeries Lafayette, a mid-range department store.
[2]In the Rue Schoelcher, overlooking the cemetery at Montparnasse.

interesting, very laborious and careful. There were also more wonderful portraits of the blue period. I came to the conclusion that he is probably one of the greatest geniuses that has ever lived. His gifts seemed to me simply amazing. We went too to Matisse's studio.[3] He now has one in Paris. There were only two things to be seen, both unfinished, which didn't seem to me as good as his earlier work, but probably they'll get better, as he seems a very slow worker. But we saw Michael Stein's collection[4] with several early things and one very large later one which was most beautiful.

We saw the Picasso you liked at Kahnweiler's.[5] I liked it too but I wasn't sure I thought it was good as you did. I don't think I liked it as much as Roger's.[6] We hesitated a long time as to whether we should buy anything or not. Roger rather wanted me to get a Vilette,[7] but I'm never really sure I like him very much. At last we got a Vlaminck,[8] a landscape which I think is very good. Perhaps you'll think it dull of us. We also saw some Cézannes at Vollard's[9] and some very fine Renoirs painted only a year or two ago. Roger offered to have a Grafton show next winter, divided into two parts—one of new people and one only of Vollard's old masters, Cézanne, and the Impressionists. It seemed rather a good idea.

We went to Copeau's theatre, which I thought very well done in general decoration—certainly infinitely better than anything here. The colour of the scenery too was what Albert[10] ought to get—greys and whites and pale tones, all really very charming. Of course Gumbo would snuff at it.

We are in a worse quandary than ever about going abroad. Lorna is to be married at the end of April and Clive says he must be there, so we must either go very early or very late. If we go early there is no one to make a fourth. The Brocks[11] were suggested but can't come. If late, Roger probably couldn't come. In fact in that case I think we

[3]At 19 Quai Saint-Michel.

[4]Gertrude Stein's eldest brother and his wife Sarah amassed an important art collection—representing especially Matisse's Fauve period—in the first decade of the century.

[5]Daniel-Henri Kahnweiler (1884–1976), art dealer and writer, had represented Picasso's work since 1907.

[6]RF owned a Cubist collage.

[7]Charles Vilette, act. 1910–20s.

[8]His *Poissy le Pont* (1909); although the painting was later sold, a copy by VB hangs at Charleston.

[9]Ambroise Vollard (1865–1939), art dealer, publisher, and writer. He presented the first important exhibitions of Cézanne, Picasso, and Matisse.

[10]Unexplained.

[11]Arthur Clutton-Brock and his wife Evelyn (née Vernon-Harcourt).

might go somewhere else than Spain. I wonder whether you would in that case come with us? Or have you any other plans by now? I suppose you have heard that Dora Sanger bought your Nepi, and Roger's sister [Margery] the Cyclamens. Nothing else much has sold, but one of Roger's pictures and several drawings by B——?jska[12] so I don't know if we shall quite cover expenses. The last few days there haven't been so many people.

I am going to Asheham tomorrow for one night and I suppose I shall be rather irritated. Virginia seems to be going on quite well. Have you done any painting? I envy you going to Tunis. I suppose it's very lovely. I have done nothing of any interest lately—mostly a lot of small things for the Omega. Except yesterday, we went down to pot without the potter! It was most exciting. We turned out about a dozen small pots, really quite passable. At first I was in despair, for we had stiff clay and I simply couldn't centre it. It needed more strength than I had. Roger just managed to and did my centreing for me but that rather hurt my pride. Then we got softer clay and I found I could manage it. Of course one couldn't possibly do anything big yet, or even do anything much but what God wills, but the feeling of the clay rising between one's fingers is like the keenest sexual joy![13] You *must* come and do it soon. Are you ever coming back? Going to Tunis sounds as if you were gone indefinitely and you'll never want to come back to England. But do come soon for you're really very badly wanted here. I'm very anxious to hear how you get on in all female society. I dare say it's better than Maresco[14] but he'd be practically female to you.

Your
VB

HENRIETTA GARNETT

[12]Henri Gaudier-Brzeska (1891–1915), French sculptor and draftsman. He settled in London in 1911 and worked briefly at the Omega. His work was included in the Vorticist exhibition of 1915. At the outbreak of war he enlisted in the French army and was killed in action.
[13]Cf. RF/DG [undated, 1914]: "We went when the potter wasn't there and got the man to turn the wheel. It was fearfully exciting at first: the clay was too stiff and V. nearly bust with the effort to control its wobbleliness—and in vain; then we got softer clay and both of us turned out some quite nice things. . . . It's fearfully exciting when you do get it centred and the stuff begins to come up between your fingers. V. never would make her penises long enough, which I thought very odd. Don't you" [all *sic*] (*Letters of Roger Fry*, 377–78)
[14]C. Maresco Pearce (c. 1878–1964), painter and etcher. Studied under Jacques-Emile Blanche in Paris, where he may have met Duncan Grant for the first time. Member of the London Group from 1929.

III-39. To John Maynard Keynes

Ap. 19 [1914]   *46, Gordon Square, Bloomsbury*

Dear Maynard,

It is plainly quite superfluous for me to write and tell you how much we enjoyed ourselves at Asheham[1] and so the only thing I can do, since you insist upon my writing, is to make my letter so bawdy that you will have to destroy it at once for fear of Lily's[2] seeing it. Did you have a pleasant afternoon buggering one or more of the young men we left for you? It must have been delicious out on the downs in the afternoon sun, a thing I have often wanted to do, but one never gets the opportunity and the desire at the right moment. I imagine you, however, with your bare limbs intertwined with him and all the ecstatic preliminaries of Sucking Sodomy—it sounds like the name of a station. (Thank you for the list and please don't forget the rhoorkees.)[3] How divine it must have been. I hope you didn't make your throat worse as you lay in that delicious drowsy state afterwards on the turf. Perhaps this is all imaginary however and it really took place in a bedroom. I wonder whose? Not Gerald's[4] at any rate, for one really couldn't have the heart to disarrange his exquisitely tight trousers. I hope they got brushed before he returned.

Well, it was a very nice interlude and I felt singularly happy and free tongued. You are rather like a Chinese Buddha as host. You sit silent, but not so silent as Saxon, and manage to create an atmosphere in which all is possible. Perhaps you talk more than a Buddha would, though. Anyhow the result is what I imagine it would be with a Buddha—one can talk of fucking and Sodomy and sucking and bushes and all without turning a hair.

Yours
VB

KCC

[1]The Bells spent Easter as JMK's guests at Asheham, which he had rented from them and the Woolfs.
[2]Lily, the new maid at Asheham, a Sussex country girl with an illegitimate child.
[3]A type of low folding canvas chair, originally from India.
[4]Gerald Shove (1887–1947), economist, educated at King's College, Cambridge and an Apostle. In 1915 he married VB's cousin Fredegond Maitland.

III-40. To Clive Bell

Wednesday [May 13, 1914]   *Hôtel du Boeuf, Le Lude [France]*

Dearest,

Isn't this an elegant pen? We have been very lucky so far. We got to La Flêche last night at about 9, having had dinner in the train, and found a most comfortable inn, all very simple, delicious coffee and bread, and the best bed I have ever slept in. I went to a solitary, soft couch, with no hint of bony and attenuated limbs to spoil its down, and slept the sleep of the virtuous from 10 to 6, when I was awakened by clattering and clanking on the cobbles below. However I dozed on till 8.30 or so. Then Roger appeared from his neighbouring chamber and we had breakfast. We started off at about 10, and bicycled slowly about 4 miles to a village where we had lunch. I am now quite at home on my bicycle and am said (by R.) to have a very neat figure. My ankle of course is seen to some advantage. The attitude is one of prim decorum, and a little strange to me at first, also a little hard on the cunt and on the muscles of my soft legs. But as we only did 10 miles in the day both parts will no doubt survive.

It was perfect weather today, warm with a light wind at our backs. We rested in a wood in the afternoon, got here before 4, found a very good commercial inn where we have just had an enormous and very good dinner—soup, chicken, omelet, rabbit, peas, cheese, sponge cakes. Now Roger is playing patience. Before dinner I had to play a game of billiards with him. He declares I am a genius at it, in order I suppose to make me play. I see it has just the amount of technique to make him happy.

Our tour as you see is being conducted on terms of modesty and propriety—how unlike your bachelor existence in Paris. I suppose you are at this moment being fondled under the table by some whore and presently you will go off with her, thankful that I'm not there to spoil things.

Do you think you or Duncan or both will meet us anywhere? Roger seems to think we could easily get to Sens about Monday or Tuesday if you cared to come there. Do arrange something.

I am longing to have a truthful account of your doings in Paris. Mind you tell me as much as I have told you. I can't give the account you wished for of the Great Man's conversation, but you can imagine our topics. Art. Gothic Art. Omeganic Art. My Art. Roger's Art. Duncan's Art. Art of the Theatre, etc. This [rough line drawing of VB and RF on bicycles] will convey more eloquently than words the spirit of our tour.

Your
VB

TATE

III-41. To Gertrude Stein

June 13, 1914   *46, Gordon Square, Bloomsbury*

Dear Miss Stein,

Instead of finding you a house and servants as I offered to do, I am writing to ask you whether you can help me to find one for ourselves. I'm afraid this will seem to you less amusing than my proposal to establish you in London! But I am still ready to do that if you would like me to.

We think of coming to Paris for 2 or 3 months next October,[1] and it seems to us possible that you might have friends who would consider a change of houses for that time. If you do know or hear of anyone who might possibly do so we should be very grateful to you if you would tell us. This house has about 8 bedrooms and 5 sitting rooms (including nursery). We should like to find furnished rooms—about 4 or 5 bedrooms and 2 or 3 sitting rooms, or if possible more sitting rooms, or a studio.

Please don't go out of your way to trouble about this. I am only writing to you on the chance that you may hear of something, but I don't want to be a bother and I hope you won't think it very cool of me to ask your help.

I wonder if you are soon coming to London and whether you'll find yourself in a Methodist hotel or in all the splendours of Knightsbridge. Please in any case let us see you and your friend whose name

[1] A plan forestalled by the outbreak of war on August 4.

I daren't attempt to spell.[2] It would be very nice if you would suggest yourselves to lunch or dine or whatever happened to suit you.

Yours sincerely,
Vanessa Bell

YALE

[2]Alice B. Toklas, Stein's lifelong companion.

CHAPTER FOUR

1914–1918

The war years were quiet for Vanessa. Few of her friends saw military service. Many opposed the war or were pacifists, actively engaged in avoiding conscription. Clive wrote an inflammatory pamphlet, *Peace at Once*, which nearly lost him his family income. Maynard Keynes' work at the Treasury excused him from military service. Lytton Strachey distinguished himself at his second exemption trial with his famous retort to the question "What would you do if you saw a German soldier raping one of your sisters?" He replied, after a pause, "I should try and interpose my own body." He was finally acquitted after a medical examination. Leonard Woolf, not a pacifist, was also excused on medical grounds.

It was felt that work of national importance, such as farm labor, might benefit a conscientious objector's case for exemption. With this in mind, Duncan went in early 1916 with his lover David Garnett (called "Bunny" after a rabbit-skin cap he wore as a baby) to work a small farm at Wissett, Suffolk, left vacant by the death of an aunt. Vanessa's priority was obvious. She had already followed Duncan to the country in March 1915, renting first Eleanor House (the country home of St. John and Mary Hutchinson) on Chichester Harbour near West Wittering, then in August the Grange at Bosham, a few miles off. Now she moved into Wissett Lodge. Her children benefited from the outdoor life, she had time to paint, and, despite material discomforts and her anxiety over Duncan's possible conscription, she was content. She bolstered her precarious position in Duncan's affections by making friends with Bunny, itself a precarious undertaking, since Bunny was principally heterosexual, and found Vanessa attractive. Frances Spalding discusses Vanessa's life with Duncan in the afterword to this volume.

As for Roger, he was inconsolable. Vanessa wrote him dozens of letters underlining her love for him as a friend. Not until 1926 did he settle into a permanent relationship, with Helen Anrep. And even so, Igor Anrep, Helen's son, believes Roger would have left Helen at any moment had Vanessa wanted him back.

Under the terms of their exemption from military service, Bunny and Duncan could not be self-employed. Vanessa already knew of Charleston Farmhouse near Firle from Virginia, who had sent an excited description of the property in May 1916. In October, after finding work for Duncan and Bunny at a nearby farm, Vanessa moved her entire household to Charleston. The house was painfully cold and inconvenient, with no electricity, water heater, or telephone. It was Vanessa's adroit management of domestic and social arrangements that made Charleston habitable and drew her friends for long visits.

In the spring of 1918, Vanessa found she was pregnant with Duncan's child. Angelica was born early Christmas Day.

IV-1. To Roger Fry

Monday [August 24, 1914]   *Asheham*

My dear Roger,

You do sound melancholy in the letter I had this morning. Here one is able to a large extent to forget the war. Yesterday of course we had no paper and this morning only the Times, which had apparently been run over by the train which brought it and was in such a torn state that one could hardly read it. But of course one can't quite forget it. I'm very sorry Goldie¹ is in such a state. I suppose he is too wretched and disapproves of it all too much also to be able to do anything, which is probably the only way of keeping going. I see that if one simply waited for news one would rapidly get into a state of melancholia, especially if one took the view that he does of the whole thing. There seems however to be nothing anyone can do just now except fight. Everyone who tries to do anything else is told they are taking someone else's living from them or making a muddle generally. Perhaps that's only an excuse for painting selfishly.

Anyhow, Duncan and I do nothing here but paint. He has started on a long painting which is meant to be rolled up after the manner of those Chinese paintings and seen by degrees.² It is purely abstract. We have also both started on a still life and on different landscapes.

¹Goldsworthy Lowes Dickinson (1862–1932), Cambridge philosopher. Educated at King's College, Cambridge. An Apostle and, though a contemporary of Roger Fry, a strong influence on younger Apostles, such as Lytton Strachey and Maynard Keynes. He was ardently opposed to the war.
²*Abstract Kinetic Painting with Collage* (1914), now at the Tate.

I don't think you need be afraid that any works of genius have been perpetrated yet, but of course I have moments of despair when I see that Duncan really does seem to be producing anything of the sort. We talk of hardly anything but painting, but haven't said anything very interesting, I think! The children take up a good deal of my time. I am now in charge of them and Duncan has gone off for a bicycle ride. Clive comes the day after tomorrow. You haven't yet told me what you're going to do in September, nor have I yet heard from Clive about our visitors. I believe we are full with Lytton, Maynard and Ellie Rendel[3] at the beginning of next week, but after that I have no idea who comes.

I think Mr R[obinson] is really rather absurd about Jessie now. What can she tell anyone that would matter? And I can't think that Lewis and Co. will still go on trying to hurt you. They'll have enough to do fending for themselves.

Roger dear, I do hope you'll enjoy your time in Wales. Don't be more dismal than you can help. One can do no good unluckily by thinking of the horrors going on and though you know I don't ignore them, it seems to me now the only thing we can do is to go on keeping some kind of decent existence going. I wish you didn't have to live in quite such gloomy company just now. I have made myself a dress, price 3/6. I wonder if you'll think it too awful! I hope my tunic is coming soon.

Your
VB

TATE

IV-2. To Roger Fry

Sep. 28 [1914]   *Asheham*

My dear Roger,
    I have tried several times to write to you. But after your letters it

---

[3] (Dr.) Frances Elinor Rendel (1885–1942), educated at Newnham College, Cambridge, daughter of Lytton's eldest sister Eleanor. After about 1924 she was the London doctor of VW, RF, and the Bells.

was difficult to write either in answer to them or just as I should have naturally wanted to write. Last night I suddenly came upon your article in the Nation.[1] It may seem rather absurd, but do you know it seemed almost like suddenly talking to you, your real self, again. I found you saying what you thought with no thought of me. I seemed to get directly again into contact with your mind. It wasn't intimate of course, but there were no surface difficulties. If only I could sometimes do that as a beginning surely it could be easy again. I didn't agree with all you said, but I wanted to disagree with you, I mean to discuss it with you.

Of course all you say is true, that it's a bad dream and that it's impossible things should come to an end between us. There is too much in us both that the other really wants.

I won't go on writing, as I shall see you soon. I come back on Wednesday. Clive will be away I expect, but I will telephone to the Omega to see if you're there when I know more of what's happening.

Your
V.

TATE

IV-3. To Roger Fry

Wednesday [March 31?, 1915]   *46, Gordon Square, Bloomsbury*

My dear Roger,

We have put off going away till Saturday, as Julian has a bad cough and cold and has been a little feverish. The children were to have gone today and we tomorrow, but I don't like to go till he is all right again. I suppose it's possible that we shan't be able to go on Saturday even, though [Dr] Belfrage thinks we shall. If we do, you know our address, don't you—Eleanor House, West Wittering, nr. Chichester. Will you write to me there?

I have been doing nothing much the last few days but try and clear

[1]"Reims," an essay deploring the artistic losses resulting from the partial destruction of Reims Cathedral (*The Nation*, September 26, 1914).

away some of the messes of the last few months. Chiefly the mari-
onettes,[1] which at last I have got moved. They now stand all against
the end wall of my room and are very upsetting to the proportion of
everything else and everyone else in the room. The odd thing is, I
think they make the room look larger and not smaller. I have cleared
out mountains of stuffs and odds and ends, but it seems very full still.
Now I have two extra days on my hands I shall I hope clear out still
more, and I am having some parasols from the Omega to do. Mr
R[obinson] says they haven't very many though, only 4 or 5.

I wonder whether you will go to Simon [Bussy] after all. I hope so.

I was here interrupted by a visit from Ottoline. She wants to come
to Wittering for a night or two. I can't think why, but it's difficult to
refuse her. Perhaps it's absurd always to suspect her motives as I do,
but I always think she has something up her sleeve.

Have you finished Virginia's novel?[2] Do tell me what you think of
it. It seems to me extraordinarily brilliant, almost too much so at
times. It makes it too restless, I think. However it is of course very
good in its description of people and conversations and all the detail.
The obvious criticism I suppose is that it isn't a whole, but I haven't
quite finished it yet so I oughtn't to make a final criticism. Lytton is
very enthusiastic and was raving about the writing and the wit and
observation and sympathy with all sorts of characters.

Novel writing does seem a queer business, at least this kind. If it's
art, it seems to me art of quite a different sort from making a picture,
but I don't think all novel writing is. The quotation from Jane Austen,[3]
even though it's only a sentence, seemed to me at once to put one
into a different world, one that's the same really that one is in when
one looks at a Cézanne. Did you feel it? I suppose it's because one
knows the rest of the book and one couldn't feel it from only one
sentence. Reading Virginia's book is much more like being with an

---

[1] On the evening of January 6, 1915, the Bells hosted a Bloomsbury play reading, featuring Racine's *Berenice* performed by Duncan Grant and Lytton and
Marjorie Strachey, with the assistance of three eight-foot cardboard puppets
made by DG.
[2] *The Voyage Out*, published March 26 by Duckworth, her stepbrother Gerald's
firm. VW herself had suffered a relapse of her 1913–14 mental illness and was
in a nursing home.
[3] From *Persuasion* (1818): "Sir Walter Elliott, of Kellynch Hall, in Somersetshire,
was a man who, for his own amusement, never took up any book but the
Baronetage. . . . There he found occupation for an idle hour, and consolation in
a distressed one"; the quotation appears on page 67 of the first edition of *The
Voyage Out*.

extraordinary witty and acute person in life and watching all these things and people with her. But that may only be because I have actually done so. I wish I could really get outside it all. As it is, I know all the people nearly and how she has come at so much of it, which makes it very difficult to be fair.

There's a great deal I want to say to you, Roger dear, only I feel as if it were rather useless to do so now. All it comes to is that I am thinking of you and do hate you to be unhappy. I feel that I care for you so much and that you do really mean so much to me and have such a special place with me that we *must* somehow get to be able to be near each other again. But I admit that for a time now I can't see the way to it, because of your unhappiness and pain. Only I can't help either feeling as if some day it would happen.

Your
V.

TATE

IV-4. To Roger Fry

Friday [April 9?, 1915]   *Eleanor [House, West Wittering,*
                                              Chichester]

My dear Roger,

I must write in pencil as all pens have vanished. I was very glad of your letter and I hope you'll write again soon. Are you now in London and working at the Omega and have you settled about going to France and about the Bussys? I do hope that can be arranged. You must let me know if there's anything special you want me to see to at the O. when I go back. I have an idea for it which I should like to know whether you think practicable, about dressmaking. I have begun to make Marjorie's dress and am going to try and get it done here, as I think she will come and stay here later. The idea is that I should make or at least superintend the making of several dresses. Ottoline heard from Duncan that I was going to make one for Marjorie and was anxious that she should have one too, and thought that if we could get several people, say her and Iris and Marie Beerbohm[1] and Marjorie Strachey and perhaps one or two others to have dresses made they could have a sort of dress parade, perhaps in Ottoline's drawing-room and have a party to see them. If this could be done at the beginning of the season, I believe it might be a great success. I don't think the cost would be much, as the actual stuffs need not be expensive, and Ottoline has a dressmaker who drinks but is otherwise capable and who could work under me. Do you think it would be a good thing if I tried to get this done as soon as I get back? I believe one could make dresses that would use the fashions and yet not be like dressmaker's dresses.

We are getting settled here now. When we first came, the oven wouldn't bake and the water was so incredibly nasty that it nearly made one sick. Clive was convinced we should get typhoid, though luckily he himself had been inoculated when he thought he was going to Italy. Also there are no coal scuttles and hardly any fire irons in the house and it's fearfully cold and draughty. Lytton and Duncan are here now and Maynard comes tonight or tomorrow. Tonks' studio[2] is much too cold to use, so we paint in a very small back room. The children are at Seend, but come here next week.

Has poor Julian [Fry] got over the chicken pox yet? I had a very nice letter from Pam thanking me for the silks, but I meant to ask you to tell her not to write. Presents from grown ups are such a curse if one has to thank for them.

I expect I agree with most of what you say about Virginia's novel, and I suppose it's true that she has genius. I'm not sure I should call it so. Can Stephens produce a genius? I doubt it. I don't think Jane Austen's art is the only kind of art and I only compared them because Woolf has always done so—of course to Virginia's advantage, or at any rate equality. But Jane does seem to me to use all her observation for another purpose and I don't think Virginia does. But of course she's an artist, though she mayn't have produced a work of art. I expect you're right in thinking Helen Ambrose like me in some way though I can't realise it. Otherwise most of

---

[1]Iris Tree (1897–1968), actress and poet, one of three daughters of Sir Herbert Beerbohm Tree, the actor-manager. Constance Marie Beerbohm (1856–1939), playwright, a half-sister of Max Beerbohm and a sister of Sir Herbert Beerbohm.

[2]A boatshed near Eleanor House had been rented by Sir Henry Tonks as a studio. It had a small bedroom and kitchen on the landward side, where Duncan stayed.

the minor characters seem to me more interesting than the principal ones.

Your
V.

TATE

IV-5. To Hilton Young

Ap. 15 [1915]   **Eleanor House, West Wittering, Chichester**

My dear Hilton,

You're quite right in thinking I'm a rotten letter writer. Then why did you write to me and not to Clive? You'll have to suffer for that now, and it was very foolish of you as he rather prides himself on his letters. But at least you've come to the right person if you don't want to hear anything about the war—perhaps you guessed that—and that may be the supreme virtue in a letter writer nowadays.

We spent a very gay winter in London, far gayer than usual. Ottoline—do you know her?—took it upon herself to keep us all merry and gave a party every week, at which you might see Bertie Russell[1] dancing a horn-pipe with Titi (Hawtrey's young woman),[2] Lytton and Oliver and Marjorie Strachey cutting capers to each other, Duncan dancing in much the same way that he paints, [Augustus] John and Arnold Bennett[3] and all the celebrities of the day looking as beautiful as they could in clothes seized from Ottoline's drawers, and Ottoline herself at the head of a troupe of short haired young ladies from the Slade prancing about. However I see it may all sound very dull, as one can't describe the queer effect all these people had on each other. Still you can imagine us doing that every Thursday evening. Then we

[1] Bertrand Arthur William Russell (1872–1970), mathematician and philosopher. He was at this time a lecturer in mathematics at Trinity College, Cambridge, and was negotiating a friendship with Lady Ottoline after the cooling of their five-year love affair.
[2] Ralph George Hawtrey (1879–1975), economist and civil servant. While an Apostle at Trinity College, Cambridge, he was friendly with most of the Bloomsbury men. In 1915 he married Hortense d'Aranyi, of the musical d'Aranyi sisters.
[3] Arnold Bennett (1867–1931), the distinguished writer.

spent another evening reading plays, which is a very good way of spending an evening, and another listening to Belgian music at the Omega,[4] which wasn't always such a good way.

When we had had about enough of all this, we came here to a funny little house by the sea, where Duncan is at this moment our only visitor. Here we live without newspapers, at least they come at moments when I at any rate can ignore them, and no horrors of any kind beyond sometimes falling into black pools. The crows get on Duncan's nerves because he takes them for boys on bicycles riding quickly past the window. Otherwise we are very calm. Our chief excitement lately has been Virginia's novel. It's a remarkable work I think, but I can't criticize it. Would you like it? If so, I will send you a copy if you'll tell me how to.

They tell me you are a lieutenant. Does one also put M.P.?[5] Yes, I suppose so, and I hope you aren't really a captain and won't take it ill. Please write again and not only to ask but to give news.

> Yours,
> Vanessa Bell

CAMBRIDGE

IV-6. To Roger Fry

May 2 [1915]　　　　*Eleanor [House, West Wittering, Chichester]*

My dear Roger,

I had written to you to Vitry le François just before getting your letter, so you may not get it. I have been trying to find a house here for the last few days without success, but have at last taken lodgings in a cottage just by this house. Clive wanted very much to stay on if possible as Mary[1] is going to spend most of the summer here and he will hardly see her in London at all. It will be nice if the weather is

[4]The Omega held concerts performed by, and for the benefit of, Belgian refugees.
[5]Hilton Young was elected Liberal M.P. for Norwich at an unopposed by-election in 1915. He was also an officer in the Royal Navy Volunteer Reserve, and later won a Distinguished Service Cross.
[1]Mary Hutchinson (née Barnes) (1889–1977), writer and hostess, the wife of the barrister St. John Hutchinson. She had recently begun an affair with Clive Bell.

fine, but otherwise I don't quite know how we shall manage, as the rooms are small and we can only just squeeze in. The children and Mabel in one room, I in another and Clive in a caravan in the garden! with one little sitting-room. However there is Tonks' studio, where Duncan is now sleeping, which I hope we shall be able to have too. Anyhow, we shall try and see what it is like. I am going up to London tomorrow for a few days to see Woolf and do various jobs.[2] I shall try to get Marjorie Strachey's dress put in hand, but I'm afraid that being away will make it almost if not quite impossible for me to do the other dresses. It seems to me one must be on the spot for them. I could do them in June but that would be rather late I suppose. However I'll talk to Mr Robinson about it.

The news of Virginia is a little better, but she still sounds pretty bad.[3]

I am sorry that the people you are with seem to be so unattractive, and it sounds very hard work bicycling over the country and seeing all the villagers.[4] You don't say what you think of doing. Has the Bussy plan fallen through or do you go there from Paris? I think you must get some time to paint as well as all this hard work, for I believe you can only get happier by painting and getting interested in it.

You say you want me to tell you what I have been feeling. It's rather difficult to. Duncan and I and Bunny have been alone here this last week since Marjorie went, as Clive has been in London. I think perhaps it was rather a difficult situation, but on the whole I am happier about Duncan and Bunny because I see that Bunny really does care a good deal for him. I had been rather afraid he didn't and that it would mean unhappiness for Duncan. I think now that he does, and that Duncan on the whole gets a good deal of happiness out of it. I can't pretend I was always happy, for it's impossible not to mind some things sometimes, but I think I'm very lucky really. I know you think so, too. But it is an odd disease we all suffer from, and I see one can't expect always to be rational, and when one isn't I think one must just treat it as a disease and wait till it gets better. But it's best to talk of it if one can, I'm sure, as then the unreal part disappears.

You know Duncan is simply amazingly good to me and puts up with a great deal I think without ever losing patience. I wish very

[2]VW was in the midst of a serious breakdown. VB went with LW to consult two doctors, Ian MacKenzie, who wished to take over VW's case, and Maurice Craig.
[3]Not until June did VW begin to recover. It was her last serious bout of insanity.
[4]RF was visiting his sister Margery, then working for the Quaker War Victims' Relief Mission in the badly damaged districts of the Marne and the Meuse.

often that I had such a nice character as his. I can't stand however thinking of myself at all. Do you know that one day Marjorie read our hands and she told me I was inconstant and cruel—I suppose it's absurd to mind such things though. But it makes me think *you* very irrational, for how easily you could find someone nicer than me to fall in love with. Perhaps you will, with some French woman. I hope so, for I'm not cruel or inconstant enough not to want you to be happy more than I want almost anything else.

I have done nothing about Doucet's pictures and won't till you tell me what to do. I often think of his death.[5] It seems to me the worst thing that has happened, for even if he wasn't a great artist it was so important that he should work in the way that he did and live that kind of life and be happy in that sort of way.

Your
V.

TATE

IV-7. To Roger Fry

Sunday [May 9? 1915]   *Eleanor Farm, West Wittering*
[Chichester]

My dear Roger,

I have only written you business letters lately. There was so much to do in London that I hardly had any time, and whenever I thought I was going to be alone someone would turn up. We never had an evening alone; people came at all hours. In fact I think London is getting quite impossible and I dread going back there. It is specially bad now on account of the war I think, but I see too that in any case it's almost impossible for me at any rate to work there. One can't refuse to see people without being a more determined character than I am, but you know what it's like, don't you? I have been seriously considering a plan by which we would give up Gordon Sq and take

[5]Henri Doucet had been killed in action on March 5 in Belgium. Two of his paintings had been left at Gordon Square.

a house in the country—not too far from London, say near Lewes. The children would live there, which would be very good for them, and then Clive and I would each have a room in London to which we could come whenever we liked quite easily. I'm not sure we shouldn't get all the good we now get out of London with the great advantage of being able to go off and be sure of being able to work in peace whenever one wanted to. Clive isn't against this, but of course it may come to nothing. It rather depends upon whether I could find a nice house.

We are now here in peace again. The Hutchinsons are at their house, I and the chidren are in lodgings 5 minutes off and at this moment Duncan and Bunny are in Tonks' studio. Clive has taken two rooms in the village ¼ of an hour's walk away, where he sleeps and has breakfast and spends the morning writing. It is extraordinarily nice and quiet and one hears as little of the war as possible. If it weren't for [the war] it would be perfect, for the weather has generally been divine, with a hot sun and everything coming out. You would like this country I think, for often it is much more like Italy than England. The estuary here looks extraordinarily like the lagoons at Venice and it is all on a very big scale just round here. Further on I believe one gets to ordinary English seaside, and the country inland is dull, but just this bit is lovely as it's not by the open sea and woods come down to the water's edge. The tide is high now and the water is only about 10 yds from where I am sitting at the great open studio. It would be fun to be able to stay here for a long time and paint, but I suppose I shall have to go back to London before long.

We have been painting a good many still lifes. I have done several very dull ones. I hope the last one or two may be better. Duncan is working at the Omega signboard.[1] On one side is a still life done from memory or out of his head, a lily and a yellow flower in a glass. It's very good I think, rather Matissian. On the other side is a huge Ω. Bunny has also taken to painting and is working at a landscape. He is amazingly skilful and not the least an artist, though sometimes he gets those odd amateur effects which one never knows about, whether they're conscious or not. You ask whether I'm afraid of hurting you by telling you about my relations with him. I'm not at all, but I don't think there's very much to tell.[2] I think you're wrong in your instinct about him. He really *is* a nice character, though he's very young and

[1]Now at the Victoria and Albert Museum.
[2]Roger expressed concern that VB might be in love with Bunny.

in some ways inexperienced. But considering how young he really is I think he understands other people's feelings very well. He's always very nice to me, and he likes I think to be demonstrative to everyone he likes, but he's not in love with me. I quite like him, but I really only see him because of Duncan. I certainly have no feelings about him that could possibly give you any pain. I wonder what you meant by saying I was a bird of prey—was that what you said? I couldn't be sure. It sounds as bad as being cruel and inconstant! However I don't often worry about my character really, but if one thought of it one would.

I am nearly always very happy with Duncan. You see I am telling you what I am really feeling. He likes being with me enough for me to be quite happy, and as you say it is so much to be able to lead this kind of life together. But we ought all to be able to lead this kind of life. I think one must do that even if it's not with the person one's in love with. You will I hope with Simon. After all, one has always sooner or later to fall back upon work and make that one's main object. But I often do so wish you hadn't had so much unhappiness because of me, Roger dear, and I often wish I could see you and talk to you and find out how you are. Perhaps when you come back things will be different in some way and we shall be able to be happy and easy and affectionate with each other, and then we could be a great deal together. You know you are very necessary to me and very necessary also to this kind of life. After all, Duncan and I can't give each other all the help and criticism we both want in our work, and you are the only other person we know who can be of use in that way.

Duncan met Etchells the other day in London. Did you know that Jessie is married and abroad somewhere? Etchells himself is much better and had come to London to look for a room in Fitzroy St. where I think he means to work for a time.

We didn't laugh at all at your being taken up as a spy.[3] It all sounded rather grim. Clive was very much impressed by its being so well written. I hope you will write some accounts for the Nation, also translations of Vildrac's letters. It's a mercy he's not fighting for the moment. Have you heard that Jos Wedgwood has been wounded in the Dardanelles.[4] I hope it's rather a good thing really. He's wounded

---

[3]In an attempt to visit his friend Charles Vildrac, who was serving at the front of Auzéville, RF had narrowly avoided arrest and imprisonment as a spy.
[4]Josiah Clement Wedgwood (1872–1943), of the famous Staffordshire family; M.P. for Newcastle-under-Lyme. He was wounded at Gallipoli.

in the thigh, I don't know how seriously. But possibly it may mean he can't fight for some time, I suppose, or even that he may be sent home.

I have now moved out to a piece of long dry grass some way from the studio because Clive and the Hutchinsons are sitting just outside it and Jack H.,[5] though supposed to be reading, never stops talking. His talk bores me to such an extent that I can't stand it. Last night we had to dine with them and if it weren't for my faculty of not listening I should have died, I think. He has that peculiar type of open minded tolerance which is more deadly than anything and he tells innumerable bawdy stories which even I can never succeed in listening to the whole of. They go on and on. I see I'm getting less and less fitted for society and I think I shall really have to retire to the country! People and arrangements and telephone bells have got on my nerves and everything seems 1000 times simpler in the country.

The children are so lovely too. Julian is the most splendid creature now, very brown and with very bright eyes, jumping about on his long legs, and Quentin is more of a character than ever and very beautiful too. He is too adorable. They're much nicer than the little Hutchinson girl,[6] at least so I think, though she's very amusing. I'm looked upon as an authority upon babies and give Mary a great deal of advice about hers. Please write again. Even if you don't much care about doing so, I like to get your letters, and tell me what you're feeling. You know I always want to hear, for I do care for you very much and everything about you matters to me. Give my love to the Bussy family.

Your
V.

TATE

[5] St. John Hutchinson, Mary's husband.
[6] Barbara, born 1911. Mary had just given birth to her second child, Jeremy.

IV-8. To Clive Bell

June 22 [1915]   *46, Gordon Square, Bloomsbury*

Dearest,

No sooner had you gone than Duncan came. Our servants seem to bear it with equanimity, even Bunny's appearance too, which usually seems to happen in your absence. But when I think of all they have stood—not to say aided and abetted—in the past, I can't imagine they will object to anything in the future.

Duncan had had an amusing enough time with Ot.[1] He says it is an amazingly beautiful house and place, not yet spoilt by Philip who is contemplating islands and hedges and walls all over the place. There is a lake in which they all bathed, Ot with a red greek headdress and hair all on end and high heeled pink satin shoes, groaning in the water that she was only decent out of the water and all naked below. But Duncan of course didn't play up and dive. Maria was there with the mature figure of a woman of 30, and Julian and a new Swiss governess of exquisite figure, and Chile.[2] They all had to gild the walls[3] in the evenings and had all meals including breakfast at 8 out of doors. Also they went and visited Nan and Ethel and found the Sickerts there. Sickert had some lovely etchings of his own to show and one he thought the best in the world by Carel du Jardin (?)[4] which Ot unluckily took for a Rembrandt. I must ask him to lunch and get him to give me the proof he nearly gave. Ot asked me and Duncan to go there next Sunday, but I thought I wasn't certain enough of being able to accept, and he thinks he ought to go to his family.

I hope you found Mary better and that you're seeing her without difficulty. Maynard has had a relapse, but not serious they say.[5] Ap-

---

[1]Duncan had just made his first visit to Garsington Manor, the Morrells' newly acquired country home in Oxfordshire. It was very near Newington, the home of Nan Hudson and Ethel Sands.
[2]Maria Nys, a Belgian refugee who later married Aldous Huxley. Julian was the Morrells' daughter, born in 1906. The Swiss governess was Juliette Baillot, later the wife of Julian Huxley. Chile was Alvaro Guevara (1894–1951), a Chilean painter then studying at the Slade. In 1916 his work was exhibited at the Omega.
[3]Lady Ottoline's exotic decorating scheme included a Venetian red dining room (painted oak paneling picked out with gold lines), described in Darroch, 158.
[4]Karel Dujardin (c. 1622–78), Dutch painter and etcher.
[5]JMK had undergone an emergency appendectomy on June 12. His recovery seemed quick, but he was in fact suffering from pneumonia, diagnosed the day after this letter.

parently poison from his appendix had got into his muscles and gave him a kind of lumbago and he had had a good deal of pain. At least that is their explanation. It sounds to me rather odd.

I haven't heard from Mrs Illingworth[6] yet.

Bunny may go to France any day,[7] though he hopes not to before Friday. I'm afraid Duncan will be rather gloomy when he has gone, but perhaps he won't. He seems to be very much interested in painting and full of schemes for new things . . .

Your
VB

TATE

IV-9. To Duncan Grant

Friday [August 6, 1915]   *The Grange, Bosham [Chichester]*

My darling bear,

I see I must run the risk of your dropping your letters about all over the place. I can't write as if I thought you just an ordinary brown bear instead of being one of the choicest and most affection-inspiring Malays. But as you'll get this in your studio, please put it into some secret hole if you won't burn it, else Gerald[1] will probably find it and not only the secrets of my heart but those of many others will become public property. That's said partly just to stir you up in case you're half asleep. I haven't really the secrets of many hearts to give away.

I have been rather melancholy since yesterday morning, having got all sorts of ideas into my head, but it's no good telling you about them in a letter because you can't answer them at once and most likely they'll subside soon. Besides I'm going to write a letter of good advice to Roger and I shall try to take some of it myself. He has written to me to say that he's overcome with shame and penitence

---

[6]Potential landlady. VB was eager to find a house large enough, and near enough Duncan at Eleanor, to settle in for a few months. Eventually, she found the Grange, Bosham, where the Bells moved in August.
[7]Bunny and his close friend Francis Birrell (1889–1935) had joined the Friends War Victims' Relief Mission and were to be stationed at Sommeilles, a war-ravaged village near the Argonne forest. Bunny returned alone in January 1916.
[1]Gerald Shove. He had recently become engaged to Fredegond Maitland, VB's cousin.

because he finds it so irritating and difficult being with someone who's in love with him[2] that he sees what it must have been for me. He dreads her coming into his studio and has got into a fearful state of nerves with her and thinks it must have been much the same for me. Perhaps it was, but it's no good thinking one person's just like another, so I shall tell him and myself.

I telephoned to him to Guildford yesterday and found he was in London, so I thought I must telephone to the O[mega]. He came round at once to Gordon Sq and I then found myself involved in deceit. I said I had been to Dorchester with you and told him about Debenham's but I thought the stay at Corfe would be too much to reveal, so I pretended I had been in London otherwise.[3] How deep you'll think me. I suppose it may come out some day but it can't be helped. I couldn't face all the revelations I should have had to make then if I had told the truth. I wonder if you saw him and gave me away, but I think we settled that was the best thing to say.

Then we came here, and who should travel down with us but Jack [Hutchinson]. I pretended to go to sleep in the train to avoid some of his conversation, but it was a depressing beginning, and the atmosphere was leaden and steamy. Bosham station looked rather dull and sordid, only enlivened by a lovely boy ticket collector, and a charming and handsome porter who rescued my gloves for me. We drove off in a shaky old wagonette and drew up at this house in about 10 minutes. Gloom settled on me. It all looked so neat and prim. The walls are grey, the paint white. All is very clean and thin and tidy and there is none of the lovely colour of the lodging house. The curtains and covers are irreproachably negative. Colour is successfully killed. The two sitting-rooms are so well furnished and spotless that I saw one couldn't possibly make a mess with paints in them. However this morning I have cheered up. Tidiness is soon done away with, after all. Then I have taken possession of the night nursery and put the children, Mabel and Flossie into the vast bedroom I had last night. I am now established in my night nursery, which is a fairly light room. The walls have a pale striped paper and there is no furniture but a

[2]Mrs. Crompton, Doucet's widow with whom RF stayed at Ste. Maxime, near Roquebrune, home of the Bussys.
[3]While RF was away in France in an attempt to distract himself from his loss of VB, she had indulged herself in many escapades with Duncan, including the outing to Corfe Castle in Dorchester, Dorset, and a visit to Garsington Manor in the second week of July. Another first-time guest on this occasion was Lytton, who became a Garsington regular. The Debenhams, a rich and cultivated family whose wealth derived from Debenham & Freebody, the department store in Wigmore Street, London, had a country home in Dorset.

bed and two sets of drawers. Then there is a balcony on which I am sitting now. I have got my painting things up here and I think one can get still lives [sic] in a good light in the room or on the balcony, so that I can have this undisturbed as a studio and bedroom. It's a great blessing to have room to paint away from the rest of the company and there'll be plenty of room for you here too.

Mabel and the children are sitting on the lawn looking too lovely and Flossie, more exquisite than ever, is busy washing my clothes, and walks up and down the garden, I can't think why. There are several painters in the place. They stand and talk in the village street. The harbour is evidently made for them. I never saw anything so picturesque. I don't really take to this place much, but I daresay one will find out its good points soon, and I mustn't tell you too much of its bad ones or you will never come here.

I am going to make myself a new dress, and would you mind if you can remember it bringing with you when you come here the yellow waistcoat Lechmere[4] made for me, which I think I can use. You will find it in one of the drawers in the small chest of drawers by the looking glass in my bedroom. You won't like the dress I'm afraid, as it will be mostly purple, but I found a bit of Broussa silk which I may as well use. Also I'm going to make myself a bright green blouse or coat, I haven't yet settled which, out of an old piece of Broussa silk.

Clive has just discovered that he has a good balance at the bank. "Of course it will soon disappear with the new taxes," he says, but still for the moment we are rich. So I shall make him give me £50, and I shall be rolling in money. So please, darling creature, don't send me any of your cheques, as you threatened to do, but tell me if you want money instead. Roger saw your picture and thought it very fine and the frame a success I think, at least he made no objections to it, and as he liked the picture I suppose the frame did what it was meant to do. So send it to him and get paid.

You know you mustn't think you've got to finish your pictures before you come here, or you'll never come, as you certainly won't ever think they're finished. Are you gallivanting every night, and with whom? I imagine you are very happy and independent, with very nice letters from Bunny to keep you going by day and I shouldn't like to say what by night, but please dear creature write and tell me. I love you so much.

Your
VB

HENRIETTA GARNETT

4Kate Lechmere, dressmaker at the Omega.

IV-10. **To Virginia Woolf**

Sunday [August 22, 1915]   *The Grange, Bosham, Chichester*

My Billy,

I am writing to you according to promise, but don't expect my letters from this place to be anything but dull and niggly and domestic little affairs. If you walked down the main street of Bosham and stopped at a gate and walked over a small rustic bridge which crosses a little stream, you would find yourself in the garden of The Grange, all neat and clean-shaven and enclosed, all the very opposite from Asheham, and all belonging to that sphere of life where servants really do their work under the mistress's eye. The garden is on the road, so all that goes on in it must be irreproachably respectable—no posing naked as at Asheham. Inside the house the walls are drab and grey, the paint pure white, the furniture gim-cracky, the pictures sham Aubrey Beardsley. A few works by me and Duncan have now been stuck over them in places in the hope of introducing a little colour. It's incredible how these people dread colour much more than our ancestors did, even with their red and peacock blue plush. However one room meant for the night nursery I have turned into my bedroom and studio and it has a large window and balcony, so at least one gets some light.

If you go beyond the village as a matter of fact the country isn't so bad. Sometimes it's very beautiful, as the estuary comes up to the village. One gets boats here and can go sailing on it. Being an estuary only it can't get very rough and even I am taken sailing. Today we are going to sail up to Eleanor, which is at the other end of the estuary, for lunch, and we often take our tea and the children to a little place called Itchenor about 2 miles off and have a pic-nic. I wish you could come and do it with us. You would like having pic-nics with the brats, wouldn't you?

Roger is staying here now and Gerald. Fredegond was to have come but was too much exhausted. I think they'll both break down if they don't marry soon, but they mean to do so about Sep. 10th, which may just save them. I am disappointed at not having her here as I wanted to find out more what she's like. They mean to live in the depths of the country and asked me if I knew of any house in the Asheham region. I kept quiet about Muggery

Poke,[1] thinking at any rate I'd try and see it first. Duncan hasn't been able to go and see it from Adrian's house as it's 8 miles off and he'd have had to walk both ways, but I daresay I shall be able to go and see it some day. I think I might at any rate put up a studio there and perhaps later make it into my country seat.

This place swarms with painters and Roger and I now join their ranks and set out with our easels in the morning. Unless he's here I'm generally too lazy to go to the painters' hunting grounds, and paint at home. His energy is still amazing and one finds he has visited the church and been bathing and all sorts of things before one gets up. I had a letter from your old friend Snow yesterday. She wants to come to London in October and paint with me for a fortnight, so perhaps you'll see her. All her relations of course have enlisted from a sense of duty and she is getting up garden parties, etc., for war charities. I see more and more that we are completely isolated from our kind. Perhaps it's a bad thing. It would be much pleasanter if one ever felt what they do, but one does so less and less.

I shall have to come up to London again in about a fortnight, so perhaps I shall see you then. Meanwhile I'll write, if my letters aren't too impossibly dull. Still, I know a dull letter is better than none at all when one is in bed, though at this moment you see far more people than I do and no doubt hear all the gossip. I wonder if you have seen Old Gumbo.

I expect I shall be alone here at the end of the week as Clive is going to stay with Ottoline and with Lytton, and then perhaps I shall be driven to be more sympathetic with my kind and pick up with some of the painters.

Your
V.B.

BERG

---

[1]Muggery Pope (sometimes Poke), a deserted farmhouse and buildings near the village of Tarring Neville in the downs east of the River Ouse. This house search eventually resulted in the Bells' acquisition of Charleston.

IV-11. To Virginia Woolf

Tuesday [August 31, 1915]   *The Grange, Bosham [Chichester]*

My Billy,

I see that the life you are leading now is a gay one compared to mine. I have been alone here with the children since last Saturday and I find it difficult to believe that my letters can be anything but dull. All the same, you see your compliments are so skilful that you induce a letter from me—not that I really believe them, but I know how insatiable your appetite for letters is. I suppose that besides seeing all the world of beauty and intellect now you also get letters from all the wits of our time—but still you haven't enough. Just because I don't happen to be in bed, my post is barren and no one comes near me. Aren't you sorry for me? Well, I don't think I shall draw any pity from you.

I have been trying to find out how I should like to live in the country and be alone a good deal, from these few days of solitude. Of course my country estate would be much nicer than this and I should have a large studio to work in. On the other hand, I should have much more solitude and it would often be winter. I don't think I should mind being alone a good deal. I always have so many jobs on hand that I never have enough time to get them done in, and I should certainly be able to work in quite a different way from what one can when one is always being interrupted. Then I see a good deal of the children in a very nice and easy way. Quentin is getting more and more charming. I suppose he is bound to get less and less so soon, unluckily. But he will be a most interesting creature even when he's less of a buffoon. On the whole, I have come to the conclusion that a background of country with easy access to London would really be very nice.

Tomorrow or the day after, Duncan is coming, so my solitude is nearly at an end, and Clive returns on Friday. After that I believe Lytton comes for a week. But we shan't have many people here, nothing like what we did at Asheham, as the house isn't nearly so big or elastic.

You ask for sketches, which I would send if I had any ready. But at present I have several begun and none finished. I wish you'd send me your copies of mine and Duncan's paintings.[1] It's a great honour to have one's works copied, and as you're the only person who's ever

[1] Not extant.

likely to copy mine, I think I ought to see it. That was a horrid picture I had at the Grafton though and not worth your attention.

Roger was rather upset at my lending you that abstraction,[2] as you know I had given it to him. He was sure I'd never get it back, but I said I could tear it from your wall at any moment and hang another instead. Roger's activities and energies amaze me more and more. One day he wanted to take us sailing. Both Clive and I were willing to go if we might take our time about it—we didn't like being hurried off after breakfast with none of the duties of the day accomplished. Roger however had to catch a train to Ford later in the day and got into a great stew. It was like our travels in Italy again, he fuming and we procrastinating. At last he got us off after we had got our way to the extent of making him do several jobs in the village while we were slowly getting ready.

Then we went down to the boat place. None were to be had. It was a blazing hot day, so Clive and I settled down very happily to watch children catch crabs and bask in the sun. But Roger was undaunted, fussed about among the boat men and eventually not only got a boat, but a very large and handsome one with great big sails and a centre-board (do you know what that is?). I have always been given to understand that sailing is a difficult and dangerous art, but Roger of course has picked it up and never takes a man.

Off we went at a terrific pace. I have never been so fast. In a few minutes we got to Itchenor and thought we would anchor while Roger had a bathe. This wasn't so easy, as first we almost ran on the mud and then we couldn't make way against the wind. Roger took off his clothes however, and at last got us anchored in safely, but happily decided in the end that he wouldn't bathe, which would certainly have been a disastrous thing to do as he could never have climbed into our boat again and would probably have been swept away by a current. (This is a long and very dull story). So we had lunch and wanted to go home, Clive and I did, that is. But Roger insisted upon going on. He hadn't yet had enough sailing.

So on we went, shooting along faster than ever, almost out to the open sea, in spite of protests from Clive, who said we should never get back. At last we turned and got back about a third of the way, when the wind dropped. The tide was against us. We talked and talked, only to find ourselves getting further and further off. You can imagine Clive's despair. It was just what we had foretold, and we might as

---

[2] A large painting that has not survived.

well anchor where we were and wait till midnight and the turn of the tide to get home. Then Roger's obstinacy triumphed. He wouldn't give in but went on tacking and tacking, until at last a slight wind sprung up and by great technical skill he sailed us home quite quickly. The whole expedition seemed to me typical of his determination to conquer men and tide and wind and come out in the end with technique triumphant. I have heard since from him that sailing a boat like that was really very dangerous knowing as little about it as he did . . .

Your
VB

BERG

IV-12. To Roger Fry

Monday [December 27, 1915]   ***Garsington Manor, Oxford***

My dear Roger,

I had your letter here this morning. I'm afraid you sound rather depressed. Will it cheer you up to think that I've been working a good deal at your writing case since I've been here, which you can look upon as a supplementary Christmas present? If you take the niceness of presents as meaning amount of affection, you ought at any rate to take this as meaning a good deal in intention, but of course it may be a failure! However, the wools are lovely, so we must hope for the best.

There is a large party here, ourselves and the children, Maynard, Lytton, Maria, J. M. Murry,[1] whom I like much better than I did at first, Ottoline, Philip, their Julian and the Swiss governess. We have had a Christmas tree and a dance and rather a good charade, the life and death of Lytton, in which the children acted and were perfectly charming. Quentin in bed as the baby Lytton, with horn spectacles on, acted most skilfully. He is quite at home on the stage. Ottoline

---

[1]John Middleton Murry (1889–1957), journalist. His lover was the writer Katherine Mansfield (1888–1923), whom he married in 1918.

is really amazing in some ways. She has all the servants in to see the acting and they are perfectly happy and enjoy it thoroughly, and the dance to which they and the villagers came was a great success. Ottoline danced with great spirit and set them all going, twirling about with the kitchen maid, so that there was none of that awful stiffness that generally comes with mixed classes. I suppose it's her aristocratic tradition that makes her able to do it. She was rather cross the first day. I don't know why, but I think she was tired with all the preparations. At the Christmas tree, every child—about 50 of them—had a separate present. But yesterday she was more amiable. Philip is fairly contented, though I think terrified of bankruptcy, and makes ineffectual attempts to economize by dividing one and a quarter chicken between 9 grown ups and 3 children! The house is crammed with objects, little boxes and tables and cushions. It will be an odd change to go to Asheham on Tuesday, though of course Virginia does rather the same thing as Ottoline in some ways on a minor and shabbier scale. We played the poetry game last night, much against my and Lytton's wishes, and as we knew it would, it turned out to be too indecent for the company, as least so Maynard thought.

On the whole it has been quite good fun here, but I shall be ready to leave tomorrow. The children have enjoyed it enormously and had almost too much excitement, but will go on to a quiet week at Seend. It has been as different from that as anything could be. Maria tells me (pen given out) that you have asked her to Guildford, but she seemed to think Ottoline wanted her to stay here. She is much happier at Newnham than she was, I think, and looks much better, though not so pretty. She'll get too fat I expect.

Backgammon has been started. Maynard seems to be a genius at it and beats them all. There is a very pretty old French table they play at and I think one might get people to sit and play while one painted them, as they sit fairly quiet for hours.

I go to Asheham tomorrow, so will you write there.

Your
V.

TATE

IV-13. To Ottoline Morrell

Friday [March 17, 1916]   *[Omega Workshops, 33 Fitzroy Square,*
Bloomsbury]

My dear Ottoline,

I am writing at the Omega, where I have to wait to see Roger. I *was* so sorry to have to say I couldn't come this morning. It sounds such a nice party, but I had promised to go to the farm[1] for Sunday. As I have never been there, I think I must go and see what it's like and what is wanted before taking the children there, and this Sunday is the only time I can go. But I should have loved to come to you.

I wish you had been with us yesterday. It was a wonderful sight when Lytton came in with his air-cushion under his arm, looking terribly dignified.[2] He put the cushion down on the chair very deliberately and then sat down and reared his head like some great sea lion and looked slowly round at all the old gentlemen. They seemed terrified by the power of the human eye and evidently only longed to get rid of him at once, and were too thankful he claimed health. They didn't at all want to hear his conscientious objections, but we were very much disappointed. However, you'll hear all about it from Lytton himself and from Philip.

It was most splendid of you to get your brother[3] to buy 3 of Duncan's pictures and I think it will tide him over many difficulties. Also, how nice of you to make him go and see mine. Did you really like any of them? I'm very glad you did, but as for wanting to buy any, it would be quite absurd for you to do so, for you know if you really did like any enough to want to have it, I should be so glad to give it to you. It would really please me so much to think you liked it, but I'm always afraid of giving people White Elephants! I know how pictures accumulate in one's house and if one doesn't like them, they're such a nuisance.

We are going to see Gertler this afternoon. He's painting a great

---

[1]Wissett Lodge, Halesworth, Suffolk, where DG and Bunny worked on the land to avoid conscription.
[2]Lytton's examination on March 16 before the Hampstead Tribunal was not as immediately successful as VB reports. His application for exemption on the grounds of conscience was adjourned pending medical examination, after which he was rejected as medically unfit for any type of service.
[3]Lord Henry Cavendish-Bentinck, Lady Ottoline's favorite brother.

picture of a merry-go-round,[4] but he won't let us see it till it's finished. He came to lunch the other day and was very amusing and intelligent. I liked him, and he's so much interested in his painting he can hardly talk of anything else, which I rather like. I think he must have been through an unattractive stage of fearful self consciousness and now he has more self confidence and is much nicer.

I hope both Lytton and Maynard won't collapse on your hands. Lytton seemed rather shattered yesterday and Maynard was starting a cold.

Your affectte
Vanessa

TEXAS

IV-14. To John Maynard Keynes

Thursday [April 20, 1916]   *Wissett Lodge, Halesworth, Suffolk*

My dear Maynard,

Do come tomorrow. We have Clive and Mary here now but they go tomorrow, so we shall have room for you and Ruth,[1] who is I believe coming on Saturday for the weekend.

You can either telegraph to the Angel Hotel Halesworth for a curious box-like omnibus, or you can telegraph to me and I will order from the village a small trap to meet you. Neither are very comfortable, but it's such a short way it doesn't much matter, only the bus is shut and the trap[2] open, so I should go by the weather.

Thank you very much for your letter and the papers. It will be very nice to see you. You'll find us all flourishing, only one of the four footed rabbits who was said to be a doe and with young has been found to have what is thought to be a penis, but no balls, and no young, and she or he buggers its mate, and one of the hens has a pale comb and the puppy has nits and Bunny has a skin disease. Duncan

---

[4]Completed 1916. Now at the Tate.
[1]Ruth Fry (1876–1962), RF's youngest sister, secretary to the Quaker War Victims' Relief Fund 1914–1918. There is no record of an Easter visit by her, however.
[2]A light two-wheeled carriage.

and I and the children are so far free from anything and we shall all be very glad to see you.

Your affecte
VB

KCC

IV-15. To Lytton Strachey

Ap. 27 [1916]   *Wissett Lodge, Halesworth, Suffolk*

Dearest Lytton,

I should have written to you before to tell you how glad I was of your letter, but in the country one's normal time for letter writing—my normal time—after dinner, is devoted to sleep, that is, after one has had one's chapter of the Fairchild Family read aloud by Duncan or perhaps read a little to oneself of David Blaize.[1] Do you know both these works? If not, you must get them at once. They are our only literature here except the volumes produced by The Board of Agriculture, over which Bunny spends many hours, though the house is full of books—you needn't bring any when you come—fascinating volumes of Temple Bar and Good Words[2] and all the Novels of the Nineties.

Today it's so hot, and I'm so lazy, that I'm sitting out in the sun and writing to you and I hope to others presently. The young gentlemen are at work somewhere, the puppy, "Little Henry," is out of sight and sound, the children are quiet, everything is rushing into leaf. If only there weren't a war and tribunals in the background it would be perfect. But perhaps one would then begin to think about fleas or money or something else and perhaps the war will soon be over and we shall all survive it. Anyhow, it seems the only thing to enjoy the present, and the only way of cheating one's fate. Are you

[1]*The Fairchild Family*, a later edition of Mary Martha (Butt) Sherwood's *The History of the Fairchild Family, or The Child's Manual; being a collection of stories calculated to shew the importance and effects of a religious education* (1819); Edward Frederic Benson's *David Blaize and the Blue Door* (1867).
[2]Both periodicals. *Good Words* was a religious Sunday weekly.

now managing to do so at Garsington? Is it true that you are going to adjoin Bertie in another cottage and shall we ever see you again if you do?[3]

I feel that all our ways are changing. We are so much overcome by the country as compared to London that I doubt if I shall ever return to Gordon Sq. The delight of having no telephone, no crowd to tea, and all the rest is so great. Then the positive delights also of flowers and trees and innumerable unexpected sights and sounds keeps one perpetually happy. It seems too absurd to spend one's days shut up from it all. We shall go to town for a delicious jaunt now and then, no doubt, and you will come and sit in the sun here, which will be much more satisfying than sitting in the dark in London. I really believe I at any rate am not fitted to be a Town Lady, and my own doubt is whether Spanish would not be preferable to English country.

Clive doesn't write at all, only a line to say he's up to his eyes in politics. Will he take to them or what? Certainly he didn't seem to like country life much. He was blinded to all else by the fleas and the cold. Also Mary I think is made for salons. Her exquisiteness is not lost upon us, but it ought really also to be seen by the polite world.

You perhaps have found the mixture that suits you at Garsington, gardens outside and town life within.

I don't see how they're all to be reconciled except by visits to each other—unless we could all inherit an estate in Spain.

After the war that is what I foresee, England abandoned to the N.C.F.,[4] who will reform her with their pink cheeks and energy and gradually bring back freedom and a fearfully enlightened and moral international state in which our grandchildren may flourish, and the flight of the intellectuals to Spain. Maynard won't approve, though I think he is now reconciled to Wissett.

I have had an amazing account of the Easter party at Garsington from Mary—purple and gold and love making everywhere, with the sudden entrance of the P.M.[5] and suite. Duncan had another from Molly [MacCarthy], who seems to have been made miserable by her

[3]Bertrand Russell and other conscientious objectors of the Morrells' acquaintance, including CB, were eagerly settling for the summer at Garsington, where they could claim to be engaged in work of national importance on the land. Lytton's taste for Garsington and Lady Ottoline was extremely suspect in the eyes of Bloomsberries.
[4]VB had been performing simple clerical work for the No Conscription Fellowship.
[5]The prime minister, Herbert Asquith, an old friend of Lady Ottoline.

deafness. I hope for other accounts from others. Also I have had one from Virginia of her party, with you as "smooth as silk"—which I hope means discreet—and Sanger in white trousers striped with black—can that be true?—and conversation about his family. But it sounded unscandalous compared to Garsington or to her talks with various family friends in London before.

This is at least a long letter, and that's all you can expect from us in the Suffolk flats. So please answer it soon.

We had a wonderful view of a Zep the other night, close down over the house on a brilliant starlight night with no one taking any notice of it beyond a feeble local searchlight which couldn't get on to it. The English seemed incredibly incompetent compared to the Germans, but I daresay they were really wise not to bother about it, and the C[onscientous] O[bjector]'s case seemed to me transparently obvious.* When would you like to come here?

Your
VB

*Perhaps this is not very clear. Please send more poems when you write them, also send, or bring if you prefer it, Florence N.,[6] which Virginia seems to have enjoyed very much.

BRITISH LIBRARY

IV-16. To Virginia Woolf

May 10 [1916]   *Wissett Lodge, Halesworth, Suffolk*

My Billy,

I'm afraid I have been a long time about your cloak, but as no doubt you have heard, we have had rather an agitating time with the tribunals, as both Duncan and Bunny were refused any exemption.[1] The tribunal consisted of perfectly bovine country bumpkins, whose

[6]"Florence Nightingale," the second essay completed for Lytton's *Eminent Victorians*.
[1]Their appeal before the Blything Tribunal for exemption was rejected despite representation by JMK, Philip Morrell, and Adrian.

skulls couldn't be penetrated at all. They would hardly listen to anything and one felt at once that it was quite hopeless. Probably you'll
have heard all about it from Adrian or someone so I won't go over
it all again. Now we have to wait for the appeal, but I haven't much
hope of that being any better . . .

Thank you very much for sending the garden book. It has been
very wet here the last few days, but now it's getting fine again and I
am going to start doing all I can. Barbara Hyles,[2] one of the young
short-haired generation, is staying here now and she is just becoming
a gardener, working at odd jobs for a nursery gardener in Hampstead
so she is useful here and can be turned on to weed, etc. She is quite
nice, not very interesting except as a specimen of the new school, very
independent and cheerful. She left home and went to the Slade and
has refused to return. She now rides a motor cycle and tried to get a
job as chauffeur, but having failed to do so is taking to gardening.

My plans are rather vague until I know what happens at the appeal.
What are you doing? Are you back at Hogarth?[3] Do write and tell
me all the gossip you can. I suppose everyone we know will soon be
either in prison or the army. Will Leonard be a C.O.? Please write
soon.

Your
VB

BERG

IV-17. To Ottoline Morrell

Saturday [May 20, 1916]   *Wissett Lodge, Halesworth, Suffolk*

My dearest Ottoline,

I couldn't send you a telegram yesterday as you will have understood, but Duncan thought Philip did so. It was rather horrid having

---

[2]Barbara Hiles (1891–1984), later Mrs. Nicholas Bagenal, a Slade-trained artist
who did some work for the Omega. She was at this time, but very briefly, involved
with David Garnett.
[3]Hogarth House in Paradise Road, Richmond, the Woolfs' home since March
1915.

to stay here as no trap turned up to take us to the station, but it was a blessing that they caught the train. These additional horrors always happen! I can still hardly believe in their good fortune, as I had quite made up my mind to a second refusal.[1] Even this seems too good to be true. Non-combatant was the most I thought possible and to be given leave to appeal never entered my head. Of course I know it may still fail, but at least one can hope, and even if it does I feel their position now is quite different from what it was, as they will get the benefit of any scheme there may be for C.O.s. We're all in great spirits and enjoying the heat and everything and wish you were all here to enjoy it with us. It is such a blessing not to have to fear the immediate arrival of the police.

Thank you so much for your letter. I was so glad to get it then.

We have Mrs Garnett[2] here now. She is just what you would imagine, and talks away steadily and continuously and sensibly exactly like one of her own translations if it weren't a translation. So she's not very exciting, but very nice, and full of valuable hints about fowls and vegetables. On Monday I believe Saxon is coming, with whom we think she would mix very well.

Your affectionate
Vanessa

TEXAS

IV-18. To Roger Fry

Friday [June 1916]   *Wissett Lodge, Halesworth, Suffolk*

My dear Roger,

I hope you'll find time to write and tell me what is happening to you in Paris. I'm afraid it looks as though the Germans were now

---

[1] On May 19, before the Appeal Tribunal at Ipswich, DG and Bunny were granted exemption from combative service, with leave to appeal to the Central Tribunal (headed by Lady Robert Cecil's brother-in-law, Lord Salisbury) regarding alternative employment.
[2] Constance Garnett (1862–1946), the prolific translator of Russian literature, Bunny's mother.

going to take Verdun,[1] but I don't know how much it matters. Is everyone very much depressed and is there anything at all going on in the way of painting?

Here we have no news. Lytton and [H. T. J.] Norton are still here but go tomorrow, I think. We have had long discussions in the old style about art, about literature especially, though Lytton really thinks me too much without sense of what it's all about, I think, to be able to argue [with me] without in the end getting very cross. We quarrelled over [King] Lear as I said it was of no interest as a story—in fact a rather mechanical and stilted affair with quite unreal relationships and feelings—and that I thought the human interest was of no value. But of course it's quite impossible to describe what it is that one does think of value. Lytton thought I had no appreciation of it and that it was really of great importance, even, that it should be actually like life. However it sounds very dull written down, I'm afraid. But Lytton admitted in the end that he had very little sense of anything but the human interest in painting. He is very suspicious of our attitude about art and thinks we don't understand our own feelings and are trying to prove a theory. I, on the other hand, think him almost entirely dramatic in his appreciations. I mean I believe he only feels character and relationships of character and has no conception of the form it's all being made into.

Then we have had long discussions about Ottoline. I believe he is very much inclined to settle down at Garsington for ever, which might I think be rather disastrous, especially as he won't really look Ottoline in the face, at least he rather resents our doing so. We disputed as to whether she had any creative gift or not. Norton and Duncan and I took the line that she was a terrifically energetic and vigorous character with a definite, rather bad, taste, which she put into practice, but that it was different from having any creative power. But Lytton thinks Garsington a creation and that she really has some. I suppose it's just as one feels it. To me it seems simply a collection of objects she likes put together with enormous energy but not made into anything. If Lytton lives there, one will never be able to see him without Ottoline's being round the corner, if not in the room, I think. However, he's very comfortable there I suppose and gets the mixture he wants of town and country . . .

[1]They did not. Though German forces had attacked Verdun in February 1916, hoping that the French would defend it to the last person and thus deplete their troops, they were surprised by stiff resistance from the French army. The battle lasted over eleven months.

I have now turned a bedroom here into a studio, as I found it rather difficult to work in the barn, which was nearly always too cold, even at this time of year. This room is rather nice, though not very big, and I have painted all the chocolate paint white and put marbled papers on some places, which makes rather interesting colour. I have been painting a picture of the pond here, but hayfever makes it almost impossible to work out of doors,[2] so I am going on with it indoors. I also want to start a rather large interior out of my head. I hope you'll see some pictures by Matisse and Picasso. It would be such a mercy to see some exciting new pictures again. I find it very depressing to see only my own works being produced, and it would be exciting even to hear what you thought of any new things you saw.

This letter is fearfully dull, but you see except for these talks which one can't really repeat one is still simply waiting. Please write.

Your
V.

TATE

IV-19. To Roger Fry

Monday [October 16, 1916]   *Charleston, Firle*

My dear Roger,

It is now 9 o'clock. We had breakfast at 7. D. and B. started for work soon after 7.30.[1] They come back for lunch at 12 and go off again immediately and finish at 5. I shall be quite alone most of the day with one girl—14 years old!—who is coming to me as servant for £8 a year! It will be an odd life, won't it, but it seems to me it ought to be a good one for painting.

You must really come and see this place soon. I wish you could think it possible to come even with D. here. You see you'd have 8

[2]VB suffered from hay fever in the early summer all her life.
[1]DG and Bunny had found employment with a Mr. Hecks, who farmed New House Farm near Firle. They lived with VB and her sons at Charleston, a farmhouse four miles from Asheham, which the Bells rented from its tenant, Mr. Stacey.

solid hours a day alone with me. It really is so lovely that I must show it to you soon. It's absolutely perfect, I think.

I wasn't quite so absurd about the house though as I seemed to be later, for as one comes to it from the front one sees the least good side of it. It has been refaced with some kind of quite harmless stucco or plaster and has a creeper over it. The other sides are wonderful. I suppose it's 17th or early 18th century (but my word doesn't go for much). Anyhow it's most lovely, very solid and simple, with flat walls in that lovely mixture of brick and flint that they use about here, and perfectly flat windows in the walls and wonderful tiled roofs. The pond is most beautiful, with a willow at one side and a stone or flint wall edging it all round the garden part, and a little lawn sloping down to it, with formal bushes on it. Then there's a small orchard and the walled garden like the Asheham one, and another lawn or bit of field railed in beyond. There's a wall of trees, one single line of elms all round two sides which shelters us from west winds. We are just below Firle Beacon, which is the highest point on the downs near, and except towards the downs the ground slopes down from the house on all sides.

Inside the house the rooms are very large, and a great many. 10 bedrooms I think, some enormous. One I shall make into a studio. It is very light and large, with an east window, but the sun doesn't come in much after quite early morning, and it has a small room out of it with another window, so one might get interesting interiors, I think. The house is really much too large at present of course, but it's nice to have space and no doubt it will get filled in time. There's hardly any furniture in it yet. I am going into Lewes today to buy a few necessary things. The Omega dinner service looks most lovely on the dresser. I wish you could come and see it all. It would be such fun to show it to you. Please write and tell me how you're getting on potting.

Your
V.

TATE

IV-20. To Saxon Sydney-Turner

Jan. 19 [1917]   *Charleston, Firle*

My dear Saxon,

I haven't answered your letter, not because I've been ill, but rather overwhelmed by domestic difficulties and visitors, which made it impossible to get the necessary quiet to consider—or at least to write about—love and friendship. I was feeling too angry with the quite inconceivable stupidities of my two 14 year olds, and too much worried lest I shouldn't provide all the necessary hot water, etc., which Clive's passion demands for his love, to be able to tell you with any coherence all I thought about your much more interesting questions. Now I have the two little Blancos (Whites) in the house, as well as all the other children.[1] But Mabel is a miracle and will I expect bring us all to a happy ending.

However you must believe I have thought a great deal about you and all you say.[2] But first I shall answer your practical letter. You can certainly come here on Tuesday, but I am not quite certain that we shan't be full for the following week end. Adrian and Maynard have both said they may want to come then and James[3] and Noel are also promised rooms some time soon. But perhaps you could if necessary go to Brighton for a day or two and come back here again. We can take in two guests at a time now, as though there's room for more, there aren't enough beds, blankets, etc. All our possible guests should let me know their plans in the course of the next day or two, and then I can tell you for certain. When you come I think it might be as well if you could bring an extra blanket, and of course your hot water bottles. Do you think also you could do one rather tiresome thing for me, which is to find out, perhaps from Oliver, whether there's a good

---

[1]VB had established a small school at Charleston which included Anna-Jane and Justine, the children of Amber Blanco-White (née Reeves). Mabel Selwood was elevated from nurse to governess and VB taught the children French and elementary music. Her "two 14 year olds" may however have been servant girls.

[2]Saxon had appealed to VB for advice regarding his love for Barbara Hiles, then attracted to both him and Nicholas Bagenal (1891–1974), educated at Kings's College, Cambridge, and at this time serving in the Irish Guards.

[3]James Beaumont Strachey (1887–1967), psychologist and translator of Freud, younger brother of Lytton.

book teaching singing in the tonic-sol-fa system,[4] as I want to teach the children? I used to know it but I've forgotten some of the details and I don't remember it all well enough to begin teaching without a book to help.

I have been reading your first letter again. I was very glad to hear what you had been thinking, but I wonder if I'm not the most incapable of all people to tell you the difference between love and the other kinds of affection. Some kinds seem so mixed. I think what one feels for one's children really is, and I think perhaps one feels the kind of tenderness you describe for them. But I think one's loves differ very much, only I believe that the difference to me between them and other affections is not simply a physical difference, but more that all one's feeling is somehow changed and influenced by one's physical feeling. I don't think however there can be any doubt you're in love, can there? It seems to me that all you say you feel about touch is quite natural, at first at any rate, and so is the not being jealous of Nick, whom you knew to be there from the beginning. Then, it seems to me that being in love is never what other people have described. It's always so conditioned by the person one's in love with.

Yes, it is very extraordinary when two people care for each other in the right way, but perhaps there's something even more wonderful in just caring without getting the exact return. One can get back and look at the other person in a way that perhaps one can't when they're feeling that about you, at least so one thinks sometimes, but I suppose one would always choose the other.

I see I'm no good at explaining any of these things. In fact, I'm always being told I don't understand my own feelings, which perhaps means that I don't know how love and other affections do differ from each other. But I think I do know when other people are in love with other people sometimes.

Write and tell me what your doctor says. How is Barbara and has she gone away?

[4]The Tonic-sol-fa Agency of London published in 1875 John Curwen's *The Art of Teaching, and the Teaching of Music: Being the Teacher's Manual of the Tonic-sol-fa Method*, a text VB may have known from HPG.

Duncan and Henry [dog] are both sound asleep. Bunny is translating a French book on gardening.[5] I am getting sleepy too, so good night.

Your
VB

Please write again whether you come or not.

MICHAEL BAGENAL

IV-21. To Roger Fry

Saturday [April 14, 1917]   *Charleston, Firle*

My dear Roger,
   I wonder if you got a letter I wrote to you at Guildford. I haven't heard from you at all since I saw you. Perhaps you're not writing on purpose for some reason. Perhaps I said something which has prevented you from writing. Please tell me what it is. You know I want to hear from you and to know how you are and what you're doing. Clive and Mary have just arrived. He says you're still at Guildford, so I will send this there.
   The only thing that has happened to us here has been that we've seen the Woolves, and Marjorie Strachey who was staying with them came on here for 2 days. She is full of her teaching, but also still very unhappy about Jos, I'm afraid, who sounds a queer character and seems to have treated her rather unkindly. I believe the Stracheys think that it has all come to an end and that it is better not to let her talk of him, but she would do so and is evidently still very much in love. I took another turn this time against dirt (perhaps Mary will now have the opposite effect again) while Marjorie was here, for really her dirt is indescribable and very unattractive. I could hardly bear to look at her with my spectacles on, and I felt cleanliness to be most necessary, at any rate as soon as one is past 17.
   I have had another child offered to me, Mrs Riviere's[1] little girl.

[5]Vincent Alfred Gressent's *The Kitchen Garden and its Management,* ed. and trans. David Garnett (London: Selwyn & Blount, 1919).
[1]Possibly Winifred Riviere (née Langdon Davies), wife of the portrait painter Hugh Riviere (1869–1956).

She wants to send her here for a month with her nursery governess, but I shall refuse. I think a boy of 9 is the thing to look out for.

I have had a long talk with Virginia the other day. She told me all about her new novel.[2] I am the principal character in it and I expect I'm a very priggish and severe young woman, but perhaps you'll see what I was like at 18. I think the most interesting character is evidently my mother, who is made exactly like Lady Ritchie,[3] down to every detail apparently. Everyone will know who it is, of course.

What are you painting? Clive seems to have been very much impressed by your copy of the Sassoferrato.[4] Mine is still getting more and more horrible and as smooth as a billiard ball. The colour is too awful. Is yours finished and have you begun the Raphael?

Your
V.

TATE

IV-22. To Duncan Grant

Tuesday [July 10, 1917]   *Durbins, Guildford*

My Bear,

I hope you're being a good bear and not getting into trouble. Trissie told me she was not going away this week, so you can ask George [Mallory] freely. I have asked Barbara for next Sunday and Norton for the 28th. When my train got to some obscure station yesterday, suddenly Roger and Goldie appeared at the window, to my surprise. I hoped Goldie was coming here but no, he went on to London. Roger and I had lunch in the train. It was cold and wet and dismal and when we got here we lit a fire and had some coffee, and then plunged into not a hot bath, but a still-life. I felt so incapable of one thing more than another that it didn't seem to make much odds, so we

[2]*Night and Day* (1919). The character modeled on VB is Katherine Hilbery.
[3]Mrs. Hilbery was closely based on VW's Aunt Anny.
[4]In May 1917 the Omega held the exhibition "Copies and Translations," to which VB contributed copies of Giotto and Bronzino, DG a Pollaiuolo and a detail of a Piero della Francesca, and RF a Cimabue, still at Charleston.

painted a madonna lily, of all things.[1] I got rather interested, contrary to all expectation, though I don't think mine's much good, as I shan't have nearly time to do what I want to do. We have been working hard all day till now when I've come out into the garden where the sun is really hot. Roger is I believe tending to the hot water arrangements. We did some weeding and a great deal of talking, but I shall tell you about it all when I see you. I mustn't spend too long writing to you. Roger is coming. I shall get back I hope for tea on Thursday. Joan [Fry] appeared last night. I asked her if she knew of a donkey and it turns out that she prides herself on being a horsey woman, but didn't know of a donkey, though she spent a long time trying to be sure she didn't. I rather like Joan. She amuses me and gives me a great feeling of security. I hope I shall hear from you tomorrow, my Bear. How I wish you were basking beside me now with your fur all warm and iridescent. Give my love to the children. Please be pleased to see me again.

Your
Rodent

Wednesday
I couldn't get this posted yesterday and don't know if I shall be able to now, nor if you'll get it before you see me. Your letter has just come, a very nice letter, darling Bear, only it makes me feel rather homesick. But it's silly, you'll think, to feel homesick in 2 days. Rodents are home-loving animals.

I suppose you had better see Lady H. de W.[2] Roger doesn't know her. He thinks she's a Jew, in which case she may have good taste . . .

I often wonder how you come to be so infinitely preferable to everyone else in the world and I meditate upon your character, also upon your extraordinary intelligence! What do you think about that? Don't you think it is very astonishing? But of course you'll only snub me and rap me down. I forgot I was to make an effort to be incoherent in my next letter, which is a pity, as it might have lent this dull letter some interest.

Goodbye,
R.

HENRIETTA GARNETT

[1]VB's painting is in the collection of the Anthony d'Offay Gallery, London.
[2]Margherita (née van Raalte), Lady Howard de Walden.

IV-23. To Virginia Woolf

Monday [July 23, 1917]   *Charleston, Firle*

My Billy,

Thank you very much for the loaf. Your example has fired me, and I made 9 loaves on Saturday which were quite successful. I find that Trissie once took a prize for bread-making, so she knows all about it and could easily do it herself, only she has so much else to do. So I expect I shall make it twice a week at any rate. We have had a terrific party here for the week-end. Clive and Mary, Saxon, who suddenly telegraphed to ask if he could come and is still here, and Barbara in her tent, who spent most of the time here. I don't know how long she means to stay there. She said a week or two, but I strongly suspect she'll stay all the summer. As long as she doesn't bring all the world about our ears I don't mind, as she's very independent, but one's rather at the mercy of people if they choose to camp at one's door.

I have had my copy of your stories.[1] You don't care what I think of your writing of course, do you Billy? So it won't interest you at all to be told that I was amused, interested and fascinated by the skill and completeness with which it was done. No doubt you are a very good writer and I shouldn't think you had much to fear from the rivalry of Katherine Mansfield[2] and Co. Why don't you write more short things? Perhaps you will now. Not that I don't want you to write novels too, but there is a kind of completeness about a thing like this that is very satisfactory and that you can hardly get in a novel.

I liked Carrington's woodcuts.[3] It has occurred to me, did you seriously mean that we might produce a book (I mean a pamphlet) of woodcuts? Both Duncan and I want very much to do some, and if you really thought it feasible, I should like to get a few other people also to produce one or two each and get together a small collection.

---

[1] *Two Stories* (1917), the first publication of the Hogarth Press, which included LW's "Three Jews" and VW's "The Mark on the Wall."
[2] The New Zealand–born writer Katherine Mansfield (1888–1923) settled in London in 1908 and in 1918 the Hogarth Press published her long story, *Prelude*.
[3] *Two Stories* was illustrated with four woodcuts by Dora Carrington, now Lytton Strachey's companion.

Could this be arranged with your new press? and if so, how many could there be and what size? I would undertake to get the woodcuts, if you think it could be done, in the course of the next few months, or whenever you hadn't anything else you wanted to print. It wouldn't mean much trouble for you, as there'd be very little letter press.

Mary gave me a queer account of your and her domestic affairs! She said the cook didn't like your basement and wanted after all to stay with her.[4] Is this true? It seems very odd after all the rows one heard they had had. If so, will you still get Ethel and another cook, or what will you do? I hope matters will soon get arranged.

Saxon has now announced to me that he wants to stay a week. I foresee endless visitors to Barbara's encampment, which is rather a nuisance. I have had a pathetic letter from Snow begging me to go and see her at Leeds in August when she'll be alone there. I think I shall have to go for a few days, but it will be a melancholy expedition and a long way to go.

How are you? Please write and tell me.

Your
VB

BERG

IV-24. To Roger Fry

Tuesday [January 1918]   *Charleston*

My dear Roger,

How extraordinary that I should sell 2 pictures. If Lala[1] pays me £6.10. altogether it's not very different from what I asked, is it? I think I only said £7. I should be quite glad to get that if you can arrange it.

---

[4]The Woolfs had attempted to replace their servants Nelly Boxall and Lottie Hope with Mary Hutchinson's servant Ethel and an anonymous cook. In the end, Lottie and Nelly stayed.
[1]Lalla Vandervelde (née Helene Frederique Speyer) (1870–1964), wife of the Belgian Socialist politician Emile Vandervelde. She was a friend of RF's and a devoted patron of the Omega.

But I'm sure my sales won't go on. If they do, I shall be delighted to exchange with you. Also, if Kauffer[2] would really like to exchange, I should be very glad to when I have anything he likes. I should very much like to have one of his water-colours, or other small paintings. Only I don't know that I've got anything that he'd care about at present. I've just started rather a large picture of the children being bathed. It's very bad at present, but I'm rather excited about it. I don't mind its being bad, as I think I see what I want to do. Also I've been working at my big bath picture[3] and am rather excited about that. I've taken out the woman's chemise and in consequence she is quite nude and much more decent . . .

Your
V.

TATE

IV-25. To John Maynard Keynes

Feb. 8 [1918]   *Charleston*

Dearest Maynard,

I hope Duncan thanked you for all the jellies, etc., you sent. I think they have made a lot of difference. Champagne I'm sure is a poison as far as I'm concerned, but your foods are most reviving.

I'm sending you a list of my investments, which the bank sent me, though I asked for the things themselves. Will this do? or shall I ask for the actual documents. Clive said he was going to ask you to consider his investments, too. I don't know if he has done so, but I also send you a list of such of his investments as he has control over. Most of his money is in trust.

The children's War Savings Certificates must I suppose just be left as they are.

Also I'm sending you Shaw's[1] bill, which will explain itself. I don't

[2]E. McKnight Kauffer (1890–1954), American-born painter and illustrator.
[3]*The Tub,* now at the Tate. See plate x, bottom.
[1]A builder engaged in repairs to 46 Gordon Square, which JMK now shared with the Bells.

know what the items are, but if you want to know he can send them of course, or perhaps Jessie will know what has been done. It seems to me rather large.

Did Duncan tell you that Tilton[2] is not to let? There's another house which is, or will be soon. It doesn't sound very attractive however, but you could go and see it next time you come.

I wonder how you'll think Duncan. There have been such storms within for the last month or two. I was really rather worried a week or two ago, since you were here, because I don't think one can go on indefinitely with such constantly recurring crises. Perhaps they'll get less. But I have also come to the conclusion that in spite of the horrors of them, these storms perhaps do relieve Duncan more than anything else would, and that he couldn't indulge in them unless he realised subconsciously that he could do so safely. I mean Bunny is too dependent on him really to give him up whatever he does. He certainly *is* a Turk. I believe Bunny and I suffer more than he does, on the whole! Still, I can't bear his getting so unhappy, but there isn't anything one can do, is there? except distract his mind.

I've had such letters from Barbara explaining her reasons for marrying Nick. They convince me more thoroughly that she has acted in complete ignorance of the probable consequences, but it's no use saying so now.[3] Please come here again soon. I hope last night's dinner with Virginia was a success.

Your
VB

KCC

IV-26. To Virginia Woolf

Feb. 13 [1918]   *Charleston*

My Billy,

How are you? Please write and tell me or ask Leonard to. It's really absurd that you should send me malt, etc., when evidently you want

[2]A farmhouse down the lane from Charleston. JMK did eventually live there.
[3]Barbara had married Nicholas Bagenal on February 1. It is said that a letter from VB advising her against it arrived on the morning of the wedding.

them yourself more than I do. But I don't follow the Fisher[1] plan of sending them back, but eat them gratefully. I am practically recovered now and am beginning all ordinary employments again. If you have really got influenza, do be careful afterwards. I got up thinking I was all right and then collapsed again after 2 or 3 days. I'm sure that's the devilish and deceptive part of that disease. Also, do feed up afterwards. I fear it mayn't be easy to do now, but you can get such things as you sent me. Here we have eggs too, and I'm going to start keeping rabbits. If starvation sets in, I really think you'll have to come and weather the seige at Asheham. I'm sure one's much better off in the country. We're going to keep all the ducks and hens we can and rabbits, besides growing potatoes, etc., all of which you could do at Asheham.

It's awful being cut off from one's principal occupation, isn't it?[2] I'm thankful to be able to paint again. One gets that tetchy without it, and off one's balance.

Do you remember your promise of coming here in February? When are you going to keep it? You'll be amused I think at the new regime. Mrs B[rereton][3] is really very nice and will I expect get the better of Julian eventually, though, as I daresay Duncan told you, they have already come to blows. However she did get the better of him then. It's amusing, if sometimes rather painful, to watch his taming. I hope one day though I shall have a pair of polite and well-behaved brats. Julian was of course very much pleased by the books you sent him, especially as he had very few presents. I hadn't been able to go and get him anything, and had made a mistake too about the day, so it all had to be rather patched up at the last moment and your parcel was very welcome. I believe he's considering a letter of thanks.

Do you know anything about Harriet Martineau and her works? I'm rather fascinated by her autobiography.[4] She was evidently so right-minded and unpleasant. You see what works one's reduced to reading in the winter evenings in the country. I find autobiographies absorbing. I wish you'd write yours.

[1]The Fishers: VB and VW's cousins on their mother's side. They were renowned in the Stephen family for their attitude of "hypocritical selflessness" (AVG).
[2]VW was unable to work due to a bad case of influenza.
[3]The children's new governess, who brought her daughter Anne with her to Charleston. She was a friend of RF's and had nursed his wife Helen (née Coombe) before her confinement to a mental hospital in about 1909.
[4]The Victorian radical Harriet Martineau (1802–76), whose autobiography was published in 1877.

I suppose if you're ill I shan't get more gossip yet, though Duncan and I laughed over the last batch until we nearly cried. Have you seen Saxon lately? He writes rather melancholy letters, poor old thing, though very high-minded of course and full of the most unselfish problems. I think your description of the conversation *à trois*[5] must have been exactly true to life. Lord, what characters. I myself think Barbara has behaved idiotically and will live to regret it, but there's no use saying so now. But how anyone with the imagination of an owl can conceive of life as she conceives it passes me—half the year with one, half with the other, a child by each, etc., and no one to have any jealousy or cause for complaint, and she like a looking-glass in the middle, reflecting each in turn. Poor old Saxon of course sees that it won't be so. He will be too like the poor old bachelor, faithful and solitary in Gt. Ormond St. long after we're all dead, supporting Barbara's children (by Nick) I daresay.

Please thank Leonard for writing to me and tell him I'd be very glad of more news, and I hope you're behaving yourself. I expect I shall come to London before long.

Your
VB

BERG

IV-27. To Roger Fry

Friday [April 3, 1918]   *Charleston*

My dear Roger,

We had great excitements about the pictures. Maynard came back suddenly and unexpectedly late at night, having been dropped at the bottom of the lane by Austen Chamberlain in a government motor,

---

[5]Cf. VW to VB, Tuesday, January 29, 1918: "Think of the three of them discussing the question over the stove in her studio and Nick saying 'No, Saxon: you must marry her;' and Saxon refusing to be happy save in their happiness, and Barbara suggesting copulation with each on alternate nights" (VWLII, 214).

and said he had left a Cézanne by the roadside![1] Duncan rushed off to get it and you can imagine how exciting it all was. Perhaps you've heard from Maynard himself by now. He wants to see you and tell you all about it. I know Holmes' purchases are idiotic considering his chances. He wouldn't hear of Cézanne and in the end didn't spend all the money, but came back with £5000 misspent and no El Greco, which he might easily have had. He did get the Delacroix portrait of the young man, an Ingres and I think some drawings, a Corot landscape (not one illustrated), Manet's lady with the cat, a Gauguin still-life.[2] I can't remember the rest. Maynard got for himself the Cézanne apples, a wonderful Ingres drawing, a small picture by Delacroix, and a drawing by Delacroix,[3] which he's given to Duncan. They are all still here and I wish you could see them. But they'll go to London soon. The Cézanne is really amazing and it's most exciting to have it in the house. It's so extraordinarily solid and alive. It's the little one of 7 apples that we liked so much, very small indeed. The Ingres drawing is one of the nudes reproduced, but it's ever so much better in reality. You'll hear all about the excitements of the sale from Maynard. It's awful to think how much might have been got, and only if you had been in London or we had known how to get at you, possibly you might have done something with Holmes. But after all it's great luck even to have got what he did. I believe it's to be kept a secret about the Nat. Gallery pictures till after the war. We must see them soon . . .

Your
V.

TATE

[1]Hearing from Duncan that the contents of Degas's studio were about to be auctioned off in Paris, JMK convinced Andrew Bonar Law, chancellor of the exchequer, to give him approximately £20,000 to buy works for the National Gallery at low wartime prices. C. J. Holmes, keeper of the National Gallery, accompanied him, wearing a disguise at the auction.
[2]Most of the works acquired by Holmes are still in the collections of the National Gallery; some drawings were given to the British Museum.
[3]Still at Charleston (a study for the frieze *Bellum* in the Salon du Roi, Palais Bourbon).

IV-28. To Virginia Woolf

July 3 [1918]   *Charleston*

My Billy,

I have written to tell Nelly that Trissie started her holiday today and I had already got a daily woman. I think in every way it's probably better now not to have Nelly here, and we can manage all right with Emily and Mrs Hoadley.[1] I won't write any more about servants. I'm feeling as if I'd rather do all myself than have these to-dos. Their conversation is more exhausting than that of all the intellectuals in London and I shall never know what happened in this affair, but I'm resigned to ignorance. I suppose really I shouldn't have sent Trissie to you and should have come myself. I would have done so if it hadn't been for the baby, but as it was I was feeling so sick I couldn't face it, and weakly gave in when Trissie offered to go.

As for Sophy, I think it's very rash of Adrian to take her on his shoulders again, but perhaps they mean to settle down to a respectable family life forever. They'll certainly have to with her, and I should find it impossible. Besides, she would ruin one in no time.

It's a relief to turn to your story,[2] though some of the conversation— she says, I says, sugar—I know too well! But it's fascinating and a great success, I think. So does Duncan. I suppose no one else is to see it yet. I wonder if I could do a drawing for it. It would be fun to try, but you must tell me the size. It might not have very much to do with the text, but that wouldn't matter. But I might feel inclined to do the two people holding the sugar conversation. Do you remember a picture I showed at the Omega of 3 women talking with a flower bed seen out of the window behind?[3] It might almost but not quite do as an illustration.

[1]This letter is in response to VW to VB, July 1, 1918 (VWL II, 256). Four months pregnant, VB was beginning to find herself overworked by the large and fluctuating household at Charleston. VW's cook Nelly Boxall had suggested working at Charleston during Trissie Selwood's holiday. Emily was the housemaid, Mrs. Hoadley the daily help.
[2]VB read her sister's story "Kew Gardens" in manuscript. It was published by the Hogarth Press in May 1919 with a woodcut frontispiece by VB. The 1927 reprint was an illustrated edition, however, with each page decorated by VB and the margins of the text altered to complement the lines of her design.
[3]*A Conversation* (1913–16), now at the Courtauld Institute. See plate vii, top.

Now do send me your theories of aesthetics and feelings on looking at one of my works. I'm longing to hear them, and it will be too tantalizing if you don't. Your description of the New English [Art Club exhibition] fascinated me and Duncan. Was it a new or an old drawing by John? Ought one to go and see the Jacques [Raverat]? But no, I know exactly what it must be like from what you say. Roger told us about it too and his account agreed with yours, I think.

I shall want also to hear about the love-birds[4] dinner. In your new Graves[5] I daresay you eclipsed the henbird. I'm glad you think her good. She's well worth going to, I think, as she's very cheap and will probably get attached to you and interested in making your dresses well.

Your account of Waller made me feel one really ought to take to him again. He sounds so broad minded, perhaps he'd even swallow this household. Old Lisa [Stillman], by the way, is going to spend the summer at Ditchling and hopes to see me very often. Luckily she can't walk a mile or bicycle. I shall say I'm going to have a baby and can't either, and that there's no kind of vehicle to be had and that we're miles from a station, and so shall hope to stave off more than one visit. Even that fills me with despair to think of. She *is* a depressing figure. She says since her nervous breakdown 8 years ago she hasn't been able to see to draw, and has done her best to fill Effie's[6] place and look after her 3 children. I send you her letter in return for Gerald's, which was almost too painful. The Duckworths must have spent many years of their lives going through tin boxes and attending funerals.[7] How they love it.

Please tell Leonard I'm very sorry if I suspected him unjustly in any way, not that I *did* suspect him of very much![8] But there, both our swan songs are over now.

Your
VB

BERG

[4]CB and Mary Hutchinson, aka "the parrokeets."
[5]Madame Gravé was a dressmaker recommended to VW by Mary Hutchinson.
[6]Lisa Stillman's elder sister, a sculptor.
[7]"Aunt Minna," Gerald's aunt Sarah Emily Duckworth, had died in June.
[8]LW had been reluctant to part with Nelly and Lottie without the assurance that they would return to the Woolfs.

IV-29. To Roger Fry

Nov. 11 [1918]   *Charleston*

My dear Roger,

We had news of the armistice early this afternoon and though one knew from the morning paper that it must come, it was still very exciting. It's extraordinary to feel that fighting is at an end. I can't quite make out why it makes so much difference to one, for one wouldn't have thought, at least I personally shouldn't, that one minded so very much what was happening to one's fellow creatures. But I think the relief now is simply in thinking that that horror has stopped, for nothing else is different from what it has been for some time. I found Bunny's state of mind rather trying and it was a relief when his emotions carried him off to London for the night to join the rejoicings of the crowd. Duncan has gone to Brighton to see if anything's going on, but returns tonight. I wonder if there's great excitement. We heard of crowds and flags and bells ringing in Lewes and everyone refusing to do any work. I hope at any rate that people generally are glad in spite of all the disappointment of the newspapers at its coming to an end.

I have done another woodblock.[1] Duncan has done 3 altogether. But we are both waiting for a fine tool with which to finish them. I hope Bunny may bring one back from London tomorrow and then we can soon get them done and send them to you. I daresay you won't want my second one or at any rate won't want the two, but in that case will you choose which you like best?

Clive was here for the weekend. I wish you could have been here at the same time. Perhaps you'll be seeing him tonight. He was very full of his after-war plans and says he means to leave Gordon Sq. and take rooms somewhere near. He thinks it won't be possible to go abroad for a long time and so he means to have rooms in London, but he thinks life with Maynard at Gordon Sq. too uncomfortable and difficult. All our doings are vague I suppose still. I feel as if I should like to go to Paris whenever it becomes possible, but otherwise I have no ideas.

It was very nice having you and Pam here, though I'm afraid you

---

[1]For *Original Woodcuts by Various Artists,* produced and published by the Omega Workshops in 1918.

came at a very uncomfortable moment for yourselves, with toothache rampant in the kitchen. If you'd have been here this week you'd have had pigs' trotters and pork pies and all sorts of things such as I can with difficulty face and which I know are wasted on me, mysterious pieces, mostly jelly it seems. I hope I'm not too bovine! I see, after country life for nearly 3 years, I shall have to take a metropolitan course. Certainly I shall give up house-keeping as soon as I possibly can.

Your
VB

TATE

IV-30. To Virginia Woolf

Friday [November 15, 1918]   *Charleston*

You wicked, wicked, extravagant and monstrous ape. You deserve a good beating and shutting up in your cage for a week, and if I were there you'd get it. How dared you send off such a parcel—cakes, soups, shortbreads, anchovies, sardines, sausages, I don't know what all. I'm simply overcome. While there you sit yourself shaking milk in a bottle[1] to keep yourself alive. It's I who ought to be bombarding you with food from the country, instead of calmly eating up a pig and eggs and honey and all. Well, I suppose I must thank you instead of merely cursing, but really you *are* wicked, Billy.

I wish peace came oftener to distract you from your duties and make you write to your poor neglected sister. I'm very much interested in the different accounts I get of the public feeling. You, I see, are fairly cynical, as I suspect I should be too. At any rate, it seems now as if the rejoicings were getting a little forced. Bunny came back after the first night of peace full of admiration for the feelings of the crowd. Duncan, at Brighton, thought the young simply very happy and re-lieved and the Metropole [Hotel] full of horrors. Duncan's mother writes ecstatically about the flags waving and crowds cheering. Roger

[1]To make butter, as the Woolfs' standard ration was inadequate.

seems unaware of any change in the situation. Mrs Garnett only wishes we could all have the advantages of defeat. Do tell me more of other people's views.

My servants went to Lewes where it was said that a "statue belonging to the Kaiser" was to be burnt, but only had to walk all the way back late at night admitting that it was a very poor show, only a rehearsal really for next week's display. There is also said to have been a burning of some mysterious object "made for the Kaiser before the war" at Firle! However, the world seems on the whole to be more peaceful in the country than in the towns, in spite of these burnings.

We are thinking of giving a weekend peace party here possibly, as I can't attend those in London. Do you think it would be possible, if Mrs B is not too much afraid of the ghost, which I think most likely, that she and the children should walk over and pic-nic at Asheham,[2] so as to leave room here? They would of course take all they wanted, and would do for themselves and leave all as they found it. The only thing would be they'd need a little coal or wood, and I don't know if you'd be able to spare any. They wouldn't of course use a very appreciable amount in 2 nights, but perhaps you'll want every scrap. So please tell me what you think. I haven't yet broached the possibility to them or Mrs B. in case for any reason you don't think it would do. If it's possible, either Dec. 1st or 8th would I think be the date.

I have altered my woodblock [for *Kew Gardens*] a good deal and am sending it back to you. I think it's better and less incoherent. I have cut 2 blocks since this one, for the book the Omega is bringing out, so I have learnt a little more about it. I am doing a small tail piece for you too, which I will send in a few days.

Duncan and Bunny have got off completely, as Mr Hecks doesn't really want them and takes the view that all that can happen to them is to become absentees, who apparently aren't going to be molested. They'll have to keep rather quite, I think, till one sees what's going to happen, but I think it's quite likely they'll simply be let alone. Bunny is working at the farm till the end of this week. Duncan isn't even doing that, but can simply stay at home and paint, which is splendid. He has gone to London now but comes back tomorrow.

Please write again soon, as I'm sure peace will continue to demor-

---

[2]The belief that Asheham is haunted persists in the neighborhood. Apparently, doors swing open and shut without human assistance. Cf. VW's story "A Haunted House" (1920), reprinted in Susan Dick's *The Complete Shorter Fiction of Virginia Woolf* (New York: Harcourt Brace Jovanovich, 1985).

alise you for some time, and writing to me is much your best employment.

Your
VB

IV-31. To Virginia Woolf

Nov. 22 [1918]   *Charleston*

My Billy,

I see that these woodcuts make almost daily letters necessary. Well, it's a good thing you still think I have some rough eloquence and vigour of style.[1] This letter is mainly on business. First, I send you the caterpillar woodcut (can you make it out?). I have managed to take fairly good prints of it, so you needn't bother about a proof if it is tiresome to send one. Then, I write also to say that if you'd really like me to do any more and think they'd add to the attractiveness of the books (which of course modesty makes me doubt), I'd be delighted to do some. I can do them much more easily now and can do them I expect up till Christmas. Only send me the stories as soon as you can or tell me what to do pictures of. As they needn't be accurate illustrations, I daresay you can tell me what to do if the stories aren't ready yet. (But I'd like to see them.)

Then, I must also tell you that our party has been given up. Mrs B. thinks it would be too difficult to take the children to Asheham. It might pour or freeze and they mightn't be able to get there, etc., which I think is reasonable considering the time of year, so I needn't bother you about that.

You've heard of course that Karin has produced another Judith.[2]

[1] Cf. VW to VB, Tuesday, November 19, 1918, regarding VB's letter-writing ability: "You possess a natural style of considerable eloquence and vigour, as I have told you more than once" (VWLII, 296).
[2] Karin Stephen (née Costelloe) (1889–1953) had married VB's brother Adrian in October 1914. Their first daughter, Ann, was born in January 1916; Judith arrived November 20, 1918. Barbara Bagenal had also named her daughter (born November 8) Judith.

They seem to be very much disappointed. I see girls are the fashion and I suppose I shall follow it too. I daresay it won't much matter. You'll think it more interesting, no doubt, and will give it your blessing. At any rate, I have two sons to console myself with, whereas I suppose the Stephens don't want to have another baby of any kind. Besides of course my daughter *would* be very nice, wouldn't she? I'm very much interested in all the writers' feelings about Peace. Of course the Stracheys are simply ashamed of having any feelings they can give a name to. Desmond's[3] seem most natural, but I see there were some advantages in not being able to join in a crowd.

You must write and tell me of the safe arrival of the [wood]block. I had a charming letter from Snow today, full of affection! Roger said in his last letter that he did not write the most interesting letter he had ever written to me all about his feelings as he knew I should not reply sympathetically. As you were just going to dine with him, no doubt you got the benefit of them. So please write and tell me all about them.

Your
VB

I don't know about papers,[4] but R[oger] will have given you advice.

BERG

IV-32. To Roger Fry

Nov. 29 [1918]   *Charleston, Firle*

My dear Roger,

I am glad I wrote and blew you up for trying to tantalize me, for I did get a most interesting reply out of you. I must tell you that of course your praise of Duncan and his genius did give me *very* great pleasure.[1] You are one of the very few people who can of course really

---

[3]After the armistice, Desmond MacCarthy had wandered London aimlessly and dispiritedly (VWLII, 297–98).
[4]For woodblock printing.
[1]Cf. RF to VB, November 24, 1918 (Tate). He had praised a DG painting called *Hat Shop* (present whereabouts unknown).

appreciate him, although most people he knows do so to some extent, but not all sides of him as you can—and I always feel I can't talk much to you about him. But when you see him alone you can enjoy him and know the extraordinary delight it is to be with someone so alive and creative. Perhaps you appreciate some things in him more than I do, for I think I'm really very dense about this curious fantastic literary thing in his painting. I know what you mean, but it doesn't seem to affect me when I look at his pictures.

Dec. 2. I had to stop writing and I had rather a tiresome day or two, so tired that I couldn't do anything but lie on the sofa. Oh Lord, I shall be so glad when I no longer enclose a baby! I had forgotten how wretched the last bit of the time is, but perhaps it wasn't so bad the two other times. One seems to be nearly always either uncomfortable or with some sort of pain, and lately I've had horrid times of feeling I couldn't breathe, and suffocated, which last an hour or longer and leave one rather exhausted. However, it won't go on much longer now. I dread the actual time, but it will be a mercy to get it over.

We've just had Lytton and Maynard for the weekend, Lytton since Friday, which has made letter-writing impossible. This is very disjointed in consequence, but I hope I shall have a little time now.

I wanted to tell you that though I suppose the past must be different to me from what it is to you, perhaps it's not so much so as you think. At any rate, all that first part of our affair always seems to me one of the most exciting times of my life, for apart from the new excitement about painting, finding for the first time someone whose opinion one cared for, who sympathised with and encouraged one, you know I really was in love with you and felt very intimate with you, and it is one of the most exciting things one can do to get to know another person really well. One can only do so, I think, if one's in love with them, even though it may be true that one's also then deluded about them—as I daresay you *were* about me. But I really loved and admired your character and I still do and I expect that having been in love with you will always make me have a different feeling about you from what I could have had otherwise, in spite of all the difficulties that have happened since. However desperate things seem sometimes, I think I always feel underneath that that is superficial, and that I can depend upon some kind of very fundamental sympathy.

Here are the children, of course.

I have been trying to read Waverley[2] to them but I find it quite

[2]Sir Walter Scott's *Waverley* (1814), his first novel.

impossible, it's so long-winded and roundabout. But I shall try another Scott before I give him up.

I wonder how wrong you were about me! I sometimes think now you don't really like me much, in spite of being still rather in love with me, but perhaps that's untrue. But I think you most likely thought me much more varied in my tastes and interests than I really am. You have got all kinds of intellectual curiosities that I'm without, and if it weren't that you're more excited about art than anything else, I daresay we should have little in common. But that's such a tremendous thing, and then there's all life apart from intellectual interests, and I expect my having read so little, etc., may even make my feelings and views about life and people more interesting to you than if we had more in common intellectually. (Dinner bell)

How amusing and incredible Mrs MacColl's[3] accounts of the cultured world are. Aren't you really at all in love with each other? At any rate, you seem to be having an amusing flirtation. But those old fogies are too much. They're much worse than the Victorians, I think, quite as prudish and with less character. It must be a relief to her to talk to you. It's a good thing perhaps that we managed to shock them so. It must have given them many a happy moment, and 5 years old gossip can't hurt the gossiped about. In 1925 they'll begin to talk about me and Duncan, and you and Nina? Lalla? Pippa? or Mrs MacColl herself.

We had Wolfe[4] here for the weekend. He was *very* nice and appreciative of the paintings we showed him, lots and lots of old things he made us rake out. He was a great contrast to Waley,[5] the only other new artist who has been here. I think [Wolfe]'s got quite definite and genuine taste and is quite honest. He made no pretence to like things he didn't like.

I'm very glad you liked my woodcut. I don't know why, but I thought it was a failure. If you don't want it, perhaps someday you could send back the other.

Would you care to come here next week end when Clive is coming? It would be very nice if you could.

[3]Andrée Desirée Jeanne MacColl (née Zabe) (d. 1945), wife of the painter and art critic D. S. MacColl.
[4]Edward Wolfe (1897–1982), a South African Slade-trained painter, at this time employed at the Omega Workshops.
[5]Hubert Waley (1892–1968), an aspiring artist who later became more interested in films. He was the younger brother of Arthur Waley (1889–1966), the poet and translator.

Please give the enclosed note[6] to Pam and *don't read it* or enclose it to anyone else.

Your
V.

TATE

IV-33. To Virginia Woolf

Dec. 13 [1918]   *Charleston*

My Billy,

It's angelic of you to have the children, and I am really most thankful to you and relieved in my mind about them.[1] I see that it is after all a great thing so to bring up an Ape that he'll come to your rescue in times of need. You know I would do the same by you, should you want it. I will give you directions about them now in case by any chance I shouldn't see you before I am laid low, but it's not very likely. Much more probably I shall be kept waiting weeks as usual.

About milk, they don't really have a great deal, and cocoa made mostly with water they can nearly always have as a substitute. Their hours and meals are: they get up about 8.30, or any time you find convenient. Blow them up if they make a noise before coming down. If Lottie will take them some hot water, they will get themselves washed and dressed. Breakfast usually consists of porridge (with a *little* sugar or treacle) and milk—that's the only time when milk seems rather necessary—a piece of bacon each, and bread and margarine. (Don't give them butter. Keep their butter rations for yourselves. They if anything prefer margarine and it's quite as good for them.) No jam or honey or anything else for breakfast. Lunch at anytime you like, simply what one has oneself, but it's usually very plain here, meat or sometimes fish and a milk pudding and perhaps a plain steamed pudding, or any kind of pudding in fact. Milk puddings are probably impossible for you and are unnecessary.

[6]Regarding VB's Christmas present for RF.
[1]The Woolfs had promised to house Quentin and Julian for a fortnight after the birth of VB's baby.

Tea: bread and honey or jam and margarine (I'll send some honey with them). They drink very little milk at tea generally, and cocoa will do instead. That's all. No supper. Bed at 7. They generally do their washing then. If Lottie or Nelly could keep an eye on them, then they can wash themselves, etc., but it may be an awkward time for them to do so. If so, they could go to bed at 6.30 instead. I daresay with the excitement of being with you, that would be as well. Then they'll be safely in bed by 7 and need not be considered again till the next morning.

Could you give Julian a 5 grain tabloid of bromide in water when he goes to bed? (I'll send some with him.) He has them from time to time and is having them now. And could someone be within ear-shot in case he should call out at night? Sometimes, but very seldom now, he can't get to sleep and then he gets nervous, but I hope he won't. As long as he knows someone would hear, he'll be all right. If this is difficult at Hogarth, perhaps Lottie wouldn't mind just looking in on him after supper, and if he's awake, then going up once more in the course of the evening. Then he'd be quite all right.

They'll be quite contented alone all the morning if they may have pencil and paper and a book or two. You needn't bother about them at all. Any small objects they can pretend are armies, such as peas or beans, or cards, will keep them happy for hours, too. Everything will be new to them and it's good for them to be left to themselves a good deal. Please don't bother about them in the least when you want to write. They're really very independent and have lots of games of their own . . .

As for not paying—it seems to me absurd not to let me, for really I've got lots of money and I shan't have them to pay for here. I wish you would let me. They will make a great difference to your weekly books, as you'll find they've got immense appetites and you're sure to give them delicious new things which will also stimulate their greed. So I really should feel happier if you'd let me contribute £2 a week to their keep.

Please be severe with them if they make too much noise. They're in quite good control at present, thanks to Mrs B., but if they get too much excited you may find them a bore. I hope Leonard won't mind having them, but I think he likes brats and they'll be thrilled by anything he can tell them about his Cingalese adventures.[2] I shall be

[2]Singhalese. LW had been assistant government agent in Hambantota Province (1908–11), Ceylon.

very curious to know what you both think of them when you see them at close quarters.

Do you think you could possibly look out the address of Mrs Lucas (?), the agent, in the telephone directory and send it me on a card? I thought I might write to her about a nurse for the baby. I haven't got one yet, but have only just begun to try seriously. She seemed so ladylike, she might have too genteel servants, but still I suppose she'd be respectable, which may be a good thing in a nurse . . .

You need never be afraid that I suffer from want of mockery. *That* is not my need in life. No. Far from it. I have no room to ask you about Shelley House. What is Shelley House?³ I say it's Elena [Richmond]'s residence, but Duncan says that's impossible. Anyhow, it absolutely fascinates us and we wish it gave a concert every week. Also, you really ought to visit Barbara oftener, to say nothing of all our relations, and it's time you went to see Violet again.

Your
VB

BERG

IV-34. To John Maynard Keynes

Dec. 19 [1918]   *Charleston*

Dearest Maynard,

This is just to say how nice that you'll come after all. It was most disappointing when you couldn't. I do hope I shall be on my legs still, or at least on a sofa, if only for the sake of the turkey and hare.

If Jessie can come by any raisins, currants or sultanas, we might have some kind of Christmas pudding. I can't get more than the minutest quantity here. We'll eat our own ham and you, at any rate,

³Shelley House, No. 1 Chelsea Embankment, the home of St. John Hornby (1867–1947), partner in W. H. Smith & Son, booksellers.

must make merry, whatever tortures I may be undergoing over your heads! But it will be a devil if it spoils my Christmas.

Your
VB

KCC

CHAPTER FIVE

1919–1925

In retrospect, Vanessa felt that Bloomsbury had died with the war. The principal reason was simply geographical dispersion. When wartime laborers like Duncan (and, nominally, Clive) abandoned their hoes and wheelbarrows, they did not easily return to the rhythm of London. Though members and friends of Bloomsbury lived in and around Gordon Square through the 1950s, it was no longer the center of their social lives. Clive, Vanessa, and Duncan spent their summers at Charleston or abroad. The Woolfs lived outside London in Richmond from 1915 to 1924 and at Monk's House, Rodmell, which they had bought in 1919 when they had to leave Asheham. In 1917, Lytton, with the help of friends, had taken on the lease of Mill House at Tidmarsh in Berkshire, where he lived with Carrington. Friends no longer shared each other's lives on a daily basis, but instead were slotted into weekends and holidays. Maynard's affair with the ballerina Lydia Lopokova also threatened the intimacy of the existing group, and when Vanessa argued against his eventual marriage, she was in a sense pleading for the survival of Old Bloomsbury.

In 1920, Vanessa was forced to articulate and defend Bloomsbury values in letters to her old friend Madge Vaughan, who had declined to rent Charleston until she had a serious talk with Vanessa about Angelica's parentage. Needless to say, Charleston was not let to the Vaughans that summer. For practical reasons, Vanessa had told no one outside her circle that Clive was not Angelica's father. The silence on this subject became habitual, then a source of embarrassment, and she put off telling Angelica herself until she was seventeen, unwittingly denying her daughter a truthful relationship with either Clive or Duncan.

During the years covered in this chapter, some lifelong patterns were established. In 1921, Vanessa discovered St. Tropez and the pleasure of leaving dark London winters for the warm and bright Midi, friendly to painters. As a result, she traveled much more frequently to France and Italy, almost always with Duncan. And with the close of the Omega in 1919, she and Duncan began to pursue joint decorative commissions. Included here are a series of letters to Raymond Mortimer, whose room at 6 Gordon Place they decorated in 1925. Her collaborative work with Duncan was an important aspect of their intimacy, replacing sexual closeness, and Vanessa took comfort in their interdependence.

In 1919 Vanessa joined the London Group, exhibiting regularly with them until her death. Her first one-artist exhibition was held in June 1922 at the Independent Gallery.

V-1. To Roger Fry

Feb. 6 [1919]   *Charleston*

My dear Roger,

I'm writing in bed at 8.30, just after breakfast, almost the only moment of the day I get to myself nowadays. I've never known such a time as we've had since you were here—absolute horror and chaos. However, it's clearing up now, at least I hope so. I haven't written a line I could help and yet I've had to write letters whenever I wasn't doing something else, nearly always either about servants or doctors— Lord! Your letters have been a great relief, showing that there was another chaotic world going on outside one's own! I'm afraid you're having rather a horrid time too now if Pam has the flu. I do hope she's better. Give her my love if you're with her, and tell her to get some beads and make some necklaces. It's the greatest fun. I'm just going to begin it, I hope, but last night Julian developed a bad cough which hurts and has been put to bed! So I can't count on it.

We've got a resident doctor[1] though now (I think she'll very likely be ill herself soon—she's got chronic bronchitis which threatens to become acute at any moment!) and the nurse is still here. All the rest of the house has had bad colds and coughs, but, after all, that's one's usual fate in this weather.

The real horror of course was feeling sure the baby was getting worse and not knowing what to do. The nurse, who's of a very worrying and timid disposition, couldn't naturally take the respon-

[1]Dr. Marie Moralt, recommended by Noel Olivier.

sibility alone if I dismissed the Lewes doctor without getting another, and I didn't see how to get another unless one had a specialist from London, which seemed rather absurd and very expensive, as I felt pretty sure that simple things like castor oil and grey powders[2] would cure the baby. They had been suggested to the doctor by both the nurse and me, and out of sheer obstinacy therefore (and fear of its being *our* remedies and not his that cured her) he wouldn't give them. When it got quite desperate I telegraphed to Noel, and she sent Miss Moralt (you know her I think, she patronizes the Omega) and she gave the castor oil and grey powders. The result was immediate improvement which has gone on ever since, though she had got so bad, poor little creature, that it will be some time before she's really right, and she's fearfully small and thin and weighs less than when she was born.

My goodness, I could show up doctors, couldn't I—all this time of anxiety and worry and the risk to the baby, because of the idiocy and obstinacy of that old man.

However, Miss Moralt is I think rather a find, as she's certainly sensible and quite easy to say anything to, which is more than most doctors are. She's a friend of Noel's and would very much like to know Bloomsbury, having never had any cultured friends of her own and longing to talk about Henry James, etc. I don't know how much one could supply that want, but I think *she* might supply the general want of an ordinarily intelligent, sensible general practitioner who'd send one to a specialist when necessary.

Of course there have been awful servant crises too, but now Emily[3] has gone (I must tell you about the final scenes with her some day) and Jenny is a changed creature, very anxious to become a good cook and to please generally (she's acquired a nice young man from Lewes) and is even trying to get me a friend of hers as h[ouse] parlourmaid. I've got a nice woman from Asheham temporarily, so those crises are over for the moment.

If you can do anything about a nurse it would be a blessing as I don't want to be longer than I can help without one.

Mrs B. was really a great blessing. She came in for the thick of the worst crisis, just before Miss Moralt appeared, and was a great help.

[2]A compound of mercury and chalk.
[3]The housemaid Emily Paton was dismissed for stealing. On her last day, VB reluctantly asked Emily to open her suitcase, and had several bars of soap and a pair of Duncan's trousers flung at her.

She's doing the housekeeping and looking after the children and talks to the nurse. You always seem to think I don't appreciate her good qualities, but I do. Only one gets irritated at times with anyone one lives with who has so little really of one's own point of view, as you know.

Do write and tell me what's happening now to you and all your various affairs. I haven't written about them as I wanted to tell you of my own, but I want to hear.

Your
V.

I've just had your letter and will write again soon. Please give my love to Mary. I'm so sorry you're ill too. Everyone is. I have no time to answer you properly now.

V.

TATE

V-2. To Duncan Grant

Monday [June 9, 1919]   *Charleston*

My darling Bear,
    . . . Will you forgive me for opening Ott's letter? It was hardly stuck up and I couldn't resist it. Will *you* resist it? Nothing could be more hellish I should think than meeting Picasso at Garsington,[1] and *I* should find no difficulty in not going to that, but I don't think she means to give you up easily.

Mme. Champco, Hope Johnson, and Mme. C.'s little girl came to tea today.[2] Hope J. had already come on Friday, but I hardly saw him as I had charge of Angelica, Nelly having gone to Brighton for the

[1]Picasso was in London in connection with his work for Diaghilev's Ballet Russe. Lady Ottoline had invited him to Garsington, but he refused since a dinner had been planned for him for that same weekend by CB and JMK.
[2]Elspeth Champcommunal (d. 1976), widow of a French painter killed in the war, and friend of Roger Fry's. She edited British *Vogue* from 1916 to 22. John Hope-Johnstone (1882–1970) was at this time editor of the *Burlington Magazine*.

day. I asked them to come hoping to do business, which I did. She said she'd buy my small still life of the coffee things on the Turkish box, which is a good thing, but no price mentioned. It's awful selling pictures in person. I asked her about hats and she said she'd talk to Mme. Reville,[3] who might take up the idea and push them, otherwise it would be best to get Mary to wear them.

She's not bad, but why when people buy or like one's pictures does one at once think they must be very foolish. Perhaps you don't. I do, and also dislike the picture they buy intensely. Oh Lord, I've been trying to paint my shop picture and it's awful and has got the upper hand of me. I've discovered the subject. Queen Mary and Princess Mary shopping. It's now just like both.

It's very melancholy here with no grown up but La B[rereton]. Henry howls most dismally and is said not to be very well. I have a lunch *en famille*. It seemed inevitable. But I have stuck out about breakfast and tea. How nice it would be if I didn't feel that everyone else in the house, that is Jenny, Nelly[4] and La B. were here against their will and would much rather be elsewhere. This makes it almost intolerable, but perhaps I've got it too much on my nerves. I am also overcome by my own inability to house-keep or dress or do anything that needs cleanliness and care . . .

Angelica is charming. She's getting quite a lot of dark gold hair. I've got some very good photographs of her and the other children which I'll bring up to show you.

Virginia has sent me the Young Visiters [*sic*],[5] which certainly is extraordinarily funny.

She says they've got the house in Lewes.[6]

Good night darling Bear, I wish I could see you now.

Your loving
R.[7]

HENRIETTA GARNETT

[3]Unidentified.
[4]Nellie Brittain, Angelica's nurse.
[5]*The Young Visiters, or Mr. Salteena's Plan* (1919), a children's book written by a nine-year-old girl, Daisy Ashford, with a preface by J. M. Barrie.
[6]The Round House, next to the Castle in the center of Lewes. The Woolfs never lived there, however, since they soon discovered and purchased Monk's House at Rodmell.
[7]For Rodent. She is also sometimes B. for Beaver.

V-3. To Duncan Grant

July 29 [1919]   *Charleston*

My darling Bear,

I think I can't come on Tuesday. I have tried hard to think [how] I could manage it, but I see it would upset too many people. Mrs Pitcher[1] wants to go to Bexhill on Tuesday for the whole day. Nelly wants to go to Eastbourne one day, probably either Tuesday or Wednesday. In any case, it would mean leaving Nelly alone here on Tuesday evening with all 3 children on her hands and her own supper to get. Mrs Pitcher does a great deal, but I have to do a good deal too, or else our fare would be *too* plain. I have to cook puddings for luncheon, cakes for tea and the evening meal for myself and Nelly. Also I have had to listen to endless stories of the horrors Jenny left behind her. In fact she did leave the larder in such a state that I had to spend all yesterday morning cleaning it out preparatory to Mrs P.'s scrubbing it. How I hate these domesticities. I can't conceive what the female mind is made of. Mrs Pitcher, admirable as she is, would very soon drive me wild if I went on seeing much of her with her incessant grumbling at Jenny's faults. It almost makes me want Jenny back again in spite of the dirt and disorder now revealed. Oh dear, how I should like to come and feel myself in a world where such things had their proper insignificant place, but it's not good, I've made up my mind not to.

I haven't been able to paint yet and I don't think I shall be able to much. It's so difficult when one can't settle down to it. This sounds very gloomy. It is impossible I think to get out of the toils of domestic life here until I have been away from it for a bit. One's had such horrors come over one again. Please don't mind my writing to you about it, my dear, though perhaps I oughtn't to.

One other perhaps gloomy subject I must write to you about because I've been thinking and thinking about it—this difficulty with Bunny. His talking didn't make any difference really. I had been worried about it before because it seems so absurd. I'm not going however to go into explanations. I see it would do no good. All I want to tell you is that I think I have behaved very badly and stupidly. I will write

[1]Daily servant.

and tell him so. Not that I want to have an emotional making up, but having thought about it all, I do understand I think why I felt as I did. It wasn't that he was on my nerves or that I was jealous of him. I think I can simply forget about it all and there's no reason for all this bother. I can behave ordinarily and as usual when we meet and I see that if it hadn't been for other bothers I could have done so before. Please don't mind my telling you about it. I think if I could have talked to you I shouldn't have got into such a state.

It's very odd being alone here. La B.'s absence is a great relief. The children are very good and have games of their own most of the time. Angelica is rampant and smiles whenever one looks at her. She's apparently more flourishing than ever on milk and her arm is practically all right again. Her hair is getting long and thick and a lovely colour, whether black or gold one can't say. I think she'll succeed in tantalizing everyone. No one ever had a more ingratiating or contented disposition. She's full of delight now because she can actually spend a great deal of her time sucking her own toes. She crams them into her mouth.

Please write and tell me all about the Picasso, also all about the party, and I want to know what compliments are paid you and by whom, for of course they're rattling on your head, you can't deny it.

My bear, don't be severe with me for writing you a gloomy letter.*
You know I'm really cheerful as a rule.

Your
R.

*Not that I expect you to be.

HENRIETTA GARNETT

V-4. To Margaret Vaughan

Mar. 10 [1920]   *50, Gordon Sq., W.C.1*

My dear Madge,

I got your two letters yesterday.[1] To be honest with you, as I always have been, I was half amused and half furious on reading them. Why on earth should my moral character have anything to do with the question of your taking Charleston or not? I suppose you don't always enquire into your landlords' characters. However, take it or not as you like. If you want it, I am ready to let it to you for 3 weeks from the middle of April as I said at 5 g[uinea]s a week (I think I can secure coal). But please let me know *at once,* if possible, as if you don't want it I think I can let it to someone else.

As for the gossip about me, as to which of course I have not been left in ignorance, I must admit that it seems to me almost incredibly impertinent of you to ask me to satisfy your curiosity about it. I cannot conceive why you think it any business of yours. I am absolutely indifferent to anything the world may say about me, my husband or my children. The only people whose opinion can affect one, the working classes, luckily have the sense for the most part to realise that they can know nothing of one's private life and do not allow their speculations about what one does to interfere with their judgment as to what one is. The middle and upper classes are not so sensible. It does not matter as they have no power over one's life. But it seems to me tragic that you should be of their mind. If you cannot accept me as I seem to you to be, then you must give me up, for I have no intention of confessing my sins or defending my virtues to you. My relations to other people are no concern of yours, nor could you possibly understand them, even if you had greater opportunities of doing so than you can have. I say this because it is evident—it must be so to you too—that our views of life are in many important ways totally opposed to each other.

---

[1]Madge Vaughan was staying at Charleston briefly and had hoped to rent it from Vanessa for a family holiday. On March 7, however, she wrote to Vanessa: "A question gnaws at my poor heart here in this house. It came stabbing my heart that day when I saw Angelica. I would like to meet you as a woman friend face to face at some *quiet place* and to *talk it out.* I don't feel I *could* come and live here with Will and the children unless I had done this" (KCC). She had written a cheerier letter, also dated March 7, which VB received with this one.

This would not prevent me from seeing you with pleasure, talking over many things with you, and even letting you my house. If you, however, cannot live where I have lived without making sure that I am fit to be invited to Buckingham Palace,[2] then it is best to realise that we are too different to see each other profitably.

I could not say more to you if I were to see you, and as I am going abroad on the 18th or 19th I have very little time and a great deal to do in it.

Please let me know as soon as you possibly can about Charleston. If you wish to take it, I will send you details about tradesmen, etc.

Your
VB

KCC

V-5. To Margaret Vaughan

Mar. 16 [1920]   *50, Gordon Sq., W.C.1*

Dearest Madge,

I daresay it was very stupid of me to get so angry with you. The fact that we differ on some important questions shouldn't make one angry. But I think if you tried to put yourself in my place and realise what you would feel if I asked you to talk to me about something that was a most intimate concern of yours and Will's—asked you to do so not because you seemed particularly in need of sympathy or help, but in order to satisfy practical considerations of my own—you would understand.

You say you offered me help, but surely that is not a true account of your motives, for had I shown any slightest sign of wishing for help or needing it? And did not you wish to talk to me really so that you might know what sort of person I was to whose house you proposed to take your children?

That at any rate was the reason you seemed to give me for writing.

[2]This is a quite specific jab. In her first letter of March 7, Madge had proudly described her own visit the previous Thursday to a tea party at Buckingham Palace, where she met the king and queen.

Nor was there even the excuse that Clive and I were known to be on bad terms with each other. In that case (though I should probably not desire it) I could understand an old friend's interference.

But whatever the gossip about us may be, you must know that we see each other and are to all appearance friendly, so it should I think be assumed that we are in agreement on those matters which concern our intimate lives. You say you tell Will everything, although your married life has been full of restraints. What reason is there to think that I do not tell Clive everything? It is perhaps because we neither of us think much of the world's will or opinion, or that a "conventional home" is necessarily a happy or good one, that my married life has not been full of restraints but, on the contrary, full of ease, freedom and complete confidence. Perhaps the peace and strength you talk of can come in other ways than by yielding to the will of the world. It seems to me at any rate rash to assume that it can't, or in fact that there is ever any reason to think that those who force themselves to lead lives according to convention or the will of others are more likely to be "good" (by which I mean to have good or noble feelings) than those who decide to live as seems to them best regardless of other standards.

One cannot judge by such things. No one can doubt surely that the best people have been of both kinds—so why consider such purely outside qualities? At least don't assume that one kind is more likely to be right than the other. The world at large does assume this, and that is why I think its judgments worthless. The longer I live, the more I am convinced of this. As you know, my life has not been free from sorrows and difficulties, perhaps greater ones than most people have to face, and I do not think that if greater still are to come they are likely to change me in this.

Surely everyone who can think at all must have had to come to some conclusion as to what they value most during the last 5 years. It hasn't been possible not to face the question.

Do not think I don't value your affection, if it is for me as I am and not for someone you would like me to be. That at any rate is surely one of the most valuable of all things, and yours for me at least has stood the test of much plain abuse from me!

So goodbye—I am starting for Rome on Friday.

Your
VB

KCC

V-6. To Roger Fry

Mar. 24 [1920]   *Hôtel de Russie, Rome*

My dear Roger,

It's very exciting to be in Italy again! I wish you were here too. I was excited enough at being in Paris, or in fact across the Channel. One is always convinced one must live in France when one gets there. So many things that have to be repressed in one seem to expand and develop when one gets into France again—but will one ever? I only had one crowded day in Paris. Duncan and I walked the streets looking at pictures in the shop windows, also we went in to Guillaume's and saw the large Derain last supper,[1] which seemed to me splendid. We lunched with Rose. Vildrac was in Geneva. Mme. Thiesson[2] was there. I thought her very charming and intelligent and beautiful. She looked rather tragic dressed in black. Rose was more voluble than ever. Lucette[3] was most attractive. We had a delicious lunch. Then we saw their pictures and chose frames for our show. Then we went on to a show of nudes Rose told us about with a magnificent large nude by Matisse, really splendid. There we met [Roderic] O'Conor, who was very friendly. I think his life has been changed by your influence. I bought some clothes and we went to return to Derain some shoes he had left in my flat last year, but he was out. We only saw Alys,[4] who was *souffrante*—with child, it seemed to me—and she couldn't think who we were or why we had come. It was all a most tantalizing rush before we started for Rome and I wished I could stay longer. Then we had to sit up all night in company with a complaining English-woman, but the next night we spent at Genoa and realised we were in Italy.

Here we are in a huge hotel of the kind I don't like. However it has a large garden and Maynard has a quiet room looking on to it. If we can get others that do so it won't matter, as by amazing good luck we have hired a studio. We were told on all hands that none

[1] Paul Guillaume's gallery was in the Faubourg St. Honoré until 1923, then in the Rue de la Boétie. Derain's *Last Supper* dates from 1913 and had been previously exhibited.
[2] The widow of the painter Gaston Thiesson (1882–1920), who had recently died of tuberculosis.
[3] Rose and Charles Vildrac's daughter.
[4] Alice Derain (née Gery.)

were to be got—not even a room of any kind—that it was as bad as Paris or London. But we got into touch with the director of the British Academy, an atrocious sculptor but a very kind little man, who persuaded a *signorina* to turn out of her studio for us. Tomorrow we take possession. It is quite large and light, very quiet, and quite near here, so we can spend all the day there if we like and have models who are very cheap. Also we can go to the British Academy for evening classes! On the whole it looks as if we should do a good deal of painting here.

Today we met Jaggers and Massine[5] in the street. They have just finished their season here and are leaving. No Sitwells[6] yet, thank goodness.

Is Lavelli here?[7]

Please write here. How are you? If you go to see Pippa, look in on Angelica and tell me how she is, also the others. I've had another letter from Madge. She says she's a Christian but that I have better brains than she has! In fact she owns she's half demented. I suppose that's the end of our correspondence. You must give me your address abroad if you want letters there.

Your
V.

TATE

[5]Léonide Fedorovich Massine (1895–1979), Russian dancer and choreographer, associated with Diaghilev's Ballet Russe until about 1928. The sculptor Charles Sargeant Jagger (1885–1934), elected to the Royal Academy in 1926, worked primarily in Rome and Venice.
[6]The famous literary siblings: Edith (1887–1964), Osbert (1892–1969) and Sacheverell (1897–1988). They shared a castle, Montegufoni, in Tuscany, which belonged to their father.
[7]Angela Lavelli, a former lover of RF's.

V-7. To Roger Fry

Ap. 27 [1920]   *I Tatti,*[1] *Settignano, Florence*

My dear Roger,

I wonder if you got my post card telling you we were coming here or if you'll ever get this either. For nearly a fortnight all our letters seem to have been destroyed *en route* to Rome. Now they're arriving again spasmodically. It seems doubtful whether we shall ever get to Paris. They say there's to be a universal strike in France from May 1st onwards, but it may have stopped by the 4th, when we mean to go. I want very much to see the children again, but otherwise I can't say I should mind how long I was kept in Italy.

Not at I Tatti however! We've been here 2 days and Duncan and I are wondering how much longer we can stand it. We hadn't meant to come with Maynard, but only at the end of his visit. However, Mrs B[erenson] wrote to say that B.B. was going to be away at first, and we thought that by coming early we should avoid him. But here he is, and now we are here it's not at all easy to get away again. If we are allowed to go into Florence in the morning by ourselves and return in the evening in time for dinner it's not so bad, as we did today.

Two old friends of yours are here also, yesterday three. The two I have come round to are Bob Trevy and Logan.[2] They are seen to great advantage here, I think. Logan shines because he's really so much nicer than B.B. and it's such a relief to talk to someone one doesn't distrust profoundly *au fond,* and Bob shines because he's kept in great order by Mary B. He hardly opens his mouth and he's well laughed at when he does, and on the whole I see he has a great deal of charm. But your third friend was intolerable, Miss Green, an attachée of

---

[1]Villa of the American art historian and connoisseur Bernard Berenson (1865–1959) and his wife Mary (née Pearsall Smith) (1864–1945). Mary Berenson had two daughters, Rachel and Karin, from her previous marriage to Frank Costelloe. Rachel (called Ray) was the second wife of Oliver Strachey; Karin married Adrian Stephen.
[2]Logan Pearsall Smith (1865–1946), essayist, Mary Berenson's brother. Robert Trevelyan (1872–1951), poet and playwright, educated at Trinity College, Cambridge and elected an Apostle in 1893. He was a close friend of RF's.

Pierpont's,[3] a most blatant American, fulsome in her admiration of Maynard of course, and really too much for my refined tastes. Do you remember her? I suppose not, but she evidently knew you well.

It's really very curious being here. I like Mrs B. She seems to me quite sincere at any rate in her human dealings, not in the least a prude, extraordinarily kind, and very sensible in most ways, and I think she must have had a devil of a time of it with B.B. He is very amusing and I enjoy listening to his talk. If only he were honestly a stockbroker one would be quite at one's ease. As it is, one never quite knows where one is with him. It seems so odd to come here and go to see pictures, which of course excite one enormously and are most important to one, and to know that he's also grubbing away in private at the same kind of thing, and yet to feel that it's a closed subject. He asks one what one has seen out of politeness and sometimes, out of curiosity to see what he'll say, I ask him a question or two, but one knows one's on very thin ice. How absurd it all is. I'm sure he has no more notion of what it is that's important in painting than a flea has. All this terrific business and income has been built up on the shakiest of foundations, but I suppose he's really supported by the stupidity of the rich, which after all is fairly safe ground.

The pictures here are most peculiar for the most part, at least so Duncan and I think. They look like quite good primitives at first, but it's impossible to believe they're even second-rate genuine paintings. Somehow they impress one as shams, got up to deceive. But we may be quite wrong. Of course there are one or two which aren't.

The house is luxurious to a degree—private sitting rooms and bathrooms, comfortable beds, endless servants, huge motors, roses everywhere, chairs, sofas, old furniture in all the bedrooms, all very American I suppose, and one can't help feeling if only they had got in an ordinary Italian workman from the village to tell them what colours to use, how different it would have been. Colour is simply non-existent as it is.

Maynard is a huge success. He has to tell them all about Lloyd George and Mr [Woodrow] Wilson,[4] and at every meal there are nondescript foreigners and millionaires who hang on his lips. I think

---

[3]Miss Green was Bella da Costa Greene, librarian of the Pierpont Morgan Library and a close friend of Bernard Berenson's. For RF's involvement with J. Pierpont Morgan and New York's Metropolitan Museum of Art, see Frances Spalding, *Roger Fry*, 81–106.

[4]JMK's account of the drafting of the Treaty of Versailles, *The Economic Consequences of the Peace* (1919), had made him famous.

he is getting tired of it, and it certainly is a lesson on the advantages of obscurity.

There is great excitement about a Russian copyist who copies old masters in their identical technique. It's really almost uncanny, but I think there can be no doubt they'd prove to be very dead affairs compared to the originals if one spent much time with them.

All the pictures here in the Uffizi and the Pitti have been rearranged very much better. The big Giotto and Cimabue have been brought from the Accademia and hung with the other primitives and look simply splendid, in a very good light. The Titians, etc., have been moved to the Pitti. However you don't want a guide book to the pictures here or a description of them, so I'll only tell you that at present Signorelli has been the greatest excitement, as one has just come from the frescoes at Orvieto and now sees the large paintings here. Also I must tell you that the Pieros at Arezzo[5] have been cleaned since we saw them before and the colour is now incredibly fresh and lovely. It has been very well done evidently and the result is astonishing. One can't make out whether the colour is really cool or warm, it seems to be both and never cold or hot.

Do you really sympathise with me about M[ichel] Angelo? I have only seen one thing of his I really admire. The unfinished Pieta (I suppose?) in the Duomo[6] here does seem to me very fine. I'm very glad I can admire it, as it makes it less likely that I am simply blind or prejudiced about everything else of his. I admit that the Sistine ceiling is pleasant colour as a whole, but it seems to me he must have done it too quickly ever to get through from his original melodramatic starting-point to anything formally interesting. However Duncan, who is always kinder than I am, has a theory that he does suggest some peculiar kind of space by these dramatic methods and probably

Sat., May 1st. I was interrupted here 2 days ago and have been carrying this letter about with me since, terrified lest I should leave it somewhere. I must put it into an envelope quickly and send it off. Since I wrote we have been to see the Castagnos,[7] which I saw before with you. They seem more wonderful than ever. But it's getting an awful strain being here, even going out all day. Yesterday we had to

[5]His frescoes on *The Legend of the True Cross,* in the choir of S. Francesco (c. 1452–65).
[6]Begun c. 1546, this is the Pietà containing Michelangelo's self-portrait as Nicodemus.
[7]Either his frescoes on Christ's Passion for the monastery of Sta. Apollonia or his works at SS. Annunziata, c. 1455.

go and hear some music at a German's called Loese, or some such name.[8] We went because he owns several Cézannes. It was really most interesting suddenly to see a Cézanne after looking at all these Italians. It seemed oddly the same thing, especially one lovely one of nudes in a landscape. There was a wonderful small still life of apples, and other landscapes. B.B. wants to have it both ways. He pretends to admire Cézanne, but at the same time to despise anyone else for doing so. His method is to be very critical of all Cézannes actually visible at the moment, implying that he knows others which really are good. As a matter of fact, some of Loese's were very good, also he had a superb Giotto, or something which he said might be a Giotto, and which certainly seemed good enough, I thought, a madonna and child, part of a larger thing. Loese himself seemed really to like pictures, and had also other quite good things, one last supper said to be an early Greco. It all seemed much more sympathetic than this house.

We are going to start for Paris on Tuesday, but it's doubtful if we shall ever get there, or if you'll ever get this letter, as there's going to be a strike apparently. I hope you'll get good food in spite of it.

I am still having neuritis, which is now said to be a result of in-oculation for typhoid. There seems to be nothing to be done for it, as it's due to a poison which simply has to be got rid of gradually. It's very tiresome.

I hope I shall hear from you soon.

Your
V.

TATE

V-8. To Roger Fry

May 17 [1920]   *50, Gordon Sq.*

My dear Roger,

I have had to steal this gorgeous paper from Maynard. I returned on Friday, thinking I should just miss you in Paris, where you are

[8]RF already knew the American collector Charles Loeser, heir to a Brooklyn department store fortune.

expected any moment. But your letter which followed me here sounds as though you wouldn't return for some time. I saw Tatlock[1] for a moment in the square, and he also seemed to be expecting your return to London almost at once. I suppose however you'll stay away as long as you can. I hope your tooth isn't very bad.

It was dreadful leaving Italy, if it hadn't meant leaving I Tatti too I don't know how we could have done it. Even France isn't the same. I don't think any people are like the Italians. They seem to me to have had art in them more completely than any other European people, for at almost every corner one comes on some colour or proportion which gives one extraordinary pleasure. I don't feel that in France. The buildings seem to me nothing compared to Italian buildings, and the people are certainly less sympathetic outwardly. Still it was a blessing not to come straight to England. My time in Paris was rather spoilt however by absurd diseases. On the train from Pisa to Paris I got most violent earache. I had no drugs with me, so I had to put up with it all night till we could get phenacetin from an English lady in the morning, and had to stand in the *snow* at Modane at 6 AM waiting for passports—in misery! It left me rather shattered and rather deaf, but thank goodness didn't return. Then I got a bad cold and cough and finally started a temperature which came on on alternate nights! Clive thought it was malaria and so did Moralt when she first saw me, but as it's stopped she says it isn't. But I was rather ill most of the time in Paris and unluckily there was a taxi strike and one had to walk miles through the streets, all buses full and the metro like hell.

However, I enjoyed a great deal. Duncan and I went to see Picasso, whom I like very much and find quite easy. He showed us quantities of his latest work and things he is actually at work on, nearly all more or less abstract designs, though I suppose usually suggested by nature. Some were amazingly beautiful. I think all gave one very definite sensations, and he was interested to find out whether they were the ones he wanted to produce. On the whole I think he was pleased by our likings. He also showed us an astonishing painting of 2 nudes, most elaborately finished and rounder and more definite than any Ingres, fearfully good, I thought. Also a very interesting beginning of a portrait of the Emperor and Empress Eugenie and Prince Imperial done from a minute photograph. Also lots of tiny watercolours, many

[1]Robert Tatlock (1889–1954), editor of the *Burlington Magazine* from 1920 to 33.

of them sketches for the curtain for his new ballet, all rejected by Diaghileff, with whom he was furious. He says he will do no more ballets.

We saw Derain only at cafés. I think it's rather a bore the way everyone expects him to live up to his character. It makes it very difficult to be simple with him. We dined with de Segonzac,[2] who was charming of course. No one could help liking him. He started a long account in the extraordinary way French men do of the joys of an artist's life, how foolish were the rich and how simple the pleasures which cost nothing and made an artist perfectly happy, the sort of thing one may agree with but could never manage to say in English. However, by way of variety I insisted upon the miseries, the horrors of letting oneself in for these awful problems and of never being able to do what one always had to go on trying to do. I really agreed with him, but I was rather surprised, as I shouldn't have thought from his painting that he had such an extraordinarily happy disposition as he seems to have.

There was a show of portraits at Cres. If it's still on when you're there do go and see it. There's an early Cézanne of the thick period. The paint is in great slabs, unlike any I had ever seen. It made everything else in the room fall flat, even Picasso's Miss Stein[3] and the Renoirs. It's in very dark colours, but I've never seen such subtle and definite blacks and dark browns. We went to the Louvre, where everything seemed in incredibly bad condition and my latest favourite Guido lost all or nearly all his point. We saw pictures at Alvorsen's and Rosenberg's,[4] but I think a stand ought to be made against dealers. They shouldn't talk about art. They should be content to be shopmen and let one see their wares while they make themselves scarce. I can't bear them. The only tolerable one is Zborowski[5] and I'd rather not see him at the same time as pictures. I think [Percy Moore] Turner is an exception.

I haven't yet done anything in London except attend to domestic

[2]André Dunoyer de Segonzac (1884–1974), a painter educated at the Ecole de Beaux-Arts under Jacques-Emile Blanche. He was a favorite of VB's and is thought to have influenced her style in this period.
[3]Now at the Metropolitan Museum of Art.
[4]Paul Rosenberg's (1881–1959) gallery was in the Rue de la Boétie. Alvorsen may be Walther Halvorsen, Norwegian artist, critic, and collector.
[5]Leopold Zborowski (d. 1932), Polish art dealer. He had assisted Osbert and Sacheverell Sitwell in organizing their 1919 exhibition of modern French art at the Mansard gallery, a show which included work by Modigliani, Zborowski's discovery.

affairs which had been in a fearful state during my absence. My little maid, Mary, had nearly gone off her head owing to the deaths of her mother, father and lover within a fortnight. Then her brother got pneumonia and nearly died.[6] Luckily he's recovering and so is she, but she terrified Sophie and the 46 [Gordon Square] servants by raving wildly all night for 3 weeks till it got so bad that Moralt had to take her to the infirmary. There she has recovered and is to return to-morrow. I don't think her state was to be wondered at. I have seen her and she is now most sensible, and anxious to return.

I found Julian very lonely without Quentin, who's at Wittering, and fearfully pleased to see me. Angelica knew me quite well and is as lovely and flirtatious and charming as ever, and trots about rapidly but rather unsteadily—a most alarming age.

James and Alix[7] are to be married, as he wants to go to Vienna to be psycho-analysed by Freud and thinks marriage will facilitate passports. Moralt has a serious affair on with a doctor and wants to set up house with him but can't find one. He's already married unluckily. That's all my news I think. Please write.

Your
V.

TATE

V-9. To Roger Fry

Monday [May 16, 1921]   *Hôtel de Londres [3, Rue Bonaparte,*
Paris]

My dear Roger,

I was so glad of your letter. It's terrible how unlucky I am when I go abroad, but this time I recovered very quickly thanks partly to the

[6]VB later wrote a Memoir Club paper (edited by Olivier Bell and published in the *Charleston Magazine*, no. 3, 1991) on "Mad Mary," who had fabricated these family tragedies and eventually bolted from Gordon Square. In June she was captured and taken to the St. Pancras Infirmary.
[7]Alix Sargent Florence (1892–1973), educated at Newnham College, accompanied James Strachey to Vienna after their marriage and also underwent analysis, at that time one of the few prerequisites to becoming a psychoanalyst. In 1926 they set up practice together at 41 Gordon Square.

many strong French drugs Duncan produced and partly to the fact that I simply had to go out to get enough to eat. They were very nice here, but evidently couldn't produce more than soup or eggs. I am all right again now. Duncan and I have spent a good deal of time sketching on the quais where I see one could go on finding new things indefinitely. The Zborowskis have lent us two rooms, very small, but light, high up, in their house, but it's so far off that we haven't used them yet. It seems more sensible to paint out of doors, at any rate while it's fine. Today however it's cold and raining and everything is shut. It's worse than a London Bank Holiday. We have been round to see Clive and found him at 10 AM just having been woken up. He had been up till 5 with Ansermet,[1] Derain, and a lot of others, drinking and talking. He does so nearly every night I think and seems none the worse for it. How the others manage to combine it with work I cannot think, but they evidently do. I suppose it's very amusing, certainly Derain can be charming and is worth listening to. But they never mention painting, which makes it less interesting than it might be from one's own point of view.

We met André Salmon[2] the other night whom I though very charming and amusing. He told endless stories about everyone. Kisling[3] was there too, and Mme. Salmon, who seemed to me tiresome. Clive's life is evidently complicated to a degree. Mary is on the scenes a good deal, but seems rather *triste*. I expect she finds it difficult to combine Clive and Jack, and I gather that Clive has got into trouble with the English contingent by saying that they were the riff-raff of the Eiffel Tower. The last complication is that Juana[4] has arrived at the Ritz! I think it's very likely that this will be the end of that affair. Evidently she couldn't combine with Clive's other companions and he has only called on her once and found her out. I suspect she will be furious, as she must have come here simply to see him. I don't believe he had given her a thought since he came here.

We went yesterday to see the Dutch show [at the Orangerie]. The Vermeers are simply amazing. There's a wonderful landscape, as fresh as if it had been just painted, with houses with dark blue roofs and

[1] Ernest Ansermet (1883–1969), Swiss conductor, associated for several years with Diaghilev's Ballet Russe. He founded the Orchestre de la Suisse-Romande at Geneva in 1918. A friend of RF's.
[2] The writer (1881–1969). Later Paris correspondent for *Apollo Magazine*.
[3] Moïse Kisling (1891–1953), French painter and graphic artist.
[4] Juana Gandarillas, a young Chilean woman with whom CB was having a brief affair.

water and a great deal of sky, and there's the head of a girl with the blue head-dress, and another lovely one of a woman at a table against a white wall. I suppose you know them all. Then there are a great many Rembrandts. The anatomy lesson with the corpse foreshortened, which I have always wanted to see. The colour is more lovely than one could imagine. There's an astonishing one of dead peacocks and several very fine portraits. There are also a great many splendid drawings. But it was so crowded it was with the greatest difficulty one could see anything.

We have also been to see the 19th century French pictures at the Louvre, where we met Simon Bussy. They were on the way to England and we lunched with them at Miss Lloyd's.[5] Dorothy is still here and we shall see her again.

Do you know I have become an admirer of Delacroix? I went to see the large decorations at St. Sulpice,[6] which I thought very fine. What do you think of them? They seem to me most interesting design and colour and I begin to understand why he must have excited other painters at that time, for the colour is so unlike all the people just before. I think it does suggest the beginning of quite a new range of colour.

I had never seen the large Courbet atelier[7] before. I don't see how all the part to the left can be taken in with the rest, but it is wonderful painting and colour, isn't it. Also one can now see his large *enterrement* properly and I think it's very fine design, too. But I expect you're rather bored by all my remarks on pictures you know quite well. I wish you were here to go and see things with.

Did I tell you about the exhibition of nudes at Bernheim's? There's a Derain which is simply superb, a woman painted almost entirely in burnt sienna, black and white I should think, rather large. There are also some very odd pastels by him, some Matisses which seemed to me too cheap and pretty, a lovely Courbet, and some Renoirs. We haven't yet been to any other dealers. The Vildracs are away. There's a show at their place of one of their usual rather second-rate painters whose names I can't remember.

Do tell me what the rest of the pictures at the Nameless Show[8] are

[5]Constance Lloyd, the painter, resident in Paris.
[6]Late paintings (1853–61) in the Chapelle des Anges.
[7]Both this painting and his *Enterrement à Ornans* are now in the collections of the Musée d'Orsay.
[8]Organized by RF at the Alpine Club Gallery.

like. Did you let in anything by Carrington or Brett?[9] You will have to tell me what you really think about this question of Duncan's and my work being so alike. There seem to me to be two things, one is worth attending to and the other perhaps not. I mean that most people are so stupid that if any two painters paint the same subject they wouldn't know their work apart. It's very tiresome, but I don't think one can help it, except by not painting the same subjects. It's a great bore often as it's so economical to share models, and if one uses the same studio it's difficult not to have the same objects in still lives [*sic*], etc. But the more important question is whether we really do have a bad effect on each other, or rather whether he does on me. My effect on him doesn't seem to count for much. I don't understand Tonks, for surely no one could think Duncan had painted the Visit[10] who knew his work at all. Nor should I have thought I could possibly have painted the standing women without being almost an imitator of his. I hear by the way that Desmond got practically every picture right! Please write again.

Your
V.

TATE

V-10. **To Roger Fry**

Wednesday [May 25, 1921] *Hôtel de Londres [3, Rue Bonaparte Paris]*

My dear Roger,

Thank you ever so much for your letter about the children. It was good of you to go and look after Julian. I feel safe with you at hand as I know you would do anything that was necessary and would let me know. How odd. I don't think I know anyone else I should feel so safe with—certainly none of my relations! not Virginia nor the

[9]Dorothy Brett (1883–1977), a Slade-trained painter. In 1924 she emigrated with Frieda and D. H. Lawrence to the artists' colony at Taos, New Mexico.
[10]Probably *A Conversation* (1913–16), now at the Courtauld. See plate vii, top.

Stephens. I am coming back on Saturday as I shall have used up all my money by then, and Clive goes back tomorrow, Thursday. From what you say there doesn't seem to be any need to return sooner, but of course if you thought it a good thing I would return at once. I only stay because one always leaves so much to be done at the last. We have to go to see the Vildracs at Valmondois on Friday. I saw Rose the other day and she rather staggered me! She shouted at me in a loud shrill voice and seemed so efficient and sharp. It would be awful to have her in the house. But I suppose she makes money.

I shall see you very soon and we shall be able to talk about all the things I would otherwise write about. The Picasso show is one of the most exciting. We went to the Private View and as we were rather early we could see the pictures at first. The two large female figures which I suppose you saw, a huge thing, seemed to me splendid. There were several other very exciting works, but in a short time the social situation became so acute that one couldn't continue to give much attention to art. Juana arrived with her aunt-in-law Mme. Arazerus (?), very charming but a little cross I thought at not having seen Clive at all. Then in came Jack and Mary and Clive! Mary was obviously very much upset at Juana's appearance, but that is the only time Clive has seen her. I had a long walk and talk with him one night when Duncan had to go to the theatre. He put me *au courant* of his affairs, and I think the Juana affair is on its last legs and that Mary will probably triumph after all. He admitted to me that he couldn't talk to Juana for long, she was really too stupid, and apparently Mary's other affair, the mysterious man she fell in love with and who didn't return it, whom I suspect of being Earp,[1] but I don't know, is the only thing that really prevents Clive from returning to her. It seems odd, but he can't get over that. Perhaps he will in time and then I daresay their affair will revive. Certainly when she was here she saw a great deal of him and was constantly going about with him. However I will tell you all the details when I see you.

We have been to see Moucha[2] twice. She has moved to quite a nice flat in a new building, where she seemed to think she would be able to paint after her baby has been born, as it's quite a good north light, high up. She was very charming and very lovely, and seemed in good spirits, perhaps because her husband has suddenly had to depart to America for an indefinite time on "spiritual business"!

[1]The writer Thomas Wade Earp (1882–1958), art critic for the *Daily Telegraph* from 1935 to 1958.
[2]Dolores Courtney, born in Russia, formerly an Omega artist.

The Zborowskis have told me of a house at a place near St. Tropez. I can't remember the name, but it's a small town or village on the sea, where Kisling had a villa last year. They think I could get it for about 200 francs a month, furnished with all one wants, a large garden shut in, no mistral. It sounds perfect, and I am thinking of writing about it at once and trying to get it from October to January. I wonder if you would come for some of the time. That is when London is so black, I think worse than after Christmas. It seems to be almost impossible to get a studio here, and unless one could do so one couldn't spend any length of time here in the winter happily.

We dined last night with the Derains, Bracque and Mme., and Satie[3] and others more or less unknown, and sat till 2 AM outside Lipps[4] talking in the end only to the Derains. All the others went. It was very hot and got delicious at that hour. Derain was perfectly charming and so was she. In fact the more I see of her the more I like her and the more am I overcome by her beauty. I think she's one of the most astonishing people I've ever met and less terrifying than she was at first. He had had a visit from Wyndham Lewis who's here. He went to him with an introduction from Kahnweiler. Derain himself wouldn't say very much about it except that he made it clear that he had disliked him very much, but according partly to him and partly to Alice, Lewis had first of all abused Clive, when Derain shut him up, then you, when apparently Derain said he didn't wish to continue the conversation and more or less showed him out. Lewis tried to pump him about the tendencies of modern art, but Derain said he knew nothing about them. Wasn't it inconceivably stupid of Lewis to try to get hold of Derain in such a way?

Well, I must tell you other things when I see you. I suppose you couldn't come to supper at 46 on Sunday, could you? It would be very nice if you could. You can telephone or send me a line there. I shall get back on Saturday afternoon.

It's very nice of you—all of you—to let the children come to you. I hope they aren't *too* messy. Please thank Margery very much from me for having them. They are nice creatures, I know—I admit I think them almost the nicest creatures on earth—but still they aren't very clean or tidy and other people can't be expected to see through the outer dirt all at once. I expect Quentin was very happy if you let him grub about with the fountain. He's getting so independent now he'll soon make his way to you alone if you encourage him.

[3]Erik Satie (1866–1925), French composer and pianist.
[4]Brasserie Lipp, Boulevard St. Germain.

I haven't seen the Times, but I'm very anxious to read your lecture[5] and hear more about it. When you're 70 the British Public will be at your feet and you'll be able to kick them nicely.

Your
V.

TATE

V-11. To Duncan Grant

Aug. 3 [1921]   *Charleston, Firle, Sussex*

I don't know if this letter will ever get to you as I have had no card giving me your address. Perhaps Grace[1] will bring it. This is much the nicest place in England, there's no doubt. We had an easy journey once we got off, though I felt as if I had left hundreds of things undone. Angelica was on the look out for us, looking most charming and very grown up. I think she's getting tall very quickly. The others are said to have been very well behaved. They look very well and are in huge spirits. Julian thank goodness is so keen about his butterflies that he walks off to Firle to get treacling materials alone and seems much less at a loose end than last year.

The house was in fairly good order. It's nonsense to say it's getting into a bad state. As far as I can see, nothing has gone wrong of any importance. The garden is dried up of course but there are masses of artichokes in flower and hollyhocks as tall as the apple trees and there have been lots of canterbury bells and columbines. There are potatoes, but not much else in the way of vegetables, and quite a lot of apples on some trees.

The chief horror is that some devils have thrown stones and smashed several panes in the studio skylight.[2] It doesn't much matter while it's

[5] RF delivered a lecture to the Royal Institute of British Architects on May 19, later published as "Architectural Heresies of a Painter."
[1] Grace Germany (1904–1983), a Norfolk girl, came to work for VB on the latter's birthday, May 30, in 1920, and was to be her principal domestic for the next forty years.
[2] The studio at this time was an old army hut; the present studio was not added to the house until 1925.

fine, and I think perhaps we can put an old frame over the broken part, but I shall wait till you come. Otherwise it's not in bad order.

I have been unpacking and setting things straight generally. I am rather astonished on coming here again to find how much energy we spent on this place, how many tables and chairs and doors we painted and how many colour schemes we invented. Considering what a struggle it was to exist here at all, I can't think how we had so much surplus energy. It is all still almost too full of associations for me, I suppose because one doesn't have much ordinary life here to obliterate them, for I don't have at all the same feelings about Gordon Sq., though I might. But also a great deal was crammed into a very short time here. I feel as if I were drowning and rapidly reviewing the different scenes! The first icy cold winter with Mabel and the Zany, Trissie, Miss Edwards [governess], La B., Emily, Jennie, horror on horror, till it really seems incredible that one should be sane and sound with Angelica running about and talking sense. I found some drawings of yours of her when she was practically a skeleton which reminded me of the chief horrors. But it will be simply too awful if one has to leave it all. I think if we do I shall really try for a house at Dieppe.

I do hope I shall hear from you how you get on with the Stephens.[3] Please don't forget about Miss Stephen and Mrs Goosens [unidentified]. Also if you can will you take a measurement of the size of the panels in Maynard's room, of the width of the yellow border and of the size the head should be. *Also* could you notice whether the background should be raw or burnt umber. I think they're alternately either.

I hope you won't be cross with me for letting Nellie go on her holiday on Saturday. She particularly wanted to see a cousin, but really I am *quite* well now and Grace will do all that's wanted. Maynard will be very much upset, as I am too rather, to find that Blanche's young man Barn is here, at the Barley Mow, and spends most of his time here. I don't see what to do as one can't treat Blanche like an ordinary servant. I'm afraid President Wilson[4] is coming too with Grace, so the children tell me. But Quentin says Blanche certainly isn't in love with Barn and that he's very useful to them as he brings sweets and can also get them rum and ale for sugaring. Perhaps however Maynard will put his foot down. I don't feel I can.

[3]VB and DG were decorating Adrian and Karin Stephen's rooms at 50 Gordon Square. But VB may also have been referring to her Stephen cousins, resident in Cambridge, since she and DG were currently engaged in decorating JMK's room at King's College, Cambridge, with eight allegorical figures.
[4]Possibly a passing attraction of Grace's.

I do hope you'll come on Saturday. It's very nice here you know, and it's very lovely now, all pale brown. There's too much wind, a scirocco, but it gets cold at night.

The peach tree is covered with peaches.

Goodbye,
Your
VB

If it's not too difficult, will you bring Aunt Julia's portrait,[5] but not if it means missing a train.

HENRIETTA GARNETT

V-12. To Clive Bell

Oct. 12 [1921]   *La Maison Blanche,*[1] *St. Tropez*

Dearest Clive,

In the chaos yesterday I couldn't send you a telegram, but I'm doing so this morning. I am still astonished to find ourselves all safely here, with all our luggage too except one package of stretchers of Duncan's. I must tell you about the journey first. The crossing was perfect, the only *contretemps* was that the people at Newhaven insisted on my registering some of the luggage, and told me I should have to re-register it at Dieppe (because I'd only taken tickets to Dieppe) and that I certainly shouldn't have time to get it out at Paris. We sat on deck in the sun having got on board before the rest of the world and ate our lunch. The sailors were French and Grace and Nellie simply turned tail when anyone addressed them in French. At Dieppe I got the luggage re-registered and through the *douane,* so that in Paris I didn't have a *douane,* and when we got there, with a friendly porter's help, we fished it out of the van and got to the Gare de Lyon half an hour before the train went. Our arrival in Paris was thrilling. You

[5]Julia Margaret Cameron's photograph of VB's mother, from which she hoped to paint a portrait. She also painted from this or another Cameron photograph of her mother during the Second World War.
[1]Rose Vildrac's villa, which VB rented from October to January.

will be sorry you missed Quentin's first sight of Paris. He and I stood in the corridor to see it and he told me he was most anxious to see what it was like as he expected to live there some day. He was wild with excitement, taking in everything with eyes staring out of his head, especially as we crossed the Seine, which did look most lovely. He thought all the colours so different from England, though it was dark and there was not much to be seen but coloured lights. Driving through the streets was a huge excitement to everyone—the cafés especially seemed to them so odd and all the sights one doesn't notice oneself now. It is really great fun as I knew it would be taking them abroad for the first time. At the station we met Duncan, who had deposited little [Edward] Wolfe in our carriage to keep the places. He had got them with the greatest difficulty in some round about way, and there were two English females in with us, so no one could lie down but Angelica, who lay across my knees and Nellie's. The state of the carriage eventually was indescribable, especially as Quentin had come by a pillow which leaked and masses of feathers were added to the other debris. The English ladies were good tempered luckily and saw that Quentin was a comic character and that we were altogether eccentric but harmless. I can't say I slept much, but the children were wonderfully well behaved and slept quite a lot. At one moment I found myself with Angelica's, Quentin's and Grace's heads all meeting practically on my lap, with bodies stretching in all directions.

At Avignon we dashed out, Duncan, the two boys and I, and got coffee and delicious rolls and butter sitting down for ourselves and brought back hot milk and rolls for the others. As soon as they see children, the French are angelic and make way for one and help one everywhere. We made everyone smile, but in a friendly way. There was no change till we got to St. Raphael, where we were caught napping. At least Duncan was sound asleep. Angelica had just gone to sleep in my arms, making me helpless, and the others were all helplessly involved in masses of small objects! With great difficulty most was got out, the guard came and raged, the train was held up, to my great relief Roger appeared in the distance, dressed in blue linen trousers and sandshoes, brown and beaming, and somehow or other all our belongings were tumbled onto the platform and Duncan was got out of the train as it moved off. Then we went to a café and had food and then went on by another little train and changed again into a sort of tram and finally arrived at about 5, and had to walk a mile up a dusty road. We were dirtier than you can conceive, even Angelica like a little gutter child, and hot and exhausted but in huge spirits on the whole.

As for this house, it is simply a *bijou* residence, but really extraordinarily nice. The rooms are large and light, all brand new and spotless, but very practical, with tiled floors. I think we shall fit in very well. Roger is not in the annexe but has managed to get a whole house to himself somewhere. He has dozens of friends here of course and although he says he has been having congestion of the lungs, it seems to have been merely an excuse for making friends with a priest who reads all the latest French writers. He looks very well and is obviously perfectly happy.

We slept like logs last night in comfortable beds. Today we have had to tackle our French cook, who is very capable and nice and I think a good cook. We have just had a delicious lunch on the terrace under a tree. The children are perfectly happy and quite rested and are busy catching butterflies. Roger's landlord, who is according to him very nice and also reads all the latest authors, is anxious to teach them French and Latin and anything else! I am to arrange with him to have them every morning and apparently he will be content with a small sum in return.

The children, Julian at least, has to come to the help of Grace with French with the *bonne*. I leave them to struggle as far as I can and hear "Julian, what is a chicken?" *"Poule."* "What is, where are the chickens?" *"Ou est les poules."* Then I tell him to say *sont* instead, and I expect they will soon pick up quite a lot. Grace is anxious to learn.

There is quite a large garden, and another small house in it with the *metayers*[2] living there, where I expect you could have the bedroom Roger doesn't use. Then there are vineyards all round. We are high up and look over the town and across the bay. The sea is very blue and today the weather [is] perfect and really not hotter than England a good deal. I think you will have to come here. It's a most sympathetic place, with everything very simple, and as soon as we have got charcoal for the kitchen stove and one or two other things to make life easy I expect we shall settle down most contentedly.

There is a lovely little Derain here, otherwise some Vlamincks, Camoins, Oeltmanns, etc., and one very nice Friesz.[3]

[2]The Santuccis, tenant farmers.
[3]Charles Camoin (1876–1965) studied at the Paris Academy (along with Matisse and Simon Bussy) under Gustave Moreau. He exhibited with the Fauves but was later more influenced by Renoir. The painter Othon Friesz (1879–1949). Oeltmann is unidentified.

Quentin looks quite acclimatised already in his blue linens. Manguin[4] lives here, also Signac,[5] and there seems to be a large floating population of other painters, but I think most of them have gone now. We are to dine with Roger at his restaurant *en ville* tonight and are all to meet him at the bathing place at 4 and have tea with him afterwards. I must say it all seems to me very much nicer and more sensible than going back to London, even in the weather I suppose you to be having there now.

I must now get ready to go to the bathing place. It's so hot that we shall go slowly. It's delicious to be in the south—one forgets how nice it is—all the colours and the light and space and everything looking so baked through—not that one didn't have that at Charleston, but by the end of October you will I hope be ready to leave the cold north. I hope my next letter won't give a blacker picture!

Your
VB

TATE

V-13. To John Maynard Keynes

Saturday [November 1921] *La Maison Blanche,*
Rte. de Ste. Anne, St. Tropez

Dearest Maynard,

Before I tell you of my doings, I am going to ask you if you could do a very tiresome job when you are next in London, which is to find out whether the [Army & Navy] Stores would send us a box of provisions. If so, could you order them and let me pay you for them? I find it rather difficult to feed the family in some ways, as there is very little variety here and on the whole things are rather expensive. What we want most of all are jam and oatmeal. If possible, would you order 10 7-lb. *tins* of jam or marmalade, and either 1 doz. pkts or its equivalent in a bag or sack of Quaker oats or rolled oats, 4 lbs.

[4] The painter Henri Charles Manguin (1874–1949).
[5] The painter Paul Signac (1863–1935), much influenced by the Neo-Impressionists. President of the Société des Artistes Indépendants from 1905 to his death.

of China Tea, 3 pkts of Cook's Egg powder, and some potted meat in whatever may be the most practical form for sending it. If they can do this without its being absurdly expensive to send, it would be a great help to housekeeping. St. Tropez is the station. Perhaps Blanche could do it all by telephone.

You'll have heard that we arrived safely, a most dirty and bedraggled party, but still all safe and sound. I felt as if I had been very clever when we all got actually into this house, got the beds made and the children into them and sat down to our first meal. But Duncan and Roger were equally responsible for the triumph really. Duncan got us places in the train from Paris and Roger had food and a fire waiting here. The house is a marvel of practical French arrangement. I rather envy its cleanliness for Charleston. All the floors are tiled and the furniture new and there are piles of linen in perfect order and every kind of cooking utensil all spotless and lots of china and glass and knives and forks—only—not a po in the house![1] One has to descend always to the lav on the ground floor, and I am wondering whether Rose would be offended if I got some for her. I think she would.

Roger is as full of energy as ever, although he says he has just had congestion of the lungs and has indigestion. But he thought he was at death's door because he could hardly walk when his lung disease was at its worst, and he is obviously in the pink of health and spirits. The first day after we arrived he simply insisted on our having tea with him, walking miles to bathe and shop and dining with him at his pet restaurant. We got back here at about 11 to find the children wide awake, terrified at being left in a strange house alone with the servants. I hadn't had a moment to unpack or anything and *never* have I felt so tired! However I have survived his first onslaughts, which are mingled with lectures on how I ought to rest of course, and except for a return of monthlies, brought on I think by bathing probably, I am all right and intend to resist all efforts to make me climb mountains and walk miles across country, bathing and painting after each 10 miles or so. It is really amazingly beautiful here and I have never seen the children so happy. They bathe in hot sea and catch butterflies and

[1]Despite improved indoor sanitation, chamber pots were still common in bedrooms, especially attic rooms far from a W.C. Olivier Bell remembers that on her first visit to Charleston, in 1950, "there was a painted washstand in the spare bedroom, and Grace would come in with a jug of hot water each morning. In the cupboard beneath the basin was a po and a slop-pail . . . The po, decorated by Duncan, had a disconcerting eye staring up from its bottom" (personal letter, November 2, 1992).

we feed out of doors. The housekeeping is now organized, only a little difficult on account of want of variety, and the fact that shops don't send. I make our French *bonne* get nearly everything on her way here in the morning, but of course one runs out of things and then one has to go to the town to get them and it's quite a climb up to this house, which is about 20 minutes walk up from the port. There are lovely sailors and half-naked youths about everywhere. I think Duncan is very happy and likes the life and is interested at beginning to paint here. There's a colony of painters, one very nice Pole who's said to be good, and others not so nice.

I have got a remarkable French woman who's going to begin teaching the children on Monday and then I hope we shall be really established.

I suppose the weather's bound to change soon. Even if it does, however, it's sure to be light, and Duncan and I each have a large room in which to paint with a very good north light.

I wish you were here. I do think so far it's a great success and I am very glad I made the effort to come. Only how absurd it seems that other people can't come too. I got a Times you sent, but otherwise have had no news of any kind since we left. Are you making or losing money? You are plunged into your beloved Cambridge of course and no doubt you're perfectly happy. Please give my love to Sebastian[2] and give him a photograph of himself from me. I meant to write and thank him for all his efforts with the children. Are there any new beauties or geniuses on the horizon?

Will you tell Sheppard[3] who sent me another wild letter about his clothes that we must really apply to Blanche direct? I can't do anything about it from here and accept no responsibility for anything that may have happened to any dark blue or other suits.

Goodbye.

Your loving
VB

Did I tell you I had a visit from Mr Stacey who said he had never written because Lord Gage hadn't made up his mind whether he was

[2]W. J. H. (Sebastian) Sprott (1897–1971), then at Clare College, Cambridge; an Apostle, and greatly influenced by JMK.
[3]J. T. Sheppard (1881–1968), a classics scholar of King's College, Cambridge, of which he eventually became provost (1933–54); elected an Apostle in 1902, the same year as Lytton Strachey. He lived for several years at 46 Gordon Square and was a close friend of JMK's.

going to farm Charleston himself or not next year. It would be settled on the 11th and he would then let me know. He said in any case we could stay in, as Lord G. won't want the house.

KCC

V-14. To Clive Bell

Nov. 21 [1921]   *La Maison Blanche [St. Tropez]*

Dearest Clive,

. . . Roger left for Paris today. You will soon no doubt have to see his works unless he leaves them all in Paris. I hope you will be as appreciative as you can, as he is really in rather a bitter state about the lack of appreciation he gets in England, most of which I gather he puts down to you and me. We have had one or two rather painful moments when I have been simply driven into a corner about his painting. Do what I will, he sees I don't like it, and now that he's such a success, a *sociétaire* of the autumn salon and all the rest of it, he seems only to resent more the fact that I can't show any pleasure in his works. When one is actually here in the midst of the country he paints it's even more difficult I think than in England to like what he does. He does manage to reduce it all to such a dead drab affair. He assures me that he knows he has really got hold of something, that he has made much more progress than either Duncan or I in the last few years, that he gets plenty of praise and sympathy from the French, and yet he's not satisfied. I begin to think that finally there'll be nothing for it but to tell him the truth. Prevarication is becoming too painful and unsuccessful. But I managed to avoid it this time.

Have you settled about America? If you take Clutton's place [at the *Times*] for a time will it make any difference to your meeting us in Paris in January? But I hope Clutton hasn't got cancer, though it sounds bad.

I have just got Julian's exam papers for Leighton Park.[1] I don't think he'll be able to do much of the Latin, but I suppose it won't matter. We shall have to spend two solid days at them and Quentin

[1] In January 1922 he was sent as a boarder to Leighton Park School, near Reading.

will have to go alone to La Bouvet.[2] She reduces him to a condition of blank obstinacy and he her to helpless fury, but all the same I think he is learning some French. I would send him elsewhere if I could, but it's not easy to find anyone else and I don't know that they'd be any better. She's evidently very stupid with him and in love with Julian, who plays up to her like anything, but it can't be helped, I'm afraid.

Today has been blazing sunshine and no wind. We have been out painting all day. When the wind blows, it's absolute hell, every pane of glass rattles and one can't go out, but even then it's light and really days like today are almost incredible at the end of November. I am getting more and more sure that one must live in France. I don't know about you writers, but for a painter, even being here is quite different from England. It's difficult to explain why, but the whole attitude towards art is so different and affects one subconsciously, and of course it is much more so in Paris. I see one will drift into it more and more.

Have you really allowed V[irginia] and M[ary] to meet again? Isn't it rash? I hear they're going to tea with each other too, or have been by now.

Do send me more London news. Mr Taylor[3] is my only informant. He tells me of the ballet and the exhibitions and says he means to spend £35 on me soon. But I should like other news. As for Paris, you told me nothing.

Give my love to all my friends.

Your
VB

TATE

V-15. To John Maynard Keynes

Dec. 17 [1921]   *La Maison Blanche [St. Tropez]*

My dearest Maynard,
    It was very nice to get more than a tiny scrap from you at last. I'm

[2] A former nun who tutored the Bell boys in French. The exam papers were presumably Entrance Exams.
[3] The rich elderly collector and amateur painter Walter Taylor (1875–1943).

glad it is drink and not work that is affecting your handwriting, but in that case I think you might find more time for un-business letters. I am alone here at the moment, with the children of course, Duncan having gone off yesterday on a little tour to Toulon, Marseilles and the neighbourhood, and then on to the Bussys. I myself have just returned from visits to them and the Raverats. The R.'s are rather a melancholy household. He is now a complete cripple. He can't walk a step but has to be carried everywhere by Gwen and a servant. Also the disease is affecting his arms and hands. He can still paint but can't write much. Gwen in consequence has to dress and undress him, write his letters, move him about, and do anything that means a movement of any kind, practically. At one moment she also had to look after a donkey and cart that lived an hour's walk away and the two children. Then she had to look after a motor. Now she is in comparative luxury with an austere but open minded Swede to look after the children and a chauffeur for the car. She still has Jacques in hand, but they both manage all the same to produce quantities of woodcuts and oil paintings of a most depressing kind. One can only admire them for doing anything but bemoan their lot, and be as appreciative as one can bring oneself to be. They are very nice, both of them. Gwen has all the incredible Darwin virtues. Vence, where they live, is a lovely place, a little too mountainous for my liking. I went on to the Bussys' and enjoyed seeing them in their little toy house in that extraordinary pastry cook's country. It was almost too fantastic to be real, and was made more so by the amazing Zoo that now exists in Simon's studio, the result of all his months of work at the real Zoo. His painting is now very intriguing and I think there is a great deal to be said for it, though I daresay the cultured world in London will hate it. It was amusing to see a little of the Côte d'Azur, which I loathe but am fascinated by. On the whole I think this place is far more beautiful and better to paint than any I have seen, so we were lucky to come here.

Two boxes of stores came—no tea in either—and enough jam to keep anyone but Quentin going for years. As it is, I don't think we shall use the golden syrup because I brought back a tin of honey from my travels, the most delicious I have ever eaten.

My plans depend slightly on Clive's, and I don't yet know his. But I have now heard from Rose that they are coming here on Jan. 4th. As they will be practically living in this house, I think we shall leave soon after—this is about the 7th, getting to Paris on the 8th. I shall send the family back on about the 11th or 12th if you can take them in at 46. Julian will be going to Leighton Park on the 19th, so he would have a week in which to get his outfit. I don't know what I shall do after that, but anyhow Duncan and I shall spend a short time, 2 or 3 weeks, in Paris. After that he suggests our coming south again, so as to put off returning to London till about the end of February, when one may hope it will be really lighter, but I don't know if that would be possible for me. It certainly wouldn't if Clive went to America, and in any case I am rather doubtful about it. But the experiment of coming here, as far as painting is concerned at any rate, has been such a success that I don't believe Duncan will ever if he can help it spend a winter in London again. We are perfectly happy here. One works all day and isn't tempted to go out at night as one is in London. Everything helps one instead of hindering one. I was afraid D. might be bored, but I think he is perfectly contented. We are both miserable at the thought of going back so soon. However for me at any rate it can't be helped. But it looks as though we should only see you in Paris. Shall you come there and for how long? I can't think why you want to get out of India, but as you do, I hope some miracle will turn up.[1] No one but yourself wants you to go except unselfishly.

I hope your finances are going to leap forward again. Duncan wants you to buy a picture for £5 by a painter here called Landau.[2] He's a young Pole and is really a very interesting painter, I think. He's the only person left here and comes to dinner sometimes. He hasn't a penny but what he makes, but he is now beginning to get on. The picture you're to buy would be a landscape done here, and is intended by Duncan to be the beginning of a collection of cheap modern works to be bought by you and housed at a public room in Cambridge, later to be housed at the Fitzwilliam, on the death of Cocherell.[3] I hope you approve of the scheme. Duncan and I of course are to choose the pictures, but all are to be cheap—£5 to £10.[4] Let me know soon if you'll buy a Landau, as he is going away for Christmas.

I had a shock about my finances as the bank wrote to say I was overdrawn, but I find the circular notes I had were debited to me, which I hadn't thought they would be till they were presented. I hope

[1]The Indian government had invited JMK to become vice-chairman of a fiscal commission. Though tempted, he did not accept the offer.
[2]Sigismund Landau, an admirer of RF's painting.
[3]Sir Sydney Carlyle Cockerell (1867–1962), bibliophile and director of the Fitz-william Museum in Cambridge from 1908 to 1937.
[4]Now about £95–£191/$166–$334.

my cheque to you for £60 was honoured. Mr Clark[5] has never paid me any rent. I've said I will wait till the end of the year if he can't pay before, but if he doesn't pay then I don't know what I can do. It's mounting up to quite a lot.

I hadn't heard anything about Lytton who sounds almost vulgarly rich.

Your
VB

KCC

V-16. To Roger Fry

Dec. 22 [1921]   *La Maison Blanche*

My dear Roger,

You ought to have had a long enough letter from me to satisfy even you by now. I was very glad of your two, especially as I have spent a solitary week while Duncan has been away on his travels. I haven't even seen Landau, who I rather think was going off to Saunarie [Sanary-sur-Mer], but I don't know whether he has come back here or gone to Paris for Christmas, which he spoke of doing. I have seen Camoin in the road and he is to come here tomorrow for coffee, with Mme. I suppose. Otherwise no one but the children and servants. I wonder what you and Virginia really said about me! Yes, all good perhaps, but wasn't I given all the dull domestic virtues with never a spark to lighten them? You see how suspicious I am—but not of you. But perhaps by now we are too old for these manoeuvres and you were both really very nice to me. I know my maternal instincts are tiresome, quite as much so to myself as to anyone else, but you must remember some of my young are soon to be taken from me and then no doubt my friends will find me quite as much at a loose end as anyone can want. I try not to bore you all with panegyrics on my young as some mothers do. I keep a great deal to myself. You get more out of me on that subject than anyone else does, but then you

[5]VB's tenant at Gordon Square.

always seem to like them so much yourself too. The doll for Angelica came at a moment when it was most wanted, as she was kept indoors with a bad cold which we have all been having. It was a lovely creature which opened and shut its eyes, to her huge delight. I'm afraid it does so no longer, but for the 3 days she was indoors it was really a godsend and is now in Quentin's charge in hospital. I see that Angelica's maternal instincts too will be the very devil. I only hope she won't have others as well.

Of course I've no news, as I have simply been painting, teaching the children and spending solitary evenings here. It has been deliciously warm on most days, even on grey ones, and I have been painting out of doors every day, doing more sketches and one bigger thing from a sketch, but I don't know if I shall have time while we are here. It's getting horribly near an end of the time, and near Rose's arrival. Mme. Santucci poured forth to me the other day. They have quarrelled with Rose who apparently wanted them to do work for her without payment. I'm afraid they will go. But I see that Rose has as bad a reputation here as elsewhere . . .

I have had another letter from Mrs Fothergill,[1] who has a ready pen I see but nothing much to say, except that she's had bronchitis and is still in Paris. Does she really think you are in love with her? It's quite possible. Women are incredible. Perhaps Landau is also an invention. As for Mme. M.[2] (who is really serious I see), I don't think I had better meet her on purpose. We might be too curious about each other. I hope you like a London Christmas. I have read all I can of Sir Edward[3] and am filled with blank despair. How did you emerge?

Your
V.

Have you seen Clive?

TATE

[1]Possibly the wife of John Fothergill, director of the Carfax Gallery.
[2]Madame Mela Muter, a Polish-Jewish painter whom RF had recently met in St. Tropez. Their affair lasted about a year.
[3]A *Memoir of the Right Honourable Sir Edward Fry* (1921), written by his daughter, and RF's sister, Agnes Fry.

V-17. To John Maynard Keynes

[May 19, 1922]   *50, Gordon Square*

Dearest Maynard,

I have had a letter from Clive. He is trying to find a house in France for the summer holidays, but so far without success. I see that it may be very difficult to find anything that will do, and so it seems to me we must seriously consider possibilities, or we may find at the last moment that we or you are obliged to take something we don't much like. Clive says he thinks it impossible for any one of us, you, he, I or Duncan, to introduce a new wife[1] or husband into the existing circle for more than a week at a time. He himself is prepared (no wonder) to abstain from doing so and sooner than make one of such a party he would prefer to go away alone. He also thinks that an annexe arrangement would really be much the same as one household and would inevitably tend to become so, and this I really agree with. In fact both Duncan and I feel that the whole question ought to be faced and that the only way is to talk quite frankly about it, only as it's almost impossible to see you in peace, I am writing to give you some sort of rough idea of what we feel, which you can consider and talk to us about when you have time.

Don't think however that what I say is any kind of criticism of Lydia, for it isn't. We feel that no one can come into the sort of intimate society we have without altering it. (She has done so perhaps less than anyone, certainly less than any other woman could have.) That is inevitable, isn't it? I think you must realise it and I think it must be taken into account, not only in its effect upon summer holiday plans, but altogether. Clive says that if any one else is to be permanently here he would have to leave the house. As you know, it would be very tiresome for me if he went far afield, but also on considering it I think it would be very difficult to give up my rooms here at No. 50 to him. It would mean having the children separated, which is very awkward for me, and would be more so of course in illness. Also Angelica and I would I think be rather uncomfortably crowded at 46.

---

[1]JMK's affair with the ballerina Lydia Lopokova (1892–1981) was becoming serious enough for him to find her rooms at 50 Gordon Square, where VB and the Adrian Stephens also lived. Her first marriage, to Randolfo Barocchi, was not dissolved until 1925.

Of course you probably don't mind if Clive does go, but unless he comes here and I move to 46 it would mean your having Lydia alone in the house (except for Duncan), which might be difficult. Don't you think the most satisfactory solution might be to find rooms for her quite near, perhaps James' at 41? She could then be quite independent and there'd be no scandal. However there is no need to decide at once about this. The only thing we want you to know is what we—Duncan and I—feel on the subject altogether. But it's very difficult to make it clear. Perhaps I've told you enough to make it easier to talk about it all when we see you.

I can't offer any solution to the summer question. We would much rather you were at Charleston of course, but I'm afraid you may be forced to choose between us and Lydia. It all seems horribly complicated and I wish it weren't.

Your
VB

KCC

V-18. To Roger Fry

[June 1922]   *[50, Gordon Square]*

My dear Roger,

I have read the whole of your article on me now and I want to thank you for writing it.[1] It makes me very happy. I hope it won't make me conceited. But—don't laugh at me—it seems to me really a very great honour to be written about seriously by you and that you should have thought it worth the trouble of trying to find out honestly what you thought about me. I think you *have* tried to be honest and not only nice to me, and I know that's very hard work. Of course you are probably too generous, but that's not important. I enjoy the nice things you say but I won't presume upon them. What really matters to me is that you take me seriously, for as you know I

[1]"Independent Gallery: Vanessa Bell and Othon Friesz," published in the *New Statesman*, June 3, 1922. This was not a joint show, but two one-artist shows.

care more for your opinion than for anyone else's. Also your hints will be useful I hope. I think it's true about my composition. Perhaps now I can try to think more of that.

Do you know when I looked at the pictures in the Second [Post-Impressionist] Grafton show years ago I came to the conclusion finally that the most important general difference between French and English art was that the English seemed to be always thinking of the pictures they were producing and the French of something else, I suppose of something they were trying to express by means of the pictures, which in themselves were unimportant to the painters. I thought then that it was very important to have the French attitude of mind. So it is odd that you should suggest now that that is more or less my attitude. Perhaps we all have it much more than we had, and it wouldn't now be the difference between French and English if one could see them together.

Is this a very priggish letter? Never mind. You'll understand I only want really to tell you how much I like you to like my work.

I hope you're feeling thoroughly romantic about Cornwall—not that I think Bertie's face will conduce to the romantic state of mind.[2]

You ought to have seen Mrs Pat as Hedda Gabler.[3] The rest were very bad, but she is really magnificent. She's amazing to look at, too. Only of course she was rather too good for the thing as a whole. But it's an astonishing play and one always gets something on the stage that one doesn't get in reading it.

Goodbye.

Your
V.

TATE

[2]RF was painting Bertrand Russell's portrait.
[3]Ibsen's *Hedda Gabler* (trans. Edmund Gosse and William Archer), featuring Mrs. Patrick Campbell as Hedda Tesman, played at the Everyman, May 22 to June 3, then transferred to Kingsway Theatre for another fortnight.

V-19. To Virginia Woolf

Monday [April 30, 1923]   *Monk's House, Rodmell*

My Billy,

I didn't know you were coming back so soon.[1] Well, we shouldn't have met you in Paris anyhow, as we only proposed to get there yesterday. I'm very glad we didn't go. This weather would have been too awful. As it is, the children have been very happy here, for which I feel I ought to be more eloquent in my thanks than I know how to be with my pen. So will you and your husband accept a work of the brush as a token of gratitude? I hope you won't spurn it, or I shall feel snubbed. Also I must pay for the coal we have used, and otherwise I don't know what depredations you may not find. I run after the brats and make Leonard out to be a terrible ogre and you, though capable of weak kindness, a she-dragon when roused, in the hope of keeping them within bounds. I don't think anything very awful has been done. Mrs Thompsett[2] says she will clean up after us.

I send you a cheque for £11. Your share of a cheque from Murray.[3] We return on Wednesday. Julian goes to school on Friday. Did I say I preferred Charleston to this? No, of course you've made it up. So I shall say nothing, except that I think both houses suitable to their owners.[4]

What company you keep in Paris! I've never met Maria Blanchard,[5] but she knows Roger well, and no doubt he's told her I take painting seriously. Do you think it's true? You had better go to the London Group and give me your views on it.

I shall I hope see you this week. I'll ring up when I get back. I hear

---

[1]The Woolfs had been to stay with Gerald Brenan in Spain. VB and family occupied Monk's House in their absence.

[2]Wife of a Rodmell farm worker. Her daughter Annie later became the Woolfs' cook and domestic at Monk's House.

[3]Royalty checks from John Murray for Leslie Stephen's works.

[4]VW was very sensitive about the comparative merits of Charleston and Monk's House. It was a recurring topic of conversation between her and VB.

[5]Spanish Cubist painter (1881–1932), aka María Gutiérrez. She had known RF since 1916 and exhibited in the 1923 London Group show.

you're going to a National[4] dinner at 46 on Tuesday. What a to-do that must be.

I think your Spring Publication[5] has come out quite well. Perhaps a little scratchier than it ought to have been, but I daresay that's my fault. Also you say it's not a good impression.

Did you know that Mr Gunn's[6] baby and the milkman's baby, born at the same time, both have webbed feet? What do you deduce? Also that Mr Shanks (1892–1953) has now divorced Mrs Shanks[7] and is going to marry the parson's daughter.

Your
VB

BERG

V-20. To Margery Snowden

May 24 [1923]   *Madrid*

My dearest Margery,

My plans were all changed after I wrote to you. It was such horrible weather that the children and I gave up our French tour and stayed on instead at Rodmell till the end of Julian's holidays and didn't come abroad till about May 8th. After a few days in Paris with Clive, Duncan and I came on to Spain, where Roger met us at Barcelona, a very dull place. We then went on to other places, some very lovely,

---

[4]LW had become literary editor of *The Nation* in March. JMK was chairman of the board. The first issue of the amalgamated *Nation & Athenaeum* appeared on May 5, 1923, and the dinner with JMK VB mentioned was perhaps related to this.
[5]Possibly Clive Bell's *The Legend of Monte della Sibilla, or Le Paradis de la Reine Sibille* (London: Hogarth Press, 1923), for which VB and DG designed the cover. The book did not appear until December, however. Perhaps the Press had issued an advance notice.
[6]The Asheham bailiff.
[7]The poet Edward Shanks (1892–1953) lived at Rodmell. His wife had left him in 1922.

on the way here, and now we've been here 3 days or so. I feel as if I ought to write to you about the Prado, as I'm sure I must have inflicted all my feelings about Velasquez upon you years ago, and you can imagine how exciting it is now to see the pictures one has known so well from reproductions for so many years. Not that I can really give you any idea of the pictures here. They are simply overwhelming and unlike any other collection of old masters I have ever seen. They are very well hung. The light is splendid. They have no glasses to get in the way as in the Nat. Gallery, and they are almost as fresh apparently as when they were painted. In fact they're very like modern painting and often give one quite a new idea of some painter whose work one has only seen before through many coats of brown varnish. Also it is the most extraordinarily good collection. Some of the best Titians are here as well as some of the finest Raphaels, Rubens and of course all the Spaniards, Velasquez, Goya, El Greco, Ribera, etc. One could spend many weeks looking at them all. I expect we shall spend about one. As for Velasquez, I feel quite bewildered. I don't yet know what I think of him except that one never seems to get tired of looking at him. His colour is most surprising. Instead of being all very subdued greys and blacks and browns, which was my general idea of it, some of the paintings here are almost dazzling, bright blues and all sorts of the gayest colours, almost like Renoir. One sees where Steer and the New Englishers got their ideas, but one also sees where Whistler and Sargent got theirs too. However, I wish you could see them all for yourself, for I can really give you no idea. There is nothing else much to do in this place but go to the Prado. It's a horrible town with no attractions of any sort. We're in the only bad hotel we've been in in Spain. Everywhere else they were very good and the people charming. The women are most beautiful often—in fact, one sees grand beauties at every moment in the street, which is a great pleasure.

This letter is very disinterested, as you can't answer me till I get back. I expect I shall be at home again about the 6th or 7th of June as I don't like to leave the children much longer. Is there any chance of your coming to London this summer? I wish you could come during June when Duncan's exhibition at the Independent will be on. Anyhow, do write to me at Gordon Sq. and tell me what you have been doing and are going to do. I suppose I shall stay at home during June and July, then go to Charleston for the summer holidays. I hope to settle down and do some work, for I haven't been able to do much beyond a few sketches at Rodmell since the children's Easter holidays began. I find it impossible to do anything while one's travelling and seeing so much.

I send you my love.

Your

VB

Please forgive pencil. I am writing in my bedroom and have no ink.

TATE

V-21. To Roger Fry

Sep. 19 [1923]   *Charleston*

My dear Roger,

. . . We have both been turning out a lot of old rolled up pictures from our stores here. I think both Duncan and I have changed extraordinarily during the last 10 years or so, I hope for the better. But also it seems to me there was a great deal of excitement about colour then—7 or 10 years ago—which perhaps has rather quieted down now. I suppose it was the result of trying first to change everything into colour. It certainly made me inclined also to destroy the solidity of objects, but I wonder whether now one couldn't get more of that sort of intensity of colour without losing solidity of objects and space. One began an astonishing number of large works which were never finished. I think one has learnt at any rate not to need such huge canvases. I seem to have thought nothing of beginning over life size full length, or nearly, portraits of Iris which couldn't possibly get finished unless she had been ready to sit for months. There are some amusing very early works of Duncan's, extraordinarily brilliant, I think, and always rather lovely colour.

I took Julian to London yesterday on his way back to school and saw the Spanish things,[1] which seemed to me most lovely, especially the carpets and great pots. I wish one could go again and get much more, though I admit I'm pretty well set up now in crockery.

[1] I.e., her Spanish purchases, just arrived.

Please write to me soon and tell me how you like La Ciotat. Perhaps next year I shall go south again, so you might keep your eyes open for a good place to take Angelica too. The one essential seems to be not too much wind.

Goodbye.

Your loving
V.

TATE

V-22. To Roger Fry

Sep. 27 [1923]   *46, Gordon Square*

My dear Roger,

I very much enjoyed your letter with its amusing account of the experts.[1] I wish I could have joined the other two ladies opposite you—you wouldn't have been more embarrassed and I should have heard your lecture and observed them. I shall have to wait till your latest—or have there been others since?—comes to London. I am rather jealous of her I think. Why does she write such good letters? It's easy to cut me out in that line. Well, I don't mind as long as you don't change your mind about me and also go on telling me all your affairs. I flatter myself that that is my special privilege, but of course you may easily find another confidante, so really I must insist on your not forgetting my other good points.

I send you a photograph of myself and Angelica to remind you at any rate that there is *one* very lovely *and* witty *and* brilliant *and* charming creature to be seen in Gordon Square. Not that she is here now. I am here alone with Quentin and the Keynes *ménage* and find

[1]RF had given evidence at the *Hahn* v. *Duveen* deposition in Paris that month. A version of Leonardo's *La Belle Ferronière,* owned by Mrs. Hahn, had been publicly denounced as a fake by the dealer Joseph Duveen, at the very moment of its sale to the Kansas City Art Gallery. RF's latest mistress, Josette Coatmellec, sat patiently observing him throughout the proceedings, though she complained of his inattention to her. Six months later she shot herself on the cliffs at Le Havre, looking toward England.

it a little trying, especially as we haven't got our separate dining room yet. I shall get it ready as soon as possible, but of course it means making new arrangements about furniture, etc.

Segonzac is in London, at least he was 2 days ago and will be again on Monday. Meanwhile he has been carried off by [Percy Moore] Turner on a tour to the north, very gloomy I should think, and on Tuesday he's going on a tour to Holland, so he won't be here long. I had lunch with him and Turner and saw his pictures which were standing about on the floor at the Independent. They looked to me very good, especially some early ones I hadn't seen before. I expect his later ones are really better though, but the best of them hadn't come. He was very nice and friendly and is coming to dine on Monday when Duncan will be here.

On Tuesday and Wednesday we shall have to hang the London Group. Are you sending, I wonder? Duncan I believe is only sending drawings and I seem to have very little finished. I have begun working again on my family group, which I think I must soon stop, as all the sitters are changing so much that I shall begin to try to keep up with them if I go on.

We had Desmond at Charleston for the last weekend I was there. You ought to have felt your ears burning, or whatever it is that happens when one's spoken well of, for all joined in your praises. You became the topic of conversation one evening and both your mind and your character got such admiration heaped on them from everyone that I should blush to repeat what was said. Desmond evidently has the greatest affection as well as admiration for you and he and I compared our earliest recollections of you. Mine was at his mother's house, when I sat next you at dinner and found to my surprise that I could say anything I liked to you. Clive also joined, but said rather to my surprise that he felt you were now rather against him. Perhaps this is very indiscreet. He thought that you felt that he laughed too much at your ideas and was too sceptical. Is this true? I mean, do you feel it? No doubt he does laugh and as you know I think he's sometimes too discouraging to any new idea or project, but I said I didn't think you minded. However he may be right.

I think Desmond himself is one of the most charming characters we know. His comments on things that happen and the way it all strikes him give me very great pleasure. He seems to me more imaginative about life than almost any of our friends. It's curious that I could no more imagine having any sort of flirtation or sexual feeling of any kind for him than I could for—Queen Mary.

Molly's reminiscences in the Nation[2] have been a great success. Constable wants to publish them and I hope she'll make some money. Also I think she will be much the happier for a little success.

Your country sounds very lovely and rather odd. Is it good for painting? It sounds very unlike St. Tropez.

Goodbye. Please write again soon.

Your loving
V.

I also send Angelica and Quentin and a rather impressionist interior of Angelica and the kittens.

TATE

V-23. To Virginia Woolf

Dec. 25 [1923]   *Charleston*

My Billy,

You oughtn't, as you well know, to inundate us with so many presents, but of course you do. The caramels which I suppose come from you and Leonard are heavenly. I didn't know such good ones could be got in London. Angelica is fearfully pleased with her doll, which is in fact dressed with such exquisite taste that I can't think how you found her. I am almost more overcome by my own life[1] than by anything else, however. Not a single word of it's true of course but I admit it made me laugh and the pictures are really lovely.

We have spent the most wildly domestic and pandemonic day you can imagine, with presents and crackers and turkey and all, ending up, just before the rain began, with fireworks.

[2]Molly MacCarthy's memoirs (solicited by LW) appeared in installments in *The Nation* from September 1, 1923 to May 31, 1924. They were published as *A Nineteenth Century Childhood* by Hamish Hamilton in 1924.
[1]"Scenes in the Life of Mrs Bell Published by the Hogarth Press Written by Virginia Woolf" was the Christmas 1923 Supplement to the "Charleston Bulletin" (an illustrated daily newspaper produced by Julian and Quentin Bell). Dictated by Virginia to Quentin Bell, who also illustrated the manuscript. Now in the collection of Quentin and Olivier Bell.

I can't think you'll much want to come over here, but I needn't say you'd be very welcome if you could manage it. If you want to get back before dark you must come to lunch at least, but it would be still better if you—both—would come to lunch and stay the night, any day and night you like after you get this. The only inducement I can offer is that you might take back some irises and any other plants you'd like.

Please arrange anything that suits you. It's just possible Roger may come here for the weekend, but not very likely I think unless he's made another miraculous recovery. Otherwise no one is coming that I know of and you'd find no one but the Bell family. Duncan has had to go to Twickenham.[2]

Also would Nellie and Lottie like to come any day? They'd find plenty of gaiety in the kitchen.

Your
VB

BERG

V-24. To Roger Fry

June 22 [1924]   *46, Gordon Sq[uare]*

My dearest Roger,

. . . I have been having rather an unsettled and worrying time here, and haven't really been able to paint much yet. Angelica has had to have more teeth out, as she still had two very bad ones and [Dr] Hamilton said her glands might get bad again at any moment till they were out. So it had to be done, though I felt very nervous. But she is none the worse. In fact, I suppose she'll be better. Then Louie suddenly had to go home as her father is dying, which has rather added to the difficulties, especially as it all happened at the moment of the Apostle dinner, when Maynard flooded the house with people from Cambridge. Then I hear that Julian has the mumps! However that isn't

---

[2]Where his mother, Ethel Grant, lived.

serious I hope, though I daresay he's rather wretched. However I hope most of these bothers are over and that I shall be able to paint this week. It is horrid not being able to.

I went and helped to hang the French show with Porter[1] and, to my dismay, Turner—I hoped he wouldn't be asked. I think it wasn't badly done in the end, though it was rather difficult to get it all in, and it took me some time to make out why Turner ever thought one thing more than another. He seemed to me to have no recognisable principle at all. But Porter and I managed to be firm about some things and I doubt anything very awful happened. It seemed to me a very good show on the whole, especially of Matisse. Also very good of Derain. I must go again as I only saw it when the hanging wasn't quite finished.

There was a great party at No. 50 in Karin's rooms the other night, given by Marjorie and Alix. Marjorie and Partridge[2] acted a play by Schnitzler,[3] the whole plot of which is a copulation scene which at first doesn't come off. It is done on the stage, though at the back, which is in darkness. It seemed to me pointless and rather painful, as they acted very realistically and rather slowly and the audience felt simply as if a real copulation were going on in the room and tried to talk to drown the very realistic groans made by Partridge! Dora Sanger was I think horrified and left at once afterwards, and I don't know what some others thought, but I don't think anyone enjoyed it. It was a great relief when Marjorie sang hymns. But I didn't think it was a very successful party.

It has been deliciously hot and fine since the first two or three days after I came back. I heard you had had Quentin out to dinner,[4] which was very good of you. Maynard has gone to Paris now and will stay there for the rest of Lydia's season.[5]

Please write again. I don't know how long you stay at St. Rémy, but I suppose you'll get this letter somewhere and I don't know where you go afterwards.

Clive has returned for his London season. The Woolves seem

[1]Frederick J. Porter (1883–1944), vice president of the London Group, later an original member of the London Artists' Association.

[2]Reginald Sherring Partridge (1894–1960), educated at Christ's Church, Oxford, and dubbed "Ralph" by Lytton Strachey. He lived at Tidmarsh, and later at Ham Spray, with Lytton and Carrington, and married Carrington in May 1921.

[3]*Reigen (La Ronde)* (1896–97).

[4]QB was at this time staying in Paris with the Pinault family.

[5]With Comte Etienne de Beaumont's company, Soirées de Paris, at La Cigalle, May 17–June 30.

very flourishing. The Stephens are constantly seen walking the streets hand in hand and seem to be inseparable. I think that is all my news.

Your loving
V.

TATE

V-25. To Roger Fry

July 6 [1924]   *46, Gordon Square*

My dearest Roger,

    ... I wanted to ask you about Souillac, because when I was hanging at Colnaghi's I met Mr Leverton Harris[1] and he told me he'd just been there. According to him, though high up, it is very sheltered. There is a very good inn, kept by a retired chef, very cheap, very nice people. Lovely country. Is all this true? And is it a possible place for the winter? It seems to me quite impossible to face another long London winter when I needn't, and I fear your desert isn't really practicable for me, so I very much want to find some place where one would have light, and if not warmth, at least no wind, and civilized enough to take Angelica to. So do tell me about it. Your people at St. Rémy sound very charming.

    July 8. I have been two days trying to finish this so you can imagine what a life one leads here. Meanwhile your letter about Ingres has come, which is most interesting. I think I see what you mean about there being something wanting. Perhaps he was too academic and dried up instead of expanding. Maynard has come back from Paris with a new Derain. It's the head of a woman leaning on her hands, with a bit of shoulder just coming in. I wonder what you'll think of it. I don't know what I think. No doubt it's very fine, yet one can't help wondering sometimes whether it's not already too much of an Old Master.

[1] Frederick Leverton Harris (1864–1926), politician and art collector. Much of his valuable collection was destroyed in a fire in 1919; remaining works were bequeathed to the National Gallery and other major museums.

I have read Morgan's book,[2] but I'm afraid if I try to tell you what I think of it I never shall finish this letter. In a way I agree with you, but I wasn't sure the rather indefinite part at the end wasn't done on purpose and that it wasn't necessary to the design of the whole that it should be indefinite. What awful people everyone in India seems to be—Anglo-Indians and Indians. The Anglo-Indians are the worse perhaps, but it seems as if India itself had a bad effect on human beings, don't you think. I enjoyed the writing very much. I should say it would be almost impossible to translate, it's so subtle. But I should say he might do still better in another book when he gets writing and ideas and construction all more of a piece somehow.

Did I tell you that Maynard has taken Tilton for August and September? We are a little nervous at having them so near Charleston, as Maynard will probably go off and leave Lydia alone there at times and she'll then be very much on one's conscience. Her divorce from Barocchi is to come about quite soon, and then I suppose she and M. will marry not long after and what will happen here I don't know. But I'm inclined to think it might be best to spend most of one's time either abroad or at Charleston, just keeping a few rooms here. Anyhow if Lydia came to live here I think it would hardly be possible to share the house with her.

I must stop if you are ever to get a letter from me and I suppose if you don't you'll write no more to me but will devote all your letter writing energies to more profitable quarters. But you don't know what London life is—or you do—so you'll understand. Really I don't think it's good enough. One is invaded day and night and has no peace. Goodbye and please write again soon, for you have no excuse not to.

Your loving
V.

TATE

---

[2]E(dward) M(organ) Forster (1879–1970), *A Passage to India* (1924), his last novel. Although friendly with the principal Bloomsbury figures since his undergraduate days at King's College, Cambridge, Forster always stood a little outside the circle. None of VB's letters to him seem to have survived.

V-26. To Roger Fry

Sep. 7 [1924]   *Charleston*

My dearest Roger,

It was a great pity you couldn't come here again, especially as this last week has really been much nicer weather. In fact, the last few days have been quite hot and sunny. As you aren't staying at Wittering I may tell you that we are now in the throes of our annual visit from Mary. Morgan, who was to have come too, has failed us, so she's here alone and it's very hard work. I know you always enjoy abuse of one lady by another, but I will only say that she does as usual strike me as a person of singularly little originative power and rather irritates me by being so self-conscious to her finger tips of what every fraction of herself is doing and looking. But except in the evenings one doesn't see much of her.

This is really a most hard-working establishment. Every morning I go off to the studio, where I now have two 5 ft. canvases on hand! Do you think me crazy? One is the children on the sand heap and the other the two nudes in your studio. I find it rather a good plan to have two, as when I've got rather stale with one I turn on to the other. But it's entirely your fault really that I embark on these works. If you hadn't bought the family group I don't think I should have had the courage to begin other large works. I think even if they come to no good it teaches one a good deal to try to push a big thing as far as one can. I have been working very hard at them. Duncan paints in his room or out of doors. He's much braver at going out than I am. We work all day till tea time, then I have the children for a bit and the time seems to rush.

The actual holidays will soon be over. Quentin will be going to Leighton Park for his first term on the 18th and Angelica will be the only one left to me. By the way, your story about me was unfortunately lost before it could be published,[1] so we have never known it. Quentin read it but can't remember the exact words, which he says are important. If it's not too much trouble do send it again, to me this time. The Bulletin has been very much to the fore lately. Large numbers appear every day and its journalese is becoming very brilliant.

[1]In the "Charleston Bulletin."

Vanessa, Stella Duckworth, and Virginia Stephen, c. 1896.

The Stephen family, c. 1894. *Front row, left to right:* Adrian,
Julia Stephen, Leslie Stephen. *Back row, left to right:* George
Duckworth, Virginia, Thoby, Vanessa, Gerald Duckworth.
Berg Collection, New York Public Library.

I

Vanessa painting her first portrait commission, of Lady Robert Cecil, at Hatfield House, 1905. *Tate Gallery Archive.*

Clive Bell and Virginia Stephen, Studland Bay, Dorset, 1911.
Tate Gallery Archive.

Vanessa and Julian Bell, Studland Bay, Dorset, 1910.
Tate Gallery Archive.

Roger Fry, 1911.
Tate Gallery Archive.

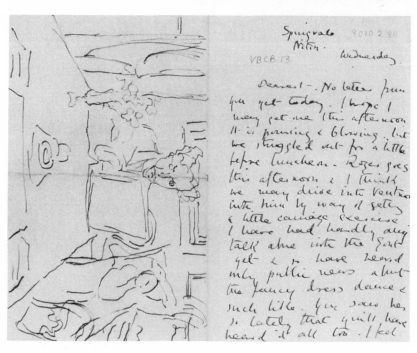

A page of a letter from Vanessa to Clive, with a drawing of Roger Fry
sketching Vanessa, 1912. *Tate Gallery Archive.*

Vanessa and Duncan Grant, Asheham, c. 1913. *Tate Gallery Archive.*

Vanessa at Brandon, Norfolk, during a neo-pagan summer camp, 1913. *Anrep Collection.*

Vanessa Bell, *A Conversation*, 1913-1916, oil on canvas.
Courtauld Institute Galleries, London.

Vanessa Bell, *Bather's Screen*, 1913, mixed media, painted for The
Omega Workshop. *Courtesy of The Board of Trustees of the Victoria
and Albert Museum.*

Left: Vanessa Bell, *Still Life by a Window*, 1914, oil on canvas. *Cheltenham Art Gallery and Museums.*
Right: Vanessa at her easel at Asheham, 1913. *Tate Gallery Archive.*

Vanessa Bell, *Studland Beach*, c. 1912, oil on canvas. *Tate Gallery, London.*

Vanessa bathing in the kitchen at Charleston, sketched by Duncan
Grant shortly before the birth of Angelica Bell, 1918.
Courtesy of The Bloomsbury Workshop.

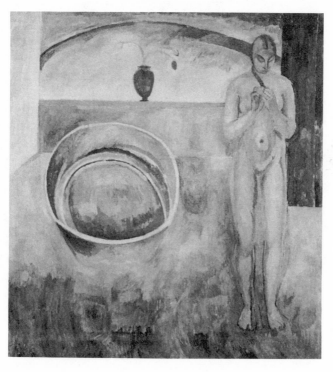

Vanessa Bell, *The Tub*, 1917, oil on canvas. *Tate Gallery, London.*

Duncan Grant, *Vanessa Bell*, c. 1918, oil on canvas. *Courtesy of the National Portrait Gallery, London.*

Duncan Grant, David Garnett,
Saxon Sydney-Turner, and
Barbara Hiles outside the
tent Barbara pitched one
summer at Charleston, 1917.
Shone, Bloomsbury Portraits.

Clockwise: Leonard Woolf, Quentin Bell, Julian Bell, John Maynard
Keynes, Clive Bell, Duncan Grant, and Mary Hutchinson,
Charleston, 1921. *Tate Gallery Archive.*

Quentin, Angelica, and Julian, photographed by Vanessa
at Charleston, c. 1921. *Tate Gallery Archive.*

Below:
Quentin, Angelica, and Roger,
Charleston, 1920s.
Tate Gallery Archive.

Above: Vanessa and Duncan's decorations of Raymond Mortimer's flat, 1925. *Shone, Bloomsbury Portraits.* *Below:* Duncan's studio at Charleston, where he and Vanessa frequently worked together (as restored by The Charleston Trust). *Courtesy of The Charleston Trust.*

Left:
Angelica and Vanessa,
Charleston, 1927.
Tate Gallery Archive.

Below:
Vanessa Bell, *Interior with
Duncan Grant*, c. 1934,
oil on canvas.
*Williamson Art Gallery
and Museum, Birkenhead.*

Above:
Vanessa Bell, *Charleston*, 1950,
oil on canvas.
Courtesy of The Charleston Trust.

Right: Vanessa Bell
at Charleston, 1960.
Courtesy of Olivier Bell.

It's odd to think of you at St. Tropez again with Rose and all the rest of them. I don't know your address there, so I must send this to Dalmeny.² How did your salon picture get on? Did you finish it? You sounded overwhelmed with people and I daresay you still are. We I hope have come to an end of our visitors. Please write soon, my dear. I hope you're fairly cheerful.

Your loving
V.

TATE

V-27. To Raymond Mortimer

Feb. 10 [1925]   *46, Gordon Sq[uare] W.C. 1*

Dear Raymond,¹

We took measurements of the room today² and considered the sofa and carpet question. We came to the conclusion that the best way of dealing with the wall would be to cover the spaces between and over the doors and that between the door and the window with canvas on stretchers. The space between the door and the book case is not so easy to deal with because it is an irregular shape. Electric light switches come into the middle of it and the book case makes it an odd shape too. So we think it would be better to leave that bit, taking the canvas in a line with the door up to the ceiling, and paint directly on the wall itself if necessary on this piece. Is this clear? The sofa seems to us all right, but we should change the places of things in the design, so as to make it a whole either with or without the sofa there.

Now as to price. We have got an estimate for the canvases and they

---

²7 Dalmeny Avenue, Holloway, the house RF bought in 1918 after selling Durbins. He lived there with his sister Margery.
¹Raymond Mortimer (1895–1980), author and literary critic, educated at Balliol College, Oxford. His first contacts with Bloomsbury came through Harold Nicolson and Edward Sackville-West, and by 1924 he had moved to 6 Gordon Place, just off Gordon Square.
²These decorations are now in the Victoria and Albert Museum. See plate xiv, top.

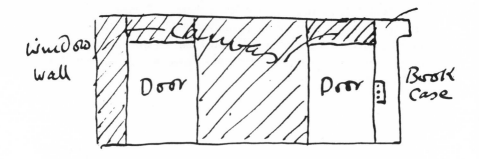

come altogether to just about £9. Our price for painting the wall, doors, etc., a panel over the mantelpiece if necessary, and doing anything else that might be wanted to make the room a complete whole would be £45.[3] This is less than it would be, but for the fact that it is possible to use an already existing design to a large extent. But it may well be more than you wish to spend, in which case please say so quite frankly. Or you might prefer to wait, for of course it could be done later quite well.

If you do want us to do the rooms I have one other tiresome announcement to make, and that is about the carpet. It seemed to us inclined to make the whole room too heavy and sombre, and that the blue in it was not very good with the blue walls. The middle part is in itself a lovely colour, but don't you think that there may be too much of that sort of colour in that room? You could I suppose change it quite easily, as it must be a very good carpet and it's lovely in itself. Perhaps however you won't agree. But if you do, when you see it in the room by daylight, possibly other carpets could be sent to try there, or you could find one rather less heavy in tone. I throw out these opinions only supposing you want us to do the room. If you don't want the wall painted, of course it would become a different problem.

I have not given you alternative estimates because I think that having canvas tacked on to the wall would be very little cheaper and not nearly so good as having it on stretchers. Please tell me if there is anything else you would like to know about or suggest.

Yours
Vanessa Bell

[3]In today's terms, about £1086/$1900.

Having no canvas between the door and window would make it about £2 cheaper probably.

V-28. To Raymond Mortimer

Feb. 15 [1925]   *46, Gordon Sq[uare] W.C. 1*

Dear Raymond,

Thank you so much for your letter and offer to make the whole amount £60,[1] which we are delighted to accept. Please do not think that we ask less from you than we should do from anyone else. The real and only reason for our not asking quite so much for this job as we might do is that the design we already have happens to fit both in design and size. This saves an enormous amount of bother and probably of time. It will of course need some adaptation, particularly in colour, but it might have taken one a long time to get the main idea settled and this is saved. I don't think it will look in the least like the panel in Mr Harrison's loggia,[2] but anyhow you do not mind the fact that both started from the same idea.

I expect the carpet will be all right when furniture is in the room. We saw it of course with nothing on it.

We hope to start painting as soon as the canvases are ready, to-morrow or the day after probably, and will let you know when they are ready to be put up. I think the space to the right of the door can probably be dealt with satisfactorily.

Yours ever,
Vanessa Bell

[1]Now about £1449/$2535.
[2]The loggia at Peter Harrison's Surrey home does not survive.

V-29. To Raymond Mortimer

March 7 [1925]   *46, Gordon Sq[uare]*

Dear Raymond,

Thank you so much for your invitation—which however a little alarms us! I hope that they will bring and instal the canvases on Monday (if that is all right for you). But you must remember that we shall most likely have to do things to them after they are in your room and we can see the effect there, also that in any case we shall still have to paint the doors and probably put a panel over the mantelpiece. Even if this is done by Thursday it is doubtful whether the paint on the doors will be dry by then. So that altogether we feel rather frightened at the thought of your asking anyone else to see them so soon. People are generally and naturally incapable of judging of unfinished works and so it seems a mistake to let them see them, except by accident. Of course you can't live the life of a hermit before we have done with them.

Perhaps you'd rather put us off therefore? and tell any of your other guests that the decorations probably won't be visible? But please do as you like now that I have given you this warning. After all, you will have plenty of other things besides our paintings to show.

I am so glad you have got the watercolours and like them.

Please let me know if you want any help about tradesmen or other local news.

Yours ever,
Vanessa Bell

PRINCETON

V-30. To Raymond Mortimer

Ap. 19 [1925]   *Charleston, Firle, Sussex*

Dear Raymond,

Thank you so much for the cheque, which covers everything. May I return your unsolicited testimonial by another to you as a patron?

I don't know how it ought to be worded, but to all artists whom it may concern, we should be delighted to recommend you as everything that is generous, encouraging and prompt. In fact, you are perfect, and I wish you could write on the behaviour of patrons in Vogue.

I hope you're enjoying yourself in Paris. Please give my respectful admiration, which is very great, to Nancy,[1] if you see her.

> *Yours ever,*
> *Vanessa Bell*

PRINCETON

V-31. To Roger Fry

Sep. 11 [1925]   *Charleston*

My dear Roger,

I suppose I can't complain of you for not writing, for I've been very lazy myself. The fact is that one hasn't had a moment to oneself during domestic life in the country. Nature is too much for me altogether, either in the shape of weeds or children, and fills up all one's spare time. Also I have been working quite hard in the studio, which has completely changed one's life here. It is a perfect place to work in, as besides having a very good and even light it is curiously quiet and removed from all the noises of house and garden. Angelica of course comes to it a good deal, and so does Judith Bagenal who is now staying with her, but one never hears a sound of anyone else. The stove has come and yesterday we lit it for the first time. It smoked rather to begin with but I think it will be all right. Altogether we are quite installed now and one feels for the first time here more or less independent of weather.

I have tried once or twice to sketch out of doors, but it seems to me impossible to do more than a very quick sketch. Duncan is

---

[1]Nancy Cunard (1896–1965), rebellious daughter of Lady Cunard. She had just published her free verse poem *Parallax* with the Hogarth Press.

more adventurous and while it was fine and hot he bicycled out and did watercolours in places farther afield and is painting from them. I cannot bear being hurried or uncomfortable as you know, so I very seldom leave the studio except to grapple with weeds in the garden.

Do write and tell me what you're doing. One reason I haven't written to you—I know it's not a reasonable reason—is that I don't know where you are or where you're going to. I want very much to hear all your news. What is happening to Helen[1] and have you managed to see her at all? Perhaps now you're at St. Tropez or somewhere in the south, or are you still at the conference?[2] I wonder how you liked that.

We have had hardly any visitors here. Saxon came for a weekend and Douglas [Davidson] for another. Molly is also coming, and Angus[3] and Lytton. The boys go back to school next week, when it will be easier to have visitors. Julian went off alone to Scotland and shot grouse and rabbits and caught fish and saw a stag killed and seems to have enjoyed it very much. Quentin refused to go and stay with Ray[4] on the broads. He remained alone here and became it seemed to me completely grown up, sitting with us in the evenings and joining in all conversations. He is really happier in grown up society than with people of his own age I think.

The Keyneses are in Russia [on their honeymoon]. We have only seen them once. Virginia has been rather ill with headaches, etc., I suspect the result of her London season, but she's better now, although she will have people like the Bruce Richmonds[5] to stay with her, enough to drive anyone silly. Please write and tell me about yourself my dear. How are you? I was so glad of your two letters and to find that I could still fish successfully for a little affection from you. I hope you're really well now and haven't started any more diseases? Even

[1]Helen Anrep and RF had been in love for nearly a year. Their affair was complicated by her husband Boris Anrep's moods and rages, but in 1926 she broke away and started a home with RF at 48 Bernard Street, Bloomsbury.
[2]The "Décades de Pontigny," an annual invitational gathering of intellectuals at the Abbaye de Pontigny.
[3]Angus Davidson (1898–1980), art critic and translator, was at this time employed at the Hogarth Press. He was a special friend of Duncan Grant's. His brother Douglas was a painter.
[4]Ray Strachey (née Costelloe) (1887–1940), wife of Oliver Strachey and elder sister of Karin Stephen. She chaired the Women's Service Bureau.
[5]Bruce Richmond (1871–1964) edited the TLS. His wife Elena was an old friend of the Stephen family. They had been to tea with the Woolfs on September 4.

being cured of them for nothing doesn't make them worthwhile. I must send this to Dalmeny. I hope you'll get it.

Your loving
V.

TATE

V-32. To Duncan Grant

Dec. 27 [1925]   *Charleston*

My darling Bear,

I had a very nice though short letter from you this morning written just before going to Twickenham. I am very glad you got your Janes,[1] which are really just as much a present to myself as to you. You mustn't send me anything else, as you've already given me a lovely green dish and I want nothing more. Your cards to Virginia and Roger came today. She was delighted, and she well may be, for they're most lovely, though perhaps I liked Roger's best. But as he's not here I shall keep it till I know what he's going to do. What a triumph to have got them done and sent off, and how did you get them so well done up? Leonard has gone today and Virginia goes tomorrow, when I hope we shall return to normal existence. I thought she'd stay longer, but she really can't bear to be parted from him a moment. To tell you the truth, though I have very much enjoyed having them, I shall find it a relief when they're gone, as one always does. Also I get very tired of the perpetual personal conversation that goes on. Yesterday Vita[2] came to lunch. Afterwards we all sate in the studio and Virginia held forth in her usual style which you know and I cannot describe, very amusing but also most uneasy, at least to my mind. The whole evening afterwards was spent in her making mock apologies for having talked so much. It is brilliant of course and I suppose one sounds curmud-

[1]I.e., trousers.
[2]Victoria Mary Sackville-West (1892–1962), writer, the wife of the diplomat Harold Nicolson. She had consummated her love affair with VW only a few days earlier.

geonly for finding any fault, but one simply gets exhausted and longs for some quiet talk that will lead nowhere for a change. I even think how refreshing some of the pure male speculations, to which as you know I cannot attend, would be. However, it's worth it of course, and I daresay it's family feeling that makes me restive.

I have been working at my carpet today and yesterday. It has become hideous and rather like a Wadsworth[3] I think. I must do another. It takes a very long time I find to carry them out indefinitely. I hope you'll do some and also stuffs. I wonder what you've decided about going to Bunny and when you'll come here. Clive goes away on Wednesday, so after that I shall be alone here with the children. We have now heard that their term begins again on Jan 15th, so I think I shall probably stay here with them till the 7th or 8th, then go to Seend for the weekend of 12th or 13th–15th to get clothes, dentist, etc., done. I shall only be here a little over a week therefore after you get this, so I hope you'll be able to come fairly soon. Did you know that Eddie S-W.[4] is desperately in love with Tommy[5] like everyone else? Please write. Angelica is looking much better and is so lovely I can't take my eyes off her. She puts your spangly stuff around her head which makes her look shingled, in the height of the fashion, and is a most ravishing elf.

Goodbye my dear.

Your loving
B.

HENRIETTA GARNETT

---

[3]Edward Wadsworth (1889–1949), hard-edge painter, one of those who defected from the Omega with Wyndham Lewis.
[4]Edward Charles Sackville-West (1901–65), novelist and music critic, son of the fourth Lord Sackville and first cousin of Vita Sackville-West.
[5]Stephen (Tommy) Tomlin (1901–37), sculptor, a friend of David Garnett, who introduced him to Bloomsbury. He later married Oliver Strachey's eldest daughter, the writer Julia Strachey.

CHAPTER SIX

1926-1931

In the winter of 1924–25, Roger Fry met Helen Anrep at a party in Vanessa's Fitzroy Street studio. She was married, like Roger, and had two children, Igor and Anastasia (called Baba). Her early history deserves a book of its own. She was born in California of Scottish parents, though her father disappeared after his entrepreneurial venture into winemaking foundered. With her mother, Helen traveled widely, staying in New York, Edinburgh, Paris, and Florence, where she learned to sing and eventually toured with a small opera company. In Paris at the outbreak of war, she entered a bohemian art world, having affairs with Henry Lamb and the Russian mosaicist Boris Anrep, with whom she settled down. He married her after the birth of their second child, Igor, in 1918. The Anreps then moved to London, where their already strained relationship was aggravated by Boris's insistence that his cousin Maroussa Volkova share their house and his affections.

Although Vanessa encouraged Roger's affair with Helen and felt genuinely pleased for him, she did miss being the focus of his affections. She remained his confidante, meanwhile pursuing Helen with fond, flirtatious letters, hoping to establish intimacy with the woman Roger loved.

Over several years, Helen became Vanessa's closest female friend besides Virginia. They were not intimate friends, however. Vanessa's only real link with Helen was their love of Roger. Helen's son, Igor, and his wife, Annabel, observing the women's relationship in the

1950s, felt that Vanessa toyed with Helen, proffering then withdrawing affection. After Vanessa's death Helen wrote to Leonard Woolf on reading the second volume of his autobiography: "What a strange man you are never to have mentioned all that time [in Ceylon]. Did you to Virginia—I can understand your not talking to Vanessa.[1] What a curious in a way self centered woman she was. [P]erhaps more family centered" (Sussex).

Vanessa had always preferred the company of men, and now delighted in Quentin and Julian as they matured. They joined her in France in 1928 when Vanessa took on the lease of La Bergère, a small stone house in the middle of the vineyards of Fontcreuse, near Cassis. Vanessa had a gift for acquiring remote houses. La Bergère was to become, as she observed, "another Charleston in France," attracting not only her family but all of Bloomsbury. Her other great acquisition, in 1927, was a secondhand Morris motorcar. After a few days' lessons, Vanessa launched into the adventurous world of driving, to the hazard of pedestrians and passing cars.

In the period covered by this chapter, three of Virginia's most successful novels were published: *To the Lighthouse* (1927), *Orlando* (1928), and *The Waves* (1931). Whatever reservations Vanessa may have had about the art of novel writing, or her sister's talents, evaporated as she read these works. Vanessa's reputation also grew. The success of her large one-artist show at the Cooling Galleries in 1930 surprised her, but not Virginia, who had written an appreciative foreword to the catalogue. "You have the children," she had teased Vanessa a few years earlier, "the fame by rights belongs to me" (VWLIII, 271).

[1] I should clarify that there's no evidence that LW withheld his past from Vanessa. On the contrary, his Memoir Club papers, which she would have heard, were more frank in some respects than his published autobiography.

VI-1. To Helen Anrep

[Mid-May 1926]   *234 S. Gregorio, Venice*

My dear Helen,

I don't see why I should sacrifice any small affection you may ever have had for me because I have the sense to go to Italy while you choose to go to France. However, as I'm of a forgiving nature, I will tell you that all your rancour is forgiven you in consideration of your having written me such a nice long letter and it will be even more so if you'll write me another and tell me at first hand about Charleston . . .

If Roger doesn't obliterate the sweet peas, I will, so you can be easy. I daresay you won't be able to keep me and my paint pots out of your rooms.[1] I warn you, as I have got several tips here regarding house decoration, some of which I think very suitable to you and which I long to try. I have been buying stuffs. Duncan and I are getting a reputation for complete insanity. He has bought a grey velvet pair of trousers with waves on it and has ordered two shirts, and I have developed a passion for cheap prints. I have to pretend they're for my *bambina,* but they're not, they're for me. I see that as usual our luggage will become a problem as the pottery question isn't even attacked yet, and there are wonderful looking-glasses with coloured edges and corrugated shapes which tempt us. I have never been so lazy in my life. I have done all the sightseeing I intend to do in Venice

---

[1]RF and Helen Anrep had been staying at Charleston while house hunting in the vicinity. Eventually they took the lease of 48 Bernard Street, Bloomsbury.

and very seldom do any painting. I read Mrs Webb[2] and French novels and eat a great deal. The only drawback is that it won't stay fine. It's no use Roger's going to France or anywhere else in Europe for climate. It's all alike everywhere. He'll have to live in England and make the best of it . . .

You don't tell me much of your practical affairs, though you hint you're in an abyss—but that's only to please me. Have you let the rest of Pond St? I see, of course, who wouldn't, that your *ménage à trois* at Dalmeny[3] couldn't last long. All my sympathies are with Margery. I'm sure such a pair of lovers must be very trying and I should be furiously jealous in no time, even if I weren't in love with you both, as no doubt she is. You'll have to be very careful or other people may share her feelings. However I hope your new arrangements won't include too much communal life. Roger always likes *combinaisons,* being so guileless himself, but he little knows even now the evil passions he arouses! I believe at one time he'd have had thought nothing of setting me and Ottoline up together with only a curtain between us and never doubted that we should bill and coo through it all day. What a comfort to be able to have so many thrusts at him. I feel he can't answer back as I'm only writing to you. I suppose this letter has lasted long enough, but you see what happens when I'm so lazy and have nothing better to do.

Do you like Bellini? and Titian? and Sebastiano del Piombo, becoming one of my favourite masters? There's no accounting for your tastes, so I have to ask.

Please give Igor my love when you go to Charleston and even though abroad I insist upon some affection being shown me (you're *not* to throw me over for Virginia, though I admit she's all very well in her way).

Your
VB

ANREP

[2]*My Apprenticeship* (1926), the autobiography of the Fabian socialist Beatrice Webb (née Potter) (1858–1943).
[3]RF had naively proposed that Helen live with him and his sister Margery at their Dalmeny Avenue home. Pond Street had been Helen's home with Boris Anrep in Hampstead.

VI-2. To Roger Fry

June 3 [1926]   *Ravenna [Italy]*

My dearest Roger,

I wrote to you the first evening of our arrival here. Since then we have got into what you may think such follies that I must confess them to you at once. Yesterday evening after a virtuous morning of sight-seeing we set out again in the evening quite intending to do some more. On our way however to S. Vitale our eyes were caught by a pottery shop and we thought we might as well look into it. Duncan is quite as bad as I am and we saw we were undone as soon as we got well inside. The owner of the shop is a charming and most friendly man whose chief joy and interest in life consists in breeding canaries. He had them at all ages, in the egg, in the nest and on the wing, and we had to look at all. But also he was most sympathetic over pottery and in the end, reckless of consequences, we found ourselves possessed of several large jugs, flasks, bowls, etc. They are really lovely, a very nice glaze, good colours and shapes, and some very odd and unusual in colour. But I quite realize our folly and foresee the mockery awaiting our arrival in London, to say nothing of the fact that we have to get them to Venice first.

But more is to come. We found out from the canary fancier that they were made quite near here, and as this morning when we got up it was raining, we decided to go to the place and find out whether anything could be done there. It seemed rather a wild goose chase. However we caught our train and went to a place called Russi, only about 1/2 an hour off. There we had a very good lunch in a *trattoria* for about 1/ each. We then hired a motor and went off at a breakneck speed through lovely country, passing most attractive looking farms and country houses, all apparently thriving. We reached a small place called Cotignola. No sign of any factory such as I had expected. But a short way beyond in the country we came to the pottery. As today is a *festa* they were not at work, but a very nice woman made us most welcome and said we could see everything. It turned out that she and her husband and daughter, a child of about 15, run the whole thing. Masses of clay which seemed ready to use are brought practically to their door by the river. Then they have another and harder clay which they get from the mountains. The daughter, Julia, does the painting.

She painted a bowl for us to see—very freely, under-glaze painting, which she prefers to over-glaze, which she also does. But it is much less free and finer and we didn't like the things nearly so much. Then the father came in and made pots on the wheel which he turned himself simply by kicking another wheel round with his foot. It was most exciting to see. He was very fine to look at, enormously solid and strong and worked with complete certainty, evidently able to do anything he liked. He made 4 or 5 pots, great big jugs and flasks, very quickly. You can imagine how thrilling it was. Then we saw a lot of the finished products and of course had to buy a lot more. However we now have so many that I think a case from Venice will be inevitable, so perhaps in the end it will be easier. We then, as well as we could in our limited Italian, attacked the question of painting there ourselves and found that they were quite ready to let us come and do so whenever we like. There is only one thorn in the flesh, a Professor, evidently an appallingly bad painter, who lives nearby, and who they seemed to think could give us a great deal of invaluable help. But no doubt he could be disposed of. The people themselves are charming, the place perfect and exactly what one wants.

So you see what your fate is by now, that I have spoken to you at such length. You needn't be alarmed immediately though. My idea is that perhaps in the autumn, after schools have begun again, we could come here.[1] We could get orders first for dinner services, etc. The potter said if we let him know what we wanted he would have things ready for us. You will be able to see the shapes of the things we bring back and get an idea of what he can do. Also you could get him no doubt to do some new shapes when you came. If we stayed a week or two I believe we could paint lots—enough to pay all expenses and something over I'm sure. Are you properly excited? . . .

Your loving
V.

TATE

---

[1] This plan was not realized, but VB and DG continued to look for opportunities to decorate ceramics. In 1929 they began to sell decorated tile tables through the London Artists' Association.

VI-3. To Virginia Woolf

June 8 [1926]   *234 S. Gregorio, Venice*

My Billy,

I will not say (which would annoy you, or would it flatter you?) that I prefer your letters to yourself. No, I don't. But you really ought to be touched if you could see how your faithful dog and cat devour them and lick up every scrap and long for more. Indeed as you probably have a pen in your hand every day I can't see why it shouldn't oftener address itself to me. As for your gossip, it's almost too good to be true. Bulley! Our old friend Bulley![1] If we had just a little more reliance on you we should send her a telegram of congratulations, but Duncan thinks it might be cruel to do so. How can anyone on earth conceive going to bed with her. But then I suppose she has a handsome dowry. As for Julian Morrell, it isn't so surprising, but very interesting.[2] I hope by the time I return you'll have been to Garsington and be able to tell us exactly how much sympathy you gave to Ott and how much to Julian. But Ott's return to Bloomsbury is rather appalling. To think she and Roger might have found themselves next door to each other.[3] I expect I shall have to quarrel with her as the only way out, and I simply can't stand the thought of the parties she'll give, nor of her coming to call on me.

Well, you'll be glad to hear that you will soon see me again. Our funds are giving out and we calculate that in a few days we must leave Italy and make for Paris. There we may stay a few days. I at any rate shan't stay very long. I shall probably go straight back by Dieppe to Charleston for a day or two, so that I suppose I shall be in London again towards the end of next week. But I'll let you know perhaps from Paris, where, at the Hôtel de Londres, I may find Clive— he never writes, so I don't know—and possibly Mary, but I hope by now she's had to return to Albert Road—and *possibly* a letter from you, if you're in a good temper.

[1]Margaret Bulley was engaged to her cousin, G. W. Armitage.
[2]Against her parents' wishes, Julian Morrell had become engaged to Igor Vinogradoff, son of an Oxford professor. They did marry, but not until 1942, after Julian's divorce from her first husband, Victor Goodman.
[3]RF had hoped to rent a house in Gower Street with Helen Anrep, but was turned down by the Bedford Estate. Lady Ottoline took a long lease of No. 10 Gower Street in May 1926 and moved there in the autumn.

When and where did I ever say that your temper was bad? My conscience is clear, at least I think it is, but of course one may say anything at certain moments and I daresay if that was the only way in which I could down you in the eyes of one of your admirers I may have said it. But I can't remember it.

Why don't you write art criticisms for the Nation instead of getting in unbalanced though amiable zanies like Mr Ede?[4] I won't say you're an infallible critic—though Duncan can tell you that as we pace the length of the Giudecca I ruminate again and again on your words and wonder if I should recast all my intentions regarding my art in consequence of them—but at least you're readable. I am glad that you approve of some of my works.[5] There seems to be universal agreement that Duncan's Twickenham is a work of genius, though his Circus apparently was the first favourite. Roger ought to be pleased, for next to Duncan he had sold most—7. I sold 6. [Frederick] Porter 5. Adeney I think 3 and Keith only 2—at least that was the last report.[6]

You're quite wrong of course not to tell me more about Monk's House, which fascinates me. I rather think you'll have to turn me into the drawing-room with a paint pot and a sewing machine and let me do my worst. I should think nothing of it after my energies at Charleston which you have still to see. I hear from Grace that we have lots of roses and that altogether the garden is a picture. What about yours? But of course I can't really compete with Leonard, I know, though I like to pretend I can.

I hear nothing of my children except Angelica. I dream that Quentin is nearly killed in a bicycle accident, but I hear no news except one letter posted a fortnight after it was written. I shall have to pay them a visit.

Mr Squire[7] of course is an old friend of ours and at one time his paintings met with a good deal of admiration, but Duncan thinks he

[4]H. S. Ede (1895–1990), collector and critic, recently hired as art critic by *The Nation* at—or so LW thought—Vanessa's recommendation. A curator at the Tate during the 1920s and 1930s, Ede is best known now for leaving his house, Kettle's Yard, as a contemporary public art gallery.

[5]At the first exhibition of the London Artists' Association, held at the Leicester Galleries. This group was managed by JMK, with support from patrons, and guaranteed a small salary (against sales) to its select artists. For VW's comments on the show, see VWLIII, 270–71.

[6]Keith Baynes (1887–1977), a member of both the London Group and the LAA. Bernard Adeney (1878–1966) was a former president of the London Group.

[7]Harold Squire had been a member of VB's Friday Club. VW met him at Edith Sitwell's party in honor of Gertrude Stein on June 1; he recalled DG as a garrulous young man.

has got into low (artistically speaking) company. He was never *very* high, and as for Duncan's past chatterings, he can remember nothing before the year 1909.

I wish you'd go to parties every night and every morning describe them to me. Everyone would then be happy, except perhaps Leonard.

Your
VB

BERG

VI-4. To Duncan Grant

Thursday [January 6, 1927]   *Charleston*

My darling Bear,

I got your letter this morning written just before you left.[1] It made me wish again that I hadn't written so as to upset you. Why does one do such things. But I had written at least 3 letters and destroyed them and at last it seemed that I must either write in that way or not at all.[2] I know I ought to have had more sense. I thought if only I could see you things would be all right and I should understand everything, and then waiting to know if I could come I suppose made me desperate for I had made up my mind I mustn't come unless you or Mayor[3] told me to. When I heard nothing on Saturday and knew I couldn't hear till Monday and then it would be too late even if you told me to come I was so disappointed I became quite idiotic and began imagining all kinds of things that I know were nonsense. But

[1]DG and Angus Davidson had left by way of Paris for the south of France, where they planned to stay at Cassis with Duncan's mother.

[2]VB's first unhappy letter to DG has not survived, and may have been intentionally discarded or destroyed by DG, since a four-letter sequence immediately following it is intact. VB followed that letter with a quick apology, conceding that "I think I know always that as far as anything can be permanent, my relationship with you is, for it seems to me to depend on things that aren't likely to change in either of us till we get old and doddering, and then perhaps it won't matter if we both are" (Collection Angelica Garnett).

[3]Probably Freddie Mayor (1903–1973), then secretary of the London Artists' Association.

my dear I hope you got another letter before you left—no, you can't have I'm afraid, though I sent one off on Tuesday which I hoped would reach you on Wed. morning. I will write of other things than my feelings now for you have had enough of them.

Roger and Julian left today so we're a very small party. I didn't really have very much talk alone with Roger as he would play chess and both Julian and I were involved. He seems to have been doing nothing but arrange his house . . .

I really don't know what to do about the Lefevre show. If there are three of us I suppose one would only have to provide about 6 or 8 instead of 12 paintings, on the other hand the prospect seems to me depressing. No one would be able to distinguish between my works and Roger's, and Porter would be bad for us both. Also it would leave one with absolutely nothing in hand either for the London Group in May or the next Leicester show in the autumn. I do wish I could have had advice from you. Roger is always so ready to show and has so many works that I don't trust him not to push me into it.[4]

I got a good deal of advice out of him about your portrait and also about Toby's.[5] You will be sorry to hear that he thought yours just not successful, and thought as I do that the head was not quite in keeping with the rest. He liked the colour and thought it very nearly good, and that possibly I might either have another try to bring the head into relation with the rest or paint another very quickly in the same position. That however I don't suppose you could face. Perhaps I could do it from this one, or almost entirely. Anyhow you can think of it calmly from a distance.

He gave me very good advice about Toby's portrait and made me square out the watercolour I am working from, with the result that I have made many small changes in the drawing of the head and have I think got it much more like. In fact at moments it seems to me almost too like. Roger himself painted a most competent still life from Quentin's subject, which is, it is true, a very lovely one in colour. You'll tell me I'm prejudiced if I say I prefer Quentin's version, so I'll say nothing.

I must break to you the fact that Angelica has wheedled me into letting her paint in oils! I know it's scandalous, but it was on a pouring wet day when she hadn't been out and was very miserable, and at

---

[4]VB did not, in the end, exhibit any paintings in this show.
[5]Joan (Toby) Cedar Henderson (b. 1916), daughter of Faith (née Bagenal) and Hubert Henderson, editor of the *Nation & Athenaeum*.

last I had to give in. Then I thought I was rescued as Louie came for her, but after tea she came in expecting to begin. In vain, I said one couldn't paint by lamp-light. She got into such despair that I had to say she could try and give her paints, etc., and draw a little girl feeding a horse for her to paint on cardboard. I have never seen any creature in such a state of intense joy and excitement. She seemed at once mistress of the technique and painted very boldly with complete certainty and no hesitation about the right way to take paint on her brush, mix it on the palette, etc. The result is really rather lovely. Don't laugh at me. I wish you could see it. As it's to be given to Louie perhaps you won't, but she is going to paint another for you and one for me. She has spent every moment since then with me absorbed in painting. She announced with triumph that *now* I could know that she was really going to be an artist. I said it was no news to me. In fact her aptitude for it seems to me almost uncanny. If she can paint like this at the age of 8 what *will* happen?

... Please tell me that you are enjoying yourself. I think you are sure to in Paris, but I hope you won't stay there too long as I shall be most anxious to hear what you think about Cassis and our coming there or elsewhere. Angelica said "I do wish Duncan were here." So do I. Goodbye my dear—what pages.

Your
B[eaver]

ANGELICA GARNETT

VI-5. To Duncan Grant

Friday [January 7, 1927]   *Charleston*

My darling Bear,

I had your card from Paris this morning. I'm afraid Julian won't have found you if you were going on at once, or anyhow you won't have had time to go and get clothes with him. Perhaps you won't regret it, for it was a tiresome job to put on you.

I am very glad you felt so happy in Paris my dear, and I was glad of your card, though I hope soon you may get time to write me a real letter, for I haven't had one for a long time. You needn't feel obliged to answer my letter of complaints which I hope you have burnt. I know you can't say anything I don't really know and I don't see why you should have to bother to say it. I am quite cheerful now and sensible fundamentally, and only wish I could promise I'd always be so.

I had a visit from Virginia today. It was a most heavenly day till this evening, when it's pouring, and she bicycled over to lunch. Angelica bombarded her after lunch and kept up such a rattle I couldn't get a word in, but when Louie at last carried her off we had a short *tête-à-tête*. You heard all her news about Ka [Cox],[1]etc., of course, and she hadn't much since they have been at Rodmell since Tuesday. I gather there has been another crisis with Angus. As usual this is in strict confidence and I think you had better say nothing, as it's no good and I think does him harm if we get mixed up in it. Virginia as you know has been asked to go to America for a month, all expenses paid and £125 extra. Leonard wants to go himself to see the political situation and defend Virginia from the Americans. I think it's quite likely they will go, anyhow they are contemplating it, and if so they feel as usual that Angus is not competent to run the press alone. It is to be discussed and settled when he returns from France. I rather guess but don't know that the affair with Tommy [Tomlin] is making him too depressed and incapable of any effort for them to be able to manage with him much longer, but I suppose nothing can help that.

Then Virginia had had an evening visit from Oliver who had been rather tipsy and had told them the story of his life. According to him, Tommy and Julia[2] have now departed to the country together, but this may be an old story. Anyhow he thinks they have practically eloped with each other and he's rather upset about it. He told them all about his marriage with Ruby and how she had a son by another man, but as he didn't know at the time the son was born in wedlock (with Oliver) and is a Strachey and St Loe[3] is terribly disturbed as

---

[1]The Woolfs had spent Christmas at Zennor, Cornwall, with Ka and her husband the painter William Edward Arnold-Foster (1885–1951).
[2]Julia Frances Strachey (1901–79), writer, only child of Oliver Strachey and his first wife Ruby Mayer, whom he divorced in 1908. Julia married Stephen Tomlin in July 1927.
[3]St. Loe Strachey (1860–1927), proprietor and editor of *The Spectator*. He was a cousin of Oliver Strachey's.

apparently he will one day become Lord Strachey. Can this be true? It sounds to me most peculiar, but I may have got it wrong. Also Oliver made Virginia very cross, so she said, by telling her he had not been in love with her—as was rumoured, do you remember, when he returned from India—but with me. Why he married Ray in that case I don't see. But perhaps his love for me—which still continues— was platonic, though I can't say it seemed to me exactly so when it came to my notice after his marriage. I can't think of any other gossip I heard. She seemed very well and as thick as ever with Vita.

Grace saw [Doctor] Masson this morning and he said she had bruised but not broken a rib. He bandaged her up and said she'd be all right in a fortnight and she can do her work, all except carrying heavy things, so it's better than it might have been. He thought she might quite easily have broken a rib. She looked most lovely half naked and I wished we could get her to sit to us.

I have been working hard at Toby, as I want to get it done before I go away if I do go. I am rather interested [in this painting]—in fact very much so, if you don't think it sounds conceited. It seems to me at present the most together of my portraits, but of course anything may happen.

Angelica spent this evening writing two poems. I am not supposed to know, but I couldn't resist looking at them after she had gone, as she had been perfectly quiet and absorbed the whole time. I think she has been led by Virginia to hope that the Hogarth Press will publish them and no doubt if so she'll make them keep to it. One is called "Spring" and it is about larks and church bells—and the other about the Queen of Night! Her painting is almost finished and I'm afraid may be slightly spoilt by the fact that as it's for Louie she will take Louie's advice, which is always bad.

Quentin is a very charming companion now we're alone together. I don't see very much of him, but he wants to learn to play chess, so we play after a fashion. Tomorrow he is going to walk over to Rodmell. In the evening we have to dine with the Keyneses, a prospect which fills us both with dismay. It will be a sad affair I expect, not even good food, as the Harlands[4] aren't there. Did you see about McEvoy's[5] death after a week's illness from pneumonia.

Please write when you can, my dear, for you seem very remote. What a fool I was not to go up and see you I often think. As it is I

[4]Mr. and Mrs. Harland, manservant and cook, respectively, to the Keyneses.
[5]Ambrose McEvoy (1878–1927), Slade-trained painter; member of the NEAC.

haven't seen you or really had more than hurried notes and cards for more than a week, and when shall I see you again?

There is so much I want to know.

Your loving
B.

ANGELICA GARNETT

VI-6. To Roger Fry

Wednesday [January 26, 1927]   *[Les Mimosas, Cassis]*

My dearest Roger,

I have sent you two cards, so you'll know that Duncan is going on all right.[1] The telegram I got in Paris was the greatest relief, but even so I was surprised when I got here to find that he was walking about and able to sit out in the sun. I suppose one always mistrusts other people's treatment of anyone one cares much about. Anyhow I am convinced that if I'd been here he'd never have been so ill and even now I feel uneasy lest they should let him recover too fast. He arrived here ill really, but they had no thermometer and evidently took it very lightly for about a week and never even sent for a doctor or got a thermometer. At last they did get the doctor but he only came in the mornings when [Duncan] was at his best and they don't seem to have made him understand how bad Duncan got later in the day. He was allowed to get up and then of course had a relapse. They only got the doctor in then by accident really as Angus had to get the key of the flat from him. (The flat is the top half of a small newly built villa near Les Mimosas.) The doctor then came for the first time in the evening and realised how bad he was and became really uneasy. I think since then he has been very well looked after and is evidently recovering very well. He still has a stitch in his side which they seem

[1]Although VB had planned to join DG later at Cassis, her plans were accelerated when she learned from Angus that DG was lying in bed at Les Mimosas (his mother's rented villa) with suspected typhoid. She left London, with Grace and Angelica, on January 22, stopping in Paris overnight, where she received news of DG's improved condition.

to think natural, and is very feeble of course and looks frightfully thin. But as he can eat and has a good appetite, I hope he'll get strong quickly.

The crowd is a little trying. Mrs. Grant, Aunt Daisy, Miss Elwes, Angus, myself, Duncan, all in the one sitting-room. I have only seen him alone once, this morning. It's difficult to make out what their plans are. But I shall try to get established at the flat as soon as possible, when I shall be more independent, and can see Duncan more easily, especially when he's strong enough to come to me or to use the studio, which they don't use at all. Here one has to sit in the salon, with English ladies and Wyndham Tryon,[2] as one's bedroom is too cold. Angelica and Grace are in a wild state of excitement and enjoy everything, food and travelling and all they see and do.

I know I gave you and Helen—Helen especially—a terrible time in London, but my dear you shouldn't both be so nice to me if you don't want me to presume upon it. Tell Helen please that she was much much too kind and weak in her treatment of me. I think she probably saved me from complete dementia, but she had to suffer for it. I don't know how I could have got through those last days if it hadn't been for you two. These things always happen in illness if one isn't on the spot, I know, but I think my worries were really not unreasonable, for Duncan has been very bad, much worse than they actually told me, and nearly as bad as I imagined. However it's over now. I still hardly know what I'm about, with nothing to do, no cupboards to fill and drawers to empty and letters to look for, or telegrams, but I am really sane again, fundamentally at any rate, though quite capable of being foolish I daresay. But I really slept last night for the first time for a week and am quite recovered. When I can see Duncan in peace I shall be completely myself again, and that I hope will be very soon.

I had quite a nice time in Paris, after I'd got news. I saw a great deal of Julian and was astonished to find that he's suddenly *really* grown up.[3] He talked to me quite freely and at great length about himself, all his feelings about poetry and other things, and also about people. He's so honest and independent in his views that I found him fascinating to talk to, and we could be quite frank with each other, which was fascinating to me. I found it almost impossible to believe

[2]Wyndham Tryon (1883–1942), a Slade-trained painter, and member of the NEAC.
[3]In the year between school and Cambridge, Julian Bell lived in Paris with a schoolteacher named Pinault and his family.

I was his mother, it was so exactly like talking to a friend of one's own choosing, only more intimate in many ways than most friends. You can imagine that he won my heart by confiding that in his opinion Mary was really exactly like the Seend people, only she pretended not to be! Of course I thought it very acute.

I saw Dr Agostini today who nearly fell into my arms when told I was a friend of yours. I hope he'll quite do so tomorrow when I take Angelica and Grace to him to be inoculated.

Don't take my criticisms of D.'s family's treatment of him too seriously. No doubt I'm quite wrong. He's certainly very well nursed now. Please write when you have time.

Your loving
V.

Dearest Helen—This is only to give you my love specially, as Roger has had all my news. I do hope I didn't tire you out and that *you* haven't had a relapse. Please be careful.

Your loving
V.

TATE

VI-7. To Virginia Woolf

Feb. 5 [1927]   *Villa Corsica,*[1] *Cassis,*
                                   Bouches du Rhône

My Billy,

I am most grateful for your letter telling me all about those extraordinary parakeets.[2] Really they are a caution. It's all most interesting. You needn't have any fears of my giving you away. Clive said he'd tell me all about it himself when he saw me in his first letter. When I heard from him again saying he wasn't coming and again

---

[1]VB's flat near Les Mimosas.
[2]CB and Mary Hutchinson were embroiled in a messy breakup. CB had involved VW by confiding in her his unhappiness and boredom. The final straw was Mary's admission that she was slightly in love with someone else.

giving no reason except that "he was a nicer character than people generally thought," I wrote to him saying I was completely in the dark and asking him to tell me a little more than those cryptic remarks. It's quite unnecessary therefore for me to tell him now that I do know any more. Probably he'll write a little more soon, but if not I can ignore the whole thing until I see him, when I shall simply ask him what it was all about as if I knew nothing. The only other person I have written to is Roger. The last time I wrote to him I asked him if he knew anything of these mysterious goings on. That's all.

But I daresay you'll get into trouble with the principals. One always does. When Clive had his affair with Juana, Mary blamed me— though I was of course completely innocent of anything beyond a liking for Juana. I expect she finds it easier to put some blame onto you and or me, and as you say, she can behave like a cook. The whole affair is very interesting.

My real opinion is that Clive ought to break with Mary. I'm not in the least anxious for him to from my own point of view, as I never see her now except for 3 days at Charleston each summer and I daresay any other mistress might be more tiresome. But I think it's quite time she stops [preventing] him from working. She may not mean to or want to, but she's so obviously really unfitted for anything but a social existence that I don't see how she can help it. I think Clive ought now to settle down and use his brains a bit. He has quite good ones and might do many things well worth doing. He could have love affairs of a milder kind which needn't interfere with work and I believe he'd be much happier. . .

Shall you really come here and not go to America, I wonder? I can't help thinking you'd like it, though it's rash to expect anyone else to like what one likes oneself. Duncan and I play with the idea of buying a house here, but we shan't really do so. We went one day to a most attractive farm with a deep well down which one looked and fields of narcissus all round and vineyards and considered how one could add a studio, but it's not for sale. We do seriously think however of trying to take rooms or studios, or something one could come to at times, for from our point of view it seems too absurd not to. Painting is a different thing here from what it can be in the winter in England. It's never dark, even when the sky is grey. The light in the Penrose[3] studio is perfect, and even now one could often work out of doors,

[3]Les Mimosas was owned by Roland Penrose (1900–84), painter and writer, and founder of the ICA.

if one wanted to. It makes so much difference to be sure one won't suddenly be held up in the middle of something by fog or darkness. Also the beauty is a constant delight. The people are very friendly and helpful and living is very cheap. I had my first household books today, and with washing and my daily's wages and all they come to just about £3.[4] One will have no gas or light to pay in addition of course, only a comparatively small amount for coal and wood. We're a small household of course, only myself, Grace and Angelica, but still I can't do it as cheaply as that in England. No doubt we could do it more cheaply still if one took trouble to—so far I have only got what seemed nicest or easiest. But I don't know whether we can find anything or what we shall do really, only it seems more and more ridiculous for painters to spend half their lives in the dark. . .

I suppose you haven't given any attention to a story for me to do drawings for? I could really do them here, as nearly all my evenings are solitary. I don't often go to the Mimosas in the evening, as I'm afraid of being a Keynes to their Charleston. I go down and work in the studio, where I'm alone with Duncan by day, but I always come back here for tea with Angelica and spend my evenings alone (that's why you have to put up with such long letters). So you see I have many hours which I could devote to trying to turn a penny or two.

While I remember it, your parcel has come. At least there's one at the station which I think must be yours. I'm very thankful for it as Angelica's underclothes are really Isabelline.[5]

Have you been to see the show at Lefevre's by Roger and Porter? You must go, and tell me what it's like. Also if they get up a show of my works at our room in Bond St.[6] soon, will you give me your criticisms—but it will only be of unpretentious sketches, if there is one.

Is Angus back all right and the better for his holiday, which wasn't so successful as it might have been, with Duncan ill.

Duncan has taken great strides the last few days and really seems practically well again. He can walk and do all much as usual and looks *much* better and is in very good spirits. Angelica is very happy

---

[4] In today's terms, about £76/$133.
[5] Isabelline: originally the name of a color, grayish yellow, but now used to describe the appearance of very dirty clothes. Legends concerning this term are dismissed by the OED.
[6] VB's one-artist exhibition at 163 New Bond Street, the showroom of the LAA. VW praised this work, telling her sister: "You are now mistress of the phrase. All your pictures are built up of flying phrases" (VWLIII, 340–41).

and getting quite pink. She spends all her days out except for a daily hour learning French with a very good little lady in the town who gives lessons in the Berlitz method. Angelica and Grace are learning together.

Your
VB

BERG

VI-8. To Virginia Woolf

Feb. 22 [1927]   *Villa Corsica, Cassis*

My Billy,

I am sorry I wrote as if I were depressed. No, I'm not, though I must say I shall be rather glad when the McNeil household breaks up. It is doing so sooner than was intended. The Penroses suddenly announced that they meant to return at once. Aunt Daisy had thought she could keep the house another 3 months if she liked and had meant to stay another fortnight and then hand it over to me. As usual in these friendly lets there was a misunderstanding, put down to Valentine, Mrs. Penrose, the Marseilles whore[1] who, everyone says, has captured Roland, and who is almost universally disliked. Anyhow they are coming back on Saturday, rather to the general upset of Aunt Daisy, Mrs Grant and Miss Elwes, who are scattered. It's also rather to my upset, as I can't have the house or the studio. That is really the only tiresome part of it as I think I can get the lower part of this house, which is now ready for habitation. We shall not have a studio, but there are 3 good rooms downstairs. Clive can live there if he likes, and also Duncan, and we shall have room for you if you don't come

---

[1]The poet Valentine Penrose (née Boue), who married Roland Penrose in 1925. They divorced, and his second wife was the American photographer Lee Miller (d. 1977). It is not clear why Valentine Penrose was called "the Marseilles whore," though one Marseilles prostitute did in fact live at Cassis, the lover of a Miss Sellers, an Englishwoman (see Gerald Brenan, *A Personal Record: 1920–1972* [London: Jonathan Cape, 1974]).

at the same time as your nephews. So it will be all right I hope and we must do without a studio.

I shall be very glad to have some grown up educated companions again, which I haven't had since Charleston early in January, not to live with, that is to say. Angelica is so intelligent and vivacious that she's much better than most grown ups in many ways, but of course no child, however charming, can be talked to equally. Since we have been here I have had practically to live with Grace—she has had all her meals with us, generally alone with me in the evenings, as it seemed too absurd for her to bring in my food and then have her own rather later in the next room. But it is curious. Though extraordinarily nice and free from any of the tiresome qualities of many of our friends, she is, like all the uneducated, completely empty-headed really, and after a bit it gets terribly on one's nerves. She either asks me questions, which it is obvious she could answer as well as I can, or she tells me things she has already told me dozens of times about the Harlands. One has practically no ground in common. I am rather interested to see what does happen with the lower classes, as Grace is a very good specimen, not only unusually nice, but much more ready than most to try to understand other things, reading all she can get hold of and making desperate efforts towards culture. But there's something I suppose in having educated grandparents, for already Angelica is capable of understanding things in a way one can see Grace never will. However my inquiries into the lower class mind will come to an end in a few days now I'm glad to say, for I shall relegate her to the kitchen again when Duncan comes here.

It has of course been rather tantalizing too to see so little of him alone, as when one's working one can't enjoy desultory gossip—this you don't believe. But he's only once, last night, been able to come up here alone in the evening and then only for a short time. Otherwise I have seen him only at work or surrounded by the ladies. Still, he's really getting quite strong again I think, which is the great thing.

I will tell you all I can unscrupulously when Clive comes, if indeed I hear anything. But I suspect it's all rather dull now. I imagine things had been difficult for some time. There was the episode of the spoilt supper party you remember, and other things of the kind showed it. Then I suppose there was a crisis, and now I imagine probably both have decided on a separation, for a time at any rate. I think Mary may mean to whistle him back in a month or two, and probably if he leads a quiet, chaste existence here for a bit she'll have no difficulty. I agree with you in a certain respect for her determination, though I think it also implies a good deal of denseness and want of sensibility.

But I expect she'll get her way. Anyhow I will tell you all I have to tell in reward for your indiscretions to me.

Clive seems to think you look young—and neat![2] So I suppose I must accept the general opinion. Duncan says however that he'll give me up altogether, far from marrying me, if I do likewise. My hair has been coming down all the evening and I feel sorely tempted. I have always thought neatness was the quality to aim at in middle age, and here I am, as you say, the worse for wear and untidy.

Do you think you'll be able to go and see Quentin soon? The wretch hardly ever writes, but I suppose he's all right. Don't bother if you already have too much to do.

I don't think Bunny's book[3] is very good, but at least it's not so bad as Eddie's, which does seem to me farcically bad. I mean the Ruin.[4] I haven't read the other, which may be better. Will the Lighthouse be worse than either? I expect you think so. But will you please take an order from me for two copies? Did I tell you that Julian gave me some criticisms on your writing? I told him he'd better tell you, so perhaps he will.

I think you had better not get too much involved with Roger Senhouse,[5] who is I should think incredibly boring, far more so than poor Philip, and not really much more attractive. His good looks quickly pall, at least I think so. He's a harmless creature of course and very well meaning, only empty-headed to a degree. Why has Lytton fallen back on him after all these years?

I hope my next letter may have more of interest to tell you. Not that I really expect much, even if Clive comes, which I shan't feel sure of till I see him.

But please in any case write to me.

Your
VB

BERG

[2]With the encouragement of CB and LW, VW had allowed Bobo Mayor to "shingle" her—i.e., to cut off her hair at the nape of the neck.
[3]*Go She Must!* (1927). According to VW, Bloomsbury agreed in finding it "unspeakably bad."
[4]Edward Sackville-West's *The Ruin* was published in 1926. His first novel was called *Piano Quintet* (1925).
[5]Lytton's latest—and last significant—love interest was Roger Senhouse (1900–70), who was to become a partner in the publishing firm Secker & Warburg. He had taken the place in Lytton's affections previously held by the Hon. Philip Ritchie (1899–1927), who died later this year of septic pneumonia following a tonsillectomy.

VI-9. To Helen Anrep

March 9 [1927]   *Villa Corsica, Cassis*

My dear Helen,

You and Roger have evidently decided to ignore me and my pride is such that I am strongly tempted to leave you in your ignoringness. But being really a very nice and forgiving character, I have decided to pocket it and address my remarks to you, as being perhaps on the whole the more likely of the two to take some notice of me. Perhaps too Roger really is rather busy for once in his life—though I must say I think it shows a wrong sense of values to consider lecturing more important than writing to me. Don't you? As for you, I strongly suspect either Faith [Henderson] or Virginia of mischief-making. I am most uneasy of your being left alone in London with that couple— for couple I believe they now are. You'll never succeed in resisting their plausible accounts of what horrid things I have written or said to them about you. You know you won't. But unless it's already gone too far do write and tell me what they are.

I'm also, in spite of my pride, really very anxious for news of you both. How are you? And how is Roger? Has he started any new disease? Also is he going to Greece? and do you approve? I'm not at all sure that I do. For one thing I hoped he might wait till next year when there might be just a chance of my going too. Then I feel very doubtful as to how he and the Woolves will get on as travelling companions, having had experience myself of both him and Virginia in that capacity. However if it's settled I'd better not throw cold water on it from that point of view. But I wonder if they'll really go and if so will he come here first? as I believe Virginia intends to do. What will you do? Shall you go to Charleston? I do hope so for selfish reasons.

We are a curious domestic party here now, Clive, Duncan, Angelica, Grace and myself. Clive still lives in the town and comes up here for meals, as the painters still occupy some of the downstairs part, but I think he'll sleep here tomorrow. Duncan lives here. We have one sitting-room, but now that we can use the lower part of the house Duncan and I have taken possession of one room to paint in.

We have had rather bad luck about weather lately. It always seems to be either pouring or blowing. I don't know which is worst. But it's not cold thank goodness. I have very foolishly begun painting almond blossom, which is being hurled to the ground now daily. I know my taste is some degrees lower than yours and Roger's and I cannot help being moved to ecstacy by pink blossom and blue sky. I was so blown up by Roger the other day for admiring a sunset that you'd better not tell him this and my pictures will evidently never be finished, so he need never know.

We have become more social since I live with males again. We made our debut into Cassis society at a fancy dress dance given by Mr and Mrs Robinson, some quite appalling Americans. However we met Roger's friend Col. Teed[1] and are to lunch with him. I took to him a good deal and found him very sympathetic and delighted to hear that Roger remembered him. We have also got to know the Currys, a half-French half-English couple, rather nice, and all the rest of Cassis society. But as I shan't call on the Robinsons one won't pursue acquaintanceship with them and won't meet most of the others again either, at least I hope not. Duncan and Angelica are dangerous. He goes to the café and so gets into touch with undesirables and she says *bonjour* to everyone who takes her fancy in the street and if she takes their fancy too, one is done for. Still I am very forbidding.

. . .What can I say to induce you to forego a gossip with Roger and gossip with me instead? Nothing but philanthropy or rage will make you do it. Please feel one or the other. Grace had a letter from Igor the other day! asking her to send him samples from the different kinds of water at Charleston! Curious child. How are he and Baba, now that they're removed from your care? That's in the hope of making you angry. You see all it implies.

Give my love to Roger if you think he's worth it.

I must admit I wish you were both coming here at once and I can't think why you aren't.

Your
VB

ANREP

---

[1]Lieutenant Colonel A. S. H. Teed (retired) and his long-time companion, Jean Campbell, kept vineyards at Fontcreuse, near Cassis.

VI-10. To Virginia Woolf

April 23 [1927]   *Villa Corsica, Cassis*

My Billy,

I'm not sure that writing in difficulties doesn't lend a certain spice to your pen[1]—at any rate you don't let them put you in favour of France at the expense of Italy. I daresay you won't understand that remark but it has a meaning. You seem to run into far more society than we do. I expect your next friend will be Bob [Trevelyan], and then no doubt Logan [Pearsall Smith]. All the schoolmasters too go to Sicily of course for their holiday.

Things, that is people, are on the point of changing here. Clive goes on Tuesday. Roger comes tomorrow. He was to have come before, but it seems that Ellie [Rendel] nearly killed him, like you, with her new brand of inoculations, and he couldn't start as soon as he meant to. Your nephews leave next Friday, just about the time I suppose when you will be returning too. Quentin will spend a few days in Paris and go back to London on May 3rd and to school on May 4th. If you feel inclined to see him, perhaps you'd get in touch with him then. He'll be at No. 50 [Gordon Square] on the night of the 3rd. Since they have been here we have had a great deal of male conversation at meals—endless discussions as to whether things fall at the same rate at which they go up and geographical questions, etc., also grand battles between the artists and the intellectuals. Julian is violently anti-artist at the moment. He and I play chess after dinner as a rule, which keeps his wits employed to some extent. I see that all will be changed by the advent of Roger, however.

We went to lunch with Bréal[2] at Marseilles one day. Do you know him? He is amusing and tells quite amusing stories. He paints, unluckily, but is really not a painter but an intellectual. We had to look at his pictures however and do the best we could, and talk to his Spanish wife who talks almost unintelligible French. We had a delicious lunch and were taken to see one of the lovely gardens that grow round Marseilles, with an old house in the middle of it. My sus-

---

[1]VW had written her a traveler's letter from Sicily on April 14.
[2]Auguste Bréal (1875–1938), painter and writer. His wife was named Louise.

pender broke and had it not been for my provident habit of carrying a supply of safety pins with me, I should have had an awkward day of it.

Tommy and Julia did not confide in me. All I heard was from Douglas [Davidson], who said they seemed to get on quite well as man and wife. They shared a room and bed and he slept alone and I suppose Julia finds Tommy more attractive than you do. They are a slightly curious couple, however. I don't think either is in love with the other, but perhaps they supply wants in each other. I should find either horribly uncomfortable to live with.

I don't know if you'll get this letter in Rome. It's rather melancholy to think that you will so soon be returning to Bloomsbury. Perhaps however excitements will be awaiting you which will seem to you to outdo the joys of chastity which you suffered from here—at least I suppose that was the cause of your back-handers?[3] Or were the Italian girls unkind? Anyhow, you see how Duncan and I smart. It is terrible to be thought chaste and dowdy when one would so much like to be neither. Perhaps Ottoline will be in full swing and provide new hunting grounds, and Vita will soon be back. So do write and tell me of all the latest scandals, also if there's any news of the parakeets' one.

. . . I agree with you in liking the Italians—only the peasant class, that is, the middle classes are absolutely imbecile and intolerable— but I like the French too. I hope we come from Patelli and de l'Etang.[4] I often feel far more akin to them than to the Stephens of Aberdeen, who would be as much horrified by us—even by me, I suppose, in spite of my chastity—marmoreal is it?—(how it rankles!) as by the Patelli.

Angelica will, I am afraid, revert completely to the lowest of her forbears. In fact Duncan fears she may take to the stage. She now does most brilliant music hall turns invented by herself and I see she'll be only too conscious of her own success and perhaps unable to resist

[3]The Woolfs spent several days in early April with the Bells and DG at Cassis. From Cassis they traveled to Rome, Palermo, and Syracuse, then back through Naples to Rome again, returning to London on April 28. Cf. VWLIII, 363, ". . . you and Duncan always seem to me, though some appearances are against it, marmoreally chaste—You have cast out so many of the devils that afflict poor creatures like me—Ever since Cassis I have thought of you as a bowl of golden water which brims but never overflows."
[4]VB's maternal grandmother was born Maria Pattle, whose maternal grandparents were Antoine, Chevalier de l'Etang, and Thérèse Blin de Grincourt.

trading on it. It might be more interesting than having another painter in the family.

Please write. I paint many pictures for you to choose from.

Your
VB

BERG

VI-11. To Virginia Woolf

May 3 [1927]   *Villa Corsica, Cassis,*
                                 Bouches du Rhône

My Billy,[1]

It is a work of absolute heroism to write to you. All my writing paper has been taken by Angelica to write a poem beginning The Robin hops on the window sill. Then having rescued one sheet I sit with moths flying madly in circles round me and the lamp. You cannot imagine what it's like. One night some creature tapped so loudly on the pane that Duncan said "Who is that?" "Only a bat," said Roger, "or a bird." But it wasn't man or bird, but a huge moth—half a foot, literally, across. We had a terrible time with it. My maternal instinct, which you deplore so much, wouldn't let me leave it. We let it in, kept it, gave it a whole bottle of ether bought from the chemist, all in vain, took it to the chemist who dosed it with chloroform for a day, also in vain. Finally it did die, rather the worse for wear, and I set it, and now—here is another! A better specimen. But though incredibly beautiful, I suspect they're common, perhaps Emperor moths. Still I know how one would have blamed one's elders for not capturing such things at all costs, so I suppose I must go through it all again. Then I remember—didn't Fabre[2] try experiments with this same creature and attract all the males in the neighbourhood by shutting up one female in a room? Just what we have done. So probably soon the house will be full of them. However you'll only tell me

[1]This letter inspired VW's novel *The Waves* (London: Hogarth Press, 1931), called *The Moths* through most of its composition.
[2]Jean Henri Casimir Fabre (1823–1915), French entomologist.

it's what comes of allowing instinct to play a part in personal relationships. What a lot I could say about the maternal instinct, but then also what a lot about Michael Angelo and Raphael. I wish you would write a book about the maternal instinct. In all my wide reading I haven't yet found it properly explored. You have many opportunities for observation and you can start with birth, which also has never been described except by men, or did a friend of Ray's do it the other day? Anyhow, they never know anything about it naturally, and I could tell you a great deal. Of course it is one of the worst of the passions, animal and remorseless. But how can one avoid yielding to these instincts if one happens to have them? Perhaps you manage to. All I hope to do is to see them for what they are, which doesn't do much good. I think however that you may hope that females, with as much good sense as your sister, will manage to be rid of the maternal instinct by the time their children are about 14—so you'll have to expect another 6 years of it from me. After that it changes, or should change—the young should be kicked out—and one's feeling becomes more rational. If not of course it's worse than ever and possibly ruins the lives of both generations. You won't want to hear any more about it at present, and you'll have forgotten Michael Angelo by now and my paper will soon be at an end, so I'll tell you such small news as we have here. Roger has arrived and seems very well and cheerful and has started several pictures, and in fact it's quite like old times. He has gone off to Marseilles to have a tooth out after a night of agony, also like old times, but he thinks nothing of it. I should be in despair.

A letter from Mary came for Clive yesterday, which I had to send on. It was tantalizing wasn't it? Evidently she didn't know he was in Paris, and I suppose she is seeking a *rapprochement*. I hope you may find out something. He says he is going back to London on the 8th. He also says Mr Bell had had a slight operation, I don't know what for, but it sounds as if he were rather ill and as he's 77 I suppose anything may be serious.[3] But they're really incredibily tough.

What other news is there? Helen threatened to settle in Flea Cottage, between us and Tilton. Luckily she can't get it, but thinks of buying land from Ld. Gage[4] and building. Will Sussex be habitable long? Where can one go?

We shall I suppose return in about 3 weeks, and except for one *or*

[3]Clive's father, William Heward Bell, died June 21, 1927.
[4]Owner of Firle Estate, encompassing several farms, and also Charleston Farmhouse.

two favourites, I can't say I look forward to meeting my kind again. It is terrible to think of plunging back after 4 months here—worse than a cold bath. I shudder at the thought. I have had a fascinating letter from Snow, full of tags and quips. She seems to be making a char-a-banc [bus] tour in France. Perhaps Clive will meet her in Paris.

The moths die around me. I can't face them any longer. When does the Lighthouse come out? *Please don't forget my order for 2 copies.* I might as well be in a lighthouse for the moths.

How are you enjoying Colefax and Co.?[5]

Did you get 2 letters from me in Rome?

I'll decorate Rodmell or a gramophone or anything you like and be most generous with my works if only you'll continue to do your part.

Your
VB

BERG

VI-12. To Virginia Woolf

May 11 [1927]   *Villa Corsica [Cassis]*

My Billy,

So I am forgiven. What a relief. Even your stony and reasonable heart would be touched I think if you knew how anxiously I looked for a letter. But I was going to write to you even if you didn't forgive me, asking for a snub though it would be. All my pride was humbled and I was eating dust at your feet in any case, and all owing to The Lighthouse.[1] I don't flatter myself that my literary opinion is really of any interest to you and it would be difficult or impossible to give it to you in a nutshell. In fact I think I am more incapable than anyone else in the world of making an aesthetic judgment on it—only I know

[5]Lady Sibyl Colefax (née Halsey) (d. 1950), society hostess.
[1]VW had sent DG and VB copies of her latest novel, *To the Lighthouse* (1927), ostensibly set in the Hebrides, but based on the Stephen family's summers at St. Ives, Cornwall.

that I have somewhere a feeling about it as a work of art which will perhaps gradually take shape and which must be enormously strong to make any impression on me at all beside the other feelings which you roused in me. I suppose I'm the only person in the world who can have those feelings, at any rate to such an extent, so though probably they don't matter to you at all, you may be interested to know how much you did make me feel. Besides I daresay they do show something about aesthetic merits in your curious art of writing. Anyhow it seemed to me that in the first part of the book you have given a portrait of mother which is more like her to me than anything I could ever have conceived possible. It is almost painful to have her so raised from the dead. You have made one feel the extraordinary beauty of her character, which must be the most difficult thing in the world to do. It was like meeting her again with oneself grown up and on equal terms and it seems to me the most astonishing feat of creation to have been able to see her in such a way. You have given father too I think as clearly, but perhaps, I may be wrong, that isn't quite so difficult. There is more to catch hold of. Still it seems to me to be the only thing about him which ever gave a true idea. So you see as far as portrait painting goes, you seem to me to be a supreme artist and it is so shattering to find oneself face to face with those two again that I can hardly consider anything else. In fact for the last two days I have hardly been able to attend to daily life. Duncan and I have talked about them, as each had a copy, whenever we could get alone together, Roger too furious at being out of it for us to be able to do so when he was there. I don't think it is only that I knew them though that makes me feel all this, for Duncan, who didn't know them, says too that for the first time he understands mother. So your vision of her stands as a whole by itself and not only as reminding one of facts.

But I am very bad at describing my feelings. I daresay you'll understand. Then of course there is the relationship between the two, which perhaps is more your subject, but it is so mixed up with the other that one can't feel only one alone. But that too is complete and seemed to me to be understood and imagined as a whole.

I agree with Leonard. I think it is your best work—you see I can't quite avoid an opinion. I know that in spite of all my personal interest I shouldn't have been moved as I was if it hadn't moved me impersonally too, only at the moment I don't feel capable of much analysis. I am excited and thrilled and taken into another world as one only is by a great work of art, only now also it has this curious other interest, which I can't help feeling too.

I daresay you'll think all I've said nonsense. You can put it down to the imbecile ravings of a painter on paper. By the way, surely Lily Briscoe[2] must have been rather a good painter—before her time perhaps, but with great gifts really? No, we didn't laugh at the bits about painting—though I'm a little doubtful about covering paints with damp cloths, but it *might* be done. But how do you make *Boeuf en Daube*?[3] Does it have to be eaten on the moment after cooking 3 days?

I wonder how Adrian will like James![4] Perhaps you'll finish his psycho-analysis for him. I shouldn't be surprised.

Now having made a sufficient fool of myself, I hope, to please even you, I will go on about less exciting subjects . . . I suppose I may stay a few days in Paris, at least I shall if I can induce Louie to accompany Grace and Angelica to Gordon Sq. I rather dread the thought of returning to Ottoline and Co. I really believe one's happier away and you'll be so occupied with admirers that you won't notice my arrival. Don't forget my expedition to the Thames with Quentin in June, to which you and Leonard are invited. The young have terribly bad taste it is true, but after all so had I—Sargent and Fred Walker still haunt me—and as for poetry it's doubtful whether I can be said to like it now. They ought to know better than we did but they have their own lapses. Quentin has written me a short stiff little letter to say he saw you and Picasso, whose latest work impressed him enormously.

I am distracted now by flies and by Aunt Daisy's sudden reappearance in Cassis—your P.S. just come. You need not fear, I send no news on to Clive or anyone else. This house is now a well of absolute secrecy, inhabited by mutes. . .

Your
VB

BERG

[2]A fictional character in *To the Lighthouse*.
[3]The elaborate dish at the center of the Ramsey family dinner. It is a Provençal specialty that, later on, Elise Anghilanti taught Grace how to make, and which the Bells often ate, both at La Bergère and at Charleston.
[4]James Ramsey, the character based on Adrian.

VI-13. To Julian Bell

July 7 [1927]   *37, Gordon Square, W.C.1*

My darling Julian,

I meant to write to you before, but I have been frightfully busy lately. Fred [Pape], Louie's husband, had 4 or 5 days' holiday, nearly all of which he has been devoting to giving me driving lessons in my own car. I have had it nearly a week now and so far have killed no one and done the car no damage. As I drive along Oxford St. at the most crowded hour of the day or up to Hampstead along the steep and winding narrow Heath Road I think it's little short of a miracle. Of course I always have Fred beside me, but still I'm getting quite confident and I think I could certainly drive alone in the country now. The car is a beauty and I think a great bargain. It's practically new, being a 1927 model, and has been very little used. It's extremely comfortable and can really hold 5 people quite well. Four would be perfectly at ease touring, even with legs as long as yours. I shall have to come back from Dieppe before the August Bank Holiday, as Fred is coming to Charleston for that weekend on purpose to teach me all he can about the mechanism and the sort of things that are likely to go wrong. So I shall return before you do, if you don't come till the 3rd.

I hope you're enjoying Gargilesse.[1] It must be rather nice after Paris.

I haven't shown your poems to anyone, but I rather wish you would show them to someone more capable of giving you useful criticisms than I am. I think some very charming, and give me the real feeling of country things. I like the one about sounds at night—the wind in the trees and that sound of the train which always makes me think of all the people in lighted carriages being carried to the sea. I am amused my dear to find that you, who say you have no aesthetic appreciations, notice colour a great deal—all your poems talk about colours. I expect that Clive or some other writer could tell you many things about the metres, etc. I know too little about it, but I have enjoyed reading them. I hope you'll write some more. They'd be easier to read too if typewritten properly. I will keep these till I see you, but won't show them if you don't want me to.

[1] The country home of the Pinault family.

Duncan and I go next Friday the 15th to Château d'Auppegard—
par Offranville, Seine Inférieure.[2]

Your loving
Nessa

BELL

VI-14. To Roger Fry

Thursday [July 21, 1927]   *[Château d'Auppegard,*
Offranville, France]

My dearest Roger,
  Please send us a glimpse of ordinary rough and tumble, dirty everyday existence. I am beginning to be in danger of collapse from rare-
faction here. The strain to keep clean is beginning to tell. Duncan
shaves daily—I wash my hands at least 5 times a day—but in spite
of all, I know I'm not up to the mark. The extraordinary thing is that
it's not only the house but also the garden that's in such spotless order.
It's almost impossible to find a place into which one can throw a
cigarette end without its becoming a glaring eyesore. Ethel goes out
at night and hunts snails till there are practically none left. Old men
come in and polish the floors, women come and cut the grass, others
come and wash, Nan makes muslin covers to receive the flies' excre-
ments (I don't believe Nan and Ethel have any—they never go to the
W.), everything has yards and yards of fresh muslin and lace and silk
festooned on it and all seems to be washed and ironed in the night.
No wonder they hardly ever paint, though, strange to say, they sometimes do. However none of this is news to you. You've seen it all for
yourself. But I remind you of it to make you see how much one wants
a breath from one's home dirt.
  We got away safely last Saturday and got all our luggage safely
here, and started work at once. Our lives are now very well regulated:
Breakfast at 8.30, work all the morning. Lunch 12.30. Siesta till 3.

2Home of Ethel Sands and Nan Hudson. DG and VB were decorating a loggia
at the far end of the house.

Work with a slight interval for tea till dinner at 7.30. So the only time for conversation is after dinner, and then we have a gramophone concert and reading aloud. At meals too we have the wireless turned on, which I think rather worrying, but perhaps one's powers of talk wouldn't last without it. The food of course is heavenly. We overeat regularly—one can't help it.

We have had to change the two smaller ovals, as Ethel thought the figures too overwhelming (Duncan's group of musicians and my dancers). Perhaps she was right. Anyhow we have had to do landscapes or rather gardens instead. I think it is better. We are getting the walls covered with a thin *couche* of colour all over, so as to get a general view and then we can get on and paint more solidly. The quality of the wax paints is rather lovely, rather like tempera, quite mat, and the wall is a very nice surface to work on, though very absorbent. I am glad to say they are having Duncan's lady over the fireplace and not the round mirror.

Yesterday Blanche and his wife came after tea and we had to come in and talk to them. He was full of his visit to you, which had evidently been the chief event of his life. He had been charmed and overcome by you and your house and all your possessions. How did you like him? He seems to be going to write about you and me and Duncan. It would have been amusing to see you together, but I'm not sure I altogether like him—or Madame. Ethel says she has never been asked to your house—as of course Helen doesn't like her—she can't think why. She always asked her to parties with Boris, but as Helen never came she gave up doing so. I am completely ignorant, have never heard Helen mention her, but there's no accounting for her tastes in people, which are most peculiar. So I try to wriggle out but I suspect I'm not very successful. Nan, who rouses my pity for some reason, is really rather a remarkable character I think, has very definite opinions of her own and is not in the least a snob. In fact I really like her. She has become very friendly with us and we're now on Christian name terms with her. She complains that people are frightened of her. Her real passion is for dogs. Give my love to that critical woman on the ground floor.

Your loving
V.

TATE

VI-15. To Roger Fry

Sunday, Sep. 5 [error for Sep. 4, 1927]   *Charleston, Firle,*
                                                   Lewes, Sussex

My dearest Roger,

I know I ought to have written to you before (not that you were
very good about writing to me) but somehow one gets no time at all
in family life in the country. I hope Vichy is doing you good and that
you've had no more mysterious or other diseases. Do let me know.
It seems such a long time since you went away. It has been better
weather lately but never really nice for long. However we have had
a few heavenly days and have been [on] various expeditions in the
car—to Bodiam Castle, which is the most romantic place you can
imagine, except perhaps Laughton, which is also a moated castle or
grange, where we had a pic-nic with the Woolves the other day, each
driving our rival cars.[1]

Cars, I see, are a mixed blessing. One's own I think, when enough
people can drive, will be almost entirely a gain, but other people's
are a terror. Now that everyone owns them one is never safe. We have
had two visitations, one from Ray [Strachey] and Dorothy Bussy, who
turned up without warning at 7.30 in the evening, just as we were
preparing for Quentin's birthday party dinner with the Keyneses and
fireworks. We had to send them packing, for the table really wouldn't
hold them. The other visitation was more terrible—Freddie Mayor,
Mr *Walter Taylor*! and Mr Coleman or Kuhlmann[2] who used to collect
pictures but has sold all or nearly all and buys no more. They stayed
hours and had nothing to say. The consequence is I have painted a
large notice and stuck it up at the bottom of the field to say

> **To Charleston.**
> **OUT**

---

[1]Bodiam Castle is a fourteenth-century moated castle, and Laughton Place, which
the Woolfs once thought of buying, is the remains of an isolated sixteenth-century
moated house near Ripe.
[2]Herbert Charles Coleman (d.c.1930), shipping merchant with Kolp, Kullman &
Co. He formed an important collection of modern art, which was shown at

Whether it will keep people off remains to be seen. Anyhow I don't think they can expect a welcome if they come. There was an extraordinary notice in the Westminster Gazette the other day headed "Bloomsbury in Sussex," saying how the Woolves had their house and we and the Keynes were near, how Duncan had a house in Gordon Sq. in which every inch was of interest and had just taken on his villa at Cassis for 5 years, Mrs Bell had 3 children all gifted and good looking, gardens which she painted, etc., etc., and a great deal about Tommy and the Davidsons. No one knows who wrote it.

Your design for the Cézanne cover seems to have come out quite well.[3] It's certainly a lovely quality, as I've always thought. I don't think I can give you any criticisms, nor would they be of any use if I could now. I hope you'll do some more lithography and find out all about it. I should very much like to do some. . . .

Did you see Blanche's article on Virginia?[4] It was wildly enthusiastic but gave one no idea of her, I thought. I wonder if he has written about us.

I have been working at various still lives and interiors, Duncan a great deal at decorating the Keyneses' gramophone and the space over the fireplace in their library. Now I am glad to say he is taking to flowers too. It hasn't been fine enough to start anything out of doors.

Angelica's spirits get higher and higher and she becomes more and more outspoken and exquisite.

Please write soon.

Your loving
V.

ANREP

Bernheim-jeune, Paris, prior to its sale. He later started another collection. Walter Taylor was a founding member of the London Group. In the 1930s his work was represented by Freddie Mayor at the Mayor Gallery in Cork Street.
[3]RF's *Cézanne: A Study of His Development* was published by the Hogarth Press in November 1927, with a cover designed by RF.
[4]Jacques-Emile Blanche published "An Interview with Virginia Woolf" in *Les Nouvelles Littéraires,* August 13, 1927.

VI-16. To Helen Anrep

Monday [November 21, 1927]   *37, Gordon Square, W.C.1*

Dearest Helen,

I send you these in fear and trembling as I know how peculiar your tastes are, far more so than mine, in the vegetable world. Probably you hate chrysanthemums. Never mind, you must take them as a sign of affection from me and Duncan. How are you? I don't suppose you want to see anyone but Roger until you return, which I advise you not to do too soon, for London is simply vile. One gets splashed from head to foot and frozen and blown away and Ottoline is at every other corner and Lydia at the ones in between.

Altogether I look forward to Cassis with relief, and I expect you and Roger to come there about a week after I get there. I am anxious to hear about all your experiences and how many nurses and doctors you have fallen in love with. I'm sure you're having a debauch of some kind.

I must now try to make myself a really smart black dress suitable for dining with Clive and going to the Sitwell play in next Sunday,[1] to which I don't look forward, as I know I shan't shine. I read in Vogue that those who dress in black must not have a suspicion of dowdiness even in their minds! so I ought to have got a colour, but it can't be helped. I shall pretend it came from Paris by aeroplane.

Do you want anything a male can't get? There are lots of such things. If so, please tell me and not Faith. Otherwise you need not write. Roger gives me bulletins quite often and seems fairly contented. I am rather relieved Bréal has gone to Kensington.

Your loving
VB

ANREP

---

[1] *(For) First Class Passengers Only* (published as *All at Sea*), written by Osbert and Sacheverell Sitwell and performed by the Sitwells at the Arts Theatre; scenery designed by Cecil Beaton.

VI-17. To Leonard and Virginia Woolf

Christmas Day [1927]   *Cleeve House*

My dearest Woolves,

I am simply overwhelmed by your presents. You have given me all
that a woman of fashion such as myself could desire, and I shall face
the world with perfect self-confidence, though why you should have
given me so many presents I can't think. Really I feel that my family
gets far too much from you. Angelica's delight over her watch is
indescribable. I had to give it to her while I was still in bed this
morning and she was so much excited that for once in her life she
remained silent. It is really a *very* pretty little watch and, as she says,
far superior to Judith's.[1] She has gone to church with Mrs Bell! fearfully pleased with herself, her watch, a new umbrella and a new bag.
Althogether she alone thoroughly enjoys herself and the whole affair.
She chatters away, entertains the Miss Boltons to tea, gets into touch
with all the servants, indoors and out, takes the dogs out, attends
family prayers, looks for first snowdrops. Quentin is bored to death,
and I am reconciled only by the relief of not having to deal with burst
pipes and missing turkeys as usual at this moment. I shall soon however be past the worst.

Tomorrow Clive and I and Cory drive over to Ham Spray for lunch,
where we shall find Lytton alone, all the rest of them having gone off
for the day. On Thursday I go to Snow at Cheltenham for the night.
On Saturday we return to London. You will have gone, I am afraid.
I imagine you now sitting comfortably over your fire, remote from
the horrors of the season, or are you setting out to dine with Gumbo
or eating a Quaker meal with Roger. Any are better than the inter-
minable meals here (though one course *has* been cut out from dinner
since Mr Bell's death, which otherwise has made no difference as far
as I can see). There is a new cook, in the same lines but not so good
as the old one. Mrs Bell objects to her because she is only 28, but as
it is almost impossible now to get a cook in the country she keeps
her. Also one under-housemaid is ill, so the staff is slightly under-
staffed in the early morning, but later in the day a woman comes to
help. Meak the parlourmaid is unchanged, so is Ellen the housemaid,

---

[1]Judith Bagenal was a frequent companion of Angelica's in these years.

so are Ovens the chauffeur and William the ancient coachman and Eyres the gardener and many underlings whom I haven't grasped. Mrs Bell rules them all and does her accounts in the dining-room in the morning and carries her keys about and locks up the house at night. I don't believe anything will ever change this house. "Could you manage to hint to the boys that there is another lavoratory they could use outside when they are in a hurry on shooting mornings?" Mrs Bell asked me in private. So I said I would try to make them understand. You, Mrs W., ought to have married Clive, not I. You would love this world. It is wasted on me. If only you could have talked to the 3 Miss Boltons yesterday. Goodbye, and thank you.

Your devoted old sister,
VB

BERG

VI-18. To Leonard Woolf

[Mid-February 1928]   *La Bergère, Cassis*

My dear Leonard,

I think on the whole you deserve a letter more than Virginia, though no doubt she'll get the benefit of this, such as it is. But until yesterday I had only heard once from her all this time and was beginning to feel rather badly treated. I admit yesterday's post made up for it and shall be replied to. Meanwhile I must first of all go into business matters with you and thank you for the cheque (which was more than my usual fee, wasn't it?) and then say that I think the colour is all right—perhaps different poets could have different colours?—but I see that the lettering is spaced differently.[1] I had put "No. 1" in the same line with the title. It is now in a line by itself. This seems to me to make the top line come uncomfortably near the top of the page and the whole thing rather crowded. Would it be possible to stick to

[1] VB designed the covers for the first eight of the Hogarth Living Poets series, edited and sponsored by Dorothy Wellesley. The first book in this series was Frances Cornford's *Different Days*, published in May 1928.

my arrangement? But perhaps it's too late to do so, at any rate for the first one or two. This is the only criticism I have to make.

We were very much amused by your letter. I see that Old Blooms-bury has lost nothing of its character and charm. It almost makes me want to be back in it in spite of the hurricanes. But I think if I obstinately stick to this country you will all be drawn after me in time and then how happy we shall be. Wouldn't you like to buy another house quite near here? There's one to be had very cheap, I'm told. It's on a little wooded hill, a most lovely position, with a small clearing round it, so sunny and sheltered that we had a pic-nic there the other day and basked in the sun. No doubt the house would want a little doing to it, but it is habitable, with a well. It is really absurd for anyone who likes the sun not to come here now. It is already so warm that one never has a fire till the evening and can easily paint out of doors except on days of mistral, and even then there's sun.

We have had terrible troubles with the car. If you know anything about the clutch of a Renault you will know that it is necessary for the "male cone to penetrate further and further into the female cone, pushing the tongues back until it is gripped perfectly." Our male cone failed to do this. The leather got worn and finally burnt to shreds. We didn't know whether to blame the cones or the road to the garage, which is certainly very bad. Experts differed of course, but we had to have a new leather and hoped for the best. To our despair, all seemed as bad as ever and the car absolutely refused to go backwards or even forwards up the steep and rather sandy slope into or out of the garage. Yesterday however a most curious character, Mr Knox, came to the rescue. He is a parachutist, or was one, also a racing motorist, and had a motor business of his own. He turned screws and induced the male cone to penetrate properly, with the result that the car took on new life, dashed about backwards and forwards, up or down, jumped out of sand pits and over stones.

Mr Knox came in and had tea with us and gave us most interesting glimpses into the studio life of such painters as Jaggers and Munnings.[2] Jaggers, he told us (the brother of the sculptor), had painted Mr Knox's "late missus" several times, "but when I say late I mean that she no longer uses me as a husband—she prefers another." He has drifted

---

[2](Sir) Alfred J. Munnings (1878–1959), later president of the Royal Academy. David Jagger (d.1958), an exhibitor at the R.A. and member of the Royal Institute of Oil Painters. His brother Charles Sargeant Jagger (1885–1934) was a successful sculptor.

here by chance and is writing a book, but confided to Duncan that he is much depressed, as he had decided yesterday that it must all be changed from the 3rd person to the 1st. He is rather a melancholy figure with sympathetic views on war, drink, Americans and such things and luckily for us a genius for mechanics. Shall we tell him to send his book to you?

We went today in our recovered car to La Ciotat, and took Grace and Elise[3] to have their hair cut and Miss [Jean] Campbell to do some business while Duncan, Angelica and I wandered about and amused ourselves. It's certainly a great pleasure driving to places when the car will go.

Except Mr Knox we have seen no one—at least I haven't. The solitude is astonishing and I must say very satisfying. I believe you think of Cassis as a hive of activity—Bloomsbury by the Mediterranean—Tommy, Julia, Douglas, Penroses, etc. There are dangers ahead of course, but so far even I have had no cause to complain. Even Aunt Daisy goes to Rome on Sunday, our only link at present with the outside world.

Tell Virginia I shall write to her in a day or two, though as you see I have no news and simply write because I have so many leisure moments and know that no bell will ring to interrupt me, regardless of the effect on the letter.

Have you ever heard from Mr Boys? I gave him your name. He's the man Haynes recommended to me. I told him we wanted to sell Hyde Park Gate.[4] We actually read books here. Can you tell me of any? I get new ones from the Times Book Club.

Quentin writes that he is extremely happy, Julian that he is rather depressed, I can't quite make out why. Angelica is in high spirits and very well and rides her donkey in great style.

I hope you'll continue to see Mary and Helen and everyone about whom malicious scraps can be wafted to Cassis.

> *Your*
> *VB*

SUSSEX

[3]Elise Anghilanti, a young woman from Cassis who shopped and cooked for the Bell household at La Bergère.
[4]22 Hyde Park Gate had been rented out for many years. There had been periodic interest from buyers, and in May 1928 it sold for £4925.

VI-19. To Virginia Woolf

Feb. 20 [1928] *La Bergère, Cassis*

My Billy,

As none knows better than you, only human news makes interesting letters, so don't expect much from me. Since Mr Knox put the car in order we have done little but use it. On Saturday we intended to go to Marseilles, but were thwarted by finding we had a puncture just as we were going to start. We could have remedied that by putting on our spare wheel, but no efforts of Duncan's or Col. Teed's could undo the nut which fastened it to the car. We had to blow up the punctured wheel and drive to the garage in the town, where we were made to feel rather foolish by finding that all our efforts had been squandered on trying to turn it the wrong way. Not quite so foolish as you will think however, for as Leonard will admit, screws all ought to turn the same way and this one didn't. By the time we got all this done we saw we should be too late for the bank at Marseilles, so we went to Aix instead, which is a large sleepy town with rows of open horse-drawn cabs and some rather lovely buildings, where we saw pictures by Ingres and others and were very happy in the sun. The drive I will not describe, so don't be afraid, lovely as it was with a baking sun and crimson earth. Duncan drove with great skill most of both ways. . .

Today we actually did go to Marseilles. Duncan drove there, managing the hills and hairpin bends with great competence, but when we got into the town he became terrified of the policeman's eye, nearly ran into a lamp post and made me take the wheel. I considered I did very well. It's true that at one moment we found ourselves in a narrow passage with no possible exit and I had to back between large heaps of stones on one side and a cart standing on the other to get out of it. We held up a good sized crowd for some time while I made my way out and received a great deal of good advice from experts who crowded round—but still we did get out without any harm done in the end. Marseilles is said to be far worse than Paris to drive in, which I think is true. No one observes any rules, there are tram lines everywhere, large horse-drawn lorries walk slowly down the middle of every street and thousands of people on foot rush in and out and are always off the pavement. It seems to me a wonder we managed at all, but we got back safe, laden with a table and a looking glass and yards of stuff for curtains. There are fascinating shops to be explored, only one never has enough time. You will have to come also to the pottery at Aubagne where I intend to spend some happy hours buying masses of things for Charleston. One can get really very nice practical things, plates and cups and jugs. . .

I shall get Jean's rooms for you, shall I? I believe she'd let them with bath and breakfast for 15 fr. a night a room, which isn't dear. You could keep the Old Umbrella[1] somewhere up here—in our garage, perhaps—and have all other meals here and the dining-room to sit in. But it's absurd to stay only a week, it really is.

What is happening to Angus? Has he anything in prospect? He hadn't when he last wrote. I don't know when Clive means to come here, if ever, but I have written to ask him. Nor Roger.

Angelica is very happy, much older and easier than last year and altogether more at ease. I think if Judith [Bagenal] does come she'll be perfectly contented. She has rather an acute religious mania on and says she'd like to spend a week or more alone with a male missionary. I don't see how it's to be managed. I can't satisfy her religious cravings I'm afraid, though I think she ought to have a glut of it really.

I suppose you won't be going to Cambridge this term and seeing Julian? Quentin sounds very happy. Do egg your husband on to write to me. It's very important to hear from you both so that I can draw my own conclusions. It's not fair to expect equally interesting replies from me. I can only do my best.

Your
VB

BERG

[1]The Woolfs' secondhand car, a Singer.

VI-20. To Quentin Bell

April 17 [1928]
La Bergère, Cassis,
Bouches du Rhône, France.

My darling Quentin,

I'm afraid I've been rather bad about writing, but no doubt you got such a much more entertaining account from Virginia than any I could have given you that it would have been a pity to destroy your impressions of life here. We had a most conversational week with the Woolves. I felt completely dissolute during and after it. Virginia drifted in and asked questions from 10 AM till midnight until Julian took to giving her such surprising answers that even she was a little held up for a moment or two. Duncan and I drove with them to Tarascon, a lovely drive without mishap. I heard from them afterwards, however, a ghastly account of their journey after they left us on their way home. They had innumerable punctures and had to drive through such driving snowstorms that they had to put the windscreen down. They ought to have got home yesterday, but I think it's very doubtful whether they did. The Old Umbrella was badly shaken on these roads and drank up several gallons of water a day, while our brave Renault is on its native heath and behaves beautifully. But no doubt you've had a prejudiced account of that.

Roger is now here and is working hard at German with a view to his German tour. I have had great difficulty in deciding what to do about going with him, but I don't see how to manage it and I am afraid in the end I shall have to give it up. Somehow or other the car has to be driven to England and Angelica, Grace and Judith also have to be got to England, but not in the car. I suspect that I shall have to take them to Paris and despatch them to England and then return here and meet Duncan and drive back with him, but I don't know. Anyhow, I don't see how I am to fit in a visit to Germany[1] in my already complicated plans. It will be a great disappointment not to see you my dear, but it is not so very long before you will be coming back, and I'm sure you are quite happy as you are. You will see Roger some time during May. I'm not sure when, but I will give him your address and no doubt he'll let you know. Julian goes back to Cam-

[1] QB was in Munich lodging with a Baroness von Massenbach in an attempt to learn German.

bridge the day after tomorrow. I'm afraid he has had rather a dull time here as the weather has been very bad on the whole. He's had a little bathing, but it's really too early in the season for it. Generally he goes out with his glasses for long walks and I suppose looks for birds. I think he'd like it if he had his little Pet[2] here and could drive himself about to out of the way places, though it's more than likely he'd break down at some remote spot and never return. The distances are so huge and the roads so bad that one might easily get badly stranded.

Roger is of course hard at work in various ways, playing chess, painting a portrait of Colonel Teed, etc. Duncan is at work on a large 3-panel screen for his own room, each panel having a nude female figure standing in an oval—I think it ought to be rather lovely. He's also doing various flower pieces and interiors, but the weather has been too changeable for painting out of doors to be possible.

I wonder how you will manage to copy Van Gogh. I should think it would be terribly difficult, as so much seems to depend on the actual handling and even brush strokes with him, which one couldn't really copy. But it will be interesting to see. When we went to Tarascon we went through St. Rémy and saw the asylum where he was shut up for a time. It's a wonderful place and Virginia hoped she'd be shut up there next time she went cracked. Certainly it looked a pleasant place to be in, with a garden and cloisters and a lovely view. I believe he could paint and do pretty much as he liked. The whole country round there is most beautiful, only in the teeth of the mistral, which was so strong the day we drove back that it really almost stopped the car at times.

I wonder if you're in the country now and what it's like. I think you'll have to come on a tour with me next year (before you forget your German) to see the pictures in Berlin, Dresden and Munich, as I can't come now. We will have a 3 weeks' jaunt in the winter and I expect Duncan will come too. You will have to do all the talking for us. Goodbye darling—I send you my love.

Your
Nessa

BELL

[2] A Baby Austin, also called "the Baby" later.

VI-21. To Roger Fry

May 4 [1928]   *La Bergère, Cassis,*
                                                 Bouches du Rhône,
                                                              France

My dearest Roger,

We have just had a week of Raymond [Mortimer] and I wonder why it is that when one sees him one is surprised to find how nice he is, how admirable in every way, but the minute his back is turned, how one begins to abuse him! However, he has gone and so has Clive and so for the moment has Duncan, to Marseilles for a night, and so I am actually alone after many weeks. We never seem to have stopped talking this last week and I haven't had a moment for writing. I wanted to tell you how horrid it was letting you go off so soon, when I really had hardly seemed to see you at all. We do seem to have managed badly this year and I think something better must be arranged. Perhaps you're right, one should come here in the summer, only I don't know about the heat for Angelica. One's always being held up by children, isn't one, but I suppose one wouldn't be only if one had children made of such clay as Judith, impervious to all variety of treatment, or so one hopes.

We drove back that day across that terrible desert, as I told you, with rain lashing us and stones on every side and underneath. What a country. It made me shiver. In no conceivable weather could it be anything but terrible. Then to my great relief we got into comparative civilization and reached Martigues for luncheon. I didn't altogether take to it—it seemed to me too much on the edge of that vast lake which is practically sea and exposed to every wind and it's too much an attempt to be a small Venice—not that it's the least like, but it seems to think it is, or such was my impression. Also I don't much like the country near. However it had got fine and we had a very good Italian luncheon with fish fished from a tank before our eyes and then we had a mostly dull drive to Marseilles.

I was very much excited by your piece of furniture and wrote for it and it's actually coming! It sounded to me very good and I think I can have it in my room and keep all my paints in it and get rid of my table. Duncan is getting a chest of drawers which we found here in Cassis.

We did dine with the Crothers[1]—you can't conceive it, or can you? But not the food, cooked by Mrs C. and really so revolting that I couldn't touch it, nor could even Duncan's politeness take him through more than 2 mouthfuls. The Grace was on completely new and original lines and ended up with some terrible snarl about "and ourselves to *Thy* service." Have you ever heard such a thing? I couldn't hear the beginning and can't conceive what it can have been to lead coherently to such an ending unless the food was to be devoted to our service and so eventually to God's. Anyhow I nearly did for myself and hope that I did quite by the end of the evening, only I think they'll forgive everything.

I saw the usual sort of imbecile notice in the Times[2] about the London Group. Do tell us what it is like. I must admit that I dread going back to London and all it means. How I wish one could avoid it. One will be out every night, unable to work, constantly asked to do things one doesn't want to do, always on the wriggle. It does seem absurd. Someday of course I shall act on my feelings and give it up or almost do so. I suppose one must keep a small hole to creep to.

You are just returning to it, but *perhaps* you'll be quite pleased to see Helen again and won't mind . . .

> *Your loving*
> *V.*

TATE

VI-22. To Virginia Woolf

June 7 [1928]   *Amboise [France]*

My Billy,

It is raining and there is nothing to do in this small place so perhaps I may write to you, though of course I have nothing to write about

[1]Possibly spelled Carruthers or Carithers. Members of the miscellaneous English colony at Cassis.
[2]A generally positive review, though the writer criticized the work of DG and RF, remarking about the latter: "He has not often painted a picture which does not give the definite pleasure that comes of a problem well solved, but often this intellectual pleasure is scarcely tinged with the emotion that enters so mysteriously into the solution of problems of sensitivity" (*Times*, April 28, 1928).

but our travels, and I'm sure travellers' tales are the last thing you'll want from me. You may be surprised to hear that we've got so far safely after our rather ineffectual start, my going without realising that Angus wasn't on board, and then Duncan's finding that he had carefully left his passport and all his money behind. Then we got held up at Arles by my getting drawn into an antiquity shop where I bought a chest of drawers for La Bergère. However after that we got on quite well and have now been more than 600 miles. Our most exciting adventure was with a carthorse driving along a flat wide road in the huge open space of the Camargues. The road was very bad and the large innumerable holes full of water. I saw a horse and cart some way ahead seeming quite quiet and with plenty of space to pass, but just as we got near them the car splashed a huge fountain of water up into our faces and as we emerged from it I saw men shouting, the horse rearing and plunging across the road, the cart coming straight into us. Luckily the road was so wide and level I could just swerve and dash by before the cart went finally into the ditch. However no harm seemed to have been done. They unharnessed the horse and we went on none the worse. Otherwise there have been no special excitements.

We have been through some very odd and some very beautiful country and some that seems as if it would give one all one could possibly want. I see that Nan is very clever, like most Americans, at finding good places and hotels. Both the places she had told us of were lovely, and at the one we stayed at, Brantôme, the inn was perfect, food delicious, hot water, electric light, people charming and very cheap. One could live there in the greatest comfort and luxury with homemade paté and truffles on about 35/–a week for everything, including hot baths . . .

It is now pouring with rain and I fear we have driven back into the usual northern summer. The climate changed completely after Perigord. The French too are another race here, far more efficient and critical. Duncan and I have both become very disreputable by now, as black as niggers and dusty to a degree. He has no ties, no buttons to his shirts and usually no socks. I have lost my only decent pair of shoes and wear red *espadrilles,* and my hat flew off yesterday and was picked up by a dog who bit Duncan when he tried to take it from him. (Thank goodness he got it however.) Angus alone keeps up to the mark. The hotels here will hardly take us in unless we drive up to the door in the car, which I insist on having cleaned occasionally to save our faces. I can't think how we shall dare to arrive in Paris.

But I am becoming shameless since I realised that one has only to change one's conception of oneself into some sort of charwoman or tramp to walk the street comfortably in rags or barefoot. Why one should ever think decency, let alone smartness, necessary I don't know, as one has no wish to hob-nob with the other decent and smart. So you must be prepared for a shabby couple. But by that time of course I shall have been able to reclothe myself in Paris.

I wonder very much what's happening to Angelica, also what you did finally about the photographs? I hope you see her sometimes. It's a blessing that you are really quite as foolish about my children as I am. In fact I don't see how anyone in their senses could resist Angelica, who is evidently the most exquisite and gifted creature of the next generation. I hope I shall get news of her in Paris.

We shall have a great deal of gossip to exchange—at least you will have a great deal to tell me. Angus has given us practically none. He seems quite contented in a mild way. I don't think he's worrying much about having no job. We sometimes suggest new professions, but I see that really the only possible thing for him is a mild office routine, nothing involving risk or enterprise. That will probably turn up one day.

We shall be in Paris on Saturday I expect and stay a few days, then drive to Dieppe, and then Newhaven and London. Shall I be able to house the car in your garage? Could you let me know about this? A line to the Hôtel de Londres would reach me.

Your
VB

BERG

VI-23. To Julian Bell

Oct. 6 [1928]   *La Bergère, Cassis*

My darling Julian.

I long to know how your journeys went off. Do send me a line to the Hôtel de Londres, 3 Rue Bonaparte, as I don't suppose you will have written here and I shall probably be there on Friday next. I was very glad anyhow that you got to Cambridge successfully, which must have been your worst journey, I should think.

You heard of course of our disasters. I cannot explain the Renault's behaviour at all. I thought it was going to start, though as usual it was a little difficult to begin with and Duncan flooded it, then it absolutely refused to begin at all. D. wound it up, we got Mr West[1] to wind it up, I could see nothing wrong, it had gone perfectly the evening before, and we were in despair. There wasn't time to investigate much and finally when we did get a taxi from Sutton and Sutton's man couldn't make it go either we had to abandon it and simply lock it up in the garage. I shall have to go down as soon as I return and get an expert from Martin's [a Lewes garage] to come out with me. But it's a great nuisance.

You heard also how I had to get across without a passport. I couldn't have done it except at a weekend, so I was successful and we got here late on Wed. night.

It is incredibly beautiful here now and so hot that one is very glad of shade to sit in. The verandah has been roofed in with canes, which is a great improvement and will almost make an extra room. There are great heaps of grape skins about,which make an extraordinary smell of something between wine and grapes. We saw the *vendange* still going on—in fact it's not quite finished yet. The great wooden tubs with handles full of grapes are most lovely. You'll have to come here for the vintage one year as it's really a wonderful sight, the grapes are such amazing colour. Forty people came to help and pick on Thursday morning, but didn't pick more than one paid man could do in half a day, and then we all had lunch on the terrace at Fontcreuse and there was a great deal of health-drinking and merry-making and finally dancing, and some of the more reckless jumped into the tanks in all their clothes and Colonel Teed was rather nervous lest there would be a free fight, especially as the sham colonel, Crothers, objected strongly to the presence of Germans! There were a good many of them whom Quentin would have liked, besides Poles and Greeks and other unknown nationalities. Now Duncan and I are very quiet, very lazy, not even painting, simply sitting in the sun.

[1]The Wests lived at Peaklets, a cottage over the field from Charleston. The men were principally farm laborers. Bessie West worked at Charleston as house-cleaner and in later years sometimes looked after VB's grandchildren for short periods.

I took Clinker to Eric's brother [a local man] and she seemed to be settling down all right there and had a meal before we left her. Also for the first time she left her puppies and went for a run in the garden. Nan Hudson thought us cracked not to have drowned them. She herself drowned all her dog's puppies (first chloroforming them and giving them a soft bed!) and said the dog didn't mind, and that if one left one puppy it was always perfectly all right. So another time it would really be the best thing to do. But I hope there'll be no more disasters.

I shall come and see your rooms as soon as I can after I get back, as I am most curious to see what they're like now, and Quentin's decorations. Do they astonish the world? Goodbye, darling.

Your loving,
VB

BELL

VI-24. To Quentin Bell

Oct. 29 [1928]   *37, Gordon Square,*
                                     W.C.1

My darling Quentin,

I suppose I can't complain of you for not writing when I haven't written myself. Still I am sure I want to hear about you and your doings much more than you do about mine. I am most anxious to know how you like working at the life class and whether you get any teaching from Marchand,[1] and generally all about you, who you see, etc. I hope you haven't got the universal cold.

When I got back here I found that the Woolves were going to Cambridge in the Old Umbrella the next Saturday for a night. They offered to take me and Angelica and she wanted to go, so I accepted. It was rather an odd expedition. First the O.U. was in a very bad way, owing they said to dirty petrol, and had to be cleaned out *en route*. However we got there at about 5, and went to Julian's rooms for tea.

[1] QB was now in Paris studying at the Académie Moderne under Jean Marchand.

He seemed to be in great comfort, with a good fire, endless cakes, hot toast and two companions, Playfair and Francis Cornish.[2] The room looked very nice, I thought, but I didn't have a good chance of looking at your decorations that evening. We had tea and Virginia had to retire into his bedroom to finish her paper for the young ladies of Newnham,[3] to give which she had come to Cambridge. Then I deposited Angelica at the Bull [Hotel] where we had two rooms, very grand in a Seendian fashion and very expensive, and then I had dinner with Julian in his room. I must say a very good dinner and all very comfortable. We sate and talked and I heard all the news, but there wasn't very much. He hadn't begun to work or to beagle, but was spending a great deal of money, he said, picking up things at sales in the Little Pet and entertaining his friends. I think he's very much happier now he's in college. He complained rather of the complete lack of interest in aesthetics and all abstract subjects among his friends. Virginia however gave a flaming account next day of the Newnhamites, their charm, beauty and intelligence, and encouraged Pernel Strachey, now Principal, to ask Julian to go and talk about French literature with them. So perhaps he'll get intellectual company there.

The next morning I had a good look at your decorations and liked the one over the fireplace very much. I think it is the most successful. I like a good deal in the others too, but have a few criticisms to make —not much good at this distance. However I'll give you them for what they are worth. I think they look rather heavy on the wall, which I think is due partly to the white picture rail just below and to the white space above. The rail could easily be coloured and I believe it would be a great help to have a little colour above, too. Then I think they'd join on the rest of the wall better. I was simply amazed at the amount you had managed to do in such a short time. I expect when you go there again you may see things yourself you'd like to alter, but for the moment it is perfectly all right.

It was most lovely at Cambridge, the light almost dazzling with brilliant sunshine. Angelica loved it and made up her mind to go to

[2]Edward Playfair (b.1909), civil servant, educated at King's College, Cambridge, a contemporary and close friend of Julian Bell's. Francis Cornish was a nephew of Molly MacCarthy's (née Warre-Cornish).
[3]A paper on "Woman and Fiction" delivered October 21 at Newnham College to the Arts Society. On October 26, VW read a second paper on the same subject to the Girton College ODTAA (One Damn Thing After Another) Society. These essays formed the basis for VW's *A Room of One's Own* (London: Hogarth Press, 1929).

Newnham. We had lunch with Dadie[4] in his rooms, where Lytton and Maynard came too, and then we returned again in the Old Umbrella and got back here about 6, and Clive turned up for supper, straight from Paris.

This last week Duncan and I have begun work at the studio, swearing a good deal at the light, which has been very bad indeed most days. I wonder if it is as bad in Paris.

There is a good deal of excitement in London over the Well of Loneliness[5]—you know the book describing Sapphic affairs which was withdrawn by the publishers. It has now been printed in Paris, where I believe you can buy it anywhere, and a consignment was sent to London and stopped by the Customs. Now either the publisher is trying to get it out or is being prosecuted for having it sent here—I am not sure which—but anyhow a case is being brought and the publishers are calling all sorts of evidence to prove that it is perfectly decent—which indeed it is, and as dull as ditch water and incredibly bad and very sentimental. Among others, the Woolves have said they'll give evidence, which I think may be very amusing, but also most alarming, as I'm sure Virginia is perfectly unreliable and can be made in cross-examination to say every sort of incriminating thing about the circles she moves in. However, we must go and hear the case when it comes on.

I will send you The Nation tomorrow. It has a review of Orlando,[6] which I believe is having a huge success, also a review on page 156 on Style and the Naturalist by Julian.[7]

Please write, darling, and tell me how you're enjoying life. I am glad you managed to see Marchand with Duncan. I rather expect Roger will be in Paris before very long on his way back from the south, but I will let you know when I hear.

Goodbye.

Your loving
Nessa

BELL

[4]George (Dadie) Rylands (b.1902), Cambridge don, poet, and theater director, educated at King's College and elected an Apostle in 1922. In 1924 he worked briefly for the Hogarth Press.
[5]Radclyffe Hall's famous novel, published in 1928.
[6]VW's *Orlando: A Biography* was published in October 1928 by the Hogarth Press.
[7]An unsigned review of *The Lure of Birdwatching* by E. W. Hendy and *Gilbert White: Pioneer, Poet, and Stylist* by Walter Johnson.

VI-25. To Julian Bell

Jan. 22 [1929]

Hotel Prinz Albrecht,
Prinz Albrechtstrasse 9,
Berlin

My darling Julian,

I have had no letters at all since I came away[1] and know nothing of what has been happening in England. Do write and tell me how you are. If you write *at once* on getting this, write to the Hotel Stadt, Gotha Schlossstrasse 11, Dresden, Germany, otherwise you had better write to 37 [Gordon Square] to be forwarded, as I don't yet know our address in Vienna. We go on to Dresden on Thursday or Friday this week and stay there 3 or 4 days I think before going on to Vienna.

Our time here has been extremely hard-working. Duncan, Quentin and I look at works of art solidly 5 or 6 hours a day. In the evenings we have been to the opera or a film or concert. How you would hate it! In fact I don't think we could keep it up for very long, but we must see all we can now we are here.

However, our lives are enlivened by a certain amount of human drama. The Nicolsons play a large part in the Woolves' existence. Vita is in a state of rage and despair. She hates the Germans, who won't let her take her dog for a walk freely, drive in her car without passing 3 medical exams or do any of the things she likes. Harold has to spend his life here in the diplomatic world. He seems to me to be well-suited to it, but she loathes it and refuses to come here more than a very short time in the year. The result is they are terribly edgy and one feels an acute crisis always going on. Then Eddy (Sackville West) comes flitting in and out irritating them both intensely. We dined together and first no table could be found for the whole party and we had to traipse through snow from one restaurant to another till at last we got room at a large and expensive one. Then the film (which I thought very good) was Russian propaganda against the English in Asia.[2] At least some thought it was and some thought it wasn't (I didn't notice particularly) and Harold's feelings ran high on

---

[1] VB, DG, and Quentin Bell had traveled to Germany to visit galleries and museums. Their visit to Berlin coincided with that of the Woolfs, who had been invited by Vita Sackville-West whose husband, Harold Nicolson, was serving as counsellor at the British Embassy there.
[2] Pudovkin's *Storm over Asia*.

the subject and Leonard was enraged by Vita who asked him six times over whether he thought the people were meant to be English or not. Altogether tempers waxed so hot that they hardly felt the bitter cold as we stood helplessly in the slush afterwards, waiting for Eddy to carry Duncan off to see night life in Berlin *without* getting involved also with Harold and the rest of the party. In vain, for Harold did accompany them in the end. Also there has been a terrible storm brewing ever since we came, for Leonard refuses to go to a lunch party specially got up by Harold in his honour, on the ground that Virginia told them beforehand (but did she?) that they wouldn't go to any parties. Altogether a lot of quiet amusement is to be got by those who are happily not embroiled. The Germans are ugly, incredibly badly dressed, kind. The food tasteless. I begin to long for France.

Your loving
Nessa

BELL

VI-26. To Virginia Woolf

[Mid-July 1929]   *[La Bergère, Cassis]*

[First page(s) missing] . . . Seend. Then he [Clive] means to go abroad, and the summer he wants to spend here with us. Well I don't know where I shall spend the summer. Anyhow it's a long way off and one has time to consider it. But I can't take Susie[1] very seriously as a possible bride—it seems to me too crazy really. He talked last year of marrying a young person, who then I imagine was Joan,[2] but why marry? I can't conceive that he'd enjoy married life really with anyone on earth, except perhaps me, and then it wouldn't be me but merely that he'd get the sort of society he likes easily and that he certainly wouldn't do with Susie or Joan. But I expect he merely plays with the idea. I myself think the only solution is work and not a bride.

How fascinating your finding Mary at Charleston. You didn't tell

[1] A fashion model, one of CB's transient and inexplicable attachments.
[2] Joan Firminger, a movie actress.

me half enough about it. You seem to go to see Raymond and Frankie[3] there far oftener than you come to see us. Yes, darling, of course I wouldn't for worlds persuade you to come, I know you have so much on your hands, only what fond delight your presence gives, my own precious, to your poor old sister. I'm glad you recognize my true character—mind you write daily.

Angelica and I should be most grateful if you'd drive us—not you, of course, but your husband, as we don't want to end in a ditch, to her school[4] if you're free then, but don't bother if you aren't. My plan is to return to Paris on Monday the 22nd (I've looked it up in a calendar many times), to London on Wed. the 24th and go to Malling (near Chelmsford, 40 miles from London) on Thursday the 25th. If that suits you, so much the better. It's a tiresome place to get to by train and I don't want to spend very long there as it's almost the end of the term and they will be very busy. So it would be very nice if we could drive and perhaps have a pic-nic somewhere—but don't bother, as I suppose in the last resort the Renault is available.

We are still labouring hard at Dottie.[5] It's an appalling job. I suppose as usual we shall come back with several tons of luggage of the most unwieldy kind.

I find it very pleasant living here with Duncan and my two sons. What odd creatures they are. Julian is really very splendid now, a deep copper colour, but so huge that he breaks chairs and all he touches and walks like a giant. It seems very familiar however. He carts a chair and table and typewriter down to Angelica's hut and sits and writes and reads all the morning. Quentin retires to the tower room at Fontcreuse and paints. They appear for meals, when we are all inclined to get slightly tipsy and rather incoherent and Julian becomes helpless with laughter. They are extraordinarily babyish and absurdly old-fashioned really, though Quentin pretends to great up-to-dateness. But he's very simple and charming here and free from mannerisms.

Have you seen Angelica, I wonder? I miss her very much. She supplies all the feminine element, which as you know is essential to my life.

Transparent green flies cling to the lampshade, the table is covered

[3]Raymond Mortimer and Francis Birrell had rented Charleston from the Bells.
[4]Langford Grove in Essex.
[5]VB and DG had been commissioned to decorate the dining room of Lady Dorothy Wellesley's home, Penns-in-the-Rocks, Sussex, a house once owned by William Penn. The panels from this room are now at Southampton Art Gallery.

with winged and six-legged creatures. I found the skeleton of the cicada who got into my room on a remote canvas the other day. So I must stop lest another comes in.

Your
VB

BERG

VI-27. To Quentin Bell

Oct. 30 [1929]   *8 Fitzroy St., W.1*[1]

My darling Quentin,

Duncan and I went yesterday to the London Group and I must tell you that I think you are quite wrong about your own work (though I know it will make you cross). But I was really surprised to see how good it looked when hung with others. I thought it looked better and not worse, as one generally expects, which is very much to its credit. Duncan liked it so much that he bought it. Your first real sale—I am so glad, and I hope you'll be pleased, for you may be quite sure he wouldn't have bought it if he hadn't really wanted to have it. We went round looking carefully for the promising young who might be considered for the Artists' Ass.[2] and marked down several.

Yesterday to my great surprise I was rung up by a complete stranger, a Mrs Woodforde, who wants me to decorate a gramophone for her. I had to go and see her today. She's rather nice, fairly young, and had a rather expensive-looking house near the Marble Arch. The gramophone is hideous, even worse than the Woolves', so I shall have an awful job.

Duncan and I are both settled in our studios now and more or less in order. His looks wonderful to anyone who used to know it, now that it's got a new linoleum. I am thankful to say furniture is still disappearing. The two R.'s[3] have taken some—Oh, they've asked us

---

[1] VB had taken the studio next to DG's at 8 Fitzroy Street.
[2] London Artists' Association.
[3] Friends of Duncan, the two R.'s were the artist Robert Medley (b.1905) and the dancer Rupert Doone.

to dine next week and I see we shall have to go. For once, we saw Robert alone, but only for a few minutes when he came to get the furniture. I rather dread a long evening with Rupert, who I am sure won't go to Riga.

I have seen the Woolves, who seem very busy and social, also of course Roger, who is broadcasting and painting and seeing so many people he says he doesn't know if they're Huns or Hungarians or what—probably all—and is going to arrange a series of lectures for Mauron, who, with Lavelli, is going to stay at Bernard St. and no one knows who'll sleep with R[oger] and who with H[elen] or whether M[auron] will sleep with L[avelli] and R. with H., but any combination seems possible and one inevitable, and also R. is arranging another series for himself, or rather wants me to do so—and then he's surprised because Helen is sometimes tired. He himself seems remarkably well, though rather lame. Well goodbye my dear. What about the Beaux Arts?[4]

> *Your loving*
> *Nessa*

BELL

VI-28. To Quentin Bell

Nov. 27 [1929]   *8, Fitzroy St., W.1*

My darling Quentin,

I'm very glad you sound so cheerful, and I long to see your view from the Pont des Arts, which evidently did its best either to be the last straw or to set the Seine on fire. Our hectic life has for the moment calmed down a little. We went to Dottie's on Friday for the weekend, taking with us the curtains and electric light fittings and our paints. We spent Friday afternoon and Saturday putting final touches—or rather, penultimate touches—to the room, for of course it's not really finished. On Saturday the guests arrived, Ethel Sands, Leigh Ashton,

---

[4]The Ecole des Beaux-Arts, the pedagogical branch of the Institut de France. QB had considered studying there.

Hugh Walpole,[1] Vita. We had a champagne dinner and everyone had to admire the room and say as many times as they could how lovely, beautiful, marvellous it was. They all played up and we had a lot to eat and drink and no one noticed the various details remaining to be done until we pointed them out. I must say that the whole effect is very luminous and atmospheric, with the 6 mirrors and curtains glittering with silk and sequins, and the electric light arrangements are I think very good. We shall have to go down and varnish the table again and put in the small tiled tables when they're ready. Meanwhile we have returned here and I have even begun to paint a still life. I had to work about 14 hours a day at the curtains for the last few days and am thankful it's over.

... Did I tell you that I saw the frieze you did in Mr Lintott's[2] (?) room at Cambridge and thought it very successful. You had got the only colour scheme which made his yellow walls into some kind of harmony, which must have been a difficult job, and I thought it very pretty as treatment too. I also saw your door at Robert's of course, and liked the colour again. Possibly it's not quite successful as a whole in design, but some bits are very good and I daresay you'd see how it could be made right after an interval.

I suppose you've given up the Beaux Arts as hopeless? What does Marchand say?

The Woolves have had another crisis with Nellie, who is said to be really leaving this time.

Do bring back all Virginia's books that I left with you. I got into some trouble for leaving them.

Goodbye, my dear. I shall be very glad to see you again.

Your loving
Nessa

BELL

[1]Leigh Ashton (b.1897), later director of the Victoria and Albert Museum. Hugh Walpole (1884–1941), the popular novelist.
[2]Henry Lintott (b.1908), a friend of Julian Bell's at King's College; later a distinguished civil servant.

VI-29. To Virginia Woolf

Dec. 27 [1929]   *[Cleeve House, Seend]*

My Billy,

The most lovely smoky blue cat's eyes pair of brooches came from you—no one else could have chosen them—which will give me the greatest air of distinction when I walk abroad. You and Leonard of course oughtn't to give me jewellery, but there's no dealing with you. Still I am very glad you have done so, I must admit. Your present of course won't reach you for a very long time, which is very dull, and I have a small present for Leonard which I think I shall bring to Charleston in the hope that you will come over to fetch it, as it would certainly get broken if sent—which reminds me that I have also got your trays at the studio and will also take them to Charleston for you to fetch, as I thought that would suit you better than having them in London. But if you do want them in London, tell me and I will leave them there instead.

I go back to Fitzroy St. on Monday and we shan't go to Charleston till Sat. Jan. 4th. Shall you still be at Rodmell on Sunday the 5th and if so will you come over to lunch with us? Please do, otherwise I shan't see you for a long time. Talking of engagements, will you and Leonard come to a children's fancy dress party in my studio on Sat. the 18th? Please keep that free. It's most important that you should come. I expect to be at Charleston from the 4th to the 16th alone more or less with Julian and Angelica. Quentin is going to be in London, and so I think will Duncan.

I don't think this establishment can last very much longer. Mrs Bell has perceptibly aged since last year. She's very weak and shaky now and must be getting on for 80. She seems to be much feebler, has breakfast in bed, and rests most of the afternoon. I suspect that one's trial at Seend will soon be over. Already it seems quite unreal and only hanging by a thread to the year 1929. It all belongs properly to 1870 and the wonder is that still servants can be found to keep up the illusion.

I have been trying to get Thoby's letters into order and have more or less succeeded, but I haven't yet read them through properly, only enough to guess at dates. I wonder if they couldn't be published, or at least privately printed? Couldn't you write a short introduction or preface? They seem to me to give such a definite idea of his character that it's a pity they shouldn't have some permanent existence. But of course I can't judge whether it's possible, but you and Leonard might consider it when they're in order and easy to read. If it's a question of privately printing and paying expenses, I would willingly contribute. Possibly they're still too personal. I don't know how Haynes,[1] etc., would take them.

Today we are going to drive over to see Dorothy, on Sunday to see Cory.[2] Such are our prospects. Otherwise Quentin, Angelica and I sit here while the others shoot. The house is cold after one's own studio. The servants are numerous and expect one to wash and change far oftener than one feels to be necessary and all is hideous. Still it will soon be over . . .

I think of you coming in from your walks in the water meadows to a delicious tea by your fire and sitting comfortably with your toes toasting, reading your books, with no thought of your poor sister sitting up as proper as may be, pouring out tea for the ladies of Seend and eating thin bread and butter, listening to accounts of Women's Institutes. A Room of One's Own lies about and they just remember my relationship in time to prevent indiscreet remarks—and so absolutely nothing of interest is said to tell you.

> So goodbye,
> VB

BERG

VI-30. To Duncan Grant

Feb. 5 [1930]   *8, Fitzroy St.*

My darling Bear,
    I'm afraid I sent you a horrid little scrap last night, but you will have realised I was too tired to write much. I went to bed before 12.

---

[1]E. S. P. Haynes (1877–1949), educated at Balliol College, Oxford; an authority on matrimonial law. Thoby would have known him in early Gordon Square days.
[2]Lieutenant Colonel William Cory Bell (1875–1961), Unionist M.P. for Devizes from 1918 to 1923: CB's elder brother.

Today I have been working from 10 to 4. If I had had my new curtain, I saw that I should have been really uninterrupted, for only Grace comes near me. So I went off to Burnet's[1] later and got 21 yards of stuff and am going to make the curtain as soon as I can. It will be odd perhaps, but I believe it may save my reason.

I am going to paint my large nudes all over again completely changing it, as I came to the conclusion I could never get the composition right with the old poses—or even as good as the original idea, which is now at my show—so I have been changing everything except part of the figure. I wish I could ask your advice. My wall-eyed model Miss Drury rang up and asked for sittings, so I told her to come on Friday and I have written to ask Brinkworth [another model] when she can come.

My dear, I have been trying to think what I should tell you I am feeling.[2] If I am honest I can say that today I have been quite calm. I have been working very hard and I mean to do so. It is the only thing to do. I feel rather half-alive still. I have seen no one, except that as I was washing my hands in my back room suddenly Raymond looked in at the window. He was on his way to see you. I said you were away and he left no message. I think probably he was going to ask you to something. Grace is out tonight and I am alone. I don't mind being alone. You sometimes seem to think I do, but I think it's more seeing people without you I mind than just being alone, which has no terrors for me, though I suppose one couldn't be so for ever happily.

I think what I feel now is that I must wait. I simply can't go on trying to be sensible. Sometimes I tell myself that I am quite unreasonable and silly and I know that when you tell me so you can generally make me quite happy for a time. But then I wonder if all my instincts are wrong—I mean my vague dread that there *is* reason in what I feel. It's all so vague. Perhaps in the end it's all because of my complete ignorance—it makes it so much worse. I suppose that need not last, but then I wonder whether in the nature of things it can be helped. However, as I said, I feel I must wait, for while I am still in the dark I can't know what to feel. I think if I can go on working hard I can wait without getting upset, and if you are happy and I am working

[1]B. Burnet & Co. ("Art Furnishers & Upholsterers"), 22 Garrick Street, W.C.2.
[2]DG was at Charleston with his lover the Russian-American artist George Bergen. He hoped in these days alone with Bergen to make a decision whether to look for a house with him.

and feeling nothing particular, perhaps that is the best thing for us both for the moment.

What else have I to tell you? I have a letter from Dottie this morning saying she wanted to buy several of my pictures, but especially of course one that was already sold, so she bought nothing, but asks me if I'd paint the children in the summer—a rather doubtful proposition. I should like to try Elizabeth if I could do it without going there.[3]

Some female, I don't know her name, editor of Vogue,[4] rang up and wants to see me about our latest decorations. I suppose I must see her, but what a bore. I don't think anything else has happened. This is more or less my new composition [sketch of three female nudes]. The middle figure is going to be a negress and I hope Brinkworth will pose for her. The others are from sketches of Drury. I've kept the curtain and dark space behind but hardly anything else. It's not quite right, of course.

Don't think I am not telling you all I feel, my dear. I have as far as I can without making myself go into it all too much, but if things change I will tell you. It seems better not to feel more than one can help.

Now I must take my letters to the post, so goodnight. I do hope you have all you want.

Your loving
B

HENRIETTA GARNETT

VI-31. To Duncan Grant

Feb. 7 [1930] *8, Fitzroy St.*

My darling Bear,

I must tell you first, because I know you will be fearfully pleased, that thanks to you and Virginia I really seem to have become some-

[3]Later Lady Elizabeth Clyde. VB did paint the Wellesley children.
[4]Alison Settle, managing editor of British *Vogue*.

thing of a best seller,[1] for the moment at least. I have sold 12 pictures
so far, amounting to £330 guineas, far more than I've ever done before,
of course. Angus said that today there was a crowd of people and
almost a free fight between who do you think?—Dottie, Sir George
Duckworth and Lady Emily someone. How he must have enjoyed it,
especially as it ended in his getting nothing. The two ladies got one
each. So really Dottie has played up. But isn't it amazing? I think it's
largely because of the Times article today, which I will cut out and
enclose. The buyer who pleases me most is a stray customer of Cooling's who wandered upstairs by mistake and bought that little grey
landscape which I rather like of the farm at Fontcreuse and said he'd
bring his wife to look at the tulips in a green jar. He can't have bought
from snobbery and he may be one of those odd Englishmen who really
like painting.

Maynard bought the large nudes—very odd, isn't it. By the way,
please tell me if you think Marriott[2] is right in his criticisms. He says
he hopes I won't carry out a larger version of that picture, so as I'd
decided not to, perhaps that is right. I daresay also he's right in saying
I couldn't do what I tried to in Quentin at sea, but if one never tried
to do what one can't, I don't think one would ever do what one can,
if you know what I mean. As for the picture of Keams [?] nude, I
defy anyone to look at her without thinking of volumes. I have been
painting all the morning at Miss Drury. Roger came too. I was rather
astonished. I saw his painting about half way through and it looked
to me almost painfully feeble and hopeless, no form properly understood and all most muddly. Yet by the end of 3 hours he had somehow
given it an air of competence which put me to shame. I can't think
how he does it.

I had my new curtains up. They have a most curious effect which
I rather like. They completely shut off the back part of the room and
will I think really solve the Grace problem. I don't mind hearing her
as long as I know I'm inviolate, and I'll take care she shall never know

---

[1]VB's one-artist show had opened February 24 at the Cooling Galleries, under
the auspices of the London Artists' Association. VW contributed an essay to the
catalogue and DG designed the exhibition poster. Angus Davidson was acting as
secretary to the LAA.
[2]Charles Marriott (1869–1957), art critic of the *Times*. Though he commented
that VB sometimes attempted effects beyond her capacity, his was a generally
positive review of her show: "This coming to herself of Mrs Bell is something
to make song about. She has always been a delightful colourist, with a fluent
style, but her pictures hitherto have been just a little priggish" (*Times*, February
7, 1930.)

whether I have a model or not. Also they make rather an odd new space and one could get a very useful background with them.

Last night Virginia dined here—just she and I—I don't know what we talked about, all the usual subjects, I suppose. She told me she was sure Julian was better as a lawyer than a poet and asked if I thought Quentin had any gifts as a painter, for though his mother, I have to be allowed to have some views on that. But of course I don't say much. They were going to Rodmell today. When she heard you were at Charleston she wanted to drive you back on Sunday, but I said it was no use. Still Virginia is capable of turning up, though I don't think she will. I let it be supposed you were alone. They asked me to go with them. But I suddenly decided yesterday to go to Tommy's for the weekend. I don't much want to, but for one thing I felt I couldn't face another Sunday in London with Frys and Woolves and without you, and for another, Tommy seemed to me the other day really rather hurt that we had never been there. So I made up my mind to telegraph and ask them to have me and they said they would. I shall return early on Monday . . .

My dear, you wrote me a very nice letter. Please don't ever be unhappy about me. As you see, I am working very hard and when I work I think of nothing else. Sometimes at night—when I used to give you such bad times—I get tired and feel melancholy. I think now the only thing I really mind at the moment is the complete uncertainty, not knowing in the least how long you will be away, nor what can happen afterwards. It can't be helped I know, but it makes it much worse. I feel all future life with you must be put aside at the moment, for I can't think of it with any definiteness. That's partly what makes it so different from an ordinary going away, when you always know more or less what you're going to do. It seems now as if everything had been blotted out in vagueness. But I don't usually feel very much. I don't want to, and I can generally switch off on to something else, for I realise one must simply wait.

I expect you are right that I shouldn't mind if I knew how you spent your time. In fact I don't think that is what I do mind. I am glad—I *really* am glad—that you should have a restful time and be contented.

Duncan dear, I don't want you to come back, as far as I'm concerned, until you come back altogether. If you needn't for other reasons, please don't. I think it would be more upsetting.

. . . I haven't heard anything about Angelica since she went back, so I hope she's all right. I meant to tell you, but I hadn't time, that I think she's really rather bored with school this term, but perhaps that always happens the second term. She seemed to me to realise how far more amusing it really was to be here than at school—not that it is of course for her in a sense, as she is far too much in need of other children, but I suspect she may be finding out that most of the girls are rather dull compared to you and Virginia (she was furious with you for not being here). She's so precocious, almost uncannily aware of what is going on.

If I have written anything stupid, please don't attend. I am alone this evening and incapable of judging, as I feel rather half-witted.

Your loving
B.

HENRIETTA GARNETT

VI-32. To Quentin Bell

June 22nd [1930]   *8, Fitzroy Street, W.1*

My darling Quentin,

I enjoyed your letter at last very much. How delicious it sounds now at Cassis in your curious household. Are you sufficiently skilful yet to fetch Elise in the mornings or how do you manage? I am glad you're learning to drive.

It has been most lovely here too lately and we have been leading rather a crowded existence one way and another. a good many theatrical entertainments have been on. In fact I seem to have been more often to the theatre than ever before—Othello with Robeson,[1] whom I thought very good and the whole thing most shattering, Hamlet also very good,[2] Yvette Guilbert,[3] almost too ancient, Revolt in a Reformatory,[4] a German propaganda play, almost too indecent as to au-

---

[1]*Othello* with the American actor Paul Robeson played at the Savoy for fifty-five performances starting May 19, 1930.
[2]*Hamlet* played at the Court Theatre from February 12 through March 1.
[3]Yvette Guilbert sang at the Arts Theatre Club from June 11 to 20.
[4]Not traced. Possibly, a private performance.

dience. We went with Raymond and met your friend (and Clive's) Sandy Baird, whom R. seemed to find dangerously attractive, Eddy Gathorne-Hardy, Bryan Howard and many more of the same kind.[5] The play was what its name suggests and I thought it rather compromising to be seen there.

I realised the other night what it must be like to be you![6] We went to a party given by Eddy Sackville-West, one of those parties where the ladies dress as men, and vice versa. I put on a lovely male mask but otherwise was very female—or so I should have thought—wearing a crinoline and red silk coat and an Italian hat. However, such was the effect of the mask that the moment I entered the room I was seized on by E. Gathorne-Hardy (whom I had never met before) and who whirled me round in the dance and was so much intrigued he tried to get the mask off. I prevented him and managed to escape unscathed and unknown, but of course had to come down to my real female self later, as masks are too hot to wear for long. The odd thing was that a moustache was enough to make several people convinced I was a man. Never shall I have such a success again, I fear!

Yesterday we went to see Angelica. We meant to go in the Renault, which had been put in order by Mr Crawford, but it absolutely refused even to start, so we had to go by train. It was a most lovely day and sight at the school as the girls acted in the garden by one of those ponds and were all reflected in it. Angelica as a boy looked extraordinary, and actually remembered her part. We were persuaded by Mrs Curtis[7] to stay and go to see the girls bathing and all went off in cars and a charabanc to a very beautiful place on the estuary where we met her boat with her son and other people on it, all a most curious party and rather fun. We had a pic-nic meal on the boat, Angelica allowed to stay with us when the others were sent home to bed. In the end we missed our last train back to London and had to spend the night at the school. Mrs Curtis seems prepared al-

[5]Sandy Baird threw a series of famous theme parties in the 1930s, one of which featured entirely white decor and costumes. He and his friends also planned but never executed a party on the theme of famous homosexual lovers through the ages. Brian Howard (1905–58), poet and aesthete, was, like Baird, an Old Etonian. Their friend Edward Gathorne-Hardy worked in the Foreign Office. He was the more flamboyant brother of Robert Gathorne-Hardy, a close friend of Lady Ottoline's.
[6]I.e., a heterosexual male in a gay circle.
[7]Elizabeth Curtis, the remarkable headmistress of Langford Grove. See Angelica Garnett's *Deceived with Kindness* (1984).

ways to put up any number of extra people and arranges everything quite competently with an air of complete vagueness. She has now bought a picture of mine, one of the landscapes at our show at Cooling's.

Maynard has returned from Spain, I hear, having been ill there. But he's all right again. I suppose we shall soon have to continue the row with him, which I daresay you have heard about.[8] When we do, I'll let you know what happens.

We've been seeing Lytton, in his most urbane mood. He and Ethel Smyth[9] came to tea together and actually got on rather well. When she's not with Virginia and has calmed down a little she can be very amusing and not so cracked.

I went to Charleton to establish Julian in his residence there, and saw a good deal of him and Helen.[10] I don't think they'll marry *yet*. One can't help being a little nervous as to the final result of this

[8]VB had protested what she felt was a hodge-podge of work by various LAA members in their projected exhibition of English landscape painting from Constable to the present. JMK was eager to display the work of the younger artists on an equal footing with more established figures such as RF and VB. Vanessa was more concerned that the works chosen best represent their time or school.
[9]Dame Ethel Smyth (1858–1944), composer and activist for women's rights. In 1929 she had written to VW praising *A Room of One's Own* and proposing a meeting, the start of a long and, on Dame Ethel's side, romantic friendship.
[10]Helen Soutar, a Girton undergraduate.

liaison, but there's no use in doing anything but encourage it at present and see what happens. I suppose Julian will certainly want to marry some day . . .

Your loving
VB

BELL

VI-33. To Clive Bell

Jan. 23 [1931]   *8, Fitzroy Street, W.1*

Dearest Clive,

I meant to write before this, but I've had a fearful rush the last two or three days. On Tuesday we had Angelica's party and yesterday she went back to school, so at last life may get more or less normal again. I rang up Raymond after I last wrote to you and he said he was writing himself. He seemed to think it possible he might pay you a visit before long and he said he had had rather a gloomy letter from you doubting whether you could stand the boredom and horrors.[1] No wonder. I don't think you need be afraid that people under-rate them or think you better than you are. Everyone is full of enquiries and sympathy and I tell them all you have told me. In fact, the general view is that it must be quite appalling and I suppose if anyone tries to make out that you're better it's only by way of an attempt to be cheerful. However, would it be of any use really if I were to come out for a little? Now that Angelica has gone there is nothing really to prevent me, but naturally I don't want to do so if it's of no use. But please say if it *would* make life more tolerable if I were to come for a week or so . . .

London isn't very cheerful. It's damp and rather cold, but not very. I haven't seen the Woolves or Roger except at our party, but I hear Helen has had to go off to Paris to nurse Igor who has influenza there, so no doubt Roger will be more visible. He's very full of the Persians[2]

---

[1]CB was being treated at a Zurich eye clinic for a disease that had temporarily blinded him in one eye.
[2]The winter exhibition at the Royal Academy.

and has Sunday tickets for them. But I don't think I want to make many more visits. Most of it seems to me very tiresome and though there are first-rate pots and carpets it's a particularly hopeless way of seeing such things, I think. However Roger is very cross when one abuses them at all and I see I shall have to pay a Sunday visit with him. When I last went to his house I was horror struck to find an enormous portrait of myself looking like a handsome but shapeless cook in a red evening dress, painted about 15 years ago, which he has raked out from Lambs Conduit St.[3] and is going to show at his retrospective show next month. He thinks it very good and so unluckily does Helen. The show will be very trying I expect. All sorts of things one hoped never to see again are being fished out and one will have to help to choose about 30 tolerable works from many hundreds . . .

I will write again soon and please send me a line or a card to say what you'd like me to do.

Your
VB

TATE

VI-34. To Quentin Bell

Jan. 26 [1931]   *8, Fitzroy Street, W. 1*

My darling Quentin,

The chief event of the week has been our party on Tuesday.[1] I think it was a success, but it was a most hectic affair. We had asked people to wear masks and the result was interesting, sometimes horrible and sometimes revolting. Roger came in his father's wig and a baboon face and when he took off the face and wore the wig only he was magnificent. So were many other people who tried it on, especially Leonard. Virginia came as Sappho I believe, at any rate a most voluptuous lady casting her eyes up to heaven. Vita wore a mask which was a terrible caricature of herself gone to the bad—so awful that it

[3]At that time the location of Stephen Tomlin's studio.
[1]To celebrate Angelica's twelfth birthday.

gave us all the creeps when left lying about afterwards. However I can't describe all—but they caused a good deal of diversion to begin the evening. Then we had supper, a huge and delicious meal with homemade game pies and lots of drink and cakes and ices and then the play—a "Quiet Morning in Whistler Studios,"[2] Duncan discovered painting Ottoline, interrupted by Tut,[3] who finally died on the stairs, by Virginia who had brought her lunch and eat it in the hall, by Roger babbling of a dark star and a black box,[4] by Julian in the hands of the police, by myself asking to be rescued from the Isle of Dogs, by the Keyneses offering a poisoned pig,[5] by Frankie asking for old clothes, by all the rest of Bloomsbury in turn, mostly on the telephone, announced by Grace (Eve).[6] Finally an epilogue spoken by Ot (Angelica) in which any stray members of Bloomsbury who had escaped mockery in the play were given sharp raps. Duncan acted himself (or Sir F. Leighton as he was called) very well, and Angelica looked most lovely as Ot. I had to be behind the scenes and had a hard time of it prompting, keeping Pinka [the Woolfs' dog] in check—she had to appear one minute—and answering the front door, so I couldn't see much, but it brought the house down, as they say, several times. We had an interval of comparative rest the next day, then Angelica returned to school. Since then it has been fine and cold and a very good light and for the first time since summer, it seems, one has been able to do a little work . . . [final page(s) missing]

BELL

VI-35. To Clive Bell

Jan. 31 [1931]   *8, Fitzroy Street, W. 1*

Dearest Clive,

Before I forget I'll give you Quentin's address, 54 Via Margutta, Rome, and tell you that Grace did find your note and the £1. It has

---

[2]Whistler had at one time occupied Duncan's present studio.
[3]One of DG's lunatics, a young man who frequented his studio and believed himself to be Tutankhamen reincarnate.
[4]An allusion to RF's faith in quacks and quackery.
[5]The Keyneses raised pigs at Tilton.
[6]Eve Younger, schoolmate and close friend of Angelica's.

turned very cold here and yesterday it snowed. I hear that Mr Harland is ill in Switzerland and I see that English people are getting killed right and left in the Alps. Here we live in the usual round, such of us as haven't got the flu. There's a certain amount of gossip, but I suspect now you are the one repository for it all. I encourage everyone I can to write to you, as I suppose you prefer some overlapping to not getting enough news.

Last Sunday we went to the Persians and there met the Frys. Roger of course was beseiged by crowds and Helen spent most of her time telling me about the latest Brock scandals.[1] She said she was going to write to you and so I daresay she has, in which case all I can tell you will fall rather flat. Also of course I take all Helen says with a grain of salt, but even so, matters sound very desperate and I think it's a pity you aren't here to be confidante to both sides. It seems that Alan, though he must really have known all for some time, was told the truth by Sheila [Sheelah] not long ago, and was so much upset that she gave up for a time seeing Peter and even I think contemplated a complete change of some kind, one way or the other. Then she got ill and had to have an operation on her ear, not a very bad one. But after it had been done she got blood poisoning and became very ill indeed. Peter heard of this and came up to see her. He wasn't allowed to, but instead had a fearful scene with Alan who threatened to make a scandal at Cambridge and said they must never meet again. Peter retired again to Cambridge in misery and came up the other day and poured it all out to the Frys. Sheila is still very ill in a nursing home and Alan is said to declare that Peter may behave well if he likes, but he [Alan] won't. Helen of course is very much down upon Alan. They all seem much to be pitied and Alan is evidently nearly out of his mind. However you probably know more about it all than I do.

On Sunday evening we went to the Camargo society,[2] a most melancholy entertainment. Some rather exquisite young ladies danced quite nicely but had nothing of any interest to dance. I saw Christabel[3]

---

[1]The critic Alan Clutton-Brock's wife Sheelah had been conducting an affair with the writer and Cambridge don F. L. (Peter) Lucas (1894–1967), who had separated from his own wife Topsy (née E. B. C. Jones, her pen name) (1893–1966), a novelist, in 1929.

[2]The Camargo Ballet Society, founded in 1930. JMK was the society's treasurer and Lydia Lopokova both performed and was a member of its committee.

[3]Christabel, the Hon. Mrs. Henry MacLaren (1890–1974), later Lady Aberconway.

who was of course almost too sympathetic about you. I mean she became so ethereal in her voice and manner that I had difficulty in living up to her. Also I saw Bea,[4] looking very charming and rejuvenated, also full of enquiries about you and very friendly.

I don't think I have seen anyone else outside the usual people. The Woolves are very full of the new amalgamated Nation and New Statesman and seem to be in the thick of all the arrangements.[5] I believe Raymond is rather desperate and thinks he won't get a job on it but surely he must be worth a good deal as a journalist.

We dined one night with the Frys to meet Count and Countess Benckendorf,[6] but only he was there. We had to put on evening dress and there was a great to-do and Helen had arranged caviare and course after course of Russian food. So it was rather a comedown when instead of the Countess, who is said to be ravishing and the best harpist in England or Europe, there was only Miss Matheson,[7] and then Desmond, who was expected, of course didn't come, and then halfway through the courses the Count was summoned to the bedside of a child with influenza, and finally old Ha [Margery Fry] appeared, having grown brighter than ever, dressed in velvet, very stout, with ropes of amber reaching to her knees and large plaques hung in the interval. I had forgotten the female Fry style of dress. Altogether the evening was rather a muddle and the next day I heard that Roger had flu. I went round to enquire and found him with no temperature, rather tired, but evidently soon about to spring from his bed. He had toothache in his one remaining tooth, to which he had been hanging on as he was due to speak at the B.B.C. that night. However as that was impossible, we decided he'd better have it out, though I gathered that all hinges on it and what meals will be like in future I tremble to think . . .

Your
VB

TATE

[4]Beatrice Howe, a writer, the wife of Mark Lubbock.
[5]The *Nation & Athenaeum* and the *New Statesman* amalgamated to become the *New Statesman & Nation* at the close of 1930. Kingsley Martin (1897–1969) was the magazine's first editor (until his retirement in 1960); R. Ellis Roberts was the first literary editor, followed by David Garnett and Raymond Mortimer.
[6]Count Constantine Benckendorff, son of the Russian ambassador to England, and his wife, Maria Korchinska, the harpist. He was a friend of the MacCarthys.
[7]Hilda Matheson (1888–1940), an intimate friend of Vita Sackville-West's, and the first director of talks for the BBC.

VI-36. To Quentin Bell

[April ? 1931]   *8, Fitzroy Street, W. 1*

[First page(s) missing] . . . all idea of a Charleston party this summer. [Julian's] plans at present are to go (with Helen [Soutar]!) to live *en pension* with the Maurons for July and possibly part of June (only Clive's Benita[1] has arranged to spend June there, which rather complicates matters!). I think he means to go straight on to Pontigny and not come to Charleston till the end of August. However I'm never surprised if Julian's plans change. But you I suppose would in that case join Clive at Cassis in June.

I went to Cambridge on Saturday to see the "White Devil,"[2] a curious affair, and spent the night in Julian's lodgings. He has rather a good large sitting-room horribly furnished in real lodging house style and on the flowery wallpaper he has hung a few works by his family and friends, among others there's a very nice still life by you which he stole from your room, he said, and which I don't think I had ever seen, some yellow flowers in a ginger jar and a coffee making machine (?) and some apples. I really liked it very much. Also he has got the horse headed female enjoying conversation with other characters of the same kind—a curious work looking even curiouser there.

We went to lunch with Bunny yesterday and then Helen drove us (rather dangerously) back to London. Oh, I forgot the event of the week, the Caesarian operation. Really it was quite the oddest entertainment I've ever been to.[3] We went to a very small underground theatre in Bush House. There was a strong smell of disinfectants or anaesthetics, hospital nurses and white coated men hovering in the background. Duncan and I took a seat at the far end near an Exit with great caution and as we arrived in good time we saw the company arrive. It consisted of the whole of Bloomsbury and most of Chelsea—

[1]Benita Jaegar, with whom CB had a long-term affair. She later married the artist John Armstrong and became a sculptor.
[2]By John Webster. Performed by the Marlowe Society.
[3]Raymond Mortimer had provided his friends with tickets to an American medical film of a Caesarian. Frances Partridge recalls that the patient was conscious during the procedure and, disconcertingly, able to converse with the doctor. "The worst moment had been the first incision, and an exclamation, or hiss, went up from the audience. There was a nurse in uniform present in case anyone should faint! The appearance of the child was a dramatic moment, received with sounds of approval" (personal letter, October 30, 1992).

no one else. Only Lytton was absent. Otherwise everyone you ever met or heard of, Morgan, his policeman,[4] Ottoline and Pipsy, the Woolves, Clive, Mary, Benita, Raymond, Fanny[5] and Partridge, Carrington, etc., etc. Then we had the film, which began with a lecture by a surgeon in an American hospital, with diagrams, etc. Then we went to the operating theatre and saw the woman stretched out, and then began the most appalling scenes. First the injection of the local anaesthetic—the mere prick of the needle turned the young man in front of us green—then the first cutting of the skin and the ripping up of the fat beneath. That I think was the worst really and must have accounted for many more victims. So it went on and became, to me, simply like a butcher's shop. However, I became callous. It seemed hardly human and one could even admire the extreme neatness and skill of the surgeon's movements. After what seemed a long time of cutting and snipping and tying one came at last to the baby, and if one had never had a baby I suppose the thrill was great. As it was it reminded me of far greater thrills, and also horrors, but I don't think it gave me any new sensation.

Then all had to be stitched up again and *then*—it was really too much—the man began all over again with a more complicated case. We left, feeling rather shattered, but on the whole quite glad to have seen it. But I heard afterwards that Benita had to be taken out fainting—Ottoline groaned audibly all through—Leonard felt very ill. There was a queue of ladies needing medical attendance. Why we were all asked is a mystery! But it was certainly a most original form of entertainment and I am glad not to have missed it!

Your loving
VB

BELL

[4]R. J. (Bob) Buckingham (1902–75), Forster's companion since 1929.
[5]Frances Catherine Marshall (b. 1900), writer, educated at Newnham College, Cambridge. Through her mother, a suffragist, she knew Marjorie and Pippa Strachey. Her sister Ray married David Garnett, who employed Frances in his bookshop, thus furthering her contacts with Bloomsbury. She had been living with Ralph Partridge since 1926; they married in 1933 after the deaths of Lytton Strachey and Carrington, Ralph's wife.

VI-37. To Clive Bell

June 14 [1931]   *8, Fitzroy Street, W. 1*

My dearest Clive,

I got your letter here last night with its rather disturbing news of Quentin's accident, not that one need be disturbed now I suppose, but it must have been very alarming to see it. Only how he did such a thing is rather mysterious to us, as presumably he was going *up* that steep hill, in which case it's usually so easy to stop very suddenly. Anyhow, as you say, it might have been much worse, and now each member of the family has had an accident that might have been worse, let's hope they've all learnt caution. I've heard from the A[utomobile] A[ssociation] (who couldn't write straight to him as he gave them an illegible address, tell him) that his *permis de conduire* is at Marseilles to be got when he's passed the test. Has he done so? I don't think he ought to drive till he does. According to Roger, it's not a difficult test. Really of course Quentin hasn't had much driving experience and all those twists and turns at Cassis and in the neighbourhood are by no means easy, so do impress caution when he drives again.

I see that our travels become confused in relating.[1] We didn't go back to Rome after Assisi, but only after our 3 days' trip to Viterbo, etc., with Roger. We had rather an agitating journey back, as when we got to Assisi we were told that, owing to a landslide, the train we had got sleepers on wasn't running, and we should either have to come by Marseilles or by a longer route through Switzerland, in either case more expensive and probably without sleepers. We had as usual not a sou too much, so we contemplated a wild telegram to you to meet us with cash at Marseilles, but I thought you mightn't have it and altogether it seemed impossible to do anything but hope for the best. So we went on to Florence, where Cook's knew nothing, and then thought we'd better go on to Pisa and see. We tried to get hold of Ethel and Nan to borrow money but they had already left. At last at Pisa we found the line had been cleared and all was in order, so we went on in very comfortable 2nd class sleepers. In Paris we found your and other letters and a telegram from Angus to say Duncan's

---

[1]VB had gone to Rome in May to meet DG, then staying with his new friend the journalist Jimmy Sheean. She and DG traveled together through Italy.

Private View[2] was the next day. He had thought it was the day after and I 3 days after, so, as he had sworn he would get back for it, after leaving all the drudgery to others, we took the night boat from Dunquerque and arrived at St Pancras at 9.30 on Wednesday morning. It was quite a good way of coming, cheap, and as it happened, the sea perfectly calm. One sleeps in berths from 1 AM to 7.30 and has breakfast on the 1 hour train journey.

Then we had a most hectic day, Mrs Grant and Virginia to lunch and at 3 the opening of the Private View by Ottoline! It was worth hearing. She was of course rapturous to a degree, but spoke really very well of her 20 years' admiration and affection for Duncan! and she looked rather fine in a white hat and black dress standing under the large portrait of me in fancy dress. She went on a little too long, but still— There was a terrific crowd of course and great compliments on all sides. Several were sold before the opening and I believe now about 18 or 19 have been sold, so I hope that even at this bad moment it may be a success. In fact it already is, but the question is whether the more expensive ones will sell and so allow Duncan to pay off his quite considerable debts to the association and others and have anything in hand. Marriot has written a quite incredibly imbecile notice in the Times, all sniping at Bloomsbury. I really think it is time someone pointed out that Bloomsbury was killed by the War. His remarks might have had some sense if made about Roger and the Omega 15 or 16 years ago, but people might be allowed to be individuals by now I should have thought. Not that it matters much, only one wonders what the cause is. Is it really hatred of Roger, or what? I can't think anyone in their senses can now lump Duncan and Roger together as artists or influences.

London is full of pictures—an idiotic (I thought) show of paintings by Sickert,[3] which fall between so many stools they hardly exist. He tries to be witty by taking these unknown Victorians as a starting point and doesn't succeed in being either them or himself. Then there's a show of "30 Years of Picasso" at the Lefevre, which I thought quite superb. It's very well arranged and one sees works of most periods, which is fascinating. One or two of about 1900 and then the very latest. They are most impressive and one gets a very good idea of him as a whole.

[2] At the Cooling Galleries and, like VB's 1930 one-artist show, under the auspices of the LAA.
[3] His "English Echoes" series, with subjects taken from the Victorians, showing at the Leicester Galleries.

I see I'm writing a very long letter and haven't told you any London gossip, such as it is. I've seen the Woolves of course, and Lytton dines here tomorrow. Wogan Philipps[4] has been cut off entirely by his father because he's painted a lady with a bush. So they are penniless and depend on her earnings. Vita's latest novel is a bestseller and she's making thousands. So is the Press.[5] Yesterday we went to see Angelica who is acting in the Précieuses Ridicules.[6] She's one of the ladies and at the rehearsal spoke in rapid French with the greatest brilliance and point, flirting her fan and making eyes. It's a pity you can't come to the Parent's Day next week.

I rather doubt also if I can go to Paris for the Matisse show as I am quite bankrupt, and after all, one has seen Matisse. One spends a terrible lot travelling, especially in Italy. The Colonel [Teed] has sent me a huge bill for wine, which I hope to pay soon. Tell him if he asks, but perhaps he won't. I have tried to write to poor Elise, but it's not easy.[7] I don't know what the French like said at such times. I'm afraid she'll be terribly upset. I suppose it wouldn't be possible, later, to get her to come to Charleston for Aug. and Sep. as cook? It might be good for her to have a complete change. You can consider it.

Did Quentin go and see Rezia [Corsini]?

Your
VB

TATE

VI-38. To Julian Bell

July 29th [1931]   *Charleston, Firle, Lewes, Sussex*

My darling Julian,

. . . I drove down today in the Baby with Angelica and Judith Ste-

---

[4]Wogan Philipps (b. 1902) was the eldest son of Sir Laurence Philipps, 1st baronet (later 1st Baron Milford). His wife Rosamond, author of the classic *Dusty Answer* (1927), was John Lehmann's sister (see letter VII-4, n. 2, p. 375).
[5]*All Passion Spent* was published by the Hogarth Press in May 1931.
[6]By Molière (1659).
[7]Elise Anghilanti's young son had died after a lengthy illness.

phen. They amused themselves by throwing banana skins at any car or walker we passed. Luckily I don't think they hit, but I had to dash by as far from them as possible to prevent it! You will be glad to hear that Fred [Pape] is here and tomorrow he is going to get the Morris out and drive it to see that it's all right. I may possibly use it occasionally if it is, which would be good for it, I suppose. Clinker came up with Eric[1] and seemed very well. The garden is looking lovely. Your room has a new floor. Everything seems in good order. Clive comes tomorrow, Duncan the next day with Peter Morris. No one else I think till after Bank Holiday. I have asked Janie[2] to come here some time after your return, so let me know when that will be—I hope in time for Quentin's 21st birthday.

I would like to know how you all get on at Cassis, and how Helen likes it. Is it very hot? I imagine the noise of the frogs and the cicadas and the general dither of everything, and rather envy it in the almost perpetual downpour here. Still I must say this place is incredibly beautiful. I suppose everyone will soon begin wishing for a "fine September." However, even if it's not fine it's a great relief to have left London, where life has been terribly hectic lately. The telephone going all the time and human beings jostling and thrusting themselves on each other. Not that my life is anything like most people's.

Tommy and I have been trying to paint and sculpt Virginia,[3] who agreed to sit to us both, but whose life clearly is so arranged that it's quite impossible for her ever to have half an hour free from her friends and admirers. Ethel Smyth even followed her to the studio and snorted like an angry bull between me and V., complaining about her operas and women's rights generally.

Please let me know what everyone intends to do and tell Quentin he's a wretch. I hope Helen keeps some kind of order in your curious household.

Your loving
VB

BELL

[1]Eric Stevens lived at Firle and had met DG at Heck's farm during the war. He worked for the railway and later gardened at Charleston.
[2]Jane Simone Bussy (1906–60), painter, only child of Dorothy and Simon Bussy.
[3]Stephen Tomlin's bust of VW, unfinished but unmistakable, can be seen at the National Portrait Gallery, London. There is also a copy in Monk's House garden.

VI-39. To Virginia Woolf

[October 15?, 1931]   **Charleston, Firle, Lewes, Sussex**

My Billy,

I have been for the last 3 days completely submerged in The Waves[1]—and am left rather gasping, out of breath, choking, half-drowned, as you might expect. I must read it again when I may hope to float more quietly, but meanwhile I'm so overcome by the beauty (Is all this what George [Duckworth] is saying to you? I expect so.) it's impossible not to tell you or give you some hint of what's been happening to me. For it's quite as real an experience as having a baby or anything else, being moved as you have succeeded in moving me. Of course there's the personal side, the feelings you describe on what I must take to be Thoby's death (though I know that is only what it means to me, and perhaps to you). But that's not very important, and it's accidental that I can't help such feelings coming in and giving an added meaning. Even then I know it's only because of your art that I am so moved. I think you have made one's human feelings into something less personal—if you wouldn't think me foolish I should say you *have* found the "lullaby capable of singing him to rest." But that's only a small bit. Mostly I am simply delighted, startled, filled with every kind of mood in turn, only one wants time to collect one's wits and realise one's feelings. I suppose it's quite idiotic to pour out one's first rhapsodies like this before one has had time to use any self control. Especially as everyone else is doubtless doing it too. Never mind, you can throw them away and laugh at them if you like. What is one to do when one wants so much to express oneself in words, which aren't one's medium. But I feel it doesn't really much matter how I express myself to you. You really understand, however much you pretend not to.

Will it seem to you absurd and conceited or will you understand at all what I mean if I tell you that I've been working hard lately at an absurd great picture I've been painting off and on the last 2 years and if I could only do what I want to—but I can't—it seems to me it would have some sort of analogous meaning to what you've done.[2] How can one explain. But to me, painting a floor covered with toys

[1]Published by the Hogarth Press on October 8.
[2]*The Nursery* (1930–32), present whereabouts unknown. Possibly destroyed.

and keeping them all in relation to each other and the figures and the space of the floor and the light on it means something of the same sort that you seem to me to mean. However, I know quite well that my painting will mean it to no one else. Only perhaps it helps me to understand what you're about. Perhaps. But you can rap my nose and tell me I'm only a sea monster and know very little about humans and had better swim off on my own back water. So I will, like a good beast. Now you can read your other letters and let mine curl up in smoke.

Your
VB

BERG

VI-40. To Dora Carrington

[December 1931]   *8, Fitzroy Street, W. 1*

My dear Carrington,

I don't want to bother you in any way—this is only a line partly to send you my love and partly to say if at any time I can be any use about household or other tiresome things, please let me be.[1] If you want a cook for instance, there is Grace, who's really very good and a most angelic character, who could come when you liked. Or if you want anything sent from London you've only to ring me up. Of course you have lots of people anxious to do things, so don't pay this any attention unless it comes in useful for any reason.

What a horrid time you must have had, my dear. I am so sorry. I fear Lytton will be a crusty patient, but I'm sure he's really got reserves of strength. I hope you look after yourself.

Vanessa

TEXAS

[1]Lytton had collapsed at Ham Spray in November. His physicians were baffled, suggesting paratyphoid or perforated colon, but after his death in January 1932 the autopsy revealed advanced stomach cancer.

CHAPTER SEVEN

1932–1937

Vanessa's reputation soared in the 1930s. She had three solo exhibitions, completed the set design for three ballets—Frederick Ashton's *Pomona* (1933) and *High Yellow* (1932), and Ethel Smyth's *Fête Galante* (1934)—and was commissioned to paint panels for a sitting room of the RMS *Queen Mary,* as well as a poster depicting a Sussex village for Shell-Mex, Ltd. With Duncan she decorated the dining room of Lady Dorothy Wellesley's Sussex home Penns-in-the-Rocks (1930), using a green and grey color scheme for the walls, ceiling, and furnishings, crowned by three large, lyrical, figurative panels along one wall. The two artists also designed and installed a music room at Lefevre Gallery (1932) and were asked to decorate Ethel Sands' house in Chelsea Square (1938).

Vanessa still disliked the publicity surrounding her artistic successes and declined many invitations that Duncan or Clive, for instance, would have happily accepted. Her financial gains too made little impact on her lifestyle, aside from foreign travel and improvements to Charleston. As a result, Vanessa never became a celebrity. On the other hand, she was no longer an artist of the avant-garde. Though she remained a thoughtful colorist, the artistic groups and movements of the day—Surrealism, Social Realism, Abstraction-Création, Unit One—washed over her. She stayed faithful to Roger Fry's belief in the irrelevance of subject matter even after he had begun to question his premise. And after her brief experiments with pure abstraction, she decided that the physical world offered more interesting compositions that anything she could invent.

Roger's interest in Duncan's and Vanessa's work continued, and he remarked to Helen:

> D. is giving free rein to his fancy which is all to the good. He is not really inspired by the thing seen. His vision has to come from some inner state of reflection but Vanessa is a realist. Her colour gets better and better. (Anrep)

In January 1932, Lytton died of stomach cancer. Though this was a blow to the heart of Old Bloomsbury, it did not compare to Vanessa's black despair at the unexpected death of Roger Fry on September 9, 1934. Roger had slipped on a rug at home and broken his pelvis, then, perhaps moved too quickly after his injury, died of heart failure two days later. The next year Vanessa received a further shock. Julian had been offered a job teaching English at the National University of Wuhan, near Hankow, China. Denied a Fellowship at Cambridge, he had tried his hand at poetry, journalism, and left-wing political activism. He was ambitious but unfocused, and jumped at the chance to work in China. Most of the letters in this chapter are "diary letters" to Julian, full of family news and affection. In March 1937, though, before his two-year appointment was over, Julian returned to England. His decision had been hastened by an unwise love affair at his university, but also by his urge to join the antifascist fighting in Spain. To appease Vanessa, he settled for a position as an ambulance driver for Spanish Medical Aid, and left England again in June. On July 18 he was killed by a shrapnel wound to the chest.

Julian's death was the most painful event in Vanessa's life. She broke down physically and emotionally, eating almost nothing during the first week and sleeping only with the aid of drugs. Virginia was at her side every day for weeks and was the only person who made any difference. There was of course no real recovery. "I shall be cheerful," Vanessa told her sister, "but I shall never be happy again."

VII-1. To Dora Carrington

Jan. 25 [1932]   *8, Fitzroy Street, W.1*

Dearest dearest Carrington,

It's impossible not to write to you, though how useless it seems.[1] But one cannot think of Lytton without thinking of you, and with all one's sorrow there is mixed the feeling of gratitude to you for having given him so much happiness. I have loved him ever since the time when Thoby died and he came and was such an inexpressible help and made one think of the things most worth thinking of. But I know how often in those years he was depressed and gloomy and unsatisfied and how later because of you he seemed to get so much more joy out of life. It is owing to you that there is nothing to regret in the past and his friends would love you for that if for nothing else.

Darling creature, come before very long and talk to us, for we loved him very much, enough to understand. I keep thinking of the many times when one could talk to Lytton and he seemed to see further into things than anyone else could. Nothing can make up for that, nothing can make the loss less great. All one can do is to be with people who know that too and try to find some way of dealing with it that he would have liked. But I know it is useless. I know that the many people who loved him cannot help you, who loved him more,

[1]Lytton had died on the afternoon of January 21.

and perhaps it is selfish to write, but I think you will forgive me and understand.

Your loving
VB

TEXAS

VII-2. To Clive Bell

Mar. 13 [1932]   *8, Fitzroy Street, W.1*

Dearest Clive,

I thought I had better write and tell you of the latest tragedy in case it gets into the papers. Poor Carrington has killed herself—yesterday. She had of course always threatened to do so and seems to have actually tried to twice, even before Lytton died, with some wild idea that if she died he wouldn't. The Woolves went down to see her on Thursday. She was alone at Ham Spray and Ralph asked them to go, trying to prevent her from being alone more than could be helped. But she wouldn't let people stay or come away herself for more than a day or two. She talked to them and seemed more cheerful afterwards, but yesterday morning shot herself with a gun she had borrowed from Brian Guinness.[1] Bunny drove Ralph and Frances and Alix down in his car and they got there in time to see her alive and conscious. Of course there will have to be an inquest and I suppose there may be rather a scandal, though the police seem to be quite kind and sympathetic. But the Woolves may possibly have to give evidence and are rather upset.

Frances and Ralph are there now, but I should think will come away as soon as they can. I believe he is in the most awful state, but evidently no one could have prevented it, and sooner or later it would have happened.

We are just off to Cambridge but I thought I had better send you

[1]Bryan Guinness (1905–1992), poet and patron of the arts, succeeded his father as Lord Moyne in 1944. He lived some ten miles from Ham Spray.

a line. I got your letter just after posting mine. I'll write when I come back.

Your
VB

TATE

VII-3. To Clive Bell

Sep. 28 [1932]   *Charleston, Firle, Lewes*

Dearest Clive,

This lot of letters hardly looks worth registering, but it's all there is. We're a very small party here now, though Julian has just returned. Angelica went back and Angus has gone to stay with his widowed sister who lives within a stone's throw of Dottie. She has just moved into her house and poor Angus' state of mind at the prospects of discomfort in a house still hardly habitable you can imagine. We drove him there and had tea with Dottie on the way. She has now got the two rugs we have had made for her by Wilton's[1] and they are an immense improvement to the room. Hilda Matheson was there, no one else. She had skidded in her baby [Baby Austin] the day before and turned upside down and said she wasn't hurt, but she looked very white I thought. The people I turned upside down are trying to get some money out of me, but so far the insurance companies are writing letters to each other and nothing has been done. Duncan's Humber[2] also is trying to get £3 or so out of me and I'm trying through Fred to beat them down. Roger writes that he has again (most curiously) knocked down a cyclist who ran, but not deliberately this time, into him. He's going to give a series of lectures at the Courtauld Institute[3] in October and sounds very well and active.

[1]Wilton Royal, a commercial carpet firm.
[2]Probably the owners of a Humber hit by Duncan.
[3]The Courtauld Institute of Art, University of London, endowed in 1931 by Samuel Courtauld, Lord Lee of Fareham, and Sir Robert Witt, located at 20 Portman Square, until the late 1980s. Now at Somerset House on the Strand.

Duncan and I are now working hard on our dinner service,[4] most of which we want to get done here, so as not to have to take it back to London again. I expect when we've done it we shall go back, though it's often still very lovely here. But winter time will be on one soon. Lottie is still here. I think I shall let her go back anyhow next week. She and Grace are starting going to whist-drives.

Tonight the Woolves are giving us dinner at Shelley's Hotel in Lewes, a curious affair. That I think is all my news.

Your
VB

TATE

VII-4. To Virginia Woolf

Dec. 29 [1932]   *8, Fitzroy Street, W.1*

My Billy,

You are an incorrigibly wicked creature and deserve nothing but abuse. You don't keep your bargains, and *then* you go button hunting. What is one to do? I give you up as a bad job and haven't a particle of affection left for you—no, not one. If you ever get a screen in return it shall express my venom and bitterest hatred, but at this moment I am so thankful to be back from Seend I cannot revile you as I would. We came back yesterday after a visit in which I must admit your letter and presents were the only bright spot. I haven't had time to tell you all about it, but I am almost become a communist. Really, the respectable rich with their dogs and their clothes and their cars all rolling in while they eat and play tennis and become soldiers are enough to make me want to revolt. They eat and eat and eat and feed their dogs as carefully, and their conversation about dogs beats any maternal twaddle I ever heard, or else it consists of nag, nag, nag, rather like Lottie at her worst. Lorna is the worst of the lot, by far,

[4]Commissioned by the Kenneth Clarks, this array of plates was decorated with portait heads of famous women, and included portraits of the two artists, with DG as an honorary woman.

and if she is some day murdered by her children no one, not even Mrs Bell, will be surprised. However, you should ask Angelica all about it. At least I have sympathy now, for she and Quentin are quite aware of all that goes on. He and I drove to Wells one day to get away from it all. Now we're back and in the thick of party preparations and also of my ballet,[1] which all has to be done within the next few days. So you see I haven't much time for letters. You'll come to the party, won't you? Neither John[2] nor Eddy [Sackville-] W. have been asked. There'll be no topical play this year as far as I know— all sweet and innocent as anything. I must stop to catch the last post. My floor is covered with huge airballs, beautiful but likely to burst.

Your
VB

BERG

VII-5. To Helen Anrep

Monday [June 12, 1933]   *Charleston*

Dearest Helen,

I found Quentin still coughing away like anything, and so we got a doctor and it turns out to be whooping cough, which is very tiresome as it's such a long affair.[1] However he seems better after nearly a week in bed, and wonderfully cheerful, and today he is up and painting in his room. Duncan and I are therefore staying on a few days. I expect D. will go back anyhow in a day or two and I as soon as Quentin can come downstairs, though I may leave Grace to look after him.

[1]VB designed the set and costumes for the ballet *Pomona,* choreographed by Frederick Ashton to music by Constant Lambert. Its brief run at Sadler's Wells began January 17, 1933.
[2]John Lehmann (1907–1987), poet, editor, publisher, educated at Trinity College, Cambridge, where he was a close friend of Julian Bell's. He had just left the position of manager at the Hogarth Press, but was to return as partner and general manager in April 1938.
[1]OB's whooping cough developed into pleurisy, which was thought to be tubercular in origin. In November VB flew with him—her only trip by airplane—to a Swiss clinic, where he recuperated through the winter and spring.

But this is to explain why I haven't rung you up. If only it were hot like last week it would be heavenly, but it's icy cold and doesn't even rain much for the good of the garden. However my roses, though not equal to yours, are better than they have ever been and I feel encouraged to go in for a complete rose bed, and shall ask your advice about kinds.

Lydia was strongly in favour of lunch to Ottoline![2] So is Virginia. Leonard of course is against it. But I shouldn't wonder if you didn't get an invitation and I shall think you cowardly beyond words if you don't come, and make Roger. Really, think of it—Henry [Lamb], [Augustus] John, Bertie, Roger, Boris [Anrep], Middleton Murry—can you resist? You with your passion for odd society and Ottoline making a speech. It will be the chance of the century for awkward encounters.

I'll let you know when I return.

Your
VB

ANREP

VII-6. To Quentin Bell

Mar 3 [1934]   *8, Fitzroy St.*

My darling,

I've been spending rather an odd day. This morning I had to go and arrange my show at Lefevre's.[1] There are about 35 paintings and they just fill the downstairs rooms. MacDonald[2] is very good at it and got it all done very quickly and I think very well. It is of course horrifying to see all one's own works laid out like corpses and makes one feel exposed naked to the world, as you will know one day, but

[2]Clive Bell, Boris Anrep, and a group of friends had proposed giving a luncheon party in honor of Lady Ottoline Morrell, but she refused the offer.
[1]A one-artist exhibition opening March 7, 1934. VW contributed a foreword to the catalogue.
[2]Duncan MacDonald, managing director and partner in Reid & Lefevre Gallery, 1a King Street, London.

towards the end of the morning Mrs Curtis appeared, so enthusiastic that, though she's such a flighty woman one can't think she knows much about it, still it was very encouraging. Especially as she bought one! A portrait of my mother done from an old photograph. She's coming to the Private View on Wednesday and is going to bring Angelica and half the school I think and they're going to have a picnic lunch here. So it will all be such a scramble that I hope I shan't have time to realise the full horrors of the occasion. Angelica also will back me up. I do wish you were going to be here—I shall make Julian come. After all this was over we went this afternoon to hear Ethel Smyth's Mass performed at the Albert Hall![3] Virginia had subscribed handsomely and been given dozens of stalls. The Queen [Mary] was there attended by Timmy,[4] and the Dame went and had a long conversation with her in the Royal Box and made her laugh a good deal. I don't wonder. The Dame was in her best wig and tricorn hat and an "Ascot frock" bought at Stagg and Mantles for 16/6. The Queen was dressed in much the same sort of way and they really made an imposing couple. As for the music, I have no views, but it seemed rather brilliantly amorphous. The oddest part of the entertainment came later when we all went on to a Lyon's Corner house[5] at Knightsbridge where the Dame had a large tea party. What the rest of the Lyon's clientele thought I cannot imagine, but there was a great crowded room and at one end a long table with all of us. In came Beecham, Lady Cunard, Lady Diana Cooper (I shouldn't think they'd ever been to a Lyon's in their lives before—they looked very out of place), Lady Lovat, our beauty's mother, Mrs Woodhouse, etc.[6] It really was a most curious entertainment. The tea was black and the bread and butter thick as at a school feast, which indeed it was exactly like. I had some talk with Lady Lovat, who said our beauty is again in a nursing home, but it's nothing much and she hopes to come and sit to us next week.

Do you know that tomorrow Lydia's fate will be decided? It's the

---

[3]Her Mass in D and other works were conducted by Sir Thomas Beecham as part of a series of events to celebrate Dame Ethel's seventy-fifth birthday.
[4]The Hon. Gerald (Timmy) Chichester (1886–1939) held an appointment at court. He was a friend of DG's.
[5]Part of the chain of Lyon's Tea Rooms.
[6]Lady Emerald Cunard (1872–1945), prominent London hostess and patron of the arts; Lady Diana Cooper (b. 1892), daughter of the duke of Rutland and wife of the politician Duff Cooper; Lady Lovat (née the Hon. Laura Lister) (1892–1965). Violet Kate Gordon-Woodhouse (née Gwynne) (1872–1948), pioneer in the revival of early music.

day of The Doll's House[7] and we are all going in the evening. We're talking Julian and Jimmy[8] and shall do our best to applaud. I'm rather nervous, as if it's a failure I don't know *what* one can say to Lydia afterwards. I believe in theatrical circles they say that it is really to be hoped it will be a marked failure—otherwise she'll never be convinced she's not an actress. But that may be female cattishness. It comes from Elsa Lanchester by way of Bunny. He had the brilliant idea (from a journalist's point of view anyhow) of asking Charles Laughton to write a review of a new work on Henry VIII and so got into touch with them.[9] Laughton was overcome with emotion at being seriously considered an intellectual and may perhaps do it.

Goodbye darling.

Your loving
Nessa

BELL

VII-7. To Quentin Bell

March 5 [1934]   *8, Fitzroy St.*

My darling,

We went last night to Lydia's performance and, wonderful to say, it was really rather good! She began I thought much too jumpily, perhaps she was nervous—anyhow, I was very conscious of its being Lydia and thought it was going to be a failure. But she was really much better at the quieter, more serious parts than she was at the very kittenish and doll-like beginning. I think she must have worked very hard at it. Do you know the play? In the scene where she dances a tarantella while she's in a terrible state of agitation she was really

[7]Performed by J. T. Grein's Cosmopolitan Theatre at the Arts Theatre Club.
[8]James Vincent Sheean (1899–1975), American journalist and friend of DG.
[9]The stage actress Elsa Lanchester had married the actor Charles Laughton in 1929. They lived in Gordon Square. David Garnett was at this time literary editor of the *New Statesman & Nation*. No book was reviewed by Charles Laughton, and in fact no work on Henry VIII was reviewed at this time in the *New Statesman*, but the book referred to is probably Francis Hackett's *Henry VIII*, published by Jonathan Cape in 1933.

very good indeed. She didn't become a professional dancer, as I was afraid she might, but danced as if that was her natural means of expression when in a state of agitation. The other people, especially the men, were very good too, and the whole thing was a success. So I suppose she will now hope to get some other part to do and perhaps she will after all disappoint all her friends and become a good actress. The part of Nora was very well suited to her and its being Norwegian somehow made it matter less that she talked with an accent. It may be difficult to find another part as good, but certainly she's far better not talking poetry, and I daresay plays can be found in which her talents will shine.

There was rather an alarming audience—Ottoline looking far more of a caricature than any I have ever done of her, and all the rest of the cultured world. I saw Geoffrey Keynes[1] who asked after you and said he hoped you would soon be quite recovered, there was no reason you shouldn't be. He gave me rather bad news of poor Dr Balfour[2] who is now in a London hospital and sounded rather bad, I'm afraid. Geoffrey said they didn't quite know what was the matter—I think he said something to do with lungs—but he is evidently worse, and they're very anxious about him. I'm very sorry.

Today I went to Twickenham for a last sitting[3] and had to take the picture afterwards to Lefevre's, where I also had to sign everything. I met Tatlock there and had to go round with him. He seemed to think the portrait of Roger very like and may be going to reproduce it in the Daily Telegraph. I had hoped the gallery would be empty today, as Press Day isn't till tomorrow, but I also had to be introduced to a female flower painter, a Mrs Engelbach,[4] a very smart Jewess in white gloves who shrank from me in horror when she found me reeking with Prussian Blue[5]—"I *know* that blue" she said! So do you.

My studio is now beautifully empty and I feel free to do whatever I like, which is a great comfort.

We had a visit from Peter Morris[6] this evening. He can't talk of

---

[1]Geoffrey Langdon Keynes (1887–1982), younger brother of Maynard. Educated at Pembroke College, Cambridge, he was a surgeon, bibliographer, and distinguished Blake scholar. His wife was Margaret Darwin, the sister of Gwen (Darwin) Raverat.
[2]One of QB's doctors.
[3]Possibly for a portrait of Ethel Grant, DG's mother.
[4]Florence Engelbach (d. 1951), a Slade-trained painter of portraits and flowers widely exhibited at the R.A. and elsewhere.
[5]Not a perfume, but a paint color.
[6]One of DG's lovers, a painter, the brother of Lady Romilly. He became a good friend of VB's, as well.

anything but his young man of the moment who's a salesman at Selfridge's tailors' department. I rather hope it won't last long as it makes Peter rather gloomy and absorbed and the young man is evidently by nature a complete womaniser. In fact he's in trouble because he's got a young woman with child and she's trying to make him marry her and he's got bored with her. No doubt Peter is very sympathetic and charming, but from the young man's point of view, that is all. So it's not likely to lead to any very great satisfaction to either side eventually. However I believe he's going to be brought to see us.

Duncan still hob-nobs with the police. In fact yesterday he had a frightfully grand head detective to sit to the artist policeman, who's done a most striking head of him. I long to meet them all but am not allowed to—yet. Darling, please tell me of your plans as soon as you know anything.

Your loving
Nessa

BELL

VII-8. To Kenneth Clark

Sep. 3 [1934] **Charleston, Firle, Lewes**

Dear Kenneth,[1]

I do not know that it is you who ought to be congratulated on becoming Director of the National Gallery. I rather suspect you are in for an awful time and perhaps your painter friends will be among the worst of your plagues. Already Duncan and I are planning all sorts of tiresome projects, such as getting you to take glasses off the pictures and getting leave to wander about with sketch books and so on. What a life you'll lead, but how splendid for us and everyone who has any real liking for painting. I cannot help being delighted that for once something so right and sensible should have been done.

[1]Sir Kenneth Mackenzie Clark (1903–1983), was educated at Trinity College, Cambridge, and worked in Florence with Bernard Berenson. He directed the National Gallery from 1935 to 1945.

Please don't answer this. I don't want to add to your troubles *yet*. My love to Jane.

From
Vanessa

TATE

VII-9. To Helen Anrep

Monday [September 10, 1934]   *Charleston*

Helen dearest,

I am coming to London with Duncan on Wednesday. If you would care to have dinner with me that evening or to see me at any time anywhere you know how glad I shall be, but don't let me be a bother. I will ring you up about lunch time on Wednesday to find out.

Please let me come with you on Thursday, my dear, unless you mind. I feel nearer Roger when I'm with you.[1] I behaved so stupidly today, but I won't. It was such a shock hearing it from Micou on the telephone that I don't think I'd recovered. But it can't have been anything else to anyone, only for what seemed a long time I couldn't get near anyone and was so faint. But I'm all right now, it's only to explain being so feeble today.

Helen dear, you know I love you very much.

Your
V.

ANREP

[1]RF had died of heart failure on September 9 at the Royal Free Hospital, London, where he had been taken two days earlier after a serious fall. VB heard the news from Micu Diamand, Pamela's husband, who had telephoned Monk's House while she was there.

VII-10. To Helen Anrep

Friday [September 14, 1934]   *Charleston*

My dear,

This is only because I'm thinking of you. I wish I could see you for a minute, but I am glad to think you are with Dorelia[1] and in the country. It can't help being nice just to be able to look at her, and I expect at her garden too. I thought yesterday it was so much what Roger would have chosen.[2] One was more conscious of the beauty of life than of anything else and it seemed enough explanation of everything. Why should one want more than that people like him and music like Bach's and such incredible loveliness as one sees all round one should exist and that one should know them. They do not really ever stop.

Please try to rest my dear and give up, *do* give up, trying to be nice to the Frys, just for a time—to please my malicious nature if for no other reason. Don't write letters. Don't go on worrying about everyone's feelings but your own. You know I'm a sensible woman and must be obeyed.

Your
V.

It is nice to be here again. It's so hot one can sit out at night in the midst of heavenly smells, and Angelica is in good spirits and exercising all her charms.

ANREP

[1]Dorelia John (1881–1969), wife of Augustus John, a close friend of Helen's.
[2]RF's funeral service was held at Golder's Green Crematorium. Music by Bach and Frescobaldi was played, and passages from Milton, Spinoza, and Fry's *Transformations* (1926) were read aloud.

VII-11. To Helen Anrep

Friday [September 21, 1934]   *Charleston*

Helen dearest,

I can't help wondering how you are. I know the Maurons are at Bernard St., so probably you are there and I'm afraid fearfully occupied and tired. I haven't written as I didn't want to make you answer, but you and Roger are always in my mind. It's still only at moments that I can realise it at all. Will one ever lose the habit of thinking one can tell him things, I wonder.

I am coming to London on Tuesday to see Angelica off to school. Perhaps I might come in and see if you're free for a minute on my way back from Liverpool St. about 4.30, but I'll ring up first and find out.

Peter Morris is here and it is nice having him. He's so alive to what one's feeling and yet sensible somehow, and I think he is good for Duncan.

I wonder if you'll be able to come here soon, before everything[1] has come to an end.

Your
V.

ANREP

---

[1] I.e., the season.

VII-12. To Patricia Preece

Mar. 8 [1935]   *8, Fitzroy Street, W, 1*

Dear Miss Preece,[1]

My sister, Virginia Woolf, wonders whether you would do a portrait drawing of Ethel Smyth (the composer) for £5. She would I think be interesting to draw. She's quite old but has a really fine head. If you would do this I would gladly lend you my studio here as I expect she'd have to be done in London, and I could arrange to leave it for you when you wanted it if I had a day or two's notice. I hope you won't think the price too low—I ventured to say I thought you would accept it—as I think if you'd do the portrait of a well-known person like that it might possibly lead to other orders, and it would certainly be seen by lots of people. My sister liked your painting, which I showed her, very much too.

Yours sincerely,
Vanessa Bell

CHRISTINE HEPWORTH

VII-13. To Virginia Woolf

Ap. 27 [1935]   *Hassler's Hotel, Rome*

Here we are for the moment, but when you write, as no doubt you will at once on getting this, send it to 33 Via Margutta, our old haunt,

---

[1]Patricia Preece (1894–1966), Slade-trained painter. Roger Fry had promoted Preece's work, and VB's interest in her was almost certainly out of respect for his enthusiasm. Recently, it has been discovered that most of the paintings signed by Preece were in fact executed by her intimate friend Dorothy Hepworth, a shy but talented painter who benefited from Preece's outgoing nature. Kenneth Pople, Stanley Spencer's biographer, is producing a study of the "Patricia Preece hoax."

Despite her need for VB's support, Preece was forced to decline this portrait commission, since she could not reasonably bring Dorothy Hepworth along to sketch Dame Ethel.

to which we move on Monday. We got here on the 23rd picking up Quentin at Roquebrune[1] as arranged. Angelica and I at any rate were quite glad to be at an end of our driving, which however went without a hitch—only one puncture all the way. On the 24th the Nicolsons arrived,[2] and the next day we had to dine with them. I hadn't seen Vita for ages. She has simply become Orlando the wrong way round—I mean turned into a man, with a thick moustache, and very masterful, and surely altogether much bigger. How have you done it? Perhaps it's partly by contrast with her absurd little lover,[3] who seemed as white as a sheet and quite unable to look after herself in any way, and altogether rather silly, I thought. Harold always seems to me to be suffering severely from [an] inferiority complex, but if one takes a lot of trouble to reassure him he gradually gets more at ease, and is rather a nice but foolish creature, I should think somewhat boring. But you don't want my views of the Nicolson *ménage,* of all things. Vita went the next day, but Harold and Nigel[4] are still here and we have to dine with them tomorrow with, of all people, Raymond, who is I hope and believe only here for one night.

Most of our time has been spent looking for a studio as this hotel, which is very good, insists on taking us *en pension* at 50 lire each a day, which seems to be too ruinous. If you only come for a short time it might be quite a good place to come to. The rooms at the back are very quiet and all one wants, and you could refuse to be *en pension* if you liked. They were very full when we came but are I think getting emptier daily. After a great deal of searching we have taken what is I think the only studio to be had. It belongs to a *commendatore* who lives in palatial apartments not far off and evidently keeps the studio for his own secret and immoral purposes. There is one immense room divided into two by a curtain, a kitchen, bathroom and WC. So Angelica and I can live in it and Quentin will get a small bedroom near and feed and work with us. I think it will be very nice when we get in. There are gardens at the back and in front a place just like the garage at Fitzroy St., no through traffic, but garages and workshops of all sorts.

[1]QB had been staying at La Souco, home of the Bussy family, while researching the history of Monaco.
[2]For VB's trip to Rome, Vita Sackville-West had offered her the use of the Nicolson's chauffeured car, which had in any case to be driven to Italy to meet Vita and Harold on their return from a Greek cruise.
[3]The Hon. Mrs. Francis St. Aubyn (née Gwendolen Nicolson) (b. 1896), sister of Harold Nicolson.
[4]Nigel Nicolson (b. 1917), writer, the second son of Vita and Harold.

You really ought to stay longer in Rome than one week. Its fascination grows and Angelica is completely bowled over by it. She's a lucky brat to see it like this instead of as I first did,[5] and she and Quentin are in the highest spirits. As soon as we get established we are going to begin Italian lessons, all of us I think. Meanwhile we wander the streets with great enjoyment and go to the Borghese gardens and poke our noses into shops. We inspect the various interesting characters who turn up at the hotel and often wonder how long it would take you to get into touch with them and why it is that you have such a passion for the elderly female abroad. There was a whole row of them at Siena, which is evidently the place for them.

When do you start and when shall you get here? and do you want me to get you rooms?

Clive gets here next week, I believe. I haven't yet come across any of his grand friends, or anyone at all in fact. It's the greatest comfort to know no one and I hope, when the Nicolsons and Raymond have gone, to disappear completely into our back street.

Have you seen Julian at all? and Duncan? and Helen? Everything seemed so chaotic just before we left and now one's ordinary life in London seems very remote. I suppose the Jubilee[6] is on you. I hope you'll see it and tell me all about it. Probably we shall see some of it in the cinema here.

We saw the Bussys of course, who had both Ellie (quite recovered, she said, and soon going back to work) and Mrs Enfield[7] with them, as well as Quentin. Simon seemed very well and delighted that his letter to the Nation[8] had attracted so much attention. Have you heard anything about Maynard's father? Whether he's alive or dead, I mean.[9] We get no news at all here except an occasional Daily Mail, and Italian papers which are quite intolerable. Have you heard also whether Grace has had her baby yet?[10] I hope I shall hear somehow when it does arrive, but I doubt her husband's capacity to write.

I find Mrs Humphrey Ward[11] fascinating in a horrid kind of way.

---

[5]I.e., in the company of George Duckworth.
[6]The Silver Jubilee was the twenty-fifth anniversary of the accession of King George V and Queen Mary.
[7]D. E. Enfield (née Hussey), wife of the civil servant Ralph Enfield. Her book *L.E.L.: A Mystery of the Thirties* was published by the Hogarth Press in 1928.
[8]"Experiences of a Hospital Patient" [from a Correspondent], published March 23, 1935 in the *New Statesman & Nation*.
[9]John Neville Keynes (1852–1949) survived his son Maynard by three years.
[10]Grace had married a local Sussex man, Walter Higgens, in 1934.
[11]VB was reading Mrs Humphry Ward's autobiography, *A Writer's Recollections* (1918).

Why is she so unpleasant? I suppose she's as pretentious as anyone could be, but perhaps she really was as learned as she makes out, and no doubt she got enough compliments from all the intellectuals of her day to encourage her to think herself a great genius. What an *appalling* set of people they were. No wonder we dodged her round the columns of the Louvre if she looked as she does in the snap shot of her and Henry James.

Please send me all gossip. But I suppose you're swallowed up by admirers and won't have any time for old crones, and I have nothing to offer in return.

Your
VB

SUSSEX

VII-14. To Julian Bell

May 5 [1935]   *33 Via Margutta, Rome*

My darling Julian,

How terribly busy you sound, with rather bothery kind of work too, I'm afraid. However I daresay a lot of it's very interesting and will lead on to other things. I had a long letter from Helen in which I was afraid she sounded a good deal tired and depressed, and I can't help feeling rather a wretch for having so to speak abandoned her and come away. But one couldn't do anything else. Quentin and Angelica are both very happy I think and we have pretty well settled down in our abode here. Clive arrived two days ago and has already taken Angelica to the Vatican. I'm terribly lazy about sight-seeing. I find it very difficult both to paint and sight-see and I want badly to paint here. There are gardens and places where one can set up one's easel without causing too much interest, and almost everywhere the light makes most interesting subjects.

We've got most of the things we want now for the leading of the sort of life we like, which won't as far as I can see include smart society. I get up at 7, and get breakfast ready while Q. plunges into a cold bath. A. is generally too sleepy to do the same, but is dragged out of bed by 8. Our Italian master comes at 9, and Q. and I have

½ an hour and A. an hour of lesson, for which he asks 2 lire 50c. and I give him 5, so he's not ruinous, poor man. We have a very nice woman, Luisa, who comes to clean and wash up. We try to go out and paint for the rest of the morning and have lunch here, at which Clive for the last 2 days has joined us, then a siesta, then we go and paint again. Then we all dine together. Angelica has become a film fan! So we have sometimes been to the cinema. Today we thought we'd go to St. Peter's and Angelica put a most becoming handkerchief on her head to keep the angels out of her hair. But we were stopped at the door by a fierce-looking man who wouldn't let us in because she was bare-legged! So perhaps my view that they regard her as a mere child isn't quite true. She certainly gets enough stared at— everyone turns around and gazes, but quite politely, and I don't think she notices. So far she has always been chaperoned by one of us.

The Woolves come here on the 16th I believe, which is getting near. I hope they'll get through Germany safely. I've heard of no tenant for Charleston, so I don't quite know what we shall do. But if we let and so don't return to England I should of course pay your expenses, my dear, so you needn't let that prevent you from coming to Cassis if other things didn't. However it's all rather vague still really, and I daresay will remain so for a time as I suppose one might easily let for August and September any time within the next two months.

I brought all Roger's letters to me here, thinking I might find time to go through them and give them to Virginia when she came.[1] But so far I have only been able to put them more or less into the right years, which is easy, as they were already mostly together and nearly all dated. I must read them myself before giving any to her, as some might easily be indiscreet. Also some are very intimate, but perhaps one oughtn't to regard that. I suppose she can be trusted not to publish things one wouldn't want published now. Anyhow I would have to see what she did. On the whole I think one ought to disregard one's own feelings of wanting to keep things to oneself. What a bore Ha [Margery Fry] sounds. It really is an awful pity Helen wasn't left literary executor. Well, remember you are mine when the time comes, but I haven't made any will yet!

I don't regret not taking a house at St. Rémy, beautiful as the country is, as evidently one would be blown to pieces by the wind. Besides I

---

[1]The Woolfs planned to spend a week in Rome with VB in May, in the middle of a month's tour of Germany, France, and Italy. VW had just begun reading for Roger Fry's biography, which Margery Fry had asked her to undertake.

think Cassis is perhaps more liveable in, with the Teeds next door, etc., and bathing to be got.

I gave your message to Q. who says he'll write to you.

I wish you were here. I feel sure you'd enjoy so much of it. One leads a very unintellectual animal life, as I think one always tends to do in the south, which I thoroughly enjoy. But one *can* get books at the two quite good libraries here, and if you were here too you and Q. could talk politics, which he feels the need of I think when alone with us ladies. Also now you'd love the wine and the macaroni and the asparagus, wild strawberries, etc. But I don't want to make your mouth water.

How are you? Have you ever done anything more about your tooth? Much love darling,

from your
VB

BELL

VII-15. To Julian Bell

May 20 [1935]   *33 Via Margutta [Rome]*

My darling Julian,

I was very glad of your nice long letter. You seem to be leading a very *mouvementé* life with a good many agitations and ups and downs of all kinds. Never mind. As long as you're doing things it really interests you to do I feel it's the main thing, and I'm sure all these curious editorial and other works will give you a lot of very useful experience and friends and reputation, which will eventually lead to your finding out just what you really do most want to do, and doing it. You're an odd mixture you know, my dear, like all my children perhaps and like me and Clive—I mean *we're* an odd mixture, aren't we? I think you've got something in you which can only be expressed in poetry. But perhaps it's a curious half-submerged bit of you which can only come to the surface now and then. All the same it's very important and really makes a great difference to everything else even when it's not apparent. But I suspect that your other writing must be used as a way of expressing ideas and theories and not as art for art's sake.

Clive paid you compliments the other day *àpropos* of your review in the Nation.[1] He's not interested of course in the art of war, but he had read it and thought it extremely well-written. He used to think, you know, that you couldn't express yourself clearly, but he says now that you have quite changed and have learnt how to do so, and that you are full of interesting ideas which you are becoming able to put down. I should think the book by conchies[2] would be rather fun to do and would bring you into touch with all sorts of rather interesting people. Why don't you get Duncan to write something? He'd be perhaps the only painter, and it might be fascinating. By the way, he's never said a word to me about an accident in the Baby, wretched creature. How did it happen? I've blown him up for not telling me, but I hope I shan't get you into trouble. I suppose he meant to keep it dark, but I'm sure one never ought to.

I have been reading Roger's letters to me and have said I'll hand over to Virginia all those I've read. So far there is very little she can't see—some remarks in later ones about Jews, but only *àpropos* of Micou,[3] etc., so I don't think they matter. I want you to see some of them (all if you like), but there are one or two which I think extraordinarily honest and disinterested attempts to analyse his own feelings about me which will throw a light on that particular quality of his mind and character which I think you want to write about. I suppose you'll have to wait to see them till V.'s done with them. No, I think I shall send you the particular letter (it's not a letter really, I don't think he ever sent it to me, it was with the odd lot of letters and papers found at Bernard St.) as you might perhaps find it useful and V. can have it later just as well. I'll give it to her when you give it back to me. I hope it won't seem conceited in me to show it! But its interest is not in the views of me but in his analysis of his own feelings.

Some of the early letters are rather painful to me to read, but

---

[1] "Incitement to Disaffection," a review of *The Army in My Time* by General Fuller and *When Britain Goes to War* by Capt. Liddell Hart, appeared in the May 11, 1935 *New Statesman & Nation*.
[2] *We Did Not Fight* (1935), a collection of autobiographical essays by British conscientious objectors in the First World War, edited with an introduction by Julian Bell.
[3] RF had opposed Pamela's marriage to Micu Diamand.

everything gets so easy and happy later that one forgets the misery and sees that it was worthwhile. Perhaps such relationships become the best of all . . .

Your loving
Nessa

BELL

VII-16. To Julian Bell

June 9 [1935]   *33 Via Margutta [Rome]*

My darling Julian,

It has at last got really hot here, so hot that one can do nothing in the middle of the day. Duncan arrived on Thursday and by Saturday was installed in a lovely studio. It is almost comic how we have found ourselves in a Roman Fitzroy St. His studio is at the top of this immense house and so he has meals with us and sleeps and works up there. It will make a great difference to us all, as his studio is so large and light that it's possible for 2 or 3 people to work together there at times. In fact it's generally used as a school and has lots of easels, etc., in it. Also at one side it opens on to a large wide roof terrace on which Angelica slept last night. There's a lovely view of the roofs and towers of Rome and we shall be able to sit on it in the evenings. The one drawback here till now has been having no good light indoors to work by and nowhere to sit out of doors. So we're very lucky.

I think our plans may now get a little less vague. Duncan has brought all the paraphernalia for doing designs for the Queen Mary.[1] It's an immense job—3 huge panels, one 18 ft. high and the other two 11 ft. high. Also he's got to do designs for carpets and stuffs, and all has to be finished by the end of November. He says he will have to go back to England by September and I expect I shall too as I also have been given a job. It's a much smaller one, but still I shan't have too much time for it as I have to do the whole of a drawing-room, with

---

[1] The R.M.S. *Queen Mary* was being built and commissioned for the Cunard White Star Shipping Company.

one large panel and some folding doors to paint and I shall be given £200 for it, which is rather nice. So it's just possible we may stay in Italy most of the time, I don't know, but if we did go to Cassis it wouldn't be for very long. However I must talk it over with Duncan and let you know, but I think whatever happens we shall probably return to England at the beginning of September, and I suppose most likely to Charleston. I think both Q. and A. will like that. She will want a little time in England before going, as I suppose she should go, to France in the autumn. She seems absolutely bent now on going on the stage and would like if possible to go as a pupil to Mme. [Ludmilla] Pitoeff or some other French school of acting. Clive said he would find out about it while in Paris.

I wonder whether it's hot with you too and you are thinking of going off to Ireland. You sounded very exhausted in your last letter, my dear. I don't believe writing really takes more out of one than painting, but it seems to, because it's all to do with life, I think, whereas in painting one seems to get into another world altogether, separate from the ordinary human emotions and ideas. Perhaps that's only an illusion, however. But it may be an illusion that helps. It seems such a relief to have this other world to plunge into. How I should like to see what you've written about Roger,[2] or rather the preliminaries that may lead to him. But I had better wait till I come back. I don't think it's very safe to send things.

I have nearly finished reading his letters. It has been an odd sensation. They made him seem *so* alive and one cannot believe that the emotions and sensations he expresses aren't still being felt somewhere. It all seems so near and I hope always will.

Have you seen Helen [Anrep] lately? She sounded very depressed in her last letter, written just before Marguerite Duthuit[3] turned up. I hope her departure may have been a relief . . .

> *Your loving*
> *Nessa*

BELL

[2]An essay eventually published in *Julian Bell: Essays, Poems and Letters* (1938).
[3]Marguerite Duthuit, the daughter of Henri Matisse, was married to the art critic Georges Duthuit.

VII-17. To Julian Bell

July 18 [1935]   *33 Via Margutta [Rome]*

My darling Julian,

You've never answered my letter to tell me of your plans, but I heard from Clive that he is coming to Cassis on Aug 1st and he seemed to think Benita would be able to come and act as chauffeur when I left, so I suppose you can be free to do whatever you like. How the Colonel will enjoy Benita's driving the car[1] I don't know. I hope it won't lead to difficulties. I expect you've seen Quentin and heard all our news from him. We miss him very much here. He is such an *incredibly* nice character! always cheerful and gay and considerate. But it seems slightly absurd to praise him to you, though I don't know why I shouldn't. It is so hot here that one has to spend a good bit of the day asleep. But it's really not too bad, as the air seems to get cool and fresh at night. Last night we went to a concert out of doors in the Forum and the moon shone brilliantly and put to shame most of the flood lighting of the ruins. It was more romantic than you can conceive. Afterwards we went into the Colosseum and looked for ghosts of ancient Christians and lions till both Angelica and I got quite jumpy.

She and I will probably leave for Cassis on the 29th so as to get there in time to have all ready for Clive and Eve, who arrive on the 1st.

I send you your cheque for £20, which you should have had before, but Clive hasn't sent me mine yet. Still, he will.

Do write some day and tell me what you mean to do. Q. will tell you all our prospects in case they affect yours. I rather hope now that you'll be in England when I return at the beginning of September.

                                        Your loving
                                        Nessa

BELL

---

[1]The Bells owned a car with Colonel Teed at Fontcreuse.

VII-18. To Julian Bell

Aug. 30 [1935]   *Charleston*

My darling Julian,

It is still difficult to believe that you are on your way and that by the time you get this you will actually be in China.[1] I don't suppose it will become real for me till I get letters from you and I mustn't hope for that for a long time. But I'm glad you promised to cable. I drove back yesterday in a kind of dream, but it wasn't an unhappy one, and everything looked so incredibly lovely. You couldn't have had a better day to see at the last. It was rather hard to come into this house with you not here, but Duncan was very nice to me and I don't mind showing my feelings to him, which is a great relief, and it seems a shame to do so to Q. and A., though I think they know very well what I feel really and they're very kind to me too. My instincts are so much the opposite to those of Queen Victoria that I immediately set about changing the state of your room, which while you're away must not be a relic of you, but take on another life and become Angelica's room. It will keep quite enough of you, but it must go on being alive. So, to start with, I tidied your books, which are now in beautiful order, even to the papers on top, leaving several empty shelves which A.'s books can come to. Your clothes too are neatly arranged about, and Duncan and Angelica full of plans for redecorating the room, which I expect they'll make very charming. One cannot be long in this house without something happening of a characteristic kind, and sure enough, we started this morning—at 9 AM—with, you'll hardly believe it, a visit from Tut. As I was coming down to breakfast I heard voices in Duncan's room and saw the door ajar, so I walked in and found Lottie looking rather frightened, talking about someone who was asking for D. downstairs. I thought it must be Rowden and Co.[2] again but no—Lottie recognised him as "the same gentleman as last year," and Grace also had seen him and fled in terror. Lottie had let out that Duncan was still there, so he had sent her back to say he was ill and couldn't see Tut. Lottie proceeded to embroider on this and said D. was very ill indeed and alone in the

[1] JB had accepted a post as professor of English at the National University of Wuhan in Hankow. VB saw him off at Newhaven at the start of his journey to China on August 29.
[2] Petty criminals whom DG had attracted.

house with her! and could see no one and Tut must go. But it took a good half hour to get him out of the hall, during which time D. and I waited in his room, expecting at any moment to have a raving lunatic on us. He must, we think, have escaped from his asylum at Brighton. It was a relief when at last we saw his well-known figure stamping down the drive. Unlike yesterday, it was a pouring wet day and one couldn't help feeling sorry for the poor man, but it would be fatal to let him in. However, Duncan has now gone back to London, so I suppose his lunatics will leave us alone for a bit. Rowden and Co. came again this evening hoping to get their clothes, but D. had gone in vain to Seaford yesterday to fetch them, as they'd already been taking by the irate father. They actually had the courage to go again to Tilton to try to borrow more money from Maynard, with what results is not known.

I drove Duncan to catch his train at Lewes today and was almost drowned, there was such a terrific deluge. The small pond is already quite full. I'll send you two photographs—the others didn't come out from that lot. But all those I did of you haven't been developed yet. Yesterday I sent off your 83 cards of change of address and now I think I have done nearly all your business except writing to Gaisberg.[3]

My dear, I forgot your bathing dress. I'm so sorry, but hope you'll get one on the boat. I don't *think* anything else was forgotten. But all this will be old history by the time you get it. Eve has come and is quite unchanged—far less grown up than Angelica. She and A. have been spending the evening undergoing a voluntary examination in history and literature by Quentin! I don't think the results were *very* brilliant—not that I could have answered any of the questions, of course. Eve did better than Angelica, who loses her head too easily and becomes wild. Q. has an amazing range of knowledge it seemed to me and could put question after question on any period with the greatest ease. To me it's a mystery . . .

8, Fitzroy St., Sep. 3

. . . I came up by train yesterday, after a hectic morning carting furniture about (my perennial occupation). I've put your writing table in Q.'s room and given him your larger chest of drawers, so he's very well off now and can house all the clothes you left. I had a letter from Clive who seems very happy on his trip, and actually found Luce[4] on

---

[3]Financial advisor.

[4]Gordon Hannington Luce (1889–1979), poet and teacher of English at Rangoon University. He was a Cambridge friend of JMK's and known to the Bloomsbury circle. Clive was on his way to the West Indies for a holiday.

board, with his family. What a lot of time he seems to spend in Europe—one's always hearing of him, it seems. Why shouldn't he visit you in China? Clive evidently thoroughly enjoys it all, though he says he is treated with such respect as an authority that he feels very old, which he dislikes.

I found Duncan here and we went round to see the Clarks, who are just off to Russia for a month. They'll be back at the end of September, so we might arrange to do Freshwater[5] early in October. They talked of some poet—Harold? Acton[6] I think—who has some teaching job in Peking which Jane [Clark] seemed to think must be very near you, but I assured her it wasn't. However, they said you must see him sometime, but I know nothing of him, do you? An Oxford poet, a friend of the Sitwells, but much younger. Kenneth has written an introduction to Roger's Cambridge lectures.[7] I'll send it to you when it comes out. He said he had got into great trouble with Margery because he had to write a very short foreword to the show of R.'s paintings at Bristol and he had to try and say honestly what he could about Roger as a painter. She was very angry, as he thinks she will be also about this introduction. They cannot bear each other, so I suppose there are bound to be difficulties. Duncan has got Charles Mauron's book[8] and is reading it and says it's very good, he thinks. I must get it too.

Darling I must stop, as I have to go and get money from the bank. Take care of yourself, won't you, and be happy and remember I love you and think of you constantly. I looked at you standing on the boat after I had left you, when you thought I had gone. You were looking down at your tickets, etc., and I can still see you so clearly.

Your loving
VB

BELL

---

[5]Virginia Woolf's play about Julia Margaret Cameron and her circle, written in 1923 and later revised but not published until 1976. VB had played her great-aunt Julia in a performance at her Fitzroy Street studio on January 18, 1935.
[6]Harold Acton (b. 1904), author and aesthete, educated at Christ's Church, Oxford. He lived in Peking from 1932 to 1939.
[7]Published as *Last Lectures* by the Oxford University Press in 1939.
[8]*Aesthetics and Psychology* (London: Hogarth Press, 1935), translated by RF and Katherine John.

VII-19. To Julian Bell

Sep. 24 [1935]   *Charleston*

My darling Julian,

A good many things seem to have happened since I posted my last letter to you, the principal and most annoying of them is a letter I had this morning from Mr Leech, calmly cancelling my contract with the Queen Mary! At the same time I had a letter from Duncan who returned to London yesterday saying he had had a "monstrous letter from Mr Leech—practically cancelling his contract." The excuse given in my case is that the Roman Catholics don't approve. But I think that's only part of the real reason. No doubt the committee of directors who have now come on the scene are horrified by our doings. I suspect they think they can down me entirely and are trying to put Duncan into a position in which he'll have to throw up the job. Mr Leech tries to apologise to me and asks me to suggest what I think would be fair compensation. I went to consult Maynard, who thinks one is entitled to full pay if they cancel the contract, or at least to what an architect would receive in the same conditions, which is two thirds. He is prepared also to write to the chairman of Cunard, whom he knows. I am going up to London anyhow tomorrow with Maynard and Lydia, and after seeing Duncan and hearing his story I hope to get further advice from Maynard, as I don't intend to take it lying down. It seems to me the most preposterous behaviour and makes me furious. Luckily we have contracts and plenty of letters from the American architect Morris,[1] with whom, and Leech, our contracts were made. No doubt they must have had authority from the company to make contracts with the artists and I don't see that they have a leg to stand on. They saw and approved of our sketches months ago and evidently considered the matter settled, and I can't conceive that they would have done all that if they hadn't full authority to. However, I shall find out more probably before I finish this letter and will tell you what happens. When I saw Maynard today he was in the throes of a short article he had just thought of for the Nation, I think about political affairs. According to him, Mussolini is now scared by the movements of the British fleet. Also, the Italians have discovered that

[1]Benjamin Wistar Morris (1870–1944).

they are so desperately poor that they are getting agitated, and he thinks they're beginning to climb down. By the time you get this, one will know, I suppose. I hope to goodness he's right.

We had our grand party on Saturday night. By miscalculating the number of grouse each person would eat and thinking two sides of a grouse went to one person instead of two people to one grouse— you see how confusing it is, don't you?—I had got 10 grouse for 10 people and then finding we should be 11 I had got Quentin to get one more from Lewes, so two enormous dishes full of grouse appeared, to the astonished delight of everyone—especially Tom [T. S. Eliot], who did eat a whole grouse or very nearly. It was a most successful party. I hadn't seen Tom for years and found him quite a different creature from what he used to be. He has become very cheerful, very amusing, quite at his ease and altogether charming. I always liked him, but he used to be so terribly slow and apparently afraid of giving himself away. He and Bunny made a very good couple, one slow in the American and the other in the English style, and both keeping us in roars of laughter. After dinner Angelica and Eve gave us a musical entertainment in the studio which consisted of their dressing up and singing such songs as Where are you going to, my pretty maid? with Quentin as the cow. However everyone enjoyed it, I think, and Tom told us the immortal story of his party with Mrs Read[2] and the German girls—which turned out to be identical with the story as told by Virginia, much to everyone's astonishment—you know it, don't you? how to make things go he bought chocolates which should have been filled with sawdust but were filled with soap, and sugar lumps with india rubber fish inside, which would have been all right in tea but were invisible in black coffee, and what a failure it all was. It seems he constantly does the same kind of thing—a curious amusement for a famous American poet . . .

Liverpool, Sep. 26. Here we are, in the huge grim place. I went to London yesterday morning in company with the Keyneses. Maynard wrote a letter to send to Sir Percy Bates, the Cunard Chairman, which I hope may have at least a good moral effect on him. I wasn't able to see Mr Leech but spoke to him on the telephone. He seemed very much upset and said he had simply had to do as he was told. I heard all about Duncan's concerns. Tully hadn't actually broken his contract, though they seem to have been on the point of doing so, but have made him change the size of his figures—what good that will

---

[2]"Ludo" (née Margaret Ludwig), wife of the critic Herbert Read.

do I can't think—and have prevented him from designing any stuffs or carpets. In fact it is evident that the Cunard people, with Maynard's friend Sir Percy at their head, have suddenly got rattled and are terrified that the ship will shock people, including it seems the Royal Family. So they have gone behind the back of the American, Mr Morris, who's in New York, and are doing their best to get rid of all the artists. We are not the only ones. I gathered most of them are being stopped or interfered with. Of course they have no excuse at all and I shall do my best to get paid in full. Mr Leech comes here, to Liverpool, tomorrow and I shall then see him. Duncan meanwhile has agreed to change his figures, but has written to say that he can only go on with the thing if he gets an assurance from the company that they will now stick to his contract. It's all very tiresome and rather a blow, but if I get paid I suppose I shall soon get interested in other work and forget about it. I daresay one is really very silly ever to expect to be able to work for such people. One had better paint quietly, as one wants to, for oneself.

We came here by a very early train this morning, having breakfast on the train, and got to this immense and very grand hotel for lunch, which we had regardless of expense (as all our expenses are paid) in what they call the French restaurant, which however is not really French but rather pretentious. Still, it's very comfortable, and it's rather amusing to see the Americans, etc., and try to make out what they're up to. We had to go to the Cunard Buildings where we were shown into an immense hall with large tables covered with every kind of stuff, and the floor covered with patterns of carpets. We each have to invent 6 different colour schemes to be used in the state rooms, for walls, carpets, curtains, etc., which will be a tiring job and will take us all tomorrow, I expect. I shall have to interview Mr Leech, so I am writing to you now in case I don't have time to add anything tomorrow. On Saturday I hope to go back to London in time to get down to Charleston the same evening, and on Monday we all leave. Next week you will reach Shanghai I hope darling, and I shall begin to expect a cable. How glad I am you arranged to cable, for I can't get a letter for a long time after that.

I went to see Janie's show in London.[3] I should think it will be a success. Duncan and I bought one together, but if I get the Cunard money I may let him have it and buy another myself. Some are really

[3] At the Lefevre Gallery. DG had been promoting Jane Bussy's work, and may have helped her set up this show.

very charming and I think have real merit—others are rather crude and superficial. But at her age that is quite understandable.

Goodbye my dearest, in case I have no time to write tomorrow. I think I must just post them then to catch the air mail to China in London on Saturday. How I long to know all about you—every scrap—and especially if you're well and happy.

Your loving
Nessa

BELL

VII-20. To Julian Bell

Nov. 1 [1935]   *8, Fitzroy St.*

My darling Julian,

The great event of my week has been your two letters, one written at different places ending at Wuhan, and the other today dated Oct 13, telling me about your being unwell. Darling, I am glad you tell me—I won't worry, I promise—and I think it's *much* better to tell me everything. One can't possibly help giving pain to the people who love one by being ill and such things, but one *can* help the far worse pain of suddenly having to spring something on them or letting them hear from other sources. I'm sure you and I must tell each other the truth. I can only feel easy if I know you do, and I will too, but as soon as it's difficult not to tell me anything, please don't hesitate. I can't help suspecting too that it's easier and better for you to tell me and not keep things to yourself. Of course it does make we want terribly to be with you. I suppose I have enough of the despised maternal instinct left to want to look after you, darling. But I know you'll be sensible . . .

Dearest, we do seem nearer each other now, and our letters will reach each other regularly and at not too impossible intervals. You *mustn't* feel too homesick! It's such a horrid feeling. I know well how wretched one can be just because one wants familiar things and people. But you will make real friends, and you will get a circle of people round you, for you know you're very good at that. Then you must remember that you've not gone away for ever and the time will perhaps pass all too quickly. I am sure you can deal with life now, and how easy everything will seem by comparison. You'll think nothing of a journey from London to Cambridge, which not so long ago used to upset you quite a lot! or even of a journey to Cassis. In fact, you'll really grow up, and many people don't do that till much later, if ever.

Darling, before I leave personal things, I wonder if you'd had a letter I wrote saying how your going away had made us both able to realise and to express something of our feelings for each other. Because you say something so like it, and it's true, isn't it, and it's really very important to us both. Oh Julian, I can never express what happiness you've given me in my life. I often wonder how such luck has fallen my way. Just having children seemed such incredible delight, but that they should care for me as you make me feel you do, is something beyond all dreaming of—or even wanting. I never expected it or hoped for it, for it seemed enough to care so much oneself. I wish sometimes I could write poems, too! I suppose it would help to crystalise some feelings one doesn't want to lose. But I can't—or even prose. Still I think you, at any rate, understand. Please, my dear, send me any new poems you write. You know they give me great pleasure and a sight of you that one can't get any other way . . .

I was rung up this morning by Peter Morris. He had been sent for from Vienna by Dora[1] because their mother seems at last to be on the point of death, though they have had so many false alarms already that this may be another. Peter was having a cure at Vienna and had got terribly involved with a young man, a friend of John Lehmann's, whose story is such that it will have to wait till one sees Peter to hear it. But he had seen a good deal of John in consequence. I hope I shall see Peter when the mother's illness takes a turn one way or the other. I'm very much attached to him. He's really a very charming person, with much more in him than one perhaps sees at first, and I enjoy his company.

Sat., Nov. 2. To my great surprise tonight, another letter from you. But when I opened it I found it was dated Sep. 27, written on the boat and posted at Hong Kong, a good fortnight before the one I got yesterday. So I shall get letters now much quicker than those written on the voyage. I shall send mine now by Siberia and hope they'll get to you in about 17 days also. In this one, of course, you say nothing about being unwell, and in the photo you send you look very splendid

[1]Peter Morris' sister, later Lady Romilly.

and beautiful—my dear, at this distance I can surely say what I like!—
and one wouldn't guess that there was anything the matter. Oh, how
glad I shall be of another letter, giving me later news of your health.
The Woolves are as usual at Rodmell till tomorrow evening, but I
hope I may see them and perhaps Virginia will have gotten your letter
about Roger and will give it to me. I think it's very likely you got
more from him than from anyone my dear, for though so much older,
it was almost uncanny how little that mattered. I've never known
anyone who bridged the generations so much. And I think his mind
and character were in some important ways so like yours and yet so
different that he was able to give you just what mattered most. In an
odd way now you and he have become very much joined together for
me. It's partly because you helped me when he died—and understood
so much—and partly your going away was like some dim reflection
of his death. Only I had to remind myself how different it was—a
beginning and not an ending. But of course there's something of death
in all partings (not an original idea, is it?). (Your letters however quite
do away with that, making me very acutely aware that you're alive
and not so very far off, even.) There's a great joy in the fact that two
people one cares for very much get so much from each other as you
and he did, and I often got acute delight from seeing you together,
hearing you talk and realising how much he gave you and did for
you.

Darling, how odd that you should tell me in this letter I've just got
that you're astonished at your good fortune and happiness, when I'd
been saying much the same to you about myself when I began to
write this last night? Perhaps it isn't so very odd, when a large part
of mine comes from you and some of yours from me.

Well, I suppose I mustn't simply write you love-letters. You'll get
plenty of them from others. I must tell you that my usual luck with
cats seems still to pursue me. Polo has disappeared, since yesterday
evening at 6. He has never been away so long before and we are in
despair. Tomorrow I intend to make a house to house visitation in
search of him, as we think he must have got into another area and
been kept by someone. Flossie is even more upset than I am, as she
adores all cats and Polo especially. I also need him badly as a model,
as I am putting him in the foreground of my Queen Mary panel, lying
on a window sill, beyond which are seen the Borghese gardens, a
fountain, trees, flowers, children, nursemaids, Dora Morris taking a
walk in a pink dress with a rather indefinite young man and a parasol,
etc. I hope it's the kind of subject millionaires will like.

Sunday, Nov. 3. I must finish this now so as to post it on my way to 50, where we are to sup and meet the Woolves and possibly Adrian. I forgot to tell you that I've got your Conchie book and am reading it with some interest, though some remind me rather painfully of the depressing atmosphere which seemed to surround most conchies at the time. I think Adrian's very good indeed, and Bunny's good though it has little to do with the subject. Also I think your introduction very good, if perhaps at the end a trifle bellicose! But I like it and thought it really made a perfect exposition of the views of your generation. I can't think how you got it all done in such a short time. It helps to show me that I'm right in thinking you must rest. I *know* you must. Lead an outdoor life if you like, but don't do anything that's too tiring, even in the way of walking or riding for a time. Believe in my good sense, my dearest.

> *Your loving*
> *VB*

BELL

VII-21. To Julian Bell

Sat., Jan. 25 [1936]   *8, Fitzroy St.*

My darling Julian,

... You say you like my chronicle letters, so I will go on telling you what happens in order more or less, beginning with the death of King George.[1] (The death of poor Mr Kipling has passed almost unnoticed.)[2] Duncan and I had a fine time of it. On Monday we thought it evident he was soon going to die and that it would be interesting to see what happened at a Cinema. So we went to one, but no news was given beyond what we already knew. However when we came out there were bulletins about "closing hours," so having the car, we thought we'd drive round by Buck House. It was rather an amazing sight, crowds so thick we couldn't get near the railings to read the

[1]On Monday, January 20, 1936.
[2]Rudyard Kipling (b. 1865) died on January 18.

bulletin and cars parked all the way along the Mall and sometimes flash lights going off. As we could hear nothing new, we decided to drive home and got back on the stroke of midnight, just too late to hear the news on the wireless, but we did hear that a bulletin would be given every ¼ hour through the night! I wondered whether I should leave it turned on, but decided anyhow to sit up for the next, and when it came there was the news of the King's death, given in extremely pompous manner and voice by Sir John Reith[3] himself. It was very badly done, a long announcement about "passing peacefully away," etc. So we heard of it exactly 20 minutes after it happened. Public life has been intolerable ever since. The wireless has practically stopped, as it won't give anything of a cheerful nature and unfortunately doesn't give all the superb melancholy music it might. I don't think the general public feels anything but mildly amused curiosity, but they have to dress in black and newspapers have practically no news. However, we went to one quite interesting occasion on Thursday, which was to see the coffin being brought from King's Cross to Westminster Hall. It actually went through Tavistock Sq. and the Woolves asked us to go and look in from the Square garden, as they said only people with keys could get in and it would be quite empty. Mrs Grant came too and my old friend Snow who happens to be in London. We went to the Woolves and already there was a great crowd and traffic held up, etc., but Virginia made us go up and talk to her, when Mabel came running in to say the crowd was climbing the railings into the square, and sure enough there they were, fighting their way in when any inhabitant opened a gate. We only got in with difficulty and only just managed to get good places. Indians in turbans were climbing the trees and altogether the grass and beds were covered by a trampling crowd. One couldn't help sympathising with them, for it did seem absurd to keep all that large space almost empty. However, we could see well, and after about half an hour's wait the procession came and was unexpectedly lovely. There were simply a few police mounted on lovely pale grey horses, walking very slowly in perfect order, and beautifully groomed. Then the coffin, covered with the Royal Standard, in a gun carriage with the crown and some flowers, all incredibly gay and pretty. As the sun came out a little I wished I could paint it, for it was such attractive colour, with a few red touches on the plumes of the riders and the brilliant red and blue and gold of the standard and the general grey and black of the crowd

[3]Director general of the BBC.

behind. Then came the new King,[4] looking utterly miserable, very small, disreputable, patchy and debauched, and his hardly handsomer brothers.[5] What a pity they aren't like you and Quentin to look at, with Ann and Judy to follow! Still you'd never get rid of royalties if they were. But the whole procession, which consisted simply of that, was as simple as it could be and very well arranged and stage managed. I expect the lying-in-state is too, but as one has to wait 4 hours in a queue, I shall leave that alone, and also the funeral. If there were to be snow, it might be worth seeing, but there won't be—it's foggy and rainy and warmer.

Well, then I must tell you about the latest London Group developments.[6] We decided on thinking things over to resign, as a protest against the methods of Cooper and Co. So we asked Keith Baynes to dinner and told him we meant to. He was very uneasy, terrified of doing so but determined to do whatever we did. It ended by our all writing letters to the new vice president to say we resigned, and he's in an awful stew, poor man, and wants us to reconsider. I expect more things will happen and it may end in a general split of the group. Anyhow for us it is rather entertaining and I think if we want to, we can arrange next year to have an exhibition at Agnew's[7] for nothing, where we can show any of the young whom we consider good. This must be kept dark at present, however, as we don't want to make anyone else resign on our account or in the hope of being provided with something else. In that way we shall be committed to no one except Keith.

Sunday. I mustn't forget that one of the principal events of the week has been your earlier letter written on Christmas Day and sounding a good deal more cheerful than you had been before, and enclosing Sue's[8] essay. First about that. Duncan and I have both read it and think it very charming with the curious Chinese charm that no other people have. It's also very interesting as giving a hint from a Chinese painter of what they're after. In a way, it makes one despair of ever

---

[4]Edward VIII.

[5]The king's surviving brothers were Prince Albert, duke of York (later George VI and the father of Elizabeth II), Prince Henry, the duke of Gloucester, and Prince George, the duke of Kent.

[6]The artist John Cooper had banded with others to oust Rupert Lee and his wife Diana Brinton-Lee from their posts as treasurer and secretary. Despite protest from VB and DG, they succeeded.

[7]Thos. Agnew & Sons, 43 Old Bond Street.

[8]JB was forming a close friendship with the writer and artist Ling Su-Hua, the wife of the dean of the School of Letters.

being able to understand and appreciate Chinese painting, for evidently one ought to understand their poetry too. But in fact one had suspected something of the kind. The little stories she tells are fascinating and the impression one gets of endless time and leisure where artists expect to spend years contemplating before actually doing. To me it seems very strange, this view that appearances are nothing in themselves, that there must always be some reference to life, held by people who have such amazing visual sensibility. They seem almost to despise our excitement about purely formal relationships. I think we have learnt largely from the Chinese not simply to represent actual appearances, but to try to convey the spirit of movement, character, rhythm, etc., and to do that one must perhaps distort and eliminate, but yet it remains it seems to me always the *visual* relationship that is important in painting. There is a language simply of form and colour that can be as moving as any other and that seems to affect one quite as much as the greatest poetry of words. At least so it seems to me, but I admit that it is very difficult to be sure of, for of course the form and colour nearly always do represent life and I suppose any allusions may creep in. However, don't think I'm disputing with Sue! I like her article and her writing and I think the best thing for me to do is to send it to Bunny and ask his advice. I don't know if it's too long for the Nation or could be published in two sections, or perhaps he'd advise one where else to send it. I can also show it to Kenneth C[lark]. In fact I'll do all I can. Whatever differences of view one may have owing to one's being a mere European I do feel a curious sympathy and liking for the attitude shown, which makes me very ready to do anything I can to help. Please give Sue some message of sympathy from me and say I'd very much like to see more of her writing.

Now for your letter darling, the one mostly about Angelica. Of course I think you're right and I certainly will take steps. I admit that I have to get over a kind of shyness about it—it's more that than anything else. Also I didn't want to rush things too much, because in those ways I believe—and have been told also by a very intelligent doctor—that girls are physically and psychologically different from men, as a rule. That is, they don't want physical satisfaction for its own sake just as a matter of growing up. Until their feelings are aroused by someone, the question doesn't occur to most normal people, and even then only when the man definitely wants to arouse it. Of course I know this may happen at any time now. But I didn't think it was very likely to happen in Paris, where Angelica is still practically at school and has no opportunities of being made love to. As soon as she returns to London, where she'll begin to lead a grown up life, I'll get in touch with the doctor and do whatever she advises. Does that seem to you sensible? I really quite agree with you all you say . . .

I expect my next letter will be posted from Paris. I am getting very hungry for Angelica.

> *Your loving*
> *VB*

BELL

VII-22. To Patricia Preece

Feb. 6 1936   *8, Fitzroy Street*

Dear Miss Preece,

Please forgive me for not answering your letter sooner, but I have been in Paris for a few days to see my daughter. You really have nothing to thank me for. The very little I have done has been simply because, admiring your work, I naturally wanted if possible to get it shown and admired by others, but there was very little I could do, unfortunately. I am delighted however that your show[1] has had some success. Everyone I have spoken to has praised your work and the sales haven't been too bad, considering the King's death which, strange as it seems, I believe has put an end to almost everything. I think you did very well. In any case, I am sure this show will have made you much better known and is a first step.

It's very kind of you to want to give me a painting, and of course I should like to have one much better than anything else. But I don't think I've done anything to deserve one. Will you let me exchange one of mine with you? It would give me real pleasure if you cared to do this, as artists whose work one likes are the only people one really wants to have one's paintings. Perhaps one day you would come and choose one, and I will go and choose one of yours, if you agree?

[1]Patricia Preece was ill, and as a result VB arranged practically every aspect of Preece's show at the Lefevre Gallery, from selecting the work to hanging it, even contributing a few titles.

I hope you are better. I shall hear from Helen, whom I haven't seen quite lately. I have things to tell you regarding your project when you next come to London.

Yours sincerely,
Vanessa Bell

CHRISTINE HEPWORTH

VII-23. To Julian Bell

Sunday, March 29 [1936]   *Charleston*

My darling Julian,

My weekly letter is late in beginning, as you see, but the last week in London was chock full, and I knew I should have free time here. Oh, it is nice to be here, alone with Angelica, but I must begin at the beginning and give you the news of the week. First of all then, on Tuesday, just when I was beginning to wonder what had happened, came a packet from you with your Roger letter. It was slightly flimsy, but to my relief I found a letter as well inside, only you hadn't pinned the M.S. pages together and one page, 46, is missing. I think you must have left it out. Well, darling, I have read it once and then handed it on to Helen. As soon as I get it back from her I shall read it again more carefully and *perhaps* be able to give you criticisms, but I saw Helen the day it came and she wanted so much to see it that I let her have it as soon as I could. Therefore I can only tell you now that so far as the first part, where it's more personal, goes I found it strangely moving and beautiful—I hope I don't sound sentimental (how afraid we both are of being that). But I do think your writing now has gained enormously and has a quality of rhythm which I like very much, as well as being much clearer and easier. You always had plenty to say, but it used to be obscure. Now you can get it across, and impress your meaning. I was of course very much moved by what you say about Roger—and that may be personal—and by the fact that *you* should feel so much about him. It seems to me what he would have chosen as the best kind of memorial, that the younger generation should have got so much from him. He really destroyed the gap between the generations more than anyone by finding their common touchstone of reason that all the intelligent can apply. It makes me incredibly happy, my dear, that it should be you who can feel and express this for your own generation and it may I think be more important even than giving a likeness of him. That you hardly attempt to do, though the few things you say do I think give a feeling of him.

I must of course read it all again and more carefully. I was hurried and interrupted. My first impression is that it is an intensely interesting exposition of your attitude to life and Roger's, and shows how his affected yours. But I know I haven't grasped it all yet and I must wait till I get it back from Helen. No doubt she'll write to you. She was so much moved by the few sentences she read I think that she couldn't go on then, but she is sure to write herself . . .

On Monday we dined with Helen and met the James Stracheys, who were nice as usual and rather melancholy as usual. Towards the end of the evening we began to talk about the possibility of publishing Lytton's letters. First the difficulty of getting anyone to type them, which James finds insuperable. I suggested Eleanor Marshall[1] (who is now married) as being the soul of honour and unshockable, and possibly we may try her. Then the awful questions of blackmail, libel, hurt feelings, etc. It seems there are a few people, Maynard and Clive principally, who would, J. thinks, be too much hurt. Perhaps—though I think James exaggerates. We all know Lytton said biting and contemptuous things about us all, but does it matter? I am out for truth, really, and think it does not matter running the risk of upsetting one's feelings about the dead. But it may be too soon. In any case, the letters should be typed and kept and then the question is who can be given charge of them. Someone among the younger generation clearly, and very likely you, I think. Helen suggested you and James seemed in favour of it, possibly with Janie. She seems to be the best person among the Strachey younger generation and you and she could work and agree together. It looks as if a great deal of work were awaiting your middle age, my dear! . . .

Then, on Friday—a day of turmoil—we had a cocktail party in the evening and had had to arrange everything for days beforehand. As I told you, I think, it was at Phyllis Keyes's workshop[2] and was intended to show our pottery, so that all had to be set out, flowers to

[1]Elder sister of Frances Partridge.
[2]In Warren Street, London. VB and DG painted ceramics of her design. The workshop was destroyed in the Second World War.

be put into some of the pots, etc. I finished my share of the work and rushed home grubby and flustered at lunch time, and then at ¼ to 3 had to go off to Victoria to meet Angelica. She arrived, very competent, very grown up, having got all her luggage through the *douane* dishonourably, relying on her charms with complete success, and we came home. Then Jimmy Sheehan and his wife appeared for tea, and then we went to the party. Angelica wore a hat which she said (and I believe it!) had caused a sensation in Paris, and its effect in Clipstone Mews cannot be imagined! I cannot draw it so as to convince you, but you must take my word for it that she looked obviously like the fashion of the day after tomorrow, and no one knew her till they spoke to her, when they found instead of a chic and affected young lady a very simple, rather childish, gay creature, delighted with her own appearance and perfectly frank and amused about it all. Only Ottoline was horrified and didn't quite see through the fashionable bluff and tried to discourage cocktail drinking. As a matter of fact, A. had made the hat herself for about 1/– and her dress also was homemade. And Duncan, who of course came late, didn't know her and was absolutely knocked down!

Well, so much for her debut in Bloomsbury. I was bombarded with compliments about her which I thoroughly enjoyed . . .

Life has been more domestic and less political this last week, which is a blessing for the moment. There seem to have been agitations about John Strachey's meeting against the Fascist one in the Albert Hall[3] which no doubt others will tell you about more than I can. Elizabeth Watson,[4] whom Duncan met, had been to the Albert Hall one, and said they had nothing whatever to suggest except the persecution of Jews, which I should think won't meet with much success in England . . .

I suppose the political situation is not really better, but here people seem to have calmed down a bit. In fact one couldn't go on being in such a state of tension—it was really like being back in August '14 at one moment. No one could talk of anything without getting on to questions no one could answer. When we met the James Stracheys we

[3]Sir Oswald Mosley led a meeting of British Fascists at the Royal Albert Hall the night of Sunday, March 22. Audience members who interrupted were roughly removed by Brown Shirts. Protestors had been warned by the government not to assemble within half a mile of the Albert Hall. With this in mind, John Strachey (son of St. Loe and Amy Strachey) planned his anti-Fascist meeting for Thurloe Square, half a mile away, but the crowd was violently dispersed by police.
[4]Elizabeth Watson (1906–55), painter and communist, a friend of QB's.

heard the "pro-German" side of it—they absolutely refused to believe in the theory of German evil intentions and think the French hysterical and idiotic. But Pippa, they said, was so scandalised by the Germans breaking a pact[5] that she simply wanted to fight them at once—quite seriously. Can there be many like her?

Oh Julian, how often I wish I could talk to you. I feel you have a saner and larger grasp of all these things than almost anyone I know and even I now cannot help wanting badly to understand something of what is happening in the world, and most people and newspapers are simply confusing.

Goodbye darling. I think of you so much here, you are essential to this place. It belongs to you and you to it.

Your loving
VB

BELL

VII-24. To Julian Bell

Saturday, June 13 [1936]   *8, Fitzroy St.*

My darling Julian,

It has been rather an agitating week, I must admit, though perhaps you'll think me foolish. Everyone assures me that if there were to be fighting anywhere near you, the British consul would insist on your being in safety, and that there's a gun-boat to look after Hankow, etc. I suppose I shouldn't worry if you were in the same position but nearer, which perhaps is irrational, but it does make it worse to know so little about your plans and position, and to have to wait so long for news. The Times has belittled the whole thing until yesterday, when even they had to admit that some sort of civil war seemed to have begun. Today however they say it has stopped again and the southern armies are retreating. One never knows from day to day what to expect. Other papers are usually much more alarmist.

---

[5]On March 7, Hitler's troops had occupied the demilitarized zone of the Rhineland in contravention of the Versailles Treaty.

I saw Margery Fry after I had written to you on Wednesday. She and Helen came to dinner. I tried to find out if she knew anything about China, but of course she didn't, though she produced a story which reminded me of some of Roger's. She said she believed that the Chinese had settled exactly what to do in the event of a Japanese invasion, down to the last detail, that they were going to retreat in a diagonal line straight across China, leaving all in the hands of the Japs, and moving all the [towns?] to pre-arranged places in perfect order. When I said that at the present moment it looked more like civil war than an invasion by the Japs she said as to that she knew nothing. We then talked a good deal about you and whether and how long you ought to stay, etc. I said I thought you found yourself rather isolated and in need of easy companionship and I wondered whether perhaps you wouldn't soon have got most of the good to be got from the place. She said of course you weren't committed to more than one year, but I don't think she really knew much about it. I said that you yourself had never said a word to imply you wanted to leave before the two years were up, and that it was only my idea that you might. Margery thought if you wanted to leave at the end of the first year it would mean giving notice at once, but she also suggested that it might not be impossible to leave at Christmas or some other time during the second year. However as to all this I really know nothing, darling. You are the only person who can tell. I suppose it is likely that either things will have settled down again for a bit by the time you begin work in the autumn or else it won't be possible to go on. I wonder if your students are striking again and what is happening. Also I wonder very much what you'll be able to do about going away. It sounded to me as though Szechewan was rather impossible, where I believe you meant to go. Perhaps I may cable later to ask about your plans.

I have been very glad that Angelica anyhow wasn't in Paris lately. It's difficult to make out what is happening there, but one prefers not to have one's family there at the moment. It's quite bad enough to have one at the other side of the world.

It is so horribly cold here still that I am sitting by a gas fire—in the middle of June—and it has been pouring with rain too. I had an absolutely nerve-racking experience the other day. You'd have thought nothing of it, I suppose. I was asked to go and criticize the works of the St. John's Wood sketch club, and thinking one ought to do what one was asked to by the young, I said I would. I didn't really envisage clearly what would happen, but before going I did ask to be allowed to have half an hour in which to inspect the works alone before giving my opinion. What was my horror to find when I got there that I should have not only to criticize the works before a large room full of students and their friends, but also that I was only allowed about 10 minutes in which to look at them first and that in company with the head master, who never left me alone for a moment. I found it was comparatively easy to know in one's own mind what one thought, but to find words and voice in which to express it before all those people was a very different matter. I managed to do so somehow or other. I then found that I had chosen the same young man[1] as being best in each of the three sections that I had to judge. This was natural perhaps, as to me he did seem to be the best, but I felt the authorities wished and expected me to divide honours more equally. However, they were all very nice to me and afterwards I was introduced to the young man I thought best and as I was told he was an admirer of Duncan's I completed my acts of favouritism by asking if I could borrow some of his designs to show Duncan and suggested he might come to tea and fetch them away again. This he did today and was so shy he could hardly get away. However, he was really a nice creature, only 19, and certainly has some gifts, so I was glad to encourage him. Angelica was at home and helped to entertain him, but I'm not sure she didn't add to his shyness . . .

Did I tell you that when Bunny last came to see me he carried off your Roger letter to read. He just began it when he was here and said it was "very well written." I hope to hear more from him soon or perhaps he'll write to you. Virginia (they're back in London and she seems much better for the time) told me she had read it rather hurriedly—and liked it—but of course began rather vague criticisms, such as that it seemed a little jumpy, and wanted pulling together. But I really doubt whether she had read the more difficult parts enough to give any real opinion. Anyhow I avoid asking her many questions as I know we shall get against each other in the queer way we always do about you. I said you wanted to know if they'd publish it and she said Leonard hasn't read it yet. I shall ask him about it as soon as I get a chance. To return to Bunny, he advised me to send Sue's stories to the editor of the London Mercury, a man called [R.A.] Scott James, saying that he, Bunny, had told me to. So I will, and will let you know what happens. Bunny seemed more appreciative of them to talk to than he had been in his letter.

---

[1] John Minton (1917–57). He later studied in Paris under Pavel Tchelitchev.

All London is now going dotty about a large French and English surrealist show,[2] much as they did about the post-impressionists. That is to say they make utterly imbecile remarks and seem to be either enraged or charmed. No doubt some are very good, as they include Picasso and other quite reputable artists, but it sounds to me (I haven't been) as though they were going back to the Victorian ideas of subject and its importance. I hope at last however to understand what surrealism is, which I have never done before. Duncan went to the Private View and found a 10/– note lying on the floor which he tried to place on a statue so as to add meaning to it. Unfortunately someone— perhaps the owner, perhaps not—came up and pocketed it. Then as he was going out Paul Nash[3] came up and gave him a herring, which he asked him to put outside, as he said some Philistine had attached it to a picture,[4] but Duncan refused. Evidently it would be easy to get up a *surréaliste* party—in fact we think our studios are full of s.r. subjects without our troubling about it, and one may find oneself one of them before one knows what's happening.

I enclose a cutting which may amuse you. The Chevalier,[5] as we now call him (behind his back) is coming to supper tonight. The Woolves may come in afterwards, I'm not sure.

Goodbye, darling. I wonder where you will be when this gets to China. But I can only trust to your being cautious on my account if on no other.

Your loving
VB

BELL

[2]The International Surrealist Exhibition at the New Burlington Galleries.
[3]Paul Nash (1889–1946) was a founder in 1933 of Unit One, and had helped organize the Surrealist exhibition.
[4]Miró's *Object 228.*
[5]CB had been made a Chevalier of the Legion of Honor by France.

VII-25. To Julian Bell

Sunday, July 5 [1936]   *Charleston*

My darling Julian,

... The most exciting event of the week was a suggestion that Angelica should play leading lady in a play to be produced at a "west-end" theatre in the autumn! It has had to be turned down however, but it was of course an exciting idea. It came from Bobo Mayor, who was asked to suggest someone by Miles Malleson,[1] who is said to be intelligent and a good actor and producer. He wants a young and inexperienced girl to take the leading part in a new Czechoslovakian play which deals with adolescence, etc.[2] Angelica is bound by contract with her school[3] not to appear in public while with them, so I had to say she couldn't do it. However I had to talk to Mr M.M. on the telephone and he was very insistent, having heard the most glowing account of A. from Bobo, and said she would learn a lot from the experience, it might be the making of her, etc., and at last I had to say I'd write to Saint Denis about it and let him know. This I have done, but I'm sure he'll refuse, and in fact I don't think it would really be a good plan. A. is too young and if she were a success it would probably prevent her from ever working seriously as she is doing now—if a failure, it would only depress and discourage her. She will only be 19 by the time her training is finished—quite time enough to start her public career. However she was thrilled by such a thing even being suggested and it was very nice of Bobo to think of her.

We went to a cocktail party given by the Bussys at their rooms at 51, and there met all sorts of people, including Mme de Margerie,[4] who was I believe responsible for Clive's French honours and who rather nervously began joking about them to me. I was on the point of taking them as a joke when I realised that perhaps it wouldn't be really tactful with the French. She's said by most to be an awful

[1]William Miles Malleson (1888–1969), actor, director, and playwright. He was especially interested in plays with social or political themes.
[2]Although Malleson produced some Czechoslovakian plays, none matches VB's description.
[3]Angelica was studying at the London Theatre Studio, founded by the French director Michel Saint Denis (1897–1971).
[4]Jenny de Margerie, wife of Roland de Margerie, first secretary at the French embassy in London from 1933 to 1939.

female, whom I've successfully avoided meeting for years, but Clive quite likes her. Then Tom Eliot, with whom and Simon I had a long and rather fascinating conversation in French, which of course Tom talks fluently, about poets and painters and originality in the arts, etc. I enjoyed listening to them, Simon exactly like one of his own birds and Tom a curious mysterious combination of American and European, but with great charm, I think. They got on very well together. Angelica came in, looking extraordinarily pretty and elegant, and Ann [Stephen] was there, magnificent and huge. But how I wish someone would dress her. Oh dear, poor child, in a pink cotton dress, badly made, the wrong colour, fussy, absurd. She could look so lovely. I think it's really a pity, for other girls are so well-dressed nowadays, probably young men are affected without knowing why. However, you probably would prefer her as she is, but then you aren't young men in general, and it would do her good to have success with them. She told me she'd heard from you lately and said she wrote to you quite often "because she liked hearing from you," so evidently your letters are a success.

On Friday Duncan and I drove down here, a horrid rainy day. We arrived at 5, had a hurried tea, then Q. drove in to meet Angelica who'd had to take a train after work at the Old Vic. They got here just in time for her to change and we all set off for Glyndebourne. I must tell you that these arrangements were necessary because Angelica insisted upon cutting a dash at Glyndebourne. She would wear, and I had to make, a dress of the most startling description. I don't suppose you remember, but I used to have a dress made from the most brilliant crimson brocade, bought years ago in Rome, a really staggering stuff. I hadn't worn it of course for years and it had been taken to pieces, but I made it up again for her, and with it she had a vermilion shawl— and roses from the garden—and red lips—and her skin looked almost green. Altogether the effect was blinding and did in fact cause a good deal of sensation. The Clarks were there and said she must come to a party to be given by Sam Courtauld, to which Duncan and I have been asked, and they'd get her an invitation to it. So I suppose she'll impress London next. Mary Hutchinson was there too and I saw her looking at her with some astonishment and perhaps not altogether approval. But most people were obviously impressed by her beauty. Christopher[5] appeared. What his feelings were I don't know, but she liked him very much and was anxious to know him again, so perhaps

[5]Christopher Strachey (1916–75), the son of Ray and Oliver Strachey.

they'll meet in London. Oliver also and James and Gumbo looking *too* peculiar, drinking brandy which Kenneth had ordered for Duncan, greatly to K.'s astonishment and indeed horror. In fact, if you could have seen Gumbo, you wouldn't have been surprised at his taking her for some drunken troll—huge and grey and untidy, sprawling over the table and tossing off brandy.

I too am said to have disgraced myself, for we brought our own dinner—the brandy episode was after dinner—and ate it out of doors in an archway. There, feeling slightly merry, I improvised a song, suitable to the occasion, "What shall we do with a broken tumbler," which I sang in a spirited manner, unaware that at the back of our archway was a door leading to the professional singers' apartments, and that through this door was peering a startled young man. The rest of the family was aware of him however and became convulsed with laughter, which I took only as a compliment to my song, and so continued gaily, till at last a whole troop of professionals came through and I had to pull myself together and behave as a polite lady making way for them past our broken tumblers and sandwiches. Altogether it was a successful evening and the music was divine.

But a terrible thing has happened in this neighbourhood and it is thought that all my powers of repulsion will be called into play. Mrs Curtis has taken a bungalow at America—on the top of the Downs above Firle, as you know, I suppose. She has actually taken it for a year, though it only came onto the market a week ago, and she has already got into possession and slept in camp beds with 3 girls and yesterday they all came to lunch here! It's really rather alarming, for she's such a terrific mad woman, there's no saying what she won't do next. She motored there, right up the Down, with beds and crockery and food and all she needed to start with and seems already to have got farmers' wives to cook scones and sell her milk, etc. I only hope she won't spend the holidays there, but there's no telling. In the [school] terms she *can* only go for weekends, but in the summer holidays it really might be serious to have her so near at hand. As it is, she carried Angelica off to tea, and we had her and 3 young women for lunch. I shall now have to draw in my horns and become discouraging.

At the same moment she arrived there was a typical Charleston scheme. Q. had just returned from a journey to Lewes with the trailer, in which was a huge barrel and case containing pottery. All was being unpacked outside, and soon the ground was strewn with pots, bowls, vases of every sort. There is lots more to come, but this first consignment is really very considerable, and at present is all laid out in the folly, where it looks very much like pottery in an Italian market place. I must say that I think it's very impressive, and Q. has really done some lovely things. He's done a lot too that he couldn't have done except by working there—things have come from being on the spot, some by accident, others because he has seen possibilities of technique and used it in a new way. Altogether I am delighted and think he must set up a pottery here and have a show in the autumn. I hope he'll do something quite his own now and different from any of our things. Already he seems to me to have got something quite original and he will I hope do still more with his own kiln and wheel. One will have to try to find the best way of selling them. Mrs C. really came at a good moment for him, for she ordered one bowl at once to be reserved for her, and she's a good patron.

I have now got the Mallarmé proofs,[6] as I am to do the jacket. It seems to me to be the most exciting book, though I've only just looked at it. I don't much like reading things in proof, but still I shall. I suppose I must do some kind of still life for the jacket.

Oh darling, I must also tell you some tiresome news. Those blessed Woolves won't publish your Roger letter. They're very tiresome. Leonard said they had given up their [Hogarth] letter series as it was a failure. He said this was too short for a book.

[unsigned]

BELL

VII-26. To Julian Bell

Saturday, Aug. 29 [1936]   *Charleston*

My darling Julian,

This week I had your short scrap from Yachow dated July 25 saying you were just off. How thankful I am that I've also had your cable from Peking, so I need not worry if I don't hear more for some time.

[6]Stéphane Mallarmé's *Poems,* translated by Roger Fry, with commentaries by Charles Mauron (London: Chatto & Windus, 1936).

I've just begun to read Peter Fleming's book,[1] which I think may be rather amusing. I wonder if you'd like to have it. There must be quite a lot that would be familiar to you in the kind of things and people he writes about and the photographs are rather fascinating. Tell me if you'd like it and I'll send it to you. Here we have been living in a whirlpool of a kind. Christopher [Strachey] came on Monday, very pleasant, very easy, with a good deal of charm and high spirits. I'm not sure how interesting I think him, but one cannot tell. He may have more in him than appears and is of course very young. I should say he has in a way rather a depressing time at home. These holidays for instance he seems to have been spending mostly alone at Mud House in company with old Mrs Berenson and Auntie Lou,[2] both quite intolerable. Oliver never goes there and Ray only for weekends. It can't be very easy for him to ask his own friends to stay with him in such surroundings and he seems very happy here. He and Angelica spend hours every day playing the piano together, which they both enjoy very much, and altogether he fits in quite easily. The preparations for our entertainment tomorrow have been terrific. Quentin and Janie had produced a sketch of Charleston 100 years hence, with a guide showing a ghastly party of ladies, American and French, the relics of this age, which gives plenty of opportunity for being nasty to everyone—Q. dressed as a stout lady in my fur coat and with a falsetto voice is very fine and Janie as an unpleasant French lady, all longing to go to the WC but forced to look at the pictures. However I think the turn of the evening will probably be Duncan's. I have never seen anything quite so indecent. He has made himself a figure in cardboard of a nude female, which is none too securely attached by tapes to his own figure, and then he wears a simpering mask, a black wig and Spanish comb and mantilla, which partly conceals and reveals the obscene figure, while a Spanish air is played on the gramophone and Duncan flirts gracefully with a fan. I can't imagine what an audience will think of it. The Keyneses are bringing the Geoffrey Keyneses—*Mr and Mrs*—and their two children, boys of about 12 and 14.[3] God knows what will happen, but Angelica says it will be good for them. I must try and get photos of all of them and send

[1]*News from Tartary: A Journey from Peking to Kashmir* (1936).
[2]Old Mrs Berenson is Mary Berenson (née Pearsall Smith), Bernard Berenson's wife. Auntie Lou is her sister Alys, the first wife of Bertrand Russell. Mud House was Ray Strachey's cottage near Fernhurst in Sussex.
[3]Geoffrey Keynes and his wife Margaret (née Darwin) had four sons, but these two were probably Quintin George and Milo.

them to you. On Wednesday Janie arrived in order to join in re-
hearsals ... On Monday all will go and their place be taken by Angus!
I fear he will fall rather flat after all these lively young, but there will
be some advantages in leading a quiet life again.

However, I must say it has been rather amazing here this last week.
For one thing, it has been really fine—absolutely heavenly summer
weather, quite hot and with the corn still in the fields, the most lovely
gold, and all the pale colours of this chalk country warm and delicious.
Everyone has been going about half naked and getting brown, Angelica looks very well and wears hardly any clothes, everyone eats
enormously and drinks masses of cider, the house seems full of young
people in very high spirits, laughing a great deal at their own jokes,
singing and playing all the time and lying about in the garden, which
is simply a dithering blaze of flowers and butterflies and apples. If
only you were here too. But we plan a tremendous celebration next
year, your return and the 21st anniversary of our being in this house.
Well—it's rash I suppose to expect anything so nice so far ahead.
Meanwhile, Duncan and I have taken to going constantly to Newhaven to paint and I am getting more and more fascinated by boats
on water—to look at—not to be in or on. We find all sorts of odd
corners to paint from and we are getting quite knowing about tides
and how they'll affect us. There is a sandy beach too, reached by a
ferry across the harbour, where Angelica and Eve sometimes go and
bathe. They go to all their usual places too quite often, but sailing
hasn't been the fashion so far without you to stir them up to it. I
think also the fact that Janie can't bear it prevents them from going.
Perhaps next week without visitors Q. and A. will try again.

I had a letter from Helen at last after hearing nothing for a very
long time, not in fact since she came back from France. I think she
had been rather worried about Gerald Brenan,[4] who is still in Málaga,
but he seems to be all right still. He has bomb-proof cellars in his
house and therefore shelters all kinds of people, including some rebels,
though his sympathies of course are all with the government.[5] Helen
as usual had plunged into every kind of trouble on returning home—
Igor ill, Baba in a very bad temper, having failed to get a degree of

[4](Fitz)Gerald Brenan (1894–1982), writer and celebrated Hispanist. His friendship with Ralph Partridge and long involvement with Carrington brought him
into contact with Bloomsbury in the 1920s. It was briefly hoped he might write
for the Hogarth Press.
[5]The Spanish Civil War had started in July.

any kind. They went down to Rodwell,[6] where Igor recovered and Helen, thinking he was better, and in spite of the fact that she was already housing a penniless artist there and had no servant, allowed Alan Clutton Brock to come for 2 nights. Ba was in such a state that she stayed upstairs and refused to see anyone, even at meals. The Benckendorfs came to dine, the Clarks turned up to lunch, Alan C.B. came to stay, Helen had to provide meals for all, nurse Igor, who had relapsed again—and Ba not only refused to appear but crept down on the sly and ate up all the food prepared for the others! What a household! Helen says she knows people will think she likes it, but she really doesn't, and in fact I can hardly believe that anyone could like such a state of things. I suppose she just drifts into it and says "do come" out of weakness and then has to take the consequences. But I must say that one would expect the wormiest worm to have turned by now—and Helen is by no means a worm. I seem amazingly lucky by contrast. I am aghast at myself for having asked the Bussys to come for next weekend, but after all I shan't have to cook for them and there'll be other people to talk to them and it's only for a weekend. If Angelica were sulking upstairs and coming down only to eat all the food I had cooked, on the sly, it would be a very different matter!

Sunday. The house has now reached such a state of pandemonium that I retire thankfully for a few minutes to my room to finish my letter to you. Presently I shall go to the post with it and also to telephone to the Woolves and find out if they are coming, which is uncertain. V. has I hope at last definitely given up trying to finish her book[7] at once, and so may recover, but any unusual effort makes her bad again. I went to tea with her one day and did my best to persuade her to put it all aside for a time and she promised she would. Oh dear, I hear the piano on the move! I've been down to see that all went well and the studio floor wasn't destroyed and was witness of what might have well been an appalling disaster. The long farm ladder which was propped against a beam was knocked against by Q. and fell to earth—but he just managed to save it from a complete crash and it did nothing more than knock a flower out of a vase—didn't even break the vase, still less kill either human being or cat. I hope now the worst dangers are over. I must stop and go to the post and

[6]Helen's country home near Ipswich.
[7]VW, who since April had been in a state nearing nervous collapse, was working on the proofs of *The Years* (1937).

in my next will tell you what happens. I send 2 photos. So goodbye, my dear. A. in trousers, and a group with Georges Duthuit, Clive, A., Duncan.

Your loving
VB

BELL

VII-27. To Julian Bell

Saturday, Oct. 10 [1936]   *Charleston*

My darling Julian,

I feel very much in touch with you at the moment, as yesterday I got your letter from Hankow enclosing photos of yourself and telling me you had at last got my letters. Haven't you got *very* much thinner? That is the chief thing that strikes one. Of course these aren't really like you, though I rather like the beginning-to-smile one—*not* the sinister Chinese one looking out of the corners of your eyes. The other, serious one, rather reminds me in some odd way of Jimmy Sheean, though you're not really the least like each other. But I am glad to have them. We all agree that it's most becoming to you to be thinner, and Angelica said you'd carry all before you, though, she added, you had already broken too many female hearts. Too true. It's very nice to be even so much in touch with you again, dearest. Didn't I tell you that Barbara Bagenal took the interiors of this house, with some wonderful German camera. She spent a week alone here in the summer. I read your letter and answer remarks as I come to them. About the swimming pool in the garden. Do you mean the walled garden? Everyone exclaims in horror! (Duncan and I have come down here for the weekend.) D. at least says "Absurd." Q. says more reasonably that he thinks the pond itself will be very pleasant to bathe in if, as he hopes, it can be got really full. I told you, didn't I, how Mr Hide [local man], too true to his name, couldn't be got to come and see about the puddling. But now another friend of Mr Dean of Rodmell has actually turned up—a professional puddler—and he says he can do it in a day.[1] That seems too optimistic and altogether unlike Sussex, but he's coming on Monday to begin work. The pond is now very low, Q. says below leak level, he thinks, so it should be possible to begin. The clay is there, all is ready, and I think with Q. on the spot it ought to be possible at last to get something done. Then we intend to get a pair of Canadian geese, nice brown creatures whom you'll approve of, I hope, and some carp, who, Bunny says, nibble the weed below water. Q. has grand projects for a stream, to meander through the orchard, making one or two large pools, by the side of which Duncan will grow water plants and one will sit and listen to the poplars, which really do now make the most delicious noise in the breeze. This stream will be the only outlet from the pond—it will eventually find its way into the field—and will be regulated by Q. who will therefore be able to get the pond very full—so he says. It all sounds perfect, if only the professional puddler will do his part and the geese and carp theirs. So you see it's thought that a new bathing pool may be superfluous, and anyhow Duncan says if you want more, why not dig a bit of the pond deeper? You can answer these criticisms at your leisure.

Yes, I am really glad you're not in Europe now. We had a visit from Eliz. Watson in London, who came to ask me and Duncan to help with a preface to a catalogue of drawings by her friend Felicia Brown who has been killed fighting in Spain. She went there before the war began—simply to work—but when it began she got drawn in, and joined the government forces. Then she wanted to leave, but it was too late. All the boats that took people off went, and there was some muddle about the friend she was with. So she was killed, which does seem a terrible waste of someone gifted, as she evidently was. I understood your wanting to go and see what war was like, and perhaps I should understand your wanting to go to Spain if you were here, only I do think nearly all war is madness. It's destruction and not creation, and it's mad to destroy the best things and people in the world, if one can anyhow avoid it. You object to cutting down trees. Isn't war that, a million times worse? I see one couldn't help joining anti-fascists if fascists started attacking, as they have in Spain. But I think you and other young people, who are the only hope of the world for the next 40 or 50 years, can do much more to help by not going out of your way to be shot. Of course going as a war correspondent is

---

[1]Mr. Dean was the Rodmell blacksmith. "Puddling" is making a watertight bottom to a (preferably drained) pond by pounding in a layer of clay.

different, but I am glad, my dear, that I don't have to try to reconcile myself to your rushing off to Spain. I think though, if it were necessary, I could find plenty of arguments against your doing so, but I wonder if they'd prevail. I haven't heard much about Ann lately. You know I hardly know Richard[2] and have no very definite opinion of him, beyond thinking he seems rather pleased with himself. He may have good reason to be, if one knew him better. It's Adrian who dislikes him so much, which is a pity. I'm glad you've written to Ann, however. I think contemporaries can do much more than anyone else on these occasions.

I will try to do something about your Roger essay when I am back in London next week. I do think there's something odd in the Woolves' attitude—which I discussed with Bunny, I forget if I told you. His theory is that V. lives so precariously (in nerves and brain) that she can't face any other writer of any real merit. The responsibility and strain of accepting them would somehow upset her own balance, he thinks. That is why she always gives absurd praise to obscure females and one never hears her really enthusiastic about any of her own generation, such as Lytton or Morgan or Joyce or Eliot, who may conceivably be of real importance. Bunny thinks it's not exactly jealousy, but some need to keep her own poise. I don't know if he's right, or if I have explained it clearly, but certainly her attitude about you is odd, I think. I believe too she affects Leonard. But he, though no doubt you're right to care for his opinion in many ways, is I think curiously narrow and limited in his appreciations. I always remember him and Roger discussing your "Good"[3] and though I didn't know enough (and hadn't read it) to follow all they said, it seemed to me strange and interesting how different their attitudes were. Roger's was so much more generous and imaginative, not uncritical, but able somehow to perceive possibilities and suggestions which Leonard was dryly blind to. Roger wasn't put off by small things from getting at the important things behind. Leonard seemed so unable to accept anything that wasn't done according to his rules. Of course I was probably prejudiced and anyhow was no judge of their arguments, but apart from that one got a clear impression of the two attitudes of mind, and I had a clearer one of Leonard's than I'd ever had before.

---

[2]Richard Llewellyn Davis (1912–1981), a Cambridge friend of JB's (and fellow Apostle), then studying architecture. He and Ann Stephen married in 1938.
[3]"The Good and All That," working title for JB's dissertation, which he wrote in hopes of gaining a fellowship at King's.

However, whether I'm right or not, I do think it's better for you to go your own way. I'm quite sure you'll get through to something eventually and very likely it's always better to be on one's own and free from family help or hindrance. I'll let you know what happens.

I must tell you something of our doings now. We went to London on Monday, leaving Q., poor creature, in bed with a bad cold. He was very sensible and stayed in bed 2 or 3 days and has now, he says, quite recovered. I didn't like leaving him, but it was all arranged and difficult to undo. In fact, I shouldn't have been much good here, as when we got to London I found I had caught the cold and was rather incompetent myself. However, I've practically recovered too. We thought A.'s term was to begin on Thursday, but it was put off till next Monday. So we had time in London to do all the jobs that invariably need doing when one moves the shortest distance. I, as often before, have changed the places of nearly everything in my studio, and am for the moment convinced that it's a great improvement. My object always is to gain space. Perhaps the only real way to do so would be to give away half one's possessions . . .

Sunday. I don't think we did much else in London of interest. Helen came in one evening, on the whole fairly cheerful. Igor has actually passed an exam! Perhaps it will break the current of not passing them. Baba is recovering from her complete failure and reading a great deal, and living at home, which is a doubtful proposition, I expect. Helen herself has been very busy gardening, as Duncan and I are here. It's a most lovely autumn day with really hot sun. There are still asters and dahlias out. Duncan has been hard at work on his rock garden, which is beginning to look less like earth works. Walter [Higgens] works under him, rather obstinate but hard-working—and completely ignorant—at any rate about flowers. Q. is doing designs for the village hall at Rodmell. I think they'll be rather good. I wish I knew just how his gifts ought to be used. He doesn't seem to me to be exactly a painter of pictures, but perhaps he'll find his *métier* as a potter and a decorator of all kinds—yet sometimes he does very lovely pictures and I don't like to discourage him. He has been elected to the Artists International[4] Committee and so will have to come up to London fairly often, which I am glad of, otherwise he might get too much buried here, I think.

[4]Artists International (later Artists International Association), a largely Marxist group founded in 1933 by Peggy Angus, Clifford Rowe, and others, mounting such exhibitions as "Artists Against Fascism and War" (1935). VB showed in their 1937 exhibition.

I am thinking of starting a weekly evening at home when we get going in Fitzroy St. It would be for "painters only" so as to avoid having all Bloomsbury [three words omitted]. Probably most of the company would be shy and not very talkative, and of course one always could ask stray intellectuals, but I don't want to have a weekly firework display. On the other hand, I want Angelica to have a chance of seeing someone besides her theatre friends. I don't say you won't be welcome to it when you return, but you won't have to be too brilliant and put us all to shame.

Now I can let myself think, this time next year you really will be here.

Goodbye my dear. This is a long letter, though without much news.

Your loving
VB

BELL

VII-28. To Frances Partridge

Nov. 20 [1936]   *8, Fitzroy Street, W.1*

Dear Fanny,

I suppose this is really a begging letter, but naturally I don't want to beg, only to make a suggestion, which you can refuse with the greatest ease. As you know, Helen has taken a flat in Charlotte St. Clive has a secondhand or rather discarded Frigidaire which wants putting in order. This would cost £19. I know what an enormous difference such a thing makes in a rather small flat at the top of a London house and it occurred to me that if 6 of Helen's friends contributed they could give it to her without making her feel that she owed too much to anyone. Duncan and I are going to contribute and I'm asking the Kenneth Clarks and I wondered if you and Ralph would like to. The amount would be £3.3.4 each. But as I said, if you aren't well enough off at the moment please say so. I can I'm sure get others, it's simply that you were the first people who occurred to me.

I'm very glad Helen is staying with you. I think she's getting absolutely exhausted between her own family and the Frys in London.

Yours,
Vanessa

FRANCES PARTRIDGE

VII-29. To Julian Bell

Sunday, Nov. 22 *[1936]* 8, Fitzroy St.

Julian Darling,

I dreamt of you so vividly one night that I thought surely there must be a letter from you in the morning—No—I was 2 days early. On Friday I got your letter telling me about the break with Sue, written barely 3 weeks before. My dear, I have thought of it all so much since, and oh how I wish I could talk to you. I *did* talk to Quentin who had come up for the night to see Charles [Mauron], and he told me he was writing to you. I have told no one else except Duncan, because I thought it quite possible that things would change in some way, and there is plenty of time yet, even if you do come home soon after Christmas, to tell people. But heavenly as it would be to have you back, I don't know what to wish or advise about it all—not that advice would be possible or useful. Still I cannot help writing and telling you more or less what I feel. You won't mind my doing so anyhow, whatever the state of things may be when you get this. At first I wanted very much to cable, but all I could have done was to urge caution, as this time last year! That gives you a sort of summary of my feeling and is not much good, I know. But I think I do feel that there is danger of your sacrificing what may be of permanent value to the exigencies of the moment. I mean it seems a pity not to go on to the end of your appointment and then have enough money to travel, all of which would be a very real experience and would probably give you more chance of getting some good job later—instead of throwing it up a little more than half way through and putting the University into rather a hole ... Well, you may have changed plans and ideas since you wrote. Anyhow, I decided to wait for your next letter and do nothing meanwhile. But darling, I also feel that you want very much to come back and mix in politics here. As to that I hope Q.'s letter may give you a better idea than I can of what is going on here. Charles also said he had written to you. I of course know very much less than they do, but I feel strongly that if you want really to do what is best for the world and not only what would relieve your own feelings most at the moment, it is clearly better to help by thinking, writing, speaking, planning, rather than by action in the field. You would be one of many in action, no more and no less valuable, but you have a better intelligence than most people, and so it should be used, and not destroyed by a chance bullet. This really isn't because I should mind it. I feel exactly the same about anyone who has brains above the average. It is I think the only hope of the world that such people make themselves felt. Don't think I don't understand and sympathise with your feelings about helping Spain and using your talents as a soldier—which I am quite ready to believe in. Only if they exist, surely my dear you should have gone into the army! If you went to Spain, not knowing the language or the people or the country and its conditions, you could only have gone into the army as other foreigners have done and been used by those in command. That is the worst of going to fight. You *must* become part of a machine and do what someone else thinks you ought to do. No one nowadays could become a general at once and decide on strategy, etc., and you'd only have to help to carry out what might seem to you a quite wrong policy. Isn't this so? In fact, in Spain, I suppose it's been want of arms that has prevented the government from winning, and that you couldn't have helped . . .

I shall be very anxious for your next letter.

Now to tell you our news. I last wrote from Charleston, didn't I, and then Angelica and I came up by an evening train. The next day I spent moving her furniture from Charlotte St. to the room at the top of this house. It always takes some time, even to move from one room, but it was habitable by the evening and she is much happier not having to go out before breakfast or at night in the cold and rain. Also the room is really nicer and she is quite alone up there. Her removing put an end to your plan of taking the room next hers, but I'm sure I could find you a room quite near here. How lovely it would be to have you at hand, dropping in when you liked. There was one tiny flat I found, with 3 small rooms, which was rather attractive, but there are sure to be lots of others.

One night we dined with the [Duncan] Macdonalds, and met a

German painter and his wife who have a grim account of intellectual life in Germany in a place like Frankfurt, where there used to be flourishing bankers who bought paintings and had a lot of music. All has come to an end. There is no freedom for artists and no money to help them. We also met Matthew Smith,[1] a good painter and odd, rather fascinating person, with whom I very much enjoyed talking pure shop. Then on Thursday we had Charles and Helen to dinner here and also Q. who came up for the occasion. I hope they enjoyed it, as they stayed till about 1 AM. Charles was very nice and amusing and seemed to be enjoying being in England. Did I tell you that Helen thinks he has fallen in love with one of the John girls,[2] but I don't know how much reason she has. Also did I tell you or has she, that Virginia is full of admiration for the Mallarmé, and for Charles altogether? He dined with them and was evidently a great success. He is giving her all his letters from Roger to read and encouraged her very much to write, regardless of the family, who will he says really thoroughly enjoy being upset and scandalised. I hope V. will take his advice. There had been a very successful party at Margery's the night before in which Charles had made an extremely good speech, followed by a debate. Only you should hear V.'s account of the food and drink, and how she tried to make Charles finish her cider, which was like ink, and how she had to conceal bits of biscuit and cake in odd corners, all brought by a small boy called Leonard, which added to the confusion of the evening. I read some of your travel letters aloud to them and Charles enjoyed them very much. Also I gave him your Roger essay to read. He was going down with Helen to stay with the Johns for the weekend and will bring it back tomorrow. Perhaps he'll be able to advise me what would be the best thing to do with it. He wants to come to see Duncan's pictures by daylight before he goes, which I think he will do one day this week. Quentin wants him to go from Newhaven and spend a night in Charleston.

My last few days have been spent in a turmoil of dress-making. We were asked to go to a party last night given by Valerie Taylor and her husband,[3] both actors and very nice people, and Angelica longed to go as we were sure to see all the actors there, but had no suitable

[1]Matthew Smith (1879–1959), painter, educated at the Slade and briefly in Paris, under Matisse.
[2]Possible. The Johns spent much time near the Maurons at St.-Rémy-en-Provence in the 1930s.
[3]Valerie Taylor (b. 1902). Her first husband was the actor Hugh Sinclair (1903–62).

dress. So I said I would make one for her in 3 days, not realizing, as I never do, what I was in for. However, by working night and day she was just able to wear it and appeared a vision of white and silver and was much admired, so it was worthwhile though I nearly expired, and after the party which lasted till 3 we all stayed in bed this morning getting up lazily for tea at about 12.30. I woke however from an awful nightmare about you, thinking you were dead, and waking saying "Oh, if only it could all be a dream."

I have had a curious proposal, to go and stay with people whose name I don't yet know, at Chester, and paint portraits of their two small children. I have said I may do so if they'll pay me £100, which would be less 33 1/3% as the offer comes through Macdonald. But I am rather nervous at the idea. Everyone tells me it would be unsporting to refuse, however. But it may not come off.

I rather hope that when your plans are quite definite about returning or not you'll send me a cable, unless indeed you are able to write and tell me some time ahead. But I don't want to be in Chester or elsewhere when you return. It's just possible D. and I might make a quick visit to Paris after Christmas to settle about furniture, etc., but I'll let you know of course. Well, I must stop, dearest. This is a long letter written mainly for my own good.

Your loving
VB

BELL

VII-30. To Julian Bell

Feb. 3–4 [1937]   *8, Fitzroy St.*

Julian darling,

I sent a cable to you at Wuchang, but I daresay it will have missed you. I said Don't decide. Letters *poste restante* Suez. Since then I have heard from you again, and so instead of writing to Suez I shall send this by air to Colombo, where it should easily reach you, and now I'll try to explain why I cabled. Two days ago I got a letter from Charles, enclosing one to you, of which I send you a copy. Helen who is staying at St Rémy also wrote. They told me you had written to Charles saying you wanted to go to Spain direct from France and asking him to help you. Have I been very stupid? I have read your letters again and again. You wrote on Dec. 24, and you said you must talk of plans. You did talk—but vaguely—saying enough to make me guess you wanted to go to Spain of course, which indeed didn't surprise me. I could see you were altogether upset, and no wonder, with no one much to talk to and only newspapers, and being ill. But although you spoke of my meeting you at Marseilles you said nothing to make me think you meant to go *at once* to Spain. It seemed to me to be a natural enough craving, but one which implied such an important decision that you couldn't think of making it very quickly or without seeing people who could give real advice. I was worried, I admit, but you were vague enough to make me hope that your own mind was not made up. Then I had another letter written on Jan 3rd, in which you seemed a little calmer, and spoke of political jobs in England, and hoped the crisis (in Spain I suppose) might be over by the time you returned. Then I got Charles' letter, and though it made me feel perhaps I *had* been stupid and blind, still even so, reading your letters again, I do not think I could have expected you to be so definite as you seem to have been to him. I cannot, my dear, help feeling as I have for the last 2 days, nor could I help letting you see it when we meet, even if I said nothing now. I can only promise you that I won't willingly let my feelings prevent you from doing anything you do deliberately and honestly feel you should do. Indeed I can promise you that they *shan't* prevent you. But I have somehow managed to think calmly and to consider *you* altogether—your character and ways of mind. I won't write you an essay about them, though perhaps someday I shall give you a lecture upon them. All I want to say now is, that though your irrational feelings have to be reckoned with, (and indeed I find them easy to understand and sympathise with) and allowed for and dealt with both by yourself and those who love you, yet they mustn't be allowed to destroy what I feel to be more real and fundamental and freer. It can happen so easily, but it mustn't happen to the really valuable people if one can possibly help it. If, when you have used your mind and understanding, you still want whatever it may be—danger—risk . . . then it's different. But I think that so much one may ask, at any rate if, as now, there is no reason that I can see why one should not.

For, practically speaking, surely there is everything to be said for your seeing people who know what is going on. You cannot have known much of the true meaning for all this so far away. It's difficult enough here—for me, at any rate. But in England you could see people who've been to Spain, people who come and go all the time, people in the centre of it all who can tell you how best to help quite disinterestedly. Surely it would be foolish to refuse to do so. If you think that once here you could not go out [to Spain] you are wrong, for everyone says it's perfectly easy. It's not even illegal, and people go all the time without question, unless they happen to be penniless and unemployed and obvious recruits.

I cannot think my darling Julian that you know how people—so many—feel about you here. Quentin for one. Do you realise how terribly upset he'd be if he couldn't see you and talk to you before you did a thing like that? For it's no good thinking you could go and return soon. It would mean a far worse separation than your going to China. I cannot write about it very calmly—and what is the good—only such things cannot, when one's grown up, be done lightly . . .

It's now past midnight, and so it's your birthday, and it seems as if therefore I couldn't say anything I more wanted to say than to wish you many many happy returns of the day, my beloved creature, and so good night.

Your
VB

BELL

VII-31. To Angelica Bell

Friday, May 6 [error for May 7, 1937]   *8, Fitzroy Street, W.1*

My own darling,

I loved your tipsy letter. You must have been sorry to leave Gargilesse, which sounds heavenly.[1] How I should like to go and paint there someday, and live quietly in the Pinaults' house or inn and do nothing but paint and eat and drink.

---

[1]QB had taken AVG to visit his friends the Pinaults in their country home at Gargilesse.

Well, yesterday was my Private View[2]—rather a failure, I'm afraid. London is simply impassable now,[3] no buses, and every street blocked with sightseers on foot and small cars very badly driven. The streets are gay with flags and rather lovely. You'll see them all next week. But no one can get anywhere. Even in one's own car it's very difficult. There is also a show of French tapestries at Lefevre's from designs by Matisse, Picasso, etc., so skilfully done one can't believe they're not painted. It was to have been opened by the French ambassador[4] who turned up very late, and as there was no one there, he couldn't open it! Some of my friends came, the Woolves, Keyneses, Mrs C. (of course), Mrs Grant, etc., and 3 were sold—one of which was of you weaving.[5] You always sell. Mme de Margerie was there and raved about you in the few seconds I spoke to her.

Well, I must hope for more after Whitsuntide. Till then all London is mad. Duncan has gone off now to a rehearsal at the Abbey.[6] I am going down to Charleston today and shall expect you at Newhaven on Wednesday unless I hear. All other news will keep till then. Give my love to Zoum [Walter] and her daughter.[7] Please tell Q. I'll write to him soon and give him my love.

Yours
Mummy

ANGELICA GARNETT

VII-32. To Virginia Woolf

May 16 [1937]   *8, Fitzroy Street, W.1*

I should have had to write to you in any case to tell you that the most heavenly asparagus arrived, to say nothing of tulips, to say

---

[2]At the Lefevre Gallery. Several paintings were sold and the show was favorably reviewed in the *Times*.

[3]The Coronation of King George VI (May 12) unluckily coincided with a bus drivers' strike.

[4]M. Charles Corbin.

[5]Bought by Lady Charlotte Bonham-Carter, and bequeathed by her to the Charleston Trust.

[6]DG had been commissioned to do a painting of the Coronation.

[7]AVG had lived with the Walters in Paris before going to the London Theatre School.

nothing of your first letter with its welcome though undeserved praises. I am writing in most unpropitious circumstances waiting for Duncan to bring his mother, possibly Aunt Daisy, possibly Miss Elwes, to tea, after driving them to see decorations in the City. Angelica is doing her best to collect oddments of jam from various pots sufficient to make one small respectable pot full. I have managed to make a cake and some scones, since we had nothing in the larder and today is Sunday. Tomorrow too is Whit Monday and altogether one feels these feasts will never cease. London is absolutely vile. It's generally pitch dark and icy cold. I have had to light my stove again after letting it out, I hoped for the summer.

I have nothing to tell you at first hand of the Coronation. At Charleston it was a fairly dismal day, beginning to rain in the morning and going on more or less all day. It was even too wet at night to go and see any bonfires, nor did they have one on Firle Beacon. I spent my day much as usual, painting in the morning. Angelica who was to have arrived at Newhaven in the afternoon didn't turn up. She had sent a telegram to say she wasn't coming till the next day, but owing to a breakdown of all arrangements in England we didn't get it. She is here now, having had a wonderful time in France, it seems.

Duncan is going to Paris on Wednesday and then may go on to La Rochelle or some such place for 2 or 3 weeks or stay and paint in or near Paris. I shall go with him, but only for 3 or 4 days, just to have a sight of Paris. Perhaps it's rather dotty to go for such a short time, but it will be rather nice to get a moment away from family life.

I was interrupted by the tea party which didn't include Miss Elwes, luckily.

I have now, late at night, just been rung up by Julian from Cambridge. He rang us only about arrangements of his own, but also told me that Maynard seems to be rather seriously ill.[1] He seems to have got much worse, with the same disease, during the last few days and is now too ill, Julian said, to be moved to a hospital. But they hope to do so soon, though it will then mean a long and serious illness at best. I must try to find out more tomorrow, as it was difficult on the telephone. Julian had seen Lydia who seemed to be very much upset.

Duncan went to the Abbey and had many amusing stories to tell, which you had better get from him direct some day. He saw it all perfectly and seems to have managed better than most people, getting away fairly easily afterwards while the peers were kept waiting hours

[1]He had had a serious heart attack.

for their carriages, and some had to stay till about 8 PM. The funniest moment must have been when he joined the cavalcade going to the Abbey, driving the Baby, which was in a very grubby state, dressed in his court clothes, while the Dukes and Duchesses in their Rolls's with their chauffeurs looked at him with astonishment and scorn. But the police were kind and he got in easily in the end. We tried to go and look at flood lighting one night, but cars weren't allowed to go anywhere near. The only tolerable view we could get was from the other side of the river, which is always lovely and wasn't very much better than usual. One could have walked, but the different places are so far apart. London is still cheerful though barriers and stands are coming down. No busses yet of course. According to Helen, [Igor and Baba] went to see the procession starting at 2 PM and got places quite easily and saw perfectly. They said the crowd wasn't nearly so large as for the Jubilee or so enthusiastic. Your Mabel also seems to have seen perfectly.

As for my show, I expect nothing has happened since the first 2 or 3 days, when I had sold 6. Nothing much can happen till Whitsuntide is over. I think I have so far made about £50 profit after paying commissions and frames.

Let me know your plans.

Your
VB

We all admit that English asparagus is better than French!

BERG

VII-33. To Julian Bell

July 7 [1937]   *8, Fitzroy Street, W.1*

My darling Julian,

At last I have a letter from you dated June 22,[1] which you must have got someone to address and post in Paris. I can't pretend my

[1] JB had left England for Spain on June 6 as an ambulance driver for the Spanish Medical Aid.

dear that I don't feel rather upset and worried that you should be in Madrid. I had hoped that to start with at any rate you'd be further from the front—Wogan seemed to think you would. I don't want to bother you, but remember it's quite impossible for anyone at home not to find it terribly agitating. It's so much easier for you, who have all your time occupied and cannot bother much about anything else. Well, it's useless—one must just put up with it. Letters take a long time and so far I don't even know if you've got mine. You seem more remote than in China. The only consolation is that you are with people you like and leading a life you like. I will try to send you all the things you want as soon as I can—according to W. the only way was by the SMA[2] people. But some of your things must be got from Charleston. We spent the weekend there and the Woolves came to dinner, V. in the highest spirits and tremendous form. I expect she enjoys making as much money as she must be doing. Quentin seemed much as usual. His chief piece of news of a domestic kind is that he thinks of cutting off his beard, because it gets in his way bathing. It's become such a handsome beard that I shall almost regret it, but perhaps not, on the whole.

July 8. I was interrupted here and go on today. Q. came up yesterday for the day and we all met at a cocktail party at the Bussys to which we were asked to meet Matisse. I don't really enjoy meeting celebrities at such entertainments and hardly spoke a word to him. But he seemed a very nice urbane old gentleman and D. got on very well with him. A. sate in a corner most of the time rather hidden from view, but had time to make one conquest in the shape of our old friend Maresco Pierce. I had a little talk with Tom Eliot, and asked if I could send him your M.S. He was very friendly and promised to read it. So I am going to do so at once before he forgets. There was slightly over-whelming Strachey atmosphere—James, Dorothy, Pippa, Janie, Pernel. Then we went in to A.'s theatre to see a dance entertainment by the school professor of dance, Q. with us, and then he drove back to Charleston. I feel rather guilty because D. and I have thrust H. [one of Duncan's hangers-on] upon him for a fortnight or so. I hope he may be useful with casting, but the main object was to provide a short respite from walking the streets half starving and looking for a job for H. It's really desperately difficult to know what to do for such people. D. has another of them who went to try for a job from the SMA people. He can drive and is interested in mechanics, so we

[2]Spanish Medical Aid.

thought it might be possible, but he was turned down completely, unless he would sign a document on the spot committing himself to them indefinitely. This seems to me unreasonable, if true, but one can't rely on reports by the semi-educated unemployed. You said in your letter than you might get P.H.[3] to ring me, but I had a letter from her sent me to read by Janet[4] written after yours—June 27th—from which it was evident she was still in Madrid or nearby. She gave a very interesting account of everything and seemed mostly struck like you by the fantasticalness of it all. I read it calmly enough at the time, not knowing you were there. But during the last few days it seems as though big attacks were being made by the Govt., so I suppose you are in the thick of it all there. Tonight it apears that the Japanese are fighting the Chinese near Peking! Well, that will be very stale news by the time you get this, if ever. Indeed I don't attempt to send you any public news at all. I wonder how much you get, and what papers. Whether you get the New Statesman or not, Maynard has an article this week which is in the nature of a reply to Auden's poem,[5] and which seems to me extraordinarily sane and unanswerable. I wish all the young (including you!) could read it and see whether you don't agree, really and fundamentally. To me it seems such a relief from the heroic view (not that I think yours is that), but I think the only adequate answer in the end to insanity is reason, and this is not politics or party or anything but pure Cambridge logic and sense, perhaps written more detachedly because of his illness. I hope you'll see it. If I can send you any papers, etc., I will, but it's difficult to find out. Also I feel that perhaps you don't want them, as I know life must be too absorbing and you too tired by the end of the day to think of anything else. I try to imagine it and then I feel perhaps I had better not, for it's easier to imagine horrors than the more cheerful bits, which must exist too.

It's dismal and raining here now. Q. has sold one picture at our Agnew show, D. also one, and I 3![6] Also I've just sold another to an

[3]Dr. Portia Holman was attached to the medical aid unit in The Escorial. She knew JB from Cambridge.

[4]Dr. Janet Vaughan (1902–1993), daughter of Madge Vaughan. VB had nearly been her godmother, but Madge reconsidered on realising VB was agnostic.

[5]In the July 10, 1937, issue. In response to Auden's poem "Spain," JMK asserted that "the claims of Peace are paramount; though this seems to be an out-of-date view in what used to be pacifist circles. It is our duty to prolong peace, hour by hour, day by day, for as long as we can."

[6]Exhibition of Contemporary Art at Agnew's, selected by DG, VB, and Keith Baynes.

American female admirer of Virginia's,[7] so I've really done quite well.

Dearest, if you can ever send me a card sometimes it will make a difference. Perhaps it's impossible to get anything sent, though. How little one really knows of a country in which war is actually being fought, or what happens to all the ordinary services of normal life. I have not been in touch with any of your friends, but Q. had lunch with Eddy, who is immensely important[8] he says and very busy over the Finance bill (?). I have some letters for you but dare not send them till I can do it safely. Tell me what gets to you if you can.

Your loving
VB

BELL

VII-34. To Ottoline Morrell

Aug. 11 [1937]   *Charleston, Firle, Lewes*

Dearest Ottoline,

I was grateful for your little note.[1] You will forgive me for not writing sooner. I am only beginning to be able to write any letters, but I wanted to thank you.

Do you remember when we first knew each other telling me of your sorrow when your baby son died—I have never forgotten it.

Yours,
Vanessa

TEXAS

---

[7]Elinor Castle Nef (1895–1953), wife of the author John Ulric Nef, a professor at the University of Chicago. In 1953 he published his wife's *Letters and Notes*, vol. I.
[8]Edward Playfair was now in the Treasury.
[1]JB had died in the Escorial hospital on July 18, 1937, of shrapnel wounds received during the battle of Brunete.

VII-35. To Vita Sackville-West

Aug. 16 [1937]   *Charleston*

My Dear Vita,

I do not find it difficult to believe that you mind about Julian and I want to thank you for telling me so. But we who have and have had so much are not really to be pitied in the end.

I cannot ever say how Virginia has helped me. Perhaps some day, not now, you will be able to tell her it's true.

Yours,
Vanessa

BERG

VII-36. To Portia Holman

[Mid-August, 1937]   *Charleston*

Dear Portia,

Forgive me, but it seems impossible to call you anything else. Virginia told me how kind you had been in going to see her and she told me some of the things you had said.[1] I was too weak at the time to take in very much and anyhow you will understand how much I would like to hear things about Julian at first hand. Would it be too much an effort to come and see me here? I shall really understand if it is and will wait quite contentedly, so don't mind saying you can't. Besides, you mayn't have time. But if you *could* come for a weekend, or a night or even a day, you'd be most welcome. Lewes is only 1 hour from London and Quentin would meet you any time. I would

[1]Dr. Holman had worked at the Escorial hospital, where JB died.

suggest coming up to save you the trouble, but I am rather unable to move still.[2]

> *Yours very sincerely,*
> *Vanessa Bell*

TATE

VII-37. To Virginia Woolf

Sep. 9 [1937]   *Charleston*

What a life you lead—as usual. Please don't exhaust yourself by coming here if it's too difficult. I really need not be visited like an invalid now. There's no reason but sheer laziness why I shouldn't go out and about and drive myself about the country.

Clive and Miss L.[1] arrive tomorrow. They don't know when, as they're driving from Dover. I hope it won't be till after tea. I fear life will be less simple after they come, but one has had a long time of ease.

I will tell Quentin to take you the Day Lewis essay.[2] We ought to have more copies typed, I think. (Don't I owe you something for

[2]Despite VB's seclusion, she was always eager to talk about JB, especially with his friends. To his closest girlfriend, she wrote: "I think there is one thing I want desperately to say to any one who will listen—if only I could—and that is simply that I am quite sure, reasonably and definitely sure, that the loss of people like Julian *is* a waste. It is not my own pain that makes me say it. In fact I am not really to be pitied—not on the whole. I never doubt for an instant that I am immensely the richer for all the feelings I have had and shall ever have about Julian. But I am old enough to know a little what he might have done and been if he had lived. I know that his life would have given infinite good and possibilities to the world which are now lost. . . . Fascism wants to destroy intelligence—we must not let it do so. The world depends upon people like Julian to help it out of its troubles later—and their memory will not help as their presence would" (August 24, 1937; private collection).
[1]Janice Loeb, an American art student. She returned to the States at the outbreak of war.
[2]QB and VB were collecting Julian's letters and papers for a book, *Julian Bell: Essays, Poems and Letters,* published by the Hogarth Press in 1938. It was to include contributions by JMK, David Garnett, Charles Mauron, C. Day Lewis, and E. M. Forster.

typing?) I'm glad you think the Morgan one good. I think we must try Chatto, partly because I know Julian wanted all three essays published together and I suppose it's possible they might do this. Anyhow, one must try. Of course I feel more strongly than he did that it's always better if one can avoid the effect of its being a family affair, but perhaps I'm wrong. Anyhow, if Bunny will write something we must see what he says.

I don't think I can paint portraits at present.[3] It needs a special kind of effort which I don't think I'm capable of. Sketching Angelica is different, as she's not sitting specially to me. But I couldn't settle down to paint Clive, or anyone, seriously as a matter of business at present, flattered though I am by the notion. It's foolish I know, but I can't help it. I'm only working at small things which matter to no one but myself.

Adrian is coming I believe the weekend after next, and Angus some day next week. So no more solitude.

Your
VB

BERG

---

[3] In an effort to help VB recover, VW had tried to commission her to paint CB's portrait.

CHAPTER EIGHT

1938–1945

The Second World War affected Vanessa much more directly than the 1914–18 war. Julian can of course be seen as an early casualty of the battle against fascism. Other casualties were Vanessa and Duncan's Fitzroy Street studios, destroyed by an incendiary bomb in September 1940. And though she lived, as in the earlier war, a quiet country existence at Charleston, Vanessa was deeply anxious for the Bussys, trapped in France. Despite the irritations of postal delays and censorship, Janie Bussy became one of Vanessa's principal correspondents, eliciting long, detailed letters in some ways similar to those she had sent to Julian in China.

A further anxiety was Bunny's courtship of Angelica, which began informally in about 1936. He was twenty-six years her senior—romantic, persuasive, experienced. He had been at Charleston on the night of Angelica's birth and, admiring the infant, boasted that one day he would marry her. At first, Vanessa discounted Bunny's advances. It seemed impossible that he was serious. Nor was she averse to Angelica's having a brief affair with an older man. Duncan was more upset, his protective feelings toward Angelica combining with jealousy. In late 1937–38, as Bunny's wife Ray was slowly dying of cancer, Bunny stepped up his pursuit of Angelica. In 1939 he rented a room opposite Angelica's in Fitzroy Street, and in the spring of 1940, after Ray's death, he and Angelica lived together in a farmhouse at Claverham, some five miles from Charleston. Nothing Duncan said dissuaded Bunny, and Vanessa, chagrined, recognized that Bunny had become her principal link to her daughter. Vanessa exhibited a curious passivity in this situation. Reading her letters to Bunny, her anguish is obvious. But her letters to Angelica are cheery and brittle. She never told her daughter that Bunny and Duncan had been lovers, perhaps assuming Angelica knew the truth. In fact, she did not, and was only baffled and repelled by Vanessa's silent suffering. "Had the situation been less fraught with unavowed emotion," Angelica recalls,

> much of it impossible for me to understand, I might have felt free to enjoy my love affair without committing myself; but the feelings it provoked floated just beneath the surface, incomprehensible and menacing . . . At the same time, Duncan, Bunny and Vanessa were too closely bound together for there to be any room for me; the last thing they wanted was an illumination of the past, of the obscure corners they hoped to forget (AVG, 153–54).

In 1942, Bunny and Angelica married, without inviting her parents to the wedding. The arrival of their first daughter, Amaryllis, in 1943, and subsequent daughters (Henrietta in 1945, twins Frances and Nerissa in 1947) reconciled Vanessa to the marriage, though she feared Angelica was submerging her artistic talents in domesticity.

After Julian's death, Vanessa and Virginia grew close again. In most of her late letters to her sister, Vanessa dispenses with conventional openings and simply begins, as if speaking to someone seated beside her, or opening a vein that runs continually between two people. But Vanessa could not prevent the gradual decay of Virginia's peace of mind. In March 1941, Virginia drowned herself in the river Ouse, a five-minute walk across the water meadows from Monk's House. Hearing the news that day from Leonard, Vanessa was stunned, but not shattered. She had been braced for such an event for over forty years.

These misfortunes, however, occurred against the comforting, rhythmic background of country life. Clive lived at Charleston during the war, bringing his usual note of luxury. Vanessa joined both the Pig Club and the Bee Club, enjoying her contact with locals, and continued to relish the slow pleasures of her garden, the Downs, and painting.

VIII-1. To Virginia Woolf

March 17 [1938]   *8, Fitzroy Street, W.1*

Here is your share of John Murray's cheque.

We're expecting you to dinner on Saturday. If you came a little early you might inspect the beauties of *our* garden.

Please tell Leonard that if he can find any use for an incompetent like myself in the political world I am willing to be used, but I know it's not much good. At the same time, when things have got to such a pass, I don't see how the least politically minded can keep out of it. I can read and write and even type-write and have no pride.

But I suppose it's no use unless one has taken part in it all for years and it doesn't seem to be much good then. Why don't you go to America, where I hear from Etty [Sands] that the whole continent worships you and that they "travel on the privilege" of knowing you. I'd send Angelica with you to keep you happy.

Your
VB

BERG

444

VIII-2. To Virginia Woolf

June 21 [1938]   *8, Fitzroy Street, W.1*

Your letter and card reminded me vaguely of the past—nor so vaguely either, now I come to think of it. I really remember the atmosphere of Corby very clearly. As for the Italian churches, etc., you meet with *en route,* I hope you're taking snaps of them.[1] I find them more difficult to believe in than the patient spinsters. No doubt they exist and I think you ought to spend a good deal of time in their company. I hope you'll also keep a truthful record of meals at British inns.

We spent the weekend at Charleston in perfect weather. Janie was there, unchanged. Today the Bussys have given their annual cocktail party, to which I didn't go, and tonight the Clarks give a party to which everyone in London except myself is going. What a blessing it is simply to have decided that one won't go to parties. The more I think of it the less reason I see for going. If one has to encounter humans, why not do so in other ways—any way that doesn't entail dressing up, at any rate when one has reached my age and dressing up is no longer a pleasure. So I sit peacefully at home and write to you. I have been wondering lately how on earth you writers manage. Getting Julian's letters ready to be printed has nearly done for me. Perhaps I am by nature too slipshod. I made the most idiotic mistakes and never have the right paraphernalia of scissors, paste, etc. However I think at last all is done and I shall send them to the Press tomorrow or the next day.

I was rung up by your John [Lehmann] the day you went. To my surprise, he began by asking me what was happening about the book, so I said "haven't you had a letter from me?" I had written the night before and sent it to the H[ogarth] P[ress] to tell him just what had happened. It turned out that the young ladies of the Press had sent it on to his country address. So then I had to tell him by telephone. I

---

[1] The Woolfs were traveling in Northumberland on their way to Scotland for a holiday. VW wrote on June 18 from the Roman Wall, reminding VB of the visit they made to it in 1897 when they were staying at Corby Castle (Jack Hills' family home) after the death of Stella.

VW's "Italian Castle" was a figurative description of the Old Hall, a large medieval house at Gainsborough, Lincolnshire.

asked if he hadn't seen Leonard and he said no, you had told him it was no good coming. I must say I thought he seemed a good deal upset—he said he was ready to see Leonard at any hour, had come back on purpose, hadn't even found a letter, etc. But I daresay it was only a momentary upset due to my telling him that Julian's letters to him weren't going to be put in. I don't know. Anyhow, you will hear. He certainly didn't approve of leaving out all but Chinese letters, but realised that it was not his affair. In the end, I simply said that I hoped all would be ready by the middle of this week and I would send the M.S. to the Press.

I had a long talk with Clive at Seend about the book and I showed him the letters after we got back. He has really been very nice and sensible about it all and I think was relieved by my talking to him. He is very much in favour of the letters and thinks them very good. Also he thinks one should not cut too much, only things that are acutally libellous or indecent. He is not as much against redundancy as Bunny is, as he says it's always inevitable in letters. He thinks too that one should not leave out intimate things which show real relationships, which is a relief to me. Sometimes I am horrified at printing so much. But I don't really mind at all. After all, what does it matter.

I forgot to tell you—you may be horrified and with reason—I have ordered from Heal's, owing to Duncan's insistence, *two* (2) chairs, price I think £3.10. each, but one only must be given by you [as a birthday present]. The other is my affair, very comfortable, up to date and nice to look at. I'm sitting now by your fan, which is invaluable.

Your
VB

The letter from Sue was enclosed in a letter to me.

BERG

VIII-3. To Duncan Grant

Aug. 5 [1938]   *Charleston*

My darling Bear,

I had your letter this morning. I can't help being rather horrified at Angelica's coming up alone to have a tooth out, or am I simply old-fashioned and fussy? Quentin says Densham [a dentist] is very cautious and Angelica very sensible, but after all one may feel very shaky after having a wisdom tooth out, and one may easily get bad later. I'm glad you happened to see her.

It has been an odd day, fine and then getting grey and close and with a little rain. This morning proofs of Julian's book began to arrive and so Quentin and I have had to begin to correct them. I am rather enraged by John Lehmann—really the more one knows him the worse, in a way, one thinks of him. He has corrected all the letters—not the originals, which he hadn't got, but the typed copies—according to his own ideas of what Julian should have done in the way of punctuation, giving us endless trouble and making it all much more commonplace. It's really very odd how he has managed to do so. Then he has done things like changing Julians' own title "Notes for a Memoir" to "Notes on my Life." Everywhere his taste is always just wrong. Also he had no business to do any of these things. It's we who have to correct the proofs, not he. As it is, we have laboriously to change it all back again! The Woolves were to have come to tea today, but never turned up, which is rather odd, or I should have told Leonard what I think of his new partner.[1] Quentin thinks their car has probably gone wrong, or they may have mistaken the day and be coming tomorrow.

Clive went off to London this morning, so Quentin and I are here alone.

My dear, I feel so sorry that I collapsed like that the other night and I'm afraid I worried you. But you mustn't let me. I think I'm better than I was—I mean more able to work. You see it's really a long time since I could be quite at ease. I couldn't really be free all that winter before Julian came home, when I was so worried about him, nor ever since then. One can't recover very quickly. But I expect I *shall*. It's difficult now to keep interested for long at a time and when one stops one feels as if that other existence were so remote— one forgets it somehow. You are the only person I ever behave so stupidly to, my dear. It's hard on you.

I suppose having Eddy [Playfair] here was difficult, though I like seeing him.

I don't think I really know how to arrange my life as regards people at all. I've often overcome by astonishment at the way in which Helen

---

[1] In April of this year John Lehmann had bought Virginia's share of the Hogarth Press and become partner and general manager.

has never let Roger's death prevent her from seeing just as many people. It may be partly that they're nearly all his friends and so can in a way keep her in touch with him. Most people, except Julian's friends, seem so remote from him to me and seem to make me feel unreal in consequence, because all that's in my mind all the time can't exist for them. I like to see his friends, but except for Eddy of course I know I'm too old for them really. I think that's why I've got so unsociable.

I don't know why I should write all this—sometimes it's easier to write than talk. But I don't want simply to become an egoist.

I shall be glad when you and Angelica are back here. You and she and Quentin make life possible, give me such intense happiness constantly. You know that is true, don't you, my dear.

Your loving
B.

HENRIETTA GARNETT

VIII-4. To Virginia Woolf

Oct. 14 [1938]   *La Bergère*

The family was enraptured by your last letter.[1] If only, Angelica said, it could go on for ever. I had to read it all aloud twice over, so you see, modest though no doubt you are, you still have some success and if you want more you know where to look for it. As for your account of the arrival of the Bag[enal]s, it simply made us squirm. We cannot be thankful enough that we escaped them. But are they camping at America [at the top of the Downs] or what? Mrs C[urtis] is known to be in Cornwall herself. Anyhow, it sounds quite appalling. Of course if one lived here long enough the same sort of thing would

[1]Of Saturday, October 8, 1938 (VWLVI, 284–89), written following the Munich crisis. Public anxiety was rampant over what appeared to be imminent war with Germany. Gas masks were issued. The crisis was averted by the Munich pact on September 29.

happen here, as indeed it used to. But nowadays one really spends days of incredible solitude. I cannot tell you what a relief it is. Of course I am the most hermit-like of the family and if it depended on me we should literally never see a soul. As it is, the rest of the family love playing *boules,* the French form of bowls, and so they have a habit of going to Cassis of an evening, where they have picked up a young man called Hare, a writer who has I believe produced a biography of Rimbaud.[2] He's harmless, rather nice in fact. Also Dick Strachey[3] and his young woman are living in Cassis, and one day even came up here, but I didn't see them. It's quite unnecessary ever to see anyone and one has no telephone. We all spend most of the day painting. In the evening we play poker and read aloud, with some difficulty, as our library is so small. The only people one sees are the peasants picking the grapes, who are much pleasanter to meet than your friend Sibyl [Colefax], and an occasional glimpse of the Teeds. But they are so busy they simply want to be left alone.

Quentin starts home on Wednesday. He's going to spend 2 nights with the Maurons and will get back about the 28th or 9th, I think. Helen looms slightly. That's to say she talks of staying with the Maurons too and possibly coming here for a night or two. But I don't know when. She takes a very gloomy view of the M.s, but her gloomy views aren't always accurate. She thinks Charles is desperately in love with the John girl, Vivian, and that Marie is very unhappy about it. I must say Quentin saw no signs of it when he was there, but I daresay he wouldn't. If you do intend ever to come and see them, it's absurd to wait till March, the worst month of all for mistral. It has been absolutely calm here ever since we came—one or two slightly windy days, but nothing worse than one often gets in England and for the most part it's like hot summer weather. We have lunch on the terrace and one could sit in the sun all day. This is almost the most beautiful moment too, with the vines now turning crimson. It's colder at night but we haven't yet wanted fires. So why not come now? It may easily go on like this till January, but after that the winds tend to rise. Talking of winds, we have terrible accounts of the damage at Charleston— our garden wall all blown down, pear trees ruined in consequence, and tool shed also blown down. Grace says we look as if we'd been bombed.

---

[2]Humphrey Hare's *Sketch for a Portrait of Rimbaud* was published in 1937.
[3]Richard Strachey, elder son of Ralph and Margaret (née Severs) Strachey, a nephew of Lytton.

I had a letter from Helen giving me her account of the crisis in London. Evidently she was terribly upset. It's interesting to see how people were affected at this distance. I shall collect mass observations.[4] So far the only person who sounds as if he'd come out badly is Kingsley Martin,[5] who really seems too hysterical both in life and in print. We enjoyed the N.S. Is Maynard's present view thought to be true? Or have any semblance of truth in it? It all sounds very depressing and as if one's relief at escaping wasn't going to last long. One's only hope is that no one really can tell anything at all, or so it seems to me.

I hear Clive has gone to Paris. We were intrigued by your account of Lydia's behaviour. Clive himself told me he had been asked to tea by you, but wasn't going, as Janice [Loeb] is painting his portrait and he wanted to give her all the daylight possible. But that may have been a mere face-saving excuse. Still I don't see why they couldn't come on their own. Janice is really more harmless than Lydia, I think.

Dear me, I wish I knew what you were saying about Roger. I meant to give you the P.I. catalogue,[6] but never did. However I don't suppose it would have been much use. But you know, one did read Cézanne and also French Art,[7] and I quite agree that he's the only great critic who ever lived—of painting, anyhow. But I think it needs the rarest of all combinations to make a great critic—great, or anyhow good, artists are far commoner. No one else comes anywhere near him. Perhaps however I can't really judge, for I find anyone else too boring to read. I hope you won't mind making us all blush. It won't do any harm and anyhow no one's blushes last long. The old Frys may perish even before we do and in any case the only important thing is to tell the truth, for the sake of the younger generation.

What are they like? In the persons of Richard and Ann?[8] I suppose they haven't much aesthetic sense, which is a pity—or has Richard any? I have had very interesting scraps of conversation with Angelica about her giving up the stage and taking to the brush. How she ever stuck to the stage so long I can't think, but she enjoyed the St Denis

[4]Mass-Observation, an anthropological study of British culture, especially of the working classes, founded by Tom Harrisson and others in 1937. The Mass-Observation archives are housed at Sussex University.
[5]Kingsley Martin (1897–1969), editor of the *New Statesman & Nation* from 1931 to 1960.
[6]VW had reached about 1911 in her work on the Roger Fry biography, and had asked VB for information about RF's Post-Impressionist exhibitions, etc.
[7]Critical works by RF, *Cézanne* (1927) and *Characteristics of French Art* (1932).
[8]Ann Stephen married Richard Llewellyn Davies in July 1938. They divorced in 1943.

school immensely for one thing and then I think being so much in the midst of painters gave her a good deal of what she wanted without the need to practice the art herself. But she's doing rather remarkable things now and is I think getting very much absorbed in it—if only the world will allow anyone to be so.

Well, as I have no news I've written quite enough. I'd like to see John Cornford's book,[9] but don't bother to send it. I can get it when I return. Thank you for giving my list to Leonard. I think Janie must be added to it, she'll be too poor to buy it, so could you have one sent to her at 40 Rue Verdi, Nice.

If you want compliments for your pen, please write again.

Your
VB

Oct. 15. Your books just come, for which we are very thankful, also Clive's pamphlet.[10] What is thought of it? No good, I expect.

BERG

VIII-5. To Jane Bussy

Nov. 28 [1938]   *8, Fitzroy Street, W.1*

Dearest Janie,

How good of you to write and tell me what you felt about Julian's book. It makes a great difference to me if you and other people of his age can get so much from it. He so desperately wanted to express himself and make people listen and I do not think it matters whether one agrees or not as long as one is forced to think. I believe your impression of happiness is a true one—I hope it is. Certainly I think it was some kind of tremendous vitality that made him want to face danger, as he himself said it was something so like one's own longing to paint that it was impossible not to give way to it.

---

[9]John Cornford (1915–1936), poet and Communist, was killed in Spain on his twenty-first birthday fighting with the International Brigade. His parents were Francis and Frances Cornford, old friends of Bloomsbury. *John Cornford, A Memoir,* by various authors, was published in 1938.
[10]*Warmongers* (1938), published by the Peace Pledge Union.

I wonder if you have seen Peter Lucas' review.[1] I don't agree with his view of Julian's reasons for going to Spain, nor above all with his impression of many love affairs and no love! That is the opposite of the truth. I do not think anyone could have had stronger affection for his friends, his family, and for so many too of the older generation—Roger whom he adored of course and others. If his letters don't imply that, it is a pity. But I think on the whole Peter's review is good and sympathetic.

Poor Sue—I heard from her only yesterday. Her letter sent by air only took a fortnight to come from West Szechwan, where she is. She sounds very miserable always, being I think the sort of person given to torturing herself, but of course with plenty of reason for it now. I can't quite make out what she is doing. She writes fairly often and seems to be very charming and in an odd way I feel I know her quite well, but she must be terribly difficult to deal with. Julian tried to make her write her autobiography and I hope she may do it. It should be fascinating, but I imagine it's very difficult for her now to settle down to anything. I'm rather nervous of the effect of the book on her with all the criticisms of the Chinese, but I've done my best to prepare her! She little knows what has been left out.

I have your letters at Charleston and will soon send them back.

My views of France are now such as would satisfy the most rabid patriot, I should think. Really the character and beauty and variety as we drove through impressed me even more than ever. As for the food, our greed nearly destroyed us, and the charm of the people and their art of living—well, Angelica has decided firmly in the end to marry a husband with about £4000 a year and make him buy a chateau in Burgundy. But this is only after being equally determined to settle in the Dordogne, near Aix and at several other places. So you may easily have her as a neighbour one day.

We did one perhaps foolish thing on our return journey—dropped all our paintings off the back of the car somewhere between Cassis and Saulieu! So there they are. However it seems not impossible we may get them back. You should have seen me and Duncan, or rather Duncan, very dapper, followed by me, very shabby, penetrating to the English Ambassadress' bedroom and then to the *chef de* something or other, M. Dubois, a French Mussolini, in search of them. It's a

---

[1] A warm review of *Julian Bell: Essays, Poems and Letters*. Lucas did write that "the letters show many love affairs but not much love," but also, "with one striking exception. The letters to his mother . . . are amongst the finest and most natural things in the book" (*New Statesman & Nation*, November, 1938).

long story, which you shall hear some day, and we hope our adventures may lead to their discovery. Certainly if anyone can find them it is M. Dubois.

Now we are settling down to London again. It's rather dreary I think, everyone still talking of the crisis and what they felt and how others behaved. That however is interesting—but the heated political arguments that follow remind me of 1914.

You heard of course how Gerald Brenan went to Ham Spray, where tempers reached such a pitch that Frances had to ask him to leave the house and he said "All right, but with my furniture," and they searched for all his old chests of drawers and armchairs all over the house and put them on his car and even that didn't seem to them funny.[2]

Angelica went to the School[3] for the first time today and seemed fairly content with it. She did quite a lot at Cassis. Quentin is buried at Charleston but we shall I hope unearth him quite often. In fact there are rumours that we may all settle down there forever. We shall at least spend Christmas there and not at Seend, thank God.

Dear Janie—I send my love to you and all of you.

Vanessa

BUSSY

VIII-6. To Virginia Woolf

May 31 [1939]   *8, Fitzroy Street, W.1*

As usual I can do nothing against your wiles, but how you and Duncan and Angelica ever managed to put your heads together to

[2]Brenan and his great friend Ralph Partridge differed on many subjects, especially the war. Having served with distinction in World War I, Partridge was now a convinced pacifist.
[3]The School of Drawing and Painting (later known as the Euston Road School after it moved to larger premises) opened at 12 Fitzroy Street in October 1937 under the direction of Claude Rogers, Victor Pasmore, and William Coldstream. VB and DG taught there briefly, without pay, in 1938. Though the school closed with the onset of war, the term "Euston Road" was applied to painting of a naturalistic bent, especially the work of Coldstream, Pasmore, Rogers, and Lawrence Gowing, for several years afterward.

this purpose[1] I can't imagine. I see I shall have to work like a nigger for 80 hours and write down every minute of it à la Leonard. Really, you shouldn't do such things. Think of Helen. She'll want another 100 or 2 before long I feel sure.[2] But it's no good complaining. I have to accept with gratitude in spite of all.

Think of me on Saturday going off to Seend with Clive. Well, it's better than going for Christmas. But the business of getting oneself into some sort of order first is appalling. I wish we were at Charleston still, only the noise there on Tuesday was too much. Nothing has happened since we returned to London. Duncan has gone off to Twickenham to take his mother to a military concert. I am alone and listening to La Traviata, I expect too low a taste for you.

I will send back your story as you want it, but I'd like to read it again first. It seems to me lovely, only too full of suggestions for pictures almost. They leap into my mind at every turn. Your writing always does that for me to some extent, but I think this one more than usual. I wonder if I could do anything though. I fear I should come a cropper by comparison, which might be inevitable because I could hardly help doing illustrations. However I'd like to try and see what happens.

How does one pronounce Ivemey? and why Ivemey?[3] But don't think me frivolous. I really only wish I could live up to it.

Your
VB

BERG

VIII-7. To Virginia Woolf

June 9 [1939]   *Charleston*

I am sitting here surrounded by great beauty but also by chaos. Piles of brick and rubble arise and then disappear and there are holes

[1]A birthday gift of money for Vanessa, specifically to be spent on models.
[2]VW had lent Helen Anrep £150.
[3]Cf. VW's story "The Searchlight" in *A Haunted House* (London: Hogarth Press, 1943).

in the floor everywhere. Baths and W.C.s sit about in odd places. If one's on the spot at the right moment one can suddenly order a wall to stop building and put in an extra door or window. You'll never know your way about here again. I dash into cupboards thinking they are passages. On the other hand the garden is snowed under by pinks and roses and irises. Angelica has just returned from France by the night boat. I got up at 6 to meet her and realised as usual how foolish one was not to do so every day. Perhaps you do on your travels.

Clive is arriving presently and I rather dread his horror when he finds what a state it's all in, though he has been warned. However it's infinitely preferable to Seend, where I spent last Sunday. There of course there's not a spot of dust anywhere and if you put down a book for 5 minutes you find it carefully put away where it belongs. But the garden calls for Mr Bell's ghost to arise. The gardener is too old and rheumatic to do anything or even to make the two under-gardeners do anything. So it's all a complete wilderness, a mass of nettles, no flowers to be seen. Mrs Bell continues to get more lively and is looked after by both a nurse and a companion and so will obviously outlive us all. She is perfectly happy, neither blind nor deaf, and sits and makes small talk by the hour. I nearly died of it—one simply feels oneself in a strait jacket—but thank goodness it's over for a year I hope. I have very little other news. We went to Simon's Private View[1]—did you know another show was on us? This time it is all of birds, fish and flowers. As usual the whole Bussy family were in attendance.

When I go back to London I'm going to begin spending recklessly on models, thanks to you. But how much nicer it is in the country—or will be once one has got rid of the builders. Do send me a line now and then to say how you're getting on. Quentin I believe will be on his way to Cassis in a day or two. They seem to have enjoyed everything thoroughly. I can't write letters here and must stop and take Duncan to Lewes, as he has to go back to London to see his mother who departs soon for Sweden.

VB

BERG

---

[1]At the Leicester Gallery, in a show including the work of Jacob Epstein, Jacques-Emile Blanche, and Doris Zinkeisen.

VIII-8. To Ling Su-Hua

June 13 [1939]   *8, Fitzroy St.*

Dearest Sue,

Your letter dated March 17 reached me a short time ago. You sound very sad—I am not surprised, it could not be otherwise, but I wish very much I could do anything to make you less so. I am relieved by what you say about Julian's book and indeed I think with all the world in such a muddle surely people wont bother very much about a scandal already more than 2 years old.[1] People's memories are short in such ways and they easily get confused. Surely not too very many people will read the book, for as you say it is expensive, I suppose more for the Chinese than the English. Even here, owing to the state of affairs, it has not been a success, though it has had many good reviews. No books have been a success since the autumn I believe. Now I think people are less nervous than they were. I cannot let myself be hopeful but I try to think of other things than possible war. All one can do is to concentrate on work and be thankful that one *has* work of such a nature to concentrate on. I really pity people who are not artists most of all, for they have no refuge from the world. I often wonder how life would be tolerable if one could not get detached from it, as even artists without much talent can, as long as they are sincere. I am very glad that Julian had that and so have Quentin and Angelica.

Virginia is at present in France. She and Leonard are motoring there. When she comes back I will ask her when she last wrote to you and also which of your manuscripts she has received. She has been very busy lately, working on the Life of Roger Fry which she is writing, but she often speaks of you and I am sure she would do all she can to help. Tell me if I can be of any use. But of course I'm not a writer and could not give advice, only I might be able to copy or show things to people. Anyhow you will let me do what I can and never be afraid to ask anything of me.

I have been at Charleston a great deal lately as we are making some changes there to make the house more comfortable and give us all more room to work. I cannot help at this time of year, especially when

---

[1] I.e., JB's relationship with Su-Hua, alluded to in the Julian Bell book.

I am there, remembering all the anxiety and sadness of two years ago, when Julian had just left me. It seems so unnecessary that he should have gone. One day he said to me "You know I could easily settle down and spend my life here if it weren't for ———" and I said "Yes, but you can't," for I knew he couldn't though even then I don't think I expected him to come back. But one simply has to remember that he wouldn't have been happy if he hadn't gone, and he wouldn't have been himself. But the beauty there is so great, and so connected with him, for me, that it is an extraordinary mixture of joy and pain to be there. Dear Sue, I hope you don't mind my writing like this. I feel you would understand more than most people, though I cannot express myself clearly. Please write when you feel inclined and tell me all you can about yourself. It is all interesting to me. Please keep as cheerful as you can and work as much as you are able to. I send my love.

Your
Nessa

BERG

VIII-9. To David Garnett

July 1 [1939]   *8, Fitzroy Street, W.1*

Dear Bunny,

I think our talk may have been a mistake the other day.[1] I at any rate couldn't talk calmly and say what I meant. I can't help being upset by some of the things you say, however foolish it may be, and then I can't explain myself. But I think it's necessary that we should understand each other because of the immediate future and I hope it may possibly be easier to explain oneself calmly on paper.

[1]Bunny had been courting AVG for over a year. While VB and DG were away from London, AVG became ill with an infected kidney. Bunny checked her into a nursing home, to the alarm of her parents.

I don't want to go into details. That is what one is always led to do in talk. Very few of the small things that have happened or been said really matter. But some things do because they imply a general attitude or feeling.

You seemed to feel for instance that Duncan and I were "touchy." This seems to me to show that you can't have any understanding of the effect of getting bad news in the way you allowed us to get it. One couldn't help feeling afterwards that it had been cruel and unnecessary. But that may not seem very important. What was more so, to me at any rate, was that, strange as it may seem to you, I have more faith in my own and Duncan's judgment and sense in making arrangements than in yours. I want it to be clear that you cannot take such responsibilities again.

As always when we talk of Angelica you told me that I consider her a child. It's no good my contradicting this because I've done so often before. All the same it's not true and I think it's a pity you can't understand what I feel because I'm sure that consciously or unconsciously you influence her view. It's so easy to make a very young person feel they're treated as a child by someone else—they're naturally very sensitive about it—and as you always accuse me of this attitude I suppose you think it and encourage Angelica to think it. That is my reason for minding it.

Your criticism of what you believe to be my relationship with Angelica seems to me a perhaps natural misunderstanding. You have seen very little of us together lately. Any human relationships, but especially those of mothers and children, are perpetually changing, developing and growing. It wouldn't much matter whether you knew the truth about mine with Angelica except that for the present naturally what you think, whether you express it or not, influences her. So it seems to me it would be better to realise that you cannot really know much about it.

These mistakes which I think you are making are what seem to me important because I think it's very difficult while you think such things for us to be at ease with each other, which is going to be necessary for her sake. I suppose she will return here on Wednesday—so Dr R. told me yesterday. You will want to see her here and I'm most anxious to make it perfectly easy for you to do so. Also I want you to be able to come to Charleston quite easily during the next 2 or 3 months. She will certainly have to lead a fairly quiet life there for some time and won't I am sure be able to come up for tiring days in London.

I have written as truthfully as I can. It seems to me the only way of clearing up misunderstandings. If you think I've made all sorts of mistakes too I hope you'll tell me. I don't want simply to have an emotional making-friends when there are real differences of attitude behind. If I'm wrong about your views, please tell me so. It's the only way out from a state of things which is making me at any rate worried and unhappy.

Vanessa

ANGELICA GARNETT

VIII-10. To Keith Baynes

Oct. 2 [1939]   *Charleston, Firle, Sussex*

Dear Keith,

I wonder how you are getting on and the only way of finding out seems to be to write to you, for I don't see much chance of either of us being able to drive 50 miles for some time to come.[1] Also I want to ask you whether you have yet experimented with an oil radiator. You said you might do so. We are beginning to consider the problems of heating. I don't know if oil will be rationed, but coal is anyhow and one must try something. It looks as though we were in for rather a dark and dismal winter, doesn't it? Have you still got refugee children with you? You heard how we got rid of ours. Now Mrs Grant and "Aunt Violet" [McNeil] have also gone. Poor creatures, it was very dull for them being here, as is inevitable if one goes to someone else's house indefinitely, and they decided it was really rather absurd not to stay at Twickenham, at any rate for the present, and departed. I must say it's a great relief to have no one.

Can you paint at all? We have begun to. Duncan in fact does quite

[1] The war had been declared on September 3, and petrol rationing was introduced on September 23.

a lot and I have worked quite hard lately in spite of lots of small practical jobs that always seem to be cropping up.

Duncan went to London for 2 nights and saw MacDonald and tried to persuade him to sell English painters in America. I think it's the only thing to hope for now, but I doubt if MacD. is the man to do it. I suspect he will always make money, having Renoirs and Cézannes, which will probably turn out to be the safest thing of all. There seems to be a certain amount going on in London—a kind of central club for artists is being started and Kenneth Clark has given up his house to it. They'll have shows and people can meet there and see all the magazines, etc. It might be quite useful. The artists of course are mostly in a very bad way but the Euston Rd. Group seem to be getting along somehow. Coldstream has a job teaching at a school in the country. Claude Rogers and Graham Bell[2] are living in Helen Anrep's house near Ipswich, sharing expenses with her and looking after the garden, etc. Pasmore has a part time job in London and paints when he can.

I hope you and Louis are at any rate comfortable and able to lead more or less normal lives. I'm sure it's really important that as many people as can should do so. How lucky at any rate that we all left London when we did! Have you any news of Dora [Romilly]? I've only heard the most depressing sounding account of her, making shrouds in company with Lady Colefax!

Yours
Vanessa Bell

BAYNES

[2]Graham Bell (1910–43), South African-born painter, had parted from his wife at the beginning of 1938. In late July 1939 he went to Rodwell, where he and several others, including Igor and Anastasia Anrep, Olivier Popham (later the wife of Quentin Bell), and Sonia Brownell (later Orwell) waited, "expect[ing] London to be bombed to bits at once," as Olivier Bell recalls. Graham Bell tried to enlist in the navy but was not called up until autumn of 1940, when he joined the RAF. He was killed on active service.

VIII-11. To Virginia Woolf

Wednesday—midnight [March 13, 1940]   *Charleston*

Since Julian died I haven't been able to think of Roger[1]—now you have brought him back to me. Although I cannot help crying, I can't thank you enough.

                                                                    VB

BERG

VIII-12. To Ling Su-Hua

March 17 [1940]   *[Charleston]*

Dearest Sue,

About 2 days ago I had your letter dated Feb. 13 which came with New Year pictures, so you see they only took a little more than a month to come. You cannot think how excited we have all been by the pictures. They are *lovely,* especially I think those on thin paper which I suppose are those of the different gods. I have never seen anything like them before. I wonder if other people in England who know about Chinese things, such as Arthur Waley, have seen prints like these. I think I must try to show them to him. They are such exquisite colour and drawing and we have all been looking at them again and again and thinking how wonderful it is that such a present should have reached us here in the midst of the war, when one seems to be completely shut out from the outside world. Dearest Sue, thank you very much.

It seems as if it were impossible at present for me to send anything to you. I tried to send you a lithograph as I told you I would in my last letter, but it was sent back to me opened by the censor. Then I applied for leave to send it again but it seems to be very difficult. One isn't allowed to send any kind of printed thing abroad without going through every kind of formality. I fear that it would be just as difficult

[1]VB had read VW's *Roger Fry* in typescript.

to send a knife as you ask, or anything else. I think it will be better to wait until the war is over and then perhaps I can give you something you will like. At present it is impossible to do anything but receive presents from you and I can give nothing in return. Even my letters don't seem very certain of reaching you. You say you haven't heard for a long time, but I hope they *do* reach you in time and that in any case you know I don't forget.

In fact lately, as always at this time of year, I have been thinking of you and of Julian even more than usual. It is just 3 years since he came home and I came here to meet him just as the spring was beginning. One cannot help feeling the waste that he shouldn't be here now enjoying it all as he might so easily have been. Well, it's no use going on with such thoughts. But we have had a terribly hard, cold, long winter. Now at last plants are beginning to shoot and birds to sing and it is difficult not to think how much happiness there could be if the world would allow it.

I have just been reading the Life of Roger Fry which Virginia has just finished writing. It is still only in type-script and uncorrected, so it is difficult to judge, but I think as far as I can tell that it will be very good. Of course to me or anyone who knew him well it is bound to be fascinating and full of interest, but I do think she has succeeded in making a portrait which will give something real to other people too. I will try to send you a copy when it comes out, if only I am allowed to. Reading it too has made me think how Julian would enjoy it. There are a few things said about him to show what Roger felt about him and what their relationship was.

I am very glad that now I may think of you living in your own house in a lovely place and able to work. You *must* work. You must write your book and paint too. It would be terrible to waste your gifts and someday I expect they will bring you happiness. I like your description of your garden with its fruit trees and the two large old trees by the gate. And I am glad that people seem generally to be kind to you and that as you say you meet good people. It often seems to me the world is full of them and yet when they try to organise and rule the world they become brutal and cruel. But luckily the people one meets in shops or the street or the country people are nearly always charming.

We go on living here quietly and are very lucky I think. So far we don't seem to suffer much from the war in any way. There is only the terrible depression that all war brings and the feeling that everything possible is done to destroy and not to create. But here we lead normal lives and do our own work as usual, all except Quentin who does farm work. But even he can do some painting now that the evenings are light.

Dear Sue, I hope you'll get this and will understand why I can send nothing to you at present but my love. That at least can't be censored! Please write when you have time sometimes and be as cheerful as you can. We hear very little of China now, but I hope that whatever is happening there you at least are peaceful. How I should like to see your home and the Western Hills.

Love from
Vanessa

BERG

VIII-13. To David Garnett

Ap. 10 [1940]   *[Charleston]*

Dear Bunny,

I am very sorry that I lost control of myself the other night and that our talk seemed to lead to so little understanding.[1] It was a great pity that we tried to talk at such a late hour and when we were all tired, and also that I couldn't see you alone. I thought I would write to you, but I find it too difficult and am afraid of only making matters worse. Isn't it possible for us to meet quietly and without bitterness or hostility? I would come anywhere you liked, but it seems to me probably very difficult for you to see me alone in London. Or I would arrange to see you here on any day at any time and could meet you in Lewes and take you back if you could come, either for a night or even a few hours. Arrange whatever suits you, but please realise that before you come to any decision which will affect Angelica's whole life it would be very cruel not to take into account our views in so far as they seem reasonable. I know that she realises this or she would not have spoken about it, but I think it is important to her as well

---

[1]Bunny's wife Ray had recently died of cancer. Free to pursue an unfettered relationship with AVG, he took her to a cottage in Yorkshire for two months, then, in October, rented a farmhouse at Claverham, about five miles from Charleston, where they lived together.

as to us that you should do so too. Please try to make possible a real opportunity of doing this.

Vanessa

ANGELICA GARNETT

VIII-14. To Angelica Bell

May 11 [1940]   *8, Fitzroy Street, W.1*

My own darling,

It was such a great blessing to get a letter, and such an amusing one, from you this morning. What difficulties you get into when you go off on your travels—but you seem to manage to get out of them. The mystery of the w[aste] p[aper] basket at No. 8 is cleared up. How we racked our brains and Mrs Farr's [domestic] over it and how suspicious we were of Pasmore,[1] etc. I must say I suspected you all along, but I thought you'd have used it to take things over to No. 13, not as a piece of smart luggage. Do bring it back—it's essential to life.

Well, so much has happened since you went, I suppose I must simply try to give you a few bits of it. First of all I went on Monday afternoon to Rodmell—alone—so I had quite a lot of conversation with the W.'s and I told them of your goings on. I don't think V. was as much upset as I had expected. She wasn't exactly pleased! but not shocked either. I think the Stephen girls have accustomed her. She was very sorry she wouldn't see you for so long or have your help with her play, which she said she had been counting on, but she was philosphically glad that you hadn't at this moment fallen in love with anyone who'd have to go to the war. As for not having been told before, I think I reconciled her to that by saying no one had been told on account of Ray and even now one was telling no one one could help. I find in fact that Duncan is rather anxious people shouldn't know in widespread fashion as he says his mother always asks after you and would probably be shocked, which would be tiresome for him. There can't be much doubt, can there, as to *my* disreputable past!

---

[1] Victor Pasmore (b. 1908), painter and founding member of the Euston Road School. He had rented Duncan's studio.

Then I went on to meet Elizabeth [Watson], who didn't arrive, so I rang up Quentin and found he'd mistaken her train, which was an hour later, so I might have had another hour with the W.'s, instead of which I looked in at the Odeon, all shops being shut, and saw the meeting of Mr Stanley and Dr Livingstone.[2] If I go on in such detail this letter will take a whole pad. So I skip to Wed. morning, leaving Elizabeth and Q. here quite happy together when D. and I went to London by the early train. We arrived at Hertford House[3] and found all his paintings already hung and Clive and an underling on the spot. My first feeling was one of horror. The paintings were so badly hung that one could see nothing. The question was how to undo practically everything, with tact. But if the show was to do any sort of justice to Duncan it had to be done somehow, so we began making small changes. Luckily Clive hadn't really any feelings and realised we had more experience in such matters and the underling who was at first horrified became reconciled and in the end we changed it all and it looked lovely. I think of writing a book upon hanging, with illustrations. Very few people know anything about it and yet there are quite a lot of rules one can follow. I wish Roger had done it.

Duncan had to do a lot of other things in London, I very little. But we went to see the Clarks in their Gray's Inn rooms before dinner and found Pasmore and the Graham Sutherlands,[4] and Jane alone. I was interested to see how those lovely shabby college rooms can be converted into the height of chic and *luxe,* rather horrifying, to my mind. I felt as I always do a revulsion towards dirt and untidyness. All the same, I spent the next morning entirely at the studio cleaning, destroying rubbish (*without* a w.p. basket!) and putting in order. The result is now really quite good and habitable. I forgot to say that one of my strokes of genius at Hertford House was the idea that that huge horse screen could be used to conceal the end of the long gallery, which was empty of paintings and spoilt the whole effect. It was carted round and made a great difference, and looked exactly right as a background at the end.

On Thursday we came back, and yesterday morning Grace had the pleasure of telling us about the German invasion of Holland, etc. It

[2]*Stanley and Livingstone* (1939), a Twentieth Century–Fox production starring Spencer Tracy and Sir Cedric Hardwicke in the title roles. The Odeon was a Lewes cinema.
[3]Home of the Wallace Collection.
[4]Graham Sutherland (1903–80), painter, designer, and graphic artist, at this time employed as an official war artist.

was all rather agitating and once more we began the listening in to news at other times than 9 PM. You must be glad to be out of it. Clive returned rather unexpectedly and we have all spent a good deal of time wondering what is going to happen. Yesterday evening we had the thrill of a real air-fight, or so it was thought. I didn't see it, but Clive, Duncan and the servants did. Puffs of smoke in the sky—anti-aircraft guns firing, it is thought. It is absolutely lovely weather though windier now. But yesterday the puffs of smoke hung in the sky quite still, they said, and it was as hot as summer.

Today I have had to go to Lewes, for, would you believe it, Mrs West burnt my car registration book and application form for more petrol, so I've had to get a new book and another form. It wasn't really her fault, as the papers must have blown into my basket from my table where I had left them, being in a hurry to catch the train. Our lives seem largely dependent on w.p. baskets.

Sunday. I began this yesterday but had no time to finish. The Woolves came to tea very late. We all talked about the war, of course. Leonard seemed quite pleased at the way things were going. I only hope he's right. Virginia produced a very amusing and charming letter from Bernard Shaw discussing a dinner party he had been to with Roger and [the composer Edward] Elgar. I think she'll quote from it in her book, but the part she really enjoyed and unfortunately can't very well quote was at the end, where he reminded her how he had written Heartbreak House[5] after staying at Asheham, where he had "fallen in love with her, as he was sure all men must have done." You can imagine how pleased she was by such a compliment.

Michal[6] rang up to say she can't come this week. She asked for your address and said you were to remember to write to her. Which reminds me, I'm sending you a pen but I'm not sure if it's yours. It wasn't in your room but in the drawing-room.

Duncan goes off to Plymouth on Tuesday and I think Elizabeth is going too, so we shall be a very small party here—if Clive goes to London, only Quentin and I. I hope you'll keep us going with letters. It has been such extraordinary weather. I hope you've had some of it. Only the garden is getting dried up. But the irises have rushed out and the tulips and wall-flowers are a blaze. Also my wisteria has one

[5]Published in 1919; the first London production premiered on 18 October 1921 at the Royal Court Theatre.
[6]Michal Hambourg, accomplished pianist, daughter of the pianist Mark Hambourg (1879–1960) and Dorothea Frances, and granddaughter of the Russian virtuoso Michael Hambourg. She was a friend of AVG's.

blossom and we have put the fruit cage up which looks very professional. The white currants are quite big, so are the gooseberries, and I regret to tell you we have eaten the last two drakes. Also I hope you won't be angry at our having had Duncan to sit today. If he goes away I daresay we shan't get him again very soon and as Michal couldn't come it was a chance.

I am having your yoghourt germs sent straight to you next time, but it won't be till the end of the week that they're done, I think.

I've had a talk with Mr White, the old man who brings the washing. He buys a new pony every week, Grace says, and he keeps hens and he's a jobbing gardener. If only I could employ him instead of the D[olt]! Isn't it tempting.

I'm glad you went to see Duncan's drawings and liked them. I'm afraid they haven't sold very well. Of course this latest crisis has put an end to everything. But there is a chance that you playing the piano may be bought by the Tate.[7] I have arranged to have a show next winter at the Leicester Galleries. Lefevre's seems to me hopeless.

This is a long and dull letter, I fear, and it must stop. But I will write often now I've heard from you, in the hope of getting answers, even though you must only expect dull domestic snippets. I hope you can paint, my dear. Your music is badly missed here and the piano looks tidy and forlorn.

> *Your loving*
> *Mummy*

ANGELICA GARNETT

VIII-15. To Jane Bussy

June 6 [1940]   *Charleston*

My dear dear Janie,

I had just been thinking I must send a letter into the blue and now your card has come. It's a mercy to have even such a scrap from you. You can imagine how much we have thought of you all especially and

---

[7] It was.

I am relieved to hear you have left Nice. I went to Vence once to see the Raverats that winter we were at St Tropez and I came on for the first time to La Souco, so I can imagine you there. In the summer I think it must be lovely and less grim than in the winter. I hope you can paint.

Well, I'll give you such news as we have. I am sitting at my open bedroom window. You can't imagine it because it used to be the larder window, but now it opens down to the ground and I look out on to the lawn which has been extended up to the terrace—Quentin's idea for making our garden a second Versailles. The monthly roses are in full bloom. It's a hot summer evening. I have pulled up the wallflowers regretfully and now the pinks are making the whole place smell. I suppose it's wicked to have flowers and not cabbages only, but I can't help preferring them. Besides I have driven the Dolt with such an iron rod all these months that we really have plenty of cabbages too. Poor man, I have no mercy on him. So you see life here doesn't seem to have changed very much. We still have good beef and mutton, though not so much sugar or butter as usual. But as far as the comforts and even luxuries of life go, we really have nothing at all to complain of. Even extra petrol is allowed us on the ground that we are 6 miles from shops and have to cart paintings to London on occasion, so it is possibly for us to pay a weekly visit to Rodmell. Also they, being so grand as to keep two cars, can come here. Clive goes to London a good deal, being on various committees concerned with the arts. I go as little as I can as I hate London as a visitor and not an inhabitant. Quentin of course can hardly ever get away. In fact at this moment he is in the proud position of Hog Master at Tilton while the usual one has his holiday. He is very well I think and a wonderful mahogany colour. With that and his flaming hair on his red tractor he is a wonderful sight. Angelica is a gad-about and off on a jaunt at the moment, also very well I hope. Duncan has lately returned from a fortnight in Plymouth where he did numerous sketches and drawings of sailors having a gunnery lesson. Luckily he has got a government job to do a painting of some such subject and so was given all facilities to do studies and had rather a fascinating time seeing life in the Navy. He came back with a great respect for their immense efficiency and charm and had most interesting stories of high and low life in Plymouth. Now he'll have to begin work on the painting I suppose, when the studies have been passed by the Ministry of Information, which seems to be partly run by Kenneth Clark and Leigh Ashton.

Virginia has finished her life of Roger. It seemed to me *extremely* good. It's very simply written—apparently absolutely straight forward, which to me is a relief, but I suppose to those who know about such things it is really done with the greatest art. What is most important is that I think it does give a true portrait and shows more than I had really expected of the fundamental things in his character. Of course it's very amusing too in places. Luckily Margery Fry raves about it, and has in fact been very amiable, and I believe the other sisters are quite pleased, though there's no mincing matters—Josette, Helen, etc., etc., etc., are all quite plainly spoken of.[1] The question now is whether to publish at once or wait till the autumn, which I expect would be wiser. This reminds me that I very much enjoyed the things about Aunt Janie[2], didn't you? It was a good idea of your dear Aunt's. It seems such years since I last wrote to you and even then— when was it—some time in the winter—one seemed to be living in such a different world—that all that has happened since comes crowding upon me and I don't know what to write about. But really we actually have been living very quiet lives—painting, gardening, keeping chickens, seeing a few people, not many. I don't think we shall get refugees again, which is one comfort. At least we are probably considered too near the coast. But we are much better off than most places, no soldiers visible unless one goes for a walk, which as you know I never do, nothing to show there's anything unusual. We try not to listen to news till 9 PM and generally succeed. Now of course the antiparachute people[3] will begin. Clive, Duncan, Quentin and the Dolt, all this household of males are joining. I offer to keep them company, but I don't think I shall be allowed to. As I gather that their principal job will be to rush back and telephone and as female eyes are as good as male ones I can't see why there should be this sex barrier. But they say the presence of females on the downs at night would lead to extra difficulties, though Clive is all for it. So far little has happened.

I hear and see very little of all your relations. Clive had an amusing letter from Frances at Ham Spray. They seem to be leading much the same sort of life there that we are here, though I expect a good deal more social. Julia she said had fled from them in terror at seeing a

[1]Though RF's romantic relationship with VB is *not*.
[2]Aunt Janie is Lady Strachey, actually Jane Bussy's grandmother. "The things" were a folder of typescript contributions *In Memoriam J.M.S. 1840–1929*. This (given by QB) is now in the Monk's House Papers, University of Sussex, Ad.25.
[3]The Home Guard.

van laden with sign posts pointing in all directions, and returned to London.[4]

The only people I see in London when I go are the Euston Rd. School who all now live in Fitzroy St. mostly in our house. Duncan let his studio to Pasmore who has now married a young woman called—Wendy Blood. Did you ever? Coldstream had the use of my studio for a time but made such a mess of it I had to turn him out and he now lives next door. They all struggle on somehow. The school of course has come to an end. Helen harbours some of them at her country house. She also harboured refugee children[5] all the winter and naturally worked herself to the bone cooking and washing and mending for them. At last they were got rid of and now refugees aren't allowed in such places.

Ba has fallen desperately in love with what Virginia calls a "buck nigger," whom she met in Paris. Therefore she longs to go back there but so far hasn't succeeded, and I should think now isn't likely to. Poor girl, she is unfortunate. [Igor] on the other hand is getting on very well and I believe has some kind of job.

As for the world of painting, as you can imagine it feels rather low at the moment. Though in fact there was a short boom about a month ago when everyone bought pictures they said and I believe even now people are buying old masters whenever they can. Are you and your father able to work? I hope so. Sometimes it seems to me very difficult but then again one gets so miserable if one doesn't that one has to make an effort and at least keep oneself sane.

This long catalogue of people and doings doesn't give you much news of interest, I fear, but you see we are complete country bumpkins. Dear Janie, you know how much love I send you all. One can't write what one is most thinking of. I wish you could in case of need turn up at Newhaven, but anyhow when you have time and inclination send me news of yourselves.

My love,
Vanessa

BUSSY

[4]Signposts had been removed in anticipation of a German invasion.
[5]Norman and Peter, nine-year-olds from Ilford.

VIII-16. To Jane Bussy

Jan. 13 [1941]   *Charleston*

[Heading:] This is the only thin paper I have—torn from a sketchbook.
My dearest Janie,

You cannot think what joy and excitement your letter caused in this household. It seems a toss up whether you will ever get this in return, but after all we have now had two from Nice, so it's not hopeless. After writing to you in June it seemed as if one could never hope to get in touch again and we have lived on occasional scraps from your family. Do write whenever you have the energy to—you cannot think how we long to hear of you all.

On the whole too you seem to be bearing up, but I wish you were here to share our puddings! They still exist—not in threes, perhaps, but quite often in twos, and on the whole we have nothing to complain of. I will give you our quiet domestic news, for it still goes on being very quiet and we don't I expect see nearly as many people as you do. The Woolves naturally are our principal visitors and we go there or they come here every week. Leonard I think adores a country life and has a lovely new blue cat. Virginia has enjoyed the success of her life of Roger. It's really had a huge success in spite of all. I hope you will like it—I do enormously. We also see the Keyneses from time to time. Clive, who is much the gayest of us all, goes off every now and then to stay with Mary Baker or at Ham Spray. Raymond is one of our few visitors but is very hard worked. I am handing on your news about his friends to Eddie West. I believe he has taken up his abode with the K. Clarks. I can't say I envy either. Also I will try to get news of the Leplats[1] for you to send on. Our chief new neighbour is Helen! Having worked herself to the bone with a house full of artists and refugees all last winter she naturally collapsed in the summer, took to her bed, was threatened with an operation, finally became a refugee herself at Ham Spray, then here. Then I think she lost her nerve about London and didn't want to return to Rodwell, and so finally found rooms in a lovely old house near here, where she is living, sometimes alone, sometimes with her fierce daughter. Igor continues to pass or not pass examinations.

[1]René Le Plat, French painter and friend of the Bussys', and his wife, née Alison Debenham, also a painter.

As for us, you will never guess what we are up to. It starts by the curious fact that Duncan is in touch with a Bishop, the B. of Chichester.[2] So friendly have they become that it seems extremely likely that we shall all, D., Q., Angelica and I, be turned into a neighbouring church [Berwick] and allowed to cover the walls with large works. What a war time occupation! It needed Hitler to bring such things to pass. We have got as far as doing sketches, which have met with approval on the whole, though D.'s Christ was thought a bit attractive and my Virgin a bit frivolous. Still that is easily changed, and on the whole we accept every suggestion and read our Bibles diligently. How we shall ever manage to paint walls 30 ft. high I can't conceive, but that trouble is in the future. Q. of course doesn't get very much time— he's planning the Wise and Foolish Virgins climbing an immense staircase seen from below—but he works like a nigger. So you see we do manage to spend a good deal of our time as usual. There have been terrific domestic upheavals. Lottie got at odds with the Higgens family (Grace and the Dolt) and our sympathies were divided. But when it came to the point of loud shrieks during dinner and terror lest a carving knife should be brought into play something had to be done. So finally Lottie went, and the Higgens family remain, but have a separate *ménage* of their own. Grace in fact has become a daily, and in consequence I cook the evening meal. The result is most of my stray thoughts are given to food, and in spite of all I must say we live very well. Clive has luckily reverted completely to the country gentleman, so pheasants, etc., come in and sit for their portraits till sufficiently high and then get cooked. I suppose their season will soon be over, but even so. With unlimited quantities of milk, potatoes, bread, vegetables, apples, coffee, etc., I don't want to make your mouth water, but one can do without Lottie's spate of iced cakes and not starve.

We were very glad of all your news, about Zoum, Matisse—that didn't surprise us somehow, Picasso, Gide, etc. What books will one day be written—are being written, I suppose. Here people are getting more sensible about refugees, thank goodness. But I won't talk even of mildly public matters for as you know I am renowned for my ignorance. Even I of course cannot help reading the papers and listening to the rumours and trying to pick up a scrap here and there,

[2]George Kennedy Allen Bell (1883–1958), educated at Christ's Church, Oxford. It was at his instigation that T. S. Eliot wrote *Murder in the Cathedral* for the 1935 Canterbury Festival.

but on the whole do manage to shut myself up resolutely and paint several hours a day, except at moments when crises of one kind or another become too acute. Quentin is the sanest of us all really I think. He is an absolute miracle of cheerfulness and understanding and sense, and never fails whatever happens.

. . . As you may have heard, No. 8 [Fitzroy Street] exists no more. It is sad, but doesn't really seem to matter very much. Only one has no *pied à terre* there now. (By the way, it is better to address letters *here*.) However I find that in my old age, even if there were no war I think, I really prefer a country life, when the small things one does seem to have more sense than the small things one does in London. I like pottering about in the garden and trying to make things grow and one doesn't waste endless time arranging to see people one doesn't much want to see. How unsociable that sounds. But shall we all flock to France again one day—oh, how nice that would be . . .

> *Your*
> *Vanessa*

BUSSY

VIII-17. To Virginia Woolf

March 20 [1941]   *Charleston*

I have been thinking over our talk today and I feel as if I hadn't made myself nearly clear enough. You *must* be sensible, which means you must accept the fact that Leonard and I can judge better than you can.[1] It's true I haven't seen very much of you lately, but I have often thought you looked very tired and I'm sure that if you let yourself

---

[1] VW had been suffering the usual danger signs (headache, insomnia, refusal to eat) accompanying the completion of a book, in this case her novel *Between the Acts*. This letter has been considered brutal by some scholars of Bloomsbury, and even a contributing factor in VW's suicide. Read in the light of VB's continual exhortations to VW about her health, however, it is more blunt than brutal. VW's response to this letter is clear from the first lines of the suicide note she left for her sister: "You can't think how I loved your letter. But I feel that I have gone too far this time to come back again" (VWLVI, 485).

collapse and do nothing you would feel tired, and be only too glad to rest a little. You're in the state when one never admits what's the matter, but you must not go and get ill just now.

What shall we do when we're invaded if you are a helpless invalid— what should I have done all these last 3 years if you hadn't been able to keep me alive and cheerful. You don't know how much I depend on you. Do please be sensible for that if for no other reason. Do what Leonard advises and don't go scrubbing floors, which for all I care can remain unscrubbed forever. Both Leonard and I have always had reputations for sense and honesty, so you must believe in us.

Your
VB

I shall ring up some time to find out what is happening.

SUSSEX

VIII-18. To Victoria Sackville-West

March 29 [1941]   **Charleston, Firle, Sussex**

My dear Vita,

Leonard said he was writing to you, so this is only because I feel I want to be in touch with you somehow, as the person Virginia loved most I think outside her own family.[1] I was there yesterday by chance and saw him. He was of course amazingly self-controlled and calm and insisted on being left alone. There is nothing I can do yet. Perhaps some time you and I could meet? It is difficult, I know, but we will manage it presently. Now one can only wait till the first horrors are over, which somehow make it almost impossible to feel much.

Forgive this scrawl.

Vanessa

NIGEL NICOLSON

[1] VW had disappeared before lunch on March 28.

VIII-19. To Victoria Sackville-West

Ap. 2 [1941]   *Charleston, Firle, Sussex*

My dear Vita,

Will you really come—you don't know how much I should like it. Any day next week that suits you would do for me. Will you come to lunch or what would be easiest for you? The only drawback to lunch is that we have to have it at 12 on account of Quentin's farm hours, but please come whenever you like.

I remember sending that message by you. I think I had a sort of feeling that it would have more effect if you gave it and I expect I was right. How glad I am you gave it. I remember all those days after I heard about Julian lying in an unreal state and hearing her voice going on and on keeping life going as it seemed when otherwise it would have stopped, and late every day she came to see me here, the only point in the day one could want to come.

Leonard is working hard, going to London to committees, etc. I think he'll simply plunge into work. He told me if he had it all over again he would do the same, and so I suppose he realises he's not to blame actually. In fact I think nothing could have prevented the possibility just then—only I wish I had realised it, but I didn't at all. Even the last time when she talked to me about herself, that possibility never occurred to me. How strange it seems.

Do you know your way here? Shall I send you a map? Don't go to Firle. We're up a turning to the right from the main Lewes-Eastbourne road, about 3 miles beyond the Firle turning and opposite a small row of cottages. Our road is simply marked Private Road and has a pillar box at the corner.

Vanessa

NIGEL NICOLSON

VIII-20. To Victoria Sackville-West

Ap. 22 [1941]   *Charleston*

My dear Vita,

It was another shock of course,[1] and one had so hoped it wouldn't happen, but I think Leonard meant it when he said, as he did to me, that it was no more horrible than all the rest. He was in Lewes that afternoon and didn't hear till he came in, then he rang me up to tell me. I tried to get him to let someone else do all the necessary things, but it was no use, he had already arranged everything. I think he really felt, as indeed I did too, that all that part of it was very unreal and unimportant. He was the only person called at the inquest, and I didn't know exactly when it was as our telephone chose to break down completely during those days. He arranged for the cremation at Brighton yesterday and didn't want me to go, so I didn't. There was no ceremony, nothing. Poor old Ethel [Smyth], who has written to me, apparently wanting a country church yard, will be disappointed, but after all anything else would have been too uncharacteristic.

I am terribly useless I fear to Leonard. It's so difficult to get to Rodmell with no petrol and buses only every two hours there from Lewes and my household here to look after. He had his odd friend, Robson,[2] for the weekend and I hope other people will come, but all our family weekly meetings are almost necessarily at an end. They would be so pointless without her. But I cannot bear to think of him alone in that house, though I know he would not stand being anywhere else.

Thank you for writing, Vita. If ever you want to, *please* write.

Love from
Vanessa

NIGEL NICOLSON

[1]VW's body had been found by children in the river Ouse on April 18, a short distance downstream from where she had left her walking stick on the bank.
[2]William Robson (1895–1980), LW's coeditor at the *Political Quarterly* for many years.

VIII-21. To Jane Bussy

Ap. 24 [1941]   *Charleston*

My dear dear Janie,

I am sending this by Lydia who is going with M[aynard] to America via Lisbon and will post it there for me and so I hope it may get to you quicker than usual. Your telegram to Quentin came. We had to answer it brutally, but it seemed better to leave no possible doubt, the worst of all things. I had been so afraid you would hear in some such way, but did not see how to prevent it. Perhaps Pippa or Marjorie may by now have told you all there is to tell. But I am writing because I know how terribly one wants details at a distance, even I think painful ones. Somehow one has to hear the truth or one may imagine even worse things. Things *could* have been worse—for us—for at least there was no suspense. For her, one knows so little. Leonard had been worried, but I, though she seemed even thinner than usual, had no idea till a week before that anything was the matter at all. Then she talked to me, and so did L., and I saw that she was in a state when rest and food were essential—as of course had often been the case before. But I had absolutely no fear of this. It simply didn't occur to me. L. had been afraid, but wasn't so at the end. He took her to see a doctor, a sensible woman whom they knew quite well, and she also thought there was no danger. So at the end it was very sudden. She simply went for a walk, leaving letters to me and L. which he found later and which made it so clear that we neither of us had any doubt what she meant. He found her stick by the river and her footsteps. I happened to go to Rodmell just afterwards. So we both knew from the beginning and had no terrible days of waiting. I think if she could have been guarded for a time she would have recovered, but there had to be these times of danger—any suspicion of being watched would simply have hastened disaster. L. himself, I am thankful to say, realises he couldn't have done otherwise. Nothing was found at first, but now it has been. I think people have been as kind and considerate as possible. Leonard is amazing—calm, sensible. I could do nothing to help him, but I think he preferred to do all himself.

Dear Janie, these are the facts. I seem incapable of writing of anything but bare facts. It seems unnecessary for us to speak of feelings to each other, and by you I mean your mother and father too. One knows it all without saying it. We are all well here, leading our usual lives. You can imagine what Quentin and Angelica have been to me. Leonard is going the same at Rodmell, and working I think even harder than usual. It is difficult to see much of him—petrol scarcity, etc. But I go when I can and he has been here several times. I feel very useless as far as he is concerned. He could not exist I think anywhere but there and yet one wishes he need not be there alone.

I know that I have told you very little of what you probably most long to know, the state of mind which led her to it. But it is still to me mysterious, for she had seemed nowhere near the state in which she had been several times before when I had dreaded this. I think she had gradually starved herself more and more, partly as always from overwork, for besides the life of Roger she had written a novel and begun other things, and partly from the difficulty of getting the usual kind of food. L. said he simply could not get her to rest. But to me she seemed perfectly normal and herself, only of course I didn't see her often enough really to judge. But I think she must have got very much worse rather suddenly at the end. She said in her letter to me that she felt she was going mad and couldn't stand it. But only the day before I had rung her up and said I was coming to tea and she had seemed pleased.

I will write again my dear when perhaps I may be able to write less matter of factly. Don't worry about any of us. We shall get on somehow. I wish last night you could have heard Angelica singing and seen her and Q. teasing and laughing at each other. The garden is a mass of fruit blossom and things coming up. How much love I send you all.

Vanessa

BUSSY

VIII-22. To Victoria Sackville-West

Ap. 29 [1941]　　　　　　　　　　　　　*Charleston, Firle, Sussex*

My dear Vita,

Leonard himself was made so angry by that idiotic letter that he rang me up to read me a reply which he thought of making which will I suppose be published next Sunday.[1] It seemed to me very good, just giving the facts very clearly and simply. Of course all the reporters got the letters wrong. Virginia really said something like "I feel I am going mad again and I can't face those terrible times again." Nothing about "these terrible times." It sounded so unlike her. But how astonishing people are. Do you know Leonard had one anonymous letter saying "The coroner has been very kind to you"—isn't it incredible. Luckily I don't think he minds the least. But he thought these untrue accounts of her ought to be denied.

As for asking him to you, I don't know, but I don't see how it could do harm and it's possible some time he might very much like to go, even if not at once. I expect that he now feels he must be with his books and his garden and all the small occupations one can only have at home, but there might come a time when he'd be thankful to get away. Anyhow he knows what you and Virginia felt for each other and I'm sure he could only like being asked. I believe the only good thing that ever comes from death is that sometimes people who wouldn't otherwise, do get to know each other.

Leonard had an appalling time I'm afraid last week. I didn't like to ask him very much about it but he said it had been horrible. He was right and she had put stones in her pockets, but as she had never moved from the place how absurd of them not to find her sooner. If they were ever going to it would have been best. The cremation sounded very odd. After L.'s asking for no service of any kind they played dance music from Orpheus![2] And then put the ashes into an ornate "casket." But none of that matters. Leonard told me that there are two great elms at Rodmell which she always called Leonard and Virginia. They grow together by the pond. He is going to bury her ashes under one and have a tablet on the tree, with a quotation, the one about "Death is the enemy. Against you I will fling myself unvanquished and unyielding, O Death!"[3]

Perhaps it would be better not to tell anyone yet. Poor Leonard— he did break down completely when he told me. He was afraid I'd think him sentimental, but it seems so appropriate that I could only

[1]Kathleen Hicks, wife of the bishop of Lincoln, had written to the *Sunday Times* remarking that many people had lost everything in the war yet continued to "take their part nobly in this fight for God against the devil." LW fired off his letter to the editor (published May 4), correcting the almost universal misreporting of VW's suicide note, but not before Desmond MacCarthy had also responded to Mrs. Hicks, with a letter in the *Times* displaying considerable violence of feeling in defense of VW.
[2]"Dance of the Blessed Spirits" from Gluck's *Orfeo*.
[3]The last sentences of VW's *The Waves*.

think it right. But he may be shy about people knowing yet. I had a long talk alone with him which I don't often manage to do, and I suppose it's a good thing he should talk. It must very seldom happen that anyone is left as completely alone as he is, but I cannot see how it is to be prevented. He wouldn't really like one to go too much out of one's way on his account and he knows what my way usually is, so that all I can do is see him there about once a week and try to get him to come here in between and sometimes telephone. I think other people will insist on coming too now the days are longer.

Dear Vita, don't talk of my being good to you. If it's ever the least help to be in touch with me you may feel sure it's the same for me.

Vanessa

NIGEL NICOLSON

VIII-23. To David Garnett

Ap. 19 [1942]   *[Charleston]*

Dear Bunny,

When I asked you to see me I did not mean to talk to you about my feelings. But I know that it is difficult in talk not to say things that are better unsaid and therefore perhaps you are right to refuse to see me. I think however that if there is a question of marriage and children there are certain purely practical matters which would be considered and I hope you would not refuse to do so. There is the question for instance of money, which could not be left quite vague, and of certain other matters of fact and not feeling. I have no doubt that if you preferred it you could discuss them with someone else (Leonard possibly), instead of me. That is for you to decide.

But I want to say this. I realise that it is entirely for you and Angelica to decide what you will do. I do not want to intend to say anything more about my feelings concerning it either now or at any time—you need not fear it. But whatever you decide I wish very much that we could try to forget these painful months of estrangement and diffi-culty—for such they have seemed to me. Cannot we try to remember only the happier times we have had and our long friendship and realise how many of the same things we must both want? Won't you some-times come here with Angelica and let me come and see you? I have talked to Duncan about this and he agrees with me in thinking it the only sanity. I feel sure that it can happen, even if it's difficult at first, if you want it as I do.

I cannot say more and can only hope you will understand that I have written this letter simply because what I feel for Angelica would not let me say less.

Your
Vanessa

ANGELICA GARNETT

VIII-24. To Leonard Woolf

Feb. 29 [1944]   *Charleston, Firle, Sussex*

Dearest Leonard,

The Press never sends me back my drawings. So they must send either the drawing or a copy of the jacket[1] to Harcourt Brace—I should think the drawing would be slightly better. I'm told by Bunny that the Americans now take a tax of 27% off one's earnings there, so perhaps the price should go up?

We have just come back from London. We were to attend the unveiling of the Cinderella decorations at Tottenham[2] but Duncan was seized with a bad cold and temperature and couldn't go. So I had to bear the brunt of it. You'd have been amused to see me intro-duced to the Mayor and aldermen, with Maynard doing the opening, but I'll tell you all about it some day. I hope Angelica is coming here

[1]For the American edition of VW's *Haunted House,* published in England in 1943.
[2]VB and DG had been commissioned to decorate the children's restaurant at Devonshire Hill School at Tottenham.

on Friday for the weekend, also François Walther [Walter] whom you probably know. Perhaps you'll come over? Also on Saturday Quentin's show at Miller's opens, which you ought to attend. I wish you wouldn't go to London during these raids. They're evidently horrible and will get worse I suppose. I hope Bunny is going to have the sense to take A. and her baby[3] to the house they've taken near his mother, but he hasn't much sense. Have you heard whether Ann is all right? We heard Paulton Sqre had been bombed. If it's true I expect you'll have her and her family on you, too. The wretched Kenneth Clarks went off to the country for a day or two, having installed his mother in their house at Hampstead because her flat has been damaged by blast, porter killed, etc. The next day, owing simply to the imbecility of electricians, a bad fire broke out in the library, lots of valuable books were destroyed, others injured, and I believe some paintings damaged. Now they have no light and hardly any heat. This house seems a paradise after London. In spite of the cold a lovely new iris has come out in front and daffodils are in bud.

I hope I may see you during the weekend.

Your
VB

SUSSEX

VIII-25. To Leonard Woolf

Friday, Aug. 5 [error for Aug. 4, 1944]　　　　　　　　*Charleston*

Dearest Leonard,

I hate getting bad news by telephone and so as I have a rather tiresome piece of news to tell you about myself I am writing. I have to have an operation—not I believe a serious one—but having had rather inexplicable pains lately I went to see Dr Tooth[1] yesterday who says I have a lump in one breast which ought to be removed—of course the sooner the better. He is putting me in touch with a surgeon

---

[3]Amaryllis, born October 11, 1943, at 41 Gordon Square.
[1]VB's Lewes doctor. The operation was a radical mastectomy.

in Brighton who is he says first rate, and I should probably have to go into a hospital or nursing home there perhaps in a few days' time. I'll let you know when I know and I hope you'll come and see me and lend me some books. But I may only have to be there 2 or 3 weeks. However it may put off my annual visit to Rodmell—what a curse it is—but I suppose one must expect such things. Everyone here has come to the rescue, Grace doing all the cooking and others coming in to help, so that I need do nothing but live like a lady if I only knew how. I fear the garden will be weedier than ever.

Whenever I can see you I shall be very glad, but don't worry about me.

Love from
VB

SUSSEX

VIII-26. To Angelica Garnett

Dec. 25 [1944]   *Charleston*

My own darling,

Thank you very much for sending me the snap-shots. I see two of mine came out, to my surprise. It's a pity they aren't better focussed as the composition is rather lovely. Some of those of you feeding A. almost had the effect of a cinema on me, one seemed to see the movement going on from one to another. Can it be possible that you will soon produce another such lovely creature, only with quite different charms and attractions? I can hardly believe it, but you will.[1]

I don't really worry about bombs, because I know if there seemed real reason to be alarmed you'd be as anxious to get your family out of harm's way as I am to have you, but I only wanted you to know for certain that you could all get in here quite easily if you wanted to. Of course you do know all I can tell you. As for Tilton, I think it was a sudden whim of Duncan on the spur of the moment. I quite realise it would be impracticable for many reasons. The Keyneses are

[1]AVG was expecting her second child.

there and giving a large party tomorrow night to which we all have to go and most people have to do a turn. Quentin is to be Father Christmas and give everyone presents. Clive and Duncan propose to act Little Red Riding-hood. What a pity you aren't coming. I believe Lydia is going to recite the Forsaken Merman[2] with 9 children in attendance! There'll be a large Christmas tree and masses of food.

I have had a long letter from Janie which you may like to read, but could you send it back soon? There are messages for you as you will see. I suppose the Stracheys have had the same account. It sounds terribly grim, but I hope is better by now. Oh, I've just done such an imbecile things—worse, far worse than Amaryllis and at my age too—upset the ink—all over my chair—that doesn't much matter—over my dress—that also doesn't much matter as it's old and dirty any-how—but worst of all over the front of my new plaid jacket, almost done. I rushed to soap and water and have done all I can, but I fear it may be ruined. How could I be such an idiot. I shan't know the worst until it's dry tomorrow.

Talking of food, we have such masses in the house we hardly know what to do. I hope you have too and that the turkey was all right. Ours is delicious. When I get a chance I will try to send you some lard, also vegetables. We have what they call a fresh ham, which is very good, but not really a ham. Also masses of brawn. To say nothing of rabbits and pheasants and a huge piece of beef. Also a parcel from Peter Morris today with a tongue, jam, orange juice, figs and odds and ends. Also a pot of honey from Leonard and another from Dick [a farmhand]! So if you feel hungry, come here.

I wish I could get the poor Bussys here. I believe the whole of England, at any rate this part of it, is in the same state as ourselves. When Quentin went to give tea to his friends he found them all busy cooking enormous Christmas dinners.

Now I have been busy routing out our old theatrical properties— a mask for Clive, and other garments to make him look like a very obscene little girl. Duncan is making himself a wonderful wolf's mask. Q.'s Father C[hristmas] is a horrible old Jew who will terrify the children.

Patricia [Preece] sends me a p[ocket] handkerchief—Helen a letter which she put into a drawer by mistake some months ago—Louie[3]— well you'll see what she sent you—mine is a "cravat" of incredible mauves.

---

[2] By Matthew Arnold (1853).
[3] Angelica's old nurse, Louie Pape, who kept in touch with the family.

If you want me to make any baby clothes you must send me instructions soon as I'm very slow. But perhaps you don't.

Much love to all.

Your
VB

ANGELICA GARNETT

VIII-27. To Jane Bussy

Jan. 9 [1945]   *Charleston*

Dearest Janie,

. . . Letters are most erratic. First came a card from you to Quentin, then a long letter to me written on Nov. 6th which came I think before Christmas, so it wasn't too bad, and then a letter to Q. and now a card to me dated Oct 29th when you had just had my letter. I would willingly make writing to you my war-work—I do no other! But we lead such secluded lives now that you must only expect the mildest of Charleston gossip, and even of that I don't know how much you may have heard from other sources. No, I didn't tell you of our operations[1] as really at such a distance it seemed unnecessary to worry you. But don't be uneasy. All I said was true, and here we are safe and comparatively sound. We really managed very well, as Q. and I went to the same nursing home at the same moment, so we had the latest news of each other and could send each other messages. One day Q.'s nurse put her head out of the window to listen to a neighbouring wireless and put it in again to say "Paris is freed." You can imagine our emotions, though of course it wasn't strictly true. However at that time, luckily for us, the news on the whole was very cheering, and we managed to get through it all very well, the chief drawback being English food at its most genteel—and even that I suppose you would have jumped at. Would you? Pink custards made of powder and dried milk and a nice cup of tea at 3.30 PM? Still Charleston provided fruit and eggs. No, we had nothing to complain

[1] QB had an appendectomy in September 1944 at the same time VB had her mastectomy.

of, and were only there less than 3 weeks. I still lead a very lazy life but I am able to paint in a small way. Quentin is back at farm work but doesn't do it all day I'm thankful to say.

You are quite right in thinking we are very thick with the church. Didn't I tell you about it years ago? It must be more than 3 years since we began our "murals,"[2] and more than a year since they were put up. Having done so much of course one wanted to go on and so various other bits are getting painted and an immense Crucifix by Duncan cut out in wood and painted in brilliant colours is now occupying most of the studio here. D. himself is *au mieux* with the clergy, especially the Bishop of Chichester who is a wily gentleman (I think) and gets round anyone. D. actually went to a conference at Chichester consisting of a week-end party with Tom Eliot, Miss Dorothy Sayers,[3] Eric MacLagan,[4] Henry Moore[5] and many more, all planted out in pubs and meeting to discuss art and religion. Can you imagine it? Some day you must hear all about it. Duncan however is now in so many committees to do with art and the children and the state that he thinks nothing of it. But his chief activity really is helping the Ladies of Miller's to run Miller's.[6] No doubt you have heard of them. They are some of the most remarkable ladies I have ever met— plain, some say ugly, shy, middle-aged, unable to speak *any* language correctly—for instance, requisition becomes requition in their mouths—they have the power to move mountains. They appeared in our lives and Lewes about 3 years ago. Their past is a mystery but it is known that they were partly brought up by Princess Louise,[7] that they have lived in Wales, Paris and Sicily, and also near Rodmell, where they kept model cows. They took a most charming little old house in Lewes and proceeded to furnish it with exquisite taste. They then built (in wartime!) a picture gallery where they have frequent and really very good exhibitions of all sorts, they have an American friend who has given them the choicest library of books of rare kinds which they have housed with the perfect taste in another small house, they took another large house and immense garden which they at

[2]At Berwick Church, not far from Charleston.
[3]The mystery writer and theological polemicist (1893–1957).
[4]Sir Eric MacLagan (1879–1951), director and secretary of the Victoria and Albert Museum from 1924 to 1945.
[5]The celebrated sculptor (1898–1986).
[6]Miller's Gallery in Lewes. "The Ladies" were Mrs. Byng Stamper and her sister Miss Caroline Byng Lucas.
[7]H.R.H. Princess Marie Louise (1872–1956), a granddaughter of Queen Victoria.

once let at a profit, reserving for themselves a studio where the younger lady (a sculptor and painter of some talent) not only works herself but at one time made me and Duncan start a school of art! As however most of our pupils were at least my age we didn't continue long. But now not having enough to do she, Miss Lucas, known to us as Mouie (don't be surprised, it's what she likes to be called), has not only started us all off doing lithographs, but has installed a press and mastered the most difficult art of printing them, even coloured ones. She and her sister (by name Bay, short for Baby I believe) have between them produced I don't know how many copies of a portfolio of lithographs which they hope [to] and no doubt will sell at a profit. Besides all this they get the elite of the intelligentsia to come to Lewes and lecture to them. Desmond, Morgan, Sheppard, St Denis, Clive of course and in 2 weeks' time Quentin is going to lecture on, what do you think, Fashions in Dress! All this is supported by the members of Miller's—about 1000 Sussex shopkeepers and yokels, all pining for art it seems. Isn't it remarkable? They are not rich, though I daresay quite well off, but it is mostly done by sheer will power. We now no longer resist anything they suggest, as one knows it will sooner or later have to be done . . .

You ask about Leonard. It has been of course very difficult to see much of him that we have no car, and buses don't fit. However a young woman has appeared on the scenes, called by the rather absurd name of Trekkie Ritchie.[8] Have you ever heard of her? She is married to someone in Chatto & Windus and is a painter herself (also a lithographer!). She is nice I think and intelligent and has a house next to Leonard's in London. (You know he has taken a new one in Victoria Sqre. The one in Tavistock was quite destroyed and the next one in Mecklenburgh Sq. badly damaged.) Well, this young woman came to stay at Rodmell when London was being fly-bombed in June, and there she still is, and that's all I know about it. But L. seems to me far happier and better and I myself think at any rate her feelings are fairly clear. I am thankful he isn't alone at any rate, and I think he really looks more rested than he has done for years. But I tell you this gossip for what it's worth. I know nothing and have heard nothing.

. . . We have heard that the Teeds are safe and back at Cassis. M[argery] Fry has heard from the Maurons. I was glad to hear Mar-

---

[8]Trekkie Parsons (née Ritchie), a Slade-trained painter. She had married Ian Parsons in 1934.

guerite [Duthuit] is safe as she was rumoured dead. Gradually everyone is emerging.

My love to you all.

Vanessa

BUSSY

VIII-28. To Jane Bussy

March 11, 1945   *Charleston, Firle, Sussex*

Dearest Janie,

You have outdone me. Your letter dated Feb. 19th arrived here on
March 5th—just a fortnight!—and unopened. So I think we really
are in touch. Somehow it is curiously difficult to write into the blue,
but now I feel there's a good chance of your knowing what we are
about before it's all a thing of the past. And I have such very trivial
domestic matters to write about that really they ought to be eaten at
once to have any flavour. (It doesn't look to me either as if this ink
would last very long.) If only we could all broadcast. It must have
been very odd to hear Clive's voice suddenly and probably much better
than we heard it here on our rickety old machine. Do you ever hear
Desmond or Morgan I wonder? Both appear sometimes about 6.30
or 10 PM.

We have been very cheerful here lately owing to the dashing habits
of the Americans—only we rather hope the English may come on the
scenes soon. Still———. We see the great gliders being towed over-
head, a fantastic sight. The most beautiful vision is on a starlight
night, when the air is filled with humming and one looks out to see
what seems to be two layers of stars, the lower one moving and almost
as numerous as the upper one. But I write as if this were new, of
course it has been going on for years. I must say the result in the
papers later fills one with horror. What an incredibly dirty and untidy
world it is becoming.

I have none but Charleston news to give you for I have only been
to London once this winter and pick up such scraps as I can from
the gad-abouts, Clive and Duncan . . . Our only visitor lately has been

Desmond, who comes for a weekend and stays a week. He is a most charming visitor. Did I tell you that we made him sit to us about, perhaps, 2 years ago? It went on and on—he didn't seem to mind—and would sit and read aloud to us and talk. At last after many visits and after several portraits had been more or less produced it had to stop because we have had to abandon the large studio owing to want of anthracite [fuel]. However, unwilling to believe that light from a different direction made any difference, he insisted on coming to sit again, but was easily diverted and taken for walks by Clive. He was made very happy the last day of his stay by the return of Dermod from the Far East[1] where he has been for 2 years.

Your account of Marguerite was fascinating. I am sure she will have been completely cured by the Nazis and in future will treat Georges (if he ever returns from the U.S.A.) with contempt. I am very glad the Master [Matisse] continues to work, even in bed. There's a very fine lithograph by him now being shown at Miller's, a portrait of a woman, hard and uncompromising and hideous and drawn in the greatest detail. By the way, I hope you know that lithographs are sure to be demanded of you the moment you reach this country, so you had better prepare your mind. All you need do at present is drawings which you can use when you are here. There is a great demand for them and I am sure lithos of Nice would sell like hot cakes. They can be either in one, two, three or even four colours. It's the kind of thing one can do sometimes when one hasn't time or materials for painting in oils. Do consider the matter.

I am glad our church relationships are dismissed as trivial. It has certainly been an odd experience coming into touch with a real live Bishop (who was at school with Adrian!). The odd thing is that it seems to be as easy as anything to get the right religious emotion into one's works—so they say at any rate and I suppose they know if it *is* right. To be sure Quentin who used Leonard as a model for our Lord in an altar-piece of the supper at Emmaus got into some trouble for making him look a middle-aged Jew, and Duncan inclined to make him too nude and attractive in his Christ in Glory, but on the whole it's quite easy to hit off a good holy atmosphere . . .

People in England seem to be getting rather agitated about the question of sending food to France and lots of ladies get up meetings to say they're willing to give up all their rations, etc., and Dame Sibyl

[1]Dermod (1911–1986), the youngest of the three MacCarthy children, was a doctor and had been stationed in the Far East with the Fleet Air Arm.

Thorndike eats nothing but a cup of cocoa to show how much she feels about it. Well, I quite agree really but what can one do? And if it *should* be made possible to send parcels to one's friends, what should one send? Tea? Coffee? Fats (but how and what to send)? Dried milk? Dried eggs? (dull but useful) Darning wool? Soap? Vitamins? Needles and cottons? Now that letters arrive so quickly it really might be worth telling me. When people have once or twice sent us things from America they generally send us tinned milk or "onion flakes" which are not exactly suitable to this household living on a farm which produces nothing but milk and onions . . .

All my love dear Janie.

Your
Vanessa

BUSSY

VIII-29. To Angelica Garnett

April 6 [1945]   *Charleston, Firle, Sussex*

My own darling,

I am sending one shirt to see if it's what you want. If so I think I could make 3 more, but tell me if it's too big or too small. I'm afraid I didn't avoid some slight stains but I hope they'll wash out. Also I had to put in a bit in the back as I couldn't get the whole out of one piece.

About the great name question. Duncan says why not Bartle[1] (or Bartholomew) as a second name for a boy? His only objection to it before was that he thought as the principal name for a first child it might be rather obvious, but it's a very attractive name we both think and would go well with Tom and with Garnett. I can't think of anything else. I agree in not liking Giles which was suggested by Clive as being after Lytton, but that's not really a good reason for a name one doesn't like.

If a girl, why not Henrietta as you suggest? I think it's a lovely

[1]Christian name of DG's father.

name and may mean such different things, either a tall and stately creature or a fantastic fluttering one. Besides, beautiful as Catherine is, I don't think you can copy Judith! It may amuse you to hear the names that Virginia suggested for you—I've been trying to get her letters to me into order and came across these—

Griselda	Theresa	Esther
Nerissa	Bridget	Vashti
Lesley	Paula (a name of character)	

Miriam (a chandelier or lustre)
Fuchsia (Leonard's favourite name)
Vanessa (splash of the sea)
Sidonia (emerald) . . .

But Angelica she says "has liquidity and music, a hint of green in it and memory of no one but Kauffmann[2] who was no doubt a charming character." So there you have plenty of choice. But I believe we did think for some time of Henrietta though she doesn't speak of it.

I have had the most difficult time trying to get the letters in order as I have so many. Unfortunately not the earliest which were stolen and destroyed, but from 1916 onwards.[3] They are fascinating, but I don't think *anyone* except my immediate surroundings could read them. Everyone else is summed up with such devastating wit, I don't think anyone could help being upset. However you or Amaryllis will be able to publish them perhaps—as long as you don't let the Bagenal family get hold of them. Clive certainly couldn't read them. Only Duncan and you children and possibly Roger escape.

. . . We have managed to find about 40 frames for Duncan's pictures which I think very clever of us. So he won't have to get very many new ones, but some need altering. Maynard appeared the other day and carried off all his loans.[4] We were left terribly bare. He said he'd lend us others instead, but when D. went round to get them there

[2]Angelica Kauffman (1741–1807), Swiss painter and printmaker who spent many years in England. A founding member of the Royal Academy.
[3]Some family papers were destroyed by strangers who rented one of VB's London houses. It is impossible to know what was lost (VB herself was wrong), but VW-to-VB letters from late 1907 on survived.
[4]Charleston had the benefit of many works from Maynard's collection. The "Renoir head" referred to is probably the plaster head of his son Coco (Claude) (1908), still at Charleston. The Matisse was a *Seated Woman* which remained at Charleston until about the 1970s, when it was reclaimed by the Keynes estate.

was Lydia in a rage saying he couldn't possibly have any. In the end he brought back the Renoir head and Matisse which Maynard had just taken away! All very dotty.

I shall try to send the bedstead, a very light and simple one, easy to put together, and the Matisse,[5] and anything else? Poetry in the Highlands?[6] by Gander [a mover] next week.

I'll make no more shirts till I hear if this one will do. It's so lovely, a mass of pear and plum blossom, wall-flowers coming out.

Your loving
VB

ANGELICA GARNETT

VIII-30. To Jane Bussy

April 10, 1945   *Charleston, Firle, Sussex*

Dearest Janie,

I have just had your fascinating letter written a fortnight ago. My letter you say only took 9 days, which surely must be a record. In case this one does the same I may tell you that if you manage to get the B.B.C. on Ap. 23rd at I think 7.30 or thereabouts you may again hear Clive, this time I believe telling the public about the use of Art— or something of the kind. It may amuse you anyhow to hear his voice . . .

There can be no doubt the war is coming to an end. Such mysteries were made about it a short time ago that large sums of money could have been made by those who doubted its immediate conclusion— all the old gentlemen at the Beefsteak Club were laying bets up to £50 or £100, but unfortunately Clive wasn't there. Still, even though we are slightly misled by the war correspondents it can't be much longer now. I myself think they're being a trifle previous in their

---

[5] A lithograph known as *Le Renard,* which AVG had purchased for £12 in 1941 with money left to her by VW.
[6] An early painting of DG's showing reclining figures under a tree, supposedly Maynard and a female cousin of DG's.

detailed plans for V-day, which I hope to pass here even out of the sound of Victory bells, but it must come soon and then surely transport of all kinds will be easier. I'm so sorry I gave you such a tantalising offer of food! One feels so much less inclined to send it vaguely to the general public, but I hope some will be sent. As for papers, of course I'll send some. I thought I had better first find out from Pippa whether and what she had sent, but as soon as I hear from her you shall have a selection, I daresay a very lowbrow one. This household has given up the Parish Mag.[1] in disgust (though Q. still hankers after it) and goes in mostly for such rags as Picture Post and the Listener, which rouse Clive's scorn every time he sees them. But I shall treat you as though you shared our low tastes. And artists' materials too. Tell me what you want and I will do my best. Some colours are strangely difficult to come by, such as yellow ochre and black, but we have never been without. I think the only things one can't get now are brushes, but things reappear from time to time. I need hardly say that we are fascinated by your description of Nice and long to paint it—at least—no, I'm not quite sure it would suit my tastes—but anyhow you must do lithographs of *anything*—still lives, your rooms, no matter what. The market is ripe. I told you didn't I that our wonderful ladies printed and produced a portfolio containing 8 lithos—2 each by D., myself, Du Plessis[2] and the younger of the ladies. Well, all have sold at £5 a portfolio and we have netted £20 each just for 2 drawings. The public is clamouring for more—in fact it seems to be clamouring for art altogether. Gowing[3]—you know, Julia's young man, who stammers, one of the youngest and most promising of the Euston Rd. Group—has just had a show at the Leicester and sold nearly all at quite good prices. They were really rather good, very serious and his own, several portraits of Julia among them. The history of the Euston Roaders is curious. Coldstream got a job as portrait painter in the army and went to Egypt (I think). There he paints very slowly and with great care portraits of gentlemen in turbans, several of which are now to be seen at the National Gallery in the otherwise intolerably gloomy and depressing show by "War Artists." I can't describe how appalling it is, but the Coldstreams have

[1]I.e., the *New Statesman & Nation*.
[2]H. E. DuPlessis (b. 1894), South African-born painter and journalist. A member of the London Group.
[3]Lawrence Gowing (1918–1991), painter and critic, curator of Royal Academy collections, who had spent the war as a conscientious objector, ostensibly as the brother of Julia Strachey, whom he later married (March 1952).

great merit of a serious kind. Fatty [Claude] Rogers, being as blind as a bat, was for a long time allowed to be a fire-watcher. Then they roped him into the army where he nearly went mad with despair, so he was let out and is now a family man, having produced a baby, and teaches in London. Victor Pasmore started by joining A. P. Herbert's boat which did something important in the Thames,[4] but was so much disliked by everyone else on the boat that he had to leave it. He then decided to be a C.O., but when that didn't convince he joined the army. However the army is so humane in this war or so sensible about not wanting incompetents that it simply let him out after a time, and there he is, also a family man, with 2 infants I believe, painting very pretty and successful pictures. I've no doubt he'll be an R.A. soon. One of the most gifted of them, Graham Bell, was killed flying.

As for Helen Anrep, she has almost given me up. She lives at Rodwell near Ipswich, and I gather that Anastasia has proved to be the one hopelessly unemployable female in England. Job after job has passed her by and really if you could see the young women of England in their uniforms you'd realise how difficult it must be to keep out of them. Helen hopefully says now she will get a job at the Ministry of Information, but as they must be on the point of dismissing all they can I have my doubts.

Igor is in Burma, having at last qualified as a doctor—a thought which fills everyone with alarm. Think of the hundreds and thousands of war doctors we shall have to attend us soon. But we may be unfair to him, probably we are. Anyhow I think it must have been very good for him to get to the other side of the world. Helen herself I haven't seen for about a year and she hardly ever writes, so I know much less of her than I do of you, but I think I must get her to come here soon . . .

Angelica hasn't been able to do much in the way of painting lately and I don't see how she can for some time to come as she does all the cooking and of course will be a good deal occupied with the new baby. I am kept busy making garments for one or other of them out of Quentin's old shirts and I often long for your talents as a cobbler and tailor. I hope you are prepared to find us all dowdy to a degree. I'm sure you French ladies manage to be smart through all, but my

[4]A. P. Herbert (1890–1971), author and wit. During the First World War he served in the Royal Navy. In September 1939, though too old for conventional military service, he joined the River Emergency Service, which operated on the Thames as part of the London defenses.

only method of having any sort of rag on my back is to buy old shawls at a second-hand shop in Brighton and try to turn them into garments of a kind. Luckily at Charleston there are no standards as you know, but I sometimes think one is unconsciously sinking to a state when one will be a shock to one's old friends. Quentin of course wears overalls, Duncan I suspect gets coupons from Aunt Daisy and has indulged in two new suits lately! Clive remains dapper as ever because he has such immense stocks, but I—don't bear looking at. However at present there is no one to see. Amaryllis I am told is extremely smart in red trousers and blue shirts. She certainly looks less like a war baby than anything you can imagine, with wonderful rosy cheeks and perfectly firm round limbs and full of every sort of vitamin.

Did you see that Mrs [Mary] Berenson is at last really dead? announced in the Times. She had been rumoured dead so often, but now I suppose it's true. They seem to have been in Italy all the time— she died at Settignano. We also had heard these absurd accounts of Picasso and his doings, but what, I wonder, is actually known about the collaborators? I can easily believe that Derain would do any sort of trick,[5] also Friesz and Vlaminck, Despiau[6] I know nothing of personally and I suppose one can't judge people from their work. But isn't Segonzac simply an old bumbler, not really interested in anything but painting, who probably may have done what came easiest without thinking clearly what it meant? I agree it's not very heroic but perhaps it's forgivable if that's what happened. At least I feel so very uncertain of how I should behave myself that I try to find excuses for people I like as I always have liked him. But then I don't know the facts. I shall try to send you an account of artists in Paris by John Rothenstein[7]

---

[5]Derain has been frequently accused of collaboration with the Nazis. His antagonist Picasso was among those who eagerly told reporters about Derain's "visit to Weimar to shake the hand of Hitler." Derain had traveled to Germany during the war with a group of artistically conservative French artists (including Vlaminck, Despiau, and de Segonzac) to attend the opening of an exhibition by the Nazi sculptor Arno Breker. This trip was "apparently made under duress, part of a deal to liberate some French prisoners of war." At the same time, Derain moved into the studio of the Jewish painter Leopold Lévy to protect it from the Nazis, while his own house and studio at Chambourcy were requisitioned by the Germans and one of his most important paintings vandalized. (Jed Perl, *Paris Without End: On French Art since World War I* [San Francisco: North Point Press, 1988].)

[6]Charles Despiau (1874–1946), sculptor. He was Rodin's assistant from 1907 to 1914.

[7]Sir John Rothenstein (1901–1992), director of the Tate Gallery from 1938 to 1964. The artist William Rothenstein was his father. This "account of artists in Paris," probably an essay, has not been traced as such.

(you know I suppose that Sir William R[othenstein] is also really dead?). It's quite well done, but may be in the nature of coals to Newcastle, or Pippa may have sent it. I think very soon you'll all be in far more of a sizzle about art and literature than we are here, for I see we're going soon to be swamped by politics. Already the Labour Party and the Liberals occupy attention and will be quite as dull as the war. However I shall insist on your coming over to rouse us out of it all and please tell your mother that she must be prepared to sit up gossiping with me till all hours of the night when you young have gone to bed.

Much love dear Janie, and please write, for your letters are a great delight.

Your
Vanessa

BUSSY

VIII-31. To Angelica Garnett

May 12 [1945]   *Charleston*

My own darling,

. . . We have had a very quiet V[ictory] week except for Maynard's entertainments. The first was a dinner party with just ourselves and Logan[1]—a chicken, champagne and very good red wine, so it was most enjoyable. I must say I was a bit shocked to find that afterwards we were expected to listen to the King's speech. All the retainers were led in and everything was so solemn that after the first moments of hysteria induced by His Majesty's stutter I nearly went to sleep and let my attention wander to Auntie,[2] whom I hope to get to sit. Suddenly wild shrieks from Lydia, to everyone's relief, and into the room dashed a tornado, a black and white puppy which rushed round, finally settling on me and nearly biting me to pieces in its joy. Maynard

[1]Logan Thompson managed JMK's farm at Tilton; he lived with his aunt.
[2]Possibly an aunt of Ruby Weller's, Lydia's former dresser who lived at Tilton with her husband Edgar, Maynard's chauffeur.

however, I suppose because he's a lord, has become completely feudal and does all the right things.[3] We had to drink His Majesty's health—it was almost like being at Seend again. Drink carried us through however, and as I don't like port Duncan and Quentin got the benefit of mine as well as their own and were very happy. Then we enjoyed open windows and lights streaming out, and fireworks in the distance and even, we thought, the lights of London—and bonfires everywhere. Finally we went home and turned on all our outdoor lights and the garden was simply fairy land—with nightingales—yes, we were sure of it—singing loudly. We walked about on the lawn and did our best to realise we were at peace. The next night looked like being a fiasco on account of rain. We went to Tilton in a downpour at 8 o'clock, an enormous straw figure of Hitler with a ghastly papier-mâché head made by Q. having been carted there earlier, and we were given beer and biscuits and cheese, and all the farm attended and the Higgenses and lots of small boys, Wests and Wellers, etc. Then songs, with a painful episode of songs by the D[olt] which reduced nearly everyone to ill-suppressed giggles. He assured us with deep passion and very flat notes that he would stand by us whatever befell. Poor Grace hid her head in the background. But almost the worst moment was when they danced and the D., seeing Edgar [Weller] waltz round gallantly with Ruby, tried to do the same by Grace, who simply sent him packing. I never saw him so crestfallen. Lydia danced and recited, everyone sang and recited, even Quentin was forced to sing a song about the One Big Industrial Union, which was a great success, and then we had the Trial of Hitler, with Maynard as judge, Q. as prosecuting and Duncan as defending counsel. He made such peculiar faces and talked such broken English that I saw Roma [unidentified] looking at him in astonishment and hardly able to keep her seat for laughing. Finally Hitler was carried off and there was a torchlight procession to the top of the hill behind the house—luckily the rain had stopped—and there we had a huge and wonderful bonfire and Hitler was burnt on it. It was the most lovely sight. I believe Q. is going to try to paint it . . .

Much love darling.

Your

VB

So you have settled on Tom? But supposing he looks Bartle all over?

---

[3]JMK was made a peer in 1942.

Do you know that Grace will have been with us 25 years on May 30th? What are we to do about it?

ANGELICA GARNETT

VIII-32. To Angelica Garnett

May 18 [1945]   *Charleston, Firle, Sussex*

My own darling,

I was very sorry not to see you again yesterday but I weakly gave in to Duncan's wish to go to the National Gallery party,[1] and in any case I could only have seen you for a very short time. I was nearly dead with heat, dirty, untidy, but Vincy[2] kindly gave us glasses of water and off we went. Of course no taxi to be had until we got one in the T[ottenham] C[ourt] Road and just as we were getting in Le Bas[3] rushed across from a bus he had been mounting and jumped in too, and off we all went. We found a crowd waiting, and inside crowds all up the steps, and Maynard and Lydia half way up and Kenneth [Clark] and his daughter [Colette] standing we supposed to receive Royalty. So we waited too until at last a friend of Le Bas came up and said Why don't you go in? It's open, no royalties have come, but the paintings are superb. So in we went and found it of course almost impossible to see the pictures, but when one *could* see them it was really most exciting. Some have been cleaned and look as if they were just painted, one Poussin especially. Hardly any had glasses on and it was a brilliant light. I cannot tell you how lovely the Piero Nativity looked, simply dazzling in its airiness and light. Titian, Rembrandt, Rubens, all one's old friends but not, like one's other old friends, 5 years older. A sham Ottoline appeared—ropes of pearls and green satin—who she was I don't know but she might have been Ottoline risen from the dead.[4] Fatty [Claude Rogers], Pasmore, Raymond,

[1]A celebration of the reopening of the National Gallery after the war.
[2]A servant of AVG's.
[3]Edward Le Bas (1904–1966), painter, and friend of both DG's and VB's.
[4]Lady Ottoline Morrell had died of heart disease in April 1938. VW wrote an obituary which appeared in the *Times* on April 28 of that year.

Waley, etc., etc., Morgan, all congratulating me on my new grand-daughter,[5] especially to my surprise Stephen Spender.[6]

Then all of a sudden the band, which had been quietly playing classical music in a far room, struck up loudly God Save The King. People were herded away from the paintings into the middle of the room, everyone dithered with excitement, and there was Her Majesty, led by Kenneth, clothed in pale blue from head to foot and ropes of huge pearls and followed by His Majesty and the little princesses.[7] It was really rather interesting to see them so near and my suspicions that Royalty is hardly human were confirmed. How they have been produced I can't think, but the Queen is really a miracle. She is absolutely smooth all over, rather like a sea-lion in contour, without a wrinkle. She looks as if she were made of cold cream and must spend hours every day being massaged, made up, ironed out and coloured. She wears an almost perpetual smile and she and K. seemed to get on very well. No doubt she asked intelligent questions, but her blue eye has a slightly glassy look and I am sure she must long sometimes to lie by the fire smoking a cigarette and let herself go. No doubt she does. The King is like a red, sandy horse—except that he barks instead of neighing. He's a coarse creature and quite uninteresting and must be appalling to live with. Our future Queen is still not quite made into Royalty, though I daresay she will become rather like Queen Victoria. She is short and unnoticeable, and her little sister is a quite ordinary human schoolgirl. Neither looked at a picture, but they were rather shy, poor creatures, and I felt sorry for the awful prospect ahead of them. But how we have managed to get Royalties to be Royalties I can't think. The Queen's clothes were unlike anything seen outside a pantomime—no human being could possibly dress like that, all in exactly one colour, feathers, veil, coat, all—really more like a Principal Boy than anything else. Jane [Clark], in a white Victorian bonnet and cotton dress was a contrast. One seemed to know almost every other person there, but I missed Colefax. Gowing and a lot of other painters were there . . .

Your loving
VB

ANGELICA GARNETT

[5]Henrietta Catherine, born May 15, 1945.
[6]Stephen Spender (b. 1909), poet, teacher, and critic.
[7]The little princesses were Elizabeth (b. 1926), who succeeded her father George VI in 1952, and Margaret (b. 1930), countess of Snowdon.

VIII-33. To Angelica Garnett

July 13 [1945]   *[Charleston]*

My own darling,

Here is your cheque,[1] late as usual, but if you only knew the life I have been leading. Pigs and red currants fill my days. When I'm not wading through masses of official papers, always of course having lost the one I want, I am wading through masses of red currants, stripping them into bottles. Six bottles take a lot of stripping and now I must do 3 more, and then the bushes are laden. But to begin with our afternoon at the church of Clayton.[2] It was pouring, dark dripping weather. Luckily we didn't have so far to go. We reached the church only to find it locked. The ladies had muddled it and never written. However I found the key on a beam outside and we got in—pitch dark, rows of electric lights, but the box of switches locked. So I tried to find that key—we all tried—but no success. I won't bore you with all the ins and outs but will only tell you that Duncan, after endless visitations to anyone who seemed likely in the neighbourhood, at last returned with Mr Allwood, famous as a carnation grower, who was also a church warden and produced lots of keys but none that fitted. Suddenly in the dark and confusion there was a wild shriek from Mouie, "Oh—I have trod on a bat—and it squeaked." It sounded curious, but sure enough there was a poor little bat sitting on the floor and Duncan had to remove it and said it squeaked again at him. Then suddenly Mr Allwood found a key and we were flooded with light. All this took hours, but at last we left, after seeing some very dim relics of ancient paintings.

The next day I went to London, where I saw first a lot of pictures, and among them one of the most exciting I have ever seen in my life. This is literally true. It was at Agnew's where there's a very good mixed show, a superb Rubens portrait, a late Titian, etc. Colin Agnew

---

[1]After the death of VW, who gave AVG a small allowance, continued somewhat spasmodically by LW, and after the birth of AVG's children, VB decided to give her £200 a year. AVG had no other revenue.

[2]Clayton is a village off the old Brighton-London road south of Hassocks. The church has a Saxon chancel arch and Norman wall paintings, photographed by Helmet Gernsheim for his book *Twelfth Century Paintings at Hardham and Clayton,* published by Miller's Press (the ladies of Miller's) at Lewes in 1947. CB wrote an introductory essay to the book.

told me he had something to show me and when he had got rid of some Jews who seemed to be buying a Gainsborough he took me into the back room and there was a fairly large painting by Giorgione. It sounds almost incredible, but apparently Colin bought it at a sale some time ago when it was filthy and very much repainted. He had it cleaned and during the war kept it in the country so hardly anyone has seen it. Of course I am no judge of its genuineness, but it seemed to me an amazing work. It's a painting of St George who is in brilliant armour, holding up a vermilion flag with one hand against a very intense blue sky and standing on a dragon. It's unfinished, very freely painted but with complete certainty, and the colour is astonishing. I wish you could see it but you probably will, for it will be there for a long time. Also I hope possibly it may get bought for the Nation, although apparently Kenneth who has seen it and agrees in thinking it by Giorgione, takes no steps to buy it because (according to Colin Agnew) he also saw it at the sale and ought to have bought it then when it was very cheap. This may not be true, but anyhow we are going to try to get Maynard to see it and perhaps a subscription could be got up. I found it very exciting. Well, then I had lunch with my old friend Snow, who really has become rather old. I suppose I am in the same boat, but it was rather a shock after not seeing her for 6 years to find she had the voice and manner of a real old lady. Still she has her charm of character, though she finds life worrying, what with traffic and a house to run and no servants. After lunch we went round to 41 which is in rather a chaotic state with James' furniture standing about. I labelled all I could see that I felt sure was ours and made a list and shall get Gander to fetch it when they bring back Duncan's pictures. I had forgotten that you had two chests of drawers of ours, but I felt sure the ugly brown one used to be here, so I labelled it.

I was forgetting to tell you that on the evening before, after our church visit, I had my first pig club meeting. You may find me in prison as a result—I shouldn't be surprised. It was amusing but rather alarming, for I realised as never before the underworld of law dodging that goes on. It happened that the Pig Council had made a mistake and sent me coupons for food for the wrong month. My natural instinct would have been to return them, but when I produced them at the meeting I found that this was far from being anyone else's natural instinct. In fact, it didn't occur to them as possible, and they simply jumped at the unexpected luck, and said what I only hope is true, that we couldn't possibly be found out. Anyhow I hadn't the courage to disagree, so there I am, committed to an offence against the law in company with Mr Toms, Mr Jordan (the barber), Becket and Dick [local working men]. Ruby our other member wasn't there, and after Mr Toms and Mr Jordan had gone, Becket, Dick and I, left over our beer, found that the coupons left to us couldn't be exactly divided between 4. So the next step was that Dick and Becket decided it was quite unnecessary to give Ruby her share! As they were a gift from the blue she need never know anything about them, they said. It then appeared that they owed Ruby a grudge because she employed Becket to look after her pig for several months and in the end gave him a one and fourpenny packet of cigarettes. So I, very weakly I suppose, agreed to the second deceit and proceeded to hear endless stories of black market transactions of every kind. Becket then suggested getting Maynard to be our President, on the ground that if we got into court he could get us out as he got Edgar³—but I hear Maynard, perhaps wisely, refuses. Don't, by the way, leave this letter to be read by someone like Eddy Playfair who would think it his duty to inform against me at once. In spite of all these doubtful transactions it was a very amusing evening and we sate on till after 11. The curious thing is that though these rustics can really hardly read or write— even Becket reads anything aloud in a very halting way and Dick was incapable of spelling anything—yet they are in some ways very sharp indeed—too sharp, you may think. But they understood practical arrangements far better than I do, at any rate more quickly. It's curious to have got into such society, for one is on quite different terms with them than one is as a rule . . .

Much love darling.

Your
VB

This envelope once enclosed a letter of the most fulsome flattery about Berwick Church from the Colebox!

ANGELICA GARNETT

³Edgar Weller, JMK's chauffeur, formerly a soldier in Jamaica, where he contracted malaria, drank heavily. On one occasion he was charged with disorderly conduct and violence. JMK hired formidable legal aid and gave evidence of good character; the malaria was blamed, and Edgar acquitted. In 1937 he unaccountably shot the gamekeeper Churchill's dog.

CHAPTER NINE

1946–1961

Although the work of Duncan and Vanessa was well out of fashion by the end of the war, interest in Bloomsbury as a social phenomenon was just beginning to get under way. Vanessa, who sometimes found herself approached by scholars, could be aloof and forbidding. Leonard was in fact supportive of many Virginia Woolf scholars, and after Virginia's death he spent much of his working life publishing her essays and corresponding with those interested in her work. The family position was that publication of a biography—or any unexpurgated Bloomsbury letters—was impossible while so many of the principals were alive, and in light of obscenity laws.[1]

Although Vanessa consented to read her Memoir Club paper on Virginia's childhood on BBC Radio in August 1956 she remained opposed to Bloomsbury scholarship in general and did not welcome the publication of her friends' memoirs. This was an aspect of her distaste for publicity. She could, however, be extremely generous with other scholars. She enjoyed talking with Noel Annan about Sir Leslie, for instance. And when the photographer and art historian Helmut Gernsheim wrote inquiring about the work of Julia Margaret Cameron, Vanessa entertained him over tea and showed him her collection

---

[1]James Strachey and Leonard did eventually publish a bowdlerized edition of the correspondence between Virginia and Lytton in 1956. And of course the question of an authorized Woolf biography was settled in the mid-1960s when Quentin Bell accepted Leonard's invitation to undertake the work.

of her great-aunt's photographs. Clarence Cline, editor of George Meredith's letters, wrote asking if she had any letters from Meredith to Sir Leslie. Vanessa willingly searched both Charleston and her London house for him.

With the destruction of her Fitzroy Street studio, Vanessa found herself without a secure London abode. She and Duncan moved several times after the war, finally settling in 1955 in the Percy Street flat vacated by Saxon Sydney-Turner when he moved into a nursing home. Charleston had become her principal residence, however. After the mid-1950s she traveled to London only for specific occasions, to meet Angelica or Quentin, for exhibitions, Memoir Club gatherings, and the meetings of The Society of Mural Artists or the committee of the Edwin Austin Abbey Memorial Trust Fund for Mural Painting, which she joined in 1949. Her last major decorative commission came at the end of the war, when she and Duncan executed decorations based on "Cinderella" for the children's restaurant at Devonshire Hill School. She also contributed tile paintings for King's College Garden Annexe, careful to avoid figural motifs which might invite emendation by undergraduates. Several attempts to sell her and Duncan's designs for wallpapers and textiles failed, though some of Angelica's designs were better received: a comment not only on their daughter's talents, but also on how out-of-date the Bloomsbury artists' work had become. Both continued to show their paintings successfully, however, Vanessa holding her last one-artist exhibition at the Adams Gallery in 1956. Of her late work, the still lifes show the most strength and continuity, faithful to her own dictum never to become mechanical, but to base each brushstroke on close observation.

Aside from her painting, Vanessa's great delights in old age were travel and her grandchildren. With rationing of some foods in England lingering as late as 1954, the everyday gastronomic joys of France and Italy took on special significance. Vanessa and Duncan made almost yearly trips abroad, returning especially to Venice. When in England, Vanessa shamelessly indulged her grandchildren, almost continually at work on some small gift for one of them. Henrietta Garnett has described her visits to Charleston, where her grandparents induced her and Amaryllis to sit to them, usually in fancy dress, for sixpence an hour each.

To Henrietta, her grandmother's physical appearance was still impressive: "Tall, thin, stooping with the elegance of a silver spoon, she had beautifully expressive eyes, the colour of grey-blue pebbles which were scattered on the paths in the walled garden. Many of the clothes she wore, she made herself. . . . She was not a good dress-maker, but, in spite of her clothes being badly cut, she wore them with a grace which defied the cobbled stitches" (*Charleston Past and Present,* 154). Yet Bernard Berenson, who saw Vanessa in Italy in the 1950s, reportedly thought she looked heavy and dirty. Angelica considered her mother's dark, untidy clothing "a further expression of her disappointment in herself," not unrelated to Vanessa's denigration of her own painting (AVG, 167).

Some late photographs of Vanessa emphasize this severity of dress and expression, especially those in which she looks directly at the camera. She is best caught in profile or near profile, relaxed, unaware she is being observed. And though it is true that the death of Julian cast a shadow over Vanessa's late years, it is impossible to read these letters without a sense of how much happiness she still had.

IX-1. To Angelica Garnett

Sunday, Ap. 21 [1946]   **Charleston**

My own darling,

You will have heard before you get this of Maynard's sudden death this morning. He came to tea on Thursday and seemed very well and in good spirits. It is still very difficult to realise.

I am going to see Quentin to tell him in case otherwise he only hears on the wireless.

Old Mrs Keynes[1] happens to be staying at Tilton which is a good thing I think for Lydia, and I believe Geoffrey is coming later.

He died this morning before getting out of bed, and Logan came to tell us.

I will write again but thought you might like to have a note and much love from Duncan and

Your
VB

ANGELICA GARNETT

[1]Florence Ada Keynes (née Brown) (1861–1958), an activist for women's rights.

IX-2. To Margery Fry

May 20, 1946   *Charleston, Firle,*
                                                              Sussex

My dear Margery,

This is to let you know that the things you lent to Miller's[1] will be returned to you by carrier on Tuesday next, May 28th. I am sending a catalogue in case you care to see it, and Mrs Byng Stamper and her sister want me to say how grateful they are to you for lending so much. The carpet especially looked very splendid hanging in the middle of one wall. It doesn't seem to be the least the worse for wear after I suppose about 30 years. I must say that after all this time I was surprised to find how good things were. I suppose one was very much excited at the time and then went through a period of being rather critical, but now after so long one can look with a fresh eye, and I think Roger's things especially, of which there are far more than there are of any other one person, are more impressive. Of course the pottery is lovely, especially the service lent by the Bethnal Green Museum, which is really exquisite. How I wish one could get more moulds made of it. But also his paintings and furniture and stuffs all come out extraordinarily well.

I wish you could see it, but I suppose you won't have time to do so. However the ladies of Miller's would be delighted if you possibly could go to Lewes any day this week and would lunch with them at the White Hart, which is in the High St., 5 minutes walk from the station. You have only to send them a card. I am at the moment overwhelmed by grandchildren who have been deposited here while Angelica has a rather badly needed holiday from them in Northumberland, otherwise I should suggest meeting you if you could get away. But they are complete tyrants, though adorable ones.

Love from
Vanessa

BELL

[1]An exhibition of work from the Omega Workshops had been held at Miller's Gallery.

IX-3. To Angelica Garnett

Tuesday, Sep. 17 [1946]   *Hôtel du Rhin, Dieppe*

My own darling,

So much seems to have happened since I sent you a hurried scrawl and a cheque last week that I hardly know where to begin. I seemed to have endless business to transact at the end concerning pig club, chicken food, ration books, etc., but I should have been ready in good time if Edward [Le Bas] hadn't turned up about 4 o'clock when I was the only person at home to entertain him, so that I didn't get all done and packed till about 1.30 AM with the prospect of rising soon after 5. However, we did get up, had some coffee, packed all our luggage, paint boxes, canvases, etc., into the car quite in the old style, and to my great relief got to Newhaven, without a puncture, before 7 . . .

Yesterday, Monday, was lovely in the morning and we all went out sketching—rather an alarming procedure always in a town, but Dieppe is really so lovely that one gets over one's nerves. I encouraged myself by remembering how I used to face the Roman crowds and used to walk miles carrying my apparatus through the Borghese gardens. Things here are much nearer at hand and the French on the whole don't bother about one much. They must be used to painters too here. The colour of everything is curiously lovely. One can see how well it suited Sickert, all these subtle greys and dingy greens and reds—nearly every street makes one want to paint it. The inside of the town behind the harbour isn't nearly so much damaged, in fact it's surprisingly little so on the whole. Sometimes one comes on little crosses saying that a Canadian soldier was killed there and bullet holes in the *pissotières*,[1] small things which seem to make the fighting more real than these great masses of ruins.

Today after sketching again in the morning until it began to pour we went off to lunch at Auppegard. That was a curious experience. The house has been terribly damaged by a flying bomb which exploded near. They have managed to repair the worst things and when one drives up to it [it] is still very lovely. But inside only the dining room is usable, and they have hardly any furniture and just enough for themselves. Poor old things—as they say, they are too old to begin

---

[1] Public urinals. The word can also mean "dribbling fountain."

all over again and they certainly do look very aged and decrepit. However they gave us one of the most heavenly lunches I have ever had. First melon—that was nothing out of the way. Then veal done in the most succulent and delicious juice with carrots, with it a perfect puree of potato and beans—done I should think with butter and cream. Masses of butter. *Delicious* butter, and bread to eat too and wine of course. Then pears cooked quite simply with a sour milk or cream with them and masses of fresh cream. Perhaps it doesn't sound very much out of the way, but the veal was so well done and so were the vegetables that one felt as if one hadn't tasted such cooking for years. After all this and liqueurs Duncan and I had to pull ourselves together and set to work to try to restore our paintings in the loggia, which had got a good deal faded and in some places been touched up by the Germans. We did quite a lot but shall have to go again. In fact we shall have to see a certain amount of them but they are really easier and nicer I think in their old age. Perhaps having to live such a much simpler life has improved them. Though Nan, or The Iron Duke as Edward calls her, is really a perfectly simple and sympathetic character. She told us an extraordinary story about her car, when they had a bad accident with it as they fled from the Germans. I think they collided with a lorry. Anyhow, the car was overturned and Ethel quite badly hurt. When Nan saw this she naturally gave all her attention to getting Ethel looked after and the car was left apparently useless and upset by the side of the road. This was in 1940. In 1941 she got a letter, very well written and charming, from a French officer saying that he had found the car when he and 3 others were trying to escape being taken prisoners and had found that though all the windows were broken, etc., the engine was all right. So they had fled in it and got to Carcassonne and escaped. The car was left there and he wrote to Nan about it and thank[ed] her for the use of it. She heard from him again last year, giving her the name of someone who might help her to find out what had happened to the car, but naturally after so long it had disappeared—only this romantic liaison between Nan and the French officer is the result, and she feels that her car has done its duty . . .

Goodnight darling,

Your
VB

ANGELICA GARNETT

IX-4. To Jane Bussy

Dec. 20 [1946]   *Charleston*

Dearest Janie,

I don't know how much family news has reached you from your own family, so you must put up with it if all I tell you is stale (I seem to have said that before?) The twins [Frances and Nerissa] of course you know about, and you can imagine that the news of two and both female was not received with unmixed joy in this house, though apparently the father at least was quite content. Still, 4 daughters, the eldest 3 years old! From a detached point of view, there were drawbacks. But when after 4 or 5 days it turned out that they were seriously ill and had to be taken off to hospital, one's only feelings were of course acute anxiety and longing to hear they were better. I was very much tied here by the other two, but did manage to get up and see Angelica who was amazingly calm and sensible and the only person able to give one a clear account of all. If they hadn't been at 51 (largely thanks to you) the elder twin, Frances, would certainly have died. It was only because the doctor was on the spot and could get all she wanted that the baby was saved. Just think if they had been miles from anyone at Hilton or high up in 2 rooms in Bond St! As it is, what a comfort it must have been to know there were kind sensible people in the house and Elizabeth[1] who has been angelic and the Gt. Ormond St. hospital[2] which is said to be the best in the world round the corner. Even so, they have been a trying time with ups and downs, but I think at last are really better, as they have been allowed to come home with a very good nurse to look after them, and Angelica will no longer have to go 3 times a day to the hospital to feed them . . .

Quentin is entering I think on an era of prosperity. His pots sell like hot cakes. He goes to London with a carpet bag full and returns with it empty and orders for more. Harrods' man wants to come here and see for himself, and there's a man in Kensington (name magnanimously given by Phyllis [Keyes] in the last encounter) who seems willing to buy any quantity of *sgraffito* work. Q. goes on experimenting all the time and I think is getting daily technically better. He always has masses of new ideas and all that is wanted I believe is that

[1]Housekeeper to Pippa and Marjorie Strachey at 51 Gordon Square.
[2]The Great Ormond Street Hospital for Sick Children.

he should get the details to have a sufficient degree of finish. People don't like roughnesses, etc. But that will come I'm sure, and we shall all be able to make a little extra cash by twiddling our brushes about on his pots. Next summer you and Angelica must prepare for hard labour in the pottery while I mind the family of 4 elsewhere. I don't say that's what I choose, but what I think likely to happen.

Is there any other news? You can't expect much as for the last 6 weeks I have been grandmother only. No more communication with P.K.[3] beyond a very short note written to Duncan reminding him that he was to paint tiles for her. I hope he'll soon do so. The Art World seems to have exhausted its rage over the question of cleaning pictures. It's odd how the R.A.'s were all in favour of dirt and the highbrows of cleanliness. But really the Nat. Gallery is now a blaze of glory. The Rubenses knock one down with their brilliance and to my mind it's all to the good. The Chapeau de Paille I am sure cannot have been spoiled in any way for the modelling of the flesh is incredibly subtle and lovely (but I expect you have already seen this?). The Rembrandt woman walking into the water is full of beauties one only guessed at before. It's true one hand looks sketchy, but I've no doubt it's true the paint removed was later touching up. The chemise, etc., are so lovely and the head most beautifully modelled. I long to see the Velasquez portrait of Philip old, which Edward Le Bas has seen half cleaned. He said it was astonishing, the cleaned part looking incredibly old—and in his view certainly much more as it must have been originally, and with the most exquisitely subtle painting of hair and side of face.

Well, I mustn't go on giving you second hand reports of picture cleaning, but the only other subject in the art world seems to be the crucifixion painted for Norwich Cathedral[4] by Mr Sutherland, with K. Clark gazing at it in a knowing way and Mr S. himself looking in awe and rapture and 2 studies beside to show how hard he has worked. Yes, I'm very catty naturally, having done rival works at Berwick, but you'll allow for that and judge for yourself. I deplore the fact, as it seems to me, that a charming, sensitive, gifted young man should be turned from his true vocation of decorating tea cups and designing cretonnes, which he really does very well, and made to think he's the

---

[3]Phyllis Keyes had shown evidence of a strong attraction to DG.
[4]Actually St. Matthew's Church, Northampton. The dean of the Northampton church was a keen collector and patron of modern art and also commissioned a Henry Moore Madonna and Child for his church.

El Greco of our age and country. But it's only Picture Post which has roused me to this tirade, and the fact that I'm in bed with nothing to do but pour out to you, and I daresay really no one will take any notice. Certainly by the time this gets to Nice it will fall very flat . . .

We are simply living on the fat of the land, you'll be surprised to hear. At this moment a turkey, a hare, a few pheasants, a present of good steak from Ireland (to be eaten tonight as a *boeuf en daube* with real olive oil presented by Clive's little Barbara⁵), besides I suppose our normal rations repose in the larder. Wines and spirits are said to be waiting to be brought up from the cottages. Last night Quentin and I indulged in a bottle of white wine. So you see a miserable pound or two of extras may well be sent to our friends in France, whom I prefer I must say to unknown Germans, two of whom, all the same, are lunching with Grace on Christmas Day.

This is a rambling dotty letter I'm afraid dear Janie, but I send all my love to you all. Any news of you will be welcome.

Your
VB

BUSSY

IX-5. To Keith Baynes

Ap. 30, 1947   ***Charleston, Firle, Sussex***

Dear Keith,

I've had a letter from the unfortunate Patricia Preece (Mrs Stanley Spencer in reality I believe)¹ asking me if I'll propose her as a member of the London Group. She says of course that it's almost impossible to exist as a painter now, she can't show anywhere or sell anything

---

⁵Barbara Bagenal had become CB's companion.
¹The painter (Sir) Stanley Spencer (1891–1959) had divorced his wife Hilda and married Patricia Preece in 1937. They did not live together, and Spencer became quickly disillusioned, his first warning being her insistence that Dorothy Hepworth share their honeymoon.
VB was unable to persuade Keith Baynes to vote this year for Preece's membership in the London Group, and in fact Preece never became a member.

and all prices have gone up so much. I quite understand no one wanting to show her and even her being refused, as I believe she was by the L.G. last year, for her pictures are apt to be most unattractive. Still I do think she has great merits and really ought to be a member. I believe no proposing is necessary, is it, and all she need do is to send works to be voted on. I have promised to vote for her, which is all I can do. Will you also do so unless you have conscientious objections? I feel that even if her work happens to be unsympathetic in many ways, still she is the sort of artist we ought to support. She is gifted and very serious and needs encourgement badly.

I shall come on the 15th to the judging and electing but may not be able to come on the 14th also.

Don't trouble to answer this.

> *Yours ever,*
> *Vanessa Bell*

BAYNES

IX-6. To Angelica Garnett

Sep. 14 [1947]   *Charleston, Firle, Sussex*

My own darling,

I had no time to write more than a card yesterday, but I thought you might want to make arrangements. We could meet you for a zoo party on either Thursday or Friday next, as you like, or you may prefer to wait till you come here. Let me know. But it seemed too much of a rush for a visit from you now. Not only must Duncan go and see his mother the day before we leave, and I have one or two shoppings to do, but Sue is coming here[1] on Monday for a night or possibly two, I'm not sure. She has been in France and all over the place most of the summer as far as I can make out, so I think I must have her now she can come. I have been unlucky in the people I have introduced her to. Waley evidently didn't take to her, pretended he was just going abroad and has never seen her again, and Old Gumbo

[1]Ling Su-Hua settled in England in the winter of 1946–47.

is horrified by her emotionalism and only accepts her as a pupil because she gets some rice out of her. Luckily Clive liked her and so does Duncan and so in fact do I—but of course it's difficult to provide a circle of friends, which is what she really wants, and one can't have her here constantly. However we shall see what happens. I hope it will be fine and she can sit and draw the willows as she did before . . .

I was fascinated by your account of Helen and her entourage. I too thought her most elegant and diminutive when she was here and she sounds gay as a lark. But no word of Ba and [Igor]. Talking of our dilapidated houses—you can't imagine what a whited palace this is becoming. I've had my 3 old men here again and the whole of Quentin's library and other possessions have been turned upside down and his room made snow white and pearl grey. I haven't dared to tell him, but I've marked everything carefully and am putting all back again, only cleaned and polished. I only hope, and expect, he won't notice. Still it really is a change for the better. Also I've had the bathroom done. So gradually the whole house will shine with cleanliness. And we haven't got a high road and railway line a few yards off, thank goodness.[2] But I must confess that our garden is a desert. I am reduced to putting seeding willow herb into vases as there are practically no flowers still alive, but it's really very beautiful. D. and I have been going mad over sketching out of doors—never have I done so much. We went to see the Constables, etc., at the Tate which rather egged us on too. They are so alive and fresh and look as if they had been done so directly. One can't see why one shouldn't do likewise.

I must some day tell you about our dinner last Sunday at Tilton to meet Sheppard. I have never known him so brilliant. He told us at great length and in minute detail the story of the Royal visit to Trinity [College, Cambridge]. He was almost reduced to tears by the emotions roused by both their majesties—especially of course the Queen—who at one moment said to him as they sate chatting in a small tent envied by all the other dons and ladies of Cambridge, "You have a very fine head of hair, Mr Sheppard. But I am sure you must be feeling the heat—take my parasol." Can you envisage Sheppard holding a frivolous parasol over his white head and almost beside himself with joy, and think of all the other dons who probably hadn't such fine heads of hair and some of whom according to him had been trying to chip

[2]The reference is to Helen's Suffolk house, Rodwell House, Baylham, which, though surrounded by farmland, does have a road running immediately in front of it, and a railway line beyond.

into the conversation. But Sheppard must be made to tell it all again. I'm sure there's nothing he'd like better. Also how at a ceremony at Eton when he had to bow to the King, he lost his balance and found himself being supported by H.M., who held him firmly and kindly while Sheppard gazed into the Royal eyes and clung to the Royal hand till he got on his feet again . . .

Your
VB

ANGELICA GARNETT

IX-7. To Amaryllis and Henrietta Garnett

Monday [December 8, 1947]   *Charleston*

My darling Amaryllis and Henrietta,

What a lovely letter I got from you today. I went into the kitchen to make tea and I looked to see if the postman had been but I didn't much expect him to have left a letter for me, and then I saw there *was* one with your names outside and you can't think how excited I was. A real letter from those two clever creatures, I thought. I showed it to Grace and she read it too. The kitchen table has 5 Christmas puddings sitting on it which she has made. I wish you were going to help to eat them, but you will have lots of your own at Hilton I am sure. Now I must think what news I have for you. It has been raining cats and dogs here. Has it been at your home? It has rained so hard that a lot of water which should have run in a drain underground from the farm has burst out and made a pond near my bee hive— quite a large pond. I expect you would try to get into it if you were here. The ducks and the geese are very happy and swim about quacking and cackling and enjoying themselves so much that they won't come home to bed, naughty creatures.

When it gets fine I do some gardening and I wish I had you to help me. Do you remember how you took all the dead plants away for me and how useful you were? That is just what I want doing now. But I daresay you have lots to do in your own garden. I wonder how much

French you can talk. *Bonjour* and *petite fille* and *petit garçon* and I expect a lot more by now.

When you write me another letter I think you must send me a drawing too.

This is Amaryllis going for a ride on a rather odd pony and on the other side is Henrietta on a *very* odd donkey

who doesn't want to go, so Amaryllis has to hold a carrot in front of his nose, but you can't see her as she keeps just out of reach.

Goodbye my darling creatures.

Your
Nessa

ANGELICA GARNETT

IX-8. To Angelica Garnett

May 9 [1948?]   **Charleston, Firle, Sussex**

My own darling,

... I believe Henrietta's birthday is next Saturday isn't it. I hope
to send off a rather peculiar present in a day or two, but I shall send
it to you and you can give it as if it came by post to her on the right
day or as you think best. The fact is it's a home-made doll and I know
your eagle eye will find much to criticize, but I hope H.'s eye may be
less acute. I thought it would be fun to try to make one, little knowing
the difficulties. So I started gaily with the idea of *papier-mâché*. Then
I found one must have a foundation and I made a doll's head in
plasticine. I got so fascinated by trying to model a head that I took
a long time over it, little realising the problems to come. However at
last I finished it and started putting on layer after layer of paper. I put
it on much too thin at first, because of course it's very small, so I had
in the end to put on what seemed endless layers of paper, then I had
to get it off the head, a desperate proceeding (with advice from Q.,
who's an expert of course). Then the real difficulties began of a body
and arms and legs. Oh dear, I fear she's no beauty in regard to figure
or extremities. I did my best however and filled her with sawdust and
she began to have a curious life of her own. I painted her head and
shellaced her, so I hope the paint won't come off too easily, and I got
some sham hair. And now I've made her a dress and pettitcoat and
knickers, and you *can* take them off and and put them on with care.
I hoped to make other things but shan't have time. Altogether I daresay
it's all been more of an amusement to me than it will be to Henrietta,
but one never knows. She *may* adore her. I feel she ought to have a
name, but I think you would be better at choosing one—Rosalba?
That is my only suggestion.

Today the poor old willow has been cut up and almost completely
dragged away by the Wests and Jack Standen [local men] with the
tractor. Axes have been ringing and saws sawing, and it all looks very
bare. Duncan and Quentin have a plan for erecting a large statue on
the site. I think it would be lovely but will make us almost too peculiar.
However I suppose that doesn't matter. Our black dining room[1] is

---

[1]The Charleston dining room has now been restored to this period. Issue 5
(Summer-Autumn 1992) of the *Charleston Magazine* reproduces the wallpaper
on its cover.

surprisingly successful with the natives, who are full of admiration, and so perhaps Antinöus[2] reflected in the pond would appeal to them too. I refuse to have Mouie's statue[3] in a more conspicuous place than it is now . . .

But we must meet soon and talk of everything. I long to show you the garden, now a miracle of beauty, flowers in full blossom and lots just about to be, the brooder full of most active and healthy chicks, the Vactric which runs about polishing the floors, my new frames, and the black dining room. But really I don't think anything has changed very much. Nothing like your vast cupboard and cow shed.

I hope Bunny remembers the Memoir Club on the 24th when he is to read Maynard's memoir I believe.

Goodnight dearest,

Your loving
VB

ANGELICA GARNETT

IX-9. To Angelica Garnett

Feb. 27 [1949]   *Charleston, Firle, Sussex*

My own darling,

. . . I seem to have an incredibly easy life now that young Mr Stevens[1] has come on the scenes. One never feels guilty because all sorts of things are getting neglected in the garden. He is a charming old man, very kind and gentle and with great character. I have fallen very much in love with him and have some hopes that it is partially returned, for the other day he told me that coming here exactly suited him and he would make my garden lovely. I can hardly believe in

[2]A plaster cast of Antinöus stood on the far side of the pond at Charleston. It eventually fell apart and was replaced in 1954 by a female figure in ciment fondu by QB.
[3]Mouie (Caroline Lucas) had given DG a small abstract sculpture that was barely visible on the orchard side of the pond.
[1]The son of old Mr. Stevens, Charleston gardener between the wars, and his wife (who lived to within a few days of her hundredth birthday). Young Mr. Stevens was about seventy years old at the time of this letter.

such luck. Also, strange to say, Quentin has taken to doing all sorts of major works in the garden and orchard by way of exercise. He is making a path, which is going to be brick, round the inside of the walled garden where there are no flower beds and which was simply weeds. So one will walk round and pick one's pears and peaches. He sprays trees and plants supports for apple trees, all in a most profound and professional manner. You'll really have to come and admire before long. Also we must soon continue the mosaic—I'm sure you'll be necessary for that.

Yesterday I went to see Leonard who never has enough petrol to come here now. He is building a studio! That's to say Virginia's old garden room began to collapse, or the roof did, and so he is now having it added on to and made about twice as long with high windows. It ought to make quite a good one and will I suppose be used by Trekkie who has no room with a good light in her own house. He had some lovely little daffodils and cyclamen, also those dark irises, reticulata, I think. He told me that when he was planting them Virginia put her head out of the window in the house and called out, "Hitler is making a speech. Do you want to come and hear him?" Leonard called back, "No, I'm planting my irises and they'll be flowering long after Hitler is dead"—very characteristic of both. He has been asked to write a life of the Sidney Webbs by the executors.[2] Of course it would be a terrific job taking about 3 years, he thought, but I think he's rather pleased at being asked and I tried to encourage him. It seems to me much better to do something like that rather than go to all these committee meetings. Beatrice Webb's diaries which he would see in full are fascinating, he says. She was completely outspoken and very biting.

Leonard gave me a box of letters which had been sent to him by those old solicitors who used to be their tenants in Tavistock Sqre. I expect lots of letters and books got scattered and mixed up during the blitz and they found these among their papers. Most are letters from the American ambassador [James Russell] Lowell to my mother. He must really have been more interesting than his letters, which are highly polished and very dull, but I think he was a good deal in love with her, which accounts I suppose for her feeling for him. Anyhow they constantly talk of her beauty and charm. I only wish one had hers to him, for evidently she wrote a great deal about her children, especially Virginia who was his god-child (so to speak) and there are

[2]He declined the offer.

tantalising references to stories about her. There are also one or two characteristic notes from Henry James after Lowell's death. Leonard so hates reading old letters that he's thankful to hand them on to me. I agree they're rather melancholy but also fascinating. I enjoy getting new lights on people's relationships in the past . . .

Now it's really time this came to an end, more than time, so good night.

All my love to the family.

Your
VB

Let me know if you think of going to London at any time. We shall be there for the night of Thursday week, March [blank in original] when Angus is dining with us at T[aviton] St.!

ANGELICA GARNETT

IX-10. To Helen Anrep

Sep. 9 [1949]   *Albergo Universo, Lucca [Italy]*

Dearest Helen,

I said I'd write to you from Lucca and as you know I'm a woman of my word. But I daresay you'd think it all very dull, and so it is, to write about. All the same, I wish you were here. We had a terrific journey out. First a day in Paris which was very hard work. We had to go to the lithographer patronised by the Ladies of Miller's and spend the morning being shown how to get the effects one wants, which is by no means easy when you're doing coloured ones. It seems to me the French print so much better than the English that I think it's worthwhile getting them to do it if one can produce enough French money to pay for it. We met Angelica up for the day from her French country house[1] which I think she is enjoying—perhaps not as much as Venice last year, but still she has a *bonne* to do everything and so she manages to get quite a lot of time for painting . . .

[1]AVG's French country house was that of her old friends Zoum and François Walter, where she was staying with Amaryllis and Henrietta.

We had a heavenly meal with Angelica at the Medicis Grill, very expensive, but such as one hasn't tasted since one was last there. The French have returned completely to their own standard of food and even coffee. They say they have no vegetables owing to the drought, but such as they have are delicious salads or other things cooked in butter. It's a comfort to find the standard kept up and not destroyed even by Hitler.

Edward Le Bas who had been touring Brittany for a week in a car with Eardley Knollys[2] said the food was wonderful and every little hotel delightful. He gave us the only piece of English news we have had—that Eddie S.-West has become a Catholic. What next? Really it seems to me almost too silly a thing even for him to do, and silly as he may be he *is* intelligent. What will Raymond and the others think of it?

Well, then we went on to Milan, leaving Paris at an unearthly hour in the morning and reaching Milan at midnight. There it was very hot and it's a horrible place. However we spent 2 nights there as E. had old friends he had to see and D. and I went to see the Leonardo Last Supper. It's a miracle it wasn't destroyed. Bombs seem to have fallen within a few feet and all round, but they sandbagged it so well that it seems unhurt and it is really very lovely. One saw it better than I remembered, by itself at the end of the long empty refectory. It is really an extraordinary composition and even still lovely colour. I was glad to have the chance of seeing it again. All the galleries were shut up or being restored. Only that horrible cathedral[3] is untouched. I suppose nothing would make us or the Americans blow it up, but otherwise there is a lot of damage. Then we went on to Parma and spent a night there and found it really too hot, and then came here by a very slow crowded train stopping hours everywhere and getting hotter and hotter but into more lovely country. At last we got here and here we shall stay, I think. There's no doubt it's a place for painters if for no one else. I suppose there's not very much to see but nearly every building is wonderful in a slightly austere way and from the ramparts all round the town one sees hills not too large or too near.

2Edward Eardley Knollys (1902–91), owner with the artist Frank Coombs of the Storran Gallery (1936–39), which exhibited work by DG and VB. He was a great friend of Edward Sackville-West, Raymond Mortimer, and Desmond Shawe-Taylor, and shared with them a country home, Long Crichel, in Dorset. Late in life he became a painter.
3The façade of the Milan Cathedral bristles with 135 pinnacles and is a fine example of the Flamboyant Gothic, a period for which VB had no sympathy.

At first the heat was terrific and one could only walk a few yards and collapse from exhaustion, but it is actually a little cooler now and I suppose it is sure to go on getting cooler. We find the only thing to do is get up at 6 and go out painting early. Then one loafs about and wanders into cool churches and buys skirts and handkerchiefs and has lunch and a siesta, and then paints again in the evening. The days seem to rush by and already one has been here nearly a week. I had a card from Quentin who sounded enraptured with Venice. I wonder if Claude and Elsie [Rogers] ever got there. Somehow I doubt it. But they really ought to go. I think more and more that painters *must* go to Italy. There's no people like the Italians for purely visual gift, even now and even in a hotel like this they still have extraordinary taste and paint their walls lovely pale greys and greens and not the eternal "cream" one always finds in England. How I wish you were doing as I am and just choosing what you'll eat without knowing how it's come by and never dreaming of doing any housework or spending your points or wondering what you'll eat when your meat ration is done. England seems to be the only country where one still has to do such things. We have met no one we know, in fact there are practically no English here, only a few Americans, and no other painters.

. . . I know nothing of news in England. Anything may be happening, but I don't suppose it is more than usual. Clive writes from Charleston which sounds as hot as it is here. He enjoyed his jaunt to Aix with Mary enormously and they saw a great deal of the Duthuits and old Mme Matisse who lives there. He went to see the Teeds at Cassis and says the place is completely ruined by huge new hotels and roads and Marseilles trippers with their cars. Fontcreuse and La Bergère however are quite unchanged.

This long letter must stop. Will you ever get through it, still more will you ever answer it? and tell me about yourself and your family. I hope they're behaving. Probably you are housing Igor's wife and family. Are you? As long as it's not Sylvia Goff[4] I'll forgive you.

Love from
V

ANREP

[4]Sylvia Gough, whom Helen had known casually for some years, had insinuated herself into Helen's London home and could not be dislodged. She was poor and, according to VB, an alcoholic.

IX-11. To Angelica Garnett

Oct. 5 [1949]   *Hôtel d'Angleterre, Rue Jacob, Paris*

My own darling,

... Well I must tell you some of our doings though I hope to see you in less than a week. We went to Siena by bus, a rather jolty proceeding but a wonderful way of seeing the country, which is incredibly beautiful. Some of it is very bare, pale brown earth with small towns perched high up. San Gimignano, the most ancient looking of all places, said to have been destroyed, was quite untouched and to D.'s great excitement Certaldo, where he had stayed at the age of 17 with the daughter of an English clergyman who lived there— the sort of thing he used to do. She must have been very nice and intelligent for she sent him off to Siena alone for a bit to see the *palio*.[1] He very much enjoyed that but actually wouldn't go and look at the great paintings by Lorenzetti because Berenson had written about them, praising them! So we saw them all this time. The Italians now seem to have taken everything from the churches and put them into museums where one sees them much better of course and so there was quite a lot to see. The first day D. had a nightmarish adventure. We all went out to look about the town and then coming back he said (as usual) he'd buy some cigarettes and follow us to the hotel, pointing out the way to us. We followed his directions and found it was wrong, but I soon remembered the right way and we (E. and I) got back and supposed D. would do the same. But he, gone wrong also, then found he couldn't remember the name of the hotel! There are quite a lot and he was absolutely at sea, not knowing where to go or what to ask for. After a time he stumbled on it, for it's not a very big place as you may remember but I can see one would feel in a dream. Siena is one of the most exquisite though very austere places as even E. had to admit. In fact he was overcome by its beauty. Then we went to Pisa by train. That also had a nightmarish quality in a different way. Never have I seen such destruction. Everything, including the station, seemed to have been laid flat. One picked one's way over rubble, and everyone looked depressed and worried, and

---

[1] Il Palio di Siena, a horse race held in the central Piazza del Campo each July and August in which the different districts of Siena compete. The winning horse attends the victory banquet and eats from its own manger.

the sky grew dark and it began to drizzle. We made our way to the Leaning Tower which would be lovely if it didn't lean and to the baptistry and all there seemed untouched. But when we got to the Campo Santo which used to have wonderful frescoes on the walls round the enclosed space it was really horrifying. The old man in charge told us that the Americans and Germans had fought each other in the air over it. It was the evening of a very hot day and everything was very dry and the lead on the roof very hot. Shells set fire to it and the roof all the way round collapsed and the lead melted—one could see where it had run. But the most extraordinary thing has happened to the frescoes. They had nearly all been destroyed but they left behind the drawings underneath. Apparently the painters—one by Giotto he said and some by Lorenzetti and others—did very elaborate but very free drawings first on the wall. Then they covered them bit by bit with fresh plaster and painted on each bit. So one now can see a good many of the original drawings which were fascinating. It is odd to think that they would never have been seen again if it hadn't been for the Germans and Americans fighting over them. Still of course the destruction is appalling and lots have vanished completely.

Pisa wasn't ever a lovely place and as it soon began to pour and a terrific thunderstorm went on all night with rain pouring from broken gutters it was rather gloomy, and Duncan and I left early the next morning for Milan. I can't bear Milan, even the ices don't reconcile me, and when we got there we had a dreary time . . .

Perhaps I shall telephone from Charleston. We go back on Friday. My love to your four.

Your
VB

ANGELICA GARNETT

IX-12. To Leonard Woolf

Jan. 26, 1950   *[Charleston]*

My dear Leonard,

I was very glad to hear from Trekkie that the [prostate] operation was safely over without complications. But I'm afraid there are always some days of discomfort and horror of one kind or another after any operation. I gather from her that one of the worst of your troubles is the skittishness of the nurses. Don't be too severe with them for you are completely at their mercy and I'm sure they'll think nothing of murdering you if you upset them too much. I had meant to come to London this week, but I'm not coming till next. Perhaps you'll be more inclined for a visit then. Anyhow I will find out.

We've had another death in the family, Cory's wife Violet, a very shy, timid creature, rather nice I always thought. The Bell family as usual have filled me with astonishment. Cory wrote to Quentin, Clive being in America, and filled the first part of his letter with apologies for not having sent some port which he had promised. Violet had been ill, he said, and he hadn't had much time. Then on the next page, "in fact she died this morning," but still the port *would* come. In fact I hear it's at the station, so no doubt Bell common sense has triumphed as usual. He was really very fond of her I think and it must be pretty gloomy alone in that huge house. Do you remember when they ordered a coffin for Dorothy in case she should be so perverse as to die at the weekend? Of course she was much too sensible to do so, though apparently at the last gasp.

What gossip to send you on your sick bed. Don't let the nurses see it.

I'll write or telephone about next week.

Your
VB

SUSSEX

IX-13. To Angelica Garnett

May 4 [1950]   *[Charleston]*

My own darling,

I was delighted to get your letter this morning with all its tit-bits about the family and the twins' most tactful remarks. I think they *did* enjoy being here, but they were certainly delighted to hear they were going home. For a first visit on their own however I consider it was very successful. How enchanting they must all have been rushing into each other's arms—at least that is how I imagine it. I often think how Virginia would have adored your having 4 daughters and have enjoyed the feminine atmosphere. Coming out of the studio I caught sight of that little drawing Duncan did of you when you were about 3 I suppose, and for the first time I saw a strong likeness between you and the twins. Please tell Amaryllis that *of course* I haven't forgotten our correspondence and I shall probably write to her tomorrow. Tell her too that Sir Ming is most anxious for an answer to his offer of his paw and wants to know whether if she consents to be his bride he will have to dye his whiskers green for the wedding. If so, he *might* reconsider the offer.

Now to talk sense. How nice it would be if you could come here for a day or two when the Mural Society[1] goes to Brighton as it will do at once when it stops in London, and we could all go and see it there and perhaps make Edward, who I believe means to spend most of May there, give us luncheon. You adore Brighton as much as he and Duncan do, so though I might feel unworthy I daresay I should see it through your eyes. Anyhow do consider this.

I went to see the M[ural] S[ociety] in London last Saturday when I had to go up to an Abbey Committee for the day, and I thought your decoration most successful. It is very well hung over one of Duncan's decorations and looks lovely. Clive, who has just returned from Paris, thought so too. In fact he admired it so much that he had to buy a catalogue to find out who had done it. The whole show seemed to me (and to Clive) very good, much better than I had expected. The general standard is quite high, though some people like Feibusch are more competent than interesting, and I think Ivon Hitchens' works are really very good.[2] I only hope it will all lead to something.

Finding myself in Picadilly at about ¼ to 1 what do you think I did? Went to the Academy! It was only just open to the public and at that hour not at all crowded, so I have done my duty. I saw your portrait [by Edward Le Bas], very well hung. It is apparently so unlike you that Barbara Bag wasn't sure it was you—in spite of its being

[1]An exhibition given by the Society of Mural Painters, of which VB and DG had been members since 1939.
[2]Hans Feibusch (b. 1898), painter and lithographer, was a member of the London Group. Ivon Hitchens (1893–1979), trained at the Royal Academy, also showed with the London Group.

called Angelica and her knowing you were sitting—rather daft, I think. It certainly isn't flattering, but I think it has a good deal of likeness of one aspect. As a painting like all E.'s work it seems to me somehow just too feeble—sympathetic and with a good deal of charm, but not enough vision of his own. In an odd way he reminds me of Roger as a painter—a great deal of taste and learning and just not original vision. I think you ought to go to the R.A. perhaps, for the huge Stanley Spencer is really rather remarkable. The detail is probably very tiresome, full of facetiousness and horrible story-telling, but I managed not to look at that and the design as a whole seemed to me surprisingly good. As a rule I simply can't bear him, so I don't think I'm likely to overrate him . . .

Your account of your farmyard dramas is really terrifying. I agree in hating hens, but I wouldn't like to see them eaten alive by geese, whom I'm not attached to either. I know they're admirable domestic characters, monogamous and maternal and paternal, but so dirty and raucous. Hens at least provide the best food in the world. The only attractive farmyard characters I think are ducks. We have none now, but I must try to get some. Did the children tell you how we went to buy "golden" fish? and how looking out of my top story window one day I saw them actually catch one in a net from the lawn pond and wave it about in glee? Luckily I rushed down and just rescued it alive— but only just.

I must in spite of the length of this letter say do you *really* think Yorkshire beautiful and paintable?[3] I can't say I know it, I've only been there once or twice, but isn't it the greenest green all over? and neither flat nor mountainous? and icy cold? and isn't Claude *without* his golden light rather chilly? You see how suspicious I am. It always seems to me it must be a writer's country and not a painter's. However if you go and do lovely works there I suppose I shall be convinced.

At this moment I am struggling in the depths with my large British Council, or is it Arts Council, work, and Duncan has got his canvas and will soon I hope actually get to work on it.

We've got Noël Annan[4] coming for the weekend. He's nearly finished the thing he is writing about my father and has sent me some

[3]The Garnetts had a cottage in Swaledale, Yorkshire.
[4]Noel Annan (b. 1916) published his first work on Sir Leslie Stephen in 1951. A reconsidered version was published in 1984. At this time he was a Fellow of KCC.

of it to see. As far as I've got I think it's rather good, certainly a great relief after Roy Harrod.[5]

Well, at last this must come to an end. If you want to go to Taviton St. you can have my room when you like, but I hope you may consider coming here.

Much love,
your VB

I am sending some sweets coupons as I don't know what to get for the family now.

ANGELICA GARNETT

IX-14. To Leonard Woolf

July 20 [c. 1950]   *Mailly, Yonne, France*

Dearest Leonard,

I have had a letter sent on to me here from a Miss Bensen who says you had a talk with her two years ago, and therefore she now writes to me wanting me to tell her about the Friday Club and the "Bloomsbury Group." She wants to come and see me at Charleston and also says Morgan told her to come to me.

So this is to warn you in case she approaches you again that I am wandering indefinitely in France and don't know when I shall be back. I have also told her that the Friday Club was a small society which didn't last very long, and implied that it was quite unimportant and that there never was such a thing as the "Bloomsbury Group."

I don't want to be brutal to the woman, but I simply cannot go on telling people about such things. They always and inevitably get it hopelessly wrong. It seems to me that if Bloomsbury is to be written about it must be by its own members (most of whom have done so). One can't tell the truth about living people and the world must wait till we're all dead. Don't you agree? I don't mind telling what I can about the past generation, but not about my own—except to my own family and friends.

[5]Maynard Keynes' first biographer (1900–1978). His book was published in 1951.

Actually we're coming back next week so I hope I may see you soon. It has been very nice to be driving about in France again, even in our poor old car which hasn't disgraced itself yet. Angelica went back two days ago. Duncan and I spent our time painting and eating—the food is as good as ever it was—and drinking. The weather is lovely and the grapes rapidly getting ripe. They grow them against every house as you do at Rodmell.

Love from
VB

SUSSEX

IX-15. To Angelica Garnett

Oct. 18 [c. 1950]   *Charleston, Firle, Sussex*

My own darling,

I send you your cheque at last. I'm sorry I've been so long about it, but I've had various accounts to do and also Cory is staying here, which doesn't really affect me or any of us but Clive very much, except that the evening is spent in conversation. However they both go off tomorrow. Cory seems very cheerful and well, though he must be very solitary in that great house alone with his dog. I think he goes to Peggy[1] quite often and she stays with him.

I long to know how the birthday party went off and if our presents were successful. Our party, the one with Simon and Coldstream, was quite a success I think. It's true Bill can hardly speak a word of French and Simon gets very uneasy when he tries to talk English, so each had to talk his own language. But luckily Simon seems to have taken a liking to Bill, which according to Janie he hardly ever does to anyone nowadays and I think Bill enjoyed hearing talk of Degas, Matisse, etc. He asked us all to go to the Slade the next morning and help him to decide which students ought to have prizes for work done in the summer holiday.[2] So we went round, including Janie who wanted to

---

[1] His daughter Margaret.
[2] William Coldstream had been appointed Slade Professor of Fine Art at University College, London, in 1949.

come too, and saw all over the Slade, which was rather fascinating. It's all wonderfully clean and in good order—it used to be dingy to a degree in my day—and a good many students were working from models in peace and quiet in very well lit rooms. Also they have a large reading room with quite a lot of art books. All seemed most luxurious—almost too much so, I thought, in Simon's view, when he thought of his own youth. There were hundreds of paintings to be inspected, but the better ones had already been more or less picked out and some were really very good. We also saw a remarkable early nude by Carrington which surprised me—I never much cared about her later things but this was really very good. Of course they also have student work by John, Spencer, etc. You ought to go there one day. It's amusing to see it all.

Your sitting to me was a great help. I've been painting your hands.

I wonder if you and Edward have arranged anything about our entertainment. Let me know.

Much love from
your VB

ANGELICA GARNETT

IX-16. To Ling Su-Hua

Dec. 7, 1950   *[Charleston]*

Dearest Sue,

I feel ashamed of myself for not having written sooner to thank you for sending me the Spectator with your story[1] in it. I thought it very good indeed. You have managed to make something lovely out of a strange and rather horrible experience and you somehow make one feel it from the child's point of view which is very rare. I hope you will publish more. I wonder whether it was Mrs Nicholson[2] who made you send it to the Spectator. If so, surely you could get other

[1]"Childhood in China" by Su-Hua Ling Chen, in the *Spectator* of December 22, 1950.
[2]Vita Sackville-West. Her husband Harold wrote for the *Spectator*.

things published with her help. You must work hard and I am sure you will succeed.

It is difficult not to be depressed by so much bad news. Also I think this cold weather makes it worse. The trees are almost entirely bare now and often very beautiful—do you remember how Julian liked the bare trees?—but all the fruit has long been picked and there are hardly any flowers. Still the beauty is very great, more so I think than when all is green.

I got so depressed and tired of my large painting, that I have put it away for a time! I hope I shall be able to come to it with a fresh eye and make it better if I don't see it for a few weeks.

I wonder how you like Picasso's plates and pots.

Love from
Nessa

BERG

IX-17. To Keith Baynes

Feb. 10, 1952   *Charleston, Firle, Sussex*

My dear Keith,

I am very sorry indeed to hear of your illness and above all of its leaving you unable to drive. I suppose from what you say that that is permanent and I can quite see how much difference it will make. One is apt to become very much isolated anyhow living in the country and without a car of course it is much worse. I hope however you'll be able to paint as usual, and will find a house in Rye with a studio or a good room, and people will no doubt come and see you there.

This household is changing a bit, as Quentin is going to be married to Olivia Popham.[1] I don't know if you know her. She's all one could

[1] Anne Olivier Popham (b. 1916), daughter of Brynhild Olivier and A. E. Popham, keeper of prints and drawings at the British Museum. Though her family and working colleagues called her "Andy" or "Anne," most friends called her by her middle name, which VB habitually spelled "Olivia." She trained as an art historian at the Courtauld Institute and worked for the Arts Council after the war. She is the editor of the *Diary of Virginia Woolf* (London: Hogarth Press, 1976–82).

wish for and everyone is delighted and they are very happy. It's not certain yet exactly what will happen as Quentin will try to get more regular and better paid work in case he has to support a family. So he may have to live in London. This would mean we were a very small party here and if only one could find studios that weren't too ruinous or out of the way Duncan and I might be in London a good deal more. Clive already has a room in Barbara's flat, so it would be easy. But studios seem impossible to find, so all is still uncertain.

As for the London Group, I'm afraid the poor old thing is tending to disintegrate. We saw John Dodgson[2] the other day and he rather convinced us that his plan is the only way of keeping it going at all. There are so many people it seems who don't pay and don't show or do show sometimes, and he said he simply couldn't turn them out, except in this way. But it seems to me that if members can only show 2 paintings each and more outsiders are shown inevitably the whole exhibition will lose character and become more of a hotch-potch— very like some of the mixed shows at dealers, only larger. If so, one doesn't see why outsiders should go on being so anxious to exhibit there. But what alternative is there? I can't see any practical one at the moment. I suspect that the only hope for the more interesting artists is to get up smaller shows among themselves at dealers—anything else seems too much risk and organisation.

Of course the whole business of giving prizes is silly. On the other hand, I think the Arts Council, etc., do do quite a lot to help painters, by sending their works about and sometimes buying them, etc. It's no good nowadays relying simply on the private patron entirely.

You won't of course be able to come to the L.G. meeting on Saturday but you will hear what happens. I hope you and Louis[3] will be on the point of setting off for the south and that the sun will do you both a great deal of good, and that we may meet when you return. Duncan and I can both still drive, but I think our difficulty will soon be that we have nothing to drive! Our poor old car gets shakier and shakier and I expect it every day to fall to pieces—and of course new ones are unobtainable.

I was sorry not to see you again in the afternoon at the L.G. meeting and very sorry to hear about Dora's illness. We saw her some time

[2]John Dodgson (1890–1969), a Slade-trained painter, president of the London Group.
[3]Louis Hoare, Baynes' companion.

later and she did look rather feeble still, but I hope she's all right now.

Best wishes to you both from

Vanessa Bell

BAYNES

IX-18. To Quentin Bell

June 9 [1952]   *Perugia [Italy]*

My darling Quentin,

It seems a long time since I had any news of you. You went to Charleston I hope. Clive wrote expecting you both and I hope you got asparagus and possibly even a strawberry or two. This has been our headquarters ever since we first got here. I forget if I told you that we had found a quiet and clean little *pension,* the food not very good, but we only have lunch here. I say little *pension,* but these Italian houses are amazing. The bedrooms aren't large and we have always eaten in a small garden, and thought there was nothing much more except mysterious quarters for the usual vague family, and a lady we take to be German who lives like a rabbit underneath all, but yesterday for the first time it rained and we were ushered into a vast *salone* for lunch, with a painted ceiling, several tables and large armchairs.

We have been for various expeditions by bus, rather uncomfortable if hot and crowded, but a wonderful way of seeing the country, which is astonishingly beautiful, with the corn almost ripe and lots of olives and vines of course. Have you been to Assisi? I forget. I'm sure all your students ought to go there.[1] One can hardly believe that ordinary mortals built and decorated such churches. The pre-Giotto masters are perhaps the most thrilling, but the whole thing is a miracle. Then in the little places one suddenly finds superb works by Perugino and others, and in one tiny place, Pienza, a church beautifully empty and

[1]After his marriage QB had taken a teaching position in the Department of Fine Art at Newcastle University.

light with about 8 works by Sienese masters painted for their places, all done with perfect taste—owing we thought to the great family, the Piccolomini, one of whom as you no doubt know was a Pope. They have a *palazzo* there which one can go into, with great books in vellum and pottery that made my mouth water, and a small formal garden with arches cut in the hedge round to show views of the amazing country all round. The mountains are at a sufficient distance to be beautiful even to me. We are starting homewards tomorrow, going to Cortona and Arezzo and Florence, which we shan't attempt to see much of, then Paris for a few days if we have enough money, and then home Saturday or Sunday the 21st–22nd. I have to be in London for *two* Abbey meetings[2] the week after, and I hope possibly you two may come to Charleston for the weekend after that. Let me know.

This place abounds in horrible pottery made at Doreto, not far off, highly ornamented and nearly all hideous. But one day some real peasant pots, mostly jugs and cooking pans, appeared in the market and of course we couldn't resist getting two or three. How we can get them back I don't know, as I've also found some very nice hand-kerchiefs and Duncan has bought some bright blue trousers, and I got lots of lovely cotton stuffs when Angelica was there to egg me on, for frocks for the children, to say nothing of *espadrilles*. But one would regret it if one didn't get them you know. Perhaps it was as well I stole your watercolour box for at least I haven't got a box like Duncan's which weighs a ton and is always falling to pieces. I do quantities of silly little watercolours while he attracts the crowds by his oils and has already found a Swiss admirer who saw his work in London. The only sensible onlooker I have had said that watercolours were *molto difficile*.

We know absolutely nothing of what may be happening in the outside world. We haven't seen a paper since we left and anyhow I think the Italian papers have only local news. The natives are very friendly to us, generally taking us for French people, but when we say we're English they often come out with long stories about the war and how much they saw of the English then. One charming old farmer said, perhaps too modestly, that the war was all their own fault, but I'm glad some of them realise that anyhow part of it was.

[2] In 1949, VB had joined the committee of the Edwin Austin Abbey Memorial Trust Fund for Mural Painting.

I long to know how you are getting on, whether you have found a flat or house yet, how Olivia is, and whether you got your car mended. I'm afraid the last 2 or 3 months of producing a baby is bound to be rather uncomfortable and tiresome, but never mind, it's well worthwhile.[3] Only make her be sensible and rest as much as possible.

Much love to you both.

from your
VB

BELL

IX-19. To Angelica Garnett

Dec. 1 [1952]   *[26 A, Canonbury Square, N. 1][1]*

My own darling,

Your letter was sent on to me here today. We came up on Thursday last week in order to go to the grand Anrep party given by Mrs Russell.[2] I was hoping you'd come on the 10th—our plans were laid to have you then. I will discuss possible entertainments with Duncan. I suppose Bunny wouldn't care to come to Charleston for a day's shooting? coming on the 8th and returning to London with us on the 10th? I fear it's rather short notice and it may be difficult for you to overlap being away, but still it would be very nice if he cared to come. Clive is in Paris I believe, having gone today, but we all return to Charleston on Friday. So perhaps Bunny could send a card either to Clive or to me. It's years, literally, since he's been there.

Duncan and I have been hard at work here painting our rooms. His have a wonderful dado—is it called?—going all round and the walls above are cinnamon, more or less. Mine I fear you may not

[3]Their son Julian was born October 1, 1952.
[1]VB and DG had moved into Olivier Bell's Islington flat when she and QB moved to Newcastle.
[2]This party celebrated the completion of Boris Anrep's mosaic on the floor of the north vestibule of the entrance to the National Gallery. Maud Russell (the wife of a banker) paid for this floor and for the party, a very large affair held in Hyde Park Gate next to Winston Churchill's house.

approve of, but we shall see. Anyhow, at worst it's chaste and cold.

The Russell party was wonderful, whether because one hasn't been to any for so long or not I don't know. But champagne literally flowed. Wherever one turned one was offered it and I at least I always accepted. The consequence unfortunately for me was that when we reached home, driven back by the Moncks,[3] who live in this square, I found I'd lost my bag, with £3 or £4, etc., in it. I thought I must have left it in the car, but it wasn't, and so I can only suppose I dropped it on getting out. I fear it has gone forever. Still the party was really worth it. Hundreds of old friends, including my old flame Freddie Ashton,[4] who flung his arms round me and I hope will come and see us. I do wish you'd been there. All the younger Anreps of course, but not Helen, who is still convalescent I believe but at home again.[5] Faith Henderson, very aged, Toby, masses of people I hadn't seen for years of a more interesting kind, such as Henry Lamb, Epstein and most extraordinary looking daughters—or models—the Partridges and Burgo,[6] rather fine to look at. But parties cannot be described. It was odd having it in a house in Hyde Park Gate, my old home.

It was stupid of me to send back your design, but I thought you or Bunny said there was some special place doing Coronation designs and that was why you wanted it. However it can easily be produced if we can get them to take any. I hope we may see Line and Sanderson[7] perhaps this week. Things accumulate so, but we must try to arrange it.

I took a great liking to Rosemary[8] when we met at the Opera, which we also enjoyed very much. I hope I shall see her again some time.

It's really terrible that all your possible servants have fallen through.

[3]Bosworth and Ruth Monck; as Ruth Beresford, she was a longstanding friend of the Anreps.
[4]Sir Frederick Ashton (1904–1988), choreographer and founder of the Royal Ballet. VB had designed the sets and costumes for his ballets *Pomona* (1933) and *High Yellow* (1932).
[5]The younger Anreps were Anastasia, Igor, and Annabel, whom Igor married in 1949. Helen had recently suffered a stroke due to a cerebral embolus. Though her recovery was quick, she continued to have the bacterial endocarditis which had caused the embolus.
[6]Lytton Burgo Partridge, only child of Ralph and Frances Partridge, was born in 1935. He married Henrietta Garnett, AVG's daughter, and died suddenly of heart failure in 1960.
[7]VB, DG, and AVG executed designs for wallpaper and took them to various manufacturers without success.
[8]Rosemary Peto, Lady Hinchinbrooke, AVG's friend and neighbor at Hilton.

It seemed more hopeful when I was with you. Couldn't William[9] be turned on to make the cottage look attractive? He can build so well, I should have thought it would be worthwile.

Our only news at Charleston was that Grace, jumping up in a rage with the D[olt] (so she said) at 3 AM, rushed to get him some dyspepsia tablets, stumbled at the top of their stairs and fell all the way down on her behind—and then fainted—and then John [her son], hearing the noise, rushed down and fainted too. The Dolt I imagine lying comfortably in bed all the time. However they came to and went back to bed, but Grace appears to have cracked her spine. Not as serious as it sounds apparently, as she has been X-rayed and is getting better. When you crack a bone it recovers of itself they say. But it was very painful for some time, especially when sitting down.

We went on Saturday to see Raymond's and Paul's new house,[10] which is simply amazing. It's like a rather large country house with a huge garden and wonderful 18th century rooms, the latest Regency style with every modern comfort and new paint and wall papers. They will out-do the ladies of Auppegard and everyone else and made us feel very small here. Quentin comes up on Wednesday this week for 2 nights which will be nice.

Much love to you all.

VB

ANGELICA GARNETT

IX-20. To Helen Anrep

Jan. 5 [1953]   *Charleston, Firle, Sussex*

Dearest Helen,

We are coming to Canonbury on Thursday this week for about 10 days so I hope I may see you. Meanwhile I wonder if you'll see Q.

---

[9]William Garnett, the younger of Bunny's two sons from his previous marriage.
[10]Raymond Mortimer and the architect Paul Hyslop (known to VB and AVG as "Curlylips") lived at 5A Canonbury Place.

and O. who went to stay with the Pophams 3 days ago.[1] They spent about 10 days here and seemed blissful. The baby of course is a wonder. In fact one hardly ever heard it make a sound and it was full of smiles and ingratiating ways and I was allowed to spoil it as much as I liked. I always knew Olivia would be very maternal and very sensible. She put the creature out in its pram all day in all weathers and feeds it herself and the result is it's immense and flourishing and will soon I'm sure grow teeth and begin to talk. But it's amusing to see Quentin with a baby, after all his objections to them all these years. He has now completely given in and obviously adores the creature who is fascinated by him and his beard in return. I must say I envy it having such a father—he'll be so good at amusing it. My only cause for complaint is that they live so far off. Angelica is bad enough but one will never see these nearly often enough and this house seems too deserted. What is one to do? Come to London a good deal I suppose, but I don't like living in two places. Everything one wants is always in the other place and one never has time to settle down before one's off again. Also the expense is great of constantly moving. Perhaps one will tend to be more and more in London as you are. I wish I knew how you are and whether you're behaving sensibly. If so it will be for the first time. Don't go looking after step-grandchildren[2] in the suburbs and do remember *one has to eat to live.*

We're going to a ghastly entertainment at Eastbourne on Wednesday—an exhibition of paintings by members of the London Artists' Association.[3] Do you remember the thing supported by Maynard and Courtauld and Hindley Smith[4] who paid us all whether we earned or not? What a world! One can't imagine such a thing now. The curator at Eastbourne [John Lake] who's rather enterprising has got up this show, which I wouldn't mind, but we—Clive, Duncan and I—have got to go to the opening lunch. Bill Coldstream is to open it! and rang up in a great stew to find out something about it. I can't bear such occasions but I can't get out of it. Otherwise we have seen no

[1]Olivier's family lived at 4 Canonbury Place, across the road from his flat in the Square.
[2]Igor and Annabel Anrep had recently produced a son, Benjamin (b. 1952). She also had a daughter, Olivia (b. 1947), from her previous marriage.
[3]"Exhibition by members of the London Artists' Association," held from January 7 to February 15, 1953 at the Towner Art Gallery, County Borough of Eastbourne.
[4]Frank Hindley-Smith (d.c. 1939), North Country cotton merchant, was a collector of modern English and French painting. He was on the committee of the LAA.

one but Lydia, Leonard and Judith Henderson[5] with her family, who were staying with him. The family, 2 little girls, rather nice and intelligent, and one rather lovely, like Ann—who is about to have her 6th baby! Well, I'll telephone one day soon.

Much love from
VB

ANREP

IX-21. To Angelica Garnett

May 13 [1954]   *La Souco [Roquebrune, France]*

My own darling,

I never hoped for a letter from you here, but here it is and a most fascinating one too with all sorts of interesting tit-bits. Dear me, what a life you lead! Almost if not quite as social as Janie's. I have been inclined to put her not painting down to having to cook, shop, look after Dorothy, etc., but now I feel it's much more owing to her social life. It's true she does cook, but usually very small simple meals, even more so when I'm not here I suppose, but she has a daily who comes morning and evening and does all housework and washing up, and nearly all food is telephoned for and arrives in half an hour. But every day she is making arrangements to see someone here or go out and long telephone conversations go on constantly. I have rather cleverly managed to appropriate the dining room which is never used and keep my painting things there and even paint there sometimes. I try to get Dorothy to sit sometimes but have only succeeded twice. I think she'd be fascinating to paint if one only had a chance. This country is impossible to paint I find—I expect you agree. However today rather recklessly I hired a cab (or got Janie to do so for me) and we all went [on] an expedition, first to see the Picassos at Antibes and then the Matisse chapel at Vence.[1] It was really fascinating. If you ever have a

---

[5]Judith Stephen had married Nigel Henderson.
[1]The Musée Picasso at Antibes and the Chapel of the Rosary at Vence, which Matisse decorated (1949–51) in gratitude to the nuns at the Dominican convent at Vence, who had nursed him through an illness.

chance of going to Antibes, *do*. The Picassos, which are paintings, drawings and pottery, are in the most extraordinary old fortress which was a museum and I imagine contained all sorts of things now turned out for Picasso. It has immensely thick walls, but very well lit rooms, all very simply arranged with rough white-washed walls and plain white cotton curtains which give a lovely light (perhaps like Mrs Jopling Rowe's?).[2] Anyhow the Picassos look simply superb in them and I was quite bowled over. I had never much liked such pottery of his as I had seen in London and Paris, but really these were most impressive, great pots and dishes with wonderful blues and blacks and less trickery than I had seen on others—I mean no realistic modelling of eggs and bacon, etc. One sees so many imitators of his that it's a relief to see the real thing at its best. I wish you and I and Duncan could go and see it all together.

As for the Matisse chapel, I don't know what to say. It's blinding in a way. It's so terrifically bright. The walls, ceiling and floor are all white as snow. On the walls are great panels of white tiles and on them he has made drawings in black only. I couldn't think them successful, try as I would. I don't think he has been able to draw on such a large scale. The small studies which are shown in another room are lovely and often as good as one expects a Matisse drawing to be, and I may be quite wrong about the others, but that was the conclusion I came to. Also I thought the stained glass windows which more or less fill the other walls and are simply a sort of abstract pattern of leaves or such like were really rather appalling colour—the brightest possible yellow, blue and green—no other colours anywhere. I know it's very rash to criticize the master so, but I couldn't help it. Again I wish you and Duncan had been there to agree or contradict. Janie I think more or less agreed but of course is reluctant to find fault. Dorothy who doesn't *really* take much interest in painting was horrified by Matisse, but for quite other reasons. She said he had no real religious feeling, which I daresay is true but I wouldn't have known it. Anyhow it didn't prevent his small drawings from being lovely. However one can't expect anyone but other painters to know anything about painting, or at least not to see them from a painter's point of view.

I hear from Duncan that most of his Dukes and Duchesses have

[2]Mrs. Jopling Rowe, painter and teacher of art in the late nineteenth century. DG may have come in contact with her in his youth. She also wrote a book on art, to which VB may be alluding.

SELECTED LETTERS OF VANESSA BELL

gone off to stay with others of their kind, and he himself was going back to London today or tomorrow. I don't know whether he'll go straight on to Charleston or wait till I arrive, which will be I hope on Thursday next the 20th, but he seems to have asked one of his aristocrats, a Miss Wynne, a cousin of Moggy,[3] to come and see us (him, as I shan't be there) at Charleston on the 19th! I suppose I shall go there too at the end of next week. You must let me know when you can come to London again and also about a visit from A. and H. I hope A. will also have got through the mumps soon, though as far as Charleston goes I don't know that it matters. But it would be a blessing to have them all clear, in spite of Fanny's most peculiar relapse.

I shall I hope spend Tuesday and Wed. nights in Paris if I can get rooms at our hotel. I haven't yet heard and Paris *may* be very full.

You must give me the full recipe for brown bread. I might be able to get Grace to make if it it's really simple, at any rate sometimes. Did I tell you that Olivia has arranged to have her [second] baby at Eastbourne in a hospital where they seemed nice and efficient. Now the difficulty is someone to look after Julian, as Grace's niece seems undecided. But I must deal with it when I get back.

Much love to you all.

Your
VB

May 15th   *Hôtel d'Angleterre, Rue Jacob*

You may be surprised at this address and date—indeed so am I. But you may have heard that Simon suddenly had a stroke and became unconscious. It is quite possible that he has died since.[4] Anyhow a telegram came from Pippa yesterday morning and they decided they must go back at once if they could change the dates for flying. There were of course lots of agitations besides the main one, for they had just got their places on the plane for a later date and Janie had sent her passport off to be renewed. I really think it was actually a relief

---

[3]Moggy was Imogen, the wife of Lord Gage, owner of the Firle estates (and all property thereon, including Charleston). She was an ardent horsewoman. The aristocratic Miss Wynne is unidentified, though in later years she often visited Charleston when she was staying at Firle Place.
[4]Simon Bussy rallied briefly but died on May 22, 1954.

after the first shock to hear about Simon. It would be much better to die than go on perhaps for years in that half-alive state—and life will be much easier for Janie I hope and think. But the worries were innumerable and as I saw I couldn't really help Janie to make all her arrangements and thought it must give her more to do to have me there I decided to go as soon as I could. So I actually left Menton yesterday evening—of course without being able to get a place or *couchette*. However though pretty full I did get a corner seat and just sate in it till I got to Paris (after a delicious dinner, regardless of expense, on the train) at about ¼ to 9 this morning. I like train journeys you know—even this one had its moments of romance and beauty—getting to Lyons in the middle of the night with the river looking immense with millions of lights all along the banks as far as one could see, and eventually coming to the familiar Yonne. Luckily the hotel here gave me a very nice quiet room at once. Paris is windy and dusty and there seems for once to be nothing whatever to see, except of course the Louvre which I went to when enough awake and a little cleaner. It's also of course absolutely ruinous and it does seem absurd to be unable to get a meal for less than £1. Would you believe it? I bought some hard-boiled eggs so as to have a pic-nic lunch— and they weren't fresh! Really nasty and dark green at the edges!

I shall go back to London on Monday. Whether I shall find Duncan there or not I don't know. But in any case I expect we shall go on to Charleston, or I shall, almost at once. It seems rather an abrupt end to my travels, but I couldn't have stayed on at La Souco alone and had really no choice. I hope I shall see you soon.

Your
VB

Do keep your press photograph for me to see.

ANGELICA GARNETT

IX-22. To Anne Olivier Bell

Oct. 7 [1954]   *Hôtel d'Angleterre [Paris]*

Dearest Olivia,

This is the only paper I have at the moment. I was most thankful for your letter this morning. It came just as we were going out. What a blessing that you are—what you are. That's all I can say. But I am so glad that Quentin has *you* and no one else to be with. I can think of him and you together, with Julian too, being happy and cheering each other up.[1] You'll have a few days with each other I hope at Charleston, and then don't go back to ordinary life again too soon, for I expect it all has been more of a strain than you may realise at once. Quentin however will look after you and he can be very severe when necessary.

Will you tell Grace that Clive returns to London on Monday next and spends a few days there before going back to Charleston. He'll let her know, but I shouldn't think it will be before Wednesday or Thursday. As for us, I am vague. Perhaps we shall get back to London while you're there or perhaps before you go there. But I'll let you know as soon as we decide. At the moment we are getting rather involved. Edward [Le Bas] and his sister have appeared, also Zoum [Walter], and Leigh Ashton and Jean Campbell and we have begun to go to draw models at [Académie] Julian's, which is rather fascinating. But I suppose want of cash will bring us back soon.

I don't think I much care about Edward's sister, Molly. She's most anxious to hob-nob with Bohemia and is even coming to Julian's to draw with us! but is really an awful snob I think. She's very smart in furs and red fingernails and I get dirtier and dirtier—how long will she stand it? Duncan's trousers almost fall to the ground and I feel disgrace is not far off. But Clive knows how to deal with her and has far more grand acquaintances than she has, which is a help. One can leave them to each other. How cattish I sound.

As usual I'm afraid I must get you to pay the rent [of the Canonbury Square flat] for me. I must also send you an enormous bill for Quentin. I suppose it's all right—he'll know. Clive will I'm sure be delighted if he finds you at Charleston and though he was of course very much

---

[1]On September 30 Olivier had given birth in Eastbourne to a stillborn daughter.

disappointed when I gave him the news and very sorry for you, yet I feel sure his one idea will be to produce something to drink! I only hope Grace will also produce enough to eat, and Julian plenty of jokes and merriment. Don't hurry off too soon. The Cézannes go on I think till the end of the month. Clive, you know, is very sane about human disasters, much more so than I am, and you'll find it easy to be with him as I hope you will be for at least some days.

Oct 8. I've just had a letter from Quentin. Perhaps he's with you now. He seems to be working so hard that I daresay he can't think of much else. As for us I get more and more dithered. Last night we dined with Zoum, who raved about you, and about Julian as far as she knew him from photographs. She said what I think is true—wicked little imp though he is—that he has a look of *goodness* which seems to have impressed her very much.

My dear, don't go and get with child again too soon. Do ask Noel [Olivier] or some doctor's advice first. Perhaps I'm ridiculous, but I cannot help wondering if your amazingly active ways and perhaps your habit of raising Julian on high—he's a fearful weight you know—mayn't have done harm in some way. I know I used to be told not to lift weights especially. Don't be cross with my mother-in-law advice, but do take advice from someone.

Don't let Quentin think he ought to have told me more at the beginning. Grace told me all there was to know then and was very kind and human. No one could have been nicer. I do hope she treated your father well . . .

Much love to you all.

Your
VB

BELL

IX-23. To Frances and Ralph Partridge

Feb. 29 [1956]   *Charleston, Firle, Sussex*

My dear Fanny and Ralph,
    Our weekend with you seems even more perfect and delightful than it would have been if we had not returned to find not a drop of water

in our pipes and the plumbers as usual in a complete state of mystification. I think they ought to be taught that water runs downhill—doesn't it?—and escapes from holes and expands when it freezes and makes an awful mess when it escapes. But they'll never learn. So today we came here—still no water. Well, I'm tired of the subject as I'm sure you are. I told Grace you had a perfect supply of boiling hot water and she wanted to know how it was done, which of course I couldn't tell her. Our only consolation is that Lydia seems to be even worse off. However we think of all the delights of Ham Spray, the delicious food, the fireside and above all sitting at ease talking to you two. It was really a great enjoyment and we send you our love and thanks. (Also Mr Bravo[1] whom I borrowed and feel doubtful about.)

> *Yours affect'ly,*
> *Vanessa*

FRANCES PARTRIDGE

IX-24. To Angelica Garnett

July 23 [c. 1958]   *Charleston, Firle, Sussex*

My own darling,

... I had such a horrible *creepy* sensation the other night. As I was sitting as usual after dinner I suddenly became vaguely aware of something, hardly enough to be sure of, yet something, under the jacket I had on, at my back, creeping up to my shoulder. Was it my imagination or not? I couldn't be sure. Yet it got more and more definite till at last I thought it couldn't be only imagination. I got up and went into my room thinking I might have to strip, when there could be no doubt—something was running or flying or scrambling up under my jacket. It sounds silly but it was horrible! Just as I was going to tear off my jacket the creature darted up into my hair—into my hair net! I tore that off and flung it to the floor with a little

[1]*How Charles Bravo Died,* by Yseult Bridges, an account of a famous Victorian murder case. Ralph Partridge used to review crime fiction and nonfiction, and VB had a weakness for both.

wriggling object thank goodness inside it. Oh, the relief. I then sought male aid from next door and the creature was seen to be a field mouse, which darted out into the room and was lost forever. I hope it soon went out of the open windows—at any rate, it hasn't been seen since. And if you think it a slight cause for so much agitation, you can't have any idea how horribly creepy the feeling was. How it got to such a position I can't imagine. But I suppose it hoped for a snug home under my jacket.

Sunday. We have had such a day of it. Edward [Le Bas] came over from Brighton, so we celebrated the opening of the Piazza[1] with champagne. Then Leonard turned up quite unexpectedly—I hadn't seen him for months. It has been so hot one could hardly go into the garden even, but rather delicious, and the Piazza with running water in it at its most Piazza-like. Only you should have been there, as everyone agreed. We shall have to have another opening one day.

The mysterious ladies have paid the option money into Dorothy's bank in Paris,[2] so they are feeling very rich and cheerful and hope it may lead to something. Janie gave us an interesting account of Barbara Bag's coming to lunch with them and when Janie went out of the room to cook an omelette—not a lengthy affair—B. poured out to Dorothy who hardly knows her all the story of her woes—how Nick has left her, etc., in tears. She must be in a very queer state. However her trips to Italy may recover her.

How exquisite Amaryllis must have looked in the evening dress I can well imagine. She is a ravishing creature. Next time I come to stay with you I think I shall bring a lot of fancy dresses and we will make the children sit properly. I'm sure they are quite equal to it and one could do quick sketches. It's always much easier if there are two or three people painting.

At last I must stop. I hope to hear from you soon.

Love from
VB

ANGELICA GARNETT

[1]An area of mosaic and broken crockery built in 1946 by QB (aided by DG, VB, AVG, and Jane Bussy) in a corner of the Charleston garden. Later (perhaps the event celebrated here) a small semicircular pool was added, with a ceramic mask that spouted water conveyed under the lawn from the house.
[2]These ladies may have bought an option to produce a motion picture of Dorothy Bussy's successful autobiographical novel *Olivia* "by Olivia," published in 1948. There was a film of *Olivia* made later in France.

IX-25. To Jane Bussy

Dec. 29 [1958]   *[Charleston]*

Dearest Janie,

I don't know whether your mother would care to have a calendar[1] this year but I send it on the chance. Anyhow I send both you and her my love. I do hope you are getting on all right and don't find life too difficult at Roquebrune, easier perhaps than it was in London. I heard a great deal about you from Barbara (of course) but I didn't see you as I had hoped to just before you departed, and now here we are listening to the rain beating down, unless there happens to be a thick fog which is even worse. Tomorrow I hope to be enlivened by the arrival of Amaryllis and Nerissa for a week or so, and then we go to the most peculiar entertainment of which you have probably heard—a luncheon party at Cambridge to be given by the grand gentlemen of King's in honour of Morgan's [E. M. Forster's] 80th birthday. His photograph now appears in every paper, he broadcasts and is interviewed and I see is so famous that it is an honour to be asked to this lunch. I only hope I shall find anything fit to wear and anything to say. Angelica and Bunny are also to be there I am glad to say. But, who else?

I have hardly been to London at all lately and as you can imagine there isn't much news to send you here. Lydia returned to Tilton after a long absence about a week ago but I haven't seen her yet. While she was away Duncan and I accompanied by Claude Rogers and Alan Clutton Brock went to Tilton to look at paintings by Duncan which might be useful for his Tate show. It was rather fascinating, also horrifying, to go all over the house as one liked, finding wonderful paintings and drawings by Ingres, Degas, Cézanne, Seurat, etc., those hung almost invisible in high dark corners. And masses of others lying on the floor in passages at the mercy of any strange dog or servant. I longed to steal some, but was virtuous. Still, something must be done. Clearly she can't be allowed to treat works of art in this way. I urge Duncan on to make a fuss and perhaps get hold of Geoffrey Keynes or others responsible for Maynard's leavings. But isn't it bad luck that of all people Lydia should have these things?

[1]VB and DG made a habit of sending painted calendars to their friends at Christmas.

We went not long ago to see the new Courtauld exhibition.[2] Don't you think it's rather wonderful that such a well-arranged and charming show should have sprung up in Bloomsbury? There are certain faults in Roger's part which I hope we may manage to get put right— one painting attributed to Duncan which certainly isn't by him, and some horrible pottery bought at Woolworth's I should think, but on the whole it's very well done. (I believe Little Ba [Barbara Bagenal] intends to instal herself there and paint the view from the window.) She and Clive seem very vague about their winter plans, but I expect you will soon have them on you. I rather wish they'd go by train or air and hire a car in Menton, but I believe B. is against that.

Dearest Janie, do take all the care you can of yourself and sometimes rest.

Much love from your
VB

BUSSY

IX-26. To Jane Bussy

Wed., Jan. 20th, 1960   *La Souco*

Dearest Janie,

Here we are safe and sound, sitting over a comfortable fire and till it gets too dark, watching the beauty outside. Even then, we see wonderful illuminated buildings somewhere up in the sky. It has been a heavenly day which I needn't describe to you as you know much better than I can tell you how exquisite the sky and sea can be, and the trees in the garden with quantities of oranges on them and most lovely flowers all coming out. Grace, who gets in touch with *everyone,* has been talking in some peculiar language to the old people below and makes them give her oranges and grapefruit and anything she wants. I have impressed it upon her that they all belong to you and not to the old couple. Mme Otto was here when we arrived and seems most amiable and brings back delicious food in the morning. Also

[2]Of Bloomsbury art, based largely on the bequest of Roger Fry.

we have got hold of the Butagaz [gas company] man who has brought a supply—in fact what more could one want? It really seems too good to be true. I am using your mother's room and Duncan I think yours, and Grace at present is in the one next it as we were afraid the one at the end might be damp. The large room with two beds is empty and can remain so for the present. I hope Angelica may come to fill it some time.

I haven't yet done any of the things you asked me to do, but I will.

Little Ba we suppose to be installed in Menton, but we haven't seen her or anyone else yet. I imagine Clive will arrive in a day or two.

Our great excitement here has been going into the studio. At first we couldn't open the door, but Duncan induced the old gardener to get hold of someone who was said to have a key (I had of course produced the one you gave me but they couldn't turn it!). However the second man did open it and we went in, and found all in good order. How you must have worked at it since I was last here. It is really very thrilling for there are so many early works of your father's that we hadn't seen. Besides the one of your mother lying on the floor there is another of her and one of the family, we supposed, standing near, and then that lovely one of you and another child, and one of you as a rather naughty looking young person which I don't think I'd ever seen. In fact there's a large collection which was *very* exciting. We hadn't time to look at more than a few, but shall do so gradually. All seemed to be in very good order though of course many want cleaning. How you must have worked to get all so straight and orderly since the time when I was last here, when as far as I remember it seemed fairly chaotic. Thank goodness we needn't hurry and feel we've got to see everything as quickly as possible.

This has been the most exciting event since we started off early on Monday morning, catching our train quite easily but feeling sure on the way to Victoria that several indispensable things, such as money and tickets, had been left behind, losing others when we had found those and had to get from the boat into our *wagon lits*—all seemed lost, but no, fairly soon we were somehow established in a carriage with some charming onion-sellers who went as far as Paris, and then our poor train wandered in complete darkness from one station to another, carriages were changed again, what had happened we couldn't tell, but did at last find ourselves in light and had a very good meal, the only and final drawback being 3 other ladies so that we were 6 somehow established in our *wagon lits!* I must say the night was not very good, Grace coughing loudly every 2 minutes just over my head, etc., etc. But at last your charming taxi driver met us and all was well. He asked most tenderly after you and pretended to remember me, and had a large and handsome car.

Dear Janie, I will write again soon and I hope tell you I have done the other things you wanted done. The beauty here is incredible.

Love from myself and Duncan.

Your
VB

TATE

IX-27. To Jane Bussy

Jan. 24 [1960]   *La Souco*

Dearest Janie,

I hope these are what you want but I warn you that I am really incredibly incompetent at all such things. Grace I think is much better and I have relied upon her as much as possible. I haven't yet given the tips to the postman and the gardener of the villa as I haven't seen them, but I will do so.

Meanwhile we live with heat and hot water at our command and are extremely comfortable, pampered in every way, and the only drawback at present being that it is raining! But that we hope won't last and anyhow you are not held responsible.

Both Duncan and I have begun to do a little painting. Today Clive and Ba came to luncheon and seemed much impressed by the luxury in which we are living. Duncan even got Ba to arrange his shaving machine so that it works from his bedside—what more can we want? Clive brought us the Sunday Times, but really one can hardly bear to look at it. We've hardly seen a paper of any kind yet, thank goodness. It's much nicer to wander in the garden and pick a few flowers which are beginning to come out in plenty—a wonderful carpet of iris, geraniums, jonquils and all sorts of lovely small things which I am too ignorant to name. As for oranges, these are the only ones I really enjoy. They always seem to me an over-rated fruit in England. Mme Otto is charming and kind and seems to understand our wants very well indeed. What language Grace talks to her I don't know, but as usual with Grace's acquaintances I expect they will become fast friends.

I do hope your household is as well as can be expected and you yourself not doing too much. Give my love to your mother if you think she'd like it, and much to Pippa and even a certain amount to Marjorie if she hasn't forgotten me.

> *Your*
> *VB*

TATE

IX-28. To Anne Olivier Bell

May 16 [1960]   *Charleston*

Dearest Olivia,

I'm afraid I must seem to you very silly. Never mind—you'll forgive me I know. Duncan and I are going to Percy St.[1] tomorrow, Tuesday. Will you let me know how Quentin is?[2] I am sitting in my studio and round me are portraits of Janie, Dorothy, Oliver Strachey, Peter's sister Dora, all dead within the last few weeks—days almost.[3] I'm not a complete idiot and I know there are many sketches of others who thank goodness are still very much alive, but one does seem to have been a good deal involved with death lately, and I suppose I have simply lost my nerve. Anyhow, do be very kind and let me know how Quentin and all of you are. Clive is in such a stew about himself that it prevents other people from being so—at any rate he saw his grand doctor when he was in London and seems to have had a good report

---

[1]VB and DG had moved into the Percy Street flat of Saxon Sydney-Turner after he entered a nursing home.
[2]QB and his family had all been having the flu.
[3]Jane Bussy's death in the bathroom of her flat at 51 Gordon Square was due to a faulty gas water heater. Dorothy Strachey, unwell and senile, was quickly removed to a nursing home, where she died within a few days, probably unaware of her daughter's death. Oliver Strachey had been in a nursing home for some time before his death.

and every possible treatment carried out. Of course he'd like very much too to see Quentin, but only when he's really recovered enough to come either here or to London, and there's no doubt that little horror B.[4] would be in evidence. It's unlucky that Grace goes on a week's holiday next week. I can't prevent it as she's going to see her old father who is I think almost at death's door! At any rate we had lots of scares about him when we were away.

Of course Quentin can easily be here when Grace is away, but Clive isn't so easy. He has lots of special dishes, etc., now. I write to you because I don't want Quentin to come here or to London till he's really well enough. But have you yourself recovered—for you had this disease too, didn't you? and the children?

Well, you see what my silliness amounts to and I know you'll forgive it. What a comfort you are.

I saw Helen when I was in London. She had been thrilled by Q.'s writing to her when in America, and she was altogether in quite good spirits I think and though *very* untidy looking, fairly well. Apparently Boris now commissions Baba to buy food and cook it and they all eat it, a very good plan I should think.[5]

The garden here is simply lovely, only things come out too quickly and are almost over at once.

Much love from
VB

BELL

IX-29. To Angelica Garnett

March 7 [1961]   *Charleston*

My darling,

I wonder what is happening to you. It seems a long time since I heard. Did you get the things you asked me to send and were they

[4]Despite VB's gratitude to Barbara Bagenal for caring so well for CB, she still found her presence irksome. According to QB, she considered Barbara "cheerful, efficient and rather boring."
[5]Since her London flat was up many stairs, Helen Anrep was living at Boris' studio with Anastasia. Boris was at this time with Maud Russell.

all right? I find it difficult to believe they were, for I feel so incompetent nowadays. I'm sure I forget everything—but on the whole I'd rather know if I do forget, so don't hesitate to say so. Duncan and I have been very quiet here, seeing no one at all, trying to keep out of the way when the rain pours in as it sometimes does and astonished when it's really fine and there's neither rain nor other things to complain of. We had a visit from Leonard the other day. He seemed very well and to be enjoying life. I've also heard from Clive who is recovering from his troubles and I think rather relieved by Cory's death. He had in fact become very difficult and one didn't quite know what to do with him when he came here, poor old thing. Yet he insisted on coming every year.

Did you send things to the London Group? And is it at all a good show? I don't suppose I shall see it. It's ages since I have been to London, and it seems so difficult to go.

Much love,
your VB

ANGELICA GARNETT

Vanessa took to her bed with bronchitis on April 4, 1961, and died quietly of heart failure three days later. Quentin and Duncan were with her. Angelica arrived soon afterwards, having been telephoned too late. When Duncan suggested she join him in drawing Vanessa on her deathbed, she felt unable to, though she kept his sketches. On April 12 Vanessa was buried in Firle churchyard. Duncan survived her by seventeen years, and they are now buried beside each other.

In April 1980, the Charleston Trust (and its support organization, the Friends of Charleston) was formed in an effort to restore and preserve the house and its decorations, both of which—after years of damp and neglect—seemed nearly unsalvageable. Following a heroic restoration, Charleston Farmhouse was opened to the public in 1986. It is the greatest surviving example of Duncan and Vanessa's domestic decoration, and a monument not only to their lives and work but to the unparalleled grace and conviviality of Bloomsbury.

VANESSA BELL
AND
DUNCAN GRANT

"As for Vanessa and Duncan I am persuaded that nothing can be now destructive of that easy relationship, because it is based on Bohemianism." So Virginia Woolf wrote in her diary in September 1930, acknowledging the success of an unlikely union, ratified neither by church nor state and one which even well-wishers may at the start have looked on askance. It is said that soon after Vanessa Bell discovered the depth of her feelings for Duncan Grant, in or around 1913, she broke down in front of her sister and wept.

He was six years younger than Vanessa, had grey-blue eyes, a full, sensuous mouth, dark hair and startling good looks. His entrée into Bloomsbury had come through the Strachey family, to whom he was related, his father being the brother of Lytton Strachey's mother. Partly for financial reasons he had lodged with his ten cousins whilst a schoolboy and student, happily becoming part of this vigorous, noisy, intellectual household. He would have learned much in the Strachey drawing room and at the dinner table, where the talk was both learned and witty. Duncan had also spent almost two years studying art in Paris, but it was the experience of two Post-Impressionist exhibitions mounted in London by Roger Fry in 1910 and 1912 that shook him as an artist and radically altered his style. When his affair with Vanessa began, he was one of the most adventurous and experimental artists working in Britain. His creative daring was for her undoubtedly a part of his appeal.

Yet her tears suggest that she embarked on this relationship, which was to be lasting, creative, and fulfilling, aware that it contained a tragic ingredient. In Bloomsbury's free atmosphere, where gossip was cultivated and nothing hidden, she knew that Duncan's loves up to that date had included two of her friends, Lytton Strachey and Maynard Keynes, and also her brother Adrian Stephen. But Duncan's homosexuality was never exclusive; he did not look at the world primarily through the prism of sexual desire. Whether abroad or at home, exploring a Spanish town or simply attending a local Sussex fête, he was acutely responsive to the life around him, to place, custom, quirks of dress, and human behaviour. His ability to involve himself in the whole web of experiences and emotions that make up the essence of life, whatever a person's sexuality, made him attractive to both sexes. After his death his correspondence revealed the huge affection he aroused in both men and women of all walks of life.

His sympathy with others enabled Vanessa always to spot the bore at any party, for he or she was sure to be found cornering Duncan. "Your loving Bear," he ended his letters to Vanessa, and this nickname, almost certainly coined by her, carried the suggestion of clumsy but very real affection. Yet in order for their relationship to remain "easy" it had to operate within very definite limits. Duncan's homosexuality did not create a bar to intimacy, but it restricted the role she occupied in his life. In turn, he accepted the responsibilities that grew alongside their relationship, the emotional demands which, though unspoken, he could not ignore.

Initially Vanessa must have offered Duncan a welcome sense of release. Among friends she was infamous at this time for her readiness to indulge in bawdy talk. It banished taboos and allowed homosexuals to gossip freely in her presence. She teased Duncan, flirted with him, and underlined their difference as painters from others in their circle. Sexual and artistic freedom became linked in her mind, and she encouraged Duncan to experiment, to rid himself of mimetic representation. "I believe distortion," she wrote, "is like Sodomy. People are simply blindly prejudiced against it because they think it abnormal." She was probably the first woman from whom he did not need to hide his sexual inclinations. She was in addition strikingly good-looking. Duncan was not insensitive to female beauty, nor averse to making a pass at a woman he found attractive. But Vanessa's feelings were intense; as her sister once observed, she had "volcanoes underneath her sedate manner." Duncan quickly saw the significance of her feelings and knew that from then on they would have to be taken into account. The decision to have a child was mutual. And on Christmas Day 1918, Angelica was born.

Soon after this the nature of their relationship altered. In order to allow Duncan the freedom to pursue his various boyfriends, Vanessa stepped back; the tone of her letters becomes more maternal; loving concern recognizes his need for independence. She begged Duncan to keep her informed about the "affairs of his heart." This frequent request suggests that the situation was bearable if she knew who was occupying his thoughts. Ironically, just as Virginia Woolf concluded that their easy relationship was indestructible, George Bergen, a young [American] painter of Russian origin, appeared in Duncan's life. His love of a *mouvementé* existence unsettled Duncan. Momentarily he became dangerously close to leaving Vanessa in order to set up home with George.

By the time this danger had passed, Vanessa appears to have re-focused her emotional life largely on her son Julian. His death in July 1937 in the Spanish Civil War left her desolate and still more dependent on Duncan. Both were by now skilled at creating harmonious living conditions conducive to the rhythm of painting, and because this was central to both their lives, it remained a major bond. The 1939–45 war kept them largely confined to Charleston in Sussex, Duncan, on his own admission, resigned and privately melancholy about the absence of any serious male love in his life. Then in 1946 he met Paul Roche, with whom he became infatuated, desire mingling with paternal feelings for the son he had never had. Though Duncan was discreet about Paul, who rarely visited Charleston while Vanessa was still alive, he could not disguise from Vanessa the importance of this young man in his life. When she caught a glimpse of the domestic intimacy the two men enjoyed in London at a flat in Taviton Street, she was upset by it. Whilst Duncan remained a dependable, deeply caring presence in her life, she must nevertheless have been aware that his mind was often elsewhere.

In 1954, Paul Roche moved to America with Clarissa Tanner, who became his wife and the mother of their four children. Duncan kept in touch by letter, writing regularly, often twice a week, during the course of the next seven years. When Vanessa died in April 1961 he suffered greatly, guilt mingling with his grief. He sent news of her death to America. Within a matter of weeks Paul returned to England in order to fulfill, for the rest of Duncan's life, the role which Vanessa's departure had left vacant.

Frances Spalding

SOURCES

Most of the Charleston Papers (once housed at King's College Library, Cambridge) were sold at Sotheby's in July 1980 to benefit the Charleston Trust, then engaged in restoring Charleston Farmhouse. The vast majority of Vanessa Bell letters in that collection were purchased by the Tate Gallery, London, and include her letters to Roger Fry and Clive Bell. Vanessa's correspondence with Virginia Woolf was among material sold by Leonard Woolf through American dealers to the Berg Collection, New York Public Library. Other important letters reside in the British Library, King's College Library, Cambridge, the University of Texas at Austin, and the Monk's House Papers at the University of Sussex. There are several smaller public and private collections of Bell letters. And many letters, including those to Duncan Grant and David Garnett, remain with Vanessa's family.

Although a remarkable number of Vanessa's letters have survived, gaps are inevitable. For instance, her letters to E. M. Forster—there may have been thirty at most—have not surfaced. And her extant correspondence with her old friend Margery Snowden comes to an abrupt stop in 1926, long before Margery's death. Saddest of all, Vanessa's letters to John ("Jack") Waller Hills, probably the first man she fell in love with, do not appear to have survived. He may have destroyed them himself after her marriage, since they are not among his few remaining papers at Halsey, Lightly and Hemsley, the London firm of solicitors of which he had been a partner. They are also not part of the "Stella Duckworth Archive" (which included her photograph album) purchased from Hills' heirs by Argosy Bookstore, New York, in 1966 and acquired by the Berg Collection three years later.

After this book went to press, Vanessa's letters to Julian Bell in China and to Angelica Garnett, previously in the possession of the family, were deposited at the Tate Archive.

Some collections of Vanessa Bell letters are cited in the text using the following abbreviations:

ANREP—Dr. Igor and Annabel Anrep

BAYNES—Lieutenant Colonel Sir John Baynes

BELL—Prof. Quentin and Anne Olivier Bell

BERG—Berg Collection, New York Public Library

BUSSY—The Bussy Family Papers, MacFarlanes, London

CAMBRIDGE—The University of Cambridge Library

HATFIELD—Cecil of Chelwood Papers, Hatfield House

KCC—Modern Archive, King's College Library, Cambridge

SUSSEX—University of Sussex Library

TATE—Tate Gallery Archive, London

TEXAS—Humanities Research Center, University of Texas at Austin

SELECTED
BIBLIOGRAPHY

Anscombe, Isabelle. *Omega and After*. London: Thames & Hudson, 1981.

Bell, Alan (ed.). *Sir Leslie Stephen's Mausoleum Book*. Oxford: Clarendon Press, 1977.

Bell, Clive, *Art*. London: Chatto & Windus, 1914.

———. *Civilization*. London: Chatto & Windus, 1928.

———. *Old Friends, Personal Recollections*. London: Chatto & Windus, 1956.

Bell, Quentin (ed.). *Julian Bell: Essays, Poems, and Letters*. London: Hogarth Press, 1938.

———. *Roger Fry, An Inaugural Lecture*. University of Leeds, 1964.

———. *Bloomsbury*. London: Weidenfeld & Nicolson, 1968.

———. *Virginia Woolf: A Biography*. Vol. 1, *Virginia Stephen 1882–1912*. London: Hogarth Press, 1972.

———. *Virginia Woolf: A Biography*. Vol. 2, *Mrs. Woolf 1912–1941*. London: Hogarth Press, 1972.

———, Angelica Garnett, Henrietta Garnett, and Richard Shone. *Charleston: Past and Present*. London: Hogarth Press, 1987.

Bell, Vanessa. *Notes on Virginia's Childhood*. Edited by R. J. Schaubeck. New York: Frank Hallman, 1974.

Bowlby, Rachel. *Virginia Woolf: Feminist Destinations*. Oxford: Blackwell, 1988.

Boyd, Elizabeth French. *Bloomsbury Heritage: Their Mothers and Aunts*. London: Hamish Hamilton, 1976.

Brenan, Gerald. *South from Granada*. London: Hamish Hamilton, 1957.

Carrington, Dora. *Dora Carrington: Letters and Extracts from Her Diaries*. Edited by David Garnett. New York: Holt, Rinehart & Winston, 1970.

Caws, Mary Ann. *Women of Bloomsbury: Virginia, Vanessa, and Carringon*. New York: Routledge, 1990.

Cecil, Hugh, and Mirabel Cecil. *Clever Hearts: Desmond and Molly MacCarthy—A Biography*. London: Victor Gollancz, 1990.

Charleston Magazine: Charleston, Bloomsbury and the Arts. Edited by Hugh Lee (since 1992, by Frances Spalding). Lewes: The Charleston Trust, 1990–.

Charleston Newsletter. Edited by Hugh Lee. Nos. 1–24. Lewes: The Charleston Trust, 1982–84.

Clark, Kenneth. *Another Part of the Wood*. London: John Murray, 1974.

Compton, Susan (ed.). *British Art in the 20th Century: The Modern Movement*. Munich: Prestel Verlag, 1986.

Cork, Richard. *Vorticism and Abstract Art in the First Machine Age*. Vol. 1, *Origins and Development*. London: Gordon Fraser, 1975.

Crabtree, Derek, and A. P. Thirlwall (eds.). *Keynes and the Bloomsbury Group*. London: Macmillan, 1980.

Darroch, Sandra Jobson. *Ottoline: A Life of Lady Ottoline Morrell*. London: Chatto & Windus, 1976.

Dunlop, Ian. *The Shock of the New: Seven Historical Exhibitions of Modern Art*. London: Weidenfeld & Nicolson, 1972.

Dunn, Jane. *A Very Close Conspiracy: Vanessa Bell and Virginia Woolf*. London: Jonathan Cape, 1990.

Fry, Roger. *Vision and Design*. London: Chatto & Windus, 1920.

———. *Duncan Grant*. London: Hogarth Press, 1923.

———. *Transformations*. London: Chatto & Windus, 1926.

———. *Cézanne*. London: Hogarth Press, 1927.

———. *Last Lectures*. Cambridge: Cambridge University Press, 1939.

Furbank, P. N. *E. M. Forster: A Life*. Vol. 1, *The Growth of a Novelist (1879–1914)*. London: Secker & Warburg, 1977.

———. *E. M. Forster: A Life*. Vol. 2, *Polycrates' Ring (1914–1970)*. London: Secker & Warburg, 1977.

Furse, Katharine. *Hearts and Pomegranates: The Story of Forty-five Years, 1875 to 1920*. London: Peter Davies, 1940.

Garland, Madge. *The Indecisive Decade*. London: Macdonald, 1968.

Garnett, Angelica. *Deceived with Kindness: A Bloomsbury Childhood*. Oxford: Oxford University Press, 1984.

Garnett, David. *The Golden Echo* London: Chatto & Windus, 1954.

———. *The Flowers of the Forest*. London: Chatto & Windus, 1955.

———. *The Familiar Faces*. London: Chatto & Windus, 1962.

———. *Great Friends*. London: Macmillan, 1979.

Gathorne-Hardy, Jonathan. *The Interior Castle: A Life of Gerald Brenan*. London: Sinclair-Stevenson, 1992.

Gathorne-Hardy, Robert (ed.). *The Early Memoirs of Lady Ottoline Morrell*. London: Faber & Faber, 1963.

———. *Ottoline at Garsington: Memoirs of Lady Ottoline Morrell 1915–1918*. London: Faber & Faber, 1974.

Gillespie, Diane Filby. "Vanessa Bell, Virginia Woolf and Duncan Grant: A Conversation with Angelica Garnett." *Modernist Studies: Literature and Culture 1920–1940*, vol. 3 (1979), pp. 151–58.

———. *The Sisters' Arts: The Writing and Painting of Virginia Woolf and Vanessa Bell*. Syracuse, N.Y.: Syracuse University Press, 1988.

Glendinning, Victoria. *Vita: A Biography of Vita Sackville–West*. New York: Quill, 1983.

Hamnett, Nina. *Laughing Torso: Reminiscences*. London: Constable, 1932.

Harrod, Roy. *The Life of John Maynard Keynes*. London: Macmillan, 1951.

Holroyd, Michael. *Lytton Strachey: The Unknown Years 1880–1910*. London: Heinemann, 1967.

——— *Lytton Strachey: The Years of Achievement 1910–1932*. London: Heinemann, 1978.

Keynes, John Maynard. *Two Memoirs*. London: Macmillan, 1949.

Keynes, Milo (ed.). *Essays on John Maynard Keynes*. Cambridge: Cambridge University Press, 1975.

Lago, Mary M. (ed.). *William Rothenstein: Men and Memories*. London: Chatto & Windus, 1978.

Lehmann, John. *Thrown to the Woolfs*. London: Weidenfeld & Nicolson, 1978.

Levy, Paul Moore. *G. E. Moore and the Cambridge Apostles* London: Weidenfeld & Nicolson, 1979.

Lilly, Marjorie. *Sickert: The Painter and His Circle*. London: Elek Books, 1971.

MacCarthy, Desmond. "The Art-Quake of 1910." *Listener,* vol. 1 (February 1945).

———. *Memories*. London: MacGibbon & Kee, 1953.

Maitland, Frederic William. *The Life and Letters of Leslie Stephen*. London: Duckworth, 1906.

Marcus, Jane (ed.). *New Feminist Essays on Virginia Woolf*. Lincoln: University of Nebraska Press, 1981.

Meyers, Jeffrey. *The Enemy: A Biography of Wyndham Lewis*. London: Routledge & Kegan Paul, 1980.

Moore, G. E. *Principia Ethica*. Cambridge: Cambridge University Press, 1903.

Morphet, Richard. "The Significance of Charleston." *Apollo,* vol. 36, no. 69 (November 1967), pp. 342–45.

———. "The Art of Vanessa Bell." *Vanessa Bell: Paintings and Drawings*. Catalogue to an exhibition held at the Anthony d'Offay Gallery, November 20 to December 12, 1973.

Noble, Joan Russell (ed.). *Recollections of Virginia Woolf*. New York: Morrow, 1972.

Perl, Jed. *Paris Without End: On French Art Since World War I*. San Francisco: North Point Press, 1988.

Roche, Paul. *With Duncan Grant in Southern Turkey*. London: Honeyglen, 1982.

Rose, Phyllis. *Woman of Letters: A Life of Virginia Woolf.* New York: Oxford University Press, 1978.

Rosenbaum, S. P. (ed.). *The Bloomsbury Group: A Collection of Memories: Commentary and Criticism.* London: Croom Helm, 1975.

Rothenstein, John. *Modern English Painters.* Vol. 1, *Sickert To Grant.* London: Eyre & Spottiswoode, 1952.

Sackville-West, Vita. *The Letters of Vita Sackville-West to Virginia Woolf.* Edited by Louise DeSalvo and Mitchell A. Leaska. New York: Morrow, 1985.

Shone, Richard. *The Berwick Church Paintings.* Eastbourne, Sussex: Towner Art Gallery, 1969.

———. "The Friday Club." *Burlington Magazine,* vol. 117, no. 866 (May 1975), pp. 279–84.

———. *Bloomsbury Portraits.* Oxford: Phaidon Press, 1976.

———. "Introduction" in *Duncan Grant, Designer.* Catalogue to an exhibition held at the Bluecoat Gallery, Liverpool, and at Brighton Museum, February 1 to April 13, 1980.

———. "Vanessa Bell." *Vanessa Bell 1879–1961: A Retrospective Exhibition* held at Davis and Long, New York, April 18 to May 24, 1980.

Skidelsky, Robert. *John Maynard Keynes.* Vol. 1, *Hopes Betrayed, 1883–1920.* London: Macmillan, 1983.

Spalding. Frances. *Roger Fry: Art and Life.* London: Elek/Granada, 1980.

———. *Vanessa Bell.* London: Ticknor & Fields, 1983.

Spater, George, and Ian Parsons. *A Marriage of True Minds: An Intimate Portrait of Leonard and Virgina Woolf.* London: Jonathan Cape and Hogarth Press, 1977.

Spender, Stephen. *World Within World.* London: Hamish Hamilton, 1951.

Stansky, Peter, and William Abrahams. *Journey to the Frontier: A Biography of Julian Bell and John Cornford.* London: Constable, 1973.

Strachey, Barbara. *Remarkable Relations: The Story of the Pearsall Smith Family.* London: Victor Gollancz, 1980.

Su Hua. *Ancient Melodies.* London: Hogarth Press, 1953.

Sutton, Denys (ed.). *Letters of Roger Fry.* 2 vols. London: Chatto & Windus, 1972.

Todd, Dorothy, and Raymond Mortimer. *The New Interior Decoration.* London: Batsford, 1929.

Trombley, Stephen. *All That Summer She Was Mad: Virginia Woolf and Her Doctors.* London: Junction Books, 1981.

Watney, Simon. *English Post-Impressionism.* London: Studio Vista, 1980.

———. *The Art of Duncan Grant.* London: John Murray, 1990.

Woolf, Leonard. *The Wise Virgins: A Story of Words, Opinions and a Few Emotions.* London: Edward Arnold, 1914.

———. *Beginning Again: An Autobiography of the Years 1911–1918.* London: Hogarth Press, 1964.

———. *Downhill All the Way: An Autobiography of the Years 1919 1939.* London: Hogarth Press, 1967.

———. *Letters of Leonard Woolf.* Edited by Frederic Spotts. New York: Harcourt Brace Jovanovich, 1989.

Woolf, Virginia. *Roger Fry: A Biography.* London: Hogarth Press, 1940.

———. *The Letters of Virginia Woolf.* 6 vols. Edited by Nigel Nicolson and Joanne Trautmann. London: Hogarth Press, 1975–80.

———. *Moments of Being: Unpublished Autobiographical Writings.* Edited by Jeanne Schulkind. Sussex: The University Press, 1976.

———. *The Diary of Virginia Woolf.* 5 vols. Edited by Anne Olivier Bell. London: Hogarth Press, 1976–82.

———. *A Passionate Apprentice: The Early Journals, 1897–1909.* Edited by Mitchell A. Leaska. New York: Harcourt Brace Jovanovich, 1991.

INDEX